French
Cinema

Jean Gabin (Jean) and Michèle Morgan (Nelly) in Marcel Carné's *Port of Shadows* (*Le quai des brumes*, 1938), (Courtesy of BIFI).

French Cinema

FROM ITS BEGINNINGS
TO THE PRESENT

Rémi Fournier Lanzoni

contin
NEW YORK

2002

The Continuum International Publishing Group Inc
370 Lexington Avenue, New York, NY 10017

The Continuum International Publishing Group Ltd
The Tower Building, 11 York Road, London SE1 7NX

Printed in the United States of America

Library of Congress Cataloging-in-Publication Data

Lanzoni, Remi Fournier.
  French cinema : from its beginnings to the present / Rémi Fournier
Lanzoni.
     p. cm.
Includes bibliographical references and index.
  ISBN 0-8264-1399-4 (hard: alk. paper)
  1. Motion pictures—France—History.   I. Title.
  PN1993.5.F7 L33 2002
  791.43'0944—dc21
                                        2002010594

À ma Kristin . . . .

Contents

Illustrations

Introduction

The present edition on the history of French cinema resulted from an increasing need for an English-language book on this history, an extensive overview of more than one hundred years of filmmaking. This volume considers motion pictures and cinematographic trends chronologically from 1895 to 2002, decade by decade, and investigates films and filmmaking within historical contexts through a diversity of disciplines such as social and political sciences. During the past few years the discipline of film studies has been the subject of growing interest among universities, especially in the humanities, traditionally involving, in its broadest terms, the study of film analysis, film history, and film theory. Unfortunately, among the general public as well as university departments of film studies, French cinema has often been restricted to the work of a few "masters," critics, and theorists. It represents, however, much more than internationally known film icons. The present book assimilates these traditional canons with often-overlooked contributions made by no less significant figures within the film industry.

Since the early days of motion pictures, when the Lumière brothers challenged the world in 1895 with the invention of the Cinématographe, France has frequently been at the cutting edge of film production. The visionary talent of Georges Méliès, who assembled the first elaborate background sets and special effects, inspired legions of filmmakers around the world. The film industry significantly benefited from the film archives movement, which originated in 1936 in Paris with the establishment of the Cinémathèque française. Later, the French New Wave granted filmmakers the exclusive authority, that of the auteur, in all areas of film production (mise-en-scène, photography, origin of the script, thematic and artistic choices). This trend, once labeled *politique des auteurs,* marked a prolific period for film production worldwide, setting a landmark in the history of filmmaking. Finally, at the turn of the twenty-first century, France emerged as the preeminent producer of European cinema and has proved its solid business and

artistic infrastructure, despite the high volume of American films in
the European market. In its contemporary context, the French film
industry stands as the champion of European cinematic creativity,
demonstrated in movies like Pitof's *Vidocq* (2001), the first all-digital
feature film.

This book treats French film primarily as a unique and powerful art
with its own traditions, history, conventions, and techniques, dispel-
ling common misconceptions—frequently found in the literature on
film history—by addressing less accessible issues and concepts. It
analyzes aspects of film form, narrative, and genre and explores major
interpretive approaches to the medium. The eight chapters in this
volume combine cultural, historical, formal, and theoretical analyses of
French films from a range of French and world cinematic sources. Each
chapter provides both an overview of French film historiography and
an introduction to specific examples and methods of historically oriented film research. One of the central goals is to introduce readers to
basic issues of the history and aesthetic appreciation of motion pictures
through the conventional aspects of cinematography, including camera
movement, montage, cinematographic expression, framing, shooting
angle and point of view, color (or black and white), sound, music, the
script, lighting, settings, costume, and makeup. Another aim is to
reintroduce film buffs to the movies they have most admired and loved.

The first chapter, entitled "The Invention of Motion Pictures and
the Silent Era of Film," investigates the development of the Cinématographe as well as the contribution of major filmmakers of the time
such as Georges Méliès, Louis Feuillade, Louis Delluc, Abel Gance,
Marcel L'Herbier, and René Clair. The chapter also highlights the
emergence of a national cinema (under the auspices of Charles Pathé,
Léon Gaumont, and others), which by the first decade of the century
had become one of the most significant phenomena, assimilating and
embodying many artistic currents, such as Avant-garde, Impressionism, and Surrealism. The second chapter, "The Golden Age of French
Cinema," centers on the numerous adjustments the French film industry had to face while incorporating in its structure the technical innovation of sound. It also describes Marcel Pagnol's successful adaptations
of regional, popular literature to the big screen, confirming its prestige
among general audiences at the time. In addition, the chapter organizes a select discussion of the principal artists and masters of the poetic
realism era, Jean Gabin, Arletty, Marcel Carné, Jean Renoir, and Jean
Vigo. Chapter 3, "French Cinema of the Occupation," narrates the
exodus of many French film celebrities at the beginning of World War
II, and the new situation imposed by German and Vichy censorship,
which included a ban in 1940 of all Anglo-American productions and
an extensive number of French films. Through the works of Henri-

Georges Clouzot, and Marcel Carné, the chapter explores the complex working conditions for most film actors and directors under the Occupation, which, although constraining, often instigated amazing ingenuity on and off the set. Chapter 4, "The Postwar Era," begins with the reorganization of the French film industry during the Liberation era as well as the Fourth Republic, with an emphasis on the difficult economic challenges of the period (e.g., the Blum-Byrnes Agreements). It presents the so-called *tradition de qualité,* represented by an old school of filmmakers, including Claude Autant-Lara, Carné, Christian-Jaque, and Sacha Guitry, as well as screenwriters Jean Aurenche and Pierre Bost, and attempts to give the reasons for its success during the early postwar era. A large part of the chapter focuses on the innovative method of filmmaking by auteurs such as Robert Bresson, Jacques Tati, and René Clément. Chapter 5, "The Years of the French New Wave," examines the situation of France during and after the explosive political events of 1958, as well as the birth of the seminal review *Les cahiers du cinéma.* The auteur theory, which asserted that the film director was the principal authority in all areas of film production, involved many young directors, such as Claude Chabrol, François Truffaut, Alain Resnais, Jean-Luc Godard, and Agnès Varda, and led directly to the explosion of the New Wave. The New Wave, which began in the mid-1950s as a reaction to a stagnating establishment, and was granted general recognition in the years 1958–59, remains to this day considered a historical landmark. Chapter 6, "French Cinema of the 1970s," offers a synopsis on the new cultural era following the May 1968 upheavals throughout France and the so-called liberalization era and cultural change. The chapter centers on the three major movements of the decade: the coming of an innovative and successful genre, the "political thriller," which gradually began to replace conventional *polars* (whodunits led by directors Louis Malle and Costa-Gavras); the arrival of talented new storytellers (Bertrand Tavernier and Bertrand Blier); and finally, a trend of humanist film directors (Truffaut, Eric Rohmer, and Claude Sautet), whose works incorporate powerful reflections on the medium itself. Chapter 7, "The Cinema of the 1980s," begins with the economic restructuring of the French film industry and its new rapport with its principal partner: television companies. These changes resulted in major transformations in the entertainment business and spectatorship behavior in general. The 1980s also witnessed the development of so-called super productions, inclined toward more profitable commercial films, as well as the out-of-control rise of production costs. In addition, the chapter examines the successful continuation of already-established filmmakers, including Truffaut, Tavernier, Blier, and Maurice Pialat, as well as myriad new rising talents, especially filmmakers such as Jean-Jacques Beineix, Luc

Besson, and Leos Carax. The final chapter, "The Last Decade and Beyond," points out the evermore central position of the French film industry, which has established itself as the largest and most successful in Europe. A unique financial-aid system, combined with the financial commitment of dynamic French television companies (led in major part by Canal+), underscores the success of a strategy initiated a decade before. These exceptional circumstances generated the realization of many new filmmakers such as Jean-Pierre Jeunet, Mathieu Kassovitz, and Eric Zonca.

I confess to the difficult task of dealing with an overwhelmingly large amount of material within a relatively confined space. It is important to bear in mind that the films I discuss represent only a fraction of the entire spectrum of French films (over 10,000 produced since 1895) and the present history is evidently and necessarily incomplete. I have tried to offer an explicit and honest investigation of the main masterpieces, directors, and actors and actresses of French cinema, combined with observations of less acknowledged but equally noteworthy works, and hope that the present volume will contribute to the understanding of French films, on their own and within the family of other national cinemas.

ACKNOWLEDGMENTS

First and foremost, I dedicate this book to my wife, Kristin, who spent innumerable hours editing the manuscript, offered invaluable advice on the organization of the text, and finally succeeded in the difficult task of coping with my French "frame of mind." Second, I would like to thank Evander Lomke, managing editor of Continuum, without whom the book would never have seen the light. Evander recognized the potential for the project and believed in it all along, working with me over the past two years. I would like to express my gratitude to Emmanuel Collin from the Archives Marcel Carné, located at the French Library in Boston, who opened the door to the filmmaker's personal archives and allowed me to have access to some invaluable materials, especially Jean Gabin's personal script of *Le jour se lève*. My sincere thanks to Nicolas Riedel from the Institut Lumière in Lyon, who was able to assemble a press kit on *Le fabuleux destin d'Amélie Poulain* in just a few minutes. I am indebted to my friend DeeAnn Memon, as well as my students Darcy Haviland of Monmouth University and Thomas Turanchik of Elon University, for their dedicated and precious editing work. Many thanks to Laura Daly for her very thorough copy-editing services, Russell Wolinsky for his proofreading skills, and Fotini Lomke for compiling the index. Mary Corliss and Terry Geesken of the Film Still Archives at the Museum of Modern

Art in New York supplied many photos. So did Cécile Verguin and Cécile Blanc from the BIFI Library in Paris. I am most grateful to Marie-Thérèse Casséus at the French Institute/Alliance française in New York City for her kind assistance and for her invaluable help in allowing me to view a great number of French films on video as well as in facilitating my research at the Institute. I am also grateful to Jean-Pierre Jeunet, Claudie Ossard, and Valerie Mullon from Victoires Productions, as well as Anne Turquet from UGC.

My everlasting thanks go to my father, Jean-Jacques Fournier, who collected abundant information and communicated his passion for cinema in my early teens. Alain Rodet, professor of philosophy at the lycée La Martinière in Lyon, was most helpful in sharing his extensive video collection of classic French films, enabling me to view several rare long and short features for the first time. Many thanks to Jane Romer, professor of French at Elon University, who indicated several publications that proved important for the final version of the manuscript. Todd May of Clemson University, whose experience in the publishing world offered me invaluable suggestions, encouraged me to organize the proposal of the book. Many thanks to Linda Alexander of Clemson University, whose extensive knowledge of American and French cinema allowed me to rediscover several French masterpieces and in particular the wonderful career of Josephine Baker.

I would also like to express my gratitude to Chad Dell, professor of communication at Monmouth University, who allowed me to share my passion of French and Italian cinema for the program of film studies at Monmouth University, as well as to Dean Kenneth Stunkel of Monmouth University, who made possible my visit to the BIFI Library in Paris during July 2001. I am indebted to Marja Warehime, Professor of French at the University of South Carolina at Columbia, whose course of French cinema between the two world wars encouraged my passion for the poetic realism era. Also, many thanks to my brother, Jérôme Fournier-Lanzoni, matte painter of *Vidocq,* who offered his sketches representing the view of nineteenth-century Paris, and Keath Pickard, who provided valuable documents on Jeunet's *Amélie.* And finally, many thanks to my friend Sandro Picchietti, who back in 1996 acquainted me with Peter Bondanella's *Italian Cinema.* His enthusiasm for that book immediately triggered a parallel interest in undertaking this project on French cinema.

Chapter 1
The Invention of Motion Pictures and the Silent Era of Film

- ➤ *France at the Turn of the Twentieth Century*
- ➤ *The Invention of the Cinématographe*
- ➤ *Georges Méliès and the Adventure of the Film Studio*
- ➤ *Growth of a National Cinema: Charles Pathé and Léon Gaumont*
- ➤ *The Invention of Genres: Louis Feuillade and Max Linder*
- ➤ *Avant-garde Cinema, French Impressionism, and Surrealism: Louis Delluc, Abel Gance, Marcel L'Herbier, Luis Buñuel, and René Clair*

FRANCE AT THE TURN OF THE TWENTIETH CENTURY

More than a century ago, the invention and early development of motion pictures heralded the beginnings of an innovation that was about to transfigure humankind's view of the world and of itself. Movies would come to generate other new and unprecedented elements of artistic creation as well. Cinematography rapidly became perhaps the most significant technical and artistic phenomenon of the twentieth century, assimilating and embodying many other art forms, yet never really imitating any of them. Specifically, it was cinematography's special rapport with theater in particular, but also painting, literature, and many other performing/lyrical arts, that made it the "seventh art" of the new century. In the 1900s, however, the new medium, soon to become a major form of entertainment, would evolve closely within contemporary artistic currents and with respect to the preoccupations of popular audiences. This in turn would guarantee its commercial viability and, consequently, its destiny. Whether labeled "motion pictures" or "cinematography," not unlike any of the other lyrical or performing arts no matter what discipline, genre, or current, audiences assimilating the films of the silent era were, as always, affected by contemporary culture and fashion, sharing many passions and events of the turn of the century.

The introduction of motion pictures in France occurred during a new prolific cultural era that promoted many important artistic currents in such fields as architecture, interior design, furniture, sculpture, and fashion. The new modern style of film backgrounds, directly influenced by the Art Nouveau movement (1890s–1910s), and later the Art Déco vogue (1900s–20s), which was consecrated at the 1925 Paris Exposition des arts décoratifs et industriels modernes, became one of the major visual trademarks of Impressionist artists. At the beginning of the century, Paris was the Avant-garde capital of the world in art, music, and literature. It was the residence of Pablo Picasso, Salvatore Dali, Igor Stravinsky, and Jean Cocteau, among many others. The yearning to explore the fields of music, painting, and poetry had now caught up with the seventh art under a quest for forms and visual images rather than meaning. In the field of poetry, the beginning of the century was characterized by a certain permanence, with the preceding current of poets such as Stéphane Mallarmé and Arthur Rimbaud, who deeply influenced newer poets such as Paul Valéry, Paul Claudel, and Saint-John Perse (pseudonym of Alexis Léger). As for the Surrealists, André Breton, Louis Aragon, and Paul Éluard, whose inspiration came in part from Guillaume Apollinaire's *The Poems of Alcools* (*Alcools*, 1913), Cubist art, and the emerging Dadaist movement, their works created a serious gap with the rest of French cultural life, isolating themselves into an artistic domain by emphasizing the subconscious aspect of the imagination against all social structures and traditional forms of expression. In the field of the novel, two of the most spectacular popular successes were Alain-Fournier's *Le grand Meaulnes* (*The Wanderer*, 1913) and Marcel Proust's *A la recherche du temps perdu* (*Remembrance of Things Past*, 1913–27). Literary reviews (*La Nouvelle Revue Française*, created by André Gide in 1908) and publishing houses (Gallimard) emerged to promote and disseminate these novelists and others of the pre–World War I era.

Following the Lumière brothers' first screening at the Salon Indien du Grand Café in Paris in December 1895, French cinema, at first a novelty, quickly progressed from popular entertainment to an art form, and eventually to a form of literature itself, as silent films reached greater complexity and length in the early 1900s and 1910s. The exceptionally profitable financial revenues that the silent movies generated permitted the French film industry to establish a sound network of distribution that gradually challenged other forms of public entertainment. At first, French cinema dominated world markets with significant inventors (Louis and Auguste Lumière), inspired artists (Georges Méliès, Max Linder, Abel Gance, and René Clair), technicians (Ferdinand Zecca), and pragmatic entrepreneurs (Charles Pathé and Léon Gaumont). However, with both the coming of World War I (1914–18) and the demands placed on all industries for the war effort, plus the rise of Hollywood's immense influence, the French film industry slowly began to recede. The war rapidly changed the direction of the burgeoning film industry, ending the period of silent pictures with a double crisis: economic, with the financial panic of 1929; and technical/aesthetic, with the development of talking pictures, which forever redefined the original concept of motion pictures.

THE INVENTION OF THE CINÉMATOGRAPHE

The last fifteen years of the nineteenth century were characterized by extraordinarily intense activity around the worldwide development of "animated photography" and mechanized entertainment. With an assortment of scientists, artists, technicians, and other innovators separately assembling their inventions at the same time in history, thus creating an unprecedented accumulation of contributions, the difficult task of attributing the exact paternity of motion pictures (for Americans) or cinema (for Europeans) remains somewhat arguable in its objectivity. In 1889, British scientist William Greene (1855–1921) invented a "chronophotographic camera" that combined animated pictures. One year later, in 1890, Herman Casler presented the Mutoscope. In France, Georges Demenÿ (1850–1917), who worked alongside Etienne-Jules Marey (1830–1904), invented the Photophone for photographing animated images in cinematographic form in 1893. That same year, Eadweard James Muybridge (1830–1904) invented the Zoopraxiscope, and in 1894, Birt Acres (1854–1918) and Robert William Paul (1869–1943) invented the Kineopticon. The same year in Germany, Maximillian Skladanowsky (1863–1939) built the Bioskop (Bioscope) and presented his achievement in Berlin in November 1895. In 1896, C. Francis Jenkins, then Thomas Armat (1866–1948), invented the Vitascope (originally named Phantoscope before being sold to Thomas Alva Edison (1847–1931).

Therefore, in light of this overwhelmingly abundant series of technical inventions, attributing the invention of motion pictures to one or two individuals, whether Edison alone or the Lumière brothers, would be rather questionable in view of the fact that cinema, by its very essence, constituted, and still does today, a multifaceted event and medium. Such an assertion would simply require overlooking the technological and scientific endeavors achieved all over the Western world (mainly the United States, France, Belgium, Germany, and Italy, however) throughout the last two decades of the nineteenth century. For all these inventors, the ultimate goal was the same: the public projection of animated pictures. The question regarding the projection of animated photographs was a difficult one to solve, causing it to become the center of research and experimentations. Establishing the perfect projection device became the next challenge, as it appeared evident after numerous defective attempts (blurriness and ripped film-strip) that the projection of the image onto the screen was actually the mandatory toll for success.

The definitive beginnings of cinema, therefore, remain highly argu-able; if anything, the genesis and early evolution of cinema underscore the seemingly universal origins of the invention, which was to give the visual element a major boom during the following century.[1]

The Kinetoscope, 1893–95

In 1889, in West Orange, New Jersey, Thomas Edison and British engineer and collaborator William Kennedy Laurie Dickson (1860–1935) developed the Kinetograph, a new system that utilized rolls of coated celluloid film to visualize animated images. The Kinetograph camera, weighing approximately 500 pounds, was built inside the Black Maria Studio, a tar paper–sealed structure with a large skylight that was adjacent to Edison's laboratory. To control light, the studio was painted in black, and the camera, mounted on a trolley, was built so that it could turn to follow the movement of the sun, allowing the right amount of luminosity for each desired subject (although never changing position during shootings). In May 1889, Edison purchased a Kodak camera from the Eastman Company that required a 2⅜-inch film stock, modified its size to 1⅜ inches (34.8 mm), and made double perforations on each side. Edison utilized the Eastman nitrate-base celluloid film stock for his commercial productions. More than a century later, the celluloid film support (35 mm) is still the standard in use, a rare example of nonobsolescence. When compared to video formats, for instance, or even international sound recording standards, Edison's film (forty-six frames per second) never experienced a contin-uing change of systems, and thus avoided delays in its international development.[2] Dickson, who had assembled the new camera, filmed his first motion picture of associate assistant Fred Ott, calling it "Fred Ott's Sneeze" (the film lasted several seconds). The sequence was dis-played to Edison, who decided to commercialize the idea. Edison's kinetoscopic record of a sneeze, January 7, 1894, starring Fred Ott as the sneezer and photographed by Dickson, became the first copyrighted film in history. Other sequences, characterized by unedited scenery and posed actions followed, such as "Fun in a Chinese Laundry," "The Gaiety Girls Dancing," "Trained Bear," "Dentist Scene," and "Bucking Broncos." Paradoxical as it may seem, Edison was more captivated by the possible application of soundtrack to the image[3] than image development itself. Dickson tried to persuade Edison to develop a projection device, but much to his dismay, the latter had a different agenda; Edison did not deem it necessary to multiply the number of spectators within the same projection. Therefore, all experiments were temporarily canceled.

In 1893, the patent was ready (but never entirely completed for the British market), and that same year the demo was finalized. Edison's first showing of the Kinetoscope viewer, as a continuous-film motion picture projector, occurred only on May 9, 1893, at the Brooklyn Institute. Rather than projecting films for large audiences, the individual viewer would put his or her eyes to the hole of a mechanism and enjoy a single strip film inside. Commercialized a couple of years before the Cinématographe, the inventor rapidly presented his "peep-show Kinetoscopes" in the United States, England, and France. Edison's invention corresponded to a peep-show motion picture that could be visualized by only one viewer at a time. In 1893, the Kinetoscope gained popularity in New York City, and in April 1894, Andrew Holland, on behalf of the Raff & Gammon Company, opened the first peep-show parlor on Broadway. For 25 cents, New Yorkers were able to share the cinematographic dream by individually viewing a series of sixteen-second films. Because Edison had underestimated the potential of motion pictures as a future industry, he failed to patent his Kinetoscope completely. Consequently, in England alone (this despite holding over 1,200 patents), Robert William Paul,[4] a British manufacturer of photographic equipment, rapidly replicated Edison's Kinetoscope in October 1894. In addition, he added the projector component that was crucially missing to the kinetograph.[5] As noted, the new apparatus was named Kineopticon. The demonstration by the Lumière brothers at the Keith's Music Hall in Union Square, New York, on June 18, 1896, as well as the emergence of the Pantopticon and the Vitascope, overshadowed the Kinetoscope whose cumbersome set could not project for public shows or entertain large audiences. Dickson created the American Mutoscope & Biograph Company, which later encouraged the directing careers of D. W. Griffith (1875–1948) and Mary Pickford (1893–1979). Along with Dickson, Edwin S. Porter (1869–1941), a cinematographer and future filmmaker, was one of the first artist/ technicians to initiate the practice of close-ups and dissolves (fade in/ out). Edison's film company survived the competition and produced films such as *Vanity Fair* (1915), *The Cossack Whip* (1916), and *Chris and His Wonderful Lamp* (1917). At the beginning of the next decade, however, the company shut down.[6]

The Lumière's Cinématographe, 1895

Louis (1864–1948) and Auguste (1862–1954) Lumière, sons of Antoine Lumière, owner of a modern-style photography factory (200 workers), specialized in manufacturing a product set up in 1881 called *plaque étiquette bleue* (photographic plates for instantaneous shots). Having assembled the different elements for printing, shooting, and projecting nineteen to twenty-four frames per second, they decided to film their very first *vue* (view) entitled *Workers Leaving the Lumière Factory* (*La sortie des usines Lumière à Lyon*) on March 19, 1895, as the well-dressed workers of the film factory came out onto the street (at the time Chemin Saint Victor, today renamed Rue du premier film).[7] Conceived and assembled by Jules Carpentier of the Lumière factory, the Cinématographe possessed a clawlike device that supplied the necessary alternating passage of the 35 mm perforated-celluloid film. The Lumières' band of film, fabricated by the Lumière factory, contained two punctures per frame (sixteen frames per second; the standard speed until the invention of sound), whereas Edison's used four rectangular perforations on each side of each frame. The composition and function of this lightweight 16-pound hand-cranked camera performed a threefold task: filming, printing, and projecting motion pictures. In addition to its phenomenally small size, permitting filming to take place anywhere, the new portable suitcase-sized camera was unique for its rapid installation and viewing, which consequently triggered a new style of filmmaking: the documentary. Thus, the operator could shoot footage in the morning, process the film print in the afternoon, and then project it to an audience that same evening.

On February 13, 1895, the Lumière brothers patented their invention, and on March 22, just a couple of days following their very first view, they organized a private projection at the Société d'encouragement à l'industrie nationale in Paris, featuring *Workers Leaving the Lumière Factory*, followed by a discussion led by Louis Lumière. Back in Lyon, on June 12, another projection of eight views for the Congrès des sociétés françaises de photographie was held, which immediately gave national fame to the invention as the members of the association saw themselves for the first time "photographed in motion." However, when compared chronologically, the 1895 Cinématographe invention already had several forerunners in Etienne-Jules Marey, whose Chronophotographe did not contain the perforated film; Emile Reynaud (1844–1918),[8] whose Praxinoscope did not in-

The Lumière brothers, Louis (1864–1948) and Auguste (1862–1954), (Photo courtesy of the Museum of Modern Art/Film Stills Archive).

clude photography, and Thomas Edison, whose invention did not incorporate public projection. In other words, the Cinématographe, which was instrumental in shaping the conventions of photographic synthesis of the movement to reproduce the reality of life, was the synthesis of three preceding discoveries. But generally speaking, December 28, 1895, corresponds to the actual birth date of cinema. It was that evening that the Lumière brothers presented their Cinématographe to a crowd of curious photographers and inventors in the Salon

Indien, located in the basement of the Grand Café, 14, boulevard des Capucines, in Paris, thus achieving the first public and paying projection in history (ten views of about fifty seconds each for thirty-three spectators in an informally assembled viewing room). Although not completely documented a century later, the program most certainly included such views as *The Arrival of a Train at La Ciotat* (*L'arrivée du train en gare de La Ciotat*), *A Sprinkler Sprinkled* (*L'arroseur arrosé*)[9] probably the first fiction film known, *Baby's Meal* (*Le repas de bébé*), and *Card Game* (*Partie d'écarté*).

For the Lumière family, who never anticipated the new invention's potentiality—having little faith in the future unfolding of a revolutionary medium—the technical progress of the Cinématographe was merely a popular entertainment destined to supply traveling fair promoters. The Lumières' prediction, "Cinema is an art without a future," became famous and by overlooking the potential of the new invention, they realized too late the consequences that their new invention would have on an entire century (as opposed to the invention of color photography, which remained their major contribution). While temporarily retooling their factory for the production and sale of film equipment, the Lumière brothers were still clever enough to instruct a group of operators on the use of the Cinématographe and sent them to capture images of the world (the locations were Venice, London, Dublin, Berlin, New York, Chicago, Mexico City, Moscow, Jerusalem, Egypt, Constantinople, Sydney, Indochina, Japan, and Africa).

After the enormous success of the first projection, the Lumières sold 200 cameras in just a few days and maintained an almost absolute monopoly on the sale of film cameras for the next two years. Although the first views displayed an obvious sign of amateurism, subsequent films included impressionistic elements, which were deeply appreciated by the contemporary public (in particular, the subtle movement of the leaves in *Baby's Meal*). The first views were shot mainly to chronicle contemporary moments or events and ran no longer than fifty seconds. During that very first year, the subject matter of each view gradually evolved from simple actions to quotidian scenes to comic films, in which a practical joke was staged as a single picture. One of the most famous films was undoubtedly *The Arrival of a Train at La Ciotat,* in which a locomotive was featured entering the station. The spectators, unaware of the cinematographic process, could not differentiate reality from this new "impression" of reality. Consequently, many of the panic-stricken audience members jumped out of their seats.

Although Louis Lumière is often referenced as the main protagonist in the invention proceedings, Auguste acted as his technical adviser. The new operators were instructed by Louis how to film, print, and

The Cinématographe (Photo courtesy of the Museum of Modern Art/Film Stills Archive).

The first film *Workers Leaving the Lumière Factory* (*La sortie des usines Lumière à Lyon*) filmed on March 19, 1895 (Photo courtesy of the Museum of Modern Art/Film Stills Archive).

project their films. In addition, they were taught how to regulate slow
or accelerated motions with their hand-cranked cameras. From now
on, the new cameramen—around fifty operators, including Félix Mes-
guich, Eugène Promio, Charles Moisson, Francis Doublier, Gabriel
Veyre, and Maurice Sestier—would command all technical processes,
since many effects required actors to perform against a background of
previously prepared film. They ventured outside to capture the real
world and brought back 1,500 films, discovering new technical skills,
such as the first traveling shots (called panoramic views at the time)
from a train platform or Venetian gondola.[10] The high quality of these
views and the technical expertise are astounding. Despite the phenomenal success of the Cinématographe, however, the Lumières ended all
productions in 1905, returning to their main activity, photography,
especially color photography[11] (1904) and the introduction in France
of the *autocrome* process (1907). In conclusion, despite the ongoing
dispute of film historians regarding the paternity of motion pictures,
chronology attributes December 28, 1895, as the starting point of the
Cinématographe's commercialization as a projection device. By 1900,
at the Exposition universelle de Paris, other manufacturers, who had
already joined the competition, such as the Pathé brothers (Charles
and Emile), Léon Gaumont, and Raoul Grimoin-Sanson, directly laid
the groundwork for the future film industry.

GEORGES MÉLIÈS AND THE ADVENTURE OF THE FILM STUDIO

At the antithesis of the Lumière cinema, which mainly focused on the
documentary and the reproduction of reality, stood Georges Méliès
(1861–1938), whose films explored new frontiers within fantasy fiction, trick film, and elaborate mise-en-scène. Despite the international
fame of the Lumière Cinématographe, film historians traditionally
consider Georges Méliès the first genuine artist of motion pictures.
Unlike the Lumière brothers, Méliès did not have a technical background, but rather a persuasive artistic inclination toward theater,
visual illusion, prestidigitation, and magic. In 1888, Méliès bought
the Robert Houdin Theatre, which specialized in magic shows and
performed numerous popular attractions on stage. It is evident that
this theatrical background coupled with a high dose of magical tricks
laid the groundwork for his future cinematic feats of skill. Although
one of the thirty-three spectators on the night of December 28, 1895,
Georges Méliès's request to purchase the revolutionary camera/projec-
tor was denied by the inventors themselves. Far from being discouraged, in 1896 Méliès turned to Englishman R. W. Paul—the Lumière
brothers' main competitor in Europe—who by then retailed his own

Georges Méliès's studio in Montreuil (1861–1938): the pioneer of special effects and film as an entertainment form (Photo courtesy of the Museum of Modern Art/ Film Stills Archive).

Georges Méliès's *Trip to the Moon* (*Le voyage dans la lune*, 1902).

version of Edison's Kinetoscope, called the Theatrograph. Eventually
Méliès rebuilt and ameliorated the camera himself before venturing
into cinematography.

During the last years of the nineteenth century, cinematographic
creativity, already debilitated by a generalized artistic plagiarism, was
at its lowest level, and the newly born cultural medium struggled to
renew its limited genres. French film, however, led by Georges Méliès's
audacious vision, breathed fresh life into the new medium and became
a popular form of entertainment in Europe. Méliès rapidly revealed the
scope of his talent and imagination by adding special effects onto the
film stock, as he developed a series of jointly artistic and technical
views in his own style. Although his very first films were merely
remakes of short Lumière-style views (never more than 60 feet), the
newcomer to filmmaking achieved his first editing special effect, in
October 1896, in a film entitled "The Conjuring of a Woman at the
House of Robert Houdin" (*L' escamotage d'une dame chez Robert Houdin*).
During the shooting, he interrupted the sequence for a few seconds
while filming the actress, then resumed without her for the second
take. This resulted in her sudden "vanishing" and inspired Méliès for
more trick films to come, for example, "The One-Man Band" (*L'homme
orchestre,* 1900) and "The Man with the Rubber Head" *(L'homme à la
tête en caoutchouc,* 1901). Therefore, by using the narrative device of the
Robert Houdin Theatre on the screen, Georges Méliès may be considered the first storyteller in film history. In 1897, he built his own
studio—the first film studio ever made—inside his house in
Montreuil-sous-Bois, as well as his own film production company
named Star-Film, whose slogan was revealing of his artistic vision: *Le
monde à portée de la main* (The world is within reach). There, between
five hundred and six hundred films were produced during the next
fifteen years (seventy-eight films in the first year alone), films that
helped shape the artistic and technical canons of cinematography.

With a myriad of special effects, superimpositions, double or more
exposure, fade in, fade out, and painted-scenery backgrounds, Méliès
generated a brand-new style. Méliès's major contribution was the organization of his fictional compositions around modern concepts of
filmmaking, such as scenario, costumes, makeup, background set, editing cuts, and, of course, actors. Since his camera was always used in
a fixed position and almost never pivoted, secured on its tripod, or
moved toward or away from its subject, its cumbersome and stationary
setup certainly could not enable viewers to enjoy different views compared with theater spectators. Well aware of his element, Méliès compensated on the visual effect of technical editing, recalling his
memorable accidental anecdote of 1898, when his film stock became
stuck inside the camera, thereby creating a sophisticated visual effect

later called "stop motion." While filming a carriage in the Place de la Bastille, the projection showed the carriage suddenly becoming a hearse. Needless to say, this involuntary editing trick inspired countless imitators. Méliès created trick photography with the simple treatment of the camera; he carried out delightful alterations by stopping it and changing the scene, and achieved the impression of backward movement by rotating the camera upside down and inverting the film. The first infatuation of the public, evermore enthusiastic for the revolutionary entertainment, rapidly evolved into an increasing demand for new visual forms (longer views, more narrative with a real story line, and increased sophistication). In 1903, the average length of film was six minutes (over 300 feet). By 1910, each film lasted an average of approximately fifteen minutes (900 feet).

However, Méliès did not take his fervent inspiration from everyday life, as the Lumière documentaries did (although he shot *The Dreyfus Affair/L'affaire Dreyfus* in 1899), but rather from a fantastic world of fairy tales and magic. *Trip to the Moon* (*Le voyage dans la lune,* 1902) constituted thirty chapters and required three months of shooting, a high production cost for a total length of eleven minutes. Méliès's film, which premiered in Paris, was the first important production in French film history. The story narrates the vicissitudes of the scientist Barbenfouillis (played by Georges Méliès himself), president of the Astronaut Club, who, accompanied by six scholars, begins his journey into space. A giant cannon projects the group in a shuttle toward the moon. Once on the moon, they are caught by a snowstorm and seek refuge within a cave. Inside, the inhabitants of the planet, the Sélénites, capture them and take them prisoner to the court of the king. Able to escape, the astronauts flee and regain their space shuttle. The shuttle falls vertically through space into the ocean and is brought safely back to port, where the heroes are celebrated. Inspired by Jules Verne's fantastic literature, the film's mise-en-scène no longer represented cinema as a show, but rather an experimental format of filmed narrative (usually utilizing a series of tableaux).[12] Faithful to its initial aesthetic, Méliès's camera, fixed in the rear of the studio, was predestined to present mainly long shots and as a result conveyed a claustrophobic sensation.

Despite an obvious but vain effort to copyright his productions, Méliès was never entirely able to control the distribution of his films in competition with larger film companies, and to his detriment, many counterfeit versions emerged all around Europe and the United States. To protect the copyrights of his films distributed in the United States, Méliès's own brother, Gaston, went to America in 1902 in an effort to represent Méliès's interests, but to no avail. His final film, "Conquest of the Pole" (*A la conquête du pôle,* 1912), clearly heralded the reason

for Méliès's decline and commercial failure. The public grew bored
with the repetitive aspect of narration and the immobility of the
camera. Overwhelmed by the illegal copies distributed abroad, in
particular in the United States, Méliès went bankrupt in just a few
years. He was forced to sell the Théâtre Houdin, his own studio in
Montreuil, and eventually to withdraw entirely from production in
1912. Méliès did not teach anyone. Although endowed with visionary
talent, he never adjusted to the rapidly evolving film industry. His
cinematographic career finished, he had to resort to selling manufactured toys in a concession stand at the Montpartnasse train station in
Paris. Nicknamed the "magician of Montreuil," or the *homme-orchestre*
(one-man band) of French cinema, Méliès opened the door to modern
cinema. His humor, juvenile passion for fictional tales, elaborate background sets, and special effects inspired many American filmmakers,
from D. W. Griffith to Steven Spielberg, making Méliès the forefather
of modern cinematic science fiction.

GROWTH OF A NATIONAL CINEMA: CHARLES
PATHÉ AND LÉON GAUMONT

French cinema was the first to organize its own film industry and with
this strength to assert itself as an authentic art form. Following the
invention of the Cinématographe, many state fairs, variety shows,
vaudeville houses, rented theaters, music halls, café-concerts, and even
fairground tents adopted the new medium to attract popular audiences.
Mainly suburban, French film viewers originated at the very beginning
from working-class origins. A decade later, French cinema slowly
turned its back on fair attractions and embraced theatrical traditions,
aspiring to reach larger audiences mainly by targeting a middle-class
audience.[13]

In 1896, Charles Pathé (1863–1957) and his three brothers, Emile,
Théophile, and Jacques, all businessmen who specialized in the commerce of phonographs, created the Société Pathé Frères Company in
response to their vision of cinema as a possible future industry. After
acquiring George Eastman's European patent right, for film-stock production, film sales soared, and the rapid expansion of the firm made
Pathé the largest film production company in the world. During the
very first years (until 1906), the principal goal was the mass production
of films, averaging six a week, mainly targeted to fairground managers
and popular audiences. While commercializing both projectors and
films, the rising company successfully persuaded most of its clients to
enter the profession of exhibition, consequently creating an increasing
demand for the Pathé product. With the collaboration of engineer

Henri Joly, the company, first located in Vincennes, then in Joinville-le-Pont, began to construct film projectors (Eknétographe).

After 1906, Pathé production was in full swing, with an average of ten films a week. With the rapid increase of public demand, many new film companies entered the motion picture business. In addition to the two giant film companies, Pathé and Gaumont (see below), several others contributed to the growth of French cinema: Eclipse, Lux, and Eclair studios (the latter stopping its production in 1919). Société Pathé Frères specialized in fast productions, then reinvested the profits in the company's agenda for the enhancement of the technical quality of the company's films. Each company strove to secure economic success through original technical innovations to develop productions. One of the major steps was to finance swiftly the establishment of film studios with the organization of professional technical crews. After 1902, Pathé developed a branch network in Europe (Milan, London, and Berlin) and the United States (New York) with its most active partner, Pathé Exchange, thus creating a formidable system for mass-producing motion pictures. Increasingly dependent on the supply of blank film stock released principally by American companies, Pathé manufactured its first French film stock in 1909. Motivated by competition abroad, Pathé soon became an important outlet for nickelodeon equipment in the United States as it made many types of phonographs and movie projector equipment.

By 1905, Pathé employed several production teams of directors, chief operators, screenwriters, set designers, and actors to make short films in an assembly line process. In August 1907, Charles Pathé decided to halt sales in favor of implementing a system of rentals through an efficient distribution network, the main concept of which is still in practice. Prior to this, films were simply considered a fair attraction, ambulatory entertainment all over France, whose exhibition concept was based on the sale of films (the price was determined by a film's length in meters). Film prints were used until they wore out. Once out of service, the film stocks were sent to the Pathé company in Joinville-le-Pont, where they were melted and recast into new film stock. From the summer of 1907 on, Pathé films screened in theaters were rented to theater management through an influential newcomer: the distribution company. Pathé also began to purchase movie theaters. This "triple organization" of the film industry also triggered the implementation of a new vertical integration of the cinema industry: production, distribution, and exhibition. The other significant contribution of the Pathé Company to French cinema was the introduction of the newsreel to theaters. A pioneer in the birth of newsreel footage, which in turn became the forerunner of commercialized current-events footage, Pathé began to screen, in 1908, the first cinematographic newsreels, through the creation of a new project labeled *Pathé-Journal*. Subsequently, Pathé's major rival, Gaumont, also implemented similar footage with *Gaumont-Actualités*.

During the years just preceding World War I, the presence of French cinema in the world market of films was enormous. According to film historian Jean-Pierre Jeancolas, the Pathé studios alone sold twice as many films to the United States as all American studios combined.[14] In addition, by 1910, two-thirds of the world film production was by French companies. The collapse of Europe, ensnared in the international conflict, as well as the rise of new West Coast investors, initiated America's slow but solid domination in film, which continues to this day. During the last years before the war, Pathé had begun to shift its commercial ambition toward distribution and exhibition, gradually reducing its overall production. The American presence in European markets became an ever-increasing reality, since most film manufacturers and crews were requisitioned for the war effort. As a result, the American branch of Pathé, Pathé Exchange, ensured the survival of the entire international corporation. After 1918, however, it began to disassemble its own multinational conglomerate by selling, one by one, its branches in Italy and the United States. It was renamed Pathé-Consortium, until it was sold to Bernard Natan, becoming Pathé-Natan. In 1930, Charles Pathé retired from the group. With the increasingly dominating presence of American films in the world market, Pathé, like Gaumont (see below), progressively limited its activity to distribution (it resumed its production after World War II). Among the most important names who worked for Pathé were Ferdinand Zecca, Albert Capellani,[15] and Max Linder.

Despite Pathé's commercial supremacy in the French cinema world, no attempt was ever made to secure a monopoly, as smaller companies such as Gaumont[16] and Eclair confidently competed. As a major rival of Pathé, although smaller in size and ambition, the Gaumont Company, founded in 1895, initially specialized in the sale of photographic cameras and projectors (Chronophotographe: a camera-projection device engineered by Georges Demenÿ) and in 1902, in a sound system called Chronophone, which was the equivalent of a record player synchronized to the action on screen. Under Léon Gaumont (1864–1946), the company immediately entered the film industry with the prospect of diversification of production (especially projection devices). From 1897 to 1907, Gaumont delegated the responsibility of film production to his own secretary, Alice Guy (1873–1968), who became the first female filmmaker (*La fée aux choux,* 1896), completing over two hundred films through 1920.[17] The company soon expanded to laboratories and movie theaters throughout France, and in the early 1900s, new movie houses began to replace popular boulevard theaters. Later, in 1906, it took the name SEG (Société des Etablissements Gaumont). In 1911, Gaumont, an industrious pacesetter in the development of motion picture equipment,[18] inaugurated what was at the time the largest movie theater in the world, the Gaumont Palace (3,000 seats). It included an orchestra pit and was equipped with two projectors, allowing a seamless transition between reels. In Paris and other large cities, the most sophisticated theaters usually included an orchestra (from a piano to a small ensemble), and, on rare occasions, some attempts were made to synchronize the dialogue with a live performance from actors or singers hidden behind the screen.[19] However, the most common practice was known as the *synchronisation vivante* or *effet de réel,* which consisted of reading intertitles to the public. The amplification of the soundtrack began in 1908 with Gaumont's Chronomégaphone, which often presented defective sound by capturing intrinsic noise that caused some disturbance during projections. Many renowned filmmakers worked under Gaumont's patronage, such as Léonce Perret (*Child of Paris/L'enfant de Paris,* 1913), Louis Feuillade, Victorin Jasset, Émile Cohl,[20] Etienne Arnaud, Romeo Bossetti, Marcel L'Herbier, and the Belgian, Jacques Feyder. Léon Gaumont finally retired in 1929, and the firm merged with two other film companies to become the GFFA (Gaumont-Franco-Film-Aubert) in 1930.

THE INVENTION OF GENRES: LOUIS FEUILLADE AND MAX LINDER

As the majority of early film artists failed to expand the scope of their production or to renew the paradigm of scenarios, the taste of popular audiences began to evolve toward more sophisticated plots and genres. Therefore, the demand for a wider variety of genres became more and more apparent among moviegoers. The pioneers of the silent era, quickly aware of the unconditional change, began to work in all different genres: documentary (Louis and Auguste Lumière), comedy (Max Linder), melodrama (Ferdinand Zecca), crime series (Louis Feuillade), historical reconstruction, and science fiction (as discussed, Georges Méliès).

The comedy genre, steadily the most popular, gave French cinema its first national and international stars, like Max Linder (1883–1925). Born Gabriel-Maximilien Leuvielle, Linder entered the acting profession through the Conservatoire de Bordeaux, under the pseudonym of Lacerda. In 1905, he moved to Paris to play his first supporting role in a full-length film with Pathé: *La première sortie d'un collégien.* After discovering that his real specialty was comedy (*Je voudrais un enfant,* 1909; *Un mariage à l'italienne, Les débuts d'un yachtman, La malle au*

mariage, 1912; and others), he created the character of Max, a young
and elegant dandy from the upper class, a womanizer on occasion, who
relentlessly found himself in trouble by indulging in burlesque chases
typically leading to a comical denouement. Like his successors Charlie
Chaplin, Buster Keaton, and Harold Lloyd, Linder was small in stature, and his tiny features enabled him to stand in marked contrast to
his movie adversaries. Max Linder wrote and directed most of his films
from 1910 until his induction in World War I (*Max, Professeur de
Tango,* 1912). Following a gas attack while on the front, he contracted
a severe pneumonia, and never fully recovered. Linder's increasing fame
in France and Europe nevertheless led to a Hollywood contract with
Essanay Studios. His image corresponded with a situational and elaborated slapstick comedy type, which mainly coincided with a parody
of romantic melodramas and classical tragedies. Endowed with a wild
imagination and an inexhaustible source of gags, Linder may accurately
be labeled the first international movie star from 1905 to 1924. In
1921, he returned to Hollywood to set up his own production company. His fragile health compelled him to spend long sessions in a
sanatorium, however, and after a last film, *Le roi du cirque* (1924),
following a crisis of neurasthenia, he committed suicide in Paris.

What may best be remembered about Max Linder's contribution to
the comedy genre was, above all, a new dimension for comic plot.
More elaborated and less vulgar, his new take on vaudeville influenced
many imitators worldwide. In addition, the chase genre, which characteristically represented a character frantically running after another,
was by far the most praised of all forms of film comedy, since it
somehow compensated for the lack of camera motions and the almost
total absence of sequence editing (at the time, one shot often corresponded to one scene, and the finished product featured a series of
scenes, not shots). Linder's legacy to world cinematography was temporarily neglected by film historians, until a rediscovery in the 1960s
placed the French actor alongside Chaplin.

The second most popular genre was represented by the so-called
historical reconstructions or period dramas. At the end of the first
decade of the twentieth century, an extraordinary array of important
feature films were targeted toward serious artistic filmmaking, gathering the most important artists of the time (screenwriters, playwrights,
actors, and composers). Because the French public displayed an obvious
taste for reconstituted current affairs, certain filmmakers did not hesitate to adopt the new genre, for example, Méliès's 1899 re-creation of
the *affaire Dreyfus* (Dreyfus scandal) in eleven episodes.[21]

In 1907, a film company labeled Film d'Art aimed to produce one
of the most ambitious historical films ever made. Because of the high
expectations of audiences, many film companies did not hesitate to

Max Linder (1883–1925), (Photo courtesy of the Museum of Modern Art/Film Stills Archive).

take a risk on their financial investments, for instance, the 1908 production by two distinguished members of the Comédie Française, André Calmettes and Charles Le Bargy's *The Assassination of the Duc de Guise* (*L'assassinat du duc de Guise,* 1908). This flamboyant production, the accompanying score of which was written by Camille Saint-Saëns, experienced national acclaim and remained a cultural landmark in French film history for many years. It ultimately failed, however, to take the necessary critical distance from the origin of its inspiration, namely, the stage (many film historians even considered it the forerunner of the future "canned theater").[22] The national success of *The Assassination of the Duc de Guise* encouraged many imitators such as Pathé's Série d'art, Gaumont's Film esthétique, and Eclair's Association cinématographique des auteurs dramatiques. However, in the 1920s, the historical genre quickly lost ground at the French box office and ended its productions with the advent of sound.

Among the successful genres of the first decade of French cinema, *drames sentimentaux,* or melodramas, were regularly praised by the public. One of its most famous directors was the Corsican-born Ferdinand Zecca (1863–1946), who entered the film industry in 1899 under Charles Pathé in the production of phonographic cylinders. Zecca is one of the most significant cinema pioneers, challenging Méliès's historic position. In 1900, when Charles Pathé moved away from his brothers and created a new studio in Vincennes, he brought in Zecca to give the young company a new stamina and flair in film design. Zecca eventually persuaded Pathé to widen the scope of the studios' film catalog (mainly documentaries) and to embrace fiction projects. Later, Zecca was designated to represent the Pathé Company at the 1900 Exposition Universelle. Like Méliès, Zecca carried his initial inspiration into the popular-theater scene, directing the crime melodrama *Histoire d'un crime* (1902), as well as the realist and moralist *Les victimes de l'aloolisme* (1902). *Histoire d'un crime* is the story of a murderer (Jean Liezer), who, after killing a bank employee, is arrested in a nearby café. While in prison, he relives his past through a series of dreams until the day of his execution. The realist element, omnipresent throughout the story line, was directly inspired by French popular theater of the turn of the century. Police authorities, however, imposed their censorship on the film, compelling Zecca to remove certain shots, in particular the final execution scene. The major innovation of the film relied on its thematic approach to the melodramatic narratives and its biting social commentary. The juxtaposition of past and present within the same scene was an important technical and stylistic innovation for the early silent film era. Following consecutive productions of a biblical narrative, *La passion de notre Seigneur* (1902), and a reenactment of true events *The Flying Machine (La conquête de l'air,* 1902), Zecca was promoted to general manager of the Charles Pathé film company in 1910. He moved to New Jersey a couple of years later to manage the American branch of Pathé Exchange, returning to France in 1920 to lead the Pathé-Baby Company, producers of cameras.

One of the most characteristic features of French cinema in the early 1900s was the interest in the so-called *ciné-romans,* also described as serials. Mostly crime serials, they were usually action-oriented narrations evolving around one type of subject matter or even a single main character. With this genre, one can easily recognize the special relationship between popular literature and the seventh art, which was one of the most significant characteristics of the early silent films in France.[23] Set designer and filmmaker Victorin Jasset (1862–1913) is the inventor or forefather of the cinematographic thriller, having taken his inspiration from the American-newspaper comic strip. He directed *Aventures de Nick Carter* (1906–11), the origin of the serial. This genre was popularized through the talents of Louis Feuillade (1873–1925), who used famous Parisian locations and evoked a new atmosphere of suburbia. Due to the ruthless (but mostly civil) competition between the major film companies during the mid-1910s, Pathé's American associate Pathé Exchange launched the American actress Pearl White with a series of films dedicated to the *Mystères de New York* and the *Exploits d'Elaine* (eighty episodes by 1915). In the meantime, American filmmaker Raoul Walsh developed the genre in America with *The Gangster and the Girl* (1914) and *Regeneration* (1915). Interestingly enough, the predominant themes of early French thrillers revolved around the representation of redemption as the criminal character begins to regret his crimes.

Eager to respond to Pathé's commercial operation, Gaumont launched its own crime-thriller series with the contributions of Louis Feuillade and his popular characters, such as the detective Jean Dervieux, played by René Navarre (*Le proscrit, L'oubliette, La course aux millions,* 1912). Journalist for the right-wing royalist press, Feuillade began writing scenarios for Gaumont around 1905 and became a director after 1906. In 1907, he was chosen as new head of production in charge of supervising all Gaumont productions. Although his career included more than six hundred films and more than one hundred scenarios, Feuillade is remembered for the Fantômas series: *Fantômas* (1913), *Juve contre Fantômas* (*Juve against Fantômas,* 1913), *Le mort qui tue* (*The Dead Man Who Killed,* 1913), *Le faux magistrat* (1914), and *Fantômas contre Fantômas* (*Fantômas against Fantômas,* 1914). In 1913, Feuillade adapted the famous serial *Fantômas,* written by Pierre Souvestre and Marcel Allain, which by then had already become a popular classic. Fantômas, genius of evil and "Emperor of Crime," was a negative hero who challenged the police authority, led by the incorruptible police Inspector Juve, and Jerôme Fandor, a reporter for the newspaper *La Capitale.* Through concealed identities and various astute stratagems, the protagonist robs, tortures, and kills countless victims all over Paris, and naturally escapes in daring rescues. Later, Feuillade continued with the new series *Les Vampires,* followed by another one called *Judex.* The prestige Feuillade exerted on the early thriller was predominant until the mid 1920s. Gaumont's *Les Vampires* responded in a way to Pathé's earlier serial, *Les mystères de New York,* produced by the American division of Pathé and released from November 1915 to June 1916. *Les Vampires* was a ten-episode serial, which namely reiterated the fantastic elements present in the Fantômas films. At the same time, it surpassed them in depth by adding a new dimension of corrosive wit, nightmarish events, filmic pragmatism, fictional horror, and sardonic humor. *Les Vampires* was a sort of criminal fresco under the form of popular *ciné-roman* and featured the exploits of bloodthirsty thieves led by the unconquerable and mysterious Irma Vep (anagram for vampire), whose erotically charged female body would mesmerize audiences. Practicing mass or serial murders, kidnapping, poison gas, and sexual domination to gain physical and psychological power over Parisian bourgeoisie, the vampires exerted, on and off screen, an unprecedented shocking fascination among the French. For instance, the corresponding role of inspector Juve (from the Fantômas series), the hero played by journalist Philippe Guérande (Edouard Maté), became even more passionate and excessive in his unpromising task eventually to capture the gang of vampires. On a purely aesthetic level, the representation of the villain itself in black tights and aggressive makeup rendered the concept of crime films even more disturbing for audiences of the 1910s. Upon the release of its very first episodes, the French Ministry of the Interior temporarily forbade a couple of sequences since the film represented the deference of organized crime. In the history of crime serial film, *Les Vampires* often triggered greater popular and critical attention when compared to the Fantômas series because of its modern mythology, which entered directly into the mass culture of the early decades of the twentieth century.

The existence of the popular series was short-lived, however, as a result of the worsening conditions of the war, as well as the need to shoot many sequences outdoors due to a serious lack of material, indirectly generating some incoherence within the story line. However, the myth of Fantômas and the vampires was seminal in the development of suspense films and thrillers throughout Europe during the 1920s. It also inspired Surrealist artists—most likely for its outward sign for provocation and disorder—and directly influenced the German Expressionist artists of the decade. Championed by the Parisian Surrealist artists for its latent anarchist look and the modernity of its plots, the Fantômas series even had its own fan club. Guillaume Apollinaire, together with Max Jacob, founded the *Société des Amis de Fantômas* in 1913. In addition to the direct aftermath of its popularity, Feuillade's adaptation commanded considerable attention during the 1920s, as writers, such as Blaise Cendrars, Jean Cocteau, and Robert Desnos, and artists, such as Juan Gris, Yves Tanguy, and René Magritte, assimilated the Fantômas motif into their work, and in particular authors with their automatic writing. This trend was all the more paradoxical, since the authors of the Fantômas series, as well as Feuillade himself, stood light-years away from the political and aesthetic belief of the Surrealists themselves. In reality, the intensely "fantastic poetics" of Fantômas surpassed the intended initial ideological limitations of its production. One of the reasons for the apparent lack of logical scenario development in the series that attracted the Surrealists was the absence of actors because of the war. Actors were mostly working during their free time before returning to the front, which resulted in a discontinued quality to films. Falling into oblivion with the coming of sound, and despite the Surrealists' endeavors to perpetuate his legacy by professing the sharpest admiration for him, Feuillade was only rehabilitated subsequent to World War II (1939–45) thanks to a group of assiduous *cinéphiles*. One of them was Henri Langlois, who rescued many of his films after 1936 with the creation of the French *ciné-club* (film club) with filmmakers such as Georges Franju (cofounder of the Cinémathèque française), Alain Resnais, François Truffaut, Jean-Luc Godard, and Luis Buñuel.

AVANT-GARDE CINEMA, FRENCH IMPRESSIONISM, AND SURREALISM: LOUIS DELLUC, ABEL GANCE, MARCEL L'HERBIER, LUIS BUÑUEL, AND RENÉ CLAIR

With the emergence of abstract art, Dada, and Surrealism—the movement founded by André Breton—in the arts and literature, the seventh art was soon incorporated as a new, experimental, yet prolific medium. One of the most significant reasons for the growing presence of French Impressionism, along with commercially oriented productions, can be explained by the difficult economic times, which penalized the French film industry. Consequently, many film producers, who had already lost their financial edge on international markets, were open to the experimentation of an alternative type of cinema. Because many French film companies were small businesses, mostly specializing in the distribution and exhibition of Hollywood product, they tended to avoid investing in problematic national productions, which, aside from facing high taxes, never guaranteed profit.[24]

Avant-garde filmmakers' main goal was to explore cinema as an art. With a new personal vision of the artist, the Avant-garde transposed through cinema the processes of deconstruction involved in literature and found its landmark with artist-authors such as Colette, Jean Cocteau, Blaise Cendrars, Guillaume Apollinaire, André Breton, Pierre MacOrlan, Cubist painter Fernand Léger, and photographer Man Ray. Although Avant-garde film theorists claimed that the new style was a synthesis of the other arts, all unanimously rejected the inspirational

potential of stage drama; their focus remained graphic and not narrative. Considered a cinema of "intellectuals for intellectuals," French
Avant-garde films—whether Impressionistic or Surrealist—represented
a collective initiative from many different artists (mostly novelists) and
were led by one film theoretician, Louis Delluc (1890–1924). Formerly
a journalist and literary critic at *Le journal du Ciné-Club* then *Cinéa*,
Delluc began to write screenplays for directors such as Germaine Dulac
(1882–1942) for her *La fête espagnole* (*Spanish Fiesta*, 1919), as well as
her best film, *The Smiling Madame Beudet* (*La souriante Madame Beudet*,
1923) and *The Little Kid* (*Gossette*, 1923), or for Jean Epstein (1897–
1953) with *The Red Inn* (*L'auberge rouge*, 1923). Although a fervent
admirer of Hollywood cinema, which at the time represented a majority of all screenings in France, Delluc's stance and crusade, much like
the *Cahiers du cinéma*'s three decades later, pleaded the cause of film
criticism and film education as well as a new cinema liberated from
the dictatorship of drama scenarios and literary adaptations. Along
with many other film critics, Delluc, who had turned director during
the war years, entertained the hope that cinema could constitute a
liberated form of popular culture mainly through symbolic expression
and psychological explorations. Using original scenarios, Delluc underscored the crucial importance of a photogenic aesthetic as filmic language; his films *Fever* (*Fièvre*, 1921), a melodramatic story ambianced
in the seaport atmosphere of Marseille, and *The Woman from Nowhere*
(*La femme de nulle part*, 1922) attested to this aesthetic. In March 1924,
Delluc died suddenly, leaving behind a small but essential legacy for
future film studies. Louis Delluc and Ricciotto Canudo were credited
with forming the first significant *ciné-club* in France, whose members
were prestigious celebrities of the film industry: Jean Epstein, Abel
Gance, Marcel L'Herbier, Germaine Dulac, Colette, and André Gide.
In 1937, his name was chosen for the prize awarded each year to the
best French film (Prix Louis Delluc).

Never able to reach general audiences because of its omnipresent
elements of dark humor, the Surrealist cinema was often scorned in its
early decades by mainstream art and literary critics. Considered a
useless demystification and an impertinent experiment meant to
merely defy aesthetic and social taboos, Surrealist and Avant-gardist
cinema was known to be an art screened for the satisfaction of intellectuals and therefore consisted of low-budget films evolving at the pe-
riphery of the industry. French Avant-garde cinema of the 1920s
usually involved a legal and cultural outcome, as filmmakers stood at
the forefront of the creative process, overtaking the credit of producers
themselves. Directors, such as Cocteau, René Clair, Marcel L'Herbier,
Luis Buñuel, and Jean Renoir, were considered the authors of the films
and could claim intellectual entitlement on the movie once released,

The new style of the Art Déco background set, in Marcel L'Herbier's *The Inhuman One* (*L'inhumaine*, 1924), (Photo courtesy of the Museum of Modern Art/Film Stills Archive).

just like any artist, painter, or musician. For this particular reason, Surrealist cinema developed a persistent nonliterary approach, which displayed an overstated tendency for psychoanalysis rather than narrative, and in some cases it overthrew the already established aesthetic. Whether the authors personalized the screenplay or not, they remained closely connected to the process of production, since they were the ones on the set who were able to scrutinize characters' performance through the camera lens. This *cinéma d'auteurs* (authors cinema), initiated in France prior to the *nouvelle vague* rhetoricians, was the symbolic icon of all great directors, from Abel Gance to Renoir. The Surrealists' enthusiasm for the so-called primitive epoch of silent films resulted in a profusion of new filmmakers, which anticipated the groundbreaking movement of the 1960s French New Wave (mainly poets and authors turned directors).

Far from secluding themselves in a cultural ghetto, the new filmmakers acknowledged the influence of other preceding or contemporary film artists, such as Feuillade's crime serials, the comedies of Charlie Chaplin and Mack Sennett, horror films such as Robert Wiene's *The Cabinet of Dr. Caligari* (1919) or Friedrich Wilhelm Murnau's *Nosferatu* (1922), and many more. With them, a new cinematic language surfaced—visual associations, sudden slow motion, overimpression, nonlinear narrative discourse, a lack of narrative sequencing, and no analytical editing—which was mainly characterized by an absence of logical causality in filmic narration and whose main distinctive feature was to separate and reassemble captured images on an imaginary level. Antonin Artaud, Blaise Cendrars, and Robert Desnos, who wrote many Surrealist film scenarios, reevaluated the conventional narrative structure and content of the interior psychological realm of the dream, and eventually offered a new king of filmmaking through their visual insolence and provocation. One of the initiators of Surrealist filmmaking in France, Luis Buñuel (1900–1983), was an active figure of both silent and sound Surrealist cinema. Characteristic of his work was the rendition of atmospheres designed to upset the so-called bourgeois cinematographic ethics (such as featuring a close-up of an eye being slit by a razor blade) as well as to mock other Avant-garde artists. With the collaboration of Salvador Dalí (who conceived the background set and the experience-dreams), Buñuel adapted to the screen his own poem, entitled "Un perro andaluz," drawn from an earlier book of poems. The short film became known as *An Andalusian Dog* (*Un chien andalou,* 1929). In his elaborated images and aesthetism, Buñuel challenged Avant-garde's emphasis on form and camera "tricks" over subject matter. The contemporary spectator was led through many detours and convoluted psychological associations in the course of this unusual cinematic odyssey, into what could be the exclusive function of a motion picture: the sanitization of reality into a few intervals of passionate desire, antagonism, and ecstasy. The critical success of *The Golden Age* (*L'age d'or,* 1930) secured Buñuel a contract with Metro-Goldwyn-Mayer, which he turned down after a visit to Hollywood in 1930. In 1946, Buñuel moved to Mexico, where many of Spain's intellectuals and artists had emigrated after the Spanish Civil War. He returned to Europe only in the 1960s (see chapter 5).

Authors such as René Clair and Marcel L'Herbier advocated for diversity in technical innovation and offered extraordinary Art Déco set productions (for example, designs by Robert Mallet-Stevens for *Money/L'argent,* 1928). This new modern look of background set, directly influenced by the Art Déco style recently launched at the 1925 Paris Exposition des arts décoratifs et industriels modernes, became one of the major visual trademarks of Impressionist films such as L'Herbier's *The Late Mathias Pascal* (*Feu Mathias Pascal,* 1925), and *The Inhuman One* (*L'inhumaine,* 1924). Background sets were designed by artists Fernand Léger and Robert Mallet-Stevens. Born Marcel L'hebarium, Marcel L'Herbier (1888–1979), a playwright, poet, and essayist, was assigned to the cinematographic unit in the French army during World War I. As an influential figure in the development of the French Avant-garde, L'Herbier's films regularly integrated works of notorious artists from other fields, including painter Fernand Léger and architect Mallet-Stevens. L'Herbier's experimental silent films and theoretical writing exerted a strong influence on cineasts, such as Alberto Cavalcanti and Claude Autant-Lara. However, with the coming of the sound era, L'Herbier's passage to the new medium proved difficult, as his apparent, solid innovative vision shifted to produce mainstream films of average quality. One of L'Herbier's most significant contributions to film history was his responsibility for the establishment of the Institut des hautes études cinématographiques (IDHEC) in 1943. There, many future celebrated filmmakers began their apprenticeships: Alain Resnais, Louis Malle, Costa-Gavras, Claude Sautet, and Patrice Leconte, to name a few.

Along with the Surrealist movement, which could never reconcile popular and intellectual audiences, many filmmakers of the 1920s followed the lead of Impressionist artists as they successfully blurred the frontier between accessible entertainment and art. Perhaps the most famous name among all French filmmakers of the silent era is Abel Gance (1889–1981). Gance began his career as a dramatic stage actor and screenwriter. After appearing in his first film, *Molière,* in 1909, and writing a few scenarios for Gaumont, Gance was drawn toward a more unconventional production type. His films were characterized by epic subject matter and historical figures. Following his first national success, *The Wheel* (*La roue,* 1923), a new style surfaced among French filmmakers, a new Romanesque eloquency through motion pictures. Adapted from Pierre Hamp's novel *La roue,* this lengthy melodrama narrated the sentimental but tempestuous relationship between two characters, Norma (Ivy Close) and Sisif (Séverin Mars), a railroad machinist who after adopting Norma as an orphan later develops a passion for her as an adult. With more than a year of shooting, an endless montage sequence (a meticulous editing procedure that trimmed the film's duration from thrity-two to twelve reels), reduced from eight hours to four hours of projection, and three years in production, *La roue* heralded Gance's future Impressionist initiatives, which shaped the last years of French silent cinema. Gance's style already had taken shape as he successfully demonstrated proficiency in new filmic techniques, introducing the panoramic screen, sound perspective, and the superimposition of shots. In addition, the characters' mental states were faithfully rendered through a series of fast-cut editing, generating an idiosyncratic visual rhythm. But for many film historians, the turning point of Abel Gance's career occurred with his masterpiece, *Napoléon* (1927), or *Napoléon vu par Abel Gance,* starring the mesmerizing Albert Dieudonné. First conceived for a triple screen, Gance envisioned, then orchestrated, an innovative version of wide-screen vision, which employed three synchronized cameras to be projected on three separate frames (triptych screen). Gance's cinematographers (among whom was the young Henri Alekan) achieved a new fluidity in their camera work that resulted in high realism and a fast editing style (for example, cameras flying through the air on wires, falling off cliffs, or strapped to a runaway horse's back during battle scenes). Gance's original story line, which was implicitly inspired by the format of D. W. Griffith's *The Birth of a Nation,* corresponded to a length of between six and eight hours and was organized around eight chapters: Bonaparte's youth, the French Revolution, Campaign in Italy, Austerlitz, Waterloo, Saint Helena, and so on. The film was all the more revolutionary because of its scope and length. Unfortunately, only the first three chapters were terminated.

With over one thousand extras and a total cost of 20 million French francs, the film severely hampered the stamina of Gance's future film career. Producers became reluctant to endorse his high-budget projects. As a result, Gance never regained any sort of creative control in future assignments. *Napoléon* premiered in Polyvision with a full orchestra on April 27, 1927, at the Opera in Paris. Interestingly enough, several versions of Abel Gance's *Napoléon* were reedited and eventually sonorized in 1935, 1942, 1955, and 1971 (at the initiative of film director Claude Lelouch, *Bonaparte and the Revolution/Bonaparte et la Révolution*). Finally, a reconstructed version of the five hours was released by film historian Kevin Brownlow at the 1979 Telluride Film

Abel Gance's grandiloquent masterpiece, *Napoléon* (1927) a.k.a *Napoléon vu par Abel Gance*, starring the mesmerizing Albert Dieudonné (Photo courtesy of the Museum of Modern Art/Film Stills Archive).

Festival. Two years later, Francis Ford Coppola also screened a longer version at Radio City Music Hall in New York City. Other significant works of Abel Gance include *I Accuse: That They May Live* (*J'accuse!*, 1937), *Blind Venus* (*La Vénus aveugle*, 1941), *Captain Fracasse* (*Le Capitaine Fracasse*, 1942), and *The Tower of Nesle* (*La Tour de Nesle*, 1954). With Abel Gance, the influence of theater obviously remained part of his inherent artistic background with sound individualistic actors' performances, but it was more the concept of mise-en-scène, which was effectively perfected, that appeared as pioneering to many.

The maturity and momentum of French Avant-garde cinema, in particular impressionistic, in the 1920s were partially the result of the growth of the French film spirit in its first and second decade of existence. The final ten years of the silent era laid the groundwork for the prolific new directing talents of the sound structures yet to come (including René Clair, Jean Renoir, Marcel Carné, and Jean Vigo). Born René Chomette, René Clair (1898–1981) began his career as an actor playing in Louis Feuillade's 1921 series *L'orpheline* and *Parisette*. Later, parallel to a writing career (as novelist and essayist), he served as assistant to filmmaker Jacques de Baroncelli. His first silent film, *The Crazy Ray* (*Paris qui dort*), was completed in 1923, but the real turning point for Clair occurred with a short film entitled *Entr'acte* (1924), featuring many celebrities of the decade (painters, writers, musicians, and journalists). The film, which initially was destined to serve as a visual intermission before features, was later screened at the famous Studio des Ursulines in Paris. Clair's *Entr'acte* was also reminiscent of the aforementioned automatic writing (*écriture automatique*) so dear to the Surrealist movement, and its techniques of intense emotional manipulation of audiences' unconscious desires. Clair's most significant silent films include *The Imaginary Voyage* (*Le voyage imaginaire,* 1925), *Prey of the Wind* (*La proie du vent,* 1926), and *An Italian Straw Hat* (*Un chapeau de paille d'Italie,* 1927), starring Albert Préjean, Olga Tchekowa, and Marise Maïa. Adapted from the famous Eugène Labiche's vaudeville, *An Italian Straw Hat* was a combination of American-style chase movies and trademark French Impressionism. The critical success of the film gave René Clair the confidence and momentum to renew an almost similar experience a few years later. At the beginning of the talking-pictures era, he directed *The Million* (*Le million,* 1931), which remains one of the very few French musical comedies. Throughout the last years of the silent era, Clair directed some of the most original and admired works of early French cinema, including another landmark musical, *Under the Roofs of Paris* (*Sous les toits de Paris,* 1930), and the great classic social satire *Freedom for Us* (*A nous la liberté,* 1931).

The silent film era would come to an end with two major events, both of which were marked by innovations or events from across the Atlantic Ocean: the invention of the first "talking pictures" in the United States after 1927 and the economic turmoil following the Wall Street crash of October 1929. This new turning point of talking pictures clearly gave the French film industry a new vitality within its creative and organizational structure and heralded the coming of the golden age of French cinema.

Chapter 2
The Golden Age of French Cinema

With the birth of sound in 1927, French cinema of the 1930s was able to reflect all aspects of French society through a major artistic current: poetic realism, a filmmaking era that began with the aftermath of the 1929 stock-market crash through the outbreak of World War II in September 1939. Shaped by seismic social and political events, French filmmakers of the 1930s created masterpieces that some seventy years later stand as landmarks of cinema. With the support of small-scale production companies whose insignificant capital base often could not contract personnel, directors nonetheless produced these great films. Jean Renoir's *Grand Illusion* (*La grande illusion,* 1937), Marcel Carné's *Daybreak* (*Le jour se lève,* 1939), and Jean Vigo's *The Atalante* (*L'Atalante,* 1934) are just a few of the great achievements of the golden age of French cinema. All were strongly influenced by the unrivaled prestige of "populist literature" (*littérature populiste*), a literary movement that included authors such as Pierre MacOrlan and Francis Carco.

THE STYLE OF THE 1930s

The origins of this passionate artistic period go back even before the crash of 1929. For a long time, these difficult years were considered ill-fated since already the cultural and creative movements linked to the 1920s' utopia had vanished with the disastrous aftereffects of World War I. The wreckage of the Great War actually served future conflicts (Hitler seized power in 1933, Franco became the Nationalist leader in Spain in 1936, Austria was invaded by Nazi Germany in 1938). These wounds were forever inscribed within each European nation, and even the most radical Avant-garde streams (Expressionism, Cubism, Dadaism), could not compete with the hastened pace of the 1930s. The hope in progress, the joining of humanism to science within the project of an enlightened new society, where artistic creation would occupy a predominant role, was no longer perceived as historically logical. Taking the long historical view, the decade of the 1930s is today often recognized as a return to order.

Despite the world crisis and the endless debate "extreme right-extreme left," France was successfully able to command international attention by dint of its many artists, scholars, and intellectuals. Above all, it was the 1937 World's Fair in Paris that epitomized the French genius. The great decade also marked the founding of the *aéropostale* (air postal service) and a generation of reckless airplane pilots. Pilot Jean Mermoz multiplied his exploits, creating a link between France and Africa, then later the Andes and the rest of South America. On the seas, the French presented the great ocean liner *Normandie* to the world in 1935. This prodigious ship, a "moving museum" of decorative arts of the time, provided a luxurious escape from the morose atmosphere of the prewar era for its fortunate clientele. French music was also omnipresent in the Western world, with singers like Maurice Chevalier and the composer Maurice Ravel. On the theatrical and literary scene, Sacha Guitry, Jean Cocteau, and Jean Giraudoux remained in the spotlight.

At the turn of the new decade, with the beginning of tragic events such as the political and financial scandal known as the Stavisky affair in 1933, which cast a cloud of corruption on the political system, the rise of fascism in Germany that same year, and the eventual eruption of the Spanish Civil War in 1936, many French Surrealist artists adopted communism or even anarchy as their political inspiration (i.e., Louis Aragon's role in the French Communist Party). In literature, the Surrealists' involvement was lead by André Breton's *Nadja* (*Nadja,* 1928) and Louis Aragon's *Le paysan de Paris* (*The Night-Walker,* 1926). In poetry, Paul Valéry, Paul Claudel, François Mauriac, Saint-John Perse (pseudonym of Alexis Léger), and Paul Eluard dominated. In the field of fiction, the literary scene saw the emergence of some of France's most popular writers, such as realist novelist Antoine de Saint-Exupéry's *Vol de nuit* (*Night Flight,* 1931), who presented a new look from the traditional diary novel form, Marcel Aymé's *La Jument verte*

(*The Green Mare*, 1933), and Jean Giono's *Regain* (*Harvest*, 1930), or spiritual authors such as François Mauriac's *Noeud de vipères* (*Vipers' Tangle*, 1932) and Céline's *Voyage au bout de la nuit* (*Journey to the End of the Night*, 1932). On the stage, the popular successes of Marcel Pagnol's *Marius* (*Marius*, 1929), a colorful comedy of Provence folklore, although ignored by the critics, triggered an immense triumph, resulting in the adaptation of his comedy to the big screen. Jean Cocteau and Jean Giraudoux's *La guerre de Troie n'aura pas lieu* (*Tiger at the Gates*, 1935) also took their work of tragedy to motion pictures. Jean-Paul Sartre's *La nausée* (*Nausea*, 1938) made him one of the leaders of the philosophy of Existentialism, which dominated the postwar era. (Sartre was later awarded a Nobel Prize in literature in 1964, which he refused.) The novels of André Malraux, *La condition humaine* (*Man's Fate*, 1933) and *L'espoir* (*Man's Hope*, 1937), combined lyricism with history, giving a dramatic picture of the Spanish Civil War.

THE "TALKIES"

The 1930s began with the sudden disappearance of silent film productions (first in the United States and rapidly all over Europe a couple of years later). With this technical and aesthetic revolution came the economic crisis of 1929 followed by the Great Depression, debilitating the American continent and resulting in a dramatic relegation of economic activities in Europe, as well as the emergence of several ominous dictatorships. As a result, in terms of the film industry, the 1930s can best be described as an era of reorganization. The industry was drawn closer each year to a government-regulated system (similar to those of Italy and Germany), and was eventually assimilated by the COIC (Comité de l'organisation de l'industrie cinématographique), during the first months of World War II. The COIC was later renamed CNC (Centre national de la cinématographie) in 1946. Within this period came the "talkies." The innovation of sound in motion pictures actually goes all the way back to the invention of the Cinématographe in 1895. The first experimentation with the synchronous dialogue system occurred when Louis Lumière filmed a conversation between Mr. Janssen and Mr. Lagrange, and later that day projected this particular shot during the Congress of the French Photographic Societies (Congrès des sociétés française de photographie) in Lyon on June 12, 1895. Using a primitive form of synchronized dialogue, the two protagonists stood behind the screen during the projection and repeated word for word their initial conversation. During the entire decade of the 1930s, French cinema did not evolve much technologically despite the dramatic historical events that served as a backdrop, but the coming of sound eventually triggered immeasurable effects. The contribution of sound required the standardization of film projection speed (twenty-four images per second), which improved the quality of projection. Film subjects evolved since dialogues allowed the spectator to penetrate the characters' psychology; as a result, the performance of the actors also had to adjust. Actors became living heroes who were known and seen in a different way by the public and served as a sort of landmark to national memory. Silent movies did not allow this "proximity": often superficial, they limited the public's credibility while the spoken word only increased it. Thirty-five years after the invention of motion pictures, actors and actresses could be heard interacting with one another on the screen. The silent era had been superseded forever.

On October 6, 1927, in a New York theater, Warner Brothers' Studios—a failing film company at the time—projected Alan Crossland's *The Jazz Singer,* starring Al Jolson, a giant step for cinematographic history with its memorable "Wait a minute! Wait a minute! You ain't heard nothin' yet!" Although including just a couple of "talking" scenes (a few synchronized dialogues and a song), the film was officially the first talking movie released to the public. In France, Gaumont Studios (with the collaborative efforts of two Danish engineers, Axel Petersen and Arnold Poulsen) had already developed sonorization, but the international marketing for this new cinematographic advancement came too late. One year later, in 1928, three giants from the electrical industry started a "war of licenses" that was resolved with an international compromise. Two American companies, RCA and Western Electric, and one German, Tobis-Klangfilm, delineated the technical standards of the new medium and became responsible for equipping thousands of theaters around the world with costly and complex equipment. In addition, all the silent film studios had to be completely reorganized and refurnished, and ultimately sound booths were now installed to shelter a newcomer: the sound operator. It was only in the fall of 1929, two years after the Americans had accomplished it, that the first studios were entirely equipped in France (studios of Epinay, with a German method, and Billancourt, with the American).

L'Argent, officially remembered as the final film of the silent era, was shown in mid-January 1929 on French boulevards and was followed at Aubert-Palace two weeks later on January 30 by *The Jazz Singer,* which was seen by half a million people during the period of its initial screening. Later that year, on October 22, the first French talking motion picture, *The Queen's Necklace (Le collier de la reine),* played. Although the designation of "first French talking film" has somehow remained a toss-up between André Hugon's *The Three Masks* (*Les trois masques,* 1929, produced in Twickenham for Pathé-Cinéma

Studios) and Gaston Ravel and Tony Lekain's *Le collier de la reine* (1929,
for Gaumont Studios), most film historians believe that the Gaumont
Studios' production was released a day earlier. Nevertheless, neither
film incorporated more than segments of dialogue and songs to accompany the omnipresent musical arrangements. Those productions were
in reality silent movies, to which a musical accompaniment and a few
hasty dialogue scenes were added. The shots were long with a primitive
set, and the camera remained fixed, just as in the time of Méliès.
Technical imperatives took over the mise-en-scène, and actors now
dealt with a cumbersome microphone usually hidden behind a seat or
in a plant. Because dubbing techniques did not benefit from any
significant technological development during the first part of the
1930s, many French as well as other European motion pictures were
filmed and produced in multiple-language versions, either filming on
the very same set with sequencing casts of different nationalities or
even, intermittently, with a single set of actors mouthing words in a
different language while the actual foreign-language speakers were
hiding on the set, out of camera range.[1] For authors and playwrights,
however, this terrible regression actually represented a period of assured prosperity since their plays were quickly adapted to screenplay
and then to the screen. In a similar fashion, songwriters and music hall
singers took advantage of this blooming revolution (it truly was not
before 1930 that French films of authentic importance started to be
produced).[2] However, a great deal of anxiety grew among actors of the
silent era, since they now had to pass the test of sound. Photogenic
presence, until the advent of sound films the only priority, suddenly
became of somewhat secondary importance to the requirement of dic-
tion. Some careers were brought to a screeching halt, such as those of
Abel Gance and Marcel L'Herbier.[3]

In the end, it was the sound operator who became the master of the
game. His judgment on the recording quality and the vocal performance of the players ultimately determined the success of the movie.
The cinematographic voice had to be harmonious, and this was what
benefited theater actors. Although it may seem almost absurd today,
one of the reasons why many critics and professionals of the cinematographic industry at the time did not welcome the new technological
change was a legitimate apprehension that sound pictures would be
artistically confined to the flawless elocution required by dramatic art.
Around 1930, immediately after the revolution of sound (depicted by
René Clair, for instance, as a "redoubtable monster"), the polemic
about its necessity and dangers was for many directors perplexing and
quite contradictory. Jean Renoir, an early supporter of the sound
system and aware of the new artistic potential it could create, was not
contracted to direct feature films between 1928 and 1931, while René

Clair, who resented it, was one of the first filmmakers to use sound resourcefully (*Under the Roofs of Paris*, 1930). Surpassing his initial struggles, Renoir, along with Julien Duvivier, became predominant directors of French cinematic masterpieces of the 1930s, while directors Gance and L'Herbier as noted earlier, among others, struggled with the new requirements imposed by the sound revolution and remained forever trapped in an outdated past. Even Gance, who envisioned *End of the World* (*La fin du monde*, 1930) as a silent movie and later incorporated technical modernization by offering an original sound angle, was unable to circumvent the evermore complicated economics leading at times to commercial fiascos. Film artists and movie critics constantly had to catch up with sound engineers and businessmen of the movie industry who controlled the technical innovations and inventions linked to sound.

Because of the sudden explosion of this new cultural environment, film historians commonly assign a premature disappearance of Avant-garde cinematography around 1930, while in reality several brilliant movies of this type were shot and produced during these very early years, including two feature films subsidized by the Vicomte de Noailles,[4] an affluent and passionate benefactor. Luis Buñuel's *The Golden Age* (*L'âge d'or*, 1930) was achieved with an unaffected independence and impudence. Acclaimed by Surrealist followers, much like his earlier work of 1929, *An Andalusian Dog* (*Un chien andalou*), *The Golden Age* unexpectedly motivated extremists to destroy the opening-night theater and caused the prefect of police to prohibit all further projections of the film.[5]

From 1929 on, French cinema required new stars. In the gigantic Paramount Studios equipped in Joinville-le-Pont, as well as in Berlin for the German film industry, teams shot up to six versions of the same movie to be spoken in different languages. It has been said that France's start was quite slow with the talkies, but no later than 1930, Avant-garde filmmaker René Clair finished *Under the Roofs of Paris* in Epinay, and in the following two years he completed *The Million*, *Freedom for Us*, and *Bastille Day* (*Quatorze juillet*, 1932). With the success of *Under the Roofs of Paris*, Clair became a director with an international reputation, above all in Berlin, where his artistic creations—admired for its dreamlike atmospheres and its technique—had an inspiring effect on a few young directors, most notably Marcel Carné.[6] René Clair's main objective with his first talking movie was to animate, through the support of music and song, the life of the *petit peuple* (middle-class Parisians), which ironically was of course anything but realistic. Scrupulously depicted in a studio by Russian set designer Lazare Meerson, photographer Georges Périnal, and composers Raoul Moretti and René Nazelles, *Under the Roofs of Paris* represented the

Annabella (Anna) and Georges Rigaud (Jean) in René Clair's *Bastille Day* (*Quatorze juillet*, 1932), (Photo courtesy of the Museum of Modern Art/Film Stills Archive).

lives of several protagonists verging on street crime and personal antagonism. Nevertheless, it must be noted that although dealing with a narrative of deep social realism, the director's interest never edged on graphically repulsive and ordinary voyeurism, but rather focused on the mode in which the camaraderie of two partners (Albert Préjean and Gaston Modot) prevailed by solving their contention over a charming but flirtatious young woman (Pola Illery). The film was first presented at the Moulin Rouge in May 1930 as an authentic talkie but did not receive any of its anticipated adulation or even popularity. As paradoxical as it may appear, the international success of *Under the Roofs of Paris* flourished (August 1930 in Berlin, and later that same year in December in New York City) because of its representation of the people of Paris, which precisely corresponded to the clichéd images of Parisian street singers, café ambience, and the popular character of French songs that eventually transformed the film into an emblematic French musical comedy.

René Clair was one of the most eminent French directors during the years of conversion from silent films to sound pictures and is still considered one of the most significant auteurs of the twentieth century. Beginning as an assistant to filmmaker Jacques de Baroncelli, Clair developed a visual inquisitiveness for the Surrealist experience while maintaining an unadulterated awareness for the more popular musical-comedy genre, as well as a real panache for social satire. Just a few years after his first sound accomplishments, characterized by an aesthetic of simplicity and classical clarity, Clair's directing career took him to England, where he completed *The Ghost Goes West* (1935), and later *Break the News* (1938), starring Maurice Chevalier and Jack Buchanan. During World War II, Clair traveled to Hollywood, where he directed *The Flame of New Orleans* (1941), *I Married a Witch* (1942), *It Happened Tomorrow* (1944), and *And Then There Were None* (1945). He finally returned to France during the 1950s and successfully resumed his directing career, as he became one of the most prominent advocates of popular entertainment (while still maintaining his auteur icon), with big-budget musical productions starring the most popular names of the times: *Beauties of the Night* (*Belles de nuit,* 1952) with Martine Carol and Gérard Philipe, and *The Grand Maneuvers* (*Les grandes manoeuvres,* 1955), with Gérard Philipe and Michèle Morgan. Clair's masterpiece of the early talkie period is *The Million,* starring René Lefèvre and Annabella,[7] a musical comedy about two penniless artists persecuted by hardhearted creditors who one day win the lottery and suddenly become millionaires. Unfortunately, the lottery ticket is in a coat that had been sold to a pawnshop dealer and which is found after countless tribulations at the opera house in an unusually happy conclusion. The story, adapted from a vaudeville sketch written twenty years earlier by Georges Berr and Marcel Guillemaud, immediately seduced René Clair with its attractive combination of traditional burlesque and Avant-garde character. During the shooting, however, the director's preference went to the musical adaptation rather than the theatrical representation. The musical element, expressed by animated popular songs, corresponded to "operetta," and thus *The Million* became a permanent reference for French musical comedies at the beginning of the sound era.

With its inventive social caricature, *Freedom for Us* may have served as the inspiration for Chaplin's *Modern Times* (1936).[8] Following his escape from jail, Louis (Raymond Cordy) develops a phonograph production technique, a highly mechanized assembly line where workers are reduced to mere robots that is just as tyrannical as the prison he just fled. Eventually blackmailed with his past, he joins up with Emile, his old cellmate, to seek new adventures on the road. Thanks to its futuristic sets, *Freedom for Us* conveys an earnest message: the challenging and ultimate negation of the concept of modern work. Clair's new vision, remote and at the same time incredibly close in its poetic sensuality, seduced the world. Other directors, including several foreigners Alexander Korda, Erich von Stroheim, and Billy Wilder, demonstrated a similar technique and talent during the 1930s. In particular, the Russian director Anatole Litvak contributed to future poetic realism in *Lilac* (*Coeur de Lilas,* 1931). This picture introduced two fledgling actors, Fernandel and Jean Gabin, who would reign over French cinema for more than forty years.

Meanwhile, French directors had to recruit new faces along with new voices, and theater logically supplied this need with new talents and, of course, new subjects. It was the age of the so-called *théâtre filmé* ("filmed" or "canned" theater), highly criticized by intellectuals for its entertainment value, yet successful among audiences. Motion pictures no longer monopolized the images; the charm of the script was uncovered, and the public now related to famous quotes in order to remember their favorite films. Among the lucky actors were Michel Simon, Harry Baur, Raimu, Gaby Morlay, Jules Berry, and Arletty.

During this shift from silent movies to talkies, an exceptional phase of concentrated technological advancement abroad, French filmmaking significantly expanded, increasing from fifty-two to ninety-four features. From 1931 onward it sustained a similar growth, producing more than one hundred motion pictures annually until the end of the decade. As a result of the sound revolution, replacement and operating expenses multiplied threefold; because of these new financial demands, most filmmakers could no longer fund and manage their own projects. The filmmaking industry had been converted to a new and powerfully lucrative investment system set in motion by a multitude of small, inexperienced businesses.[9] The struggle for cinematographic preeminence between Hollywood and the European film industry implicated all production activities. As a result of this international tension, exceptional motion pictures were shaped and achieved by small producers, who frequently had to fight their way through the byzantine world of financial backing with often derisory financial assistance. What is most significant are the different strategies adopted by the two giant systems, German and United States studios. The American market produced an overwhelmingly large number of motion pictures for instantaneous local screenings, while the German, and to a lesser extent the European market, intended to fashion a "prestigious product" to be promoted internationally. The foundation of these colossal European productions (twenty-four films a year with Paramount) consisted of simple adaptations of existing narratives or plays, and gradually imposed the authority of the multifaceted and stylistically complex art of talking movies. The invention of sound immediately impacted French cinema, now at the mercy of German or American patent holders and cinematographic equipment manufacturers. From the turbulent promotion of the Joinville studios, where film manufacturing was terminated in 1933, in favor of the postsynchronized dubbing system, practically no film legacy was ever maintained subsequent to Marcel Pagnol's first film, *Marius* (*Marius*, 1931). As paradoxical as it may seem, directors such as Jean Grémillon (also known for his antifascist positions), René Clair, and Julien Duvivier directed in German studios (between 1930 and 1932, whether in Berlin or in Epinay, at the Tobis Studios in Epinay on the outskirts of Paris) to make some of their quintessentially Parisian films. After establishing connections in France with modern sound systems, Tobis-Klangfilm Studios supplied other studios, such as the French competitors Pathé and Eclair. Despite the fact that several movies characterized a genuine French milieu, the French production sponsorship came from other European countries as well as the United States.

FRENCH CINEMA AND ECONOMIC RECESSION

By 1932, the rippling effects of the Great Depression impacted France's cinema industry just as much as any other part of the national economy. Investments diminished dramatically, and countless actors and technicians joined the millions of unemployed. Due to the frequency of demonstrations from both political borders, 1934 marked one of the most volatile years of a volatile decade. The outstanding quality and authenticity of French national cinema at that time was due to the pressure and weight of that troubled period. The economic and political upheavals in this second half of the decade unquestionably contributed to the approach taken by numerous filmmakers to indulge in adventurous productions, which brought into high relief a rare poetic, philosophical, psychological, and intellectual substance. Brilliant screenplays coupled with outstanding theatrical presentations resulted in what is acknowledged as the golden age of French feature films.[10] Though heavily influenced by both a painter's tradition (treatment of colors) and the Surrealistic overtone of the Avant-garde heritage, French productions quickly embraced literary and theatrical projects by authors such as Stendhal, Honoré de Balzac, Gustave Flaubert, Emile Zola, and Guy de Maupassant. Elaborate scripts of writers such as Jacques Prévert, Charles Spaak, and Henri Jeanson, all of them coming from literary backgrounds, defined an era. Although the first effects of the depression reached France only after 1932, the cinematographic industry was far from being safe since it often depended on a multinational agreement to finance future projects. The American competition was revivified with a technique called *dubbing*. This new technological innovation was first considered doomed because of the language barrier it would have to face, but it brought forth the unthinkable—American actors spoke in different languages on screen. Indeed, in 1932, James Cagney, Greta Garbo, and eventually all of Hollywood spoke French in movie theaters worldwide.

The gargantuan transformation of movie theaters and film studios as well as the construction of new and luxurious cinemas (such as the famous Rex in Paris) created huge debt in the movie industry. In 1933, bankruptcies erupted and unfortunately continued to prevail during the remainder of the decade. During the summer of 1929, Gaumont joined a holding company, GFFA (Gaumont-Franco-Film-Aubert). Two years later, the major financial investor for GFFA, Banque National du Crédit, was in difficulty and needed financial endorsement from the government. As a result, the French government indirectly became a major partner of GFFA. Despite financial assistance, GFFA went out of business in the difficult climate of scandals and corruption in July 1934. Gaumont followed GFFA in 1938 and was immediately bought by a financial group, the Havas agency, which prior to the war created a new company called SNEG (Société nouvelle des Etablissements Gaumont), which is still active today. These examples illustrate the fragility of the French film industry of the 1930s, constituted by small companies, often in fiscal trouble and always at the mercy of financial disaster, which frequently resulted in the production of one unique film. The precarious economic situation was addressed by the French parliament in March 1939 to regulate and reorganize the industry, but it was too late to restructure the financial framework of French cinema.

Despite its weak and disorganized financial system, between 1934 and 1940 France saw a handful of productions that elevated the image of its cinema to worldwide recognition. Not only the importance and the prestige were immense, but this period, more than sixty years later, remains a high point. One of the many explanations for this overwhelming avalanche of talent is to be found in the passage (sometimes extremely brief) of some foreign contributions to artistic and technical work. The first wave of foreign technicians who arrived in France took place in the early 1920s immediately following World War I, at the very time when Paris was considered the world capital for artists of all sorts. Among those foreign technicians, many Russians came to France fleeing the Soviet regime, and contributed mightily to the prestige and fame of the Montreuil studios. The tradition began in the 1920s, when Russian immigrants (Ladislav Starevitch, Victor Tourjanski) became well known among French popular audiences before the advent of the sound. Jacob Protozanoff's *L'Angoissante aventure* (1920), starring Ivan Mosjoukine and his wife, Nathalie Lissenko, was one of the most important productions of the 1920s. Besides the Russians, Danish filmmaker Carl Dreyer (1889–1968), who had already worked in several different European countries before coming to France, directed one of the most celebrated French silent films, *The Passion of Joan of Arc* (*La passion de Jeanne d'Arc,* 1928). Following a long career around the world, and more precisely in Mexico, Spanish director Luis Buñuel would return to France three decades later with *The Diary of a Chambermaid* (*Le journal d'une femme de chambre,* 1963), starring Jeanne Moreau, and *Belle de Jour* (*Belle de jour,* 1969) with Catherine Deneuve. From Carl Dreyer to Luis Buñuel, Billy Wilder and Fritz Lang (who fled the Nazi regime in Germany), among others, all of them expressed a preference for the French creative and production system. But with the increasingly rising threat of Nazi Germany, many filmmakers stayed in France just in time to make a single motion picture before embarking to Hollywood. Others, like Max Ophuls, remained in France until the debacle of May 1940 just preceding the German Occupation. Some productions already had a sizable European market, such as *Carnival in Flanders* (*La kermesse héroïque,* 1935),[11] which was shot in two unconnected-language versions, both under the direction of the same filmmaker, Jacques Feyder (1885–1948), even before their distribution. This professional collaboration explains why after the rise of the fascist regime many professionals of the German cinema industry fled into exile, choosing Paris and its studios to continue their careers before reaching Hollywood. Not all of them were directors. One could also find technicians, background designers, and light operators, such as Curt Courant (1899–1968) and Eugène Shufftan (1893–1977), who offered their knowledge of "dark" lighting directly imported from the set of Babelsberg; they contributed to the immortal and gloomy atmosphere of Marcel Carné's *Port of Shadows* (*Quai des brumes,* 1938) and *Daybreak* (*Le jour se lève,* 1939).

Unlike its American and German counterparts, the French film industry of the postwar era did not thrive. In the United States, the studios were organized according to a "vertical monopoly,"[12] which ensured effective distribution, compensated for high production costs, and permitted export at a reduced rate to Europe. The pace of the patent competition between the United States and Germany left France behind. Paramount, in the meantime, supplied enormous funds for their studios in Joinville, which revealed the extent of their objective to make over a hundred motion pictures annually. As a result, many French filmmakers were compelled to move to England and Germany to rent foreign studios that were equipped to produce feature sound films (in 1929, only five fully synchronized films were completed). However, by 1932, the production, which by now was taking place in France, reached 150 films per year. Because of the ever-increasing cost of sound equipment, many Avant-garde and experimental filmmakers (mostly the Surrealists of the 1920s), who usually operated on a minuscule budget, were, for the most part, not able to have their new projects subsidized.

Beyond financial difficulties lurked another major obstacle to film production, censorship. The decree that established censorship goes back to July 25, 1919; it stipulated that "no cinematographic film, with the exception of newsreels,[13] could be shown in public if the film and its title had not obtained the visa of the Ministry of Public Instruction and the Beaux Arts."[14] Needless to say, sound on the screen reactivated the relevance of censorship by the French government's Censorship Commission, and a more sophisticated control was adequately organized. Luis Buñuel's *The Golden Age,* initially approved by the commission, triggered protest among the right-wing political movement and was ultimately banned from screening. Jean Vigo's *Zero of Conduct (Zéro de conduite,* 1933) was also not granted a visa due to its numerous satirical allusions to the French educational institution.

The isolation of artistic French filmmakers from more-commercial productions was an active factor in the creation of an important new organization, Ciné-Liberté, the main objective of which was to preserve the independent nature of cinematographic creations as well as bring together independent film directors. Up to the rise of the Popular Front in the mid-1930s, political cinema feebly conveyed dogmatic propaganda (in comparison to literature and theater) and was often neglected by political parties as an alternative support for their campaigns. The PCF (French Communist Party) was therefore the first party to solicit intellectuals and artist-filmmakers for the reputation of their political actions. In November 1935, Louis Aragon, who had been elected as the new secretary-general of the AEAR (Association des écrivains et artistes révolutionnaires), was present for the inauguration of the ACI (Alliance du cinéma indépendant), an organization whose main goal was to defend and promulgate artistic culture in France (music, theater, plastic arts, architecture, and, of course, cinema). Along with him, an impressive group of well-known intellectuals, such as novelists André Gide, André Malraux (who had recently won the 1933 Prix Goncourt for *The Human Condition*), Jean-Richard Bloch, and Jean Cassou, supported the event. ACI's first project was the production of *People of France (La vie est à nous)* in February 1936. Though never affiliated with the PCF, Jean Renoir was chosen to direct the innovative feature film *People of France,* an hour-long documentary made with the PCF's financial support. An enlightening endeavor but almost unknown, it united a well-edited newsreel subject (principally social current affairs), discourses from party leaders, and publicized cinematographic views in which several renowned actors of the decade appeared in small roles (including Marcel Duhamel, Gaston Modot, Jean Dasté, and Madeleine Sologne).

The PCF delegated to the ACI the responsibility of creating *People of France* for the forthcoming elections, and while producing the film, the young organization members realized the true sense of their mission and the immense potential of their action, which contrasted with traditional commercial cinema. The ACI, cinematographic division of the AEAR, had no administrative and financial link with the PCF, and became Ciné-Liberté[15] shortly before the making of *People of France* and continued to produce several movies until early 1938. *La Marseillaise,* which received the help of the CGT (Confédération général du travail, the largest trade union in France), was estimated to be "the" film of the Popular Front and symbolized leftist filmmaking and the mobilization of its people. The film indirectly memorialized the role of the people during the French Revolution and consequently their essential responsibility in maintaining democratic values in a society constantly harassed by extreme right-wing engagements: Prussians standing as a direct reference to Hitler's Germany, and French nobility as French Fascist factions. *La Marseillaise,* a classic homage to the grandeur of the French Revolution, represented Renoir's commitment to the ideas and ideals of the Left and his support of the newly elected Popular Front. Fundamentally optimistic by nature, Renoir often asserted his disagreement with the pessimistic message of Carné and Prévert's *Daybreak* and *Port of Shadows*.

The political scene of the 1930s is principally remembered for the triumph of the Popular Front in 1936 and its cultural policy (social and economic reforms voted by the parliament, such as the forty-hour work week and the first paid vacations), early filmmaking projects, as well as leftist radio organization. By 1934, the unstable conservative government was deeply affected by the Stavisky scandal (a financial affair that tainted the credibility of important leading radicals). Consequently, antiparliamentary factions of the Right took advantage of the incident to protest against the government. On February 6, a large gathering near the Parliament building ended in a tragic clash with police forces, during which a dozen protesters were killed and over a thousand injured. Soon after, France's conservative campaign was overpowered by unity of action on the Left that resulted in the creation of the Popular Front in 1935. In the spring of 1936, the first socialist government in French history came to power. The Socialist Party became France's leading political force for the first time, although the biggest political growth was in the Communist Party, the representation of which in the Parliament soared from ten to seventy seats. During the two previous years, the successful political movement had slowly gathered national interest, sparked by the tragic riots of 1934, which had startled the various leftist factions against a possible fascist menace. Just a few months after French Premier Léon Blum completed his new government, the Spanish Civil War erupted in July 1936, leading to the question of intervention for countries such as France and England and posing a serious problem of conscience for Blum's government toward the Spanish Republic, the only other Popular Front regime in Europe. But after much indecision, the French government, fearing a possible civil war at home, reluctantly called off the military aid project and allowed private initiatives to take over (the radical members tenaciously opposed any kind of military involvement and threatened to bring down the coalition).

At the same moment, French cinema of the 1930s looked for a mode of diversion without social implications, and filmmakers who sought to give active support to the Popular Front received little encouragement from politicians. From June 1938 until January 1939, André Malraux (1901–76), novelist, historian, and outsider to the French film industry, shot *L'espoir* (*Man's Hope,* 1945), rare footage of the Spanish Civil War in Barcelona with the International Brigades, which despite precarious conditions managed to capture on film reportage that helped the Republican cause. It is important to observe that despite the tragic subject matter of this enterprise, the film set itself apart from the defeatist French mainstream features of the period.

VERBAL CINEMA OR FILMED LANGUAGE? MARCEL PAGNOL

Many of the filmmakers with a theatrical background who surfaced in the early 1930s were highly criticized for "misusing" the cinematographic medium in order to serve a certain ideal of the so-called filmed theater. One of them, Marcel Pagnol (1895–1974), began his involvement with the film industry in 1930. A former schoolmaster, he became a nationally famous playwright in the late 1920s and was contacted by Robert Kane, an American executive for Paramount Studios in France, who wished to give his studios a Parisian accent and intellectual flavor. Pagnol, dramaturge above all in his hometown of Marseille, considered the cinematic medium a great tool with which to promote his theatrical oeuvre. With the introduction of sound feature films and the prolific transformation of plays to the big screen, Pagnol's stage productions were logically sought out by film producers, and in three years all three of his big stage triumphs had been filmed: *Marius* by Alexander Korda for Paramount in 1931, *Fanny* by Marc Allégret in 1932, and *Topaze* by Louis Gasnier in 1933 (starring Louis Jouvet, with screen adaptation by Léopold Marchand). Needless to say, it was his extraordinary regional success that permitted him to enter directly into the movie industry. Instead of enjoying the mundane Parisian life, Pagnol spent most of his time on the sets and in work-

shops in Joinville in order to study this new medium. There he met
Alexander Korda (1893–1956), an exiled Hungarian, who later became
one of the most prominent directors of British films. In 1931, Pagnol
took *Marius* to the screen with the same actors who performed in
Marseille. Marius (Pierre Fresnay), a young bartender in Marseille, is
torn by a harsh dilemma: he must choose between a tranquil life ashore
with his fiancée, Fanny (Orane Demazis), and running off to sea on a
ship to explore the world. Desperately in love with the young man
since her early childhood, Fanny pretends to accept the favors of the
old widower Panisse, a rich sailmaker (Fernand Charpin), in order to
prompt Marius's jealousy. Pushed by despair one night, Fanny comes
to the bar after hours to declare her love for Marius and her false desire
to marry old Panisse. In response, Marius reveals to her the true nature
of his thorny alternative, especially since a ship is leaving port that
evening. The plans for embarkment are thwarted at the last minute,
and the enamored couple spend their first night together. As the
months pass, Fanny prepares for the wedding, but the call of the sea
comes back to haunt Marius's fragile mind. Meanwhile, Fanny's
mother, Honorine (Alida Rouffe), visits César, Marius's father (Raimu),
to discuss their children's awkward state of affairs, and they finally
agree on a dowry. But one night before the wedding, Piquoiseau
(Alexandre Mihalesco), a local sailor, informs Marius that a ship, the
Malaisie, is heading off the next morning and that he could join the
crew. Fanny overhears their conversation and realizes that as long as
Marius stays ashore, he will never be happy. As the departure of the
ship approaches, Fanny uses subterfuge to persuade Marius to leave for
his dreams. Because Marius refuses to leave her alone, she announces
to him that she will eventually marry old Panisse for financial reasons.
The infuriated Marius believes her account and immediately walks out
to the ship. The sequel of the movie and second chapter of the trilogy,
Fanny (*Fanny,* 1932), narrates the return of Marius after Fanny has
married Panisse and reared Marius's child, Césariot. Many years later,
Césariot reunites his parents after the death of Panisse in *César* (*César,*
1936), the second sequel. Seven decades after the making of the first
part of the Marseille trilogy, *Marius,* it still seems remarkable that one
of the most provincial works in French cinema, full of the flavor of the
Midi of France (in which actors and actresses converse in picturesque
dialect), should be an international accomplishment. The trilogy *Marius–Fanny–César,* combining comedy, melodrama, romance, and all the
energy and flavor of Marseille, generated worldwide and long-lasting
reception.

The predominance of narrative and theatrical values characterized
the cinema of Marcel Pagnol, who at an early stage of his cinemato-

Marcel Pagnol's *Marius (Marius,* 1931) directed by Alexander Korda starring Pierre Fresnay (Marius) and Orane Demazis (Fanny), (Photo courtesy of the Museum of Modern Art/Film Stills Archive).

graphic career openly declared his attachment to the text, a key element to "filmic dramaturgy." Pagnol's straightforward chronicles of
Provençal people progressed effortlessly between sagacious comedy and
frivolous melodrama, delighting in vividness of language but always
attentive to the variances between words and actions. The many verbal
disputes between Marius and his father, César, which used an uninhibited exercise of language, accurately portrayed Pagnol's affection for
the Provençal lifestyle, its values of family, honor, happiness, and
idleness. Distancing himself from the synthetic environment of the
Billancourt and Joinville studios, Pagnol returned to his native Marseille, acquired a soundtrack from Philips, and put together his own
three-stage film studios outside the city. Many brilliant stars
immediately followed him: Raimu, Fernandel, and Pierre Fresnay, to
name a few. Pagnol, however, maintaining a critical distance, realized
that the only way he would be able to control his work on screen was
to select future actors, hire a crew, and direct the shooting—all himself. The young director disregarded all the conventions of studio
sound still prominent in Paris and permitted his camera to tag along
with the actors and to shoot on location. Pagnol chose his own property as the shooting location for many of his films; the influence and
magnificence of the surrounding Provençal landscape served as background and functioned as his own outdoor laboratory. Between the
delicate fragrance of the hills of Provence and the entertaining lifestyle
of the fishermen at the Canebière in Marseille, the three films had a
common effect, a French-style "meridional" commedia dell'arte that
instantly charmed audiences. Although Pagnol's early career as a director of plays had a classical edge (similar to the style of Emile Augier
and Courteline), he soon understood that the best source of inspiration
was literally in his own backyard. He collaborated with the novelist
Jean Giono, also from Provence, to produce *Harvest* (*Regain,* 1937) and
The Baker's Wife (*La femme du boulanger,* 1938).

   Best known for his distinctively Provençal quality, Raimu was unquestionably one of the best comic actors of the decade. Although
quite different from Chaplin in physical appearance and style, Raimu
could embody comic and tragic characters in the same sequence. *The
Baker's Wife,* a narrative borrowed from an episode in Jean le Bleu's
novel, featured Raimu as the village baker, deceived by an adulterous
wife who runs off with a shepherd. Since he no longer wants to make
the bread, the people of the village gather to persuade the "unruly"
wife to come back and to ascertain a tolerable arrangement. Ginette
Leclerc interpreted the idyllic, sultry spouse, and Raimu, assisted by
Pagnol's dialogue, made one of his most outstanding performances,
though his refusal to play dialogue scenes in the open air resulted in
an odd and rather inadequate mixture of location and studio work for

Marcel Pagnol's *Marius* (poster by
Albert Dubout, © Jean Dubout).

The legendary "partie de cartes" in Marcel Pagnol's *Marius,* (Courtesy of BIFI).

the film. After *The Baker's Wife,* Pagnol's movies resulted in successful careers for actors Fernandel (*Le Schpountz/Heartbeat,* 1938, *La fille du puisatier/The well-digger's daughter,* 1940) and Raimu (*Marius, Fanny* and *César*), among others.

Pagnol was nevertheless severely criticized for the Marseille trilogy. The devotees of "pure" motion pictures reproached him as merely a "lost" playwright whose personality and talent were incapable of adapting to the laws of the screen. According to contemporary critics, he conveyed a "false" cinematographic language, much too close to theatrical eloquence, and most works conveyed an apparent contradictory form, combining a traditional-conservative moral tone with an innovative structure. Still, Pagnol's contribution to motion pictures was to assert the preeminence of narrative values and his attachment to the text as well as the spoken word. His invaluable efforts resulted in the international dissemination of the folklore of Provence. The public, unlike most film critics, manifested a warm enthusiasm for this "sunny" work. Pagnol's films promoted the eloquence and generosity of the heart, the inspiration of the word, and the necessity for a peaceful life balanced by the natural rhythms of existence far away from the disquieting influence of the city.

Though of short duration, Pagnol's contribution to French cinema (1931–52), along with Jean Renoir and Marcel Carné's participations in the 1930s, remains significant. He served as an inspiration for many future young directors and authors (Claude Chabrol, Eric Rohmer, and the Italian director Roberto Rossellini). Marcel Pagnol's movies were condensed samples of effervescent humanity; his characters were authentic archetypes, and his art remains alive due to his sincere contemplation of reality. In the early 1930s, Pagnol vigorously promoted the leadership of sound in cinema and advocated the idea of film as "canned theater," declaring that "silent film was merely the art of printing and distributing pantomime, the sound film was the art of printing and distributing theater."[16] Envisioning sound feature films as an actor's means of expression (for supporters of talkies, sound was far more significant than any series of visual metaphors), Pagnol considered his technical crew and actors part of one big enterprise involved in a joint venture.

During the years that the sound system rapidly expanded, Sacha Guitry (1885–1957) and Marcel Pagnol, among other playwrights, dynamically contributed to the coalition of cinema and theater, eventually using motion pictures as a successful extension of theater. Guitry, an indefatigable and self-centered playwright who remained indifferent to artistic techniques, assembled in film a series of his reworked theatrical productions and imaginative plays written for the screen, resulting in a blend of sophistication and humor, beautiful

Raimu (Aimable) and other supporting actors in Marcel Pagnol's *The Baker's Wife*
(*La femme du boulanger*, 1938), (Courtesy of BIFI/© Roger Corbeau).

actresses, and an overall salient discourse. Strangely enough, Guitry's
most remarkable and identifiable realization on film, *Story of a Cheat*
(*Le roman d'un tricheur*, 1936), represents a performance without a
specific channel of communication. In this film, he prefigured Alain
Resnais's innovation of interchange, connecting text and image, a
sharp communicative strategy for a storyteller's interpretation. Although reprimanded for his alleged allegiances and conduct during the
later Nazi Occupation, Guitry reemerged after World War II and
completed many noteworthy commercial productions of popular romanticized historical subjects, such as *Royal Affairs in Versailles* (*Si
Versailles m'était conté*, 1953) and *Napoléon* (*Napoléon*, 1954).

BEYOND FILMED THEATER: TOWARD POETIC
REALISM

Although poetic realism dominated French cinema of the 1930s, only
a minority of the entire production of French films from that era
could be considered part of the "realist" current. In fact, the 1930s

were a complex period that included comedies, "filmed theater," literary adaptations, and exotic and colonial adventures. Many financially
insufficient film budgets generated mediocre scenarios, and the mise-
en-scène often resulted in a poor display of actors. Poetic realism, by
contrast, was a creative effort to reconstruct commonly accepted representations of life through the perspective of an artistic medium. The
director's purpose was to convey his own, honest, and objective outlook
on life. "Literary realism," initiated as a European literary movement
in the eighteenth century, occurred as an insurrection against the
classical standards of art, which held that human existence was more
predictable and structured than it actually appeared. Furthermore, it
was an insurgence against romantic conventions, in which life appeared
more enjoyable than it was in reality. Cinematographic realism universally expanded together with the progress of modern science in its
detailed social observation, precise footage, and new perspectives on
human experiences. In addition to the image of life, authors as well as
screenwriters began to develop a social conscience, representing the
evils of society and insinuating radical transformations. Poetic realism,
also labeled *social fantastique* (or *cinéma du désenchantement*), brought a
new aesthetic to films. The aim was to show real life and represent a
reality detached from the mundane trepidations and clichés of bourgeois drama. With its heavy atmosphere of *banlieue* (suburban) landscape, new film subjects of everyday popular culture were revealed and
defined: naturalistic reflections on wet cobblestones, suburban com-
muter trains in the early morning, factories' smoke mixing with fog,
small cafés in popular districts—in short, realism.[17]

Poetic realism can also be described as "cinematographic expressionism" refined in textured facades, gradation of grays, and a graceful
equilibrium between naturalism and stylization. Poetic realism came
directly from realism followed by the literary movements of naturalism, represented by the social novels of Honoré de Balzac (*Le père
Goriot*), Victor Hugo (*Les misérables*), Eugène Sue (*Les mystères de Paris*),
and Emile Zola (*Germinal* and *La bête humaine*). The essence of the plot
focused on the working-class individual whose existence corresponded
to a series of lost illusions, love deceptions, and existential disenchantment. The bourgeois psychology of the silent era was finally cast aside
as the new kind of realism became part of the populist, artistic expression. Although literary critics invented the formula of poetic realism
during the 1930s to distinguish so-called works from populist literature, it only became linguistically prominent after the war in an
attempt to identify French films of the 1930s. The implicit contradiction of the terms *realism* and *poetic* explains the fate of the phrase, since
it represents both the dramatic and urban concept of the plot as well

as a dreamy and lyrical dimension of quotidian life. However, the image of tragic destiny that came out of the new poetic realism was far from entirely negative and pessimistic, since beyond their profound distress, characters displayed new strength, which eventually led them to the quest for happiness and ideal love. A succinct summary of major themes in poetic realism could be presented as follows: the representation of the popular hero, the pessimistic atmosphere, the (doomed) quest for happiness, and finally the tragic destiny. The chiaroscuro lighting, background artifices, evocative visual imagery, and wittiness of dialogue resulted in a distinctive lyrical style. This cinematographic stream was characterized by its unity, its codes, and its very artifices. Only the actors, however, often prisoners of an image required by the public, were the main center of interest. In 1934 and 1935, several movies welcomed the dominating ideology: a slight dose of anti-Semitism or Parliamentarism, and occasionally, a reminder that the only solution for order was a strong political power. With the Popular Front's victory in 1936, these threats were set aside, but only for a while.

ARTISTS AND MASTERS OF POETIC REALISM: JEAN GABIN, ARLETTY, MARCEL CARNÉ, JEAN RENOIR, AND JEAN VIGO

The same realism, labeled as poetic, became even more pessimistic by 1939 with the failure of the Popular Front and the impending threat of war. Jean Gabin, (1904–76), the popular hero par excellence, dies at the end of most of his films: *Escape from Yesterday, Pépé le Moko, Port of Shadows, Daybreak,* and *The Human Beast.*[18] The stereotype of the characters played by Gabin during the 1930s often corresponded to the archetypical proletarian, the working-class protagonist who met his tragic destiny and ultimately became a victim, a representative of the syndrome of failure: failure to love, failure to dream, and failure to succeed. It was because he was able to reconcile contradictory elements (ordinary and extraordinary, poor and rich, proletarian and individualist bourgeois) that Gabin became a true movie star and was able to continue his career until his death in 1976. The "Frenchness" of Jean Gabin, besides his visual intensity, comes from the fact that he was the principal actor during the decade of realism, which perhaps more than any other cinematographic period, concentrated on the detailed representation of real and contemporary characters. This is also the reason why French cinema of the 1930s is often spoken of as the *cinéma d'acteurs* (actors' cinema). The sociopolitical climate of the Popular Front and the atmosphere of impending War forced the end of poetic realism. Its influences, however, remained predominant for the rest of the century and confirmed the identification of the 1930s as the golden age of French cinema.

At the beginning of poetic realism, the social milieu was a fundamental criterion for determining the sequence of events, as seen in *Under the Roofs of Paris, The Crime of Monsieur Lange (Le crime de Monsieur Lange,* 1935), and *Freedom for Us,* but toward the end of the 1930s, and especially after the fall of the Popular Front, protagonists became more self-governing characters, unconstrained by social environment (as seen in *Daybreak* and *Port of Shadows*). Because of the minor importance of the star system in prewar France, "commercial" norms were less perceptible and less important than they were for Hollywood cinema. Cinematic representation evolved from a tradition of character types and set design that foreshadowed the influence of society and environment toward psychological and more idiosyncratic films, which favored individualized characters and unambiguous subjects. As noted, French cinema of the early 1930s relied a great deal on actors and actresses who were competent in a variety of theatrical backgrounds (operetta, cabaret, and boulevard),[19] and this movement built up their presence in terms of fixed-character roles.

Jean Gabin, something of a mythical actor and perhaps the only "star" in French cinema, received his first major acting role in 1930 for *Chacun sa chance,* but was only truly discovered in 1934, when he was introduced to filmmaker and producer Julien Duvivier (1896–1967). Although his national fame came after several years, Gabin's career proved to be rapidly prolific. Between 1930 and 1935, he acted in twenty films. He consequently appeared in a great deal of mythical and tragic movies in which he played a tough, introverted character haunted by a tragic fate: *Escape from Yesterday (La Bandera,* 1935), *Pépé le Moko (Pépé le Moko,* 1936), *Lover-Boy (Gueule d'amour,* 1937), *Port of Shadows, The Human Beast (La bête humaine,* 1938), and *Daybreak.* His character often evolved in a hostile urban underworld usually ruled by mobsters. As a main protagonist, typically an outsider, the personage temporarily relied on a line of work to unravel his own obstacles and confronted the criminals in a breathless finale, which ultimately resulted in the reestablishment of a moral order. After a series of successful films, Gabin and actress Viviane Romance were the most popular actors in France during the second part of the decade. Gabin's doomed characters included young lovers, bad boys, manual workers, soldiers, and gangsters. Thanks to his famous role as a pacifist deserter in *Port of Shadows,* he quickly became connected to the symbol of the Popular Front. Gabin stands as a monument of French cinema and his impact on the French collective imagination is enormous.

Jean Gabin's cinematographic icon displayed a permanence that is difficult to define, an alliance to a particular aesthetic style consistent enough for the public to recognize him but offering enough diversity to avoid loss of interest. The numerous roles of gangsters and murderers contributed to build his great success and eventually his myth. According to Ginette Vincendeau,[20] the movie star was defined through a triangular rapport among actor, man, and character, which evolved altogether from movie to movie. *Escape from Yesterday,* far from being one of Gabin's best pictures, gathered all the ingredients of the myth, representing the protagonist through a variety of social, political, and cultural discourses. Gabin's performances were characterized by straightforwardness and bluntness, carefully crafted to convey an impression of "nonacting."[21] Although this trend changed dramatically after his return from Hollywood, when he interpreted characters with social status (rich gangsters, poised bourgeois, a president), Gabin is best remembered for his roles as a proletarian with a tragic destiny.

Gabin projected a sense of belonging to a unique symbolic community. (In the movies, Gabin wore the famous *casquette,* symbol of the French working class.) *Port of Shadows* provided Gabin the famous line *T'as d'beaux yeux, tu sais* (You have pretty eyes, you know) and another in *Daybreak:* "Listen . . . you're a charming girl, but when you've finished doing your washing, let me know."[22] The performances of Jean Gabin related to a masculine stereotype: motionless and silent, he represented the man who mastered his every gesture and emotion. Gabin's characters manifest virility and masculinity as well as emotional turmoil. It is because he was able to incarnate both features simultaneously that the myth came to life. The essence of Gabin was the inherent compromise between two different compulsions: the honest man and the brave proletarian. What most characterized Gabin's cinematographic performance as an actor was the absence of "behavioral motion"[23] (with the exception of his ritual burst of wrath on the balcony facing the crowd in *Daybreak*). However, the national fame, which quickly made Gabin a national icon, created an ambiguous rapport with the social structures. Not only his status as a movie star and an "extraordinary" actor, but also the original disposition of the populist ideal conveyed the image of the ordinary working man. This emerged from the trend in French cinema during the 1930s, which represented the individual within the community; in direct contrast, Hollywood privileged the individual, regardless of the social community. When in a group, Gabin was intuitively placed at the center; he had more close-ups than any other actor of the 1930s, at a time when most close shots were made at half the distance of today's (unlike Hollywood film, with its fervent use of close-ups during that decade). This innovation, identified as a modern photographic tool for the first time, allowed access to the characters' internal individuality.

When World War II broke out, Gabin left France for Hollywood, shot a couple of movies, and returned to Paris. Compared to the American star system, which financially compensated actors, European stars did not have access to similar means (Gabin was in fact under contract with the French studio Pathé-Natan). In France, the first few years following the war were problematic, and it was a good decade later that Gabin regained his star status, incarnating new characters— older, more experienced, and authoritarian—such as those in Marcel Carné's *La Marie du Port* (1950), Jacques Becker's *Grisbi* (*Touchez pas au grisbi,* 1954), Jean Renoir's *Only the French Can* (*French Cancan,* 1955), Claude Autant-Lara's *Four Bags Full* (*La traversée de Paris,* 1956), and *Love Is My Profession* (*En cas de malheur,* 1958).

Often associated with Jean Gabin as one of the *montres sacrés* (true stars) of French cinema is Parisian actress Arletty (1898–1992). Profoundly Parisian middle-class and street savvy, Arletty had one of the strongest personalities in French films of her era. Her first performance, as a parachutist in Jacques Feyder's *Pension Mimosa* (1934), led to some success, but it was her entertaining performance in Marcel Carné's *Hôtel du Nord* (*Hôtel du Nord,* 1938) whose famous line *Atmosphère . . . atmosphère . . . est-ce que j'ai une gueule d'atmosphère?* and her glowing charisma in *Daybreak* that brought her to the attention of the French public and made her legendary. Still loyal to Marcel Carné, her performances in both *The Devil's Envoys* (*Les visiteurs du soir,* 1942) and *Children of Paradise* (*Les enfants du Paradis,* 1945) have remained among the greatest in French cinema and unquestionably triggered her international stardom.

Sharing a great deal of success with Arletty was actress Simone Simon (born in Marseille in 1911), who first worked as a fashion designer and a model before becoming a film actress. She began in Marc Allégret's *Ladies' Lake* (*Lac aux dames,* 1934), which brought her to the attention of the French public. In 1936, Simon went to the United States when American producer Darryl Zanuck hired her for Twentieth Century-Fox. Two years later, she returned to France to star in Jean Renoir's masterpiece, *The Human Beast,* and also featured in other European cinemas, including two movies by Max Ophuls in the 1950s. As an actress, Simon benefited from her unique quality, a blend of innocence and sex appeal that often featured her characters as young, elegant, and erotic seductresses. Simone retired from movies in the 1950s, having accomplished such films as *The Human Beast,* Maurice Tourneur's *Cat People* (1942), *The Curse of the Cat People* (1944), and also Max Ophuls's *Roundabout* (*La ronde,* 1950) and *Pleasure* (*Le plaisir,* 1951). She lives in France to this day.

The distinction of French actors and actresses of the 1930s that characterized French cinema was not only the result of brilliant per-

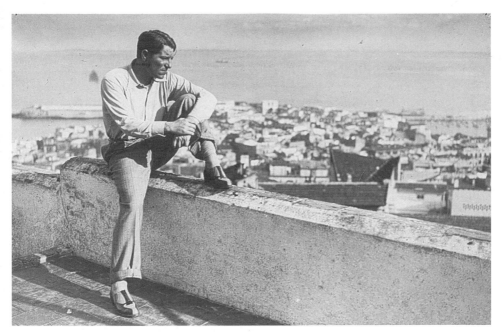

Jean Gabin (Pépé) in Julien Duvivier's *Pépé le Moko* (*Pépé le Moko,* 1936), (Courtesy of BIFI).

Jean Gabin (Lucien) and Mireille Balin (Madeleine) in Jean Grémillon's *Lover-Boy* (*Gueule d'amour*, 1937), (Courtesy of BIFI).

formances but also the fruitful collaborative efforts of film directors with outstanding artistic and technical crews. Marcel Carné (1909–96), one of the preeminent directors of poetic realism, established himself during the 1930s by completing a short film, *Nogent — Eldorado du Dimanche* (1929), which so overwhelmed René Clair that he appointed Carné his assistant in *Under the Roofs of Paris*. Carné then collaborated as assistant to Feyder on *Pension Mimosas* and *Carnival in Flanders*. From 1930 to 1935, while working as an assistant to Clair and Feyder, Carné rapidly acquired his own cinematographic technique, learning from both veteran directors the notion of a motion picture as a pattern to be tailored within the film studio. During this time he also made publicity shorts and wrote film criticism, occasionally under the pseudonym Albert Cranche. Shortly after his involvement with Jacques Feyder, Carné supervised his first motion picture, a classic melodrama entitled *Jenny* (*Jenny*, 1936), which was written for the screen by Jacques Prévert. Prévert, a poet whose considerable magnetism originated from an exceptional arrangement of wit, sentimentality, and social parody, was often affiliated with the Surrealists as well as the politically active Popular Front. Carné's astute direction and Jacques Prévert's rigorous and poetic texts destined both men to have highly successful careers. Prévert and Carné met during the *Front populaire,* and in view of their very different personalities, no one could have ever predicted their long and fruitful collaboration. Carné's compassion went toward the marginalized groups, like homosexuals, and his style borrowed the technical approach used in German Expressionism and American thrillers. His domain of predilection was undoubtedly *atmosphère*. Prévert's background in Surrealist poetry and the Groupe Octobre (a communist-oriented theatrical group) contributed to his refinement of poetic realism's tragic pessimism and sociopolitical satire. The viewpoint that considers the success of Carné's work solely through his alliance with Prévert, however, is erroneous and unfair. The achievements of both writer and director (when operating on their own after they had split up) proved to be harmonious in the fundamental domains of the protagonist's social function, the emphasis given to human obsession, and the outcome of destiny in everyday life. The only true discrepancy in their work was their method of production and certainly not their philosophies and artistic schemes.

The road of poetic realism widened as the general public in France reconsidered their reaction to the Popular Front, moving from cheerful optimism to the anguish of the latent occupation. Characteristically, the collaborative work of Carné and Prévert showed signs of apprehension that vacillated between pragmatism and the metaphysical. Spectators perceived the apprehension through the combination of prominent lyrical speech, a pessimistic backdrop, and an exhaustive

Two French actresses go to Hollywood: Simone Simon and Annabella (Photo courtesy of the Museum of Modern Art/Film Stills Archive).

representation of tangible social situations. Their style, framed by populist poetry, singularized itself with emphasis on the actors' roles, their witty dialogues, and a chiaroscuro lighting that nuanced the characters. Carné realized his own personal style in the 1938 film *Port of Shadows,* which was quickly followed by *Hôtel du Nord,* inspired from a novel by the populist writer Eugène Dabit, as well as *Daybreak.* In *Port of Shadows,* the collaboration between Carné and Prévert reached its peak and gave birth to one of the most admired films of French cinema. A similar situation occurred in *Hôtel du Nord*, which benefited from Henri Jeanson's dialogues, an avalanche of witty cinematographic citations. Prévert and Carné reunited for *Daybreak*. This picture, released June 7, 1939, remains one of the most celebrated examples of film noir.[24] André Bazin considered *Daybreak* and *Port of Shadows* two of the most successful dramas of the decade, possessing "the ideal qualities of a cinematic paradise lost."[25]

The pairing of Jean Gabin and Michèle Morgan in *Port of Shadows* powerfully represented the feeling of a heavy and impending doom. Adapted to the big screen by Jacques Prévert from Pierre MacOrlan's novel, the script possessed a subtle duality, coupling romantic myth and eternity much like that of Tristan and Iseult. The attention to visual and intellectual parallels gives Carné and Prévert's work the richness and complexity of the original novel. *Port of Shadows* is one of the best examples of poetic realism, featuring the archetypal Jean Gabin persona as it constructs a character of experience who appears skeptical and suspicious of everyone, but proves to be inspired by a highly developed moral code when the moment occurs. In these productions, it seems as though central characters are resolute to tempt their already doomed fate at any cost. Significantly, all of Carné's leading actors (in particular, Jean Gabin's roles) were alienated individuals, abandoned in a merciless cosmos and alienated from any social or intellectual order, and whose redemptory way out was to come through self-dependence. *Port of Shadows* narrates a love story between the sensual Nelly (Michèle Morgan) and Jean (Jean Gabin), a deserter from the French Foreign Legion in search of a secure haven. They encounter one another in the foggy port of Le Havre at a dockside back street, late at night in a brooding atmosphere, and immediately both destinies become tragically linked. Their brief moments of hope and happiness are interrupted by the presence of the villainous characters Zabel (Michel Simon), Nelly's criminal guardian, and Lucien (Pierre Brasseur), a local mobster. Jean engages in violent altercations with both of them, which highlights Gabin's legendary charismatic, masculine, stoic persona, and he is unpredictably murdered at the end of the movie. Jacques Prévert's inspirational dialogue and Alexandre Trauner's (1906–93) set design greatly enriched Carné's authentic filmic discourse, through the characteristic blend of words and images, which has come to be its trademark. *Port of Shadows,* like *Hôtel du Nord* and *Daybreak,* fits into the category of the archetypal French melodrama of thwarted passions and entangled providences. Because of its predisposed melodramatic surroundings, the stylistic approach of the film mirrors French emotional responses to the political, social, and cultural events of the 1930s. Carné's films typically feature people who are suffering from an existential angst: despondency, isolation, dishon-

Jean Gabin (Jeannot) and Viviane Romance (Gina) in Julien Duvivier's *They Were Five* (*La belle équipe*, 1935), (Courtesy René Chateau).

esty, disillusionment, pessimism, and psychoses. Carné's poetic realism portrays a humanity where people were not fundamentally good, but rather devious and manipulative. With subtle insight, the film perfectly expresses the leading actors' emotions and depicts the tender feelings of a pair of young lovers lost in an evil and pessimistic world. Today, *Port of Shadows* is widely recognized by film historians as the seminal example of French poetic realism.

As revelation or confirmation, actors' stares became legendary, and their love stories conveyed an impression of mystery thanks to Carné's talent. A year later, his perseverance and belief in cinema as a medium to communicate basic truths of human condition allowed his films to overturn censorship and to bring *Daybreak* to the forefront of pre–film noir. UFA (Universum Film Allgemeine) decided not to pursue the production of the film based on the subdued and overly pessimist nature of the script. In reality, Carné's notorious "artistic melancholy" was not any more pessimistic than that of Julien Duvivier or even Jean Renoir. For both filmmakers, the inspiration of unattainable love and the desire for a blissful getaway were consistently exemplified in their script, in order to generate unadulterated feelings. *Daybreak* is a psychological as well as social drama, the major quality of which resides within its characters. François (Jean Gabin) kills a man named Valentin (Jules Berry). He shoots him in his hotel room, and the body rolls down the stairs just before the police arrive. Barricaded in his room, François, chain smoking because he is out of matches, contemplates one by one all the events that led to the tragedy. The story line is structured according to a series of emotional flashbacks that reconstruct the itinerary of the murder and the solitary days preceding it. Interspersed with each flashback, the narrative returns to the barricaded room where François, the alleged murderer, reflects on his past while a crowd gathers on the street outside begging him to surrender peacefully. The first flashback reveals how François meets a young-and-mild florist, Françoise (Jacqueline Laurent), at the factory and how they both realize that not only do they have the same name, but also that they are both from the same orphanage. As François gets to know Françoise, he discovers, much to his dismay, her odd fascination for Valentin, a manipulative dog trainer who exerts an outrageous influence on her as well as his assistant, Clara (Arletty). Clara eventually leaves Valentin for François, who offers her protection without romance. As the four destinies become emotionally intertwined, Valentin attempts to corrupt François, who ultimately kills the immoral perpetrator. Facing the inevitable, François commits suicide.

The emblematic *Daybreak* was produced entirely in the studios. Scenes of suburban architecture were cleverly re-created by the decorator Alexandre Tauner and magnified by artificial light. Carné's polished mise-en-scène, which benefited from chief operators Eugène Schufftan and Curt Courant, and composers Maurice Jaubert and Joseph Kosma, displays the most lifelike and meticulously detailed representation of reality, and paradoxically elicits the poetic course of action. It was, as André Bazin said, "written in verse or at least in prose which is invisibly poetic."[26] In addition to this scenario, the legendary screenwriter Jacques Prévert (1900–1977), formed a monologue of poetic words for the protagonists, resulting in a literary language tailor-made for Gabin, Arletty, Jules Berry, and Jacqueline Laurent. The representation of François, sitting alone in his room while outside an apprehensive crowd eagerly awaits the outcome of this

Jean Gabin (François) and Arletty (Clara) in Marcel Carné's *Daybreak* (*Le jour se lève*, 1939), (Courtesy of the Archives Marcel Carné).

Annabella (Renée) and Louis Jouvet (Monsieur Edmond) in Marcel Carné's *Hôtel du Nord* (*Hôtel du Nord*, 1938), (Photo courtesy of the Museum of Modern Art/Film Stills Archive).

hopeless impasse, provides an introspective metaphor for the entire nation's desperation on the eve of the war.[27] Through a deep awareness of the meanings produced through fashioning the individual images (with light and, for the most part, darkness), Carné shaped a highly subjective cinematographic style in which these elements were combined to reflect the mental state of his main tragic hero.[28] His cinematographic viewpoint managed to assemble the artificial and constrained studio style with his own experience of realism to eventually shape a unique visual quality. The consistent use of the deep focus, wide-angle lenses, night-for-night photography, and low-key lighting characterize a unique film noir quality.

Carné's style, described by others as the essence of the genre, could be defined as a combination of faultless atmospheric studio realism with compactness of action and a strong use of half-light. His finest movies were always a result of a rigorous partnership, which assembled a talented and experienced technical team. By the end of the 1930s, Marcel Carné's control of technical modus operandi had resulted in the making of films whose cold formal magnificence, logical dimension, and meticulous narrative rhetoric firmly stood at the vanguard of a future "tradition of quality" in filmmaking. *Daybreak* already prefigured the future characteristic features of film noir in the next decade through the physical and moral traits of Jean Gabin versus his characters: a doomed protagonist, with a strong personality and a generous heart, surrounded by an unsympathetic and hostile universe, usually a suburban area or possibly industrial port, and who is generally involved in ill-fated plots such as organized crime or corruption schemes, out of which comes a final attempt to secure social justice revealing through the device of social realism the depth of the hero's human nature.

Jean Renoir (1894–1979), consistently regarded as the greatest and most "authentically French" of all filmmakers, had a reputation that coincided with Marcel Carné's. While Carné mastered filmmaking in the studio, Renoir developed artistic aspects of cinematography on location. Son of the Impressionist painter Pierre-Auguste Renoir, Jean Renoir worked within all cinematographic genres: acerbic comedy, *The Bitch* (*La chienne,* 1931); literary adaptations, *Madame Bovary* (1933), *A Day in the Country* (*Une partie de campagne,* 1936; released in 1946) and *The Human Beast;* entertaining improvisation, *Boudu Saved from Drowning* (*Boudu sauvé des eaux,* 1932); social chronicals, *Toni* (*Toni,* 1934); solemn meditation on war, *Grand Illusion* (*La grande illusion,* 1937); political manifestations, *La Marseillaise* (1937) and *The Crime of Monsieur Lange;* and social satire, *The Rules of the Game* (*La règle du jeu,* 1939). Renoir's active artistic involvement in his film productions

Elle se tourne vers
François et l'interpelle
directement.

        ... Vous avouerez qu'il faut a-
        voir de l'eau dans le gaz et des
        papillons dans le compteur (<u>el-
        le se tapote la tête</u>) ...pour
        être restée trois ans avec un
        type pareil !

I55- <u>PLAN RAPPROCHE</u>

    François, de face.
    Clara, en amorce, de
    profil.

        <u>FRANCOIS</u>, très calme :

        - Ecoutez... vous êtes bien gen-
        tille, mais quand vous aurez
        fini de faire le ménage, vous
        me le direz ?

        <u>CLARA</u> :

        - ... le ménage ?

        <u>FRANCOIS</u> :

        - Parfaitement !... Vous arrivez
        là ... vous videz vos tiroirs...
        vous battez vos tapis ...Je ne
        vous ai rien demandé, moi !
        Pourquoi que vous me racontez
        votre vie ?...

I56- <u>PLAN RAPPROCHE</u>

    Clara, de face.
    François, en amorce,
    de profil.

        <u>CLARA</u> :

        - Oh !... Faut pas m'en vouloir
        ... Si je vous parlais, c'est
        histoire de ne pas causer toute
        seule... Ce soir, je suis telle-
        ment heureuse... vous pouvez
        pas savoir... la liberté, ...
        c'est pas rien!

    François, tout en écoutant
    Clara, continue à surveiller
    Françoise ... Clara le regarde
    et sourit.

        <u>CLARA</u> :

        - Tout de même, vous n'êtes
        pas très aimable... Vous fe-
        riez mieux de m'offrir quelque
        chose...

    Elle se retourne face au bar.

Jean Gabin's script in *Daybreak* (*Le jour se lève*, 1939), (Courtesy of the Archives Marcel Carné).

following 1931 increased his esteem among French film critics (as opposed to the general public), who early on identified him as an essential and perceptive filmmaker. Renoir's sound films immediately demonstrated an obvious openness to the new standards of talking pictures; *Toni* and *The Crime of Monsieur Lange* exemplify the eclectic nature of Renoir's films, underlining that his artistic concerns prevailed over the actual subject matter; *Toni* demonstrates Renoir's early artistic vision. Set in the south of France, the film chronicles an Italian immigrant (Charles Blavette) in love with a Spanish girl (Célia Montalvan) who, failing to prove his innocence in a murder case, is killed for a crime that his young lover committed. Considered one of the early prototypes of neorealism in its social observation and pessimistic outlook, *Toni* departs from this genre in its lack of both authenticity and proper social perspective.[29] A film like *The Crime of Monsieur Lange* provides a link between an anarchist period of Renoir's early years and a militant interlude that brought Renoir closer to the PCF (French Communist Party). The movie, shot during the incipient months of the Popular Front, epitomized with joviality the confounded but truthful social point of view of the Left in 1936. Built around Jacques Prévert's scenario, the story shows how a common man in a collective society can conquer despotism. The employees of a small printing press collaborate to collect money and take over as publishers of the popular novelettes, *Arizona Jim,* after the owner, Batala (Jules Berry, the most insufferable "bad guy" of the 1930s), has fled to avoid facing his creditors. Unfortunately, the former proprietor revisits the business to maintain control of the now-flourishing publishing company. To defend his collectivity's autonomy, Lange, one of the publishing company's employees, guns down the old manager and becomes a fugitive from justice. In this film, the plot is almost secondary to the sense of atmosphere just prior to the establishment of the Popular Front.

Between 1936 and 1939, Renoir directed his best movies. *A Day in the Country,* a narrative by Guy de Maupassant that tells a touching, sensual, and emotional love story, ushered in a new epoch of filmmaking for Renoir. Using a technique comparable to Impressionist painters, Renoir focused on motifs to recapture original impressions. A year later came *Grand Illusion,* a film in which Renoir's militant spirit came to light. Having experienced World War I as an airplane pilot, he was part of the veteran group for whom war was never to happen again. It was a pacifistic movie with a certain dose of nostalgia and mystery. Although the audiences preferred Marcel Carné's films for their refined style and completed narrative structure, Renoir's *Grand Illusion* drew universal enthusiasm for its remarkable set of actors (Pierre Fresnay, Erich von Stroheim, Marcel Dalio,[30] and Jean Gabin), as well as its

Jean Gabin (1904–76), (Courtesy of the Archives Marcel Carné).

technical team. The story takes place during World War I, when the Germans capture two French Air Force officers from very different backgrounds. Captain de Boeldieu (Pierre Fresnay), an aristocrat, and Lieutenant Maréchal (Jean Gabin), a mechanic before the war, join other prisoners and comrades-in-arms such as Rosenthal (Marcel Dalio), a well-off Jewish banker, in the prisoners' camp. Several months later, after a first and unsuccessful attempt at evasion, they are sent to the remote fortress of Wintersborn, which is ruled by the upper-class German camp commander Von Rauffenstein (Erich von Stroheim). Because of the deference given to his aristocratic lineage,

Captain de Boeldieu is given courteous hospitality; as a result, he initiates an amicable rapport with the German officer to aid Maréchal and Rosenthal's preparations for escape. To conceal their departure, de Boeldieu volunteers to serve as a decoy and distracts the guards by playing a tune on a flute while running on top of the fortress walls. He eventually gets killed by Von Rauffenstein, who, beseeching him to surrender, is forced to obey the military code and orders the guards to fire. Maréchal and Rosenthal, who twisted his ankle in the fall, manage to escape from the fortress, but they must reach Switzerland before the troops catch them in the exposing snowbound landscape. However, both their tempers rise when Rosenthal can no longer walk. Maréchal explodes: "Yes, a parcel, a ball and chain tied to my leg. I never could stand Jews for a start, get it?"[31] They finally seek refuge at a German farm, where a young widow, Elsa (Dita Parlo), with whom Maréchal falls in love, shelters them before they cross the border. Along with this final optimistic reflection on Franco-German relations, the story concludes with a message of anticipated hope, heralding the decline of the old aristocracy and the coming of a modern era, symbolized by the two prisoners' escape.

There is no doubt that this film, loosely based on Renoir's experiences in World War I,[32] provided an exceptional unity of purpose and drama. The message is clear: the rhetoric of war is deceptive, and patriotism is an illusion. The camera work in the film is expert, causing the viewer to move constantly along with the image (though not a single war combat is shown; most of what happens takes place offscreen). In addition to the cinematography, Charles Spaak (1903–75) contributed an extraordinary screenplay. Considered one of the leading scriptwriters at the time, Spaak had already collaborated with Renoir on *The Lower Depths* (*Les bas-fonds,* 1936). The true energy of *Grand Illusion,* however, was in its intimate relationships. In an understated denunciation of war, Renoir not only emphasizes the disintegration of a social idyll but also the primacy of the individual being above anything that is artificially created: the restrictions and conflicts between nations were shaped by outside influences and therefore were not significant, even in a world at war. This film, unlike *The Rules of the Game,* made just two years later, proved the best international accomplishment of Jean Renoir's career.[33] During the 1958 Exposition internationale de Bruxelles, the Cinémathèque Royale de Belgique conducted a survey among the most prominent film historians around the world to designate the list of the twelve all-time greatest motion pictures. The result of the referendum, although remotely objective in its proceedings, included Renoir's *Grand Illusion.* Shortly after *Grand Illusion,* Renoir also directed *The Human Beast*[34] in 1938 in a twentieth-

Jean Gabin, Marcel Carné, Jacques Prévert, and Alexandre Trauner (Courtesy of BIFI).

century adaptation of Emile Zola's novel. In *The Human Beast,* Renoir, who by then was in the vanguard of militant filmmaking, began to move toward Carné's well-known pessimism, and the film was indubitably part of the poetic realism experience.

Although highly criticized before World War II for his indecisive and contradictory positions, Renoir is considered one of the greatest directors of French cinema. André Bazin viewed Renoir as the most accomplished filmmaker of the 1930s and considered him a generator of influence for directors of the next twenty years. His artistic concepts were exemplary, and his mise-en-scène triggered constant technological inventions. Although often believing in a method of improvisation to direct actors best, Renoir's influence was corroborated by a significant and lifelong love for the dramatic stage. During the 1930s, his attachment to acting was obvious. Because of their unprompted performances, Renoir's actors skillfully exceeded a sense of improvisation to communicate a dimension of stark reality and tangible authenticity. On frequent occasions, Renoir performed as an actor in his own films, with his most noteworthy theatrical role as Octave, the unsuccessful conductor in *The Rules of the Game.* Because the human condition as a theme was constantly reflected in all the elements of poetic realism, Renoir's films sought to be as authentic as possible, circumventing the practice of using studio set backgrounds to ultimately enhance the naturalness of actors' performances and credibility.[35]

A synthesis of all Renoir's previous works, *The Rules of the Game* had a complex structure and an elusive message that the public and critics of the time never fully understood. This fantasy is a mundane massacre, and a sharp vision of prewar social degeneration, with a hint of several theatrical traditions (Beaumarchais, Musset, Marivaux). The complex mise-en-scène setting, though somewhat experimental, was far ahead of its time, influencing a number of later directors, François Truffaut in particular. Although now considered by many his masterpiece, *The Rules of the Game,* released on July 7, 1939, was commercially unviable despite its influential emotional charge and the genuineness of its outlook. After the public attempted to set a theater on fire, the film was screened for only three weeks. This comedy, which veered inescapably into a dramatic finale, illustrated a series of ruptures in the social order. For example, the scene showing the senseless carnage of rabbits in the forest became an omen for the disproportionate combats that occurred a few weeks later all over Europe, and it exemplified society's plunge into pointless violence. Although malicious and totally useless, the hunt that is depicted has its conventionalized forms and procedures. Serving as accomplices, the servants beat the trees, driving the rabbits out of their retreat and into the open, where they are slaughtered. Rarely surpassing an ambiance of compelling pessimism, *The*

Alexandre Trauner's background set and Jean Gabin in Marcel Carné's *Daybreak* (*Le jour se lève*, 1939), (Courtesy of the Archives Marcel Carné).

Rules of the Game is less a formulaic kind of plot than it is a testimony to the perennial nature of human vulnerability, insatiability, and cruelty. The story begins with André Jurieux's (Roland Toutain) triumphant arrival in Paris following his transatlantic flight and his expectation of seeing Christine de la Chesnaye (Nora Grégor), the woman for whom he achieved this heroic act, among the huge, enthusiastic crowd. Immediately interviewed by a journalist, André makes his secret disappointment public on the radio. The next day, Octave (Jean Renoir), a friend in common, invites André to a party at Robert and Christine de la Chesnaye's at La Colinière. As the other distinguished guests arrive at the chateau, André Jurieux cannot identify with this entourage of conspiracy and deception. The following day on a hunt, Christine discovers, through her binoculars, the secret relationship between her husband, Robert, and Geneviève (Mila Parely), his longtime mistress. At the same moment, Schumacher (Gaston Modot), the janitor, finds his wife (Paulette Dubost) in the arms of the house servant, Marceau (Julien Carette),[36] and threatens to kill him. André sees his chances with Christine vanish when Christine elicits a new romance with another guest, Saint Aubin. Later that evening, she changes her mind and declares her love to André, and runs off with him. But Robert apprehends both and starts a fight with André. As the evening party comes to an end, Robert makes peace with André and agrees to let his wife leave with the famous aviator. Christine and Octave peacefully walk in the park reminiscing on their mutual childhood until they arrive at the greenhouse. Octave leaves to get his coat from the chateau, but decides to tell André the truth and persuades him to run to Christine. But when André is close to reaching her, Schumacher, the janitor, angered by his wife's deception, who in the darkness recognizes André as Marceau, mortally shoots the pilot. The story ends abruptly with the mourning of the intrepid hero.

The Rules of the Game clearly illustrated the social and moral decadence of French upper-class society before World War II. By radically turning his back on his former "humanist" films, Renoir engaged in a forthright satire of French society, which, a few weeks before the outbreak of the war, exemplified, through a notoriously intricate plot, its citizens as socially egotistical and mentally convoluted, desperately trying to escape a doomed reality. Throughout the film, viewers can feel that the rise of the impending threat of a possible world conflict, coupled with a deep apprehension of hostile foreign neighbors, had generated a defeatist mind-set about the prospects for the future of France. Indeed, the typical hero in Renoir's point of view unquestionably did not long for the future and only attempted to endure the present moment. His atypical use of the camera—overly long shots and extreme wide-angle compositions in unusual depth—is an indirect

Jean Renoir among the actors of *Grand Illusion* (*La grande illusion*, 1937), (Courtesy of BIFI/© Sam Lévin).

Pierre Fresnay (Captain de Boeldieu) and Jean Gabin (Lieutenant Maréchal) in *Grand Illusion* (*La grande illusion*, 1937), (Photo courtesy of the Museum of Modern Art/Film Stills Archive).

allusion to the commedia dell'arte, and consequently designed to capture what happens to all the guests of La Colinière without interrupting their frantic performance. With a pervading atmosphere of paranoia, suspicion, and intrigue, the main characters of *The Rules of the Game* seem equally perplexed about the plot as the audiences were on a first viewing. In 1939, aesthetic references to classic Hollywood movies were solidly established in Europe and usually stipulated the need for a strong story line, several main protagonists with an easily comprehensible outlook, and respect for the genre and other cinematographic codes. Commenting on what appeared to be a disappointing film, André Bazin observed the following: "But this was certainly not the principal cause for the commercial failure of the film. As a conventional love story, the film could have been a success if the scenario had respected the rules of the movie game. But Renoir wanted to make his own style of *drame gai,* and the mixture of genres proved disconcerting to the public."[37] Nevertheless, Renoir's picture stood as the antithesis of American definitions and broke the "rules" and principles of narrative continuity to express a more compelling assessment of French society gone astray on the eve of world conflict.[38] More than sixty years later, the film is still considered one of the most charismatic directing experiences of the prewar. It has been rediscovered by *cinéphiles* around the world and revalued for the eminence and the many strengths that make it one of the great movies of the thirties. Unfortunately, the film was rapidly withdrawn from distribution during the summer of 1939, and consequently was altered and then reedited for its too "depressing" content. It was not until 1965 that the original version was even found. Renoir went on to serve in the film unit of the French army in the first weeks of the war, but was lucky enough to reach Portugal and then the United States after the debacle of May 1940.

Unlike Renoir and Carné, whose prominence benefited from extended and prosperous careers, Jean Vigo (1905–34) directed only four movies, dying at the age of twenty-nine from septicemia. He inaugurated his cinematographic career as an "adolescent performer," in other words with an almost juvenile amusement in the potential of trickery (reminiscent of Georges Méliès), not with a typical and predicable filmmaker's aesthetic. He overlooked the traditional pattern of mainstream cinema and instead assembled his movies according to his perception of the misunderstood poet. He also had a compulsive fascination with the role of the artist and his sources of inspiration. Vigo replaced temporality and the conservative codes of objective realism with personal references to his own life and sentiments. Following his direction of several short documentaries, such as *A propos de Nice* (1930), contrasting the life of the grand hotels and the city's casino with the adjacent urban poverty, and *Taris, roi de l'eau* (1931), Vigo

Jean Renoir (Octave), Roland Toutain (André Jurieu), and Nora Gregor (Christine de La Chesnaye) in Jean Renoir's *The Rules of the Game* (*La règle du jeu*, 1939), (Photo courtesy of the Museum of Modern Art/Film Stills Archive).

rapidly began to shape an unparalleled cinematographic style that would establish his "outsider" status. *Zero of Conduct* (*Zéro de conduite*, 1933),[39] independently produced at the GFFA studios, subversively portrayed the authoritarian boarding school institution to which Vigo had been subjected during his disturbed and painful childhood. The central theme of the film is obvious: the suffocated childhood oppressed by a contrived adult world. Though deprived of visual brilliance and often difficult to follow, the technical value of both picture and dialogue in this study of a disjointed, claustrophobic, and fantastic boarding school remains a youthful innovation of uninhibited excitement. Vigo's cinema can be defined as the meeting point between social cinema and the poetic Avant-garde experience. It had many followers, among them, again François Truffaut.[40]

A year later, Vigo would direct *The Atalante,* filmed mostly on location in France but occasionally on studio interiors, intending to re-create identical conditions found on location. Jean (Jean Dasté), captain of a barge on the Seine River, marries a country girl, Juliette (Dita Parlo), in a small Normandy village, and together they start a new life on the water. Reluctantly, she accepts the monotonous life on board a ship and immediately resents the close cohabitation with Jules (Michel Simon), an old eccentric. Following a fight with her husband, she decides to head to Paris, only to experience a much more difficult lifestyle than she had ever imagined. Resigned to her own fate, she relinquishes her desire for freedom and returns to her husband and an unvarying existence. In the movie, when the character of Juliette is alone in the city, the viewers are shown an exceptionally rare image of France during the post–Great Depression era that included prostitution, the lines of downhearted and unemployed, and a famished, hopeless robber beaten by an elegant, well-fed bourgeois. Vigo approximated his vital characters with the same judgment for realistic analysis, filming the discomforts of thwarted dreams and the ineffective relationship of two simple characters from completely different worlds.

Despite the restrictions imposed and the editing it received from French censorship, *The Atalante* was a film of exceptional authority. Jean Vigo presented a persuasive picture of the adult world in its deep responsiveness and recognition of sensual love. The film can be regarded as an Expressionist archetype, where action was interpreted as if emerging from inside a besieged individual's mind. By illustrating the individual's struggle with sensual love and nature, Vigo suggested an unusual complicity between the sailors of the barge, as the story imparted several fantastic episodes pictured during the scene under water. Far from functioning like most realist directors, Vigo's Surrealist rendition of a dream world was never remote from his story lines. He exemplified both the ecstasy of life and his own inner emotional impetus, and he transmitted images with an infinite assortment of contrasting styles, affectionate but acerbic, in order to invite the audience to reach his foremost objective, the poetry of the "unreal." In addition to being one of the precursors of the *ciné-club*[41] movement in France, Vigo was an authentic and sincere director who set the tone for poetry and realism of the 1930s. It is important to note that both commercial failure and the death of the author-director resulted in the cancellation of the film's forthcoming screenings. French censorship banned Vigo's movies until 1945, and it was only in 1990 that a thorough restoration of *The Atalante* made the film available in its intended version.

Finally, in addition to filmmakers such as Clair, Renoir, Carné, Vigo, and Feyder, it is impossible to omit the role of director Julien Duvivier. Although Duvivier's cinematographic career lasted several decades, he nevertheless remains associated with a particular style and time period. The positive reception of his movies was in large part contingent on the inspired coherence of his screenplays, whether created by himself or by an expert scenarist. Duvivier's pictures from 1934 to 1937, along with acting performances by Jean Gabin and screenplays by Charles Spaak, greatly appealed to French audiences. These films include *Escape from Yesterday* (*La Bandéra*, 1935), a romanticized adventure movie with a Foreign Legion presence in North Africa. Adapted from Pierre MacOrlan's novel, *They Were Five* (*La belle équipe*, 1935) is a film about a group of five unemployed men (Gabin, Charles Vanel, Aimos, Robert Lynen, and Raymond Cordy), living in a rundown hotel, who after winning 100,000 francs in the lottery try to manage an open-air café-restaurant on the banks of the Marne River, only to split their friendly group. Finally, there is the well-liked *Pépé le Moko*, adapted by Henri Jeanson from Roger d'Ashelbé's novel, which offers interesting imagery of exotic lands that identify the depth of France's self-image as a colonial power. Gabin plays an expatriate Parisian mobster gone underground in the Algerian Casbah who slowly loses his willpower when challenged by the graceful Gaby (Mireille Balin), a Parisian seductress. An ominous ambiance full of darkness beautifully coincides with the figure of Pépé, the outsider who, after a romantic interlude with Gaby, attempts to flee with her, only to see her run away. His plans are further thwarted by police officer Slimane (Lucas Gridoux) in a typical spine-chilling ending—encircled by the police forces on the wharf, Gabin stabs himself. The unruly Algerian collective order, with its multiracial faces, serves as a fine parallel to the presence of the stylish but equally uncontrollable Gaby. Inspired by Howard Hawks's *Scarface* (1932), the film succeeded in France and resulted in the 1938 American remake *Algiers*, directed by John Cromwell.

All three of these productions by Duvivier had noticeably benefited from the Jean Gabin myth: the hopeless hero obligated to a life of crime who is, ultimately, callously eradicated. One of Duvivier's rare artistic limitations was the inaccessibility to the intensity and profundity of his characters' emotions. Thanks to Charles Spaak, Duvivier's movies presented custom-made parts not only for Jean Gabin, but also for actors and actresses such as Françoise Rosay, Viviane Romance, Charles Vanel, Harry Baur, Raimu, and Pierre Blanchar. It was *Escape from Yesterday* that truly established Gabin's national standing. He plays Pierre Gilieth, a man running away from a murder accusation in Paris. As he reaches his destination in Barcelona with no money, he desperately struggles to forget his past by enrolling in the Spanish Foreign Legion. His days become complicated as new friendships with fellow countrymen, Mulot (Raymond Aimos) and Lucas (Robert Le Vigan), and a love affair with Aischa (Annabella) make him want to fight against the violence of war.

In his films, Duvivier visualized leading roles as irreversibly spellbound by their existence and their social environment with little faith in collective accomplishment. In addition, the predominance of indi-

vidual vulnerability and suspicion is perceptible even in films whose
conclusion offers a rare uplifting ending. More than a half century
later, Duvivier could be considered a predictive reporter rather than a
"committed celebrant" who involuntarily represented the (projected)
downfall of the Popular Front.[42]

CINEMATOGRAPHY AND THE POETICS OF IMAGES

In the early 1930s several important cinematographers, such as Curt
Courant and Eugène Schufftan, came to France and rapidly contributed
to the growth of French cinema, thanks to their inspiring knowledge
of the manipulation of light and framing. In addition to the expressive
purpose of their assignment, one of their most important contributions
was recognition by directors of the cinematographer's decisive responsibility in the creative process. The dilemma between actors and set
was an eternal source of tension among technical crew, cinematographers, and directors. Often based on the hierarchy and the order of
appearance in the pictures, the set designers argued the fundamental
importance of an appropriate atmosphere for the actors. In other words,
as Colin Crisp explains, the actors' photographic glamour and photogenic style could never be privileged at the expense of the set: "The
unjustified use of close-ups, rare angles, and camera movements has a
great disadvantage: it destroys the illusion of participating in the
narrative; instead of believing in the film, the spectator focuses on the
way it's put together."[43] So-called European lighting style, in contrast
with Hollywood, did not emphasize the physical features of the actors
in their most complimentary light. Throughout the 1930s, the preeminence of the artistic background over the light of the actors confirmed the minor attention given to movie stars in general and the
greater importance given to the portrayal of French society over the
actors' beauty or virility. The lighting setups, chiaroscuro, and knowledge of different hues of gray were crucial artistic mechanisms for the
illusion of depth and relief, and were the most important aspects of
the European scene.

Before the coming of sound, the debates between on-location shooting and studio reenactment had always been a dilemma with which
directors and producers had to deal. According to André Bazin, the
two types of French filmmakers of the prewar decade can best be
described as follows: Jean Vigo, Jean Renoir, Jean Grémillon, Marcel
Pagnol, as filmmakers utilizing real decor, and Marcel Carné, René
Clair, Jacques Feyder, and Julien Duvivier as filmmakers more inclined
toward synthetic decor. The role of the set had primary importance
since it could either establish the artistic style of the film or incorporate the backdrop in the action. Some of the major problems encoun-

tered by technical crews with on-location shooting was dealing with the public on the set, clearing traffic, handling unwanted noise, which deeply affected the quality of direct recording, maneuvering cameras for preferred angles, and obtaining ideal lighting. Some directors, less interested in visual and artistic meticulousness, shot exclusively on location since it provided a higher degree of authenticity. The majority of early set designers' artistic backgrounds came principally from their experience in the theater, with its strong emphasis on colorful, spectacular, extravagant, and luxurious settings. Designers were suddenly compelled to modify their expertise to fit the designs characterized by the restricted symbolism of poetic realism. The primary importance of the background, originating from the theatrical tradition, came into the consciousness of directors in the early 1930s and served a double purpose in creating a film: contributing to the fashioning of a unique atmosphere and facilitating the "sympathy," and plausibility, of the characters. One of the drawbacks that emerged with motion pictures and that was irrelevant in theater backdrops was the function of close-ups, which divulged any scenographer's imperfections. Consequently, set designers had to focus to an even greater degree on their precision and realism.

> Set designers were faced therefore with a set of tensions, of contradictions. Trained as artists, and seeing themselves as engaged in an artistic undertaking, they were constrained to suppress any inclination to realize their artistic aspirations in the ways their fellow artists in other media realized them. Conditioned to an ideology of individual self-expression, they had to recognize the supremacy of a teamwork and collaboration in which, if there was a directive personality, it was not theirs. Given the supreme creative task of designing and building a world, they found themselves restricted to building one that would be a credible replica of the real world. The décor must pass unnoticed, yet determine the mood and atmosphere of the film. A décor which obtruded to the point of being symbolic would mean fewer spectators, financial crisis for the producer, and no more work for the set designer.[44]

The key decorators of the decade include Lazare Meerson (1900–1938) and his protégé, Alexandre Trauner. Meerson built the set representing the futuristic factory with *Freedom for Us* in the Epernay studios, as well as the extraordinary set representing the Renaissance city of Boom in *Carnival of Flanders* (1935). Trauner[45] was also well known for his reconstruction of Canal St. Martin in *Hôtel du Nord,* and the suburban working-class edifice decor built in false perspective to intensify the impression of solitude in *Daybreak.* Born in Hungary, Trauner arrived in France in 1929 and began his film career as assistant to Lazare Meerson. Then, in 1932, he met poet and screenwriter Jacques Prévert. Later, he went to Hollywood, working in turn with

Howard Hawks, Gene Kelly, Anatole Litvak, David Lean, Orson Welles, and finally Billy Wilder, with whom he won an Oscar for *The Apartment* in 1960. After his return to Europe in 1974, Trauner worked with directors such as Joseph Losey in *Monsieur Klein* (1976) and *Don Giovanni* (1979); Bertrand Tavernier, in *Round Midnight* (1986), Claude Berri in *Tchao Pantin!* (1983), and Luc Besson in *Subway* (1985).

The goal of set designers of the classic period was to guide the audience to an analytical reading of the picture without transcending into a symbolic or conceptual process of abstraction, which in the postwar era would set the tone for aesthetic convention (as the antithesis of originality and art in general). This explains why after the war, numerous decorators suddenly decided to abandon studio shooting for preexisting location shooting, such as Italian neorealist films *Open City* (*Roma, città aperta*, 1945) and *The Bicycle Thief* (*Ladri di biciclette*, 1948).

Chapter 3
French Cinema of the Occupation

With the beginning of a global conflict that rapidly resulted in the enforced censorship of most commercialized productions in Europe, the makers of French cinema, already debilitated by the industry's own structural organization (or rather from the absence of it), could not possibly detect any optimistic sign for the future. Notwithstanding the importation of hundreds of German productions, the ban on Anglo-American movies unpredictably encouraged French filmmakers. And while the sudden vanishing of foreign competition, in terms of cinematographic productions, coupled with the massive exodus of its most celebrated stars, could have quite realistically reduced the economic impetus and artistic vigor of the French film industry, the actual consequences proved just the opposite. The Nazi Occupation, with its compulsory need for pleasure and inherent escapism, saw an outburst of original works, the rise of first-time young directors, and the creation of a cinematographic school that lasted until the era of the French New Wave in the late 1950s. During the Occupation, more than two hundred films were directed and released in France. Today, many of them belong to what film historians as well as typical moviegoers consider classics; for example, Marcel Carné's *Children of Paradise* (*Les enfants du Paradis*, 1945).

FRANCE IN 1940

France and Great Britain reluctantly declared war on Germany on September 3, 1939, two days after the invasion of Poland and the annexation of Danzig. On May 10, 1940, after a seven-month hiatus from military combat (what the French called the *drôle de guerre*), came the first wave of Nazi invasions in the Netherlands, Belgium, Luxembourg, and later France. Following the collapse of the French army, the German Wehrmacht crossed the French border using blitzkrieg tactics and entered an undefended Paris on June 14. Unlike the dramatic events of the preceding year, which occurred during the first hours of World War II on French territory, the year 1940 was an economic loss for the French film industry.[1] From May until October of that year, due to various military interventions and civil evacuations, all movie productions were stopped and existing distribution instantaneously dried up. The German invasion indirectly forced the already weakened French Parliament to find another strategy and leader. Numerous well-known politicians, such as General Charles de Gaulle, Edouard Daladier, and Pierre Mendès-France, had already left for England and North Africa to set up a government in exile. In his famous radio appeal on June 18, 1940, de Gaulle attempted to persuade French partisans to resume combat on the Allied side (although the French army was reduced to 100,000 soldiers and the navy was neutralized in all its ports). While many French citizens gathered to listen to de Gaulle's appeal, however, Marshal Philippe Pétain, hero of World War I and eighty-four years old at the time, had already persuaded a French majority to collaborate with the Germans occupying France in a publicly broadcast appeal. As a result, Pétain remained the principal political figure for France. De Gaulle became the head of the Resistance movement outside France, involving the Free French forces and a French National Committee, to which some colonial territories rallied.

An armistice accord between the German high command of the armed forces and French government representatives took place near Compiègne on June 22, 1940 (in the very same railway car that had been the scene of the French and Allied forces' triumph in 1918). Compelled to immediately cease fire against German troops in France as well as in French colonies and territories, the French government also had to face many difficult stipulations of the armistice; this included the immediate selection of the seat of its future government in unoccupied France. The country was separated into two different zones, which delimited the northern part of France as the "occupied zone," where the German army exerted strict control over the administration, and the southern part as the "free zone," an area that nevertheless remained under the control of a collaborationist government located in Vichy. Caught by intense panic, the French Parliament met in Vichy on July 10 to desperately organize the remains of the devastated country. The debates were clearly dominated by Pierre Laval, at the time Pétain's prime minister, who genuinely persuaded the rest of the legislative body that France had lost the battle and consequently saw it as his duty to settle the country within the new Nazi guidelines. By dint of Laval's persuasion, the parliament voted full power to the *maréchal,* marking the end of France's prewar government as well as the termination of the Third Republic. Marshal Pétain's close collaborators, with the exception of Laval and a few others, rapidly gathered right-wing conservatives and traditionalists, whereas real pro-Fascist activists, such as Jacques Doriot and Marcel Déat, who aspired to an authentic Fascist regime, left Vichy for Paris, where they used German funding to conspire against Pétain. While Vichy's actual power still included unoccupied France and numerous colonies, Laval's administration was never recognized by the Allies, and instead functioned as a puppet government for Nazi authorities.

Before the coming of pro-Nazi propaganda in 1940, no politicians of the Third Republic wanted to fight for the film medium, which for them was considered no more than a common form of entertainment for merely popular exhibitions. What had characterized the French film industry during the preceding decade was its total lack of structure and regulation as well as its inclination toward amateurism and improvisation. Film historians agree that the German invasion of France occurred at a significant time for the always-struggling French film industry, which had neither technically nor financially improved from the setback inflicted by the American talkies of the early 1930s. The mobilization of French troops put the country in suspense, and the film industry, much like other sectors of society and the economy, was no exception. More than twenty films were interrupted with the outbreak of war.

Although diminished by the exodus of its most notorious talents of the late 1930s (Jean Renoir, René Clair, Julien Duvivier, Max Ophuls, Jean Gabin, Louis Jouvet, and Michèle Morgan, among others), French cinema was in fact on the threshold of one of its greatest periods. The lack of activity and numerous restrictions imposed by the war as well as the difficult living conditions drew large crowds to movie theaters (which were often heated during the wintertime).[2] With the recognition of the film medium as a new and efficient weapon of propaganda, it was decided by the Nazi administration on September 9, 1940, to prohibit British and American films in occupied Europe, which indirectly facilitated the production of new French films. European spectatorship then had the choice between German, Italian, and French movies. Not surprisingly, the "captive French public" overwhelmingly preferred French films.

As early as July 1940, the German management for French cinema in France intended to create extremely favorable conditions for the German film market at all levels of productions (distribution, management, technical industries, and actors). Along with the creation of new German movie companies in France, the new regulations enslaved the entire profession to the mercy of the Propaganda Abteilung (propaganda department), and the development of the German film market in France imposed the establishment of new economic structures, such as participations to the capital of preexisting French film companies, the "aryanization" of film companies, the creation of new French film companies with German capital, and the hiring of the best French directors, technicians, actors, and actresses of the moment.

THE EXODUS OF FRENCH CINEMA CELEBRITIES

Numerous young emerging actors and actresses of French cinema, such as Michèle Morgan, Danielle Darrieux, Micheline Presle, and Michel Auclair—often called "Left Bank celebrities"—established themselves at the Grand Hotel in Cannes or in the outskirts of Nice, appearing to have left behind the rising political tension of the summer of 1939. The first Cannes Film Festival, slated to begin on September 1, 1939, the day Poland was stormed, was irrevocably canceled (it officially came into being on September 19, 1946). For those who decided to flee abroad, the road to Hollywood was far from easy. In addition to having a required visa from the French authorities and one from the country of destination, candidates for departure had to cross the Pyrenees and Spain to reach Portugal (a neutral country at the time) because all the Atlantic ports had been closed.

Françoise Rosay, actress and wife of film director Jacques Feyder, fled with her husband to Switzerland. Erich von Stroheim, Marcel Dalio,[3] Jean-Pierre Aumont, Julien Duvivier,[4] and Max Ophuls embarked on transatlantic voyages. Pressured by the German ambassador to set up a play in Germany, Louis Jouvet pretended to be involved in a theatrical tour in Switzerland in order to flee occupied France and go to South America for the next four years. Following in the footsteps of several of his fellow countrymen, Jean Gabin turned down an offer from Continental, a newly created German film company based in France, to avoid the drastic working conditions of the Nazi occupation. He instead expatriated himself to the United States, ultimately signing with Fox Studios. Although already a national celebrity in France and one of the best-known media magnets of the big screen all over the world, Gabin's American film experiences in *Moontide* (*La péniche de l'amour,* 1942) and *The Impostor* (*L'imposteur,* 1944) did not succeed and did not meet the actor's prior level of prestige (though directed by prominent directors such as Fritz Lang and Archie Mayo, respectively). In 1943, following a brief romance with Marlene Dietrich[5] and discontented with his American interlude, Gabin first enrolled in the Free French navy, then in the Free French forces, and ended the war as a tank driver in the Second Division Blindée. It was only in the 1950s that Gabin, away from the French screen for more than ten years, regained his reputation as a top actor in French cinema. Unlike the suburban proletarian or mobster roles of his prewar films, he was now used for experienced, successful middle-aged men of confidence and authority in such films as Marcel Carné's *La Marie du Port* (1949).

In 1940 Gabin's "lover" in *Port of Shadows,* the young Michèle Morgan, also fled to Hollywood, where she married actor William Marshall and signed a contract with RKO. Unfortunately, like most of her compatriots in the United States, her films were mediocre and her luck was often bad. Even in Tim Whelan's *Higher and Higher* (1943), starring the young Frank Sinatra, the femme fatale image imposed on Morgan failed. Chosen by Warner Brothers' Studios for the leading role in *Casablanca,* RKO would not release her for the suggested compensation, so the part went to Ingrid Bergman. Michèle Morgan did, however, appear with Humphrey Bogart in Michael Curtiz's *Passage to Marseilles* (1944), a substandard continuation of *Casablanca.* Her Hollywood feature films included Robert Stevenson's *Joan of Paris* (1942) and Edwin L. Marin's *Two Tickets to London* (1943).

Another French actress who got her ticket to Hollywood was Danielle Darrieux (b. 1917). Her career extended from the beginning of French sound pictures. Starting as one of France's most celebrated artists, she starred with Charles Boyer in Anatole Litvak's *Mayerling* (1936). Danielle Darrieux embarked for her Hollywood sojourn in 1937 and was quickly contracted by Universal Studios. After the release of Henry Koster's *The Rage of Paris* (*Coqueluche de Paris,* 1938), she returned to France unexpectedly (Universal Studios filed a suit for contract violation, but the quarrel fell into oblivion with the outbreak of the war). During the Occupation, she worked for Continental and, in particular, got involved with fellow actors Viviane Romance, Suzy Delair, Junie Astor, and Albert Préjean in a *tournée de galas* organized by studio manager Alfred Greven in Germany (March 18–31, 1942), which brought suspicions of collaboration against her in 1944. In the 1950s, Danielle Darrieux no longer played the French coquette and wild adolescent but rather mature roles such as Emma in Max Ophuls's *La ronde* (*La ronde,* 1950), an adaptation of Arthur Schnitzler's *Reigen,* and Madame Rosa in *House of Pleasure* (*Le plaisir,* 1951). Her most famous films are the above-mentioned as well as *The Truth of Our*

Marriage (*La vérité sur Bébé Donge,* 1951), *Napoléon* (*Napoléon,* 1954), *The Red and the Black* (*Le rouge et le noir,* 1954), and *Pilgrimage to Rome* (*L'année sainte,* 1976).

Actors were not the only professionals of the French film industry to flee the Nazi invasion. Directors like Jean Renoir also chose the American alternative. Renoir's situation in France, similar to Carné's but more pressing, was precarious because several of his films were fiercely disapproved by the new regime (*The Crime of Monsieur Lange* and *People of France,* both in 1936).[6] He also had signed several articles with a strong emphasis on his anti-German sentiments. Renoir directed six films during his Hollywood interval. Between 1940 and 1946, his movies received a tepid welcome by American audiences. One of the main objections Renoir had to face in the United States was the strong aversion for his new creations involving French themes presented through a Hollywood perspective and technique. This alleged artistic "duplicity" clearly disoriented the French public, which did not recognize the creator of *Grand Illusion,* the film that brought Renoir international attention and acclaim from American producers.

When the German army invaded France, Renoir, while directing *The Story of Tosca* (*La Tosca*) in Italy, called off the shooting of the film. Later that same year, encouraged by other filmmakers residing in the United States to join the Hollywood experience, he embarked for New York, where he arrived in December. In California, he signed a short-term contract with Twentieth Century-Fox. Darryl Zanuck wanted Renoir to remain within a strictly French background by showing a typical French story in an emblematic French landscape for the American public. But Renoir intended just the opposite: to present American subject matter through a privileged foreign eye. Renoir's legacy included *Swamp Water* (1941) and *This Land Is Mine* (1943), his biggest success. In March 1944, Renoir was asked to shoot a short film entitled *Salute to France* for the American GIs just prior to their landing in Normandy. At the end of 1944, Renoir directed *The Southerner,* the release of which in 1945 dismayed the American public in the South, but won the prize for Best Actor and Best Director at the New York Film Critics Awards, as well as the Golden Lion of Venice that same year. Finally in 1946, Jean Renoir completed *The Diary of a Chambermaid,* followed by *Woman on the Beach* in 1947. With *The Diary of a Chambermaid,* the "Frenchness" of his talent was for the first time fully revealed on screen, as Zanuck had expected from the beginning of Renoir's American sojourn. Renoir's penchant for creativity and original cinematic techniques gave him a new dimension and style once in Hollywood. Greatly captivated with water imagery and symbolism (like his father), Renoir repeatedly used the element as a symbol of eternal life. In 1951, in India, he shot a motion picture entitled *The*

River, an inspired color production (before making his comeback in Italy in 1952 with *The Golden Coach/Carrosse d'or*). Yet, in taking a critical distance from Renoir's overall career, all of his Hollywood movies can be ranked among his least memorable works as a result of the significant obstacles he faced in adapting to the American production structure.

The same certainly could not be said for actor Charles Boyer (1897–1978), whose career blossomed in Paris during the 1920s, and who rapidly became a popular actor on stage as well as on screen. Constantly in search of the latest European rising talents, MGM invited Boyer to Hollywood and shortly offered the ambitious actor a contract. The main ambition of MGM was to make a star out of the young French talent. To charm and persuade American spectators, however, Boyer, although already speaking several foreign languages, had to be fluent in English. He had to learn rapidly in order to survive the fast production pace of Hollywood studios. While Boyer diligently worked on his English, Irving Thalberg, MGM's legendary vice president, took a personal interest in the young actor, offering him roles in French versions of MGM's films for European markets. Boyer costarred with the most famous actresses of the time: Ingrid Bergman, Marlene Dietrich, and Greta Garbo. Following his marriage to British actress Pat Paterson,[7] Boyer also worked in Europe, most notably with his performance in *Mayerling*. At age thirty-nine, during the first hours of the war, Boyer joined the French army and fought until the defeat of 1940. Nevertheless, he maintained many contacts with the Free French units of the Resistance throughout the Occupation. Boyer's movie career remained successful; he made more than eighty films, including famous American dramas such as *All This and Heaven Too* (1940) with Bette Davis and *Gaslight* (1944) with Ingrid Bergman, as well as remakes of French blockbusters such as *Algiers* (1938), adapted from Duvivier's *Pépé le Moko; The Thirteenth Letter* (1951), adapted from Henri-Georges Clouzot's controversial *Le Corbeau* (1942); and his last feature performance in *A Matter of Time* (1976). Boyer's soft and languorous voice completed to perfection the romantic image of "Frenchness" that Hollywood conveyed for decades on the screen.

Another image of the French that Hollywood proudly paraded on screen—though less romantic but with abounding gusto—was the one created by Maurice Chevalier (1888–1972). Parisian by birth, and from the most Parisian of all districts, Ménilmontant, Chevalier became an international show business legend over several decades, beginning in the 1920s with his music hall successes, such as "Mimi" and "Valentine," at the Casino de Paris. He signed with Paramount Studios and landed his first role in Hollywood for a musical entitled *Innocents of Paris* (*La chanson de Paris,* 1928), just one year after Alan Crossland's

The Jazz Singer, starring Al Jolson. Chevalier embodied the stereo-
typical Parisian with his distinctive *gouaille* (verbal stamina), cheerful-
ness, and, of course, heavy French accent. During the Occupation, his
tour through Germany in support of French prisoners of war later
attracted suspicion of possible indulgence toward the German regime.
He was nominated for Academy Awards for Ernst Lubitsch's *The Love
Parade* (*Parade d'amour,* 1929) and Hobart Henley's *The Big Pond* (*La
grande mare,* 1930). In 1958, his performance in *Gigi* reactivated his
Hollywood career following the McCarthy era, during which he had
been explicitly labeled a communist. Maurice Chevalier retired from
the theatrical stage in 1968.

Because of the numerous voluntary and involuntary precipitated
departures to Hollywood (and other destinations), several assistant
directors rose to become directors. Although they started their career
under extremely difficult conditions, the new generation of filmmakers
already had extensive training in the cinematographic industry, contrary to their predecessors, who had learned from the outside.[8] Most
saw their cinematographic careers soar. These included Jacques Becker,
for *It Happened at the Inn* (*Goupi-Mains-Rouges,* 1943); Robert Bresson,
for *Angels of the Streets* (*Les anges du péché,* 1943) and *Ladies of the Park*
(*Les dames du Bois de Boulogne,* 1945); Clouzot, for *The Murderer Lives at
Number 21* (*L'assassin habite au 21,* 1942); Louis Daquin, for *Portrait of
Innocence* (*Nous les gosses,* 1941) and *Premier de cordée* (1943); and André
Cayatte for *Shop-Girls of Paris* (*Au Bonheur des Dames,* 1943). Along
with these new directors came new actors, such as Suzy Delair (b.
1916), Jean Marais (1913–98), Alain Cuny (1908–94), Serge Reggiani
(b. 1922), Gérard Philipe (1922–59), Martine Carol (1920–67), Danièle Delorme (b. 1926), Maria Casarès (1922–96), Paul Meurisse
(1912–79), Daniel Gelin (b. 1921), Marie Déa (1912–92), Micheline
Presle (b. 1922), Odette Joyeux (b. 1914), and Madeleine Sologne
(1912–95). Although most entertainment activities were slow during
the first months of the war, movie theaters and music halls were almost
always sold out because they offered a depressed and discontented
population an immediate escape from the reality of the Occupation,
hunger, and endless material struggles. During the entire period of the
Occupation, the French public enjoyed some of its most celebrated
actors: Fernandel (1903–71), Raimu (1883–1946), Saturnin Fabre
(1884–1961), Pierre Renoir (1885–1952), Albert Préjean (1894–
1979), Robert Le Vigan (1900–1972), Pierre Fresnay (1897–1975),
Fernand Ledoux (1897–1993), Jean-Louis Barrault (1910–94), Viviane
Romance (1909–91), Arletty (1898–1992), Mireille Balin (1909–68),
Edwige Feuillère (1907–98), Harry Baur (1880–1943), Charles Vanel
(1892–1989), Michel Simon (1895–1975), Jules Berry (1883–1951),
Gaby Morlay (1893–1964), Madeleine Renaud (1900–1994), Ginette

Leclerc (1912–92), and others. Not surprisingly, the most popular movie genres, mainly of the "escapist" variety,[9] were comedies, costume dramas, romantic comedies, thrillers, historical productions, and legendary tales. According to film historian Jean-Pierre Bertin-Maghit, French movies eagerly dodged the reality of life since audiences equally wanted to escape the reality of war. Among the 220 films produced during the war years, only a handful reflected a contemporary situation dealing with the war and the reality of the Nazi Occupation.[10]

FRENCH CINEMA AND VICHY

Although Vichy's spirit constantly strived to invest in French cinema and its industry, it never quite succeeded in maneuvering its works of art during the four years of the Occupation. And as paradoxical as it may appear, much of French filmmaking took shape during this tormented period. The slogan *Travail, Famille, Patrie* (Labor, Family, Homeland) illustrated an entire symbolist paradigm of family values, the joy of labor,[11] and craftsmanship that became the content of documentaries. It was also the occasion for the extreme right wing to create a climate of expiation for all the "mistakes" made during the preceding decade (allegedly caused by the Jews and left-wing Republicans with Masonic connections) and to eventually censor the best French productions from the preceding years: *Hôtel du Nord, Grand Illusion, Port of Shadows,* and *Daybreak,* among them.

A fervent anti-Semitism emerged following decades of politically right extremist activities coupled with thae pressure of the occupying forces (Referat Film cinema services as well as the Propaganda Staffel directed at the time by Dr. Dietrich). Marshal Pétain, who never tempered his political position against "too much" Jewish influence in the Third Republic, certainly capitalized on the indistinguishable ill feelings held by many toward political leaders of the Popular Front and its successors, such as former premier Léon Blum and Edouard Daladier (Jewish and non-Jewish, respectively), who were speedily put on trial by the Vichy government for their political ties with the former administration. In this context, Vichy presented the German presence as a just and logical punishment. Subsequently, Jews and communists were the principal guilty icons. Many directors, caught by this hostile momentum, published articles about the negative presence of Hollywood productions on French soil.[12] Marcel L'Herbier himself, a pioneer of French silent films, indulged in a critical discourse that left no doubt about the political climate of the Occupation: it clearly represented French cinema as the victim of American and Jewish economic powers. Indeed, the presence of Jews, much more important on the production side of the cinematographic industry than on the acting scene, had inherited a bad reputation following the scandalous bankruptcy of the Pathé-Nathan company in 1936 (see chapter 1). The Third Republic's low "cinematographic standards," represented and influenced by the American "enemy," were regularly identified as the source of the disaster and placed in opposition to the moral order.

Subsequent to the creation of a new commission, labeled the Commissariat général aux questions juives (Commission for Jewish Affairs), French authorities undertook a legalistic process to authenticate different origins and proof of "Jewishness" or "non-Jewishness." On October 3, 1940, Vichy introduced, on its own volition, the articles of the new racial laws: any individual who had two Jewish grandparents or who was married to a Jew would fall into the category of Jewish. With the immediate implementation of these decrees Jews, or categorized Jews, were no longer allowed to exercise the professions of film directors, administrators, business managers, company and theater owners, cameramen, and journalists.[13] Prohibiting Jewish participation in any of the film industry's activity began the long and latent "purification" process of the cinematographic profession. But the role of Vichy in the massive arrests and deportation of Jews created dismay and to this day remains controversial. The silent and systematic repression exerted by the French public administration in tracking down the "unwelcome" foreigners throughout the 1930s is an essential component without which an understanding of the actual preestablished process would not be possible. In 1940, the representation of Jews as the enemy of France was already widespread and therefore did not break new ground. One could argue that the version, according to which Nazi pressure railroaded the Vichy government to enact anti-Semitic laws and to establish a process of "aryanization" of Jewish property in France, remains somewhat unverified.

Following the declaration of war, many foreign Jews who were involved in French cinema were arrested and sent to French camps; others were able to flee abroad, or for a few, to work underground under a different name (for example, Joseph Kosma who worked under the pseudonym of Georges Mouque and Alexandre Trauner, who, unlike many eastern Europeans, had chosen to remain with his prewar crew). The witch hunt had begun. The participation of French police in virtually all anti-Semitic apprehensions, both in the occupied and free zones, facilitated the events of the Vélodrome d'Hiver of July 1942, which sent thousands of Jews to deportation and death camps.[14] Vichy's policy seemed to be a vindictive enterprise of the late anti-Dreyfus activists more than an enactment of allegiance to the occupying forces. Actors themselves, though safeguarded by their national fame and deference, could not elude the unremitting allegations of an anti-Semitic press. Harry Baur, one of the most reputable French actors, who starred in Maurice Tourneur's *Volpone* in 1940, also had one of the most tragic destinies. After his participation in Continental's first production with Christian-Jaque's *The Murder of Santa Claus* (*L'assasinat du Père Noël*, 1941), the actor was suddenly accused of Jewish origins by the collaborationist review *Je suis partout*. While firmly defending himself about his identity, he was forced by the Nazis to play a role in *La symphonie d'une vie* (1942), a German musical comedy. But after shooting the film, the accusations came back to haunt him. Following his return to France, authorities declared him an English agent who had provided help in the escape of several prisoners.[15] Baur was immediately arrested and sent to prison. He died a Nazi prisoner, worn out by the physical, psychological, and moral tortures he underwent in 1943, just a few days after his liberation on April 8.

How well organized was the French film industry before the advent of the war? From the early years of the Lumière brothers' Cinématographe in 1895 until Renoir's *The Rules of the Game* in 1939, its history had been, even for its greatest masterpieces, an endless epic of adventurous enterprises that conjoined financial scandals with artistic feats, and bankruptcy with unprecedented creativity. For the first time, despite all the social upheavals, French cinema was contained within a firm political and economic structure. Consequently, the government was finally able to take command of the industry and of the distribution of motion pictures. The war was also a good occasion for the government, and indirectly the industry, to unconditionally regulate the economic and logistic flaws[16] of the past and ultimately to impose administrative guidelines on a profession that for decades had produced a certain customary negligence. The film industry was now attached to a ministry called the General Secretary of Information, and Cinema Services became the central organ of its management. The government was concomitantly in charge of censorship commissions, propaganda initiatives, production assessments, negotiations with the Propaganda Abteilung and the decisions of a new structure, the COIC, or Comité d'organisation des industries cinématographiques (Organizational Committee for Cinematographic Industry). Created on October 26, 1940, the COIC was directed by Jean-Louis Tixier-Vignancour and Raoul Ploquin.

The new COIC put up countless obstacles to French filmmakers. One of the first resolutions of the committee was to impose the use of the famous *carte professionelle* (CIP, or professional card) without which no actor, director, cameraman, or set assistant could possibly work. To be able to begin the shooting of a movie, producers had to obtain a triple license for all stages of production. A production visa (mandatory until 1942), a management visa (*visa d'exploitation*), and finally, if necessary, an exportation visa were attributed by the Referat Film and distributed by the newly created COIC. Needless to say, only non-Jewish and experienced directors were the recipients. In addition to that obstacle, directors had to deal with the shortage of film stock, which consequently reduced the number of allocated licenses by half (not including the numerous power cuts that choked production until 1944). German control and power over French filmmaking rapidly increased. On October 17, 1940, the Nazi military command intercepted all existing negatives of films made after January 1, 1939, and later on May 21, 1941, it confiscated all films whose initial screening was prior to October 1, 1937, as well as films that "ostentatiously" exalted French patriotism.[17] (Once the films were destroyed, the recovered nitrates were reused to make blank-film stock.) After the disappearance of all Anglo-American movies on European soil, German productions started to invade the French market in 1941, growing from twenty percent of the market to saturate the screens completely.

Another restrictive outcome was the abolition of double programming in theaters. Before the advent of the COIC, French audiences used to enjoy for the price of a ticket the so-called double programming which included two movies back to back, one of which usually corresponded to a B-picture feature film, plus newsreels, a documentary, and several live attractions. But with the limitation of film and power, and the introduction of curfews, the new commission imposed the *programme unique,* which now included one feature film, one documentary, and a single newsreel. It was during the projections of the Wochenschau (weekly show) that most of the mockery came from spectators who were outraged by the level and content of the Nazi propaganda. As expected, when appearing on screen, the Germans were immediately booed, whereas the English and Americans were acclaimed. Nevertheless, not all new measures emanating from the COIC were to be considered restrictive and punitive. Several new measures benefited the film industry to such a degree that some are still active today. These include the establishment of a censorship system to protect viewers under the age of sixteen, the normalization and uniformity of ticket prices (which finally regulated box office statistics and compelled theater managers to be accountable for their profits), the establishment of advances to anticipated productions starting in May 1941 and financial assistance to short film productions[18] (because of the prohibition against double bills, which indirectly benefited the shorts), and the creation in January 1944 of the prestigious Institut des hautes études cinématographiques (IDHEC/French Institute of Advanced Film Studies, which has since become known as FEMIS), presided over by Marcel L'Herbier.[19]

PROPAGANDA AND CENSORSHIP: THE CASE OF HENRI-GEORGES CLOUZOT

In October 1940, a German regulation banned Anglo-American productions and a large number of French films. At the time, there were an estimated 75 million francophone spectators in 5,000 theaters in the world compared to the anglophone market, which counted 225 million spectators in 30,000 theaters. According to the CNC, among 572 films projected throughout France in 1933, 230 were American. Under the German occupation, censorship authorities silenced cinematographic creation. The interrelationship between the Vichy government, German authorities, French Republic institutions, and religious authorities was a complicated one. The COIC, acting on behalf of the Vichy government, fervently controlled the production of cinematographic subject matter. It prohibited films from conveying themes such as the traditional representation of the working class, unequivocal allusions to contemporary events, and distinctive features of the German Occupation. To them as well as to extreme-right followers, French cinema of the 1930s was guilty of constantly representing its main protagonists as evil social characters. In addition, the plot almost always evolved in a decadent background such as crime, murder, and places of ill repute. As a result, most films of poetic realism as well as other masterpieces of the 1930s were rigorously banned by the COIC. These included Renoir's *The Human Beast, Grand Illusion,* and *The Rules of the Game* plus Marcel Carné's *Hôtel du Nord, Port of Shadows,* and *Daybreak.* In no instance could any authority figure be ridiculed or demasculated. The recurrent backgrounds evolving in the lower depths of society (with characters like prostitutes, pimps, callous crooks, and demimondaines, adulterous relations, and the mafia) were no longer to be depicted. In addition, all vulgarity and slang were banned.[20] As Pierre Darmon described it, the Vichy regime was deeply involved in a *pudique* campaign: "Kisses on the big screen being shortened, the ones inside the movie theater were to be forbidden."[21]

The exportation of French films was declared illegal after 1942. Cinematographic and media censorships were directed by the Referat Film, which also indirectly controlled the COIC, the production and attribution of films, and the process of manufacturing. The Occupation authorities had three main goals: the avoidance of any intellectual reflection on current conditions of the Occupation, the "purification" of existing motion pictures, and the liquidation of the French cinematographic patrimony, which concomitantly eased German competition on the European market. However, the real collaboration sought by the Germans, the only efficient one known at the time, was based on the establishment (created by the French themselves) of sound economic structures made solely for the purpose of facilitating their control toward a more lucrative exploitation. Several films such as Clouzot's *The Raven* and Albert Valentin's 1944 *La vie de plaisir*[22] which would have been banned from screening during the 1930s by the administration of the Third Republic were surprisingly granted a distribution visa, despite compelling criticisms by French society and the wide freedom in their study of local customs that pervaded those films.

Unlike what one would expect, French cinema of the Occupation (with the exception of rare "vindictive" and isolated projects produced by the Propaganda Staffel, such as *Les corrupteurs* in 1942 and Paul Riche's *Forces occultes* in 1943)[23] did not indulge in explicit or exuberant figurations of the multiple "enemy" (Jews, communists, the Anglo-American menace, or Freemasons). This absence of fascist imagery, however, disappeared with Vichy's emerging political doctrine and its racial laws. Between 1940 and 1944, the impact of political propaganda on the French public was nonexistent. It is safe to conclude that the cultural colonization enterprise undertaken by the Nazi authorities as well as the Vichy government was eventually an utter failure because all nationalist productions, except for a few productions highly endorsed by Josef Goebbels, such as Veit Harlan's *The Jew Süss*[24] (*Le juif Süss,* 1941) and Joseph von Baky's *Münchhausen* (*Les aventures du Baron de Münchhausen,* 1943), were almost completely severely rejected by the public.

Also disregarded by French audiences were the world newsreels of the Deutsche Wochenschau projected in the occupied zone. During the years of the Occupation, a major focus of attention by the German authorities was the vigorous implementation and maintenance of the newsreels between projections in theaters. Needless to say, because of its content as well as its mandatory screening, the Deutsche Wochenschau became so immediately unpopular that French police officers had to be present during screenings to monitor aggravated movie audiences. Before June 1940, companies such as Pathé, Gaumont, and Eclair edited newsreels in France. After the arrival of the Germans in Paris, screening of a single broadcast of German news in the occupied zone was imposed with the Wochenschau, also distributed throughout thirty-five countries. To edit world news in French, the Occupation forces created a film-press company during the first summer of the war known as the Alliance cinématographique européenne (ACE), the main task of which was the distribution of German films in France. Later in 1942, the Nazis negotiated with the Vichy government for the production of a single news program, which would replace both the world news in occupied France and the single news program that Pathé and Gaumont had produced for Free France since October 1940. Though predisposed by the Vichy collaborationist endeavors, led by the royalist review *L'Action française,* as well as Nazi propaganda, news relating to France was gradually incorporated. The program, *France Actualités* (France News), stopped showing in August 1944 with the Allied troop movements in Europe.

Paradoxical as it may appear, French productions, unlike German and Italian national cinemas, never openly reflected any major theme of Vichy propaganda that was usually broadcast by Radio-Paris or by the Parisian press. Although dealing with a constant assault of German and Vichy propaganda, concluding that the French population had been truly swayed by its seditious rhetoric and content still remains arguable. During the first months of the Occupation, the Vichy administration owned the editorial management of the popular *France Actualité* newsreel that accompanied every film screened in French theaters. But with the organization of the French Resistance movement, and especially the transmission of radio broadcasts from England, the occupying authorities, fearing loss of command over French popular audiences, began to assemble and edit their own current affairs footage with a rigorously German partiality leading to believe that "the war was over" (then later "far from being over"). In fact, French audiences were in large part ignoring the effort for misinformation (also found in the press, current affairs footage, and radio broadcasts); and due to their individual concerns with the struggle of their everyday life, most French civilians actually never came close to enrolling in the Resistance movement or to participating in collaboration operations. As a matter of fact, the French people were known for their legendary, and self-imposed, *attentisme,* a "wait and see" state of mind.

Before the war, German films made up twenty percent of the films shown in French theaters. During the first years of the Occupation, seventy-five percent of projected films in France were of German origin. To position Germany as the only promoter of European cinema as well as to replace Anglo-American productions, German authorities had to establish a powerful and efficient film company on French soil. The first steps were to ascertain what was taking place in the French film industry, ensure control, and, if required, supervise all aspects of production. Shortly after German authorities intervened, they efficiently implemented a new organizational structure. On October 3, 1940, Continental Studios was established, with ostentatious headquarters on the Champs-Elysées. Created out of two German companies (UFA and Tobis), Continental Studios' exclusive mission was to produce French films. Needless to say, for both German distributors, the eradication of French cinema was a good idea, since by now two-thirds of Parisian theaters showed only German productions.

Alfred Greven, who already had extensive experience with the German film industry, managed the new studios. His previous position as producer for UFA had enabled him to work with French directors in Berlin studios who had come to produce multilanguage film versions. For instance, Henri-Georges Clouzot, Jacques Feyder, and Henri Chomette all worked in Germany between 1931 and 1938. When Greven arrived in France, he understood immediately that the small, fragile size of the existing French production companies, aside from Gaumont and Pathé, did not correspond to the scale of other European film studios. He soon developed a vertical concentration of cinematographic companies. Just one month after the establishment of Continental, Greven created SOGEC *(Société de gestion et d'exploitation du cinéma),* a distribution company whose main goal was to purchase and control new theaters. Although Continental Studios did grant a certain margin of artistic freedom to the film directors, actors, and technical crew it hired,[25] the company mostly did not attract distinguished French actors or directors, with the notable exceptions of Pierre Fresnay, Raimu, Maurice Tourneur, Marcel Carné (who never directed any film for Continental), Christian-Jaque, and Georges Lacombe.

As a direct representative of the German authorities in France, Alfred Greven's offers for roles or participation in productions had to be understood as resolute commands. Consequently, many artists, such as Louis Jouvet and Françoise Rosay, who were opposed to the Vichy regime, insinuated fake motives such as prior engagements, poor health, or retirement to make themselves unavailable for any acting role with Continental. Despite the sudden exodus of French actors abroad and into the Resistance, Continental remained the major film company of the Occupation, with a total of thirty films among the two hundred twenty films produced by French and German companies in France (among which fourteen for Pathé-Cinéma and ten for Gaumont).[26] Despite the highly criticized reception of these films, in 1943 Continental produced one of the most famous and controversial motion pictures of the Occupation period, a suspense/psychological thriller entitled *The Raven (Le corbeau).* The motion picture, directed by Henri-Georges Clouzot,[27] possesses a solid, almost "mechanical," plot, around which is based an enthralling study of French provincial customs. The screenplay was adapted from a script by Louis Chavance, a master of the hard-boiled novel.

The story line, inspired by a true story (the anonymous letters of the city of Tulle), was judged defamatory by producers during the 1930s, since French provincial life was mainly represented in a gloomy manner. The facts went back to 1917 when in Tulle, a small provincial town, Angèle Laval overwhelmed the town with poisonous, anonymous letters to seek revenge following a romantic disenchantment. Once the vindictive rage was unleashed, the outcome of the frantic storm resulted

Micheline Francey (Laura) and Pierre Fresnay (Dr. Germain) in Henri-Georges Clouzot's 1942 *Le Corbeau* (Courtesy of BIFI).

The Victorine Studios in Nice and the gigantic set designed by Georges Wakhevitch and Alexandre Trauner for Marcel Carné's *The Devil's Envoys* (*Les visiteurs du soir*, 1942), (Courtesy of BIFI).

in three suicides. At the time of the Third Republic, the Censorship
Commission, fearing a scandal from this tense thriller, never deemed
the script tolerable. In a reversal, the project ended up five years later
in the hands of Alfred Greven, and Continental endorsed the project.
The story opens with *Une petite ville, ici ou ailleurs* (A small town, here
or elsewhere), anticipating a portentous conclusion. Somewhere in
France, a small, peaceful town is swiftly overwhelmed by a campaign
of anonymous letters. The unknown author, who signs his missives *Le
corbeau,* initially accuses the new doctor in town, Dr. Rémy Germain
(Pierre Fresnay), of adultery, and abortion, and soon broadens the range
of his victims, sparing no one. Humiliated with their most intimate
secrets and betrayed by outrageous allegations, the citizens begin to
doubt one another, and the fragile social harmony seems to be irrevocably plagued. With the presence of the unknown (the reason for all
the turmoil), the anguished citizens start to liberate their true feelings
about their enemies as each day brings new letters and new denuncia-
tions. Long-term personal hatreds, family feuds, adulterous relations,
suspicions, and jealousies are all revealed behind the mask of hypocrisy.
Dr. Germain is accused of engaging in an adulterous relation with
Laura (Micheline Francey), the attractive young wife of Dr. Vorzet
(Pierre Larquey). Given his old age, Dr. Vorzet appears to be a father
figure within the community, but he is also clever and eventually gives
signs that he is slowly identifying the author of the letters, the crime,
and exactly how it was committed. Meanwhile at the hospital, a young
cancer patient is mysteriously informed (through another anonymous
letter) of the terminal nature of his illness and commits suicide the
next day. Marie Corbin (Hélèna Manson), a nurse working there, is
immediately accused of the homicide, and the entire town hopes desperately that she is the source of all their torment. But during a service
at church, another anonymous letter flies down the vault. Its contents
clear Marie of any role in the death or the letters. Dr. Germain and
the township officials, exasperated by the gloomy plot and the intangible nature of the crime, decide to gather all the suspects in a
classroom and force them to write for hours in order to discover the
authentic handwriting of the mysterious author. This is to no avail,
since the author of the letters is still free. One day Dr. Germain
discovers Laura, emotionally unstable, with a stain of ink on her
thumb, and realizes that she has been writing the letters all along.
After Laura is sent by her husband to a mental institution, Dr. Germain relates his discovery to his colleague, and comes to understand
that Dr. Vorzet is the real *corbeau.* When Germain enters Vorzet's
office, it is too late. He finds Vorzet dead, his throat cut by the same
razor that killed the young cancer patient. While all the elements fall
into place and put an end to the satanic puzzle, someone steps out of

the home. The murderer, the mother of the young cancer patient, walks slowly away under the powerless gaze of Rémy Germain.

To deconstruct the story would be to miss the cinematographic nuances that make *Le Corbeau* tantalizing. Standing back from the film and what it expected audiences to assume, one can see that Dr. Germain is not engaged in unethical behavior or scandal, but in a quest for truth. *Le Corbeau* has one of the most familiar film noir themes: the hero is not a criminal, but an isolated character who, despite being tempted, betrayed, and humiliated, finally succeeds. In this "double" relation (Rémy/Denise and Rémy/Laura), women and men tempt one another; neither would have acted alone. Both are attracted not so much by the crime as by the thrill of committing it with the other person (Rémy, Laura, and Denise, played by Ginette Leclerc, are pulp characters with little psychological depth, and that is the way Clouzot wanted it). In the world of *Le Corbeau,* heroes and villains constantly struggle to survive, as Dr. Vorzet's philosophical discourses to the townspeople convey a peculiar tone of guilt.

> DR. VORZET: Since this whirlwind of hate and calumny started, all moral values have suffered; yours like others. You too will fall. I don't say you'll strangle your mistress, but you'd go through my papers, if I forgot them on the table, and sleep with Rolande if she wanted to. There is no choice.
>
> DR. GERMAIN: I can see you're used to mad people.
>
> DR. VORZET: At your service . . . [He exits the classroom] and good night.

The explanation given by Dr. Vorzet illustrates a mechanism Clouzot often used in his films, and his inclination for a persuasive Manichean mise-en-scène rather than academic technique. The internal convulsions of the city and the epidemic nature of the letters are all perfectly represented in its finest symbolic contrasts. The photography by Nicolas Hayer helps to develop the film noir style of sharp-edged shadows and shots, strange angles, and lonely settings. Imagery is the movie's other great strength, more immediately apparent to viewers than the subtle remodeling. As a director, Clouzot was not an artist who framed his shots eccentrically or cut for shock effect. Instead, chiaroscuro, shadow projections, and shafts of bright light entering the frame were among Clouzot's favorite devices.

As his second film, *Le Corbeau* represented a first full-scale orchestration. The visual element of the film expresses its literary style. It is no more realistic than its dialogue, but it is not quite expressionistic either: stylistically, the film extends imagistic conventions of contemporary American movies by further inflating stylization. Few other directors have made so many taut, savvy, cynical, and, in many differ-

ent ways and tones, witty films. As a film director, Clouzot was rarely
patient with long takes and slow-paced action; instead, he emphasized
psychological tensions with deliberate and well-timed cuts. The audience is involuntarily engaged by the subtleties of character, the psychological tensions that evolved through complex relationships, the
ambiguities of human behavior, and the interpersonal relationships.

With its constant gloomy atmosphere, *Le Corbeau* offered a perfect
blend of form and content. The desperation and hopelessness of the
townspeople were reflected in the visual style, which saturated the
screen with shadows and only occasional bursts of sunlight. Enthralling
but occasionally acerbic and cynical, *Le Corbeau* portrayed for the
French audiences of the Occupation a series of anxious characters (Laura
and Dr. Germain) trying to elude some mysterious past that continued
to haunt them. They are hunted down with a fatalism that taunted
and teased before delivering the final, definitive *coup de théâtre*. The
decor was the right fit for the hard, urban context and dialogue created
by Louis Chavance, who elevated chiaroscuro in motion pictures to a
metaphorical representation of both truth and dishonesty. Following a
tiresome oral dictation inflicted on the town's suspects in order to
identify the handwriting of the *corbeau,* Dr. Vorzet reminds Dr. Germain of the impossibility of his quest: "You think that people are all
good or all bad. You think that good means light and bad means
night? [He swings a ceiling light between him and Dr. Germain.] But
where does night end and light begin? Where is the borderline? Do
you even know which side you belong on?"

Fate will not permit the protagonist to escape his past. After losing
his wife and newborn baby at birth, Dr. Germain decides to be at the
service of pregnant women; he inhabits a world that constantly pulls
people back into the chaos of existence and eventually suffocates them.

At the time of its release in 1943, a large number of viewers were
reluctant to praise the film, some because they had trouble categorizing
it, while others were morally offended by it. *Le Corbeau* was indeed
besieged from both sides of the political scene. The anti-Nazi activists
and members of the Resistance considered *Le Corbeau* pro-Nazi propaganda and fiercely fought (in the clandestine press) against the screening of the film. To them, it exemplified a collaboration with and
submission to the German authorities by portraying a gloomy image
and the malicious character of French people. The choice of the small
provincial town was comprehensible since it accentuated the dramatic
background of the plot. Isolated from the rest of the country, the
tragedy occurs step by step without any exterior pressure, as the destructive presence of madness slowly pervades the screen. For the
Resistance, the final message, despite revealing a tormented epoch, is
often underestimated: anyone can become a *corbeau* in order to free

oneself from any agonizing obsession. The right wing and Vichy supporters also demanded the film be banned for its immoral values. For them, it stood as the antithesis of the National Revolution and violated the ethics of a fundamental morality (as it indirectly reminded audiences of the epidemic scourge of anonymous letters that was widespread in those days in occupied France).

The years during and after the liberation of France, the Comité de libération du cinéma français (CLCF), a newly created committee that supervised the reorganization of the French cinema industry from 1944 until 1946,[28] left no ambiguity about *Le Corbeau*. Clouzot, the director, and Chavance, the screenwriter, had made an anti-French movie, directly commissioned by Josef Goebbels. This accusation would be one of the main grievances retained against the filmmaker. Louis Chavance, however, was able to disprove the accusation by justifying the date of the project (*L'oeil du serpent*, 1937), well before the German presence in France. After the Liberation, the case of *Le Corbeau* vehemently impassioned public opinion. On October 17, 1944, as Clouzot stood in front of the Comité de Libération du Cinéma, formed to judge film directors and their productions during the Occupation, the main accusation was related to the intended message of *The Raven*. According to *Les lettres françaises* and its violent article entitled *"Le corbeau est déplumé"* ("The Crow Is Unfeathered"), the film had most likely been shown in Germany under the title *Province française* (*French province*). But, according to Clouzot, because the film was not dubbed, it was shown only in Belgium and Switzerland, never in Germany. During the hearings, Clouzot took advantage of the climate of denunciation to remind his judges of the poisonous atmosphere of anonymous letters, which overwhelmed France at the Liberation.[29] Behind Clouzot and Chavance's hearings was a political agenda to sanction Alfred Greven's closest collaborators. On May 7, 1945, Clouzot was condemned to a lifetime professional suspension. One year later, however, the sentence was reduced to two years even though *Le Corbeau* was still considered in part an anti-French movie. The committee never expressed a clear verdict on the film, leaving the impression that the main accusations were leveled toward the director and his close working relationship with Greven.

If it is true that *Le Corbeau*[30] exposed a darker side of small-town chronicles in France, balancing the optimism of Hollywood melodramas by focusing on squalid criminals and doomed atmospheres, the question of whether or not the film is fundamentally anti-French or anti-Occupation remains arguable. Whereas Hollywood strove to maintain high public morale during the war years, film noir gave viewers a peek into the alleys and backrooms of a world filled with corruption. *Le Corbeau* undoubtedly made Clouzot a leading authority of French film noir during the postwar era. The French public, which eventually forgave Clouzot's entanglement with Continental, appreciated his later darkly pessimistic psychological thrillers, such as *Wages of Fear* (*Le salaire de la peur,* 1953) and *Diabolique* (*Les diaboliques,* 1955), which are discussed in the following chapter.

WORKING CONDITIONS UNDER THE OCCUPATION: MARCEL CARNÉ

The four years of German occupation resulted in a time of extensive rationing all over France. (Shortages actually began with the first hours of the War in May 1940 and lasted until the late 1940s and the first fruitful results of the Marshall Plan.) While food appeared to be the most important article in demand (75 percent of French household revenue was spent on food), many other resources were in short supply such as gasoline and diesel for vehicles, coal, spare parts, paper, wood, and fuel for domestic heating. Because fuel and vehicles were regularly requisitioned by the German forces, a large percentage of the population was suddenly compelled to use other means of transportation such as bicycle or *gazogène,* a vehicle with a mechanical gas converter affixed to the rear. In addition, the scarcity of vacant apartments, caused directly by the destruction of the war and later aggravated by the Allied bombing raids, deteriorated the situation of populations in all major European cities. The outbreak of the war and the rapid globalization of the conflict distressed all French economic activity, with more than two million men forcefully sent to Germany. Following the appalling consequences of the war in the Soviet Union, the German Wehrmacht was short of manpower for its own war factories. Consequently, under intense pressure, Vichy incited the mobilization and recruitment of the male population between the ages of eighteen and fifty to work in Germany, and at the same time liberated prisoners of war. The service was known as STO (Service du travail obligatoire/ Forced Labor Program). During certain weekdays (nonholidays), German authorities started to take into custody idle young men whom they found attending movie theaters and sent them to Germany for the STO. Needless to say, this new development immediately created a desertion of movie theaters among the young adult population of France. For all these reasons, and as a direct result of the STO, after 1942, film companies, laboratories, and shooting studios had to face a drastic shortage of personnel.

In addition, the French cinematographic industry had to surmount an eight-month interruption during the Nazi invasion followed by a difficult restart period after the Occupation. But even after restarting, the disquieting context and a series of innumerable regulations resulted in much improvisation. Dealing with the new occupying forces as well as the new Vichy government was no easy task. Once financing issues were resolved, censorship avoided, authorizations granted, and the Nazi authorities' suspicions assuaged, the road to the final completion of the film was far from easy. The next serious obstacle was the scarcity of materials. The German authorities imposed extensive film stock restrictions, and Kodak factories present in France, at the time the primary manufacturer of film, were forced to direct seventy percent of its production to Germany, leaving French producers in an abrupt state of panic. In addition, German authorities confiscated twenty of the eighty contact printers[31] running in France. Raw material shortages caused by the war made cinematographic projects a precarious business for producers as well as for crews. Intermittent power cuts, air alerts and raids, and strenuous night shifts that exhausted actors affected most of the artists' performances and memories. Toward the end of the war, over one hundred theaters in Paris alone were destroyed by Allied bombing raids, more than four hundred throughout France. Consequently, actors and directors were compelled to perform perfectly in the first shoot in order to save supplies. From film stock to lights, from nails for sets to fabrics for costumes, from food for hungry crews to the number of extras on the set, nothing could be wasted. According to Jean-Pierre Jeancolas, the Pathé Film Company had to appoint a special employee to collect, straighten, and recycle every possible nail from used sets.[32]

Interestingly, the difficulties often instigated ingenuity in order to maneuver within guidelines and restrictions. For example, the poor quality of film stock during those years of frequent requisitions compelled directors and cinematographers to discover and utilize new lighting techniques. In his autobiography, Marcel Carné also remembers shooting *The Devil's Envoys* (*Les visiteurs du soir,* 1942) and the cruel dilemma of displaying a bountiful amount of food for the banquet scene in front of starving actors who had to pretend to be enjoying a *gargantuesque* feast.[33] Although set assistants relentlessly reminded the extras not to eat the food displayed on the extravagant silver platters, one by one fruits of all sorts were disappearing by the minute. Carné himself had to redo a shot since a particular loaf of bread was in the camera field. As he removed it, he was surprised by the very light weight of the loaf. Much to his surprise, a hole had been secretly dug out by some hungry actor, who meticulously emptied the center, leaving the crust intact. Someone from the technical crew finally came up with the idea to inject phenol in all the pears and apples to avoid temptation. After warning the crowd of extras, the scene was at last completed. But food was not the only center of preoccupation for directors; fabrics for costumes and decoration, such as silk or velvet, were significantly in short supply in those years, especially when designed to represent medieval court splendor. Once again, artistic and technical ingenuity prevailed over the adversity of the war, and costume designers were compelled to dress extras with rougher fabric, requiring cinematographers to use long shots. In his overview of French cinema during the Occupation, Pierre Darmon recalls how the fear of wasting film stock turned into an authentic nightmare. While shooting the scene of the prenuptial festivities in *The Devil's Envoys,* Carné had all actors standing "frozen in time" when inadvertently a greyhound (also starving) ran across the set, ruining the cut and forcing a retake.[34] Due to the shortage of electricity, and therefore any heating system on the sets, many directors accelerated the shooting process in order to finish projects before winter. For most well-known actors used to traveling in style, with comfortable cars, their first challenge was reaching the shooting location or studios, whether by public transportation, bicycle or even foot.

Many employees of the film industry had to work clandestinely within the studios because of their affiliation with the Resistance. In Nice, the Victorine Studios[35] became a center for clandestine workers, usually confined and protected by those who worked legally. Georges Wakhevitch agreed to direct the set of *The Devil's Envoys* under the control of Alexandre Trauner. At the same time, Maurice Thiriet (1906–72) composed the film's orchestral score and agreed to accept credit for the three ballads written by Alexandre Kosma. For the epic production *Children of Paradise,* a gigantic set was build at the same studios in Nice that represented a feat of almost unparalleled skill at the time of the Occupation: 3,000 square yards, 150 yards long, over 50 building fronts, 12 to 18 yards high, and 2,000 extras for the opening and closing scenes, many of whom, engaged in the French Resistance, were using their employment as a daytime cover. But it was during those hard times of deprivation and day-to-day struggle toward the end of the Occupation that the most spectacular productions were completed. Marcel Carné's *The Devil's Envoys* and *Children of Paradise* manifested on a grand scale the difficult move many directors of poetic realism made in order to dodge Vichy's disapproval for the movement by transferring the plot into a world of dreams or into a past historic mode, temporarily relinquishing the contemporary themes and settings of their earlier movies. This new "poetic" genre not only deceived censorship but also enabled Carné and Jacques Prévert to blossom in the darkness of the Occupation as they painted a masterly portrait of romance.

The Devil's Envoys, produced by André Paulvé, was released in December 1942 and received a warm welcome. Because of its medieval background, Carné was somehow able to dodge censorship, as Jean-Pierre

Jeancolas recalls: "The 'realists' of 1939, as embodied by Carné and Prévert, were the architects and builders of a fictional universe which they synchronized with the times, with real life. But they were better equipped than others to transpose their work into a temporal 'elsewhere,' when the constraints of the Occupation required them to do so."[36]

The year is 1485, and the Devil (Jules Berry) sends two envoys, Dominique (Arletty) and Gilles (Alain Cuny), to earth under the guise of serene troubadours with the mission to sow anarchy, corruption, and despair among the human race. They go from castle to castle propagating a romantic psychosis, which incites anxiety for their victims. As they arrive at the castle of Baron Hugue (Fernand Ledoux), they find a citadel celebrating the future wedding of the lord's daughter, Anne (Marie Déa). The unexpected visitors are invited to attend the prenuptial festivities along with the court, acrobats, tumblers, minstrels, and other musicians. Satan's plans are quickly disrupted as one of his messengers, Gilles, falls in love with his intended future prey, Anne. Meanwhile, Dominique beguiles both baron and fiancé, the egotistic knight Renaud (Marcel Herrand), instigating a feudal rivalry between them. Since the two envoys have lost sight of their mission, Satan arrives in person in diabolical fashion to put an end to his envoys' unexpected romantic escapades. He is announced as a lost traveler caught by a storm and is welcomed into the castle. When asked to declare his identity, he replies that he is "forgotten from his homeland, unknown elsewhere; this is the destiny of the traveler."[37] In the main room, while Baron Hugues and Renaud play chess, the devil approaches the fireplace, and, as he caresses the fire, says with a demonic grin: "Look at how those flames like me . . . They lick my fingers just like a puppy would do."[38] Gilles is finally discovered by the lord of the castle with the bride-to-be, Anne, and ends up hastily thrown in the castle dungeon, awaiting sentence. Meanwhile, the baron and his prospective son-in-law, madly in love with Dominique, decide to settle their quarrel in combat, which results in Renaud's death. Now comes the turn of the devil himself, who is seduced by the pure and chaste Anne. To her, he offers a pact: though deprived of his memory, Gilles will go free if she agrees to come with him and to love him (and therefore never see Gilles again). Much to the devil's dismay, she lies to him when she accepts. But after several unsuccessful attempts to dissuade her, the devil changes the two lovers, Anne and Gilles, into eternal stone as he comes across them holding each other by the fountain. As he nears the immobile couple, he realizes too late that their hearts are still beating inside their petrified bodies. Satan's compelling power has failed in the face of true love, and his triumph is shown to be relative and limited. Good and evil constantly fight, but love ultimately conquers all.

Audiences at the time witnessed a modern society, distanced in time by the medieval background, completely inclined toward entertainment and legitimately unaware of the impending danger surrounding the feast. This flamboyant feudal society appears without any contradiction, and only the stranger, the unknown, the unusual, can trigger woe. Behind the selected choices appears occupied France. Indirectly, the film related the prewar situation, and the story unfolds to show the incapacity of Baron Hugues to resist the process of destabilization generated by the satanic envoys. He even challenges his future son-in-law and wins the duel with the help of one of them. In this allegorical tale of eternal love, many critics envisaged a metaphorical fiction relating the presence of the Germans in France to satan (much to Carné's dismay). The last scene in the movie, depicting satan's recognition of the power of love, may be viewed as a depiction of contemporary events in France; it reveals the state of mind of this tormented *époque,* since the devil, the symbol of oppression, is unable to terminate the ardent passion between the young couple.

Although many critics immediately believed Carné's film to be a masterpiece, many others, far from being persuaded by the experience, underscored the atypical slowness of the film. For them, the tale predicted another solution: moral resistance, as Gilles and Anne surpass the contradiction of the "occupying force." Through a series of "cryptic messages,"[39] the characters of the castle could be viewed as the French people during the Occupation, watching their life blossom while the fantastic element dispelled the oppressive confusion experienced by the whole country. *"The Devil's Envoys,"* Edward Baron Turk observes, "is a story about freedom of choice in selecting one's partner. It openly disparages the institutions of family and marriage. It tampers with conventional distinctions between masculinity and femininity. Such themes ran counter to Vichy's ideology. But the prejudices that made these themes offensive to the Vichy establishment have outlived Vichy."[40] The Occupation authorities were so focused on present difficulties that they could not comprehend that the remote medieval past could imply the present. French film cameras never captured true life more confidently than the characters of *The Devil's Envoys,* who represent good and evil simultaneously. Alain Cuny's marble facial expression also accentuates the impenetrable features of mystery in this deeply allegorical tale.

Following the triumph of *The Devil's Envoys,* the team of Carné and Prévert renewed their success with *Children of Paradise,* which is considered by many film historians the greatest French motion picture ever made—and also considered Carné's last great picture. This film endured trying times following the suspension of the production, most notably with the invasion of the Allied forces in Sicily and the damage

Jules Berry (the Devil) in Marcel Carné's *The Devil's Envoys* (*Les visiteurs du soir*, 1942), (Courtesy of BIFI).

Arletty (Dominique) and Alain Cuny (Gilles) in Marcel Carné's *The Devil's Envoys* (*Les visiteurs du soir*, 1942), (Courtesy of BIFI).

caused to the gigantic set of the boulevard du Crime[41] (erected at the same location where, a year earlier, stood the white castle of *The Devil's Envoys*) by winter weather. The repair of the set was more difficult than expected after the authorities prohibited night shifts. Special authorization was required for a wartime film of such dimension (its two parts totaling over three hours), and production was stalled several times, sometimes by Marcel Carné himself, who was determined to premiere it months later for the Liberation. Due to its unusual length and cost for the time (originally more than four hours and reduced substantially to three hours and fifteen minutes), the film was presented in two separate parts: *Le boulevard du Crime* and *L'homme blanc*. The premiere of *Children of Paradise,* deliberately intended as an ostentatious international display of French savoir faire at its height, took place at the Palais de Chaillot in Paris on March 9, 1945, in an almost totally liberated France. With this visual and cinematographic feast, Marcel Carné clearly presented to the world—Germany and, indirectly, Hollywood—what France was able to achieve under even the most difficult conditions. Parker Tyler describes it as a will to survive: "Beyond the cameras stood monitors, sleepy-eyed with self-importance and the thrill of victory: the Germans who had humbled Paris itself, who controlled a city and a nation in all ways but the essential, the governance and proliferation of spirit."[42] The film paid homage to the theater with its title *Paradise,* which makes reference to the theater's worst seats (an ironical French epithet), farthest from the stage, where the audience responded honestly and boisterously to the actors below. The inspiration for this ostentatious depiction of the life and background of Jean-Baptiste Debureau, one of France's greatest mimes, came from actor Jean-Louis Barrault, who met with Carné and Prévert in Nice during the summer of 1943. Prompted by the box office success of *The Devil's Envoys,* the team was eager to embark on an ambitious new project, recognizing the cinematographic profitability and scope of their subject matter.[43]

Set in 1840s Paris and centered on the Théâtre des Funambules on the boulevard du Crime, home of Parisian popular operettas at the time—where mimes and burglars rubbed shoulders with aristocrats and assassins—the narrative relates the vicissitudes of four men whose existences are intertwined through their irresistible passion for the same woman, the attractive yet free-spirited actress Garance (Arletty). Garance truthfully loves only one of them, Baptiste (Jean-Louis Barrault), but their plans are relentlessly thwarted by an unsympathetic fate. Baptiste has loved Garance since the day she threw a rose at him while performing on stage; Frédérick (Pierre Brasseur) flirts with her as much as his ego and wit allow him; the count of Montray (Louis Salou) seeks in her a glamorous mistress; and finally Lacenaire (Marcel

The boulevard du Crime in Marcel Carné's *Children of Paradise* (*Les enfants du Paradis*, 1945), (Courtesy of BIFI).

Herrand) envisions her as a malicious but providential muse. All four men are mesmerized by Garance's indolent glamour (Arletty was forty-four years old at the time of the film), who seduces them, and eventually gains the protection of her most powerful, suitor, the count. The opening scene occurs in medias res among the spectators when Garance, surrounded by the carnival crowd, is accused of having stolen a spectator's watch. Baptiste, a young artist longing to love, who at this very instant is performing on stage, seizes the opportunity to prove Garance's innocence in an entertaining and astute "reconstitutive" mime, at the end of which the police, clueless, in their perplexity, let her go. Baptiste instantly falls in love and finds Garance a job at the Théâtre des Funambules. Their idyllic romance is shortened following the arrival of a new and promising actor, Frédérick, who quickly seduces her. Garance resigns herself to the dazzling virility of the new upcoming actor. One night Frédérick, Garance, and Baptiste are involved in a pantomime performance on stage as, respectively, Harlequin, Colombine, and Pierrot. They repeat the events that occurred between them the night before. Pierrot fails to charm Colombine, and, disappointed, he slowly falls asleep next to her while the audacious

Harlequin, who comes by unexpectedly, seduces her by his gallantry
and together they flee in the night (offstage). As a result, Baptiste/
Pierrot attempts to hang himself, but he is saved *in extremis* by Nathalie (Maria Casarès), who realizes at this moment in the performance
that the play is becoming a real charade about what had probably
happened to Baptiste. Because of her love for him, Nathalie breaks the
sacred rules of mime and calls his name on stage, generating a misunderstanding of the silent and theatrical genres: the play within the
play. Later in the film, Garance seeks the protection of the count of
Montray following another murder accusation committed by her forlorn friend Lacenaire, a Parisian dandy but also a malicious criminal.
As a result, she leaves Paris for several years. By creating a social
barrier between herself and her old accomplice Lacenaire, she unwillingly revives and rekindles the blaze of his final project. Consequently,
Lacenaire, pictured as a "living embodiment of the connection between
art and crime,"[44] promptly prepares the count's murder in his elaborate
stage management. Meanwhile, Frédérick has become a talented and
famous actor, and Baptiste marries Nathalie: she had loved him before
he even met Garance. At the end of the film, Garance and Baptiste
meet by chance, and immediately the old flame is revived. Forced to
accept the impossibility of their happiness, the enigmatic Garance
ultimately flies away in a carriage through a crowd, while Baptiste,
desperate and alone, inconsolably—and ironically, since he works in
silence—calls her name.

   The characters Baptiste Debureau as the mime, Pierre-François Lacenaire as the cynical dandy, and the actor Frédérick Lemaître were
based on historical personages, but the story and the fourth character,
the disdainful count Montray, who anticipates an undivided protection
of Garance, remains fictional. Through Jacques Prévert's screenplay,
which is rich in its sharpness, eloquence, and wittiness, Garance best
symbolizes an uninhibited and sophisticated woman, mercilessly dis-
posing those who attempt to possess her. Garance's mysterious charisma makes her an oversized character corresponding to the classic
femme fatale of film noir. Her accomplice, Lacenaire, plays a parallel
role, a character who seems to come directly from the Paris of Eugène
Sue's *Les Mystères de Paris,* with its mysterious streets and perilous
alleys. In a discussion about his tormented childhood, Lacenaire elo-
quently discloses his future plans (through the screenplay authored by
Jacques Prévert and Pierre Laroche):

> Even when I was a child I was more intelligent, more logical than the
> rest of them. They never forgave me for it. They wanted me to be like
> them, to think like them. . . . A fine childhood I had: my mother, my
> worthy mother, who preferred my idiot of a brother, and my confessor,
> who repeated to me without ceasing "You are too proud, Pierre-

Maria Casarès (Nathalie) and Jean-Louis Barrault (Baptiste) in Marcel Carné's *Children of Paradise* (*Les enfants du Paradis*, 1945), (Courtesy of BIFI).

François, you must take a serious look at yourself." So I took a serious look at myself, and I've never wanted to look at anyone else! Fools! They left me alone with myself, and yet they tried to keep me away from bad companions! What idiocy! But what a prodigious destiny . . . to love no one . . . to be alone . . . to be loved by no one . . . to be free.

The reciprocal rapport between reality and representation of reality on stage, real and fictional characters, tragedy and pantomime, and silence and the word are the recurrent themes of the movie. *Children of Paradise* is Prévert's richest script, where the words, along with eloquent lyrics and mime, beautifully merge and fuse with visual opulence. Never had a "period piece" been so impeccably accomplished, and with a cast without equal, *Children of Paradise* remains one of the greatest French motion pictures ever made (which interestingly enough never ostentatiously materialized into a costume nor historical picture). Was Carné's success as a filmmaker mostly due to the steady teamwork of Prévert, Trauner, and Kosma? If Carné stood at the forefront of French creativity during the period of poetic realism, his methods of work and organization were now comparable to the Hollywood studio system. One of the biggest assets of the film is the use of the silent era's lessons as reproduced through the mime of Baptiste—and, indeed, illustrated by the choice of a mime as the main protagonist, whose sensitivity produced the emotional key of the film. In her study of *Children of Paradise* for the British Film Institute, Jill Forbes summarizes the preponderance of the choice of pantomime by Carné and the ironic recognition of the social significance of performance: "Although *Les enfants du Paradis* is not a conventional narrative film, it nevertheless makes magnificent use of the facility of sound. But it equally celebrates all the lessons of the silent cinema in placing a mime performer at its center and making him the key sensibility in the film, underlining the cinema's reliance on appearance, gesture and expressivity of the body."[45] The multilayered contemplation of the different natures of theatrical performances—mime, comedy, vaudeville, romance, melodrama, and tragedy, extending from a glowing image of conflicting dramatic modes and a reflection of the interchangeability of theater and life—was at the heart of the project. The film is a colossal tribute to the theater. The photographic performance, directed by Roger Hubert, achieves rare lucidity thanks to its seamless scale, and succeeds in representing an unparalleled eloquence of facial expressions. André Bazin said of Marcel Carné's legacy that "to the memory of these films are linked the most moving images of the only two real stars of French talking cinema: Jean Gabin and Michèle Morgan."[46] Along with Renoir, Carné remains one of France's very greatest film directors.

Jean-Louis Barrault (Baptiste) in Marcel Carné's *Children of Paradise* (*Les enfants du Paradis*, 1945), (Courtesy of BIFI).

Arletty (Garance) and Pierre Brasseur (Frédérick) in Marcel Carné's *Children of Paradise* (*Les enfants du Paradis*, 1945), (Photo by Roger Forster. Courtesy of the Archives Marcel Carné).

RESISTANCE AND LIBERATION

During the first year of the war a kind of quiescent dismay prevailed in France, and filmmakers frequently debated between going back to Paris to fight or not. For the Left, the discouragement was even more dramatic with the recent failure of the Popular Front, the bitter defeat of the Republicans in Spain, the treason of Munich, and the German-Soviet nonaggression treaty. Toward the end of the war, however, Vichy's slow erosion was challenged by the upsurge of the French Resistance (also known as the Maquis). After 1940, small groups of French citizens, little by little, organized all over the territory against the occupants and the Vichy regime. Their activities concentrated on sabotaging German installations, assembling strategic information for transmission to London, prearranging getaways for British Air Force pilots who had been shot down, and coordinating disruption operations of railways. The French Resistance was strengthened by Vichy's agreement to send French workers to Germany. As a result, countless numbers of recruited men entered the underground units, winning the support of an ever-larger part of the population. But the peak of the underground fight came with national unity in May 1943, when General Charles de Gaulle's most prestigious delegate in occupied France, Jean Moulin, was parachuted over France and succeeded in uniting the main Resistance organizations into the National Resistance Council (CNR), finally connecting all the most important isolated units into one federation. At the same time de Gaulle, now headquartered in Algiers, set up a temporary command of the French Republic from the alliance of the CNR. The Resistance also actively existed in the cinematographic profession. Many professionals of the film industry delayed material deliveries, slowed down the frequency of productions, limited the quantity of apparatus for German companies, and finally, falsified their production costs and sabotaged equipment. Even though they demonstrated what they believed to be acts of the Resistance, a few years later the *épuration* commission (cleansing committee) stated that the only real and heroic act of resistance would have been never to work with the Nazis.[47]

In November 1942, all of Vichy's remaining sovereignty, authority, and declining prestige were shattered, as the direct consequence of the Anglo-American landings in North Africa, which compelled Hitler to send German troops into occupied France. The year 1943 was the turning point of the war. The repeated defeats of the Wehrmacht triggered the reawakening of hope and a vision of future liberation. Men and women joined the French Resistance, many factions of which united for the long overdue final insurrection. The CLCF (*Comité de libération du cinéma français*) was created and included citizens from many political and professional backgrounds: from the followers of the National Front to the communist activists, from the patriotic militia to the major trade union representatives. Meanwhile, the Resistance had significantly expanded all over French territory. At the time of the Normandy landing on June 6 and the landing in Provence in August 15, 1944, the armed forces and Free French units participated in the liberation of Paris, which organized its own successful insurrection led by General Jacques Philippe Leclerc on August 25, 1944. French Resistance also had an important enough role to play in the battles by targeting retreating German forces and sabotaging bridges and railroad networks. Members of the Vichy government, arrested or in retreat, were instantly replaced without procedure. The Resistance's responsibility in the victory was acknowledged by the Allied forces and earned France a seat at the signing of Germany's capitulation on May 8, 1945, as well as a permanent seat in the United Nations Security Council. Now officially accepted by the United States, British, and Soviet governments, de Gaulle's interim government took advantage of its uncontested influence in liberated France. But for four years, the Nazis had emptied France of crucial raw materials and food; the road networks were relentlessly interrupted by air offensives and sabotage; over two million French prisoners of war, STO workers, and deportees were still in German camps; and the responsibility of eradicating Vichy's legacy endangered the nation with critical internal controversies. In the summer of 1944, summary executions by Resistance groups appeared to have exceeded 10,000 during the unceremonious and impulsive cleansing of Vichy officials. In addition, to expedite justice, special courts were set up to try citizens charged with collaborating with the enemy. The courts dealt with over 125,000 cases during the following months. Among the accused, 50,000 wrongdoers were sentenced to "national degradation" (suspension of civic rights), some 40,000 received jail terms, and less than one percent were condemned to death.

All employees of the movie industry were called to respond before the CLCF. Because of the great number of cases, many sentences were decided within a few minutes after a brief interrogation, at the end of which, if considered innocent of any participation or collaboration with the enemy, the individual received a certificate of good standing (*certificat de "bonne conduite"*). This document consequently authorized the individual to regain the professional card indispensable for work in the film industry. In contrast, if the defendant was judged guilty of collaboration (the charge of collaboration could be evoked simply if the suspect was alleged to have been at the German embassy, or had had personal relations with any German), the files from the case were sent to another committee (Commission des Onze), which could order suspension from work. On October 4, 1944, the CLCF published a list of film technicians, among whom were filmmakers who had worked for Continental, including Henri-Georges Clouzot and Marcel Carné. Over one thousand files were examined, and professionals were cross-examined at all levels of the film industry: directors such as Marc Allégret, Claude Autant-Lara, Carné, Louis Daquin, and Marcel L'Herbier; screenwriters such as Jean Cocteau, Jean Anouilh, and Jean Aurenche; and producers, technicians, and even anonymous theater ushers were all scrutinized. Among the artists and technicians alleged to have collaborated with the enemy, two categories of crimes were recurrent: antipatriotism and pro-Nazi activity.

Among all the artists connected to activity with the occupying force, actor-author Sacha Guitry triggered the most heated debate, having been charged with supplying intelligence to the Nazis. At the time of the Liberation, more than half the French population approved of his arrest.[48] Guitry's encounter with Hermann Goering, Hitler's right-hand man, remains the most regrettable episode of his career.[49] The case of Arletty seems simpler. It was a known fact that the French actress was for a while the mistress of German Luftwaffe officer Jürgen

Soehring from 1941 to 1943. When facing charges of collaboration with the enemy after the Liberation, Arletty, along with Sacha Guitry, reminded accusers of their patriotic efforts. The two were released, along with fellow actor Tristan Bernard. Pierre Fresnay also received numerous accusations from the CLCF for his intellectual closeness to Marshal Pétain as well as his generally right-wing inclination. Among all French actors who performed during those difficult years, however, the case of Robert Le Vigan remains one of the most tragic and regrettable.[50] Despite many brilliant performances throughout the 1930s, which included work with the directors Jean Renoir (*The Lower Depths*) and Marcel Carné (*Port of Shadows*), Le Vigan's career terminated with the end of the Vichy regime. Due to his repeated and open expression of fascist ideologies, he was compelled to flee to Germany at the end of the war. Eventually, the French courts sentenced Le Vigan to a ten-year sentence of hard labor, resulting in his permanent exile in Argentina.

The philosophy of the so-called *épuration* involuntarily established some paradoxical and contradictory criteria against the accused persons. Often, convicted artists were sanctioned more for sharing political ideas with the German authorities than those who actually participated directly in German productions. The Court of Justice in Paris condemned twelve persons to heavy sentences; this group included scenarist Jean Marquès-Rivière, condemned by proxies to the death penalty, and director Paul Riche (*Forces occultes,* 1943), who eventually was brought before a firing squad and executed on March 29, 1949. Also executed was film critic and historian Robert Brasillach (author of *The History of Motion Pictures,* 1935), who vigorously corroborated anti-Semitic and fascist decisions in the collaborationist reviews *L'Action française* and *Je suis partout,* often describing the Vichy regime as guilty of moderation.

Meanwhile French cinema was finally nationalized, and with the help of the state was heading for a safe and sound future. At the Liberation, many intellectuals and employees in the film industry understood that the war offered the opportunity to change radically the face of cinema in France and to elaborate a new program for true social progress, eliminating bourgeois influences and capitalistic practices. One of the results of this initiative resulted in productions like René Clément's *Battle of the Rails* (*La bataille du rail,* 1945). The CLCF became the CNC (Centre national de la Cinématographie) in July 1946, as the United States and French governments struck a deal and negotiated the importation of Hollywood films in France without the presence of French film industry representatives. With this feeling of betrayal, French cinema did not actively pursue the reforms as planned. For the newly formed CNC, the goals were quite clear: to eliminate

the system of control established under the Vichy regime, to assist
French productions and distribution abroad, and finally to limit the
power of censorship in the arenas of morality and public order. Unfortunately, French cinema of the postwar era did not turn out to be what
was hoped during the first hours of the Liberation. Economic activity
was now in the hands of the government within a plan of national
economy. The postwar era therefore assured the impossibility of a
return to the 1930s, when small businesses and amateurism reigned.

French filmmakers and actors of the early 1940s gave cinema a
unique artistic identity and commercial scope. One must bear in mind
that from a political or academic point of view, historical documenta-
tion of the facts can only be fully understood and mastered several
decades after the events. Film historian Roy Armes argues that any
hasty judgment about a particular director or career can lead to serious
misconceptions.[51]

To a considerable degree, it is inadequate or unfair to base judgments
on extrapolated plot synopses or the details from carefully selected
moments of a film. To be understood, films need to be seen in terms
of their makers' overall philosophy, as expressed in a wide range of
pictures. Without such a perspective, Jean Delannoy, the patriot,
speaking out boldly for the Resistance in *Pontcarral* in 1942, inexpli-
cably becomes Jean Delannoy, the Aryan apologist, of *The Eternal
Return* (*L'éternel retour,* 1943) the very next year. But if we consider the
director's whole career as a skilled but routine filmmaker without a
deeply felt range of subject matter, this shift becomes more easily
understood, and the superficiality of both approaches can be appreciated. Along with Marcel L'Herbier's *The Fantastic Night* and Marcel
Carné's *The Devil's Envoys, The Eternal Return* was one of the greatest
commercial successes of the Occupation period. Premiered in Vichy in
October 1943, *The Eternal Return,* an idealistic mythology adapted to
the circumstances of modern times by Jean Cocteau, transformed Jean
Marais and Madeleine Sologne into heroes of a generation. Director
Jean Delannoy, one of the forerunners of the future *cinéma de qualité,*
assigned the set to Georges Wakhevitch and the photography to Roger
Hubert, who intriguingly was able to keep the predominant themes of
the legend without affecting its enthralling atmosphere. Besides the
presence of the protagonists' unexpected blond hair and a certain
amount of ambiguity in the young leading performers, the film offered
a lucid version of Greek mythology while allowing audiences to escape
daily concerns. A modern version of the famous Tristan and Iseult
myth, the story transfers the love between Patrice (Jean Marais) and
Nathalie (Madeleine Sologne) to the eternal dimension. The account
begins with the friendship and affectionate relation between Patrice

Jean Marais (Patrice) and Madeleine Sologne (Nathalie) in Jean Delannoy's *The Eternal Return* (*L'éternel retour*, 1943), (Courtesy of BIFI).

and his uncle Marc (Jean Murat), who owns the castle in which they both live. With time, both men have developed a mutual and sound friendship. Although being his protégé, Patrice becomes enamored with Marc's wife, Nathalie, but cannot communicate his love for her due to his loyalty toward Marc and the profound faith Marc has in him. Likewise, Nathalie loves Patrice, but she is afraid to display her affection explicitly. To make matters worse, a malicious dwarf named Achille (Patrice's cousin, played by Pierre Pieral) who also resides in the castle, wanders around the dwelling, thwarting all possible future plans of the couple, stealing their little remaining privacy, and consequently preventing any chance for intimacy. One night, the young couple is caught in Nathalie's bedroom. Patrice is immediately expatriated to a small town, where an old friend of his (Roland Toutain) works as a mechanic. Once again, passions take control of his destiny, but this time he is loved by his friend's young sister, also named Nathalie (Junie Astor). Patrice can no longer express love for anyone, however, since his heart belongs to his true love. Slowly, he begins to lose faith in life and with a broken heart lets himself exist aimlessly. Alarmed by the depth of Patrice's despair, the sister calls upon Nathalie to come to Patrice. Before dying, Patrice at last confesses to his beloved Nathalie the immense love he always has had for her. Too late, death takes Patrice away, as Nathalie admits her reciprocal love.

The oneiric panache of *The Eternal Return* is due more to the participation of screenwriter Jean Cocteau than director Jean Delannoy, and can unquestionably be interpreted as a precursor to Cocteau's next film, *Beauty and the Beast*. Celebrating for several decades the great myths of humanity, Jean Cocteau was certainly one of the most prolific French auteurs of the century. With contributions in a variety of fields, such as poetry (he wrote a first volume of poems, *Aladdin's Lamp* (*La lampe d'Aladin*, at eighteen), theater, cinema, essays (a friend of Raymond Radiguet and Guillaume Apollinaire), and painting (he worked with Pablo Picasso and Amadeo Modigliani), Cocteau displayed a rather sophisticated artistic taste and most importantly an extraordinary scope for creative talents. His first full-length film, entitled *The Blood of a Poet* (*Le sang d'un poète,* 1930), an interpretation on his own personal mythology, promoted him to one of the most prominent figures within the growingly popular Surrealist field. Deeply attached in the reworking of Greek mythologies and other popular "fantastic" tales by sponsoring an ethic of straightforwardness and of orthodox imagery, he wrote the script for *The Eternal Return,* then directed *Beauty and the Beast*. But it was in 1949 that Cocteau truly achieved his greatest movie with the adaptation of the myth of *Orpheus* (*Orphée*), a play he had first performed in 1926, and for which he cast his favorite actor (and life companion) Jean Marais, followed a few years later by *The Testament of Orpheus* (*Le testament d'Orphée,* 1960), a deepened exploration of the nature of the poet.

Proclaiming French cinema of the Occupation as profoundly predisposed toward the Vichy government and propaganda—the way Italian cinema was in fact with Benito Mussolini's control over the media—can be misleading, since it is now clear, more than half a century later, that the vast mainstream of French productions indeed escaped censorship, thanks to the depth and fullness of their very creativity. Eventually, by 1944, in an effective consensus, the French public and filmmakers defeated the propaganda of Vichy's ideology. Although most directors represented on the screen the ubiquitous *attentiste* attitude characteristic of the French themselves during the Occupation (underscoring the avoidance of strong ideologies and often refusing to recognize the depth of the atrocities committed), neither Vichy nor the Nazi administration was able to eradicate the creative resilience of French cinema.

Chapter 4
The Postwar Era

The conclusion of World War II, ending six years of material devastation and human loss, gave France the opportunity to reorganize the slow internal reconstruction process of its national territory and the restructuring of its sociopolitical framework.[1] Despite numerous shortages, austere rationings, and dramatic political events, the postwar era is remembered as an exciting period for the French film industry, with the introduction of color as well as the wide-screen format of Cinemascope. Even though American films flooded European markets, as a result of the four-year ban during the war and the ratification of the Blum-Byrnes Agreements (see below), the French film industry experienced one of its most prosperous periods ever. With a record annual attendance of more than 400 million (until 1957), the film industry finally gained the financial stability and, in turn, better management, it had always sought.

French productions of the postwar era can be classified into three distinct categories: the cinema of the so-called *tradition de qualité*, perpetuating the academic concept of filmmaking generated in the 1930s; the development of film noir, which, despite a restrictive aesthetic, involved many productions; and a new cinema "in transition" heralding the incipient phase of the future French New Wave, which

exploded in the late 1950s. The French tradition of quality, represented by the old school of filmmakers, including Claude Autant-Lara,
Marcel Carné, Christian-Jaque, and Sacha Guitry, as well as screenwriters Jean Aurenche and Pierre Bost, corresponded to mainstream
cinema of the postwar era. Although it featured traditional genres—
almost exclusively comedies, period dramas, and literary adaptations—
the tradition of quality did manage to achieve numerous box office
hits, including Christian-Jaque's *Fan-Fan the Tulip* (*Fanfan la Tulipe,*
1952), René Clair's *The Grand Maneuvers* (*Les grandes manoeuvres,* 1955),
Autant-Lara's *The Red and the Black* (*Le rouge et le noir,* 1954), Carné's
The Adulteress (*Thérèse Raquin,* 1953), and Julien Duvivier's *The Little
World of Don Camillo* (*Le petit monde de Don Camillo,* 1951). This so-
called academic filmmaking, which advocated studio work, sophisticated lighting, and affected mise-en-scène, primarily relied on the
biggest stars of the decade (Gérard Philipe, Martine Carol, Michèle
Morgan, Fernandel, and Micheline Presle). Concerning film noir/thrill-
ers and their characteristic pessimistic vein, it is interesting to note
that the new *polar* genre, which was perfected in 1940s Hollywood,
made a successful development (or comeback) in France in Yves Allégret's *A Woman of Antwerp* (*Dédée d'Anvers,* 1947), Duvivier's *Panic*
(*Panique,* 1946), Henri-Georges Clouzot's *Diabolique* (*Les diaboliques,*
1954) and *Wages of Fear* (*Le salaire de la peur,* 1953), and Jacques
Becker's *Golden Marie* (*Casque d'or,* 1952) and *Grisbi* (*Touchez pas au
Grisbi,* 1953).[2] An innovative method of filmmaking announced its
arrival immediately after World War II with films such as Jacques
Tati's *Holiday* (*Jour de fête,* 1948) and *Monsieur Hulot's Holiday* (*Les
vacances de Monsieur Hulot,* 1953), Max Ophuls's *Roundabout* and *Lola
Montès* (*Lola Montès,* 1955), Robert Bresson's *The Diary of a Country
Priest* (*Le journal d'un curé de campagne,* 1951) and *A Man Escaped* (*Un
condamné à mort s'est échappé,* 1956), Becker's *The Night Watch* (*Le trou,*
1959), and René Clément's *Purple Noon* (*Plein soleil,* 1959). Of particular note are the films of Alain Resnais, one of the very first filmmakers
to embrace the cause of the future New Wave, especially *Night and
Fog* (*Nuit et brouillard,* 1955).

THE FOURTH REPUBLIC AND POSTWAR FRANCE

Although many politicians from the prewar era reemerged as cabinet
members, the disposition of the Liberation era was characterized by a
popular aspiration to social and political reforms. These anticipated
circumstances accounted for the economic expansion that marked the
later years of the Fourth Republic (for a time, the speed of industrial
development in France equaled Germany's postwar effort and surpassed
most other European countries). At the Liberation, the scope of the

government's administrative power, omnipresent in the reconstruction process in France, surfaced stronger than ever.

The Fourth Republic was formally decreed in 1946. Although similar to the constitution of the Third Republic, the new constitution focused on the reorganization of the colonial empire. Vincent Auriol was elected president of the Fourth Republic by Parliament in January 1947 and was succeeded by René Coty in December 1953. Although limited in power, the government made some essential resolutions during these years, including the modernization of the country, the organization of health insurance, the nationalization of strategic areas of the economy, and, most important, the ratification of the Treaty of Rome, which established the European Economic Community on March 25, 1957.[3] Following the Liberation, the political parties that emerged directly from the Resistance forces (Christian Democrats, Socialists, and Communists) and that had supported the interim government established in 1944 were predominant in the constituent assembly, representing three-fourths of Parliament members. They rapidly experienced severe dissensions, however, particularly on constitutional issues. Consequently, against all odds, Charles de Gaulle left the government in January 1946. The cold war, the bipolarization between the United States and the Soviet Union, along with world decolonization, soon instigated fierce disagreements with dramatic consequences for both British and French colonial territories. France consented to the financial assistance of the United States' Marshall Plan, introduced by Secretary of State George Marshall on June 5, 1947, to secure the reconstruction of battered western Europe.

The question of decolonization brought serious setbacks to the Fourth Republic and resulted in costly efforts to maintain the French colonial empire. Following the example of the British Empire, the populations of French colonies in Indochina felt entitled to request new political status with France. Most French leaders, including de Gaulle, however, were not ready to consent to any incursions on French colonial prestige; the prospect of a weakening empire was unimaginable, and to them any idea of colonial independence could potentially result in another foreign imperial power taking control. But what was destined to happen happened: France dispatched thousands of soldiers in an attempt to overpower the emergent Nationalist-Communist factions led by the Vietnamese political figure Ho Chi Minh. The enterprise dramatically failed with the French defeat at Diên Biên Phu on March 13, 1954, following eight years of appalling hostilities. Immediately after the defeat, decolonization began in Indochina. Pierre Mendès-France, newly elected président du conseil (prime minister), terminated the war within an international framework and endorsed the agreement of the Geneva Accords of July 22, 1954. The new decree established a transitory separation of North and South Vietnam into separate states. Two other subdivisions of French colonies in Indochina, the protectorates of Laos and Cambodia, were finally transformed into autonomous monarchies to conserve minimal French influence.

The turmoil of the decolonization process did not stop with Indochina. Just a few months after the Geneva Accords, on October 31, 1954, Algerian nationalists officially initiated a widespread insurgence against the French administration within Algeria. More than half a million French soldiers were sent to Algeria within three years (the largest overseas expeditionary force in French history). France's firm resolution to maintain Algeria as part of its empire was principally motivated by the presence of a million European settlers (colloquially called *pieds-noirs*) along with the discovery of oil in the Sahara desert. By contrast, the French government granted Morocco independence on May 26, 1954, as well as Tunisia on March 20, 1956, while in sub-Saharan Africa a diplomatic course of action took control of decolonization.

Right-wing politicians and militants led by General Jacques Massu, infuriated by the increasing doubts surrounding decolonization among the French population, chose to conspire against the government. Both in Paris and in Algiers, armed rebel groups headed by army officers plotted the eradication of the Fourth Republic to be replaced by a new regime led by de Gaulle. On May 15, 1958, de Gaulle declared to Parliament that he was ready to reenter the political arena if solicited by the French people. The vast majority of the Fourth Republic's officials unenthusiastically recognized that de Gaulle's comeback was the only solution that would prevent a military coup. Consequently, on June 1 of the same year, the National Assembly voted to confer absolute power for six months to de Gaulle as the new head of the French government, indirectly terminating the Fourth Republic and its ineffective and countless ephemeral coalition governments. The process of decolonization would continue.

With the cold war in the background, the postwar era was certainly a challenging period for French filmmakers and artists in general. Although the political phenomenon triggered anticommunist witch hunts in the United States but not in France, the cold war divided French intellectuals into antagonistic factions. The political circumstances compelled many French filmmakers, actors, and other artists to reorganize their professional careers, much as it was for actors in the United States during the "Red Scare era." Nevertheless, the 1950s were also a great era of rediscoveries in filmmaking. Due to the harsh censorship of the Third Republic, some unseen movies like Jean Vigo's *Zero of Conduct* were finally accessible to general audiences. Jean Renoir's *A Day in the Country* (*Une partie de campagne,* 1936) was released more than a decade after its production, and Orson Welles's *Citizen Kane* (1941) came out in France in 1946, along with all the other big Hollywood movies prohibited in France during the years of the Occupation. Those films included such classic masterpieces as Victor Fleming's *Gone with the Wind* (1939), John Huston's *Maltese Falcon* (1941), Michael Curtiz's *Casablanca* (1942), Billy Wilder's *Double Indemnity* (1944), and Howard Hawks's *The Big Sleep* (1946).

The intense intellectual activity in the humanities, with prestigious literary and critical reviews such as *Temps modernes* and *Les lettres françaises,* led Existentialism to become perhaps the major literary and philosophical current of the postwar era. Novels, theatrical plays, and films began to portray the human race as isolated in a "godless" cosmos, the coherence of which relies heavily on the free will of the individual, as humankind determines its own fate. After the Liberation, Albert Camus's and Jean-Paul Sartre's existentialist concepts set the tone for an entire generation that gathered in the cafés of Saint-Germain-des-Prés. Paris had once more become the great incubator of ideas for the Western world. The mood of this disenchanted generation—its innocence, its jazz clubs, its veneration of Sartre himself—was captured in Boris Vian's 1947 novel *L'écume des jours,* (*Froth on the Daydream*). Sartre's essays and novels made him one of the most celebrated intellectuals of the postwar era and won him the Nobel Prize in literature in 1964, which he refused. His distress over the war in Algeria and many other conflicts made him one of the most influential figures of the last century. In 1947, Albert Camus wrote *The Plague* (*La peste*), an allegory set in a town infested by the plague, and gave a universal dimension to the awareness of current dilemmas. He also received the Nobel Prize in literature, in 1957. French poetry gained a large readership with the works of Jacques Prévert,[4] Simone de Beauvoir, and Louis Aragon, who had been associated with the Surrealist movement in the 1920s. Aragon's poems were often used as rallying cries through the Resistance in the occupied zone. One of the major literary innovations was the appearance of the *nouveau roman* (new novel), particulary Alain Robbe-Grillet's *Jealousy* (*La jalousie,* 1957) and Michel Butor's *The Modification* (*La modification,* 1957). Both authors methodically declined the conventional framework of fiction as well as the omniscient narrator-author. The *nouveau roman,* demanding more from the reader, presented condensed, recurring, and partially elucidated events from which the significance had to be determined by the reader. French readership could now enjoy the first *Livres de poche,* and in 1947, Maurice Duhamel published the famous *Série Noire* with Gallimard. Painters Henri Matisse and Fernand Léger, fashion designer Christian Dior, and the larger-than-life singer Edith Piaf, who emerged from a new generation of musicians and whose notoriety endured for the remainder of the century, seemingly influenced the world. Among popular audiences, Piaf, along with her contemporaries Charles Aznavour, Georges Brassens, Gilbert Bécaud, Yves Montand, and Jacques Brel, would be the most celebrated singers of the decade.[5]

The 1950s in France can be most accurately described as a humanizing and modernizing decade (although not yet prosperous). Noteworthy indications of the nation's new optimism could be seen in the spectacular demographic surge of the postwar era, with an increasing birth rate. Also, due to the rapidly changing socioeconomic environment, French cinema remained an authentic, popular form of entertainment and the product of an industry in the flush of expansion throughout the 1950s. The year 1957 actually saw an attendance record, with more than four hundred million spectators (by comparison, three hundred seventy million in 1958). As early as 1950, television slowly drew the attention of the French public, invading the first homes in 1952. Although experiencing a lengthy progression, French television appeared to be cinema's most serious competitor. By the close of the decade, just over ten percent of French households owned a television set (40,000 TV sets in 1953, compared to 700,000 in 1958).[6] In addition, many films started to be shown on the small screen, and this novelty indirectly reduced the incentive to go to the movie houses.[7] In 1952, French television broadcast over two hundred films, the majority of which were French productions.

THE BLUM-BYRNES AGREEMENTS

In May 1946, French prime minister Léon Blum went to Washington to sign with his American counterpart, Secretary of State James F. Byrnes, a series of commercial agreements concerning the future of the French national economy, including a series of commissions to reorganize and enhance the standing of its film industry. The main goal was to eradicate France's debt to America and to obtain new credit. In return, France agreed to open its market almost entirely to American products, in particular, film productions. The American counterparts, visibly anticipating the future General Agreement on Tariffs and Trade (GATT), which were approved in 1947, came to the negotiation table with the firm intention of implementing a system based on the principle of free competition within the European film market. Consequently, the continuation of commercial quotas on film productions would be eliminated, and a reduction of tariff duties in Europe would ensue. The number of American productions was almost unlimited (before the war, the commercial agreement stipulated a limit of 200 US films per year in French theaters), and American film companies, having already absorbed the cost with strong box office hits, were finally able to successfully reconquer European markets at a very low cost. Over two thousand unseen American films, backlogged due to four years of Nazi occupation in Europe (see chapter 3), were waiting to "overflow" French theaters. Anticipating the impending effects of the cold war in Europe, this was the ideal commercial opportunity for the United States to display "the American way" to a divided and spellbound Europe in search of new socioeconomic models.

French theaters and distribution networks faced a difficult dilemma. Should they support French productions, which encountered endless difficulties, or endorse American films, with their unbeatable prices and guaranteed commercial success that they had already experienced in the United States? The competition was unequal because of the number of American films ready to flood the market. The vast majority of these films had already amortized their cost in the United States, so they could easily be sold inexpensively before reaching France. As a result, in 1945, 60 percent of the films in French theaters were actually American. For the recently created Committee for the Defense of the French Cinema (December 1947), the newly signed settlement instituted unfair stipulations under which French cinema could never recuperate its full power of production; immediately after, the committee vehemently reacted to the French-American agreements. French producers, as well as personnel of the film industry, were prompt to call for a control to ward off the impending crisis and in due course organized, on January 4, 1948, a demonstration involving several thousand technicians, writers, and actors, including Simone Signoret, Jean Marais, Raymond Bussières, Madeleine Sologne, Jacques Becker, and Louis Daquin. Six months later, on September 23, 1948, the agreements that had been ratified a year before and that had allowed over two hundred American films to be distributed in France each year were suddenly revised by the French government under pressure, and the number of American (dubbed) films authorized in French theaters was reduced to 130.[8] In addition, the new commercial quota, which defined the amount of time French movie theaters were to reserve for French productions, increased to twenty weeks per year, instead of the previously agreed upon sixteen.[9]

Meanwhile, the Centre national de la cinématographie, created on October 25, 1946, principally sought to control the financing of French film productions, the exhibition profits, the organization of a professional education system, and the financial aid to production.[10] In 1948, the project was realized, and the government started to assist the French film industry indirectly; it established a tax included in the entrance fee for all featured movies. However, the profit was directed to build up funds to assist future French productions exclusively. It was indeed a concealed way of having American "super productions" financially assist a convalescent French cinema. At the end of the 1950s, a new system was established by the CNC, which provided an advance based on prospective profits. As film historian Colin Crisp described it, the system was "extraordinarily effective in introducing new blood into the industry, and must be considered a key factor in the development of a Nouvelle Vague of young filmmakers."[11] As early as the first year of the postwar era, the French government supplied substantial financial aid that eventually prompted the development of small theaters outside Paris, the initiation of the Avignon Festival, which was launched in 1947, and the establishment of significant and pioneering theater companies, such as the Théâtre National Populaire (TNP) and the Compagnie Jean-Louis Barrault–Madeleine Renaud.

When recentered in a global perspective, France was by this time unquestionably the European country that best protected itself against an American cinematographic hegemony. Hollywood films represented more than 75 percent of Italian and British markets, whereas in France, they did not reach 50 percent. The coming of Italian neorealism, led by Luchino Visconti, Roberto Rossellini, and Vittorio de Sica, only confirmed that European cinema, despite the austerity of its subject matter, continued to be vital. The immediate postwar era also represented the materialization of continental coproductions, especially between France and Italy.[12] The coproduction initiative had already proved beneficial during the Occupation years with Carné's *Children of Paradise* and Jean Delannoy's *The Eternal Return*. After 1946, a long list of Franco-Italian productions began to flourish, including such films as Christian-Jaque's *Fan-Fan the Tulip*, Autant-Lara's *The Red and the Black*, Carné's *The Adulteress*, and Duvivier's *The Little World of Don Camillo*.

THE PRESTIGE OF FRENCH CINEMA OR CINEMA OF PRESTIGE? JEAN COCTEAU

One of the most essential issues for the cinematographic industry during these years of national reorganization was to decide whether to maintain the liberal policy of the prewar years or to instigate a more controlled structure. For many members of the Resistance, the winds of change brought by the Liberation were supposed to trigger a rebirth of the French economy and to inflict formal sanctions on the "collaborationist bourgeoisie." Therefore, after the war, the concept of nationalization and general reforms was widely accepted, while the structures installed during the Occupation, combined with prewar aesthetics, were maintained. In addition to the success of *réalisme noir,* literary films, and the newly introduced *réalisme psychologique,* French films of the postwar era, except for a few examples, such as Jean Renoir's works, did not look much different in content or form from the prewar era. They continued the tradition of genres, the conventions of which did not evolve significantly with time. Poetic realism was the predominant current of the prewar era; after the Liberation, its new term, psychological realism, suggested a similar high degree of blackness. This lack of cinematographic creativity and narrative discourse is the main reason why the 1950s usually appear to many film historians as a period of transition rather than a solid and prolific cinematographic decade. Postwar French cinema can also be characterized in terms of obsessive doom and gloom, much like Italian neorealism of the late 1940s. It remained somewhat different from Italian films in its realistic method, as Gerald Mast explains: "The postwar Italian film sprang from the reality which the director sought to capture with camera and film; the postwar French film sprang from the director's stylistic concern with the way a camera can capture reality."[13] Therefore, one may well ask the following question: What social and intellectual circumstances motivated such numbers of French film directors to approach the depiction of reality, while defending a creative and artistic initiative, without also experiencing a real sense of self-limitation?

One of the closest and most significant examples mirroring the Italian neorealism experience remains René Clément's *Battle of the Rails,* usually considered a rare authentic voice of the French Resistance. Promoted by the Conseil national de la Résistance and Resistance associations such as Résistance-Fer and Ciné-Union, the film represented more of an epic than a simple war documentary. Few "Resistance" films resulted in high-quality cinematographic achievements, since in postwar France, the need to rebuild and modernize the nation was often used as a reason to overlook past division to unify the population.[14] Because of its affinities with Roberto Rossellini's *Open City,* the film was considered the equivalent of Italian neorealism on a truly epic scale. Like his Italian neorealist counterpart, René Clément (1913–96) strengthened the representation of war reality by filming on location with authentic train conductors, railway employees, and Resistance fighters. Set in the region of Chalon-sur-Saône between 1940 and 1944, *Battle of the Rails* was built in two distinct parts: the first, a documentary on the underground sabotage actions and the tragic aftermath with the massive and random executions of hostages, and the second on the actual German convoy en route to the D-Day front. Clément's unobtrusive plot and assiduous planning of every sequence resulted in a film that incorporated an even greater sense of realism than the average war movie, disguising the careful artistry behind it and maintaining an almost documentary impression in its realistic nature. Through the fluid use of the camera by cinematographer Henri Alekan (1909–2001) and the dialogues of Colette Audry (1906–90), the story portrayed the audacious underground efforts by French railway workers to sabotage Nazi reinforcement-troop trains, which contributed to the Allied victory in June 1944. The association between historical testimony, contemporary footage, and tragic human epic catharsis with the derailment of the train itself, made this one of the landmark war films of all time. The most memorable scene is the execution of the hostages by the Nazis as seen from the last hostage's point of view, while in the background the engine conductors blast their locomotives' whistles to protest and to salute those who are about to die. This inspired moment, glorifying, even deifying, the anonymous martyrs of the war, is one of the greatest scenes in all of French film. During the first edition of the Cannes Film Festival in 1946, *Battle of the Rails* received the award for Best Director and the Prix spécial du jury (Special Jury Prize).

At the same time as *Battle of the Rails* and in a radically different genre, René Clément codirected with Jean Cocteau (although officially his assistant) *Beauty and the Beast*. After a thirteen-year interruption in the film industry, Jean Cocteau (1889–1963), who was involved as a novelist, poet, and dramaturge in the Avant-garde movement of the 1920s, devoted himself to writing scenarios for other French films, including Jean Delannoy's *The Eternal Return,* Serge de Poligny's *The Phantom Baron* (*Le baron fantôme,* 1943), and Robert Bresson's *Ladies of the Park* (*Les dames du Bois de Boulogne,* 1944). Above all, he aspired to find a new artistic structure, not just a new cinematographic technique: a new thematic and graphic system that communicated his fascination with the arts in an understandable form for the public. Able to intervene in numerous artistic domains such as painting, opera, ballet, the novel, and drama, Cocteau began the postwar era with a colossal literary adaptation, *Beauty and the Beast,* perhaps his most popular film. Cocteau's 1946 production was a remarkably faithful version of the 1756 fairy tale by Jeanne-Marie Leprince de Beaumont. Along with the presence of Josette Day (Beauty) and Jean Marais (the Beast), the memorable dark and romantic set, which intensely implicated Surrealist elements and heavy symbolism (the Beast's castle), was the highlight of this impressionistic tale. In competition during the 1946 Cannes Film Festival, *Beauty and the Beast* won the Prix Louis Delluc during the same year partly due to the creative efforts of Cocteau's cinematographer, Henri Alekan,[15] whose cinematic tricks included slowing the motions of the camera (or accelerating them) to create dazzling visual effects and accentuate the presence of the supernatural and storybook elements: the enduring enchantment of the main entrance of the Beast's castle, the human candelabras, and the "living" caryatids of the fireplace.

Josette Day (Beauty) and Jean Marais (the beast) in Jean Cocteau's *Beauty and the Beast* (*La belle et la bête*, 1946), (Photo courtesy of the Museum of Modern Art/Film Stills Archive).

René Clément's *Battle of the Rails* (*La bataille du rail*, 1945), (Photo courtesy of the Museum of Modern Art/Film Stills Archive).

Three years later, in 1949, Jean Cocteau directed *Orpheus* (a projection of Cocteau himself through Jean Marais), a faultless marriage of the Greek myth and the director's poetic language, which undoubtedly appeared as a substantial improvement on *The Eternal Return*. By no means can Cocteau be considered a prolific filmmaker, with a total of only six long feature films. He was also involved with poetry, novels, and the theater. It is noteworthy that his films, in contrast to many contemporary filmmakers, proceeded not from commercial impulse but from the essence of his personal, Surrealist imagination. For Cocteau, rewriting poetry with a prescribed amount of cinematic magic was the ideal way to convert the ancient Greek myth of Orpheus into a motion picture.

The story of *Orpheus* begins in an imaginary Paris, at the peaceful Café des Poètes favored by young Avant-garde artists. Orpheus (Jean Marais) is a young, successful Parisian poet who, fascinated by the prospect of everlasting notoriety, confesses his secret desire to renew himself, to go beyond the limits of human experience, and to reach the unknowable, the mystery behind mortality. Hindered by the notoriety of his poems, he feels the bitterness of the younger generation of artists, perhaps invigorated by their own lack of success, and he understands that to be esteemed, he must astound them.

While sitting at the café's terrace, a couple of motorcycles followed by a dazzling Rolls-Royce unexpectedly appear on the square, running over a fellow poet, Cégeste (Edouard Dermithe), and eventually killing him. Out of the mysterious car comes a seductive and enigmatic young lady in black, known simply as the Princess (Maria Casarès),[16] who orders Orpheus to put the wounded young man in the back seat and to accompany her as a witness. Confused, she appears to be in command of the motorcyclists who have run over the young poet. Instead of a hospital, the car, driven by the chauffeur Heurtebise (François Périer), takes them to the Princess's home, which is eventually revealed to be the underworld. There, much to Orpheus's surprise, Cégeste is brought back to life after the Princess says to him: "Do you know who I am? . . . You are my death." They all step through a mirror except for Orpheus, who cannot follow them. Orpheus is escorted home the next day by Heurtebise (Françoise Périer) but remains oblivious to his wife, Eurydice (Marie Déa), distracted by his encounter of both the enthralling Princess and a mysterious radio broadcast, which transmits cryptic segments from enigmatic fractured poetry. As he goes back to his bedroom to sleep, the mysterious Princess appears to him. Unwillingly in love with Orpheus, she orders her motorcyclists to take the life of Orpheus's own wife, Eurydice, to entice him back. To bring his wife back from the underworld, Orpheus must learn from Heurtebise how to go through the mirror. Heurtebise indeed reveals to him that "mirrors are the doors through which death comes and goes. Look at yourself in a mirror all your life and you'll see death at work, like bees in a hive of glass,"[17] giving him the key that leads him to the underworld. They both depart for the journey, but Orpheus's heart is now divided between the Princess and Eurydice. There, a supreme court rules that the Princess, though a mythical representation of death herself, has selfishly killed only to satisfy her own desire and that Eurydice must return to the real world with the condition that Orpheus never sees his wife again. With this precarious limitation, which turns out to be impossible to keep, the young couple awkwardly deals with the strenuous constraint until the day when both, sitting in their car, fatally violate the sacred agreement by casting a look at each other in the front mirror.

Cocteau's "personal mythology" surreptitiously explored the dark side of his innovative mind with considerable flamboyance as he investigated the myth of Orpheus on three occasions: *Blood of a Poet* (*Le sang d'un poète,* 1930), *Orpheus,* and *The Testament of Orpheus* (*Le testament d'Orphée,* 1960). Wistful and compelling, *Orpheus* depicts an under-

Jean Marais (Orphée) in Jean Cocteau's *Orpheus* (*Orphée*, 1949), (Photo courtesy of the Museum of Modern Art/Film Stills Archive/© Ariane).

world that is not too different from everyday life. The special effects are simple yet ingenious (actors penetrating and reemerging from mirrors thanks to a still pool of water that reflects their faces; rubber gloves leaping onto hands, broken glass flying back into frames through a reverse photography process),[18] rendering the film inventive, enigmatic, and dreamlike. Film historian Roy Armes celebrated Cocteau's extraordinary representation of death as "totally lacking in irrevocability or awesomeness."[19] Nevertheless, the story line was not only about love, death, and cupidity, but also about how poetic inspiration could beguile the artist away from everyday life (after Orpheus unexpectedly returns from the underworld, he is more engrossed with the irrational radio signals than with the presence of his lost spouse). *Orpheus* is a film that lends itself to many different interpretations and is a doorway for any viewer into Cocteau's oeuvre. One of the strong points of the film, probably Cocteau's finest, was the fact that, despite all its heavy and intricate metaphysical elements, it nevertheless fully succeeded in captivating the general public's imagination and inquisitiveness.

A CERTAIN *TRADITION DE QUALITÉ*

In the postwar French film industry, two radically opposed groups began to surface: those preoccupied with the artistic component of the medium (a small minority) and those more interested in developing a conventional narrative format and remaining in touch with the market and its requirements. Three different types of films were regularly shown to the French public: the comedy, the costume drama/literary adaptation, and the thriller (in French, called the *polar,* short for *policier/noir,* which was heavily influenced by the 1940s Hollywood thrillers).[20] Yet all these filmic genres contented themselves with a preexisting repertoire and thrived within a purely academic cinema. In addition, many filmmakers were confused with the notion of literary adaptation and its subsequent cinematography requirements, resulting in long screenplays burdened with a pseudophilosophical message that rendered films impossible to enjoy. Aside from the unique interest toward the novel and drama, the main grief that the insurgents of the New Wave expressed a few years later was the lack of original thought and the relatively limited expression of cinematographic discourse. For instance, despite a prolific series of masterpieces in the 1930s and early 1940s, Marcel Carné produced an overdose of décors and studio sets, with such films as *Gates of the Night (Les portes de la nuit,* 1946) and *Juliette ou la clé des songes (Juliette ou la clé des songes,* 1951), which consequently accentuated the decline of indoor shooting. Despite his sound technical skills, as well as his popular achievement and critical success of the prewar and Occupation eras, by the 1950s Carné's modus operandi unfortunately lacked a sense of renewal and was never quite as convincing. The same phenomenon occurred with filmmakers/authors Marcel Pagnol and his *Manon des sources* (1952), a rural epic of fortitude and revenge directly adapted from his novel *The Water from the Hills,* and Sacha Guitry with *Napoléon* (1954), who by the mid-1950s began a visible decline.

Fifteen years after its beginnings in the United States, color arrived in France. Yet despite its obvious groundbreaking appearances and the hopes it procured with avid audiences, very few French directors took immediate advantage of the technique. In 1953 French cinema, which had been in no rush to adopt this newest technological innovation, was quickly dominated by two American processes, Technicolor and Eastmancolor, plus the German Agfacolor.[21] Color, which was first developed in the early 1900s, surfaced at a commercial level in the United States after the mid 1930s. In France, because of the reluctance to change the aesthetic standard of cinematography, color films were extremely rare before and after the war; it was only in 1953 that some important productions were made in Technicolor, such as Christian-Jaque's *Lucrèce Borgia* (*Lucrèce Borgia,* 1952), Jean Renoir's *The Golden Coach* (*Le carrosse d'or,* 1952), René Clair's *The Grand Maneuvers* (*Les grandes manoeuvres,* 1955), and Claude Autant-Lara's *The Red and the Black* (*Le rouge et le noir,* 1954). Then in 1956, France experienced a short-lived color boom. This transient introduction was due to higher financial costs during the post-production phase as well as the rise after 1958 of the New Wave, a genre partly defined by reduced production costs. For the majority of French filmmakers in the 1950s, color was only suitable for certain types of productions, mainly period films, historical reconstructions, and costume dramas. For the new filmmakers of the late 1950s and early 1960s, as well as for many directors working within the *tradition de qualité,* black-and-white composition corresponded with the best visual definition as it inexorably granted a much more persuasive and dramatic sense of realism than color composition could ever achieve. This disaffection with color lasted until the late 1960s, when, for instance, Robert Bresson finally used it in 1968 with *A Gentle Creature* (*Une femme douce*).

Released to the French market in 1953 by Twentieth Century-Fox, Cinemascope was already a long-used invention (an anamorphic procedure, employing a lens compressing a widespread image onto a regular 35 mm film stock; when projected, the image is decompressed through another lens on the projector). The audacious director Roger Vadim, however, started with both Technicolor[22] and the new wide-screen Cinemascope, offering panoramic framing in his film . . . *And God Created Woman* (*Et Dieu créa la femme,* 1956). Colin Crisp describes the significance of color for a whole generation:

> As a final hypothesis concerning the odd shift in views about color production in the Western world, it is worth considering the very general sociological transformations that were taking place over this period. By the 1960s, capitalism had transformed itself into a consumption-based economy, which had begun to provide its citizens with a significantly greater quantity of domestic industrial goods. For

the working classes, it is doubtful if the quality of life had ever transformed itself so radically in so short a time. Information, mobility, comfort, control of one's destiny, were significantly more within each citizen's control. Reality was no longer a thing to be endured, self-denial and delayed gratification were no longer such necessary elements of mass ideology. Fantasy and escape were realizable, rather than a compensation for reality. The representation of reality as colored could more readily be accepted than in the early 1950s (let alone the Depression or war years), when the residual morale of delayed gratification and of endurance was still powerful. While this hypothesis would be risky as an isolated explanation of such a fundamental media phenomenon, it might take its place beside others as a supplementary factor, rendering the shift (from color as fantasy to color as realism) that much more appropriate.[23]

The so-called *qualité française* may sound abstract and overly comprehensive, but in fact it included mostly prestige productions (classic literary adaptations, costume dramas, and historical reconstitutions), whose actors, principally from dramatic schools, were adorned with elaborate attires and surrounded by magnificent studio sets. The works of the directors who emerged from the dark hours of the Occupation had become, by the middle of the next decade, quite imposing in the number of their achievements and the prestige of this so-called quality. They contributed significantly to the reputation of the French film industry throughout the world. As the years went by, however, most of these experienced filmmakers progressively lost their own idiosyncratic artistic creativity and cinematographic originality, which had been their determining trademark fifteen years before. They had simply fallen prey to their own triumph due to the constant demand from film producers for bigger budgets and an invariable need to satisfy the expectation of new spectatorship. French cinema focused less on its spiritual and moral correlation to viewers and more on its own methodology to engage a subject matter. Although the works they performed were ingenious and academically stimulating, there was little change in the concept of cinema itself. This was a scenarist cinema, the genre and rules of stagecraft seemingly fixed within an agreed perception of what constituted literature, history, or vaudeville. The films of Claude Autant-Lara (1901–2000) epitomized the literary adaptation trend of the late 1940s and mid 1950s. Many of the literary adaptations of the postwar era were inspired from realist or contemporary literature, such as Raymond Radiguet's novel *Devil in the Flesh* (*Le diable au corps*), André Gide's *The Pastoral Symphony* (*La symphonie pastorale*), and Jean-Paul Sartre's *The Chips Are Down* (*Les jeux sont faits*). The ringleader of the *qualité française* was Autant-Lara, with adapta-

tions of Colette's *The Game of Love* (*Le blé en herbe*), Stendhal's *The Red
and the Black,* Georges Simenon's *Love Is My Profession* (*En cas de
mahleur*), and Marcel Aymé's short novel *Le vin de Paris.* Honorable
attempts to transfer the involvements and density of classic French
novels to film were sporadically made but logically remained incapable
of capturing, entirely and in depth, the full dramatic fortune of the
novel. French cinema was focused too much on an imaginary past
(adaptations of literary classics) and remained clearly disconnected from
France's current events and its preoccupations. For film historian Roy
Armes, the constant dilemma for directors was between realist venture
and quality impulse:

> French cinema has always been at its richest when it has direct contact
> with the world of the arts in general, but the major currents of thought
> and literature hardly find their reflection in the cinema of the 1950s,
> whose concerns remain, essentially, professionalism, attention to detail
> in setting and acting, and commercial viability. In this sense it was a
> cinema without risks, which could hardly attract the young aspirants
> who were nurtured by the growth of the *ciné-club* movement in France
> after 1945, by the activities of the *Cinémathèque française,* which main-
> tained a lively and eclectic approach under Henri Langlois, and by the
> new generation of film critics.[24]

The *cinéma des scénaristes* reached its heyday with productions such as
Children of Paradise (premiered in 1945), thanks to the team of Marcel
Carné and Jacques Prévert, clearly experiencing its slow decline by the
beginning of the 1950s. A new team of scenarists, Jean Aurenche and
Pierre Bost, marked the soaring postwar era. Their specialty was the
adaptation of literary oeuvres labeled *de qualité.* Unfortunately, although many of the works produced reached a high level of quality
(such as *The Pastoral Symphony* and *Devil in the Flesh*), they generated
an overly academic approach, the rigidity of which hampered the
creative process that indirectly opened the door for the future New
Wave of 1958–59. Representative directors Autant-Lara[25] and
Christian-Jaque removed themselves from France's current preoccupations by their impersonal works and their rejection of the ecumenical
character in their films. Although assisted by expert technicians—
Jacques Natteau, Robert Juillard, Oswald Morris, and Louis Page, to
name a few—they were unable to capture any sense of rejuvenation
within their visual style. In 1954, a young journalist named François
Truffaut wrote what remains today a landmark in cinematographic
history, an article entitled "Une certaine tendance du cinéma français"
in *Les cahiers du cinéma,* which vehemently recvaluated the *cinéma de
qualité* and all other concepts of film studies of the 1950s. Truffaut
accused directors and scenarists of the *qualité française* of conforming to
established standards so closely that they eventually destroyed the

spirit of their original work. This devastating position would essentially give the world the New Wave. The evolution toward a new concept of filmmaking had become a necessity.

Among a myriad of new talented actors, it is worth considering several heroes of the 1950s generation. One of the best known illustrations is, of course, Gérard Philipe (1922–59), who died at the age of thirty-seven (a fate similar to American actor, James Dean), but whose few roles made him one of the most identifiable icons of postwar French cinema. Although many have argued that his celebrity status came from the simple fact that his image of rebel youth remained untarnished by age and universally appealing for future generations, Philipe proved on many occasions the extent of his repertoire and the depth of his acting potential. He is described by film historians Olivier Barrot and Raymond Chirat as a "hero to whom the gods of the arts as well as the public, have bestowed . . . a legendary providence."[26] Autant-Lara's *Devil in the Flesh* led Philipe to become the most celebrated of all French actors following his first success, which garnered the Grand Prix for Best Actor at the Brussels International Festival in 1947. Philipe concomitantly pursued a second career in theatrical drama and was consecrated with national glory at Jean Vilar's TNP in 1951. During the 1950s, thanks to his seductive talent and panache in popular cape-and-sword productions (reminiscent of Errol Flynn's performances), he became the enchanting emblem of the *cinéma de qualité* as well as the favorite male actor among the French female public. His most memorable roles include Roger Vadim's *Dangerous Liaisons (Les liaisons dangereuses,* 1959), Autant-Lara's *The Red and the Black,* Christian-Jaque's *Fan-Fan the Tulip,* and *The Charterhouse of Parma (La chartreuse de Parme,* 1948).

Along with the "French James Dean," Marie-Louise Mourer, a.k.a. Martine Carol (1920–67), can be considered French cinema's leading sex symbol, much like Viviane Romance in the 1930s and Brigitte Bardot in the late 1950s and early 1960s. A voluptuous blond with outrageous, yet in some ways conventional, beauty, Martine Carol hypnotized male audiences throughout the 1950s with a series of historical costume dramas characterized by their bountiful production resources and sophisticated eroticism. Under the pseudonym Maryse Arley, Continental Studios hired her for secondary roles in films such as Georges Lacombe's *Le dernier des six* (1941) and Henri Decoin's *Strangers in the House (Les inconnus dans la maison,* 1942). She later changed her name to Martine Carol in honor of her favorite star, Carole Lombard. In 1950, Richard Pottier adapted Cécil Saint Laurent's historical novel *Dear Caroline (Caroline chérie),* a Jean Anouilh–scripted story of a young aristocrat, Caroline de Bièvre, living on her wits and physical charms while sacrificing her virtue to survive Revolutionary

162

FRENCH CINEMA

France. The popularity of *Dear Caroline* was not due to its cinematographic quality, nor to Martine Carol's artistic talent. Far from it, her
numerous pseudo-nude scenes, which unveiled an agreeable *plastique,*
mesmerized French audiences of the Fourth Republic. More importantly, the image of the stylish libertine institutionalized the genre
with which she was most intimately associated, the multihued erotic
"costume melodramas."

By the late 1950s, Martine Carol's national gleaming notoriety was
fatally hampered by two major obstacles: first, by the emerging New
Wave and its fierce aspiration to eradicate expensively produced historical and literary adaptations by a more unprompted directing method;
second, and more seriously, by the rise of sex kitten Brigitte Bardot as
the new look of femininity for French cinema. Martine Carol attempted a second career in Hollywood but made only three films with
minor roles: Michael Anderson's *Around the World in 80 Days* (1956),
the Jack Palance vehicle *Ten Seconds to Hell* (1958), and John Ainsworth
and Bernard Knowles's *Hell Is Empty* (1966).[27] Other notorious French
movies featuring Carol include André Cayatte's *The Lovers of Verona*
(*Les amants de Vérone,* 1948),[28] Christian-Jaque's *Lucrèce Borgia* and
Nana (*Nana,* 1954), René Clair's *Beauties of the Night* (*Les belles de nuit,*
1952), and Max Ophuls's *Lola Montès* (*Lola Montès,* 1955). "With
Martine Carol," said French film historian René Prédal, "motion pictures are in the street, with its magic, its mythology and its show."[29]

If the first half of the 1950s was devoted to Martime Carol's glamour, the rest of the decade as well as the 1960s shifted to Brigitte
Bardot. Although rarely noted for her association with the quality
tradition, Brigitte Bardot (b. 1934), Parisian by birth, was without
doubt the only French actress who could claim absolute world fame.
She quickly became the French symbol of enlightened sexuality and at
the same time the female sex goddess of the 1950s. Ginette Vincendeau describes her persona as the ultimate "sex-kitten, wedding natural
and unruly sexuality with childish attributes—slim but full-breasted,
blond with a girlish fringe, the pout and the giggle."[30] Before becoming the new myth of youth, Bardot began her professional career as a
fashion model in the late 1940s. Soon after being noticed by future
husband Roger Vadim, she made her first film appearance as Javotte
Lemoine in Jean Boyer's *Crazy for Love* (*Le trou normand,* 1952), opposite comedian Bourvil.[31] A year later, in 1953, her international notoriety became reality with her first US production in Anatole Litvak's
Act of Love, starring as Mimi opposite Kirk Douglas. The year 1956
marked a revolution in the sexual visual ethic of the 1950s, with
Bardot's steamy performance in Vadim's . . . *And God Created Woman,*
just three years after her appearance at the 1953 Cannes Film Festival,
which promoted her starlet image to international proportions. Despite

Martine Carol (1920–67), (Courtesy of BIFI/© Guy André).

her worldwide success—she was enormously popular in the United States—she was, and always would be, an entirely French actress.[32] As Jacques Siclier put it, "Bardot exhibits her nudity without chastity, without complex, as a normal thing. She makes love whenever she feels like it. Able to have feelings, passion, she claims the right to choose her own men."[33] What disarmed her rivals (Martine Carol, in particular) was that "BB" did not act: she was simply herself on the screen. In addition to her powerful look, temperamental outbursts, and modern haircut, her overall voluptuous mannerism influenced enumerable copycats on and off screen.

Vadim's . . . And God Created Woman, despite a rather unadventurous setting, is notable for several reasons: its numerous "pre–New Wave" aspects and qualities (cinematic novelty), its tempestuous scuffles with censorship, the use of Cinemascope and color, and a prefiguration of the future liberalization of sexuality in the dawning decade of the 1960s. Although not especially innovative in its form and mise-en-scène, Vadim's film was revolutionary for its emancipated erotic and sexual content. Juliette, a young orphan in Saint-Tropez, creates scandals everywhere she goes with her outrageous look and behavior. Her love affair with two brothers, Michel (Jean-Louis Trintignant) and Antoine (Christian Marquand), triggers an abrasive rivalry by her unrestrained conduct. The character of Juliette was more than just a sexual symbol. It broke new ground within the myth of conventional youth, which was for the first time not bound to social taboo or traditional morals, and it further anticipated the erotic explosion of the 1970s, with such scenes as the wedding lunch in which Juliette and Michel first consummate their marriage in the upper bedroom while the family waits for them to begin the wedding banquet. The success of . . . And God Created Woman persuaded even the most reluctant French producers, who hung onto the aesthetic and strategy of the qualité française, that a new approach to picture making might also generate profits. The Bardot phenomenon put an end to the moral, suggestive, erotic tone of the 1950s and "desacralized" the Hollywood mythical sex symbol by displaying sensuality in quotidian décor, in the street, through realistic photography: "Eroticism leaves the dream to join reality."[34] It is, however, important not to neglect other valuable films that Bardot made, such as Autant-Lara's Love Is My Profession (En cas de malheur, 1958), in which she costarred with Jean Gabin; Henri-Georges Clouzot's courtroom drama The Truth (La vérité, 1960); Louis Malle's A Very Private Affair (Vie privée, 1962), which used some elements of the actress's own life and stardom; and Jean-Luc Godard's Contempt (Le mépris, 1963).[35]

Another significant female star of the 1950s, not only in France but also in the United States, was Simone Signoret (1921–85). An unusu-

Jean-Louis Trintignant (Michel) and Brigitte Bardot (Juliette) in Roger Vadim's
... *And God Created Woman* (*Et dieu créa la femme*, 1956), (Photo courtesy of the
Museum of Modern Art/Film Stills Archive/© Ariane).

ally beautiful and accomplished actress who cast a spell over numerous talented directors, Signoret was a genuine movie star whose complex personality has never been completely revealed. Born Simone Kaminker, she started her acting career during the Nazi Occupation under precarious conditions (without a working permit) as an extra in Jean Boyer's *Le prince charmant* (1941) and Marcel Carné's *The Devil's Envoys*. Simone Signoret married French director Yves Allégret in 1944 and landed her first leading roles in 1946 with Jean Sacha's *Fantômas*, and Allégret's *A Woman of Antwerp* and *The Cheat* (*Manèges*, 1949). In 1951, Simone Signoret remarried singer-actor Yves Montand: a perfect movie couple for the newspapers' headlines, just as Madeleine Renaud and Jean-Louis Barrault were at the time. Because of Signoret's powerful personality and sheer outspokenness, her marriage survived Montand's notorious affair with Marilyn Monroe[36] and became one of the myths of the twentieth century. In the 1950s, Signoret's major roles were as the scheming mistresses in Clouzot's thriller *Diabolique* and Jacques Becker's 1952 *Golden Marie*. She received international recognition in this film for her most seductive role as Marie, a tenacious prostitute facing bleak circumstances while under the spell of a jealous and possessive lover in 1900s Paris.

Because of their open left-wing political views and active militant presence, their film and theater careers, their intellectual interests and friendships, Signoret and Montand were denied entry visas to the United States during the McCarthy era in the 1950s. However, only a few years later, in 1960, Signoret won the Oscar for Best Actress for her performance in Jack Clayton's *Room at the Top* (1959). This was the first time the Oscar was awarded to an actress with no Hollywood experience (contending for the Oscar with actresses Doris Day, Audrey Hepburn, and Elizabeth Taylor). That same year she was also awarded the Grand prix d'interprétation at the 1959 Cannes Film Festival for *Room at the Top* as well as the British Film Academy Best Foreign Actress award for *Golden Marie*. She continued her career in Hollywood with the role of La Condesa opposite Vivien Leigh in Stanley Kramer's *Ship of Fools* (1965) and with James Caan in Curtis Harrington's *Games* (1967). Her most memorable role was unquestionably as the charismatic woman of the French Resistance in Jean-Pierre Melville's *The Shadow Army* (*L'armée des ombres*, 1969). She received the French César for Best actress for Moshe Mizrahi's *Madame Rosa* (*La vie devant soi*, 1977). Her autobiography, *La nostalgie n'est plus ce qu'elle était* (*Nostalgia Isn't What It Used to Be*), was published in July 1976. Widely regarded as a fine example of the genre, it became a bestseller in France.

Failing eyesight in the early 1980s hampered Signoret's film career, though she continued to write and to campaign for humanitarian causes (for example, with philosopher Michel Foucault) until her death in 1985. In the opinion of her directors and most critics, Signoret had perfect intuition for acting before the camera. Her talent, her great beauty, and her indifference to public opinion made her career unique in the history of French cinema.

COMEDY À LA FRANÇAISE: CLAUDE AUTANT-LARA

Despite its status as the most popular of genres throughout ten decades of French film history, comedy has concomitantly been, among film critics and historians, the most overlooked and underrated of genres. It is indeed commonplace to see that the French public consistently underestimates the importance of actors' performances and usually expresses injudicious assessments about the overall impression of comic movies and their hypothetical contribution to cinema. Movie critics have always emphasized the lack of social issues, emotional depth, and artistic elements in most comedies, which irrevocably condemns the genre to a cultural ghetto. Apart from rare exceptions such as Max Linder, Marcel Pagnol, Sacha Guitry, Jacques Tati, and more recently Coline Serreau, the genre's advocates have consistently been ignored for national awards and other prizes of recognition—a fact not altogether untrue for the Oscars as well. Promoters of a national identity as well as powerful cultural icons (even more so since successfully exporting countless comedies to Hollywood), those burlesque vaudevilles, sarcastic farces, and other parodies have shaped and financially facilitated the development of the postwar-era cinema. With well-wrought comical scenarios, popular comedy of the 1950s was unquestionably the only genre to be indistinctively acclaimed by all audiences throughout decades safely guaranteeing a profit each weekend at the box office.

In the 1950s, three comedians were at the top, tirelessly entertaining several generations of French audiences. Fernandel (1903–71), born Fernand Joseph Désiré Contandin in Marseille, was, along with Bourvil and Louis de Funès, one of the most popular comic actors of French cinema. He starred in over 150 films, including Gilles Grangier's *L'âge ingrat,* (1964), Claude Autant-Lara's *The Red Inn,* (1951), Julien Duvivier's *The Little World of Don Camillo,* (1951), and Marcel Pagnol's *Harvest (Regain,* 1937) and *The Well-Digger's Daughter (La fille du puisatier,* 1940), and his popularity lasted over four eventful decades. From the *comique troupier* (military vaudeville) to *provençal* folklore, his physique, graciously described by Ginette Vincendeau as having "horselike features, especially his huge teeth, and a strong southern accent,"[37] made him famous, especially in the Don Camillo series, in which he played the memorable role of a parish priest who battled the communist town mayor (Gino Cervi). Fernandel performed one of his best roles with Bourvil, the other grand comic actor, in Grangier's *My Wife's Husband* (*La cuisine au beurre,* 1963). As for Bourvil (1917–70), he began to write songs for the music hall, making a name for himself (as André Raimbourg), and like many comic artists, he eventually became a stand-up comedian. Autant-Lara's *Four Full Bags* (*La traversée de Paris,* 1956), one of the most memorable satirical comedies of the time, launched his acting career, revealing Bourvil's wide-ranging potential as a movie star. The 1960s were the years of his biggest success with two films that remain the most popular French comedies of all time: Gérard Oury's *The Sucker* (*Le corniaud,* 1964) and *Don't Look Now We're Being Shot At* (*La grande vadrouille,* 1966).

Four Full Bags takes place in 1943 Paris, as Martin (Bourvil), an unemployed taxi driver, is involved in the black market under the German Occupation. His duty consists of smuggling large quantities of pork in "four full bags" through the streets of Paris during curfew. This smuggling job works well until the day he meets Grandgil (Jean Gabin), an aging, debonair painter in search of an adventure. Martin, who unexpectedly needs a partner (his former partner had just been arrested by the Gestapo), proposes that Grandgil join him in the endeavor. But when Grandgil meets Jambier (Louis de Funès), the ruthless black market grocer, he attempts to pressure him for more money by screaming his name aloud, an act that threatens to wake up the entire district. Jambier quickly agrees to double his fee, and both men go on their way. After innumerable other twists and turns, mostly of a comic nature, Grandgil and Martin are apprehended by the German authorities and are brought in front of the German commander. The officer immediately recognizes Grandgil and sets him free because he is a great admirer of Grandgil's paintings. As for Martin, he is sent with the rest of the unfortunate suspects to an unknown destination. A few years later, after the war, both protagonists coincidentally meet at a train station in Paris. The one who escaped from the turmoil of the Occupation now travels in first class, and the other, who survived the death camp, ends up as a baggage porter.

This cynical comedy, which ran countercurrent to postwar patriotic and bourgeois conventions, can be viewed as a subliminal indictment of the suspicion, with all its excesses, engendered by the Occupation. The principal asset of the film, aside from denouncing the despondency of human nature and its cruelty, was its revelation of a too-often-concealed side of the Occupation (an era that mostly extolled the value of an undivided Resistance): the "innocuous" side of the collaborators, the gloomy reality of the black market, and the war pilferers. It also virulently criticized the victims themselves, French police forces, middle-class, law-abiding citizens, and even Jews, with Gabin's famous

Jean Gabin (Grandgil) and Bourvil (Martin) in Claude Autant-Lara's *Four Full Bags* (*La traversée de Paris*, 1956), (Courtesy of BIFI/© Teledis).

quote, *salauds de pauvres.* Director François Truffaut warned viewers, "Don't laugh too loudly when you see *La traversée de Paris*, first of all so your neighbors can hear the dialogue—but even more because Martin and Grandgil could be you and me."[38] From a picaresque story and a suspenseful scenario, Autant-Lara slowly developed characters and an inimitable atmosphere prior to the dramatic climax at the *Kommandantur*'s headquarters. The choice of Gabin was surprising: the common image of the actor, now transformed from the proletarian hero to the solid and stable bourgeois or gangster boss, was the antithesis of the insidious anarchist painter. This may be the reason why Bourvil received the Volpi Cup for Best Actor at the Venice Film Festival in 1956 (Gabin had received the same international recognition two years earlier for Jacques Becker's *Grisbi*).

Heavily reliant on the quality of the script for commercial success, Autant-Lara, like numerous old-school directors at the time, used the services of team-scenarists Jean Aurenche and Pierre Bost to adapt a short story of Marcel Aymé, *Le vin de Paris* (1947). *Four Full Bags* covered the subject matter of the Occupation in nonsplendid, unheroic terms for the first time, denouncing the French who were involved in the black market, who profited from the shortage of food and the distress of the population—the hidden face of occupied France. Nicknamed the *bourgeois anarchiste* for his literal "assault" of his audiences with his abrasive style and uncompromising viewpiont, Autant-Lara started in the cinema industry as a set designer with Marcel L'Herbier, then went on to Hollywood (1930–32) to complete French versions of minor films (including one with Buster Keaton). His celebrated career was considered one of the indomitable forces of French cinema of the 1950s—before the young critics of the future New Wave began to reassess representatives of the traditional *cinéma de qualité*.[39]

FILM NOIR OR *FILM D'AMBIANCE:* HENRI-GEORGES CLOUZOT, JACQUES BECKER, AND RENÉ CLÉMENT

An innovative aesthetic of filmmaking, film noir is a product of the early 1940s, a very fruitful epoch in American cinema history. The term *film noir* (dark film) originated from Marcel Duhamel's *Série Noire,* a series of French translations of detective fiction in the 1930s that included American authors Raymond Chandler and James M. Cain. The label *film noir* was used during the 1940s to describe a darker thriller. The murder plot, suspense investigation, and heavy psychological implications were typically set against a particularly mysterious and gloomy urban background accompanied by violent gangsters and loners. Hollywood thrillers from the late 1930s on, although standing at the antithesis of family values and traditional morality, were consequently closely interrelated with the new code of the time. At the center of the new trend was a specific atmosphere, preferably a dark and pessimistic frame of mind, where crime, murder, and corruption systematically prevailed, leaving hardly any space for human sympathy. Soon after the end of World War II, French audiences enjoyed noir films for the first time (they had been banned during the war), such as Billy Wilder's *Double Indemnity* (1944), John Huston's *The Maltese Falcon* (1941), Otto Preminger's *Laura* (1944), Fritz Lang's *Woman in the Window* (1944), and Alfred Hitchcock's *Rebecca* (1940) and *Suspicion* (1941).

A question remains: Is film noir really a genre? or a trend? Although not a genre by definition, film noir could be categorized according to tone, theme, and atmosphere, which consistently pervaded the screen. However, because film noir was deeply influenced by several subjects and forms, such as the American gangster film of the early 1930s (for example, William Wellman's *The Public Enemy,* 1931), German Expressionism, and French poetic realism, film noir can best be described as the assemblage of several genres, a blend of suspense films, B-rated movies,[40] gangster films, and psychological dramas. What fascinated

French audiences as well as future French filmmakers during the first years of the postwar era was the presence in those films of an incomparable new representation of violence (whether shown on screen or evoked offscreen) and the depth of the characters' hopelessness. Film historian Robin Buss described the classic film noir protagonists as individuals who "seem to be trying to escape from an over-regulated society toward more primitive times; their rule is the survival of the fittest (and, consequently, the elimination of the unfit)."[41] On a purely technical level, the new visual style, with its chiaroscuro lighting and fast-paced camera work, flawlessly suited the dark mood of the underworld and immediately seduced moviegoers all over Europe. Film noir reached its apotheosis when one of its best examples, Billy Wilder's *The Lost Weekend,* stole the show at the 1945 Academy Awards, winning Oscars for Best Picture, Best Script, Best Director, and Best Actor (Ray Milland). Although the popularity of film noir increased among general audiences on both sides of the Atlantic, the content seemingly remained unchanged. By contrast, its artistic form steadily evolved toward more visual violence, emphasizing murder over corruption and the disregard for human life over human despair. The popularity of film noir reached another peak in the mid-1950s and soon after declined with the indirect but growing competition of television, which was slowly siphoning movie audiences, as well as the great popularity of color movies, especially in Cinemascope and Panavision. Color and black-and-white aesthetics could no longer coexist, as color pictures introduced new technology to the film industry and steadily captivated viewers.

In France, the most successful author whose novels (around forty) were regularly adapted to the screen was Belgian writer Georges Simenon (1903–89).[42] Simenon occupied a privileged position among Francophone authors, as his numerous novels and psychological thrillers, although never considered "pure" or academic literature, were often praised by some of the most important novelists of the century (including Henry Miller, Max Jacob, and even André Gide, who once said that Simenon was the "greatest novelist ever"). Simenon was best known as the creator of Paris police detective Inspector Maigret, the legendary investigator in France. (Among the hundred Maigret novels, approximately fifty thrillers were produced for either television or film.) Simenon's crime novels, over 400, have sold more than 500 million copies worldwide, and have been translated into fifty-five languages. His amazing production as well as the scope of his entire body of work challenged the laws of writing in the field of literature. (His detractors like to assert, however, that Simenon never wrote the one great novel that many expected of him.) After spending a few years in New York, from the late 1940s until the early 1950s, which inspired him to write one of his most famous novels, *Trois chambres à Manhattan* (1946),[43] Simenon returned to Europe in 1955 and declared residence in Lausanne, Switzerland, where he died in 1989.

Simenon used countless "static" moments to describe states of mind and emotional feelings, a problem for the cinematographic concept of movement. The core of his story lines relied heavily on observation and atmosphere rather than a logical course of events. As a rule, French thrillers of the 1950s required credible plot development with successively coherent situations and, more importantly, a constant evolution in the scenario and mental state of the protagonist's character. Typically, fidelity to the original work led to failure and betrayal of the film. But for this impressive number of adaptations, only a handful of films appear in the anthologies of French cinema. Simenon's most memorable screenplays and novels were adapted in such films as Jean Renoir's *Night at the Crossroads* (*La nuit du carrefour,* 1932), Henri Decoin's *Strangers in the House* (*Les inconnus dans la maison,* 1942) and *The Truth of Our Marriage* (*La vérité sur Bébé Donge,* 1952), Julien Duvivier's *Panic* (1946), which also was remade by Patrice Leconte as *Monsieur Hire* (1989), Marcel Carné's *La Marie du Port* (1949), Jean Delannoy's *The Baron of the Locks* (*Le baron de l'écluse,* 1960), Claude Autant-Lara's *Love Is My Profession* (1958), Bertrand Tavernier's *The Watchmaker of Saint-Paul* (*L'horloger de Saint-Paul,* 1973), and Pierre Granier-Deferre's *The Widow Couderc* (*La veuve Couderc,* 1971).

Along with the name of Simenon, one associates Henri-Georges Clouzot (1907–77, cf. chapter 3), known as the "French Hitchcock," with the development of psychological thrillers in France during the postwar era. Like Robert Bresson's, the career of Clouzot included a small number of feature films, eleven in all. Relentlessly solicited by Hollywood, Clouzot turned down many lucrative contracts because he refused to compromise his control over production and cinematography. In 1942, Clouzot undertook his first feature film, *The Murderer Lives at Number 21* (*L'assassin habite au 21*), and immediately won great popular support. (The film was from a script by Georges Simenon.) In 1947, following his two-year professional exile as a result of the controversy surrounding *The Raven* (see the discussion in chapter 3), Clouzot reestablished his success, standing, and popularity with *Jenny Lamour* (*Quai des Orfèvres*) an inspiring crime story. By the early 1950s, Clouzot's contribution to the noir genre had proved essential, as his crime thrillers were highly regarded by film historians like Georges Sadoul, who considered Clouzot to be Hitchcock's alter ego. In 1953, *Wages of Fear* (*Le salaire de la peur*), which starred the young Yves Montand, made Clouzot an international celebrity. The darkness of the film penetrated the chilling suspense that built and unfolded only at the end. One year later, *Diabolique* (*Les diaboliques,* 1954)

Yves Montand (Mario) and Charles Vanel (Jo) in Henri-Georges Clouzot's *Wages of Fear* (*Le salaire de la peur*, 1953), (Photo courtesy of the Museum of Modern Art/ Film Stills Archive).

Véra Clouzot (Christina), Simone Signoret (Nicole), and Charles Vanel (Inspector Fichet) in Henri-Georges Clouzot's *Diabolique* (*Les diaboliques*, 1954), (Photo courtesy of the Museum of Modern Art/Film Stills Archive/© Ariane).

confirmed the national and international stature of his filmmaking and style. Clouzot's feverish intensity and his unbearable scenes of suspense were by then the hallmark of his style. This was followed by a few less well known, but highly regarded, works, including *Le Mystère Picasso* (*Le mystère Picasso,* 1956) and *The Truth* (*La vérité,* 1960). Emblematic of many French films of the 1950s, Clouzot's technique was indirectly influenced by American film noir[44] and its hard-boiled detective stories (in contrast to French New Wave films a few years later), chilling atmospherics, bleak marriages, sexual frustrations, macabre intrigues, and inhibited lives: everything seemed to be present and influential in the plot construction and its dramatic function.

Adapted to the screen from Georges Arnaud's novel *Le salaire de la peur, Wages of Fear* takes place in South America and narrates the odyssey of four men (Yves Montand, Charles Vanel, Folco Lulli, and Peter Van Eyck) compelled to transport highly volatile nitroglycerine shipments by truck across mountainous terrain. The film, filled with tense interactions and distressing anxiety, seduced the jury at the 1953 Cannes Film Festival, winning the Grand Prix as well as the award for Best Actor (Charles Vanel).[45]

Diabolique also revealed a strong combination of disquieting atmosphere, sexual maneuver, morbid tempo, and prominent horror-plot construction (for example, the camera framed and stopped on less significant features, such as dead leaves floating in a swimming pool). The cinematographer, Armand Thirard, was careful to focus menacingly on the characters' facial expressions when they were stunned or distressed. Unlike many noir thrillers of the time, *Diabolique* took as much time defining and refining its characters as developing its plot. Details of shooting of the film went undisclosed as journalists were prohibited from coming near the set. At the time of its release, theaters immediately closed after the beginning of each projection; an announcement came at the end of the film asking the public not to reveal the ending in order to spare the suspense for those who had not seen the film. The entire publicity campaign resulted in a significant commercial success. Although severely criticized by numerous film critics for being too close to the traditional thriller with its usual multilayered intrigue and for overlooking the psychological development of its characters, the film won the prix Louis Delluc in 1954 as well as the Best Foreign Film Award at the New York Film Critics Circle in 1955.

An adaptation from Pierre Boileau and Thomas Narcejac's *Celle qui nétait plus,*[46] *Diabolique* blended the horror, mystery, and thriller genres. The intrigue takes place in a boys' boarding school run by a callous and brutal headmaster, Michel Delasalle (Paul Meurisse), who tyrannizes his weak and defenseless wife, Christina (Vera Clouzot, Henri-

Georges Clouzot's spouse), and an icy teacher, Nicole Horner (Simone Signoret), who has until recently been his mistress. He repeatedly slaps his wife, abuses her psychological and physical fragility (she has a heart condition), and displays his conquests in front of her. Eventually, both his wife and mistress, who have become close in their common distress, fabricate a Machiavellian stratagem of murder. Nicole suggests a plan to get rid of Michel: they will visit Nicole's home in Niort, entice Michel to come over, drown him in a bathtub, then clandestinely return to the school to dump the body into the school's filthy swimming pool. Christina calls Michel on the phone and pretends to file for a divorce. Due to the rash nature of his personality, Michel immediately heads over to their home to violently discourage her. There, the women place a sedative in his drink, and he soon falls asleep. While Nicole drowns him in the bathtub, Christina gets a tablecloth to wrap up the body and ultimately places it in a wicker chest. Back at the school, they both empty the chest in the pool in the dead of night. The viewer assumes that once the body is discovered, it will appear that Michel was a victim of an accident or even suicide. But when the pool is finally drained, the corpse has disappeared.

Michel's presence is felt more and more in the school, which drives his killers (and the audience) frantic with almost unbearable suspense. The body simply goes missing from the murky pool, and the suit the victim was wearing that night is unexpectedly returned from the cleaners. Anomalous developments occur one after the other. The presence of the deceased headmaster is terrifying; his features seem to appear in the school photograph, and a young student confesses to having spoken with him recently. When a retired police inspector (Charles Vanel) enters the story to cross-examine Christina, her already frail sangfroid turns into something bordering on psychosis, as both she and Nicole are at a loss. The simple murder plot has gone beyond their imagination.

Michel's disappearance prompts mysterious rumors of his reappearance, which grow more and more substantial in Christina's fragile mind. One night, as she hears a noise in her former husband's office, she walks along the dark corridor to discover Michel's body in the bathroom tub. As the ominous body slowly rises from the water, she collapses dead on the floor. Suddenly, Nicole enters the room and hugs Michel, appeasing him for his insurmountable physical efforts: the original plot for murder worked, and both lovers are now free. But their idyll is short-lived, since the police inspector, who had never left the building, has overheard their confessions. Once they are arrested, the monotonous life at the institution can resume.

With similar visual panache, director Jacques Becker (1906–60) attained national visibility and notoriety in the early 1950s. Becker's reputation for perfect mise-en-scène and cinematography was in large part due to the success of *Golden Marie,* which for many was considered his masterpiece, receiving the award for Best Foreign Actress (Signoret) at the British Academy Awards in 1952. Becker underscored the atmospheric environment, the decorative charm of the period in the lower depths of Parisian life, and focused less on the psychological development of the main characters, disgruntling film critics but gaining the sympathy of future New Wave proponents.

The story, reminiscent of Eugène Sue's *Les Mystères de Paris,* is set in Paris at the turn of the century, in a world of terror and violence. One Sunday afternoon at an open-air *guinguette* (dance hall), Marie (Simone Signoret), nicknamed *Casque d'or* for her flamboyant blond hair, who is dissatisfied with her man, Roland (William Sabatier), a cold-blooded Parisian mobster, agrees to dance with a stranger, Manda (Serge Reggiani). Manda is a carpenter but also an ex-con and friend of one of the gangsters of the group, Raymond (Raymond Bussières). Resentful and malevolent, Roland decides to humiliate the newcomer in front of the squad. But Manda and Marie are already in love. Meanwhile, Leca (Claude Dauphin), the gangster boss, is also interested in Marie. To get rid of his two opponents, Leca sets up a jealous machination. He pushes both of them to fight a duel to the death, which eventually leaves Roland dead and Manda on the run. Marie follows Manda, and they live peacefully on a farm outside Paris, sharing fleeting moments of romantic passion. Persistently, Leca imagines a new subterfuge to eliminate Manda. Aware of the solid friendship and loyalty between Manda and one of his best men, Raymond, Leca denounces the latter to the police as the murderer and gives the news of Raymond's arrest to the young lovers (knowing that the carpenter will boldly accept the blame). Manda cannot bear to have his best friend condemned for his crime and gives himself up. This leaves Marie alone, which is what the iniquitous Leca wanted. While being transferred to prison, Manda escapes with Raymond, who is killed during the getaway. Aware of the diabolical stratagem, Manda tracks down Leca and corners him in a police station, where Manda kills him. Arrested and condemned to death, Manda dies on the guillotine at dawn under the eyes of the crowd, while Marie watches from a neighboring balcony.

In the great tradition of naturalist authors, Becker's approach conveyed the impression of fate and the impossibility of changing one's destiny, already inscribed by the conditioning of society. Surprisingly enough, the opening reception of *Golden Marie* was cold at best, despite the intense emotion that emanated from the French public. Popular audiences anticipated more action scenes (many fewer when compared to conventional American noir films) and never identified with the intricacies of the intrigue and the remarkable arrangements of suspense

Simone Signoret (Marie) in Jacques Becker's *Golden Marie* (*Casque d'or*, 1952),
(Courtesy of BIFI/© Studio Canal).

in the visual rendition. As a result, they were unresponsive. The aesthetic approach of *Golden Marie,* despite the reaction of the public at the time, demanded detailed photography to mirror its author's emotional response as closely as a novelist's prose technique would emulate the creation of the mind. This is what was projected on the screen, making the film one of the most persuasive crime movies of the decade.

After the release of *Golden Marie, Grisbi (Touchez pas au grisbi,* 1953) was Jacques Becker's first national success. In *Touchez pas au grisbi* (French slang for "Don't touch the dough"), Becker, much as in *Golden Marie,* created a compelling story, told in a laconic style, about two men in the mob milieu and their undivided loyalty to each other, comradeship, elderliness, and the internal conflicts of the individual. Two aging gangsters of Montmartre, "Max the Liar" (Jean Gabin) and his longtime friend Riton (René Dary), decide to retire in style from the mob by taking 50 million francs in gold bars left in a safe (a fortune robbed years ago from the Orly Airport). The boss of another mob family, Angelo (Lino Ventura),[47] gets wind of Max's plans. One night, as Max leaves his usual club, he remarks that Angelo's men are following him. Without delay, he calls Riton to warn him not to talk to Angelo and to stay away from Angelo's men. Shortly after, Max takes Riton to a private residence and reveals where he hid the gold bars. Later on that same night, Riton, left alone, makes the mistake of going back home to see his girlfriend Josy (Jeanne Moreau), who seduces Riton and hands him over to Angelo. The rival gang eventually kidnaps him in order to have the booty in ransom. The twenty-year friendship between Riton and Max compels the latter to be magnanimous. Because he cannot abandon his friend Riton, Max undergoes a crisis of conscience and ultimately gets the gold to deliver it in person to the other gang. Angelo, however, has secretly planned an ambush to eliminate Max, Riton, and his lieutenants after gaining possession of the gold. The exchange takes place on a dark country road outside Paris. Yet, as the finale unfolds, the suspense deepens, until Riton and Angelo die in an exchange of grenades. The surprise climax is truly disquieting. In the end, Max manages to turn the odds against Angelo, but his hopes of a peaceful and luxurious retirement quickly vanish.

Although judged too damaging for the prestige of French cinema (the film was overlooked for selection before the Cannes Film Festival), it did manage to make the official selection of the Venice Film Festival in 1954, before it went on to become a colossal success and a source of inspiration for a wave of new noir films, including Jules Dassin's masterpiece *Rififi (Du rififi chez les hommes,* 1955) and Jean-Pierre Melville's *Bob the Gambler (Bob le flambeur,* 1955).[48] Based on the thriller

Lino Ventura (Angelo) and Jean Gabin (Max) in Jacques Becker's *Grisbi* (*Touchez pas au Grisbi*, 1953), (Courtesy of BIFI).

series *Touchez pas au grisbi* by Albert Simonin, a specialist in Parisian and underworld slang of those days, *Grisbi* profoundly renewed the scope of French film noir by eluding any reference to the French police force, its justice system, or its institutions. It was not a *film policier*, but a film noir as a gangster movie: that was its "Frenchness."

Jacques Becker started his career as an assistant for many of Jean Renoir's films, including *Night at the Crossroads* (*La nuit du carrefour*, 1932), *The People of France* (*La vie est à nous*, 1936), *A Day in the Country* (*Une partie de campagne*, 1936), and *Grand Illusion* (*La grande illusion*, 1937). Film critics, mesmerized by his immaculate style and formal photographic technique, have regularly placed Becker among the very best filmmakers of the postwar era, and his accomplishments extended over a vast horizon of different skills: commercial productions, cinéma d'auteurs, genre cinema, and mise-en-scène. Thus, Becker unpredictably reconciled the commercial schemes and auteur initiative. His genuine passion for directing actors combined with his preference for involved rehearsals ultimately resulted in characters that embodied coherence and truth. One of Becker's most important contributions to world cinema was his creation of a new cinematographic language that eventually influenced directors such as Federico Fellini, Michelangelo Antonioni, and even Max Ophuls, all of whom were inclined toward circumvolutions of viewpoints and experimental cinema. Consistently concerned with the predominance of realism and truth for his characters, Becker was often described as an unclassifiable artist. With respect to the charisma he carefully crafted in his characters, François Truffaut stated, "The beauty of the characters in *Grisbi,* even more than those in *Casque d'or,* comes from their quietness, from the economy of their movements."[49] Representative of one of the prominent characteristics in French cinema, Becker's directing principally focused on the individual psychology as he repeatedly showed each character at his or her most sensitive state, confronting his or her own predetermined fate.

Despite René Clément's (1913–96) three consecutive successes at the first three Cannes Film Festivals for *Battle of the Rails* (*La bataille du rail,* 1945), *The Damned* (*Les maudits,* 1947), and *The Walls of Malapaga* (*Au-delà des grilles,* 1948), his next film, *Forbidden Games* (*Jeux interdits*) was excluded at Cannes in 1952. That film, however, did receive an impressive list of prizes during the year, including an Academy Award for Best Foreign Language Film, the New York Film Critics Award for Best Foreign Language Film, and the Venice Film Festival Golden Lion Award. *Forbidden Games* was often misconstrued as a simple tale about childhood and an antiwar statement with powerful allegories about the waste of warfare (without actual battle). Although the film was made in a rather extemporaneous manner (two children were first-time actors), the script was vigilantly written by Jean Aurenche and Pierre Bost. In addition, Clément, who had originally planned to produce a scene film, decided during the shooting to keep only the first story, adding several scenes to reach the necessary length of a *long métrage.* The dramatic buildup (war), the emotional patterns (the loss of the dog), and the fatalistic overtones (the loss of the parents and adopted family) emphasize the core of the film: the world of adults as seen through children's eyes. The realistic depiction of war was used only as a narrative background; it gradually emphasized the psychological rapport established between the two children.

The story, drawn from a novel by François Boyer (*Les jeux inconnus,* 1947),[51] is set in May 1940. The film opens in the midst of an exodus of Parisian refugees fleeing a Luftwaffe air raid. As the German planes plunge in formation against the defenseless column of refugees, people panic, leaving their carriages, cars, and luggage to dash under the trees or hide in ditches. A six-year-old girl, Paulette (played by Brigitte Fossey),[52] gets up and wanders aimlessly; her parents lie dead. Lost and alone, she holds her dying puppy in her arms and joins the hundreds of refugees who start moving again. Shortly after, an insensitive peasant woman considers the little dog dead and brusquely throws it into the river. Paulette, horrified by the gesture, immediately leaves the column of refugees and desperately runs to the river to fish the corpse

Brigitte Fossey (Paulette) in René Clément's *Forbidden Games* (*Jeux interdits*, 1952), (Courtesy of BIFI/© Studio Canal).

out of the water. In tears, she tries to revive her puppy but to no avail. There she meets Michel Dolle (Georges Poujouly), a ten-year-old boy who works at a nearby farm with his family. He takes the girl home with him, and eventually, his parents temporarily adopt her. When Paulette is told that her parents are soon to be buried, she wants her dog to be buried in a grave with a cross, too. Oblivious to the human massacre around them, the children become good friends, and Michel offers to lay Paulette's dog to rest in an old uninhabited mill, reassuring her that it will not be lonely. After having watched the adults bury their dead, they begin to assemble their own cemetery. Both wander in the countryside to pick up dead creatures for their secret cemetery for animals including baby chickens, moles, earthworms, even insects. The two children pilfer fourteen crosses from the village church, from another cemetery, and even from Michel's late brother's hearse to properly adorn the grave sites. The missing crosses, however, make the local population panic, and soon neighbor turns against neighbor. The peasant family with whom Paulette lives has an ongoing feud with their neighbors that eventually leads to violence. The impending discovery of the children's secret creates a heartbreaking culmination. Michel is forced to confess, and Paulette is immediately removed from her new family. She is taken by the police to a Red Cross camp, where she is lost in a crowd of thousands of war refugees. As she hears someone yelling "Michel!" she dashes through the crowd as the camera fades out.

Although *Forbidden Games* opened with outwardly realistic turmoil—the exodus with its death toll and disquieting representation of human tragedy—it offered a nonconformist vision and an authentic look at childhood and children's desires to construct their own fantasy world away from adult supervision. The visual approach of the film and its story line created a series of persuasive arrangements between documentary, idyllic neorealism, and film noir. Perhaps considered too manichaeistic in its contrast of the forbidding adult world and the innocence of childhood (especially among coldhearted and belligerent peasants), the story denounced the adults, often depicted as harsh, callous, and even cruel. *Forbidden Games* was not subject to the restrictions of production (mainly economic) that predisposed early neorealist films to explore the extent of realism, yet it was the practice of analogous investigation that in the end made the identity of the movie so persuasive. Although limited by technical constraints, Clément's unsophisticated and outspoken style was well esteemed among the public and emerged as one of the closest productions to Italian neorealism. By 1951, the conventional cinematographic point of view, which represented the horrors of war and the deceitfulness of the adult world through the eyes of children, was nothing new. In fact, Italian neorealist filmmakers directed their work as major authors with productions such as Vittorio de Sica's *The Bicycle Thief* (*Ladri di biciclette*, 1948) and *Children Are Watching Us* (*I bambini ci guardano*, 1943). Nevertheless, with Michel and Paulette, the exploration of war went beyond the innocence of childhood and its helpless observation, and created a world that gave total freedom to the formation of children's own playful world of death. Although the game of imagination and friendship appeared gruesome and monstrous to adults, they were the ones who lacked discernment and regard. Paulette felt more grief for the loss of her dog than the death of her parents since the concept of death did not have any real significance to her. The children's objective of putting together a secret memorial was sincere and outspoken. Paulette merely wished to do what was right for her little dog, and Michel only attempted to please his new friend. It is obvious that the communicative actors ultimately endowed *Forbidden Games* with its true emotional core. Interestingly enough, the memorable musical score (composed by Narcisco Yepes with a single Renaissance guitar melody), unlike most films of this time, did not offer any musical cues or direct connection in relation to the image or to the plot. This pragmatic quality, present in the style of René Clément's vision, and his relentless affinity with managing inventiveness (mainly audiovisual modernism) constituted a facet that a few years later was unconsciously to be reused by young authors of the next generation.

TOWARD A NEW CINEMA: ROBERT BRESSON, JACQUES BECKER, AND RENÉ CLÉMENT

A paradoxical decade, the 1950s witnessed the birth of a new era, immediately following World War II, and at the same time represented the end of an old-value system with the coming of the 1960s. A young clan of new film critics and future filmmakers reproached the "old school" that prevailed in the 1950s, believing that everything was "outdated" within the *qualité française,* including its aesthetics of studio, and its pseudo-Expressionist aesthetic. Most of the current filmmakers, screenwriters, and producers had begun working in the 1930s, and most film studios were built at the time of the silent era. For the younger generation, access to job openings was extremely difficult. It was a road strife with obstacles regulated by one insurmountable condition, time. Sometimes it took fifteen years for an assistant to begin shooting a motion picture as a director. As René Prédal described it, "Between the ages of twenty and thirty, the future director unfortunately plays messenger during the most creative period of life. Talent and ideas only remain within the old school. Between the ages of thirty and forty, he is promoted to second, then first, assistant, or possibly co-screenwriter, a position in which he must display technique, skill, efficiency, but still no creativity."[53]

The 1950s experienced an explicit stagnation of the mise-en-scène. The "dictatorship" of the chief operator (just like the sound operator in the 1930s, with the implementation of microphones on the set) forced directors to remain within studio boundaries due to the precision of such effects as diffused floodlighting and focused spotlighting. Consequently, the mise-en-scène was directly reduced in importance, and the director was considered more responsible for the final project than its "author" and initiator. The New Wave evidently ran against the 1950s' despotism of the "great technicians" and expressed aversion to the psychological approach and traditional narration. These filmmakers did not believe in the so-called *grand sujet* that required overwhelming financial means, such as historical reconstitutions, period movies, and literary adaptations. For them, French cinema was in a fossilized state, and ultimately remained prisoner of rigid formulas of its own making, and as a result failed to demonstrate any risks or innovations. New filmmakers used a preexisting reality to profile their own vision of reality (while preserving their creative control), mostly with small-budget films and little-known actors. Jean-Luc Godard, François Truffaut, Eric Rohmer, and Alain Resnais,[54] among others, contrasted the *cinéma de scénaristes* with the *cinéma d'auteurs*. This opposition derived its full meaning from the very perception of the use of the cinematographic medium and ultimately brought a much greater scope to French cinema. A few years earlier, Alexandre Astruc's concept of *caméra stylo* (writing through motion pictures) threw into high relief the conventional, long-established, backward-looking implication of the huge majority of French productions of the late 1940s. Among all the filmmakers who worked in the 1930s, only artists such as Jean Renoir and Jean Cocteau were able to adapt to this new era, positioned between the outburst of new talent from the Occupation and the latent creative era of the 1960s. Their predominant position in the *cinéma d'auteurs* allowed them to use different genres simultaneously by mixing thrilling action with both myth and supernatural adventure (Cocteau) or humanistic will with prolific creativity (Renoir).

Representing the antithesis of the tradition of actors' performance and dialogue-based story lines, Robert Bresson (1901–99), more than Jacques Tati or Jacques Becker, stood alone in his field of endeavor. Combining intellectual integrity with artistic honesty, he is one of the most studied film artists in world cinema. As an authentic artist, Bresson was among the very first directors quoted by François Truffaut as an auteur because of Bresson's revelation, manifest to the younger generation, of the infinite possibilities of using cinema as a resourceful intermediate for personal inspiration. For Bresson, who trained as a painter[55] before moving into films as a screenwriter, cinematography did not necessarily equal entertainment. Instead, it was a mode of expression that conciliated image and sound in the form of a slow, visual, and meditative narration. In sum, cinema was "interior movement," to use Bresson's own celebrated phrase. Jack C. Ellis described Bresson's films as minimalist, unembellished representations of spiritual life, relying on a rigorous series of stripped-down shots: "While Bresson's films have never been widely popular with audiences nor noticeably influential on the work of other filmmakers, he has emerged as one of the rare examples of a consummate individual stylist. His search for ever greater clarity and simplicity of visual-aural statement, his concentration on only those themes that most deeply concern him, place him among the very select company with which he is being considered."[56] For Bresson, actors' performances were critical to the interpretation of the theme and to the style of the resulting story line.

In 1950, returning to the screen after a five-year absence since *Ladies of the Park,* Bresson's next project was the adaptation of Catholic writer

Georges Bernanos's *The Diary of a Country Priest*. Bresson eventually received approval from Bernanos's attorneys, who had previously turned down earlier script proposals by several screenwriters (Jean Aurenche and Pierre Bost) upon the writer's death. This introspective film succeeded in deciphering the essence of George Bernanos's novel into cinematic language. It traces the anguish and torments of a young priest (Claude Laydu) in Ambricourt, a gloomy Normandy village, where his emotions and despair are subtlety revealed. This confessional first-person narration portrays the interior itinerary of the feeble and unnamed priest during his first assignment, and the torment of his soul through Christian symbolism. He attempts to accept the parishioners as they are while struggling with a life of poverty. His acquaintances and environment are hostile: a cynical doctor who callously reveals to him the terminal nature of his illness, a coldhearted count who does not keep his promises for help, a fanatical daughter who incriminates him in her mother's death (the countess), and the indifference of his parish. The priest fails to change the town's resentment. His only achievement is to bring peace to a withdrawn countess the day before she passes away (after a long hatred for God as a result of the tragic death of her son). Only an old vicar from a nearby village sporadically shows paternal interest in him. The story continues with the priest's forlorn combat against sickness, dejection, death, and the cruel tribulations with his parishioners, who neither welcome nor acknowledge his profound conviction and his great effort to stay alive. Slowly making his way toward grace and saintliness, he finally finds transcendence through death. His last words, *Tout est grâce* (All is grace), epitomize the priest's spiritual strength and devout constancy with the world's fear and doubt. The austere visual representation of the film prompted the presence of the invisible spiritual life, and with it Bresson accomplished what, cinematographically speaking, was impossible to render: a straight path of diegesi, a linear intrigue, filled with an almost obsessive desire for abstraction. This perfectly corresponded with a personal quest for the truth of a tragic and lonely destiny. "Bresson's films show little but suggest much," explain Kristin Thompson and David Bordwell,[57] and therefore require extreme attentiveness on the part of audiences. *The Diary of a Country Priest* received the 1951 Grand prix du cinéma français and shared the International Prize at the Venice Film Festival with Akira Kurosawa's *Rashomon*.

Bresson's next picture, *A Man Escaped* (*Un condamné à mort s'est échappé*, 1956), confirmed his tendency for an uncompromising independent and "pure" cinema, the antithesis of mainstream narrations. Like Jacques Becker's *The Night Watch* (*Le trou*, 1959), the story line begins with "This is a true story. I render it as it is, unadorned."

A *Man Escaped* is based on the memoir of André Devigny (1918–99), who had escaped from prison thirteen years before in 1943. The author was on the set to assist Bresson in reenacting the plot as well as in demonstrating the different tricks in the getaway scene. The main protagonist of the film, Lieutenant Fontaine (François Leterrier), a French Resistance activist spends his last hours planning a highly crafted breakout. For days, he gradually carves an imperceptible hole in the cell door with a sharpened spoon handle and assembles a rope and a couple of hooks out of bedsprings and torn blankets. Just before the critical departure, a young man (Georges Poujouly), known to have collaborated with the Nazis, is thrown into his cell. The crucial dilemma compels Fontaine to trust and consequently confide his plan, instead of eliminating the new stranger. Both men eventually succeed.

Shot at the Montluc Prison[58] in Lyon, with Devigny on location, the representation of the disquieting fortress constituted an impersonal and mystical universe, secluded from reality (like Franz Kafka's *The Castle*). In 1943, Devigny, a French army officer, was tortured by the Gestapo and kept handcuffed in a small cell. After four months, he was sentenced to death by Nazi leader Klaus Barbie and was to be shot, but managed to escape. Clearly, Devigny was a crucial consultant in the making of the movie, which in part was shot inside his own prison cell. Ironically enough, almost thirty years later, Barbie was incarcerated in the same prison. The Court of Justice in Lyon convicted Barbie of crimes against humanity and sentenced him to life imprisonment.[59]

Although during the ninety-nine minutes of the film viewers were never left in the dark about the final outcome, the scheme and technique of escape constantly kept them apprehensive and unresolved. Interestingly enough, Bresson was not concerned with the development of the action but rather with the spiritual outcome of what happened. When Fontaine entered his new cell, the camera (unlike, for instance, Becker's *The Night Watch*) is limited to close-ups of objects and faces and offered no descriptive panoramic shot, which immediately conveyed in masterly fashion a claustrophobic impression of the penitentiary milieu. In addition, the whole movie materialized into recurrent scenes, for the most part composed of a single long shot. Bresson's camera dwelled on Fontaine's hands holding the few objects that were to assist him in the breakout attempt.

In *A Man Escaped,* Bresson favored the presence of a "psychological being," as opposed to the determination of a character based on his eloquence.[60] His dominating relationship with his actors was notorious, since for him, actors had to be substituted by their own "presence," which eventually led the spectator to the real character in question. On the set, Bresson was known to rigorously dissuade his

Claude Laydu (Priest of Ambricourt) in Robert Bresson's *Diary of a Country Priest* (*Le journal d'un curé de campagne*, 1951), (Photo courtesy of the Museum of Modern Art/Film Stills Archive/© Studio Canal).

Francois Leterrier (Lieutenant Fontaine) in Robert Bresson's *A Man Escaped* (*Un condamné à mort s'est échappé*, 1956), (Photo courtesy of the Museum of Modern Art/ Film Stills Archive).

actors from any individual expression or touch of acting eloquence by
dint of constant repetitions and takes. His personages were rarely the
conventional, readable figures of traditional dramas, but rather characters who did not disclose emotive signals, such as speech intonation
that disclosed feelings. To heighten the tension, Bresson used the
protagonist Fontaine for voice-overs to connect the scenes to one another as inauspicious sound effects (the slamming of cell doors, the
jingle of the warden's key) are heard in the background. For Bresson,
the discourse of the film had to be "devoiced" of superfluous acoustic
components that could affect the escape's fragile passage of time, as
François Truffaut explained: "The suspense—there is a certain suspense
in the film—is created naturally, not by stretching out the passage of
time, but by letting it evaporate."[61] Bresson went on to earn the Best
Director Award at the 1957 Cannes Film Festival. His uncompromising methods rarely consented indulgences to film producers, refused
commercial cinema and professional actors, and at the same time
required total control over the production. This helps to explain why
he directed only thirteen films in his career. The first and last film for
which Bresson worked with professional actors was *Ladies of the Park,*
in 1944. Although his productions did not achieve great popularity,
he nevertheless ranks as one of the greatest artists in the history of
international cinema. Some of his most brilliant films include *Pickpocket*
(*Pickpocket,* 1959), *Mouchette* (*Mouchette,* 1967), *The Devil Probably* (*Le
Diable probablement,* 1977), and *Money* (*L'argent,* 1983).

Along with Bresson's *A Man Escaped,* Jacques Becker's *The Night
Watch* (*Le trou*) was responsible for raising the stakes for all future
prison films by way of its rigorous camerawork, use of real sounds that
produce a remarkably authentic sense of locale, and visual intensity
with respect to character development. Made only three years apart,
these two classic prison dramas/thrillers were both brilliantly staged,
capitalizing on the tension normally found in such a claustrophobic
place and amplifying it greatly, as each cellmate had to search within
himself for answers. What was created in these flawless pieces of
suspense was a real phenomenon of simplicity and understated relationships, showing how uncertain it was to trust an outsider with one's
life. *The Night Watch* was in competition during the 1960 Cannes Film
Festival and received the prize for Best Film at the 1961 British
Academy Awards. In the early 1940s, Becker shot his first real *long
métrage* as a movie director with *It Happened at the Inn* (*Goupi-Mains-
Rouges,* 1942), and quickly moved with apparent success from intimate
dramas (*Edouard et Caroline,* 1950) to tragic romance (*Golden Marie,*
1952) to crime films (*Grisbi,* 1953). As Truffaut once observed,
"Becker works outside all styles, and we shall place him therefore at
the opposite pole of the major tendencies of French cinema."[62]

Charged with a premeditated manslaughter attempt on his "well-off" wife, Claude Gaspard (Marc Michel), a twenty-seven-year-old well-mannered car salesman, is locked up in the Parisian Santé Prison in 1947. His wife accuses him of having attempted to murder her during a domestic dispute, when his gun (un)intentionally discharged and the bullet hit her shoulder. One day, while his cell undergoes maintenance, Gaspard is relocated to a different cell block already occupied by four hardened convicts, Roland (Jean Keraudy), Manu (Philippe Leroy), "Monseigneur" (Raymond Meunier), and Jo (Michel Constantin). His arrival is met with manifest skepticism. Having already decided to plan an escape, the four cellmates are not enthusiastic about Gaspard's arrival, but the present circumstances compel them to reveal their project to the outsider. They choose to go on with their plan, considering it too late to turn back. They have admitted Gaspard as one of them into their circle, since there was no apparent reason not to (they even recognize that Gaspard will have done his share in helping them excavate the tunnel). They start to dig a hole underneath the wooden floor. Since ongoing construction occurs all over the building, the noise made by their digging goes unnoticed. Each night, according to Roland's plans, they use every ounce of perseverance and ingenuity in an elaborate attempt to connect their underground passage with a second, already-excavated tunnel that reaches the city sewer. One morning, however, Gaspard is called into the office of the prison director to learn that his wife has dropped the murder charges against him; he should be a free man within weeks, maybe days. The simple convocation, however, turns out to be much more than a succinct discussion. The meeting lasts more than two hours, and when Gaspard returns to the cell, his companions presume that something is up since no prisoner stays for such a long time to be updated on trial procedures. Still, he agrees to take part in the breakout with his accomplices. It is only on the verge of freedom that the prisoners find out that Gaspard has betrayed them in exchange for a reduced sentence. The lights are out, and the group is ready to escape when suddenly the cell is invaded by the prison warden, who instantly catches the prisoners red-handed. The despair can be seen on their hardened expressions as Gaspard is led away to another cell. As the four unfortunate escapees are lined up against the wall, Roland addresses him one last time: "Pauvre Gaspard" (poor Gaspard).

The Night Watch, a French–Italian coproduction, was Jacques Becker's last film. He died during the film's post-production in February 1960, one month before its commercial release, leaving final details to his son Jean. Writer José Giovanni, whose novel *Le trou* inspired the film, was an actual ex-con who took part in an escape attempt from the same prison in 1947; one of his cellmates, Jean

Keraudy (Roland in the film), the so-called King of Escape, performs as himself and opens the film: ". . . My friend Jacques Becker re-created a true story in all its detail: my story. It took place in 1947 at the Santé Prison."[63] Beyond the opening statement, the presence of Keraudy was an extraordinary guarantee of authenticity. In addition, Becker insisted that all his characters were to be interpreted by non-professional actors, much like the approach of Robert Bresson.

Although not fully associated with the new trend of filmmakers (due to an artistic rigor reminiscent of the *qualité* tradition), René Clément's *Purple Noon* (*Plein soleil,* 1959)[64] became a classic of the French tradition called *réalisme psychologique*. The theme of identity transference occurred frequently in *réalisme psychologique,* and many contemporary critics did not hesitate to compare Clément's skills to Alfred Hitchcock's. The screenplay was based on (not adapted from) Patricia Highsmith's novel[65] *The Talented Mr. Ripley* (the film was quite different from the famous novel, the first of the Ripley series in the 1950s).[66] In both story lines, one protagonist is intensely fascinated with the other, and reveals his obsessive fixation through crime, the murderer in both cases essentially wanting to become the other man.

In *Purple Noon,* Tom Ripley, played by Alain Delon, (b. 1935), who starts out as the secondary character, is sent to Mongibello, near Naples, by a wealthy industrialist, Mr. Greenleaf, to persuade his financially spoiled and globe-hopping son, Philip (Maurice Ronet), to return home to San Francisco. For the service, Tom will eventually receive $5,000. Shortly after his arrival in Italy, Tom meets Philip in Rome and reveals to his longtime friend the true purpose of his journey. The news is welcomed with laughter, since Philip enjoys a hedonistic lifestyle in Rome. Instead of persuading him to return home, Tom settles in to stay among the well-dressed jet set on the Amalfi Coast, putting off the father's mission for updates. Philip even plays with Tom's patience, by changing his mood daily about a possible departure. In reality, he has no intention of leaving his fiancée, Marge Duval (Marie Laforêt), to honor his father's request.

As the days and nights of the Roman *dolce vita* go by, Ripley becomes more and more drawn into Philip's lifestyle of wealth and womanizing in the restaurants, clubs, and yacht basins along the Italian coast. (In one of those social encounters, sharp-eyed viewers may spot a then-unknown Romy Schneider in an opening-scene, one-line appearance.) Both young men share the affections of Marge and even each other's wardrobes. Tom begins to covet Philip's life as a rich playboy until the day he receives a letter from Mr. Greenleaf, who, considering the assignment a fiasco, decides to terminate Tom's financial subsidy. Nevertheless, Tom chooses to maintain his new way of life and quickly begins to conspire: if Philip's outfits, fiancée, and

Philippe Leroy (Manu Borelli) and Jean Keraudy (Roland Darbanin) in Jacques Becker's *The Night Watch* (*Le trou*, 1959), (Courtesy of BIFI/© Studio Canal).

standard of living better fit him, why not permanently remove Philip from the picture? Following a navigation dispute, an increasingly tense series of mind games takes place between the two young men, who begin to adopt a mean disposition toward one another until Tom murders Philip onboard his yacht and takes over his identity. Tom wraps the body in a sail and throws it into the sea, where he is sure it will vanish. (After being momentarily retained by the anchor, the body disappears.)

Back on land, Tom begins a long sequence of sophisticated lies. He first announces to Marge that Philip has returned to Rome and wants

to remain alone for a while. Tom departs to Rome in order to rob
Philip of his possessions. After meticulously forging Philip's passport
and signature, switching identities, and checking into the luxurious
Excelsior Hotel in Rome, he sends typed letters to friends and family
(on behalf of Philip) to reassure them about his sudden desire for
seclusion. People begin to wonder about Philip's absence, however,
and their search unavoidably leads to Tom. A few days later in Rome,
Philip's old friend Freddy Miles (Bill Kearns), suspecting Tom of foul
play, shows up at Tom's hotel room, discovering the fake letters' real
author. Tom feels as if he has no alternative but to commit another
murder to cover his tracks, and so he eliminates Freddy. Meanwhile,
step by step, the police close in and begin to pursue him from hotel
to apartment and town to town. When Tom realizes that his plans are
seriously compromised, he goes to Mongibello one last time with the
remaining loot and secretly relinquishes it to Marge as Philip's will
(theoretically to dissipate all suspicion). But as he is near the end of
this sequential nightmare, the yacht finally comes on display for sale.
As the boat is raised out of the water, a gruesome bundle is attached
to the rear of the boat. It is Philip's body, still wrapped up in
the sail.

The mechanism of intrigue, filled with ingenious turns suggestive
of Hitchcock's greatest thrillers, becomes increasingly more intricate
as the story unfolds and creates an involuntary uneasiness among
viewers. The suspense deepens until the twist ending successfully
manipulates the visual medium. René Clément, often described as a
motivating force for the future New Wave, did more than draw the
spectator into a well-written scenario of psychological suspense; he also
focused the entire film on Tom's narcissistic progression to such a
degree that it became difficult for the spectator not to wish for Ripley
to go free. In *Purple Noon,* the rapport mise-en-scène/cinematography,
with its deep panoramic shots of the Mediterranean that accentuate
the young men's idleness and lack of benevolence, is comparable to the
visual focus of Michelangelo Antonioni's *L'avventura* (*L'avventura,*
1960). In conjunction with an intense Nino Rota score, the photography of cinematographer Henri Decaë, who compiled most of his shots
with idyllic saturated colors of the Mediterranean sun, includes a long
series of close-ups focusing on the eyes of Alain Delon, which divulge
the ominous astuteness behind his deceptively candid appearance.

Tom Ripley, the antihero par excellence, forced the admiration or
perhaps the fascination of viewers but never their sympathy. As Patricia Highsmith herself noted: "From a dramatic point of view, criminals
are interesting; at least at one [particular] moment they act with a free
mind, and [feel like they] do not owe anyone an explanation. I find

Alain Delon (Tom Ripley) in René Clément's *Purple Noon* (*Plein soleil*, 1959), (Photo courtesy of the Museum of Modern Art/Film Stills Archive/© Studio Canal).

the general public's interest for Justice rather dull and artificial, since neither Life nor Nature are concerned with whether Justice has been rendered or not."[67] *Purple Noon* represented a new type of examination of near-perfect murders and a compelling look at the amoral and self-indulgent killer who commits them.

Chapter 5
The Years of the French New Wave

- *France during and after the Events of 1958*
- *The Signs of Change: Louis Malle*
- Les cahiers du cinéma *and the Auteur Theory*
- *The Emergence of the New Wave: Claude Chabrol, François Truffaut, Alain Resnais, Jean-Luc Godard, and Agnès Varda*
- *The Return of Commercial Movie Successes*

In the late 1950s, the emergence of the film director as the undisputed authority in all areas of film production (mise-en-scène, photography, script, thematic and artistic choices) was a direct result of a growing trend called *politique des auteurs* (authorism) that proclaimed the future predominance of a new cinema. Although often misunderstood and abused, this creative concept in filmmaking was the direct aftermath of that trend, which clearly emerged with the explosion of the New Wave in 1958. The years of this movement—which actually began in the mid 1950s as a reaction to a stagnating establishment, only to become recognized in the years 1958–59—can best be described as an innovative era, setting a historical landmark in world film history. The changes created a sense of diversity in cinema. Never before had an artistic movement revealed itself to be so seminal and influential, creating breathing space for creativity both in France and abroad.

The New Wave camera work represented a radically different concept both in content and form. The traditional perception of cinematography, held by the *tradition de qualité,* which corroborated a visually flawless photography and concealed to audiences the work of true film artists, vehemently resisted the new trend. Throughout the years generally considered the postwar era (1945–58), French film directors used equipment that facilitated the interconnection between action and narrative leaps. As technology improved in cinema, it gradually gave mainstream filmmakers more freedom in their procedural and artistic choices (more mobility for the cameraman, and as a result more interest and comfort from the spectator's standpoint). Their style, however, remained surprisingly unchanged in the storytelling process and so-called filmic grammar. This lack of artistic renewal explicitly set the future young directors of the New Wave on their "revolutionary" agenda. What they sought was simply the utilization of an innovative narration, entirely freed from conventional Hollywood-style storytell-ing and offering an ensemble of images and sounds. The audience would be required to participate in the narrative process and conse-quently had to develop an understanding of the function of cinemato-graphic language.

Apart from the visual revolution of cinema, the 1960s entered a new phase in the advancement of the French audiovisual industry (film and television). The *avances sur recettes* system (financial aid or Federal loan) was a unique government funding program whose aim was to support the film industry, which, without such financial aid, was doomed to stagnation and bankruptcy. By the early 1960s, this pro-gram had assisted many first-time directors of feature films. The newly created organization guided certain aspects of film culture as it took risks in such high-budget productions as Yves Robert's *War of the Buttons* (*La guerre des boutons,* 1961), which otherwise would not have been made. This special financial allocation was granted by the Minis-tère de la Culture not only to film directors but also to many producers and scriptwriters from the European Union.

Finally, the 1960s witnessed the full emergence of important new acting talents such as Anouck Aimée, Michel Piccoli, Alain Delon, Jean-Paul Belmondo, and Catherine Deneuve,[1] as well as the promo-tion to the status of movie star for actors such as Brigitte Bardot, Yves Montand, Bourvil, and Jeanne Moreau.

FRANCE DURING AND AFTER THE EVENTS OF 1958

The 1960s in France was a period of constant conflict between the old dispensation and the new.[2] Politics, like the French film industry, had to change with the moods of the times and respond to the needs and desires of people in their everyday lives. Taking form at the end of the 1950s, the new decade emerged in a country rife with colonial antag-onism, deep sociopolitical divisions, and a series of inefficient coalition governments. In December 1958, Charles de Gaulle instituted a new constitution and became France's first president for a seven-year term. The Fifth Republic was established on January 8, 1959, when de Gaulle appointed a new government. Unlike the constitution of the Fourth Republic, which gave more power to the French Parliament, the new political structure guaranteed full power to the president, simultaneously giving the executive branch considerable importance at the expense of the Assemblée nationale. Thus, de Gaulle had created an era, later labeled by historians the "golden years of the Gaullist episode," by operating as an elected "sovereign" while at the same time being widely esteemed as a world statesman.

Following his famous vow, *Je vous ai compris* (I understand you now), the president quickly adopted a more pacifying tone, to the dismay of hundreds of thousands of *pieds noirs,* settlers from Europe descent as he led the discussions on Algerian self-determination despite a fierce terrorist campaign fomented by the Secret Army Organization (OAS, Organisation de l'armée secrète) of the extremist French military. In 1961, in the midst of a war that had continued since November 1954,[3] General Raoul Salan and other commanders of the French army attempted an unsuccessful coup d'état in Algiers, triggering a series of terrorist acts in France as well as several murder attempts on the president himself. A few months later, a referendum on April 8, 1962, overwhelmingly supported the Evian Agreement (by 90.6 percent), settling the thorny Algerian conflict and giving Algeria its independence on July 5, thus ending 132 years of French domination. Consequently, a massive immigration movement was set in motion, with close to a million French settlers immediately repatriated to France, the majority of whom had never set foot on French soil. Although the financial cost of such a resettlement movement was beyond measure, the French economy was able to supply housing and jobs as a result of the exceptionally favorable economic situation of the early 1960s.

Despite the tragic events during the eight years of conflict in Algeria, which claimed the lives of one million victims (among a population of ten million at the time), relations with Algeria, as with most of the former African colonies, remained cooperative primarily because of the strong economic state of affairs. Free of colonial entanglements, France enjoyed growing economic strength and wealth and became a nuclear power in 1960. Six years later, to the world's surprise, President de Gaulle decided to remove French forces from NATO integrated command, obligating all US troops to exit France. Another of de Gaulle's political bombshells occurred during his visit to Montreal on July 24, 1967. His stay ended precipitously, after he declared in front of a euphoric crowd of 500,000 (much to Canadian officials' disbelief) "Vive le Québec . . . vive le Québec . . . libre!"

The so-called golden years came to an end with the dramatic events of May 1968. By that year, French companies felt growing pressure for labor reforms and a more significant improvement in working conditions. The dissension was especially forceful in France (among western European nations), with passive forms of censure (for example, absenteeism—

up to 30 percent by 1968—and strikes). Workers' dissatisfaction became a major issue throughout France, and at this time the question of labor reorganization and collective conventions took up an unusual postponement when compared with other European counterparts.

In the 1960s, working conditions in French companies worsened a great deal, which led to the riots in May 1968. Trade unions responded with a new concept, "qualitative demands," which aimed to enhance working conditions and democratize the workplace. This initiative was principally endorsed by the CFDT (Confédération française Démocratique du travail), a union that emphasized the concept of *autogestion* (workers' control). On May 3 of that year, students in Parisian universities (mainly at the Sorbonne and Nanterre) started the largest insurrection ever organized in the century. After French police brutally retaliated during the initial upheavals, the rest of the student body joined the confrontation, and as barricades were set up all over the Latin Quarter, street riots quickly broke out. Students, who reorganized themselves into a large commune, annexed the Sorbonne on May 13. The student protests, mainly targeted at the conservative government and against an obsolete educational system, infiltrated other sectors of French society as factory workers and farmers answered the call, and precipitated large national strikes. What had unobtrusively started as a local and constrained demonstration escalated to paralyze a nation (close to nine million workers went on strike). On May 27, following an entire month of intense and difficult negotiations, the Agreements of Grenelle were finally signed by Premier Georges Pompidou granting trade-union organizations improved wages and working conditions and a modernized restructuring of the French education system, among other reforms. Throughout the crisis, de Gaulle seemed powerless and revealed at several public occasions his inability to tackle the crisis. Unable to comprehend its nature, he clandestinely flew by helicopter to West Germany to confer with French army commander General Jacques Massu about possible strategies for dealing with a hypothetically threatening insurrection. If not entirely destabilized, de Gaulle's government was undeniably weakened (although successful during the June 1968 legislative election), which consequently precipitated his retirement. De Gaulle's successor, right-wing moderate Georges Pompidou, also a Gaullist, was elected president in June 1969.

During these difficult years of transition, the French film industry was far from being absent from current affairs. In addition to state censorship, moral, political, and self-censorship prevented references to the war in Algeria, leaving the nation deeply divided into two equally disheartened sides. Unlike the war in Indochina, where only a professional army was sent to fight, the draft involved almost two million young Frenchmen in Algeria, consequently drawing greater negative public opinion and concern. In this particular emotional climate, and as paradoxical as it may seem, French cinema of the late 1950s and early 1960s could not provide criticisms or eloquent commentaries on the dramatic events that involved the daily horrors of war, such as the practice of torture in the French army and many FLN (Front de libération nationale) prisoners who were condemned to death in French prisons. Among the few filmmakers who bucked censorship was Jean-Luc Godard, who shot *The Little Soldier* (*Le petit soldat*, 1960). Godard had expected the film to be released in the fall of 1960, but French censors prohibited its release because of its numerous indirect allusions to the events in Algeria,[4] especially the references to torture. The film was finally screened after the conclusion of the conflict in 1963. The noticeable absence of political commitment by French artists was particularly evident when confronted with the situation in Algeria. Ironically enough, one of the most important historical authentications adapted to the screen was directed by an Italian director, Gillo Pontecorvo, in *The Battle of Algiers* (*La bataille d'Alger,* 1965), which portrayed in a vivid documentary style the struggle of the FLN against French paratroopers in Algiers. Prohibited for obvious political reasons, the film was finally released in France in 1972, ten years after the independence of Algeria.

It seems evident that the Algerian war caused a deep scar in the French psyche with no remedial healing process throughout the 1960s. During these poisoned years, countless young artists and intellectuals began to raise their voices in protest against the war, the result of which was already known to be a failure. On September 5, 1960, they organized a manifesto including the names of 121 personalities. Calling for civil disobedience, and instigating a national refusal to "wage war against the Algerian people" as well as a demand for Algerian independence, the document, baptized *L'appel des 121,* was signed by some of the most prominent actors of the time (Simone Signoret and Alain Cuny), directors (Alain Resnais, Alain Robbe-Grillet, Claude Lanzmann, Claude Sautet and François Truffaut), novelists (Nathalie Sarraute, Edouard Glissant, Marguerite Duras, Simone de Beauvoir, and André Breton), and philosophers (Jean-Paul Sartre), making history despite the timid participation of the directors of the *nouvelle vague* (New Wave).

In the arts, the 1960s are remembered for an explosion of new values and radical changes in clear contrast with the ubiquitous classicism of the postwar era. Whereas French intellectuals achieved original contributions to almost every field of the social sciences and humanities, French culture preserved its distinctive disposition as it attempted to withstand the powerful transatlantic competition coming from the United States. In literature and philosophy, Existentialism was slowly supplanted by a new intellectual trend identified as structuralism led by Jacques Derrida, Jacques Lacan, Roland Barthes, and Michel Foucault. In 1964, the Nobel Prize in literature was awarded to Jean-Paul Sartre, but, to the world's astonishment, the philosopher refused it, claiming that becoming a Nobel recipient compromised his intellectual integrity as a writer. Inspired in part by the thesis of anthropologist Claude Lévi-Strauss, the adepts of structuralist discourse underlined the existence of "deep structures" at the basis of all human cultures subsisting through the course of time, which, unlike the Existentialists, were not much affected by historical transformation and even less by human resourcefulness.

The face of western Europe changed quickly with the emergence of new entertainment avenues. At the beginning of this evolution in the film and entertainment industries, many American jazz musicians, often underappreciated in the United States, flourished in European clubs. With them, America brought many of its popular myths to France, such as actors James Dean, Marilyn Monroe, and Marlon Brando, as well as rock 'n' roll. Along with the traditional cinema, new possibilities came along for leisure, as the use of the automobile was no longer a sure sign of opulence for a select few. In addition, the increasing presence of TVs and stereos in almost every home—at least by the end of the decade—became a major cultural and economic factor of the 1960s. The trend initiated in the late 1950s intensified to become an increasing challenge for the French film industry: 1960 was the first year to see more than a million television sets in homes. The development of television's broadcasting capability as well as its growing communication scope also contributed to the widespread change all over the nation. Unlike television in the United States, the powerful and conservative ORTF (Office de radio-télévision française), created in 1964, was endowed with a strong state monopoly, and was able to exert power on the medium's panorama until the state-controlled networks were split into several companies—eventually becoming separate private and public entities—in 1982. As a result, the film industry had to face a growing negotiating power from television producers, who were more and more in a position to open doors for filmmakers. Unlike American studios, which rapidly absorbed television studios, and thus controlled TV's growth, the French film industry was no longer fully independent. A more "noninterventionist" television slowly began to play an increasingly influential role in cultural life, as new approaches toward problematic or taboo themes, like open sexuality and even brand-new types of subject matter, were envisaged.

THE SIGNS OF CHANGE: LOUIS MALLE

Although successful at the box office, many older directors such as Marcel Carné, Claude Autant-Lara, René Clément, René Clair, Henri-Georges Clouzot, Christian-Jaque, and Henri Verneuil remained unchanged in their approach to cinema. Increasingly, the younger French film press criticized them for their lack of cinematographic innovations. Only a few skilled filmmakers, such as Robert Bresson, Jacques Becker, and Jacques Tati, were able to stand apart from the old-school group, not by the number of their productions but rather by the high quality of the few films they produced. Most of the leaders among French actors of the postwar era were now middle-aged (Jean Gabin, Fernandel, Bourvil, Danielle Darrieux, and Michèle Morgan), leaving a serious gap between them and a younger audience. One of the rare examples of celebrated youth that could have rejuvenated the 1960s generation disappeared with the unexpected death of Gérard Philipe in 1959. A whole new generation of actors was long awaited.

The new trend in filmmaking initiated by the critics-turned-directors generation suggested a more "unsophisticated" technique generally predisposed toward the documentary aspect of filmmaking, the aim of which was to establish an implicit (rather than unambiguous) unadulterated narrative. One of the first filmmakers of the French postwar era to delineate the new approach was Jean-Pierre Melville. In his 1947 directing debut, *The Silence of the Sea* (*Le silence de la mer*), Melville used a drastically different approach. With a minuscule budget, unknown actors, and limited crew, he is considered the forerunner of independent cinema as well as one of the spiritual fathers of the New Wave. Melville's theories on location shooting and smart use of budget and actors foreshadowed the renewal brought by the New Wave ten years later. With *Bob the Gambler* (*Bob le flambeur*, 1955), Melville finally revealed the impending breakthrough, by amalgamating American-style film noir with documentary-fiction plot through an unconditional realism. His contribution was "compassionately" recognized when he appeared as Parvulesco, a world-renowned novelist interviewed by Patricia Franchini (Jean Seberg) in Jean-Luc Godard's *Breathless* (*À bout de souffle*, 1959), which recognized his prestige among the emerging young directors of the New Wave. Melville launched the career of future cinematographer and collaborator Henri Decaë (1915–87), one of the most prominent cinematographers in French cinema, who, although often solicited by commercially inclined directors, was also frequently contracted by many New Wave filmmakers because of his technical expertise in fluid panning and tracking shots. Decaë contributed to the production of more than seventy films, including Melville's *Le silence de la mer*, *Bob the Gambler*, *The Samurai* (*Le samouraï*, 1967), and *The Strange Ones* (*Les enfants terribles*, 1950); Louis Malle's *Elevator to the Gallows* (*Ascenseur pour l'échafaud*, 1958) and *The Lovers* (*Les amants*, 1958); Claude Chabrol's *The Cousins* (*Les cousins*, 1959), *Bitter Reunion* (*Le beau Serge*, 1959), and *The Girls* (*Les bonnes femmes*, 1960); François Truffaut's *The Four Hundred Blows* (*Les quatre cents coups*, 1959); René Clément's *Purple Noon*; Henri Verneuil's *The Sicilian Clan* (*Le clan des Siciliens*, 1969); Gérard Oury's *The Sucker!* (*Le corniaud*, 1964), *Delusions of Grandeur* (*La folie des grandeurs*, 1971), *The Vengeance of the Winged Serpent* (*La vengeance du serpent à plumes*, 1984), and *The Adventures of Rabbi Jacob* (*Les aventures de Rabbi Jacob*, 1973); and Claude Zidi's *Inspector la Bavure* (*Inspecteur la bavure*, 1980).

Another significant cinematographer, Raoul Coutard (b. 1924), served in many *nouvelle vague* productions. He was known to operate promptly, especially on the low-budget films of the New Wave, and preferred the spontaneous mobility of a handheld camera to the cumbersome powerful pieces of traditional equipment. Because of his own idiosyncratic visual style (using faster film stock that required less light), Coutard can be labeled one of France's most innovative cinematographers of all time. Generally underestimated when compared to the work of filmmakers, the cinematographers' contributions often match those of the film auteurs in significance. Using sharp creativity and intuition for exact framing, camera angles and movements, scene composition, and integration of special effects, Coutard's trademark technique profoundly marked the French New Wave with his own recreation of the spirit of the times. His most important films included art direction for Godard's *Breathless, A Woman Is a Woman* (*Une femme est une femme*, 1961), *The Little Soldier, Contempt* (*Le mépris*, 1963), *Crazy Pete* (*Pierrot le fou*, 1965), and *First Name: Carmen* (*Prénom Carmen*, 1984); François Truffaut's *Shoot the Piano Player* (*Tirez sur le pianiste*, 1960), *Jules and Jim* (*Jules et Jim*, 1961), *Love at Twenty* (*L'amour à vingt ans*, 1962), and *The Bride Wore Black* (*La mariée était en noir*, 1967); Jean Rouch's *Chronicle of a Summer* (*Chronique d'un été*, 1960); Costa-Gavras's *Z* (*Z*, 1969) and *The Confession* (*L'aveu*, 1970); Pierre Schoendoerffer's *Drummer-Crab* (*Le crabe-tambour*, 1977); Richard Dembo's *Dangerous Moves* (*La diagonale du fou*, 1984); and Philippe Garrel's 1996 *The Phantom Heart* (*Le coeur fantôme*).

In addition to these key technicians, it is worth mentioning the contribution to the emerging French New Wave of filmmaker Jean Rouch, (b. 1917) who, along with Jean-Pierre Melville, directly influenced cinematographers' use of handheld cameras. Rouch was one of the first directors to employ the newly developed lightweight handheld cameras with direct recording and natural lighting. This so-called *cinéma vérité* is characterized in two ways. First, there is the capturing of reality through the cinematographic medium, thereby avoiding conventional documentary journalism. Second, cinéma verité makes noninterventionist use of interviews in films. Unlike the traditional documentary, in which the images and sound were recorded simultaneously, the new approach suggested the predominance of the oral text as the starting point, and recorded conversations prior to the actual shooting. Ad hoc footage was regularly recorded, showing evidence of the technical malleability of the latest television handheld cameras in combination with the use of post-synchronization for dialogue. As a result, the films usually gave a striking effect of realism combined with an evident ethnographic background. At first criticized for lacking artistic interpretation and favoring a journalistic approach to images, the cinéma vérité, or "direct cinema," of Jean Rouch (who directed over one hundred films) unpredictably influenced other filmmakers of documentary chronicles.

Film historians have often neglected to credit the quintessential influence of the Italian neorealist style, in conjunction with the British "free" documentaries, without which French cinéma vérité may not have inspired so many future young filmmakers to enter the field. For this new trend, the expressive force was also to be found behind the camera as these filmmakers involved poetic energy as much as others did with fiction. Overlooked by popular audiences due to its journalistic visual format rather than imaginative fiction, cinéma verité introduced a pioneering style to documentary cinematography. The most important achievements were Rouch's *Moi, un noir* (1957), which earned the Prix Louis Delluc in 1958, *Chronicle of a Summer,* and Chris Marker's *Le joli mai* (1962).

Often associated with the French New Wave movement, Louis Malle (1932–95), whose film performances were considered tangential and not seminal to the emerging trend, maintained a rather atypical and personal place within French cinema of the late 1950s. After some studies at the Sorbonne and IDHEC (Institut des hautes études cinématographiques), Malle worked as a cameraman with Robert Bresson in *A Man Escaped* (*Un condamné mort s'est échappé,* 1956) and co-directed Jacques-Yves Cousteau's undersea documentary *The Silent World* (*Le monde du silence,* 1956). This experiment with Cousteau proved pivotal for his career, since the film not only won the Palme d'or at the Cannes Film Festival but also, a year later, Malle achieved his first long feature film, *Elevator to the Gallows* (*Ascenseur pour l'échafaud,* 1957; Prix Louis Delluc in 1957). Following the success of his first psychological thriller, Malle directed *The Lovers* (*Les amants,* 1958), which established Jeanne Moreau as the emerging female star of French film (along with Brigitte Bardot). At the time of its release, *The Lovers* was a graphic sexual experience that explored the sensually explicit, erotic world of a frustrated upper-class housewife who realizes the futility of her bour-

geois existence, and as a result indulges in an extramarital affair with
a last-minute encounter, only to leave both her husband and suitor.
The unambiguous love scenes, tracked with clever timing, revealed the
young director's impulsive management of erotic themes. In the
United States, *The Lovers* was severely criticized by film reviewers
and censored for its unequivocal love scenes (apparently too far
ahead of their time). From that time on, Malle's versatile yet marginal
filmmaking seldom received the same critical attention as his New
Wave peers.

As usual with Malle's versatility, his next film was radically different
in tone and genre. *Zazie dans le métro*, (*Zazie dans le métro*, 1960) is an
effervescent comic tale in which a young girl plans to travel on the
Parisian subway. Moving toward more difficult subject matter, such as
The Fire Within (*Le feu follet*, 1963), a forlorn yet influential investigation of an author on the brink of suicide, and *Lacombe Lucien* (*Lacombe
Lucien*, 1974), a contentious portrayal of collaboration, resistance, and
childhood corruption during the Occupation, Malle progressively distanced himself from the circles around the *Cahiers du cinéma*. The
following decade was the beginning of the second chapter of his career,
as he continued to direct feature films in America such as *Pretty Baby*
(1978), a narrative about a photographer and a preteenage prostitute
(interpreted by Brooke Shields in her first major role), and *Atlantic
City* (*Atlantic City*, 1980). In the late 1980s, Malle made a successful
comeback in France with *Au revoir, les enfants* (1987), an autobiographical account of childhood and solidarity during the tracking of Jews of
France through World War II, followed by *May Fools* (*Milou en Mai*,
1989), a cheerful and sardonic comedy whose main point of interest
illustrated the bourgeois sense of self-righteousness during the 1968
events in France. Malle married American actress Candice Bergen and
died in 1995 at his home in Beverly Hills, following his direction of
two more American movies: *Damage* (1992) and *Vanya on 42nd Street*
(1994), an adaptation of Anton Chekhov's play *Uncle Vanya*.

In *Elevator to the Gallows*, Malle imposed a new aesthetic on film
noir by combining the visual liveliness of cinematographer Henri
Decaë with a melancholic yet highly energized musical score by the
renowned jazz musician Miles Davis. Faithful to his passion for jazz,
Malle asked Davis and his quintet to improvise the sound track of the
film. This inspired a trendy edge that gave the film a more enlightened
and modern countenance when compared with earlier examples of film
noir. Although disclosing its noir heritage with its numerous formulaic
outlines (Billy Wilder's 1944 *Double Indemnity* and Tay Garnett's 1946
The Postman Always Rings Twice), *Elevator to the Gallows* was a unique
allegory of a period in transition, the end of the 1950s and the

beginning of a new era, an innovative look just before the advent of a new cinema.

The story line of the movie, a rather formulaic outline for Malle's first feature film, begins with a classic plot. Julien Tavernier (Maurice Ronet), an ex-paratrooper officer and veteran of colonial wars in Indochina and Algeria now working for a munitions corporation, plans to murder, with the help of his mistress, Florence Carala (Jeanne Moreau),[5] her rich and tyrannical husband, Simon Carala (Jean Wall) the owner of the company. After climbing up to the balcony to enter the boss's office unnoticed, Julien takes Carala's gun, shoots him, and leaves a note to insinuate suicide. He soon begins to encounter a series of complications as he realizes once outside the office building that he left behind the hook dangling from the balcony, which allowed him to scale the wall outside Carala's office. He rushes back inside only to get stuck in the elevator while the janitor of the building turns off the electricity for the weekend. Over the next few hours, Julien tries desperately to escape and finally, despite the dangerous situation, manages to exit using the elevator. Meanwhile, Louis (Georges Poujouly)[6] and Véronique (Yori Bertin), an idle young couple in search of adventure, steal his luxurious convertible car, which was parked downstairs. Florence, who happens to see the car driving by, mistakes Louis for Julien. Bewildered, she hopelessly wanders around .town fearing the worst. Using Julien's identity, the young couple decide to spend the night under his name in a suburban motel, where they meet wealthy German tourists. Invited for a drink, Louis and Véronique take photographs with Julien's miniature camera and give the roll of film to be developed and printed to the same motel. Sensing some suspicion on their new acquaintances' part, they decide to run away in their sports car. As they start the engine in the garage, Louis and Véronique get caught by the German tourists but retaliate by gunning them down using a revolver they find in Julien's glove compartment. They go on the run. Florence, who waited all night for Julien, first believes that Julien changed his mind for another woman as she remembers the car with Véronique. A few hours later, Julien's picture appears on the front page of the Parisian newspapers as the prime suspect in the motel murders. Arrested shortly after, Julien is charged with the murder of the German couple. Florence, who traces the young couple, investigates the motel and finds them with the help of the film from Julien's camera. Inspector Chérier (Lino Ventura) waits in a dark room and arrests Louis. Unfortunately, the roll of film also has previous pictures of Florence and Julien taken in happier times, which present the necessary indication of the plan to murder her husband. Ironically, Florence, who manages to track down the real murderers and gain the specifics necessary to clear Julien, inadvertently incriminates him in the murder of her husband.

The transformation of the old French political and cultural décor of the late 1950s, including the burgeoning of decolonization and modernization, is explicitly shown in the film, as Robin Buss describes:

> Many heroes of classic film noir (who are in conventional terms villains) seem to be trying to escape from an over-regulated society toward more primitive times; their rule is the survival of the fittest (and consequently, the elimination of the unfit); and it is not only the left that despises the bourgeoisie. In this sense, film noir may become a sort of urban Western, with an underlying nostalgia for a mythical past. Julien, in *Ascenseur pour l'échafaud,* is applying the simple morality that he has learned in the jungles of Indochina to the concrete jungle of contemporary Paris, and his defeat by fate can almost be seen as tragic, as well as just.[7]

It is also noteworthy to remark that the characterization of Julien and Florence is explored with depth; they are persuasively depicted as victims rather than murderers. Jeanne Moreau would soon become one of the favorites of other New Wave directors, especially François Truffaut. Without ever fully endorsing their style, Moreau's acting talent was particularly well exploited in Malle's film, as her apprehension during the early morning search in the streets of the capital, while her lover is trapped in the elevator, remains one of the most characteristic suspense scenes in all of French film.

LES CAHIERS DU CINÉMA AND THE AUTEUR THEORY

In 1951, Jacques Doniol-Valcroze (1920–89) and André Bazin (1919–58), along with a group of young film critics, most of whom were under thirty at the time, founded *Les cahiers du cinéma,* which quickly became the major reference for French film studies. Initially inspired by Alexandre Astruc's[8] concept of *camerastylo* (cinema as an autonomous language, with the author "writing" with a camera), the review divulged new standards for French cinema and limited its esteem to a few old-school film directors such as John Ford, Alfred Hitchcock, Howard Hawks, Orson Welles, Fritz Lang, Nicholas Ray, Billy Wilder, and Luchino Visconti—ironically, most of them working within studio systems making genre pictures. Throughout the different cinematic currents of the twentieth century, French filmmaking had always profited from its inherent resourcefulness to deepen its connection with the public: interactive storytelling, montage, an identifiable approach to divulging a narrative's intrigue, the interaction of plot, black-and-white aesthetics, and so forth. In its quest for constant renewal, the young French cinema indirectly reproached Hollywood's long-established narratives and restricted story line subterfuges. Narratives, necessarily unsophisticated, were to satisfy spectators and produce an impression of cerebral control and visual omniscience via an unchallenged mind. As for French inspirational models, only a few directors stimulated the new school: the austere classicism of Robert Bresson with *A Man Escaped,* the "absurd" comedy of Jacques Tati (1908–82) with *Monsieur Hulot's Holiday* (*Les vacances de Mr. Hulot,* 1953), and *My Uncle* (*Mon oncle,* 1958), and the early works of Jean Renoir with *Toni* (1934), *The Lower Depths* (*Les bas-fonds,* 1936), *Grand Illusion,* and *The Rules of the Game.*

In the early 1950s, this untested inclination for a new filmic language was at first more a tribute to *cinéphilie* than an actual film theory itself. Later, in January 1954, a young critic named François Truffaut made history when *Les cahiers du cinéma* published his article in volume 31, entitled "Une certaine tendance du cinéma français."[9] It attacked the old guard of French film directors, such as Jean Delannoy and Claude Autant-Lara, and scenarists Jean Aurenche and Pierre Bost, along with their "fossilized" production system, the predominance of scriptwriters, the lack of imagination, the theatrical concept of cinematic discourse, material comfort, and dependence on commercial success. For Truffaut, the old-fashioned concepts of literary adaptation were no longer functioning: "Ordinarily, Aurenche and Bost adapt novels by turning them into theater pieces rather than screenplays, using standard dramatic procedures: cuts and summaries, ellipses, three acts, ingenious flashbacks, commentaries, etc."[10] As for the rest of the group—Eric Rohmer, Claude Chabrol, Jean-Luc Godard, Jacques Rivette, and others—young directors were to offer a new look on filmmaking and especially at scenario with a fluid filmic narration inspired from their own personal reading and not the same old literary canons. In addition to the authors' radically new subject matter, the techniques were meant to turn their back on the traditional use and abuse of studio shooting, its almost motionless camera movement, and traditional *champ-contrechamps* (shots–countershots).

The *Cahiers's* unique spirit of collective encouragement, which alleviated obstacles of future productions, challenged established conventions, and fiction no longer appeared to have a privileged place in literary culture (although literary cinema was still the bottom line of the *Cahiers*). In addition, the New Wave directors' expertise in film theory and criticism during the 1950s was a decisive advantage in their battle against traditional cinema. A year later, in 1952, another influential review called *Positif* was founded in Lyon. A battle of concepts was waged between the two magazines, which conveyed radically different ideas, content versus form. What was reproached in the *Cahiers* was a recurrent obscurantism, a tendency to promote some minor films in an intellectual manner (often calling their competitors *les enfants du paradigmes*). This obscurantism became even more challenging in the 1960s with the coming of new critics like Christian Metz, who "grandfathered" semiology in film studies. Interestingly enough, all the critics were assiduous members of the Cinémathèque française, an institution founded by Henri Langlois (1914–77) in 1936 and considered by international film historians a monument to *cinéphilie* and the most important film archive in the world. This private institution, whose main objective was to assist filmmakers who came to find their inspiration, idols, models, and future projects, also organized within its walls the information and critical reflection on film studies as well as encouraged the distribution of lesser known films. To date, its archives hold over forty thousand films, fifteen thousand scenarios and other manuscripts, two million stills, and several hundred costumes. In addition, the Cinémathèque française edits and publishes manuscripts, biographies, studies on critical theory, and rare cinematographic documents.

Long before the advent of the *Cahiers du cinéma*'s promotion of authorism, French cinema had always celebrated groundbreaking authors who expressed a literary penchant for analysis rather than action, respecting a theatrical, or even Romanesque tradition for their study of custom. While observing human souls and passions through the motion of their cameras and the network of light, which depended directly from their personal choice, French directors have always taken advantage of the free will they were given to represent in their characters the world in which the plot evolved. Champions of individual creativity (first-person narration through the lens of the camera), Robert Bresson, certainly one the most studied and celebrated film authors, as well as filmmakers Abel Gance, Jean Renoir, and Jean Vigo were the real inspiration not only for the young directors of the 1960s but also for more current artists such as Claude Sautet, André Téchiné, and Eric Zonca. Regarded as unsuitable in the context of commercial cinema, the notion of the auteur was first officially claimed in André Bazin's theories of the early 1950s. He promoted the idea that directors, who watched over all written, sound, and visual fundamentals of the film, were now to be measured more in term of "author" of the film and not, for instance, the screenwriter or textual author. Such elementary visual constituents as camera motions, lighting, and photography, rather than traditional story line, communicated from now on the profound implications of the film.

In the category of auteur one can include Alain Resnais, Agnès Varda, Chris Marker, Alain Robbe-Grillet, and Marguerite Duras, among many others. Unlike the *Cahiers du cinéma* and the New Wave directors, the so-called Rive Gauche (Left Bank) group indirectly inspired the political and social upheavals of May 1968 as it enthused the culture of French cinema and its intellectual content from the late 1950s until the end of the next decade.[11] Generally older than the New Wave neophytes, members of the auteur movement were already either successful novelists (Duras, Robbe-Grillet) or collaborators of the renowned Editions du Seuil. Often labeled *cinéastes rive gauche* for their attachment to an intellectual and literary background, these insurgent filmmakers remained faithful to a long literary tradition in which novelists expressed their inclination for the seventh art. Although the young critics and commentators of the *Cahiers* shared a similar conviction in the future of French cinema, several key dissensions occurred on a theoretical level. Unlike the New Wave cinema, the auteur theory did not advocate or prompt a severe fracture with the past, nor did it take inspiration from foreign cinema (Hollywood films, for instance). Instead, it took its narratives directly from the eclectic concept of the arts as well as the mental and intellectual processes of French literature. In a certain way, the mise-en-scène became "mise-en-phrase."[12] Just like the *Cahiers du cinéma* group, these filmmakers were categorized as auteurs because of the characteristic themes that could be regularly distinguished throughout the essence of their filmic language. Through their choice of a literary scenario (although opposed to the traditional literary adaptations), the *groupe rive gauche* paved the way for a conversion of film studies into a field as esteemed as any other academic field in the arts.

But the real innovation of the auteurs lay in their theory on montage (mainly a denunciation of temporal continuity), rather than a direct intervention of the director's intellect, which best illustrated its radical change for visual input (absence of the use of wipes or traditional filmic punctuation, juxtaposition of contradicting shots, and so forth). The revolutionary "editing" point of view broke new ground with its visual discontinuity, spatial-temporal ellipses, and the absence of logical connections, thus indirectly reminding the audience of the inevitability of an active spectatorship. For the promoters of authorism, the new concept of editing was to differentiate cinema from traditional filmed epics, and, in general, the conventional Hollywood linear narrative. According to them, film authors had to manipulate the actors' presence as a basic material, which, once assembled in a nonlogical order, could eventually trigger many unusual dramatic effects. Therefore, what the new concept implied was a substitution of the editing process with a more important function given to camera positioning and movement, and consequently suggested the eradication of montage aesthetics with its accurate and undetectable cutting, and of a

Hollywoodian concern for emotional stability. The room for improvisation on the set was extremely limited among the auteurs and contrasted with the loose approach favored by the New Wave. Consequently, the mise-en-scène process became more and more intricate as director-authors endeavored to translate thought, memory, oblivion, and imaginary and psychological processes into the medium.

THE EMERGENCE OF THE NEW WAVE: CLAUDE CHABROL, FRANÇOIS TRUFFAUT, ALAIN RESNAIS, JEAN-LUC GODARD, AND AGNÈS VARDA

The first great surge of change in French cinema took place with the New Wave, which swept across the industry, eventually engendering an emotional impact even on the seemingly unshakable attitudes of Hollywood. The term *New Wave* is applied to the period of French cinema, that covers the years 1959 to 1965. However, it survived the following decades and transcended its spectacular explosion in 1959. Even today, many filmmakers are labeled auteurs either directly or indirectly in reference to the innovation of the late 1950s. The breakthrough occurred concurrently with technical advancements and favorable economic changes that deeply renewed the practice for the pre-existing medium. The French weekly *L'Express* first came up with the phrase *nouvelle vague* in the early 1960s, correlating to a generation of young artists and critics to whom France looked for renewed energy and innovative ideas. What unveiled in these last years of the decade—and to this day still stands as the last period of revolutionary creation—was a radical split that ushered in a mythical cinematographic battleground. The realistic approach of the French New Wave and its constant obsession to render a truthful version of fiction ("immediate truth") ought not to be confused with the Italian neorealist movement of the 1940s, which did not include inherent romanesque elements.[13]

A common fascination for American cinema was clearly displayed among the majority of young French directors for its prestige as an inventive national cinema, its predilection for location shooting, and its constant genius in attracting young, new talent (although simultaneously against the genre convention and the rigid distinction between styles). In opposition to the old school of French cinema, trapped in the literary-dominated cinematographic tradition of the adaptation, new directors advocated freer structures, more innovative subject matter, and an immediate emancipation from the predominance of scriptwriters that was long overdue.[14] Although lacking aesthetic cohesion in the late 1950s, an exceptional visual current seemed to connect the young creators during the early 1960s, a sort of common thought with similar preoccupations and sensitivity toward contemporary situations, narrated through personal themes and an ostentatious subjectivity, making the spectators not passive participants implicated only emotionally, but an active force, analytically assuming the film's sequences.

In the beginning, the core group of French New Wave filmmakers supported each other, resulting in the growth of a collective use of cinematic structure, style, and language that would make their work easily identifiable. A reexamination of the rules of this so-called filmic grammar was the primary step New Wave directors took toward a "new cinema." The authors narrating their story meant that they knew fully about it (from a personal viewpoint) and used actors whose lives were closely connected to the fiction they embodied. In other words, New Wave directors talked about themselves. Being rarely engaged politically and socially on the screen, many contemporary critics reproached New Wave filmmakers for turning their backs on political cinema or systematically avoiding religious subject matter. The story lines typically began within or against a realistic background before evolving toward fiction documentary, the thriller, or the fantastic, and they usually developed an emblematic narration mode free from regulations and spatial-temporal cohesion. The use of interior monologues emphasizing the first-person point of view and unstated responses to questions was also frequent and added to a sense of art-for-art's sake.

Existentialism as developed by Jean-Paul Sartre and Albert Camus, was one of the key inspirations for the themes of French New Wave since it emphasized the importance of free will and the absurdity of human existence in its rational attempt to comprehend the world. Many characters in French New Wave movies were frequently outcasts, antiheroes, and loners (Antoine Doinel in *The Four Hundred Blows* and Michel Poiccard in *Breathless,* for example), living according to a carpe diem itinerary and performing according to their own intuition rather than a role attributed by society (or, for that matter, the film director). With the breakthroughs in the expression of physical love and the explicit contemplation of sexuality as an acceptable subject matter, new characters developed into a representation of "modern romanticism" with the reverence of nature and its use of outdoor location shooting.[15]

On a technical level, French New Wave was predominantly artistically oriented filmmaking with countless improvisations and other artistic directional features, which in the long run clearly differentiated the movement from the *cinéma d'auteurs.* Because of its rapid international success, many filmmakers and producers, already battling competition and eager to recover a young audience, criticized the elements of the new cinema, using the phrase *nouvelle vague* in such a derogatory way as to designate a simplistic cinematic character, undaunted editing, and artistic carelessness. In fact, in contrast to the heavy style of traditional filmmaking and its ostentatious technique, New Wave no longer used well-defined photography that left room for free stylistic considerations based on intuition and nature, as, for instance, the famous use of freeze frames in Truffaut's *The Four Hundred Blows* (the final shot being singled out in post-production). Jump cuts were frequently used to ease montage difficulties, which dramatically increased the number of shots in a film. The methods used by young directors were unheard of to this point. It was indeed their deliberate choice to combine practical necessity with strong professional and artistic conviction that made almost all of them establish their movie careers in a climate in which there was no room for mistake.

Most cinematographic innovations had to allow the spectator, for main purpose and effect, to feel the presence of the filmmaker behind the camera and no longer consume the "visual product" from a distance. The technical improvements of location shooting allowed audacious cinematographers to experiment with exterior shots using natural lighting.[16] Since new cameras were more silent, they allowed high-quality direct sound and recording.[17] This new technique was also significantly less expensive than the traditional heavy equipment of the film studios. As for extras, directors often used their own crew, friends, or anyone willing to participate for almost no remuneration; even the actors themselves were sometimes hired on a deferred-remuneration basis. These economic and artistic alternatives—smaller budgets, smaller crews, nonprofessional or untrained actors, shorter shooting time (for instance, Jean-Luc Godard's *Breathless* was completed in just four weeks: August 17–September 15, 1959), light-weight equipment, natural background with natural lighting—drastically lowered production costs and thereby allowed directors to improve their often antagonistic relations with their own producers. The minimization of costs encouraged film investors to venture on contracting beginners, or even at times anonymous artists, as the minimalism of technical resources and financial elements granted the young filmmakers an unconditional command over every facet of the creative process.

From a historical viewpoint, it is hardly arguable to assert that the impact of French New Wave on cinematographic history quickly modernized international filmmaking as no other national current, leaving a choice between fiction-film and essay-film for another generation. From a commercial point of view, the accomplishment of the new cinema triggered an upsurge of fresh talent inside the French film industry until the 1960s, as myriads of young *neophytes* finally directed low-budget independent films. Although never officially classified as a cinematographic movement, the French New Wave inspired everlasting academic as well as nonacademic debates about the essence of modern cinema and conciliated the endless dilemma between commercial and artistic filmmaking as it proved that artistic films could survive at the box office.

In the 1950s, making a first movie without prior training on the set of a major motion picture director was almost impossible. The postwar era, known for its spirit of continuity in artistic as well as economic achievements (see chapter 4), never put the organization of its structures into perspective. The way to access the cinematographic profession (from set operator and cinematographer to film director) remained practically unchanged since the 1930s (with the exception of the four years of Occupation). Each year, only a handful of new directors could make it to the top. But for those select few, the road was rife with ambushes. As a result of the long training period, which in some cases took more then a decade, young filmmakers' dimension for creativity or vision for change remained dramatically reduced, locked up in an artistically stagnant industry, concerned with the popular audiences' demands. And what the popular spectatorship primarily enjoyed was France's biggest movie stars, acting within a perfect scenario, containing a tight and memorable dialogue. Consequently, the "critic-turned-directors" unmistakably understood that trying to beat the system from within was doomed to failure and quickly worked their way outside the traditional path, eventually reintegrating it with significant experience on their résumé. But not all young directors of the New Wave were beginners. Some filmmakers already had prior experience, such as Alain Resnais, Chris Marker, Jean Rouch, Georges Franju, and Pierre Kast.

Then came the year 1959, which turned into the moment of revelation. Claude Chabrol (b. 1930), first among the group to secure triumph with *Bitter Reunion* (*Le beau Serge,* 1958) and *The Cousins* (*Les cousins,* 1958), received the Jean Vigo Prize in 1959 and the Golden Bear at the Berlin Film Festival that same year. The major revelation, however, occurred at the 1959 Cannes Film Festival with the prize for Best Director awarded to François Truffaut for *The Four Hundred Blows,* while the Prize of the Critics went to Alain Resnais for *Hiroshima, Mon Amour* (*Hiroshima, mon amour,* 1959). During that same summer, several other groundbreaking projects were being completed, for example, Jean-Luc Godard's *Breathless.* Although successful at the box office, the films of the new cinema still did not surpass the traditional commercial productions of the *qualité française.* Most of them, however, became better commercial deals since costs were lower. If one considers Chabrol, Truffaut, Resnais, and Godard the first directors of the New Wave, in a chronological sequence, their contributions can be grouped, respectively, into different categories: *Bitter Reunion* and *The Cousins* as the "giant step" against an old production system; *The Four Hundred Blows,* crowned by the most important film festival in the world, as a technical discovery as well as a media revelation; *Hiroshima, Mon Amour* as an intellectual renewal; and *Breathless* as the cinematographic event of the next decade.

At the 1959 Cannes Film Festival, a private meeting was organized in La Napoule, gathering seventeen directors, (Roger Vadim, Edouard Molinaro, Marcel Camus, Jacques Rozier, François Reichenbach, François Truffaut, Claude Chabrol, Louis Malle, Jacques Baratier, Robert Hossein, and Jean-Luc Godard, among others) all coming from different directions within the young French cinema, each seeking under the aegis of Jacques Doniol-Valcroze to announce publicly his own dedication to the free spirit of the New Wave. They also sought to defy the film industry and to find a definition of the future "new cinema." Although symbolic, the temporary union did not last (and never was intended to), but it did play the role of a cinematographic Magna Carta of French New Wave, setting the necessary tone for the coming decade. The movement had no preestablished theory, but Truffaut rapidly differentiated the two main currents in cinema, the documentary (labeled the Lumière) and the fictional (the Méliès).

Much more than the first years of the Occupation, the early years of the New Wave experienced an unprecedented explosion of new talent. Some thirty young directors constituted this revelation usually with a first film:[18] Louis Malle (*Elevator to the Gallows*), Jean Rouch (*Moi, un noir,* 1958), Pierre Kast (*Love Is When You Make It/Le bel âge,* 1959), Jacques Demy (*Lola,* 1961), Jacques Rivette (*Paris Belongs to Us/Paris nous appartient,* 1961), Eric Rohmer (*The Sign of the Leo/Le signe du lion,* 1959), and Jacques Rozier (*Adieu Philippine,* 1963). The success of the New Wave at the 1959 Cannes Film Festival, extolling the ever-compelling myth of youth for the entire decade to come, almost undervalued the Palme d'or awarded to Marcel Camus's *Black Orpheus* (*Orfeu Negro,* 1959), which also received the Oscar for Best Foreign Picture in 1960.

When released in June 1958, Claude Chabrol's *Bitter Reunion* (*Le beau Serge,* 1958) was the first feature film of the *Cahiers* group. At the age of twelve, Chabrol (b. 1930) had even created a *ciné-club,* and carried out his old project to become a film director until he became a public-relations man for Twentieth Century-Fox Studios in France. As he learned the language of film with a sharp visual sagacity, he completed his first feature film despite the fact that he was not able to contract a deal with a distributor. (He therefore had no guarantee that the film would be screened.) Unlike most young directors of the New Wave who had to use ingenious stratagems to persuade producers to finance their projects, Chabrol was not only able to produce and direct his first film (with the money bequeathed from his wife's family), but also able to produce Rivette's *Paris Belongs to Us,* Philippe de Broca's *The Love Game (Les jeux de l'amour,* 1960), and Rohmer's *The Sign of the Leo.* Once established, Chabrol exhibited an attraction for the visual grotesque in his many films, wherein incongruity of situation and derision of tragedy echoed a style inspired by director Alfred Hitchcock.

Le beau Serge tells the story of François (Jean-Claude Brialy), a theology student and tuberculosis patient in convalescence who returns to his native village of Sardent,[19] located in an isolated rural community lost in the center of France. There he encounters his old childhood friend Serge (Gérard Blain), who has become a relentless alcoholic through the years and is trapped in a bad marriage. He finds Serge in a bar with his father-in-law, old Glaumaud, just as Serge's wife, Yvonne (Michèle Méritz), and her friend Marie (Bernadette Lafont) take them home before they collapse. François is deeply disconcerted by the cruelty with which Serge rules over his pregnant wife, following the premature death of their first child (who had Down syndrome). As he attempts to dissuade Serge from drinking, François realizes that his enterprise is doomed to failure, just as the local priest had failed years ago. Meanwhile, Marie falls in love with the newcomer and reveals the considerable gossip of the town. Although affected by his disease, François refuses to surrender to the dreadful circumstances. He understands that the true cause of Serge's sporadic follies is the remorse of his first child's death. One winter's night, as Yvonne is about to give birth alone, François runs out to find Serge and takes him back to his wife just in time for his son's birth. Released in Paris in February 1959, the film was a compelling investigation of the theme of care and nurturing in friendship, particularly one that has declined with distance and time. It received national and international recognition, before any other of the New Wave, with the Prix de la Mise en Scène at the Locarno Festival in 1958 and the Jean Vigo Prize the following year.

During that same year Chabrol's second feature film, *The Cousins,* was released starring the same actors, Gérard Blain and Jean-Claude Brialy, who quickly became international celebrities. The story is about Charles (Gérard Blain), a timid but earnest young bourgeois who comes to Paris from the provinces with high hopes of finishing law school. While staying in the lavish apartment of his rich and rather decadent playboy cousin Paul (Jean-Claude Brialy), he is confronted by the reality of an overactive Parisian *dolce vita* lifestyle. Despite his condescension toward his fellow students, Paul places himself at the center of student social life with his genuine aptitude for meeting and entertaining attractive girls and his suggestion of a certain sophistication. During the extravagant parties organized by his successful and charismatic cousin, Charles naively encounters love at first sight with Florence (Juliette Mayniel). In a romantic conversation, he confesses his respect for women and his desire for marriage, as well as his moral obligation to please his mother by doing well in school. Warned of this change in Charles by his loyal parasite friend Clovis (Claude Cerval), Paul breaks the incipient romance and seduces Florence shortly after. Inconsolable, Charles seeks refuge in Balzac novels and the hope that the final exam will procure him redemption. Ironically, Charles fails the bar exam, despite conscientious but gullible efforts in his studies, whereas Paul, who did not spend much time preparing, receives his diploma. In a desperate move, Charles secretly seizes Paul's gun and places a single bullet in it. He approaches the sleeping Paul and wants to measure his luck once more. But when he presses the trigger, the shot does not fire. In the morning, Paul finds the gun on the chair and involuntarily points the gun at Charles, accidentally killing him.

The great camera work of cinematographer Henri Decaë accurately depicted Parisian student life: a cynical but fair look at how Parisian society operated and how young people could suffer from the spitefulness of youth, sometimes even in a deadly manner. The rendering of Charles's character was quite radical and severe, and consequently conveyed the feeling that what was conventionally right may have very well been a moralistic trap. The character of Charles, at first detached from the stakes of sophistication and the mundane, was depicted as a crushed and perplexed being, unable to know how to express himself adequately to anyone his age, or to communicate with his peers what he saw as the problematic ethics for the spontaneous generation of the early 1960s. The enigmatic moral fable of good and evil, which finally surfaced at the end of the film, can also be seen as a compelling investigation of the corruption of an unspoiled and innocent mind, how society is based on the principle of the survival of the most resilient. Some critics have repeatedly asserted that most of Chabrol's movies did not incorporate a significant content with them, or in other words had little to say in their substance. Although the depth of their subject matter may be arguable at times, it is undeniable to notice that the absolute freedom of Chabrol's vision enriched the quotidian style of the period. The neoromanticism of Chabrol's first films was often compared to the depiction of the misunderstood characters of Alfred de Musset's dramas and poetry (i.e., "La nuit de mai"). *The Cousins* won the Golden Bear at the 1959 Berlin Film Festival.

Not as successful as his first two productions, Claude Chabrol's *The Girls* (*Les bonnes femmes,* 1960) narrated three days in the lives of four young working-class Parisian girls, through several nights of debauchery. Jane (Bernadette Lafont), Ginette (Stéphane Audran), Jacqueline (Clothilde Joano), and Rita (Lucile Saint-Simon) are all employed as sales assistants in a light fixture and appliance store that is owned by a male despot (Pierre Bertin). Each evening, at precisely seven, their time comes around, the end of the day and the beginning of nightlife in Paris, as they rush to go out on the town. They all fantasize about romance, though they can foresee doomed attempts at true romance. Jane is the flirtatious type, Rita falls in love with Henri, and Ginette dreams of becoming a singer as she sneaks out at night to practice in a substandard music hall, not wanting her friends to know. Jacqueline, the least fortunate of all, meets a motorist who, after a short idyll, ends up strangling her in the park. The final scene is an unconventional one as it represents a "fifth" girl who evidently has accepted a dance with an unobserved man. As she stares at the camera, the spectators look into her eyes for a final message of hope: life goes on. Once again in this middle-class *dolce vita* chronicle, the four young women live in a world that mocks them, uses them, and heartlessly exposes their hopes as desperate fantasies with constant overtones of free sexuality. Most of the film actually narrates events offscreen, but the viewer does not need to know the surroundings to be enthralled by the diverse relationships that give the sense of decadence and wastefulness. The strip-club sequence, a freewheeling montage of faces and bodies inflamed by lust and alcohol, seems to have influenced many films of the 1960s. In banal existence or collective nightmare, Chabrol poises a mix of realism and symbolism, for example, the shots of the women doing their makeup in the reflection of the store's blank television screens. Discovered by American critics in the mid-1960s, *The Girls* was never released in the United States (except for a few cities in 1966).

Moving slowly toward more commercial assignments, Claude Chabrol's *The Does* (*Les biches*, 1967) revealed the multifaceted talent of its director as the New Wave gradually settled down with the return of more commercial cinema. *The Does* disclosed the relation between women, the stylish and devious "does," and the male hunter, as they all strive with the fantasies and uncertainties of their sexual desires.

On a Parisian bridge a young sidewalk artist named Why (Jacqueline Sassard) is noticed among the fascinated crowd by Frédérique (Stéphane Audran), a rich, sensuous, and idle woman with an implicit lesbian penchant, who on the spur of the moment becomes strongly attracted to her physical beauty. As Why finishes her drawing, Frédérique approaches her in a predatory manner. At first, the contact is awkward, but soon enough she persuades Why to stop by her apartment, offers her a nice hot bath and coffee, then seduces her. An enigmatic relationship and sexual romance begin.

Frédérique takes her new girlfriend to her huge villa in Saint-Tropez, and there they spend their days of lavishness in an indolent fashion. Frédérique introduces Why to the wealthy lifestyle of French decadence until one night, at a party Frédérique had organized, an attractive young architect named Paul Thomas (Jean-Louis Trintignant) becomes intensely mesmerized by Why. They wind up spending the rest of the night in his apartment. But Frédérique's jealousy is relentless, and it forces her to intervene in the least opportune moment, only to lure Paul into her own arms. She decides to see Paul in person at his workplace and seduces him as she tests once more her incomparable sexual powers. Her expectations confirm her self-confidence, and consequently Paul forgets his rendezvous with Why. Paul displays evidence of his interest in having a bisexual ménage à trois, but Frédérique is resolute in keeping Paul for herself. Paul moves into Frédérique's home in Saint-Tropez, and the new couple compel Why to become an indoor-love satellite. As the days go by, Why becomes more and more fascinated with the physical image of her rich and powerful friend and begins to change identity. Frédérique and Paul decide to move to Paris and leave Why behind by herself. Desperate, she catches up with Frédérique and ends up face to face in her Parisian apartment. Frédérique reveals to Why her embarrassment at having Why as a burden and repudiates her immediately. Why then stabs her in the back with a knife.

The thematic and visual impertinence of the film was to intertwine an account around three characters, each exploring something inside his or her body and mind that remains inscrutable. Here, Chabrol deliberately neglected his habitual suspense ending for developing an innovative propensity for adult drama, as the visual enlightenment about the changes of present-day French society were revealed. Although sexual relationships were not unequivocally illustrated, the film's plot and apprehension became that of sexual obsession itself. For her role as Frédérique, Stéphane Audran, Claude Chabrol's wife at the time, received the prize for Best Actress at the Berlin Film Festival in 1968.

It is true that Chabrol's first films chronologically preceded Truffaut's *The Four Hundred Blows,* but the prime importance of the latter in film history remains hardly arguable. An influential film critic, François Truffaut (1932–84) set himself apart from his contemporaries by his almost total self-absorption in the cinematographic medium. Truffaut grew up in difficult circumstances, which created in him a singular yearning to seek refuge in books and movie theaters. The cinematographic presence in his life emanated from an act of personal relationship with the aesthetic image and not an attraction to technical feats of skill. Truffaut acquainted himself with cinema through an intensive confrontation with films, as he recalled in interviews his

Stéphane Audran (Frédérique) and Jacqueline Sassard (Why) in Claude Chabrol's *The Does* (*Les biches*, 1967), (Courtesy of BIFI/© Artedis).

Albert Rémy (Mr. Doinel), Claire Maurier (Mme Doinel), and Jean-Pierre Léaud (Antoine) in François Truffaut's *The Four Hundred Blows* (*Les quatre cents coups*, 1959), (Courtesy of BIFI/ © André Dino-MK2).

innumerable attempts to sneak out as a child to see night shows. Reminiscing on his turbulent teenage years, Truffaut explained in his autobiographical collection, the vicissitudes he had to endure to enter movie theaters: "I saw my first two hundred films on the sly, playing hooky and slipping into movie houses without paying—through the emergency exit or the washroom window—or by taking advantage of my parents' going out for an evening (I had to be in bed, pretending to be asleep, when they came home). I paid for these great pleasures with stomachaches, cramps, nervous headaches and guilty feelings, which only heightened the emotions evoked by the films."[20]

At the age of twelve, he was determined to become a filmmaker. His friendship with the usual adepts of the Cinémathèque in Paris, and especially film critic André Bazin, greatly influenced him and his attitudes toward film. (Bazin bailed him out of a predicament on two occasions: once as a schoolboy, the second time during his military service as his regiment was preparing to serve in Indochina.) Whether as an outspoken film critic for the influential *Cahiers du cinéma* in 1953 or as a young cineast, Truffaut always retained his *cinéphile* attitude, as he once described his dedication to the visual medium: "Sometimes I saw the same film four or five times within a month and could still not recount the story line correctly because, at one moment or another, the swelling of the music, a chase through the night, the actress's tears, would intoxicate me, make me lose track of what was going on, carry me away from the rest of the movie."[21]

Deeply influenced by the work of such pioneers as Jean Renoir, Jacques Becker, Jean Vigo,[22] Ernst Lubitsch, Alfred Hitchcock, and Orson Welles, Truffaut's early films were immediately characteristic of the coming New Wave visual revolution. In 1956, he assisted Italian filmmaker Roberto Rossellini in several productions before marrying Madeleine Morgenstern, the daughter of a powerful film entrepreneur, and establishing his own production company, Les Films du Carrosse, named for Jean Renoir's great film *The Golden Coach* (*Le carrosse d'or,* 1952). Later on, Truffaut participated in the establishment of the *nouvelle vague* with filmmaker Alain Resnais (*Hiroshima, Mon Amour*), Jean-Luc Godard (*Breathless*), and Claude Chabrol (*Bitter Reunion* and *The Cousins*).

His first full-length feature, *The Four Hundred Blows,* dedicated to his spiritual guide, André Bazin, who died in November 1958 at the beginning of the shooting, took considerable advantage of exterior scenes (streets and schools of Paris) combined with hand-held camera shots. By dedicating *The Four Hundred Blows* to Bazin, Truffaut revealed his critical views through a partly autobiographical motion picture that disclosed the roughness and frustrations of childhood.

Initially intended as a regular short feature, the film was eventually lengthened with the addition of numerous autobiographical scenes. Truffaut essentially investigated his own troubled childhood[23] through a series of rapid anecdotes in poetic but also dramatic points of view.

The plot narrates the numerous delinquent exploits of twelve-year-old schoolboy Antoine Doinel (Jean-Pierre Léaud), also remembered as Truffaut's preteen alter ego. Ignored and admonished at home by his parents and underestimated in school by his unsympathetic schoolmaster (Guy Decomble), Antoine skips school with his friend René (Patrick Auffray) to wander the streets of Paris, stealing milk bottles at doorsteps and venturing into movie theaters in Place Clichy. His parents do not get along very well at home, and one day Antoine catches sight of his mother (Claire Maurier) kissing a stranger on the street. Antoine and René decide to steal a typewriter from the office of Antoine's father (Albert Rémy), eventually to sell it and make some money. No one seems interested in buying it, so they take it back, only to be caught by the janitor. Once arrested, Antoine spends the night at the police station before being punished for his misbehavior. He is sent to a correctional center for juveniles with the agreement of his dismissing parents. His mother, who comes to visit him at the center, announces that his father no longer wishes to see him. The disciplinarian life is tough for young Antoine, and one day, taking advantage of some confusion during a soccer game, he runs away, ending up on a Normandy beach, aimless but free. The celebrated closing shot of the film is an unexpected freeze frame photographing Antoine from the back at the edge of the water, facing the infinite sea, his whole life before him. Truffaut's suspension of little Antoine in an indeterminate future would spawn numerous imitations.

Beyond the launching of his career, the success of the film, first screened in France in March 1959, proved that from now on it was possible for a young critic-turned-director to achieve fame by means other than the byzantine and financially weighted film industry. Just one year after banning Truffaut for his violent condemnations of the commercial exploitations of the Cannes Film Festival, this same festival in May 1959 awarded him with the Prix de la mise en scène (Best Director). He also won the award for Best Film at the New York Film Critics Circle, Best Film at the British Academy Awards, and the Prix de l'Office Catholique International du Cinéma. In addition, the film earned a nomination for Best Original Screenplay (François Truffaut and Marcel Moussy) at the 1959 Academy Awards.

In contrast to the vision of Italian neorealist directors such as Roberto Rossellini and Vittorio de Sica whose representations of children usually contrasted images of childhood purity versus adult corruption,

Truffaut's rendering of youth was quite the opposite. In his nonsenti-
mentalized view of childhood, Truffaut powerfully underscored the
other side of a child's ingenuity as well as innocence. A child's world
may not be as tarnished as an adult's, but the juvenile quest for escape
can lead the child along hazardous paths filled with corruption and
cynicism, as the interview between Antoine and the psychiatrist reveals
at the end of the movie. In the center for delinquents, Antoine has an
interview with a child psychiatrist who evaluates the young boy's
predicament, which is revealed in a disjointed series of question-and-
answer monologues. The innovation created by Truffaut with this
particular scene was the memorable use of jump cuts at the moment
that Antoine reveals himself. The child's future motivations were left
to the audience to analyze. Truffaut directed the shot so that Antoine
is seen facing directly into the camera, opposite the psychiatrist, whose
questions come offscreen. The effort to render truthful the fictional
element of the story was rewarded by the strength and energy of the
boy's answers, and although the edited version of the interview did not
promote the sequencing of the events, it added an extraordinary humanistic feel to the character of Antoine. The same character is also
found in later films directed by Truffaut, as an older teenager in *Love
at Twenty* (*L'amour à vingt ans,* 1962), as a young man in *Stolen Kisses*
(*Baisers volés,* 1968),[24] as a married man in *Bed and Board* (*Domicile
conjugal,* 1970), and as a divorcé in *Love on the Run* (*L'amour en fuite,*
1979).

For his second feature film, *Shoot the Piano Player* (*Tirez sur le pianiste,*
1960), Truffaut adapted, in atypical fashion, pulp author David
Goodis's novel *Down There.* Although perplexing at times (if compared
with *The Four Hundred Blows*), this film captured the true essence of
the French New Wave, mainly through its frequent unprompted shifts
of atmosphere from comedy to melodrama. The story line was rather
inconsequential, and its content persistently scrambled as it frequently
remodeled its tone, intermingling elements of two classic American
genres (the gangster film and film noir) with an energetic new cinematic style. Therefore, a plot synopsis does not give an adequate
picture of *Shoot the Piano Player,* given the nonlinear scenes that appeared even remotely pertinent to the film (much like Quentin Tarantino's 1994 *Pulp Fiction*).

In a small Parisian bar, a piano player named Charlie Kohler
(Charles Aznavour) entertains crowds at night while seeking anonymity. Suddenly, a chain of events begins that forces him to protect his
brother Chico (Albert Rémy), who, after a mix-up with the local mob,
is tracked down by a rival gang. Each new experience brings disaster
upon disaster. Although the events entangle Charlie in his brother's
problems, the focus is more on his relationships with women, from his

prostitute neighbor Clarisse (Nicole Berger) to Lena (Marie Dubois), the bar waitress who, intrigued with Charlie's secret past, finds out that he was a talented and famous musician once known as Edouard Saroyan. In a flashback, Charlie reveals the reason why he renounced his former life, and why he decided to begin a self-imposed exile (his former wife had committed suicide following an affair with his manager). Meanwhile, Charlie's address is turned over to mobsters Momo (Claude Mansard) and Ernest (Daniel Boulanger) by the jealous club owner (Serge Davri). The two thugs pursue Chico, who has double-crossed them. In a skirmish with the bar owner, Charlie stabs him in the back. Lena drives Charlie to his brother's mountain hideout to escape from the police, but when the gunfire breaks out, she is shot dead.

Following the huge success of his first feature film, Truffaut anticipated the difficult challenge of maintaining his success by radically changing the subject, filming a tribute to American B-picture gangster movies.[25] Against the academic structure and form of conformist cinema, Truffaut's low-budget black-and-white film (shot in just six weeks) was an insightful inner meditation on cinematographic conventions. Along with *The Four Hundred Blows,* one can easily consider *Shoot the Piano Player* as Truffaut's most highly experimental film. The use of different cinematic devices—such as Jean-Luc Godard's use of mobile hand-camera shots, sweeping camera work, and profusion of location shootings—simultaneously suggested a free-associative meditation on the gangster film and noir genres, far from being concerned with plot mechanisms or well-defined subject matter. This collection of skillfully scripted and photographed moments also serves to articulate Truffaut's melancholy realism and distinguishes his style from the other New Wave directors. On the actors' level, the characterization was in general relatively low, especially with respect to the main protagonist, Charles Aznavour, one of France's most popular singers at the time, who ultimately lacked the necessary magnetism to draw the audience's attention fully and to sustain dramatic momentum. However, the score by Georges Delerue, who consistently provided Truffaut with evocative refrains, and the unforgettable guest feature, Boby Lapointe, a real-life Parisian club singer with his famous fast-paced song "Avanie et Framboise" were memorable. Truffaut's *Shoot the Piano Player* was a tight, high-speed melodrama, very much like the American ones he admired, with the exception that Truffaut gave considerable attention to character development and transformed the gangster convention to impart a distinctive French flavor.

Sensitivity can be defined as the dominant trait of Truffaut's next feature, *Jules and Jim (Jules et Jim,* 1961). Part of the reason for its immediate success among audience and film critics was the innovative freshness and overall fluidity of the direction, utilizing hasty camera work (mostly long takes) in a moving hymn to love and friendship. When Truffaut discovered little-known writer Henri-Pierre Roché's semiautobiographical novel *Jules et Jim,* he considered the project for the next six years, even after the death of the author in 1959.

The story of this ultramodern romance on love and friendship takes place between 1912 and 1933 in Paris, and depicts the sentimental tribulations of a love triangle between two friends, Jules (Oskar Werner) and Jim (Henri Serre), and a young woman named Catherine (Jeanne Moreau), who combines astuteness with an ostentatious erotic spell. Although the two men give the film its name, the obsessive and multifaceted Catherine actually dominates the story. Jules and Jim both fall in love with her since her smile reminds them of the face of an enigmatic yet beautiful Greek sculpture. Despite the war around them, Jules and Jim worship Catherine incessantly and unfortunately underestimate how unconditional her refusal to choose between them will be. Both uninhibited artists, although inseparable, sharing their time, experiences, and love, they live a ménage à trois that is doomed to failure. The months go by, and Jules marries Catherine before the outbreak of World War I. After the war, Jim visits Catherine and Jules, who live in Austria, and soon realizes that the couple do not love each other any longer. Catherine indulges in an affair with Jim and suddenly expresses a desire to have a child with her former lover. Wise and tactful, Jules accepts the divorce, but Catherine finds out that Jim is still in love with his French mistress, Gilberte (Vanna Urbino), as he rushes back to her while visiting Paris. Jim and Jules decide to go to France, as in the old days, but begin to evaluate their failed romance. Catherine's failure to decide between the two leads to tragic consequences for all three lovers, as she commits suicide with Jim by driving her car off a bridge into the Seine.

With the character of Catherine, a woman entertaining several lovers, and even leaving for weeks at a time in her bemused desire to behave with the free will of a man, the film was indirectly perceived by the new values of the 1960s as a cinematic model of feminist thought and free love. In reality, the film took on a more universal, somber tone in its meditation on the possibilities of love. *Jules and Jim* divulged the restrictions placed on a woman's freedom by men's projection of what perfect love ought to be. Therefore, the feelings of free will and expansiveness of the movie—beautifully filmed by photographer Raoul Coutard—can also be seen as feelings of doubt, enigma, and isolation.

Next to Truffaut and Chabrol, Alain Resnais (b. 1922) is most often associated with the New Wave, with his haunting *Hiroshima, Mon*

Amour (*Hiroshima mon amour*, 1959) released the same year as Truffaut's and Chabrol's first films. However, one should consider him more an author whose talent regularly elicited phenomenal polemics, the same way Michelangelo Antonioni's *L'Avventura* (*L'avventura*, 1960), screened at the Cannes Film Festival, triggered strong protests from conservative spectators, thus setting off one of the most passionate disputes of modern cinema. Among all the young directors of the new cinema, Resnais was one of the very few to be experienced in filmmaking (*Night and Fog*, 1955; see chapter 4). His highly personal films were distinguished by a groundbreaking methodology of style and narrative structure as he applied techniques that entirely transformed the long-established procedures of movie editing.

His first full-length feature, *Hiroshima, Mon Amour,* represented an absolute transformation of cinematographic language. The film took viewers to new intellectual grounds, as the plot must be re-created according to each individual's capacity of imagination and fantasy in the manner of an abstract mobile-art form. Following his contribution to the tenth anniversary of the liberation of the Nazi death camps, Resnais was solicited by Japanese producers who expressed their desire to subsidize a documentary-fiction film to show the world the state of Hiroshima more than a decade after the detonation of the atomic bomb. Resnais was granted total freedom in his interpretation of the original project under the condition that two main protagonists would be Japanese and the other French, with a story line based in Japan as well as in France. As a result, the film was shot in France and Japan (in Hiroshima for exteriors and in Tokyo for interiors). Delayed in its screening due to pusillanimous distributors, however, the film had to wait for the 1959 Cannes Film Festival in the spring to become a cinematic revelation.

Hiroshima, Mon Amour's story line, aside from its Surreal imagery and heavy symbolism, follows a nonlinear sequence of events, using interior monologues, frequent flashbacks and cuts, a voice-over, and parallel tracking shots of Hiroshima and Nevers. The eloquent (but also frustrated) love story takes place in Hiroshima during the summer of 1957. In their hotel room, a French actress, Elle (Emmanuelle Riva), and a Japanese architect, Lui (Eiji Okada), are engaged in a love affair that appears ideal, but the romance is doomed. In fact, this is her last day in Hiroshima; the actress must return to France. On location to play in an antiwar film, she narrates all the scenes she has witnessed during her visit—the pictures in the museum of the bombing victims and the deformed children. But the man keeps reminding her, "Tu n'as rien vu à Hiroshima!" (You didn't see anything in Hiroshima!) In the morning, while he sleeps, she contemplates his features, which remind her of the German soldier she loved (Bernard Fresson), who was killed by a sniper during the first hours of the liberation of Nevers. By indulging in a new love affair, the young actress experiences feelings of betrayal toward her former love interest. Simultaneously, she recalls that the harm of her first love was the source of excruciating physical and psychological pain. This intense flashback triggers a narration about her nightmare of Nevers as she shares with her new companion what she never had with anyone before. The mental wound left on her by the inflicted distress is such that, although tempted thirteen years later into another love affair, the old hallucinations reemerge like a nemesis that precludes her from loving again. She also reveals her imprisonment for having loved a German soldier and the subsequent public humiliation. Her self-conscious parents, ashamed of her betrayal, had kept her confined in her bedroom and the cellar before sending her off to Paris. The day she arrived in Paris was the day the bomb was dropped on Hiroshima. As the meeting intensifies, the story of Nevers resurfaces each time with even more emotion. Now sixteen hours separate them from the actress's departure and serve as the agonizing struggle between the two since the last hours of her stay are going to be an incessant "run-and-chase" through the streets of Hiroshima, its cafés, and its train stations. The architect finds her later on the set of the film that she is working on and takes her back to his apartment, telling her his wife is out of town for the weekend. He tries to persuade her to stay, but she runs away again. Through this poetic evocation of time and memory, an abrupt conclusion stresses the magnitude of human harmony through the metaphor of an interracial romance. At the moment of departure, she finally stares at him and says: "Hiroshima . . . c'est ton nom" (Hiroshima . . . is your name). He replies: "C'est mon nom, oui. Ton nom à toi est Nevers. Nevers en France" (Yes, it is my name. And your name is Nevers. Nevers in France). Both protagonists simultaneously want to interchange Nevers for Hiroshima, but to no avail. Both will, in time, forget each other, but both cities will remain their symbol of love. The viewer is compelled to leave the film in suspense: Is the power of love ruined by humankind's killing of itself? The last shot of the film seems to imply this question.

In most of Resnais's films, the course of events is revealed in quick flashbacks (juxtaposing scenes of tranquility with graphic-documentary footage of the aftermath of the bomb in contemporary Hiroshima), all alluding to the concepts of time and memory. Here, as in Resnais's *Last Year at Marienbad* (1962)—see the discussion below—the conflicts between the central characters' respective pasts, between both concepts of time and identity, and ultimately the dimension of memory in human experience, define the film. With interrogations such as how does man absorb the memory of an event or its oblivion, Resnais

Eiji Okada (Lui) and Emmanuelle Riva (Elle) in Alain Resnais's *Hiroshima, Mon Amour* (*Hiroshima, mon amour*, 1959), (Courtesy of BIFI/© Argos Films).

and scriptwriter Marguerite Duras conceived a multifaceted story using inventive techniques to imagine the unimaginable: a highly referential and symbolic love affair (with a thread of unobtrusive eroticism) that exposed a complex philosophical discourse about the horrors of the atomic bomb and its temporal and eternal consequences. What Resnais sought in *Hiroshina, Mon Amour* was less a reenactment of the experience of the horror of the bomb and its atrocities than a narrative expressing the survivors' nightmare through their emotions and dialogues. And it is precisely those dialogues about love and death—under an existential, almost subliminal form—those multilayered allegories, the nonlinear storytelling techniques and its juxtaposition editing that ultimately contribute to the filmmaker's deliberate compositions (which consequently set Resnais apart from most of his New Wave peers and at the same time confused many filmgoers and commentators upon its first release). By means of intermittent long-tracking shots, enhanced by the musical score of composer Giovanni Fusco (with whom Antonioni also worked), Resnais rearranged the visual enunciation of time, thereby giving new significance to the scenes set in the present. He also used a single voice-over dialogue, which connected the characters to scenes of the past. This particular double use of the tracking shot and commentary–voice-over represented a completely new form of cinematographic expression at the time.

Resnais's "rhetoric" corresponded in both films (*Hiroshima, Mon Amour* and *Last Year at Marienbad*) to a series of assorted fleeting images and allegorical concepts (usually on temporal motifs), as critic James Reid Paris explains: "Here is a cinematic use of the Proustian device of recapturing the past fragmentarily through the operation of involuntary memory by which an object or bodily attitude in the present can accidentally trigger off a recall of past feelings or incidents associated with it."[26] Resnais's new editing style can best be characterized as a sort of cinematographic language punctuated by conflicting combinations, the main impression of which is the interruption and disorientation of the conventional narrative progression. His use of uncompromising angles consisted of numerous swift cuts, sudden close-ups, and war footage interwoven with love scenes, bewildering long takes, and so forth. Aside from the notion of time, the other important theme of the film is memory and doubt as suggestive faculties, which even the most mature and philosophical human being is powerless to control (the stranger himself in *Last Year at Marienbad* was not quite sure of certain details). All perceptions are subjective and suggestive. Every instant of memory experience triggers a multitude of connections to other senses, to previous experiences in memory, and to particular thoughts and emotions. "Resnais," explains Wolfgang

A. Luchting, "does not wish the past to reside in the present, he pushes it back into its own realm. . . . Resnais believes one can keep on living only by forgetting, no matter how important is that which we have experienced and are going to forget—sooner or later."[27] The main goal is to create a new language based on the interrelationship of time, memory, and imagination through a cinematic eye. The scenario at times challenges intellectual acceptance with its numerous riddles of seduction and cryptic dialogues, yet still has enough implications in its emotional momentum to allow each viewer to deduce the central enigma. The audience was offered a puzzle to put together, the numerous pieces of which must be assembled in order to create a complete picture.

Considered either futile exercises of style or, on the contrary, masterful experimentations by contemporary critics, *Hiroshima* and *Last Year at Marienbad* gained strength due to the predominance of a sophisticated montage. For this reason, they are probably the most enigmatic films in motion picture history, as Parker Tyler observes: "Love in the *Marienbad* film becomes absurdly ambiguous through the imagination's illusive faculty, love in the *Hiroshima* film cruelly clears through the same faculty."[28] Interestingly, the repeated denial of the Japanese lover, who reminded the actress that she did not see anything at the Hiroshima museum, indirectly suggests the inability of filmmakers to represent fully the atrocity of the bomb.

For unspecified diplomatic reasons, *Hiroshima* was temporarily barred from participating at the Cannes Film Festival for fear of disconcerting the US delegation at the competition. It was finally presented in the *hors competition* category and managed to win the Prix de la Fédération internationale de la presse cinématographique (the Film Writers Award) at the festival, along with a nomination for Best Original Screenplay (Marguerite Duras) at the 1960 Academy Awards, the award for Best Foreign Film in the 1960 New York Film Critics Awards, and the Best Foreign Film at the British Academy Awards.

A couple of years later, Resnais again contracted stage actors with distinctive photogenic features for his next feature, *Last Year at Marienbad (L'année dernière à Marienbad,* 1961). The film, to an even greater degree than *Hiroshima, Mon Amour,* transfigured viewers' cinematographic reaction and brought a new concept of scenario and image reception to them. Not only did viewers have to supply their imagination, but they also had to apply their faculties of creation to assemble the story. According to Alain Robbe-Grillet, filmgoers, just like readers of the *nouveau roman,* were to find the true reality from the form of the fact and not from its content.[29] Although more rewarding to talk about than to watch, Resnais's *Last Year at Marienbad* was one of the most essential and influential films to emerge from the early 1960s.

This new genre demanded that the viewer become an active observer and contributor in the deciphering process of the story line, and no longer a passive consumer.

The story line became the object of a more scrupulous assessment. It is difficult to outline, since it is the spectator who must bring his or her own sensibilities to the understanding of this cinematic puzzle. Unlike *Hiroshima, Last Year* corresponds to a mental structure, without a frame of reference. This makes the film one of the most enigmatic and atypical movies ever made. During a theatrical show at a luxurious baroque hotel in Germany, an unknown Italian man (Giorgio Albertazzi) is staring at a nameless elegant young woman (Delphine Seyrig). He tries to persuade her that they already met a year ago and were romantically involved, and the love that was born at the time is still very much alive between them. A new universe imprisons the man's mind within the rational limits of reason. At first reticent to the unknown man, the young woman adopts a lighthearted attitude to the new situation, which appears to be more realistic as the minutes go by. Mental icons are intermingled with eloquent shots of the magnificent park, endless halls, and rooms.[30] In a continuum of abstract time, which obscures the representation of the grand hotel, words deeply resonate inside the endless corridors.

Gradually, the suspense unfolds through a world of illusions and tension between the lover, the woman, and the implicit husband (Sacha Pitoeff), creating a mystifying love triangle. The film characters, just as in a game, come to life at the beginning of this enigmatic dream and disappear at the end of the film in austere visual beauty. The long-established pragmatic narration was therefore replaced by an internal unfolding (usually as a voice-over), which joined together images of the real and the imagined. As the camera wanders about the endless corridors of the hotel, the voice-over dialogues convey the idea that the narration is perhaps a rendering of episodes just as they occur inside the suitor's mind. Therefore, the real subject of the film is the imagination, itself a metamorphosis of time. After repeatedly shifting the temporal focus, the narrative settles on Resnais's fertile imagination and mood of abstraction, connecting an implicit tendency to digress with an obsessive power to recollect (also to be found in *Night and Fog* and *Hiroshima, Mon Amour*). The investigation of the love affair from "last year" was one of sincerity in memory and imagination. This retrieved past, however, may only happen to those select few capable of investigating their own lives with sincerity. More difficult for the viewer was the evocation of dreams and the acceptance of a constant new reality. It was a domain where the viewer did not quite belong, and his or her vision, as ephemeral as it may be, must inevitably involve a trompe l'oeil perspective (between real time and psychological time).

In *Last Year at Marienbad,* mental space and mental time were created to involve the presence of dreams and voluntary memory, accompanied by a somber score.[31] Some critics at the time had noted its parody of Hollywood romantic narratives in an attempt to divulge a new form of melodrama, liberated from the yoke of Hollywood. This, by itself, was an underestimation of the original intent and goal of Robbe-Grillet. The content of *Last Year at Marienbad* corresponded to its form and could not otherwise be deciphered, as explained by film critic Jacques-Bernard Brunius: "It happens to be a very unconventional film where the content can only be discovered by consideration of the structure."[32] Since Resnais had signed the petition against the war in Algeria, his film was excluded from the Cannes competition in 1961. Instead, it received the Golden Lion at the 1961 Venice Film Festival, the award for Best Film at the 1962 British Academy Awards, and a nomination for Best Original Screenplay at the 1962 Oscars.

Finished in September 1959, Jean-Luc Godard's (b. 1930) first feature film, *Breathless (A bout de souffle),* was premiered in Paris in March 1960. Following the success of *The Four Hundred Blows,* it gained an enormous triumph both with critics and at the box office, and instantly became a seminal film in French cinema. Taking many of its cinematic references from American cinema, particularly with its amicable allusions to Humphrey Bogart's style (as Jean-Paul Belmondo reminded viewers of Bogart with his use of hat and cigarettes), its jagged editing and its overall romantic and *cinéphile* approach to filmmaking were far from the usual Hollywood film noir. With its temperamental and impulsive lines, often commanded by improvisation, the film, written by Godard from a subject by François Truffaut, was essentially about vulnerability, premonition, betrayal, and ultimately death.

Michel Poiccard (Jean-Paul Belmondo)[33] a small-time thief without scruples, is wanted for the murder of a police officer following a car theft in Marseille. On the run, he arrives in Paris, where he is supposed to collect money for an undisclosed job. He then meets his friend Patricia Franchini (Jean Seberg), a young American woman who sells the *New York Herald Tribune* on the Champs-Elysées. He is in love and wants to take her to Rome. Their relationship develops as she reveals to Michel that she is pregnant. Once again, Michel steals a car to go for his suspicious appointment, but by now his picture has been plastered on the front pages of the local newspapers. While the police are closing in, agents pressure Patricia to reveal Michel's hideout. Ultimately, she turns him in, and while running away, Michel is shot in the back. Reminiscent of the final scene of *Port of Shadows,* the film ends with a striking dialogue as Michel agonizes in the middle of the street:

MICHEL:	*C'est vraiment dégueulasse!* (It's truly disgusting!)
PATRICIA:	*Qu'est-ce qu'il a dit?* (What was he saying?)
POLICE OFFICER:	*Il a dit: vous êtes vraiment une dégueulasse.* (He just said: You're really a bitch.)
PATRICIA (staring at the CAMERA):	*Qu'est-ce que c'est: dégueulasse?* (What does it mean?)

Along with Chabrol's *Bitter Reunion* and Truffaut's *The Four Hundred Blows*, *Breathless* stands as a landmark of creativity. Once again, the director is quintessentially the author of the project. Godard also broke new ground with innovative techniques such as handheld camera work, willfully restless jump cuts, and outdoor shooting in natural light with the sound postsynchronized, as well as improvised dialogue, loose narrative form, and references to the history of cinema (especially American thrillers). Because the film was directed without a definite script, and because Godard himself often outlined and altered the dialogue in the course of a take, Belmondo and the other actors were on occasion expected to improvise their lines. This could explain the long takes, inconsequential gestures, and striking exchanges.

The restless portrayal of Michel (which was Jean-Paul Belmondo's first significant role), who is living on the edge on a daily basis, reflected the state of mind of those troubled days and the moral, political, and social disorder characterized by them (characters and extras frequently stared directly into the camera). The sudden shifts in Michel's voice and intonation often communicated the necessary attentiveness that anything could happen at any time. During the long tracking shots, the camera technician was sometimes pushed around in a wheelchair to follow the actors down the street. The editing contributed to the groundbreaking format of the film, especially the countless use of jump cuts that connect two shots of the same subject with a striking image skip on the screen.

Often considered the most innovative film of the New Wave, somewhere between a replication and an impersonation of American film noir, *Breathless* offered a thoughtful homage to contemporary directors of film noir genre, American pop culture, and contemporary art. *Breathless* garnered the award for Best Direction at the 1960 Berlin International Film Festival and the Jean Vigo Prize.[34]

Godard's next significant success, entitled *Contempt* (*Le mépris,* 1963), was an adaptation of Alberto Moravia's 1954 psychological novel, a modern tragedy based on a misunderstanding but ultimately a movie about filmmaking. Starting from a conventional story as an initial frame within which Godard could maneuver and exhibit his own personality, the protagonists were shown secluded, vulnerable, and

Jean-Paul Belmondo (Michel) and Jean Seberg (Patricia) in Jean-Luc Godard's *Breathless* (*A bout de souffle*, 1959), (Photo courtesy of the Museum of Modern Art/Film Stills Archive/© Studio Canal).

ultimately betrayed by their closest peers in a society degraded by the power of money and the quest for lust.

Set in Rome, the film revolves around the disintegrating relationship of a young couple and their emotional vicissitudes as they reach the point of no return. Paul Javal (Michel Piccoli),[35] a talented film scenarist, is asked to participate in the making of the latest film of Fritz Lang (playing himself), an adaptation of *The Odyssey*. Lang's project is to maintain the story within a literary tradition, whereas American producer Jeremy Prokosch (Jack Palance) wants just the opposite, looking principally for a commercial success. After formal presentations, Prokosch asks Paul and his wife, Camille (Brigitte Bardot), to come to Capri to be on the set of the film. Camille, after being humiliated by the lack of protection from her husband, later cedes to temptation. After a series of emotional discontents, her frustration presses her to leave with Jeremy, abandoning her husband on the set, until both lovers find death in a fatal car accident. The Italian co-producer, Carlo Ponti, wanted Sophia Loren and Marcello Mastroianni, but ultimately Bardot and Piccoli pulled off the deal. Furthermore, Ponti asked Godard to add an erotic episode once the film was finished, which he did, and it is still today one of the most memorable scenes of the film.

The restrained dialogue—one of the most revealing of the spirit of the times—along with the convulsive attitudes of Camille, gives *Contempt* its strength and illustrates the eternal conflict between artistic expression and commercialization:

> CAMILLE: Do you like my eyes?
> PAUL: Yes.
> CAMILLE: Do you like my mouth?
> PAUL: Yes.
> CAMILLE: Do you like my breasts?
> PAUL: Yes.
> CAMILLE: Do you like my ass?
> PAUL: Yes.
> CAMILLE: So you love me, then?
> PAUL: Yes.[36]

Less concerned with character and story than with ideas and analysis of social issues, Godard's movies were also often misunderstood by audiences. From the inside, *Contempt* was about a certain death of a certain type of filmmaking: high-budget, conservative motion pictures, a sort of analytical deliberation on the hegemonic Hollywood institution. Another of Godard's artistic trademarks was the presence of long tracking shots accompanied with a quivering camera. A device for some or discovery for others, it served the purpose of emphasizing the fiction-documentary factor or communicating the apprehension of the personages by replicating actual movements more truthfully than could be produced by the steady motion of much heavier equipment. Besides representing sequences in self-effacing or conspicuous light, Godard's montage procedures united sequences into larger sections and, as a final product, corresponded to a unique structure of narrative rhetoric. In fact, not much consequence was given to timing promptness and the actual duration of the takes since the subsequent montage was regularly a matter of mid-scene cutting sessions. From the outside, *Contempt* was an introspective assessment of the contemporary filmmaker's standpoint in a resurging commercial cinema that ultimately brought a critical awareness of the medium itself. (Godard was personally challenged by similar circumstances since Carlo Ponti had granted Godard the largest budget of his career, compelling him to direct a star of Bardot's importance for the first time. This may explain why *Contempt* was far from being Godard's best movie.)

One of the most interesting auteur filmmakers is Agnès Varda (b. 1928), the first woman in French film history to direct a full-length film entirely and alone. Prior to her first feature, *La pointe courte* (1954), Varda had never worked in the film industry and confessed to having barely seen a handful of films. A photographer at the TNP (Théâtre national populaire), working with Jean Vilar from 1948 until 1960, Varda used the medium to express the existential dimension of the chronicle, often filled by the obsession of time. Her acute sense of social observation and her intellect draw many obvious comparisons to Alain Resnais.

In 1962, Varda wrote and directed her masterpiece, *Cléo from 5 to 7* (*Cléo de 5 à 7*), presented in competition at the 1962 Cannes Film Festival. The film was a time capsule of Paris in the early 1960s. Its wide range of inventive techniques and unprompted, authentic, almost documentary style seized the new sense of modern life in Paris.

Cléo Victoire (Corinne Marchand), a trendy Parisian pop singer on the decline, is awaiting the results of a test for cancer. While spending two frantic hours contemplating doom, she must face the most difficult moments of her existence. The results of the test, which undoubtedly will come as an unsympathetic verdict, are not available until seven that evening. Dreadfully superstitious by nature, Cléo immediately consults a fortune-teller, who, using tarot cards, announces a bleak future. Cléo must draw nine cards, three for each marker of time: past, present, and future. The cards disclose the forces of evil and an already instigated fight, a disease in all probability. As far as her future goes, there seems to be no wedding in sight, just the profile of an impending voyage or departure. Confused, the fortune teller asks Cléo to draw four more cards to fathom the future, but this time one of them is the card of Death itself. The fortune-teller, however, does mention a young man, quite talkative, who may very well be a surprise in Cléo's life after all. The plot is in real time: the couple of hours of agony that constitute the entire story line—the total running time is actually ninety minutes—ultimately opens up the protagonist to a new rapport with friendship and love, life and death.

Throughout the tribulations of the young artist, Varda translated into visual impressions the numerous torments of her character. The camera did not desert Cléo's footsteps for the entire time as she runs away from death.

To ease her disquiet, Cléo buys herself a hat, then decides to rush home and receives, as the diva she really is, a visit from her older wealthy lover (José Luis de Villalonga) in her lavish white Parisian apartment. Later, her musician and songwriter come to review some new material. A series of unsolicited practical jokes forces her to walk out on them, to desperately put her worries out of her mind. She once again wanders the streets of Paris, walking through a park, watching a silent film short, and listening to the news on a taxi radio. In a park she meets the stranger announced by the fortune-teller, a young soldier named Antoine (Antoine Bourseiller), who is on leave from the war in Algeria. He approaches her, and soon in the conversation she confesses:

CLÉO: Ah, men, it's not the same. They would wait for any women. They approach them and then they talk to them. Usually, I don't answer, but this time I forgot. My mind was somewhere else. Plus, you look so peaceful.
ANTOINE: I am on leave.
CLÉO: And this uniform?
ANTOINE: You see, I am half on leave. Half gone, so to speak. I'm leaving tonight. Yes, tonight it's over. I had three weeks, but I did nothing, it was too short. I like talking with you. Are you married?[37]

Unfortunately, Antoine reminds her that the date is June 21, which also happens to be the longest day of the year, and at the same time the beginning of shortening days as well as the first day of the astrological sign of Cancer. Although this sudden revelation comes as a shock to Cléo, the pair quickly befriend each other, and Antoine, aware of Cléo's anguish, agrees to accompany her to the hospital to help her. At this moment, Cléo understands that Antoine can be considered her own alter ego before Death, since he is only hours away from what could be his fatal destiny as he departs for the front.

ANTOINE: For me, it's more the thought of dying for nothing that saddens me. It's sad to give your life for war. I'd rather give it for a woman, to die of love.
CLÉO: Have you ever been in love?
ANTOINE: Oh yes, many times, but not as much as I wanted, because of girls, you know how they are. They're in love, and then suddenly they love to be loved. They are afraid of everything, to commit, to lose something. Their body is like a toy, it's not their life. So, me too I stop and take a break. Sorry to tell you all this, I don't even know you.[38]

After a long bus ride through the streets of Paris, Cléo finds the comfort she needs to while away the time and experience a new kind of hope. While both ride at the back of the bus toward the hospital for the test results, Antoine snatches a flower and offers it to Cléo. They stare at each other while the bus nears its final destination. At

Corinne Marchand (Cléo) and Antoine Bourseiller (Antoine) in Agnès Varda's *Cléo from 5 to 7* (*Cléo de 5 à 7*, 1962), (Courtesy Ciné Tamaris).

the hospital, the doctor lets Cléo know that indeed she will have to go through treatments. As far as the nature of the cancer goes, the audience is not told.

The actual time of the film corresponds to the time of the story. However the shooting, arranged chronologically in thirteen chapters, lasted two months. (Varda's directorial style is characterized by an obvious penchant for linking elements in a scene via jump cuts.) In an emblematic New Wave tactic, Varda combined any approach that suited her needs: subjective point-of-view shots, a soundtrack that captured secondary characters' conversations, an open ending with the denouement left unsettled, and an earnest desire to let the course of suggestion and ambiguity became part of the viewing. The early scenes with Cléo persuasively establish the main character, and clarify the nature of her despair, as Varda conjures up a variety of current tragedies (for example, events in Algeria) that gradually offer the spectator a new sense of perspective. Ultimately, the young pop singer stops playing the roles her admirers expect of her, when she finds out about the nature of her cancer and begins to live realistically: "Cléo is shown trapped, reflected in the image construction of others who narrate her. This is an image construction in which she in fact colludes by talking about herself in the same terms and by her constant self-referentiality through mirrors. By the end of the film, however, she asserts herself and abandons the rhetoric of both language and reflection that would fix her by leaving behind those who narrate her through their portraits of her."[39] One of the greatest thematic renditions of the film is the gripping representation of a female protagonist whose identity is epitomized by a simple visual icon perceived by others (men staring at her because of the popularity of her songs). The narrative represents Cléo's pursuit of her real individuality, eventually to find her real self despite the adversity of her state.

In a film full of extended silences, one aspect rings with significance: the deliverance from fear. *Cléo from 5 to 7*'s artistic tone noticeably underscored the visual representation, since the screenplay was frequently organized more as a visual inventiveness than as a conventional dramatic composition. The film also deconstructs the traditional sequence of events, which had never been contested since the invention of motion pictures, and fashioned a new cinema, with a kind of self-referential critical awareness of the medium itself. Varda found the perfect equilibrium between the spoken word and the power of the image, making her one of the top directors of the 1960s generation. (In 1964, Varda directed *Le Bonheur/Happiness,* an abstract and compelling representation of happiness, which turned out to be her most controversial film.)

Cléo from 5 to 7 is accompanied by Michel Legrand's memorable composition. Son of music composer and conductor Raymond Legrand, Michel (b. 1932) secured national fame with his work in French film. With the rise of the New Wave, particularly his work in Jacques Demy's *Lola* (*Lola,* 1961), Legrand became one of the most popular film composers of the second half of the twentieth century. In the field of musicals, an area to which the French never much contributed, he flawlessly arranged the dialogues of *The Umbrella of Cherbourg* (*Les parapluies de Cherbourg,* 1964), as well as those of *The Young Girls of Rochefort* (*Les demoiselles de Rochefort,* 1967). But Legrand's greatest contributions were his brilliant orchestral compositions for Demy's *Bay of the Angels* (*La baie des anges,* 1963) and *Cléo from 5 to 7,* (in which he appeared as Cléo's accompanist). Impressed by Legrand's personal style, which was deeply influenced by jazz expressions of musical elegance and eloquence, American filmmakers began to solicit him for movies—including Joseph Losey's *The Go-between* (1971); Norman Jewison's *The Thomas Crown Affair* (1968), for which he received an Oscar nomination for Best Original Musical Score; and Robert Mulligan's *Summer of '42* (1971), which gave him the Oscar for Best Original Dramatic Score.

THE RETURN OF COMMERCIAL MOVIE SUCCESSES

Around 1965, the French New Wave, suffused by the momentum of aesthetic reaction against the *tradition de qualité,* lost ground after several years of transformation. This significant deceleration of the free artistic spirit occurred with the return of the French public's interest in big commercial productions (especially when filmed in color and Cinemascope), a sort of second wind for the French cinema of *qualité,* all of a sudden rejuvenated with big economical and technical means. After the mid-1960s, the fundamental experimentations of the New Wave slowly began to be incorporated into more "regular" productions, including some commercially oriented movies, each usually gathering in one feature film several of the most popular actors of the time. Examples include Georges Lautner's *Monsieur Gangster* (*Les tontons flingueurs,* 1963), starring Lino Ventura, Bernard Blier, Francis Blanche, and Jean Lefèbvre; Gilles Grangier's *The Old Guard* (*Les vieux de la vieille,* 1960), with Jean Gabin, Pierre Fresnay, and Noël-Noël; Henri Verneuil's *The Sicilian Clan* (*Le clan des Siciliens,* 1969), with Jean Gabin, Alain Delon, and Lino Ventura; Gérard Oury's *The Brain* (*Le cerveau,* 1968), with Jean-Paul Belmondo and Bourvil; and Claude Lelouch's *A Man and a Woman* (*Un homme et une femme,* 1966), with Anouck Aimée and Jean-Louis Trintignant.

Directors like Claude Lelouch (b. 1937) diverged in style and developed a distinct cinematic image as other filmmakers, like François Truffaut, remained more identifiable in their films (and also still commercially successful). This was unlike Jean-Luc Godard, who maintained an increasingly political flavor in his direction. Inspired by commercial ads as an art form and format, *l'image pour l'image,* the cinema of Claude Lelouch can be defined in terms of a free technique associated with a natural style.

Lelouch's most famous film, *A Man and a Woman,* incorporated several innovations inaugurated by the New Wave: photographic aesthetics, a free camera motion, spectacular view angle, intervention in the speed of the film, fluidity, and a spontaneity in keeping with the life and character of the protagonist. Lelouch supplemented a multifaceted soundtrack that combined different dialogues, sometimes spoken concurrently with the music, into an inventive assembly. The chief operator (Claude Lelouch himself) also provided a mode to light sets by strengthening the meaning or implication of a given shot or scene. For Lelouch, film composition was to be cinematic rather than static. The composition within any take or sequence was less imperative than the relationship of that sequence to those that preceded and followed it. In 1966, when the Cannes Film Festival opened, Claude Lelouch was still virtually unknown. With the awarding of the Palme d'or, he gained recognition, and *A Man and a Woman* became one of the most prominent productions of the decade outside the French market.

This flawless love story between a man and a woman, despite their past wounds, took the viewer through several levels of enchanted *roman populaire*. Jean-Louis Trintignant, as a race car driver, and Anouk Aimée, as a scriptwriter, are haunted by the memory of their respective lost loves (both are widowed). The music score became one of the most emblematic of the 1960s, (especially at the time of the popular "scopitones," the ancestor of the video clips) with its catchy tune from Francis Lai sung by Pierre Barouh and Nicole Croisille.

Lelouch's countless technical abilities rapidly combined to become his own personal style, recognizable in the most daring projects throughout the 1970s and 1980s. Although using movement and constant hand cameras, he never quite fit into the category of New Wave directors since his thematic approach was not utterly part of a reaction. Lelouch initiated a long series of feature films, all highly praised for the flamboyance of his improvisatory filmmaking procedures, the techniques of which alternatively scrutinized reality or presented his own idiosyncratic visualization of it (ultimately interconnecting the two to create a uniquely abstract effect).

Although unremittingly attacked by the New Wave, commercial cinema reemerged in the 1960s with the same genres and predominance for literary adaptations. On the screen, Georges Simenon remained the favorite for thriller movies now interpreted by Jean Gabin. One of the countless examples of popular gangster movie revivals was *Any Number Can Win* (*Mélodie en sous-sol,* 1963) by Henri Verneuil (1920–2002), which was the very first collaboration between Alain Delon and Jean Gabin (they would renew the experience in *The Sicilian Clan,* again directed by Verneuil).

Adapted from John Trinian's novel *The Big Grab,* the story begins with the release of professional gangster Charles (Jean Gabin) from the penitentiary. Once at home, where his wife Ginette (Viviane Romance),[40] has been waiting for his return, his new ambition is indeed quite ambitious: Cannes's Palm Beach Casino. Charles has already designated two accomplices, Francis Verlot (Alain Delon), a young, idle delinquent whom he met in prison, and his brother-in-law, Louis (Maurice Biraud), a mechanic who will serve as chauffeur during the operation. While in Cannes, Charles organizes the robbery and begins to familiarize himself with the schedule and every move of Mr. Grimp, chief accountant of the casino. The turnover of each night is placed in a safe in the basement of the casino. Francis's mission is to gain access to the backstage of the music hall. For this, he must seduce one of the young dancers in order to enter the theater freely. He will then have to scale the rooftop, get into the air vent in order to make his way

Jean Gabin (Charles) in Henri Verneuil's *Any Number Can Win* (*Mélodie en sous-sol,* 1963), (Courtesy of BIFI/© Roissy Films).

down to the basement level without making any noise. However, the young gangster does not turn out to be as skilled as planned. He wanders aimlessly between the rich and famous customers and ends up being photographed by reporters. Eventually, Francis reaches the basement and places himself on top of the elevator. When the accountant comes out he jumps into the elevator and pointing his gun at them, gets the money, and takes off. The next day, the newspapers have front page photos showing customers gambling at the casino a few hours before the holdup. In one photo, one can clearly see Francis in the background. In a panic, the gangsters must leave immediately. They take two bags containing the loot across the hotel swimming pool area, where at that moment the police are conducting their investigation. The police get so close to Francis that he is forced to discretely release the bags into the pool to avoid drawing attention. The result is just the opposite; the bank notes begin to float out of the bag and fill the entire pool.

With more than 500,000 tickets sold in Paris during its first week, the commercial success of *Any Number Can Win* was guaranteed as it secured a selection in the 1964 Cannes Film Festival. The scenario by Albert Simonin, with dialogue by Michel Audiard (1920–85), included such memorable lines as Jean Gabin's explanation of the success of the future robbery: "Dans les situations critiques, quand on parle avec un calibre bien en pogne, personne ne conteste plus. Y'a des statistiques là-dessus,"[41] Francis's description of the honesty of his brother-in-law: "Louis? Il est d'une honnêteté monstrueuse, un vrai pervers, enfin je veux dire . . . il n'a jamais eu une contredanse quoi."[42] Audiard's other commercial successes included *The Magnificent Tramp* (*Archimède, le clochard*, 1959), *The Old Guard, The Counterfeiters of Paris* (*Le cave se rebiffe*, 1961), *A Monkey in Winter* (*Un singe en hiver*, 1962), *The Gentleman from Epsom* (*Le gentleman d'Epsom*, 1962), *Monsieur Gangster, 100, 000 Dollars au soleil* (*Cent mille dollars au soleil*, 1963), *The Professional* (*Le professionnel*, 1981), and *Under Suspicion* (*Garde à vue*, 1981).

The return of the *tradition de qualité* was also due to the solid performances of several box office hit comedies. French comedies of the 1960s, such as Phillipe de Broca's *That Man from Rio* (*L'homme de Rio*, 1963) and *Chinese Adventures in China* (*Les tribulations d'un Chinois en Chine*, 1965), and Edouard Molinaro's *Oscar* (*Oscar*, 1967), were more than ever based on the world of vaudeville. The phrase *cinéma de boulevard* was even created during the return of the popular comedy. One of the most spectacular comic outbreaks was the case of comedian Louis de Funès (1914–83), who benefited from his association with the other great comedian of the time, Bourvil (1917–70) (de Funès appeared as Jambier, the crooked butcher, in Claude Autant-Lara's *Four Full Bags/La traversée de Paris*, 1956, which starred Bourvil). Having played innumerable supporting roles during the 1950s in French and Italian films, de Funès was finally able to see his career rewarded with Gérard Oury's *The Sucker* (*Le corniaud*, 1965). On stage, de Funès gained additional fame for his work in the comedy *Oscar* (1967), which was eventually adapted to the screen from Claude Magnier's play, *Oscar* (1958). Following these double successes, he appeared in commercial hits such as Oury's *Delusions of Grandeur* (*La folie des grandeurs*, 1971) and *The Adventures of Rabbi Jacob* (*Les aventures de Rabbi Jacob*, 1973), Claude Zidi's *The Wing or the Thigh* (*L'aile ou la cuisse*, 1976), and Jean Girault's *The Miser* (*L'avare*, 1979) and *La soupe aux choux* (1981). In 1965, *Le corniaud* created the biggest box office revenue since Henri Verneuil's comedy *The Cow and I* (*La vache et le prisonnier*, 1959).

In *Le corniaud*, Antoine Maréchal (Bourvil) gets involved on his way to Italy in a car accident with a rich and obnoxious businessman, Saroyan (de Funès), owner of a large import company, who invites

Louis de Funès (Saroyan) and Bourvil (Maréchal) in Gérard Oury's *The Sucker* (*Le corniaud*, 1965), (Courtesy of BIFI).

Louis de Funès (Stanislas) and Bourvil (Augustin) in Gérard Oury's *Don't Look We're Being Shot At* (*La grande vadrouille*, 1966), (Courtesy of BIFI).

Maréchal to his office the next day to settle the matter. Indeed, to assuage Maréchal's troubles (he has lost his Citroën 2 C.V.),[43] Saroyan offers Maréchal a one-way plane ticket from Paris to Naples on the condition that, for the return, Maréchal would drive Saroyan's Cadillac to Bordeaux. In reality, Saroyan is a gangster trying to smuggle drugs and diamonds into France inside his luxury car. He and his accomplices, as well as a rival gang, follow the car at a distance, while Maréchal, too busy enjoying Italy and its young female hitchhikers, does not bother to look back as an extravagant gangster chase rages behind him. After innumerable escapades, Maréchal finally arrives in Bordeaux with the Cadillac in one piece, outsmarting the gangsters who would exploit him. The quality of the script, the liveliness of the dialogue, the frequency of the gags, and the hilarious confrontations between the honest Mr. Nice and the cunning manipulator made this burlesque farce one of the most popular with French audiences.

Following the national success of *The Sucker,* Oury once again teamed Bourvil and de Funès in another commercial coup, *Don't Look Now We're Being Shot At* (*La grande vadrouille,* 1966). The story takes place during the Nazi Occupation, when an English fighter plane is shot down over Paris. The three parachuted fliers land in three different places. While German police pursue them, Stanislas (Louis de Funès) and Augustin (Bourvil) accomplish feats of skill to conceal the Englishmen. After numerous adventures, they decide to smuggle the three Englishmen out of the occupied zone, at times disguised as German soldiers. With the help of a glider, they eventually pass the frontier. To this day, *Don't Look Now* remains the most popular movie in French film history, with more than seventeen million spectators (not including its innumerable reruns on television). The success of the film was due mainly to the success of *The Sucker* the preceding year and the association of two radically different comic types, Bourvil and de Funès, who were the most popular comic actors in France at the time.

Chapter 6
French Cinema of the 1970s

Numerous film critics and historians have maintained that French cinema after 1968 was visually overpowered by a nostalgia for the New Wave and the veneration that movement elicited from the media. The visual prominence of the New Wave and the revelations it brought to world cinema were a landmark in modern filmmaking. Indeed, for the new filmmakers of the 1970s, taking over its legacy was a difficult task. The three major movements which occurred during the post-1968 era can be described as follows: first, the coming of a brand-new genre, labeled the "political thriller," which gradually began to replace conventional *polars* (crime movies) born three decades earlier; second, the emergence of newcomers such as Bertrand Tavernier and Bertrand Blier, who gave a fresh start to a new generation of young filmmakers (many of whom are still active in film production today);[1] and third, the ascension of humanist film directors such as François Truffaut, Eric Rohmer, and Claude Sautet, whose successful rendition of one of the most prolific periods in film history incorporated powerful reflections of the medium itself. Because the 1970s were characterized by an unprecedented liberalist wave (1974 represented the last year for cinematographic censorship), three decades later many film productions of that period appear forever modern, relevant, and truthful in their representation of the spirit of the times.

Aside from mainstream cinema, the development of the erotic and pornographic film industry characterized a cultural transformation in the post-'68 era. The last bastions of "correctness" and conservative values ceased to be obstacles to physical representations of the body as well as the mental dimension of sexuality. Born with the events of the late 1960s, one of the most popular and powerful slogans associated with the concept of freedom was *Faites l'amour, pas la guerre* (Make love, not war), which indirectly contributed to the gradual rise of erotic[2] filmmaking (Just Jaeckin's *Emmanuelle*[3] in 1974 initiated a series of soft-core porn movies known as "Emmanuelle films," starring Sylvia Kristel).[4] Although already present during the initial years of cinema as a form of entertainment, erotic and pornographic film productions[5] increased dramatically and developed as a money-making industry in the mid-1970s. This trend, evolving apart from mainstream cinema, serves as a reminder that the real era of liberalism started in the 1970s and not in the 1980s. The phenomenally successful trend of liberal and progressive movies of this period can be considered the direct outcome of a social and political sea change in attitudes toward sex and other taboo topics. (Some film historians argue that it was the consequence of an ill-fated reaction toward a society in decline, the main escape of which was a creation of artificial desire.)

MAY '68 AND AFTER: A NEW CULTURAL ERA

The events of May 1968 were a turning point in French history. On May 3, 1968, police forcefully evacuated more than 500 striking students who were at the time occupying the Sorbonne. On May 13, workers joined students in the protest with a revealing slogan undeniably capturing the spirit of the times: *Dix ans, ça suffit* (Ten years are enough). For many, it was the beginning of a new era, culturally, socially, and politically. After an entire month of general strikes, the Agreements of Grenelle were signed by Premier Georges Pompidou, who consented to raise the minimum wage by 35 percent: life could start anew. On May 30, close to a million Parisians walked down the Champs-Elysées in support of Charles de Gaulle's regime and indirectly heralded a large right-wing victory in the coming elections. Although de Gaulle had dissolved the National Assembly, the conservative majority not only claimed victory at the legislative election in June 1968 but also gained an unanticipated absolute majority. However, the signs of rejuvenation within French society corresponded to the end of the Gaullist era.

Following the rejection of his referendum for regional reorganization, de Gaulle resigned in April 1969. From that moment, many political observers anticipated that the Fifth Republic would quickly disintegrate since the configuration of the presidency had been tailor-made for de Gaulle. Nevertheless, after de Gaulle's death on November 10, 1970, Georges Pompidou replaced the former president with no trouble at all, despite the oil crisis of 1973 that was sparked by the Arab-Israeli conflict. The unexpected death of Pompidou in 1974 corresponded to the end of a period commonly called the Trente glorieuses (the Thriving Thirty).

The conservative Valéry Giscard d'Estaing, Pompidou's former finance minister, was elected president in 1974, defeating Socialist leader François Mitterrand in a close election. For the first time since World War II, industrial production began to decelerate, unemployment suddenly became a growing political and social issue, and inflation became widespread. The new government, led by the young president, carried out a reform program that immediately favored young voters; it changed the voting age to eighteen and partially legalized abortion. Meanwhile, Mitterrand, who had already lost two presidential elections (1965 against de Gaulle and 1974 against Giscard d'Estaing), persuaded the Communists to merge with the Socialists in drafting what was to be called *le programe commun*, a project that united the parties in future elections and in an eventual coalition government. It quickly occurred to political observers that the Socialists had made considerable improvements at the Communist Party's expense, and consequently many Communist leaders felt left behind in the "common program." The repudiation of the agreement came at the worst moment for the Left since the dissensions enabled conservative forces to keep a majority in the National Assembly in the 1978 legislative elections. On the conservative side, political dissension also existed, as Prime Minister Jacques Chirac resigned in 1976 from his position to create a new Gaullist party called the Rassemblement pour la République (RPR), appointing himself its general secretary. Mitterrand's victory in the presidential elections on May 10, 1981, broke new ground in the country's political landscape and terminated a long and eventful decade, which began and ended with cultural euphoria. In a way, the 1970s were born in the events of May '68 and can be seen today as a cultural benchmark in French history; the decade ended in May 1981, which can be considered one of the major political landmarks of twentieth-century French history.

The 1970s can best be described as one of the most sensitive periods, reflecting the anger and impatience of the post-'68 era.[6] Outside the political realm, the 1970s were an extremely prolific period in French cultural history (as seen in the 1977 inauguration of the Centre Georges-Pompidou, most commonly called Beaubourg). The explosion of new values infiltrated many different sectors of society such as social laws, trade unions, language, education, sexuality, and family values.

In 1972, one of the most significant trials of the century was at the center of a media storm, as judiciary, political, and medical institutions were vehemently contested. Divorce (by mutual consent) was finally authorized by law, and the controversial Veil Law was passed, which considerably improved access to birth control for women and legalized abortion.

This was a prolific time for women, particularly in the film industry. Women could now advance in a profession that had been heavily influenced and controlled by men. As film historian Susan Hayward stated, "The improvement of women's legal status and the legalisation of abortion certainly reflected Giscard's heeding of the claims of the women's movement in France which post-1968 had become extremely vocal and consolidated in its demands. Directly within cinema there is a manifest attestation to the presence of women on a political front by the greatly increased number of women making feature films, particularly in the second half of the decade. During the whole of the decade, some thirty-seven women filmmakers made their first feature films."[7] The 1970s also witnessed the first MLF (Mouvement de libération des femmes, equivalent to the American National Organization for Women) demonstrations.

In literature, Jean-Paul Sartre's ideas, although no longer as highly regarded by French intellectuals, allowed him to remain hugely popular among the young, the working class, leftist intellectuals, and especially the media.[8] Paradoxical as it may seem, Sartre's own persona surpassed his ideas. Structuralism, led by philosophers Jacques Derrida and Michel Foucault and psychoanalyst Jacques Lacan, became the prevailing intellectual school in France and abroad. It gradually resulted in doctrines designated as "poststructuralist." In addition to new intellectual and philosophical concepts, May '68 triggered an awareness of third world problems, anticapitalistic and anti-American points of view, the beginning of ecological alertness, and the development of environmental organizations (especially those against nuclear-power plants, such as in the Larzac region).

The post-'68 era allowed the French to take advantage of the return of consumerism generated by a leisure society (by the end of Pompidou's term, two-thirds of French families owned an automobile).[9] An authentic national transportation network became a reality on October 29, 1970, with the inauguration of the long-awaited first interstate, labeled Autoroute du Sud Lille–Marseille. More than three decades after the first paid vacation granted by the Popular Front in 1936, which sent thousands of French workers to discover the countryside, French vacationers were able to enter the modern age of highway travel. But a thriving economy (unemployment rarely exceeded more than two percent) came to a screeching halt in France with the first oil crisis[10] in 1973. If the previous decade was dominated by economic prosperity and surplus, the new one is remembered for the international economic problems that were triggered by oil crises, the beginning of gradual and massive unemployment, and the paradoxical but insidious growth of inflation.

ECONOMIC ASSESSMENT OF FRENCH CINEMA

In May 1968, the professionals of the French film industry organized themselves under the title Etats généraux du cinéma (General Estates of Cinema), a designation reminiscent of the idealistic pre-revolutionary concept intended to herald major political and economic reforms. A few years later, the first signs of change in film productions became noticeable. In addition, the CNC (Centre National de la Cinématographie), on which authorization visas as well as censorship committees depended, centralized all cinematographic activities and productions around the Office radio-télévision française (ORTF). The conservative state monopoly, which served as a direct division of the government to determine the visual culture for the nation, had begun to modernize its policies. However, French television began its race for power as the ORTF was split into four different companies TF1, Antenne 2, FR3, and the SFP (Société française de production)—all of which later became major partners in film production.[11] During the second part of the decade, the four companies steadily increased their activities in film as the number of movies screened on national television as well as films made for television grew annually.

The *avances sur recettes* (financial advances) program continued to grant loans to producers of full-length feature films based on screenplays. After a film generated profits, the loan was to be paid back directly to the state. This financial aid was usually earmarked for newcomers to the film industry, who without this particular type of loan did not have the funds to complete their first assignments. One of the changes in French cinema in the new decade was the emergence of different types of financial sources. No longer waiting for financial assistance from large film companies, many young directors (as well as other auteurs) financed feature films (for example, Robert Bresson's *The Devil Probably/Le Diable probablement,* 1977) with the assistance of corporations, such as smaller film production companies, and eventually French television itself.

One of the very first agreements between French television and the film industry was to establish the feasibility of their future cohabitation within the so-called PAF (Paysage audiovisual français, the authority in charge of official statistics for the film and audiovisual industries). With a maximum of 10 percent of the entire broadcast dedicated to film projections (half of the 500 films broadcast were to be French productions), the French film industry halted the decline in production, especially in comparison to Italy and England in particular. However, the situation was far from economically secure for new producers and filmmakers. Although at first appearing to be a fearful competitor of the film industry, French television contributed in a not negligible way to the resuscitation of the *cinéphilie*[12] movement. In 1971, the first *ciné-club* was created on channel Antenne 2, which was followed in 1973 by an analogous program entitled "Cinéma de minuit" on FR3. Each week, both programs screened French film classics and other world masterpieces. The majority of viewers were new, having never set foot in a *ciné-club*.[13] In addition to the late night shows, French television, with the assistance of advertising tycoon Georges Cravenne and under the presidency of Jean Gabin, started to broadcast in February 1976 the newly formed French Academy Awards ceremony, created for the occasion, called the Césars (Académie des arts et techniques du cinéma).[14] Similar to its American counterpart, the French Academy Awards ceremony attracted record audiences and undeniably served as a great commercial opportunity for the industry.

If the means of production underwent many changes, the distribution networks remained unaffected in their organization. By the 1970s, most movie theaters in France were located within city limits and were owned by large distribution companies. Beginning in the early 1970s, many of the older theaters began to be divided into two or more smaller theaters because of decreasing attendance (an indirect cause of free television as a new device for home entertainment). The number of large theaters, which had been extremely popular during the postwar era, decreased dramatically and left the space wide open for smaller-size theaters. For exhibitors, the advantage of smaller auditoriums was the speedier rotation of feature films, as opposed to larger theaters, which were obligated to screen films for a longer period of time. The declining situation was all the more difficult to manage now that French audiences attended movies an average of a couple of times a year as opposed to the immediate postwar era, which experienced at least three times more attendance. When theater viewership slowly began to resume in the mid-1980s, multiplexes became the standard and quickly expanded in urban and suburban shopping malls. As far as the exhibition companies were concerned, the situation in the early 1970s became alarming. Despite the huge changes in the cinematographic and economic landscape, the internal structure of movie theaters never quite adjusted to the changes and as they diminished in size and numbers, filmgoers' attendance lessened.

Did French moviegoers recognize themselves through French films in the post-'68 era? Probably. Most New Wave films rarely chronicled the *faits de société* (real-life chronicles), nor did they make faithful representations of everyday life. Once the wake of the French New Wave dissipated among general audiences, French cinema of the 1970s appeared as a much more transparent medium since its thematic content translated not only the state of mind of an eventful era but also, uniquely, the physical and emotional background of contemporary society. Despite the huge transformations generated more than ten years earlier by the directors of the New Wave, French cinema did not fundamentally alter its cinematographic standards or the modes of visual consumption. The attempt to transform French cinema radically and exclusively into a full-fledged medium of the Seventh Art failed as audiences expressed renewed interest in commercial films[15] (without denying nevertheless the appreciation for the New Wave). Consequently, literary adaptations and big-budget comedies were favored by investment companies—the *qualité française* was back. But despite popular demand and sudden mood variations the spirit of May '68 and its aftermath remained very much alive in French cinema of the 1970s. Militant cinema, new types of commercial cinema, and theoretical discussions captured for the first time the curiosity of accomplished filmmakers. Although not always reliable in format, French films were politically thorough, regularly intervening at every level of society, such as social reevaluation, political contestation, and cultural interrogation (for example, Jean-Luc Godard's *Tout va bien*, 1972). The numerous *films militants* were, however, limited in their audience appeal and did not last long at the box office.

One of the biggest headaches of militant and out-of-the-mainstream cinema was the financial distance separating production and actual distribution. The risk run by a distribution company was always great, and the only guarantee for a filmmaker to have his or her film commercialized was to secure a distribution deal before shooting. For the new filmmakers of the post-'68 era, unlike the young directors of the New Wave ten years before them, the approach to cinema represented a different reality in comparison to the obstacles filmmakers such as Jean-Luc Godard, François Truffaut, and Alain Resnais had to face. Their auteur "responsibility" was an already endorsed factor this time with no establishment to challenge and no respectability to secure. In fact, the 1970s turned out for many New Wave directors (with the exception of several films made by Truffaut) to be a decade of fruitless productions for aesthetic and professional reasons since most of them did not follow the main current dictated by popular audiences. Alain Resnais did not produce any significant pictures aside from *Stavisky* (*Stavisky*, 1974) and *My American Uncle* (*Mon oncle d'Amérique*, 1980);[16] Claude Chabrol mainly produced run-of-the-mill commercial assignments such as *The Twist* (*Folies bourgeoises,* 1975) and *Innocents with Dirty Hands* (*Innocents aux mains sales,* 1975), the exceptions being serious accomplishments such as *Violette* (*Violette Nozière,* 1978) and *The Horse of Pride* (*Le cheval d'orgueil,* 1979); and Louis Malle, excluding *Lacombe Lucien* (*Lacombe Lucien,* 1974), did not produce representative artistic contributions and eventually left for the United States.

THE "SCANDAL" OF THE CINÉMATHÈQUE FRANÇAISE

Founded by Henri Langlois (1914–77) in 1936, the Cinémathèque française (see the discussion on page 208) rapidly became the most important film archive in the world. At a time when movies were considered an inconsequential entertainment medium, the Cinémathèque found them a sophisticated art form and sought to preserve them. The Cinémathèque gradually gained financial security through regular government subsidies in order to maintain good care of its enormous volume of stock and state of preservation. Eventually gaining a majority of shares in the institution, however, the French government decided on February 9, 1968, to replace Langlois as its head with Pierre Barbin, a more financially responsible civil servant (in direct opposition to Langlois's lack of organization that was described by his detractors). Part of the allegations against Langlois involved negligence, not only with respect to financial matters, but also at the level of institutional organization. On several occasions this negligence led to the deterioration, or even disappearance, of films, as well as other negative financial aspects. Indeed, the problems were numerous, from decisions on the films to be purchased to the storing of new acquisitions under difficult conditions (light, temperature, and humidity) and classifying them into records in order to allow them to be viewed without damaging the copies. André Malraux, at the time the Ministre de la Culture (secretary of culture), was severely criticized by the press, in particular by *Les cahiers du cinéma,* for the sudden decision and more importantly by the entire French-film industry. On February 12, 1968, more than three hundred filmmakers demonstrated their dissent with the government's decision to eradicate Langlois's leadership in what, in their minds, was the founder of the greatest film institution. A couple of days later, several thousand demonstrators gathered in support of the movement (as a prearranged rehearsal of the future events of May) in the garden of the Trocadéro in Paris. The confrontation with the police resulted in several injuries (Jean-Luc Godard even lost his glasses that day).

Immediately aware of the scope of the movement, a number of French directors founded the Comité de défense de la Cinémathèque

(Cinémathèque Defense Committee), including the omnipresent François Truffaut, Jean-Luc Godard, and Claude Chabrol, as well as old-school veterans Marcel Carné and Jean Renoir. On April 22, after countless hours of negotiations between the government and film-industry representatives, the government hastily reinstated Langlois as director of the Cinémathèque. A few years later, on June 14, 1972, Langlois achieved his lifetime goal: the creation of a museum dedicated to film (Musée du Cinéma) at the prestigious Palais de Chaillot in Paris.

After Langlois's death in 1977, the Cinémathèque went through another major crisis. A fire in 1980, in one of its stock rooms, led to the loss of several thousand reels. (Subsequently, the Cinémathèque budget increased from seven to twenty-three million French francs.) The question of film conservation and restoration was once again raised. This time the answer was a new type of film preservation: cellulose acetate and polyester-film base. Despite the fact that film can be indefinitely duplicated, few have been preserved to this day and many are still in poor condition.[17] The difficulty in maintaining film stock contributed to the film industry's negligence in preservation.

The Langlois case was long remembered since it concomitantly came to symbolize the unavoidable disconnection between the French government's rigid administration and the unpredictable evolution of a nation's artistic creativity. In such a difficult context, French cinema proved once more, just as it did on January 4, 1948 (see chapter 4), a deep kind of collective vision regarding the future of the medium. Jean-Luc Godard said about Henri Langlois that without his precious concourse, "Lumière, Méliès, Griffith, von Stroheim, and others would have died twice." On the other hand, the cost of the victory was for this prestigious institution to see state subsidies gradually diminish during the coming years. Although more remote in chronological comparison, the history and vicissitudes of the Cinémathèque are not directly linked with the events of May '68, despite the presence at both rallies of personalities like political activist and student leader Daniel Cohn-Bendit, who like many professionals of the French film industry continued to support the cause of cultural integrity.

POLITICAL CINEMA AS A NEW GENRE: LOUIS MALLE, JOSEPH LOSEY, AND COSTA-GAVRAS

According to film historian Jacques Siclier, "French society of the 1970s resembles that of the victorious Second Empire. It is dominated by the cult for money, extensive urbanism, and financial greed generating real estate scandals in which the political class in power becomes entrapped."[18] It seemed as if French cinema's creative innovations stalled after 1968. The great explosion of new talent and approaches to filmmaking did not survive into the next decade. However, with the subsequent social makeover triggering innumerable changes of thought and behavior, the post-'68 era gave birth to a new cinematographic genre: the politically oriented narrative.

The primary goal of political films was to represent French society realistically, including its social injustices. At the same time, it attempted to invent a new cinematography, a new kind of coherence linking extreme political ideology (mostly leftist) with a highly intellectual cinematic discourse. As film historian Jean-Michel Frodon defines it, "Within this narrative cinema, the authentic new 'politically oriented' films that characterized this period were no longer the quest for narrative pleasure in collective values but rather in the appreciation of individuals—what can be understood as a linguistic manipulation is eventually considered revolutionary."[19] In its exclusive format, French political cinema was en route to a thorough examination of the social structures of society and of the redefinition of individual rights versus the social order. In the post-'68 era, movies and politics were immediately put in the spotlight with the success of Costa-Gavras's Z, followed by The Confession (L'aveu, 1970). From now on, political movies were also successful among popular audiences as they showed signs of crystallizing into an ideology or worldview.

Within the French film industry, one of the most significant initiatives of this period was the creation of a politically oriented parameter, the Société des réalisateurs de films (SRF). This new association promoted filmmakers to a more recognized status within the industry (in comparison with, for instance, technicians and producers). It also established its own film festival, called the Quinzaine des réalisateurs, in 1969, which to this day functions as a preselection phase for the Cannes Film Festival as well as a "detection apparatus" for new talent. This parallel film festival offered more ambitious choices, as feature films chosen by their thematic content were openly more politicized as a direct result of the new consciousness that surfaced after 1968 (e.g, in comparison with Cannes, there was a larger number of young directors and easier access to the competition among a wider number of countries).

After 1968, Jean-Luc Godard, who was noticeably no longer willing to bear the emblem of authorism alone, began to shun a certain mode of filmmaking that he considered intellectually and politically "comfortable," thereby initiating an almost silent crusade in militant filmmaking (Tout va bien, 1972, starring Yves Montand and Jane Fonda). In his attempts to define his new political filmmaking, Godard developed the idea of experimental work, but this time not conceptually nor technically. The goal was to research and no longer to deliver a

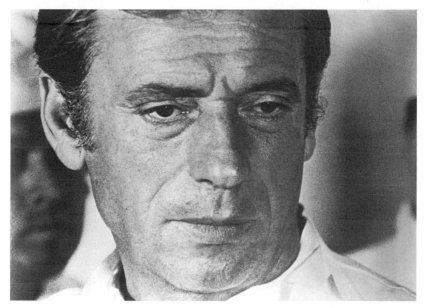

Yves Montand (the deputy) in Costa-Gavras's *Z* (*Z*, 1969), (Photo courtesy of the Museum of Modern Art/Film Stills Archive/© KG Productions).

cinematic message. Despite the risk of a certain dose of incommunicability, which ultimately permeated his narratives and discouraged many of his admirers, Godard's militant cinema remained vital for film studies throughout the decade until his comeback in the 1980s. His professional itinerary recalls the trend adopted by the *Cahiers du cinéma* at the same time. William Luhr thus summarizes the financial and mental situation in the editing room of the *Cahiers*:

> Along with the total radicalization of Godard was the leftward slide of *Cahiers du cinéma.* By 1969 [François] Truffaut and [Eric] Rohmer, formerly the cornerstones of this most famous of film journals, found themselves completely alienated from its positions. Truffaut ceased giving it financial support. Rohmer excoriated it in several interviews. *Cahiers,* like Godard, was committed to a Marxist position, to such an extent that it excised from its pages everything that had as its goal the reflection of cinematic pleasure. Out came photographs and reviews of popular films. Out came the interest in American cinema or in the New Wave. Soon advertising was dropped. Consistent to the end, it had to withdraw from the standard distribution companies that had seen to its popular diffusion. For four years *Cahiers* followed this ascetic policy, returning by degrees to the popular journal it once was. The results have been mixed. Its theoretical rigor utterly renewed the study of cinema in France, Great Britain, and the United States. And its team of editors, like their predecessors, ten years earlier, fought their way

into the margins of the cinema while striving to maintain their political purity.[20]

One of the most common flaws among the leading directors of the New Wave, in their desperate attempt to shift toward a more politicized and radical view in filmmaking, was the absence of a strong and perceptible storytelling device. Reality through a transparent medium could no longer motivate crowds intellectually, much less attract audiences to revisit movie theaters, unless along with this coherent realistic discourse movies combined accessible cinematographic language. This explains why most of the time popular audiences preferred films featuring streets, cities, and life in general that would be as easily recognizable as their daily routines. Protagonists had to resemble closely those who shared their quotidian existence, namely, the audience. In the early 1970s, Godard was unwilling to compromise for public consumption his longtime professional friendship with François Truffaut, since both directors took very different approaches in their film careers (Godard reproaching Truffaut for doing "commercial" cinema and thus betraying the ideals and foundations of the auteur theory). Although Truffaut was by then clearly preaching for intellectual independence, Godard's strategy was entirely opposed to the intellectually compromising and pragmatic trajectory of his former colleague and friend.[21]

The canon of this politically inclined cinema often represented fictional narratives involving outcast characters as in films like Louis Malle's *Lacombe Lucien* (*Lacombe Lucien*, 1974). Twenty years after Claude Autant-Lara's *Four Full Bags* (*La traversée de Paris*, 1956), Louis Malle's *Lacombe Lucien* again attempted to reevaluate the glamorous and undisputed image of urban resistance during the Occupation. Based on a script written by Patrick Modiano, *Lacombe Lucien* sought to re-create another reality that was radically opposed to the heroic concept of patriotic duty.

Based on Malle's own experiences in France during the Occupation, the film narrates the difficult choice seventeen-year-old farmer Lucien (Pierre Blaise) must make during the last days of the Nazi presence in France. Disturbed by the absence of his father, a prisoner in Germany, and the infidelity of his mother with her employer, he now works for the German police, after having failed to join the Resistance. Unluckily, he falls in love with a young girl, France Horn (Aurore Clément), who is the daughter of a wealthy Jewish tailor, and consequently attracts the wrath of the Gestapo as well as the unsympathetic Resistance fighters.

In Malle's film, there is no longer innocence or guilt but simply mistakes in each individual's existence, a sort of predestined and insurmountable pathway. Severely criticized for its ambiguous position toward the responsibility of those who enrolled as collaborators, *Lacombe Lucien* took the defense of what had never been questioned before. Far from staining the heroism of the French Resistance, the film put into perspective, through emotional dissociations, the entire function of the Resistance's cause without ever making a moral or value judgment. As a result, its screening, although three decades after the events depicted, remained controversial for years since it altered the traditional rendering of the glorious accomplishments of the Resistance. *Lacombe Lucien,* with a score by Django Reinhardt, which was by contrast universally esteemed and very popular, earned a nomination for Best Foreign Film at the 1974 Academy Awards and won the prize for Best Film at the 1974 British Academy Awards.

Also offering a retrospective investigation of an atypical approach to the Occupation was a film directed by Joseph Losey (1909–84) entitled *Mr. Klein (Monsieur Klein,* 1976). Controversial yet extremely coherent in the development of its story line, the film recounts the incredible vicissitudes of Robert Klein (Alain Delon), a successful Parisian art dealer who suddenly sees his cozy life come to an end when he realizes that another Robert Klein "hides" in Paris, a man with rather inexplicable underground connections. As a businessman, the first Klein does not mind taking advantage of the Parisian Jews who have to sell their possessions to survive. Far from being a crook, he is, however, an authentic, self-centered, and unscrupulous character. Ironically, Klein is himself mistaken for a missing Jew, a man who has been using Mr. Klein's name as a cover for his secret operations. One day, just as he concludes a deal with a Jewish man on a Dutch painting, he receives a newspaper from the Jewish community in France. Intrigued by the fact that his first and last name appear on the address, Klein conducts his own private investigation and learns from the newspaper's editor that his namesake, who lives at another address in Paris and subscribes to the newspaper, has replaced his address for the protagonist's own. Since the police control the Jewish residents of the capital, Robert Klein is now, to his dismay, officially registered as a member of the Jewish community. But the more he investigates, the more he sinks into this quicksand. The price of truth, justice, and peace of mind will be for Mr. Klein to assume the identity of his namesake. As Klein progresses toward the truth, he also locks himself into a fatal destiny. Because of his French Catholic ancestry, he goes back to his native Alsace to locate the family archive and obtain his certificates of family origins. His desperate quest to find his detrimental alter ego leads Klein from apartments to country castles and ultimately to the Vélodrome d'hiver (a bicycle-racing track). Since the official documents never arrive, he is temporarily de-tained with more then 16,000 Jews, moved to the camp of Drancy near Paris, and ultimately sent to a German death camp.

At first glance, *Mr. Klein* appears to take the same approach as most Resistance movies. The film objectively represented the struggle and the dilemma of the French Resistance, but instead it makes a U-turn, indirectly denouncing the narrative structure of its predecessors. Unlike most Resistance films of the era, which focus on a collective representation of the tragedy (even when through the eyes of a single protagonist), *Mr. Klein* is entirely centered on a single individual without developing any other protagonist. The question of the shadowy "other" in one's existence, represented by the emblematic and nonexistent other Mr. Klein, who deliberately discharges his own identity on his alter ego, eventually leads to ruin. Constantly addressing the theme of the shifting relationship between victim and oppressor, Losey's film is directed with tremendous care and subtlety. Losey[22] directed a work more intellectually than emotionally involving. The end result is a devastating picture of the French authorities during the Nazi Occupation. The film is furthermore a serious reflection on human identity and human destiny, the state and condition of the individual within a community in danger. At the 1977 French Academy Awards, *Monsieur Klein* received the César for Best Director, Best Film, and Best Production Design (by Alexandre Trauner).[23]

The character of Robert Klein is unforgettably interpreted by Alain Delon. Following service in the Navy in Indochina, Delon began his film career in the company of little-known actor Jean-Claude Brialy, who invited him to attend the 1957 Cannes Film Festival. Immediately noticed by several film directors at the time, Delon made his cinematographic debut with a small part in Yves Allégret's *When the Woman Gets Confused* (*Quand la femme s'en mêle,* 1957), followed by an appearance in Marc Allégret's *Be Beautiful but Shut Up* (*Sois belle et tais-toi,* 1958). His first lead role in a picture came in René Clément's stylish thriller *Purple Noon.* A year later, Delon appeared in Luchino Visconti's *Rocco and His Brothers* (*Rocco e i suoi fratelli,* 1960), then in Michelangelo Antonioni's *The Eclipse* (*L'eclisse,* 1962), and again in Visconti's masterpiece *The Leopard* (*Il gattopardo,* 1963).

With so many renowned filmmakers after him, the young actor became one of Europe's most popular cinematic figures. In 1969, Delon and wife, Nathalie, found themselves at the center of a crime scandal when their bodyguard was found dead outside their home. While many dire predictions announced the possible end of Delon's film career, the tabloids weighed in on the Delons' side. To the French public, however, accustomed to seeing the actor in mobster roles, Delon's film personality took on a new and intriguing reality in light of the scandal. Nevertheless, Alain Delon spent much of the 1970s as

France's biggest star, performing in important films such as Henri Verneuil's *Any Number Can Win* (*Mélodie en sous-sol,* 1963), Jacques Deray's *The Swimming Pool* (*La piscine,* 1969), Jean-Pierre Melville's *The Red Circle* (*Le cercle rouge,* 1970), Pierre Granier-Deferre's *The Widow Couderc* (*La veuve Couderc,* 1971), José Giovanni's *Two Men in Town* (*Deux hommes dans la ville,* 1973), Volker Schlöndorff's *Swann in Love* (*Un amour de Swann,* 1984), José Pinheiro's *Cop's Honour* (*Parole de flic,* 1985), Jean-Luc Godard's *New Wave* (*Nouvelle vague,* 1990), Agnès Varda's *A Hundred and One Nights* (*Les cent et une nuits,* 1995), and Bertrand Blier's *Actors* (*Les acteurs,* 2000).

Since the beginning of the postwar era, French cinema had never fully produced a "politically" oriented national cinema (for reasons of political censorship as well as lack of political commitment), except for notable but sporadic examples such as René Clair's *Freedom for Us* (*A nous la liberté,* 1931), Jean Renoir's *The People of France* (*La vie est à nous,* 1936), and Alain Resnais's *Night and Fog.* The achievement of Greek filmmaker Costa-Gavras[24] was therefore all the more impressive since his project was conceived during a period little inclined toward political change. Born Konstantinos Gavra in 1933, Costa-Gavras moved to France in 1952 to study French literature at the Sorbonne and later switched to film studies, entering the IDHEC (graduating in 1958) where he became assistant to such prestigious directors as René Clair, Henri Verneuil, and most notably René Clément, who, according to Costa-Gavras, profoundly influenced his professional career.

Z chronicles the fraudulent process of politics in Greece, which resulted in the defeat of the democratic government with a coup d'état on April 21, 1967, led by military insurgents (the colonels' dictatorship lasted for seven years). When Costa-Gavras embarked on the film project, the military dictatorship was already in place in Athens, and it became obvious that finding another country for outdoor shootings was imperative. Algeria was the first choice as a substitute since the working conditions in Greece made filming there no longer an option. The problems Costa-Gavras had to face were immense. Because of the intense political nature of his film, as well as the recent date of the actual tragic events, many producers turned down the project with a similar reply: "Too political to be commercial." Finally, producer Jacques Perrin, who also played the role of the young reporter in the film, found a compromise solution by having the project coproduced in France and Algeria (most exterior scenes were shot in Algeria and interiors in France during the summer of 1968). Thus, *Z* became a Franco-Algerian production.

One of the very best political films of the decade, *Z* was inspired by the actual events that occurred during the 1963 assassination of Gregorios Lambrakis in Thessalonica (interpreted by Yves Montand), a popular leftist-liberal member of the Greek Parliament, whose growing popularity challenged authorities by organizing a rally against the future installation of Polaris missiles in Greece. During a peace demonstration, he was knocked down and killed, while the police not only failed to protect him, but also tried to cover up the murder. The examining magistrate in charge (Jean-Louis Trintignant), despite numerous attempts by the police authorities to close the case, acted as a detective and eventually managed to solve the mysterious nature of the accident, thereby unveiling the political conspiracy. It soon became clear that Lambrakis had fallen prey to a scheme triggered by officials of the Establishment. The closing credits reveal that although the perpetrators were put on trial and condemned in 1966, they were eventually reinstated in their respective functions after the military coup a year later.

Costa-Gavras's film represented for the first time a new cinematographic genre: the political thriller. Both scenario and editing successfully combined to present the course of events without falling entirely into the thriller category. Many European filmmakers, who first had not anticipated the popular and commercial success of the project, took Costa-Gavras's lead, in a different style. They included Italian directors such as Francesco Rosi and his rendition of *The Mattei Affair* (*Il caso Mattei,* 1972) and *Illustrious Corpses* (*Cadaveri eccellenti,* 1974), as well as Elio Petri for his films *Investigation of a Citizen above Suspicion* (*Indagine su un cittadino al di sopra di ogni sospetto,* 1970) and *The Working Class Goes to Heaven* (*La classe operaia va in paradiso,* 1971). Costa-Gavras addressed the urgency of political issues of the early 1970s with perhaps a more flamboyant sensibility and style than others.

With its concentration on the theme of injustice, *Z* brought contemporary European audiences to the conclusion that cinema, as a medium, had a crucial role to play in the history of human ideas. Its opening credits could not have been more direct: *Toute ressemblance avec des événements réels, des personnes vivantes ou mortes, n'est pas le fait du hasard. Elle est volontaire* (Any similarity to actual events, to people living or dead, is in no way the result of coincidence. It is intentional). The original screenplay of *Z*, adapted from Vassilis Vassilikos's novel, Raoul Coutard's rousing cinematography, the lively music score by Mikis Theodorakis (a Greek musician whose work had been banned by the military regime in Greece), the kinetic editing, and clear-cut figures, all placed the film at the antithesis of traditional gangster pictures, to make it an unambiguous political statement, and contributed to the success of the enterprise. Its innovation was to combine European political awareness and commitment with the vigorous, dynamic, well-paced style of Hollywood action movies. Winning the Jury Prize at the Cannes Film Festival in 1969 and Best Actor award for Jean-Louis Trintignant, the film was screened for thirty-six weeks in France and enjoyed considerable success in the United States, where it received Oscars in 1969 for Best Foreign Language Film and Editing (Françoise Bonnot), as well as an Oscar nomination for Best Picture. Capitalizing on a sincere sense of political commitment and narrated in an unforgettable style, *Z* remains Costa-Gavras's most popular and influential film. Far from being prisoner to dogmatic concepts, Gavras's oeuvre questioned the frightening possibilities for perversion of ideologies when held in a nondemocratic way.

With his next picture, entitled *The Confession* (*L'aveu*, 1970), Costa-Gavras took on another kind of forceful condemnation: the Stalinist purges in Czechoslovakia of the 1950s. Here, he explored the nature of true believers in communism. Adapted from Artur London's autobiographical novel (which was published in 1968), *The Confession* retraced the difficult years of this hero of the Czech resistance, who devoted his entire life to the communist cause and at the end finds himself imprisoned with many other political activists from all over the Eastern block. Considered too intellectual for the Stalinist regime, the hero is forced to render prearranged confessions and consequently is sentenced to prison in 1951. The film was shot more than a year after the invasion of Prague by Soviet tanks in the spring of 1968. The depth and intensity of Yves Montand's performance directly suggest the possible redemptive act that the artist took upon himself for his past moral support of the Soviet regime. The dramatic function of the plot, although devoid of all the twists and turns present in *Z,* conveys a simple but moral emotion, powerful enough to attract audiences that over the years have been larger than the wildest predictions of its authors and investors. By indirectly denouncing the control of the "progressive" intellectuals by the PCF (French Communist Party), the story actually anticipated that political party's irremediable and gradual decline throughout the decade. With its horrifying evidence, the film expressed a solemn condemnation of the use of moral turpitude, falsified trials, artificial confessions, and Stalinist terror, as well as the approval of French communists at the time.

Back in France, Costa-Gavras's popularity experienced several ups and downs, since many political figures of both the Right and Left were outraged by the director's lack of patriotic consideration. But those attacks were easily silenced since Gavras never had a political agenda of his own. His true and observable lack of aspiration for a political career gave him the credibility he needed in France and abroad. His only agenda was his professional itinerary. Two years later he completed *State of Siege* (*Etat de siège,* 1972), a film that dealt with activities of the CIA in Uruguay during the Mitrione scandal[25] while exploring dramatic problems of conscience and of moral ambiguity. Ironically, it was made in then-democratic Chile, just before the fall of Salvatore Allende. The success of the film encouraged the director, who ten years later made *Missing* (1982), starring Jack Lemmon and Sissy Spacek, a story about the political dictatorship in Argentina. (*Missing* received the Palme d'or at the 1982 Cannes Film Festival.) Despite the depth of the political message that Costa-Gavras's film conveyed at the time, his main cinematographic interest was to combine the best features of at least three different genres: the lurid atmosphere of film noir, the standard action-oriented melodrama, and the basic gangster picture.

With the critical reception of *Z* at film festivals around the world, it became clear that one of the most important, as well as enduring, qualities of the Cannes Film Festival was to promote and preserve the admiration of the art of film. Additionally, its role had often been to call attention everywhere to the social dimension of film in the general culture, using movies as vital parameters for the examination and propagation of moral and political ideas. The true wind of change at the Cannes Film Festival occurred in the spring of 1973 and brought new orientations for the rest of the decade. A year before, the French selection process was severely criticized for a predominance of commercial productions. The commission took note of it, and consequently opened its doors to a more apparently cultural and diverse cinema. The 1973 selection of the highly controversial French-Italian film *La grande bouffe*,[26] directed by Marco Ferreri, with a spectacular cast including Philippe Noiret, Marcello Mastroianni, Michel Piccoli, and Ugo Tognazzi, marked this change.

THE LAST DAYS OF THE FRENCH *POLAR:* JEAN-PIERRE MELVILLE AND HENRI VERNEUIL

Based on Joan McLeod's novel *The Ronin*, Jean-Pierre Melville's *The Samurai* (*Le samouraï,* 1967) was released shortly after its writer and director—the great maverick of French cinema—had made two other fatalistic crime thrillers: *Le Doulos* (*Le doulos,* 1961) and *The Second Breath* (*Le deuxième souffle,* 1966), both a dozen years after his classic noir thriller *Bob the Gambler* (*Bob le flambeur,* 1955). The richly textured story of *The Samurai* focused on the life and schemes of the professional hit man Jeff Costello and concentrated on relationships and human intrigues rather than violence. A particular atmosphere often enveloped the urban backgrounds of Melville's psychological thrillers. They featured deserted streets, steamy subways, seedy hotel rooms, and aban-

Alain Delon (Jeff Costello) in Jean-Pierre Melville's *The Samurai* (*Le samouraï*, 1967), (Courtesy of BIFI/© 1967 Filmel Production).

doned police stations, as well as some clothing fetishism (Jeff Costello's raincoat). Melville's script was on a different level than most gangster films, offering much more than just crime and bloodshed. Jeff Costello (Alain Delon), a solitary professional hit man who lives in a one-room Parisian apartment with only a caged bird for companionship, is hired by a nameless Parisian mob to assassinate a nightclub owner. Shortly after accomplishing his task, the police apprehend him during a routine check of known criminals. He successfully goes through a police line-up identification thanks to the false testimony given by Valérie (Cathy Rosier), the piano player who saw him stepping out of the victim's office. In addition, his loyal girlfriend, Jeanne (Nathalie Delon), provides him with an unbreakable alibi by maintaining that he spent the night with her. Although no one can recognize him officially, the police are determined to nail him sooner or later. Constrained to release him, the inspector (François Périer) begins to tail him through the streets of the capital. Double-crossed by the mobster who hired him, Costello tries to discover the source of his betrayal, and at the same time becomes fascinated by a nightclub musician who purposely failed to finger him to the police. Although cheated out of his reward, he must threaten to kill his contact, who reveals to him the real name of his chief employer. Jeff once more receives a new mission. This time he must eliminate the only eyewitness, Valérie, the piano player who saw him entering the club on the night of the crime. As Costello approaches her, the police shoot him down. Much to their surprise, his gun was not loaded.

Commercialized in the United States in a seriously abridged, re-edited, and poorly dubbed version entitled *The Godson,* the film was finally rereleased thirty years after its initial public airing in its intended form. Considered a seminal work by many film historians, *The Samurai* anticipated many American films, among them Martin Scorsese's *Taxi Driver* (1976), Quentin Tarantino's *Pulp Fiction* (1994), and John Woo's 1989 remake *The Killer* (Woo once declared *The Samurai* a movie that is close to perfection).

Known for his low-budget productions, location shooting without film stars, self-written scripts, and complete artistic control during the immediate postwar era, Jean-Pierre Melville moved from independent art films to big-budget productions with internationally famous actors. In this European film noir, Melville consciously adopted the classic Hollywood style of his favorite directors, exploring the moral code of mobsters while confessing to be strongly influenced by the work of American filmmakers such as John Huston and Billy Wilder. Melville's clichés of the American version of film noir include the requisite nocturnal, bleak atmosphere; wet, gray, and gloomy Parisian streets; expressionless jazz nightclub musicians; and deserted police offices. Commenting on Melville's overpowering and absorbing thriller, director Henri-Georges Clouzot once said: "In this film void of soul and flesh, realism is then absent. It is rather the thriller's mechanism that is the real subject of *The Samurai.*"[27]

In a film that omitted car chases, explosions, and other eye-catching effects, Melville's opening shot successfully established the existential nature of this gangster drama. *The Samurai* was about survival (as in the scene showing Jeff's punctilious technique for stealing a Citroën DS). At the same time, Melville's gangsters reflected a European sensibility, reminiscent of the existential gangster films of Jean-Luc Godard as the protagonists talk all night seemingly about every possible subject, voluntarily eluding the actual matter of the imminent plot. In addition, the film's opening quote was said to be taken from *The Book of Bushido* (it is actually an invention of Melville) and clearly set the tone of the main character: "There is no solitude greater than a samurai's, unless perhaps it is that of a tiger in the jungle." What ultimately emerged in this character study was an elaborate series of traps and double-crosses. Melville's nonromanticized view of Costello's professional obligation as a mob executioner was quite mesmerizing. The film was as much an interesting exploration of the human spirit and its failings as it was a story about crime and moral turpitude. Although

The Samurai is a bleak movie, both in tone and morality, the intrigue surrounding Costello sustained an exciting tale whose hero was repeatedly compelled to improvise in order to protect his cover. Thus, the outcome of Costello's conflict became far more than a foregone conclusion and was genuinely compelling to watch. The intense emphasis on Delon's impassive face created a sense of style. His stoicism actually elicits passion, heightening the psychological tension of the film, while the austere dialogues accentuate the introverted nature of the antihero character. Together, they render the protagonist passionless. Although the inclusion of the relationship between Costello and Valérie represented a redundant occurrence in the film, it did work with the rest of the narrative. It also brought some humanity to the tale, providing the vehicle for an explosive climax. The entire movie corresponded to a series of mini-climaxes, all building to the devastating, definitive conclusion.

The grim and dark passages of the film, in contrast to the rare, bright exterior scenes, were all part of the beautiful cinematography of Henri Decaë. The existential themes of alienation, solitude, and apprehension were particularly well illustrated through the Expressionistic lighting and framing techniques reminiscent of German Expressionism. To exclude the predominant and omniscient existentialist blackness of most film noir, the visual tones evolved around three colors (ice blue, cool gray, and murky green). Decaë's cold but stylish monochromatic photography, with its gloomy exteriors and dim interiors, nearly brought the movie to a black-and-white picture. Alain Delon's blue eyes and almost angelic features appeared so irrelevant with respect to his profession that the viewers were unexpectedly daunted, just as they were a few years earlier when he played the role of a boxer in *Rocco and His Brothers*. Melville claimed to have studied color for years before venturing to make his second color film,[28] *The Samurai*. The impeccable cold beauty of the bright-blue seats and walls inside the police station contrasts dramatically with the sickly grays and greens of the rest of the film, and the scarce presence of daylight accompanied with the omnipresence of closed doors, all to complete the feeling of entrapment.

This same feeling of entrapment is found in Melville's next feature film, *The Shadow Army (L'armée des ombres,* 1969). Widely regarded as the most historically accurate screen version of the French Resistance, the film (it was never shown commercially in the United States) chronicled a rare portrayal of authenticity. The vicissitudes of the story line and the vital performances of the actors combined for an atypical dramatic impact in this tale of the French underground during the Occupation.[29] Inspired by Joseph Kessel's 1943 novel *The Army of Shadows*,[30] *The Shadow Army* revealed from an internal point of view fictionalized accounts of the lives of members of the Resistance: their tragedies, their solitude, their suspicions, and most of all the inhumane choices they had to make in order to survive. Set from October 1942 to February 1943, as noted the story depicts the plight of the French Resistance. The Gestapo in Paris arrest Philippe Gerbier (Lino Ventura), one of the Resistance's chiefs, and sends him to a concentration camp for political prisoners. Soon after, he manages to flee by killing a guard during an inquisition in Paris, and he later joins his group in Marseille. There, the conspirator Dounat (Alain Libolt), who had denounced Gerbier, is discretely executed by the Resistance survivors. He hides in Lyon, the main center of the French Resistance at the time, and organizes the expatriation of several members and downed pilots to England. Meanwhile, Felix (Paul Crauchet), another Resistance fighter, is arrested and tortured by the Gestapo. So is Gerbier, a few days later. Both men are condemned to death by firing squad (at the moment of execution, the condemned are led to believe that they may save their lives by running away, unaware that this is actually a trick to train the firing squad for moving targets). Mathilde (Simone Signoret), a Resistance chief, manages to save Gerbier at the last second, and together they escape. But fate mercilessly falls prey on each member of the group; Mathilde is eventually captured herself. She is released, but as "bait" to capture the rest of the underground organization. Her choice is simple: if she does not disclose all the names of her Resistance group, her daughter will be immediately sent to a brothel for German soldiers in Poland. Later, the group discovers that two members have been arrested the same day Mathilde was released from the Gestapo headquarters. Heartbroken, the other members have no choice but to liquidate her. As they face her from inside their car, she seems to give her final agreement to her destiny, and they shoot her. None of the members of the group will survive the war, as the closing credits reveal the dreadful fate of each of them.

As a member of the French Resistance, for two years, who later moved to England to join the Free French forces, Melville dedicated two other feature films to the period of the Occupation: *The Silence of the Sea* (*Le silence de la mer*, 1949) and *Leon Morin Priest* (*Léon Morin, prêtre*, 1961). But for this assignment, he had waited twenty-five years to make the project come true. *The Shadow Army* was actually Melville's personal memoir, and it captured an honest look at the dignity of the French Resistance in its difficult missions of sabotage and spying for which its members were rarely prepared. Avoiding war clichés and a banal melodramatic background, Melville offered an altruistic view of the French Resistance, which contradicted other attempts to evoke the movement as downhearted and selfish (e.g., Louis Malle's *Lacombe Lucien*). For film Historian Freddy Buache, the greatest quality of the film in relation to the rendering of human courage was to "express a certain idea of this fight motivated by conviction, with no concern for possibilities of success."[31] This appreciation of genuine "feel" of the movie was apparently not shared by many French-film critics. At the time of the movie's release, they declared that Melville's characters ironically lacked emotion, the human touch, and a sense of life in general. Although in essence these assertions may be true, it is important to remember that the most significant intention of Melville's *The Shadow Army*, despite its cold historical reconstitution, was the deliberate absence of dramatization, which, by conveying a singular spirit of the Resistance struggle, revealed a psychological mood with no exaggerated characterizations. The war or Resistance anecdotes, relegated behind a mood of abstraction (long shots with no sound), played a much greater role in the viewers' mind. Melville drew his actors out of diverse figures and deliberately rearranged and disguised events to prevent the movie from being classified a "historical reconstitution." Also worth noting is the musical score (Eric de Marsan), which was eventually used in "Les dossiers de l'écran," one of France's most popular TV shows of the 1970s and 1980s.

Director Henri Verneuil is also known for his contributions to *polar* or thriller/noir film, French style. Born Achod Malakian in 1920 in Rodosto, Turkey, Verneuil moved to France in 1924 and grew up in Marseille. Following the Liberation, he developed an interest in cinema. With the assistance of comedian Fernandel, he began directing several shorts in the late 1940s, and a few years later, he made several of the most popular feature films of France, such as *The Sheep Has Five Legs* (*Le mouton à cinq pattes,* 1954), *The Cow and I* (*La vache et le prisonnier,* 1959) with Fernandel, and later *A Monkey in Winter* (*Un singe en hiver,* 1962), *Any Number Can Win* (*Mélodie en sous-sol,* 1963), *100, 000 Dollars au Soleil* (*Cent mille dollars au soleil,* 1963), *The Sicilian Clan, The Body of My Enemy* (*Le corps de mon ennemi,* 1976), *I . . . comme Icare* (*I . . . comme Icare,* 1979), and *Mille milliards de dollars* (1981).

Drawn from a novel of Auguste Le Breton, Verneuil's 1969 *The Sicilian Clan* made history in the thriller genre since it gathered three of the most prestigious film stars of the moment: Jean Gabin, Alain Delon, and Lino Ventura.[32] Needless to say, for the French film industry as well as the French public, this international crime drama was the equivalent of a Hollywood blockbuster. Adapted to the screen by José Giovanni (*Le trou, Le deuxième souffle, Le ruffian*), the story begins with convicted murderer Roger Sartet (Alain Delon), who, after escaping from prison, joins his clan, the Sicilian mafia, led by Vittorio Malanese (Jean Gabin). While in detention, Roger concocts a plan: to steal a precious jewel collection in exhibition at the Villa Borghese in Rome. The ultimate coup is to skyjack the plane that transports the

Lino Ventura (Le Goff), Jean Gabin (Vittorio Malanese), and Alain Delon (Roger) in Henri Verneuil's *The Sicilian Clan* (*Le clan des Siciliens*, 1969), (Courtesy of BIFI).

valuables. Under suspicion and tailed by Police Inspector Le Goff (Lino Ventura), Roger assumes the identity of a professional jeweler specializing in diamonds. His recalcitrant quest ultimately ends with the disastrous division of the family and the arrest of the patriarch Malanese himself.

This gangster film reinvented the classic gangster genre, elevating it to a higher level with its hard-boiled acting, deep character studies, and attractive photography. *The Sicilian Clan* can be viewed as an insightful sociological study of violence, power, corruption, and assassination, with the crime "family" serving as a metaphor for the way business is conducted in capitalistic, profit-making corporations and governmental circles. On many levels, Verneuil's film provides equal satisfaction for viewers in search of a good story.

Ten years later, Verneuil renewed his success with *I . . . comme Icare,* starring Yves Montand. *I comme Icare*[33] looked at human behavior in opposition to established power and revealed the reason why people comply with almost every form of order, even murder. Following the assassination of a US president, (presumably JFK), district attorney Henry Volney (Yves Montand) refuses to sign the final report, which holds a mental patient responsible for the murder. Volney is given the task of investigating the crime scene. He and his assistant have little evidence, aside from a seven-second tape from a security camera. However, this tape contains precious information: the features of a man filming the scene. The investigating team compare evidence and identify an eyewitness, and as the assistant tracks him down, there is a resulting series of crimes. One night, Volney enters the office of Mallory (Jacques Sereys), the head of the Secret Service, hoping to find a clue, and discovers proof of a cover-up. But once again he arrives too late; Mallory is no longer in the office. The plot continues with an overambitious attempt to scrutinize and ultimately to lash out at the government and Secret Service scandal behind the president's mysterious assassination and its cover-up. Unfortunately, at the very moment that Volney unveils the truth and obtains proof of the conspiracy, he is coldly assassinated.

Uniquely blending myth and reality, *I . . . comme Icare* reinforced the prevailing attitude on the issue of assassination and openly embraced the idea of conspiracy. The use of pseudoarchival material gave the film, through a series of rapid and striking editing techniques, an almost documentary character. Leaving aside all of its drama and emotion, the movie was a masterpiece of film assembly. The writing, the editing, the music, and the photography were all used to weave a persuasive tapestry out of an overwhelming mountain of evidence and testimony. Other than the obvious dramatic impact of the political puzzle, the film offered a minor melodramatic subplot in which the character played by Montand alienates his staff with his monomaniacal approach. This subplot was superficially added and resolved just as superficially. The detail of the investigation was narrated in such a way as to allow the individual viewer to decide what to believe following the depth of revelations on the assassination. Vaguely inspired by the details of the Warren Commission report, the movie somehow triumphed over the inundation of odds and ends and rendered a suspense thriller that never failed to disturb the moviegoer. One can argue that because *I . . . comme Icare* was never intended to be viewed as a documentary, it did not have to be historically accurate. Certainly, a film does not have to be historically correct to be entertaining.

Other important contributions to the thriller genre during that decade were José Giovanni's *Two Men in Town (Deux hommes dans la ville,* 1973), Jacques Deray's *Cop Story (Flic Story,* 1975), Verneuil's own *Night Caller (Peur sur la ville,* 1975), Alain Corneau's *The Case against Ferro (Police Python 357,* 1976) and *A Choice of Arms (Le choix des armes,* 1981), and Claude Miller's *Under Suspicion (Garde à vue,* 1981).

THE HUMANISTS' SCHOOL: CLAUDE SAUTET, FRANÇOIS TRUFFAUT, AND ERIC ROHMER

Heirs to the humanistic, cinematic tradition of Jean Renoir, filmmakers such as François Truffaut and Claude Sautet (1924–2000) made movies that reflected three professed passions: a love of cinema, an interest in male–female relationships, and a compassionate obsession with midlife crises. It may be said that Sautet's earlier inspiration was embedded in the reminiscence, melancholy, and despair of his middleaged stance, and with success he matured into an experienced filmmaker and storyteller. Although his films lost their lyricism, they maintained their fidelity to life's prosaic side. But the "discoloration" and monotony of life were chronicled with a sense of resignation and quiet achievement quite distinct from the banality of traditional autobiography. Truffaut, who collaborated on occasion with Sautet, considered him the most "French" of all French filmmakers and explained the quintessential quality of the French director in his memoir, *The Films in My Life*:

> To love American cinema is fine; to try to make French films as if they were American is something else again, very much open to argument. I am not going to attack anybody for it, having myself fallen into that trap two or three times. Jean Renoir learned a lesson from Stroheim and Chaplin when he was making *Nana* and *Tire au flanc*, that is to say, he reinforced the French side of his films while he absorbed the Hollywood masters. In the same way, Claude Sautet understood, after the unavoidable detour through the crime films,[34] that he should, in Jean Cocteau's words, be a bird who sings in his own genealogical tree.[35]

A former graduate of the prestigious IDHEC, Claude Sautet did not enjoy immediate success in the early years of his career. Mostly known as an excellent technician (due principally to his editing skills, Truffaut baptized him the "patcher-upper"[36] of screenplays, as he was able to bring a mediocre film back to life via his great talent of montage), Sautet's contribution to French cinema was far from substantial in films such as *The Big Risk (Classe tous risque,* 1959) and *The Dictator's Guns (L'arme à gauche,* 1964). Unlike many other directors of his generation, Sautet never pretended to fight for a political or social cause. What Sautet is remembered for is his faithful and sincere portrayal of the French upper-middle-class bourgeois[37] (doctors, lawyers, businessmen, and architects) experiencing a reevaluation of their place and purpose in society. Sautet's cinema was centered on a meticulous yet humanistic study of the evolution of modern lifestyles, couple values, and society in general, as in *César and Rosalie (César et Rosalie,* 1972); *Vincent, François, Paul and the Others (Vincent, François, Paul . . .*

et les autres, 1974); *A Simple Story (Une histoire simple,* 1978); *Waiter!* *(Garçon!,* 1983); *A Heart in Winter (Un coeur en hiver,* 1992); and *Nelly and Monsieur Arnaud (Nelly et Monsieur Arnaud,* 1995). Popular audiences clearly understood Sautet's discourse since he transmitted the credible dimension of a pseudoautobiographic depiction and a self-critical rendering of the society of his time. (In many ways, one could easily draw a parallel between Sautet and Woody Allen if the latter did not often play his own character.)

Faithfully adapted from Paul Guimard's novel *Les choses de la vie, The Things of Life (Les choses de la vie,* 1969) was an immediate success and launched Sautet's career. The narrative expressed the fundamentally absurd nature of human existence as well as the consequences of the "little" moments in life that make up its essence. Although the story line featured an ensemble cast with multiple overlapping plots, the scenes were organized chronologically, including sporadically inserted conversations unrelated to the film. Through numerous flashbacks, the story describes the last moments of Pierre (Michel Piccoli), a forty-year-old architect, as he is killed in a car accident. During the last moments of his life, he reviews his intimate past, especially with his lover Hélène (Romy Schneider), for whom he had left his wife. Pierre is separated from his wife, Catherine (Léa Massari), and lives with Hélène, a young German architect. Trying to take a major step forward in his life, Pierre decides to terminate his relation with Catherine. To this end, he has written a letter that he intends to mail the next day. But at the last moment he changes his mind while at the post office, puts the letter in his pocket, and calls Catherine to arrange to meet her in Rennes. The accident occurs shortly after. As the car rolls over, Pierre relives the most important episodes of his life. On the brink of death, he sees all the various protagonists of his own existence gathered around a banquet table, silently accompanying him to his death. While peacefully expiring, he continues to perceive the discontinuous reality of his present situation, which triggers a series of mental images.

Although the narrative technique, intermingled with flashbacks, was not new at the time, the real innovation of the film relied on the characters' depiction through a sharp sociological eye and a constant hidden fascination for an existentialist vision of middle-aged happiness. In addition, the essential characteristic that set this film apart from its many predecessors and later imitators (in 1994 Mark Rydell directed *Intersection,* the remake of the film) was its weaving of often disparate layers of the story into a coherent whole. Each and every individual strand of *The Things of Life* was strong enough to form the foundation of a movie. Rarely would a film depict as many assorted chronicles, yet interconnected personal stories and tragedies.

Michel Piccoli (Pierre) in Claude Sautet's *The Things of Life* (*Les choses de la vie*, 1969), (Photo courtesy of the Museum of Modern Art/Film Stills Archive/© Studio Canal).

The different stages of *The Things of Life* were not compiled to satiate the sentimental appetite of the theater masses; rather, the film was carefully and painstakingly crafted to substantiate every character's tragedy and eventually mold them into distinct, complex individuals. The slow camera movement possesses a dreamlike power, and, when combined with the intensity of the accident motions, gives a somnolent impression to express mental recollection or even, at times, hallucination. In fact, Sautet's cinematography communicates a sudden surge of emotion, a contemplated action, making strongly rhetorical points by juxtaposing shots. The overall impression Sautet conveyed derived from the use of a seemingly floating camera to join not only elements within a scene but also the scenes themselves. In Sautet's filmmaking, the cinematography in motion, one of the strategic indicators of the existence of the narrator (Piccoli as Pierre), moved independently from the actions of the narrator, poetically reacting to them or commenting on what happens. Sautet's viewpoint progresses to keep the action in view and to follow as many elements as possible. The storyteller could well be considered a novelist investigating, but not commenting on, what was shown.

The actual meticulous montage of the film, which took nearly three months to carry out, was what essentially placed it above the ordinary.

Sautet's editing prompted a succession of resourceful tricks that allowed a passionate or catastrophic incident (a car accident, for instance) to appear as a very natural occurrence. For Sautet, the conception of common visual artifice in *The Things of Life* depended on the editing process for its force and excitement, since its plot would stay within the bounds of illusion and reality.[38]

Sautet and his cinematographer, Jean Boffety (1925–1988),[39] developed or enhanced already established techniques for allowing the drama to develop on multiple planes of vision and sound. Deep-focus photography, which Boffety had used in a more restricted manner in earlier films, permitted actors and objects to stay in focus regardless of their distance from the camera. Using this particular technique, multiple sequences could be staged within a single frame and remain intelligible, allowing for multifaceted interactions between a subject and his or her—or its—surroundings. Boffety's camera captured the spontaneity of life and the passion of lust.

Out of an almost banal event, a man in his prime hit by tragic fate, Sautet was able to touch on universal themes and concerns. *The Things of Life* was one of the great popular successes of the decade, as it was awarded the Prix Louis Delluc in 1969. For Sautet, cinema had to be, on the one hand, personable, and on the other, a splendid spectacle. His style as seen in *The Things of Life,* at once delicate, lyrical, and exceptionally fertile in its cinematographic invention, would become, partly by design, more prosaic and conventional with Sautet's later projects. As a result, some elements of controversy developed regarding the extent to which his later films involved a sense of ostentatious militant conservatism, such as in *César and Rosalie* and *Vincent, François, Paul and the Others.*

On a stylistic level, one can locate a diverging strain that characterized most of Sautet's work from the early 1960s on. The director celebrated life in the humanistic tradition of Jean Renoir, which includes the masterwork of 1970s cinema *César and Rosalie.* This film defined the modern romantic triangle for a generation. It is the bittersweet story of Rosalie (played by Romy Schneider), a woman who dominates others' lives and is at last free to choose her own. This sentimental drama-comedy must be seen as a contemporary novel. Self-made businessman César[40] (Yves Montand) and his amicable wife, Rosalie, have a happy marriage until an artist, David (Sami Frey), Rosalie's ex-lover, comes back into her life seeking to reclaim her. César comports himself like a friendly bourgeois who believes he has succeeded in life. Financially successful, he never misses an opportunity to boast about it. As the presence of David becomes a tangible reality, Rosalie realizes that she is still in love with him. At first furious, César understands the nature of the situation and decides to allow David to share their happiness. As the friendship between the two men grows stronger each day, Rosalie begins to feel differently about the arrangement and eventually leaves both men and their friendship.

Yves Montand and Romy Schneider (1938–1982) were Sautet's favorite actors. Montand worked for film directors such as Claude Sautet and Costa-Gavras at the peak of his career in the early 1970s. Along with Jacques Brel, Georges Brassens, and Léo Ferré, he was also one of France's most popular singers in the twentieth century ("Les feuilles mortes," "La bicyclette," "C'est si bon," "Le temps des cerises"). Born Ivo Livi near Florence, Montand, came with his parents to France in 1923 and grew up in Marseille, working as a docker at an early age. In 1944, sponsored by the legendary French singer Edith Piaf, he began a singing career, which quickly took him to the big screen where he landed his first role in Marcel Carné's *The Gates of the Night* (*Les portes de la nuit,* 1946), a role which was prior assigned to Jean Gabin. His major breakthrough was with Henri-Georges Clouzot's *The Wages of Fear* (*Le salaire de la peur,* 1953), which won the Palme d'or at the 1953 Cannes Film Festival. In 1951, as noted, Yves Montand married Simone Signoret (see chapter 4), and their marriage lasted until her death in 1985. Montand's national fame took him temporarily to Hollywood, where he starred as Jean-Marc with Marilyn Monroe in George Cukor's *Let's Make Love* (*Le milliardaire,* 1960).

Throughout his life, Montand was involved in various political and humanitarian campaigns. Along with countless artists and intellectuals, he petitioned against the atomic bomb in March 1950. The conservative press severely attacked him for his position against the deployment of troops in Indochina and Algeria, and especially for his support of socialist regimes. Years later, Montand recognized the mistake that led him to underestimate the reality of political trials in Prague and Budapest, and the restriction of human rights in the entire Eastern bloc. Following the invasions of Budapest and Prague, he stepped out of the political arena but never relinquished his support for politically oriented films. Montand acted for the most prestigious American and French directors: Vincente Minnelli, Joseph Losey, Costa-Gavras, Jean-Pierre Melville, Alain Resnais, René Clément, Claude Lelouch, Jean-Luc Godard, Claude Sautet, Pierre Granier-Deferre, Alain Corneau, and Henri Verneuil. With Sautet, Montand was able to communicate his showman talents as well as his joviality, particularly in *Garçon!* After his most memorable roles in the 1970s, Montand experienced a second wind not only as president of the 1987 Cannes Film Festival but with his performance in *Jean de Florette* in 1986. Yves Montand died at age seventy while finishing Jean-Jacques Beineix's *IP5: The Island of Pachyderms* (*IP5: l'île aux Pachydermes,* 1992).

The role of Rosalie, one of the most influential in all of French cinema, was interpreted by one of the great French actresses of the 1970s, Romy Schneider. Schneider was born Rosemarie Albach-Retty in 1938, in Vienna. After working in films directed by prestigious filmmakers such as Luchino Visconti in *Boccacio 70* (1962) and Orson Welles in *The Trial* (1963), the young actress settled in France in the 1960s and became one of the country's most respected actresses. Far from being a classical beauty, she sometimes appeared glowing (in Jean Girod's *The Woman Banker/La banquière*, 1980) and sometimes morose (Bertrand Tavernier's *Deathwatch/La mort en direct*, 1980). But once her character was engaged, viewers had the impression of an intelligent, intuitive actress wanting to commit herself to the inner rhythm of her role. At her best, she was riveting, capable of persuading spectators that she was beautiful and able to vary her own appearance according to the mood of the film, as for instance, in her performances in *The Main Thing Is to Love* (*L'important c'est d'aimer*, 1975) and *A Simple Story* (*Une histoire simple*, 1978), (she won Césars for Best Actress for both films). Above all, she bared a vivid but vulnerable soul.

No film better expressed Schneider's persona than the moment in *The Things of Life* when she glares at Pierre (Michel Piccoli) and says: *Tu m'aimes parce que je suis là, mais si il faut traverser la rue pour me rejoindre, tu es perdu. Tu es comme un vieux. Les avions s'en iront sans toi; en fait tu n'as plus d'espoir.* (You love me because I am here, but if you have to cross the street to meet me, you're confused. You're old. Planes will take off without you; in fact you have no hope.) Those words embodied not just the sensual dominance of the actress herself but also a residual sadness inherent to her personality. Like Catherine in *Jules and Jim*, Romy asserts her presence in a way that shows a woman encouraged to experiment in front of the demanding camera. Rosalie may be her most intense role, but it involved the greatest risks as well as the greatest triumph. Sautet was not renowned for his depiction of female characters, but Rosalie comes to life with Schneider's emotional pragmatism and her instinctive, dour fun. The long sequence in which she departs is a perfect expression of spitefulness and playfulness.

In her later years, the actress experienced several personal tragedies, including the accidental death of her fourteen-year-old son. A few months later, Romy Schneider was found dead in her Paris apartment. The official cause was heart failure, though friends of the actress believe that she committed suicide.

Following the success of *The Things of Life* as well as of *César and Rosalie*, Claude Sautet's *Vincent, François, Paul and the Others* (1974), one of the rare Sautet films in which Romy Schneider did not star, renewed his favorite theme—the relationship between men and women over forty. All the different aspects of existence are scrutinized in a

Romanesque manner: love, work, friendship, ambitions, and disillusionment. A group of middle-aged, long time friends face midlife crises. Although sharing common social successes, Vincent (Yves Montand), the owner of a small company, sees trouble in his life as he faces bankruptcy, the sudden departure of his lover, and the relentless desire of his wife for divorce. François (Michel Piccoli), a successful physician, has lost his ideals in medicine and simply works for money as he entertains a tumultuous relationship with his wife, who does not hide her relation with another man. Paul (Serge Reggiani), a thriving journalist, struggles with a never-ending novel he has been writing for twenty years. One day, a sudden heart attack sends Vincent to the hospital, strengthening the friendship among the friends. The realistic depiction of the group's plight, the disappointment in their lives, and the loss of their youthful dreams to change the world, despite their social accomplishments, carries along with the simple story line a heavy burden of human failure, the price of which seems high. In theory, the friends would all seek to help one another, but when money creates conflicts, the friendships disappear until reconciliation (re)occurs. The group of friends see Vincent's heart attack as an ineluctable stage of life that awaits each one of them; it symbolically represents the end of youth.

Similarly, in *A Simple Story* Romy Schneider plays Marie, an independent, forty-year-old, middle-class woman who chooses to rule over her dull existence as she seeks separation from Serge (Claude Brasseur) when Georges (Bruno Cremer), her former husband, comes back into her life. The film is a description of the characters' struggles, an examination of their behavior as they make the transition between youth and their future.

Jean-Loup Dabadie, who authored the script for *A Simple Story* in collaboration with Claude Sautet, played a major role in Sautet's success. *A Simple Story* earned an Academy Award nomination for Best Foreign Film in 1979. François Truffaut described him as one of the most influential screenwriters of the postwar era: "The common denominator [. . .] is Jean-Loup Dabadie, a true cinema writer, quite simply an excellent writer in any case, a musician of words that sound like what they are, modest and mischievous, scrupulous and inspired, a daring young man on the flying typewriter, and trained in Sautet's school."[41] The strong performances, the solid directing, and the tightly structured script all contributed to the film's success. Romy Schneider, despite her prestige in the French cinema of the 1970s, was convincing in her rendition of an ordinary woman emotionally affected through her own personal and professional struggles. The framing device worked to make Marie a gentle character and worthy hero. Once again, Sautet depicted the dead-end lives of a series of characters from a humanistic perspective. Romy Schneider, Michel Piccoli, and Yves Montand were undeniably the speakers for Sautet at his best, a constant visual movement between character studies and social chronicles.

In the early 1970s, François Truffaut, who, after a phenomenal first decade of filmmaking in the 1960s, was reaching a turning point in his career. Following more or less successful films such as *Wild Child* (*L'enfant sauvage*, 1970) and *Day for Night* (*La nuit américaine*, 1973), Truffaut's second international breakthrough occurred with *The Story of Adele H.* (*L'histoire d'Adèle H.*, 1975), an openly humanistic film that narrated Adèle Hugo's secret diary. The mesmerizing Isabelle Adjani played Adèle, a young woman crushed by the weight of her famous father figure, the writer Victor Hugo, and the sudden death of her sister Léopoldine (who drowned in 1843). Under a false identity Adèle arrives in Halifax in 1863 to find her English lover, Albert Pinson (Bruce Robinson), the Hussard lieutenant with whom she was madly in love. The two met on the Channel Island of Guernsey, where Victor Hugo lived in exile after Napoléon III overthrew the French Republic. In order to survive, Adèle constantly has to solicit the financial help of her father. Adèle receives her father's consent to marry, but the young officer does not return her affections and eventually turns her down. The consequences are dreadful for Adèle's young, sensitive mind. The unbearable solitude, the need to relentlessly imagine new impostures, and the repeated lie to her parents who think that she is indeed married all work to entrap her in a swirl of revolt and, ultimately, madness. She is eventually taken back to France in 1872 and sent to a mental institution, where she dies in 1915 at the age of eighty-five. Somber and romantic, passionate and obsessive in love, Adèle self-destructs. The 1975 New York Film Critics' Circle awarded Isabelle Adjani the prize for Best Actress and Truffaut the prize for Best Screenwriting.

Isabelle Adjani (b. 1955), whose glamorous French femininity attracted and still attracts the attention of many French and foreign directors, is undeniably entitled to the status of international stardom. In 1977, *Time* magazine dedicated its cover to the twenty-two-year-old who quickly drew attention with her emotional sincerity and rare dedication to dramatic acting. Adjani's first important movie role following her apprenticeship at the Comédie-Française, was in Claude Pinoteau's *The Slap* (*La gifle*, 1974) revealing another aspect of her intriguing individuality. The depth of her acting talents was further demonstrated through intense, self-destructive, and passionate characters in love stories like Jean Becker's *One Deadly Summer* (*L'été meurtrier*, 1983). Later, Bruno Nuytten's *Camille Claudel* (*Camille Claudel*, 1988) confirmed Adjani as one of the most talented French actresses of all time. She received Oscar nominations for her performances in *The Story of Adele H.* due to the dramatic intensity of the film, which also revealed her talent as unclassifiable, as well as *Camille Claudel,* and in the 1990s she won the César for Best Actress in Patrice Chéreau's *Queen Margot* (*La reine Margot,* 1994). She also starred with Sharon Stone and Chaz Palminteri in Jeremiah Chechik's *Diabolique* in 1996, a Franco-American coproduction (and remake of Henri-Georges Clouzot's *Les diaboliques*). Other significant films include Alain Berbérian's *Paparazzi* (*Paparazzi,* 1998), Luc Besson's *Subway* (1984), Werner Herzog's *Nosferatu the Vampyre* (*Nosferatu: Phantom der Nacht,* 1979), and André Téchiné's *Barocco* (*Barocco,* 1976) and *The Bronte Sisters* (*Les soeurs Brontë,* 1978).

In his numerous explorations of psychological truths, Truffaut has rarely disclosed a need to limit himself to what can be considered "realistic." With *The Man Who Loved Women*[42] (*L'homme qui aimait les femmes,* 1977), Truffaut depicted a man whose main passion in life was concocting elaborate erotic intrigues, and who dedicated his adult life to an unremitting courtly pursuit of female lovers, none of whom could fulfill his aspirations. Suzanne Schiffman, in collaboration with Michel Fermaud and Truffaut, wrote the script.

The story begins in Montpellier with the funeral of the main protagonist, Bertrand Morane (Charles Denner), a forthright gentleman who preys on female hearts and minds for personal pleasure. Attending the funeral are dozens of female companions, all of whom he had loved at a moment during his life. The forty-year-old engineer Bertrand, who does not find much satisfaction in his professional career, cannot keep his eyes and mind off women. For this modern-age libertine, the only real passion in life is the pursuit of women. Although dealing with an old theme—Don Juan and his sexual exploits—the film relentlessly examines the central subject matter in every scene. The character of the "traditional womanizer" is portrayed differently since the story glorifies not the protagonist but instead the intricacy of his strategies, the man's forged destiny, and his unavoidable series of elaborate lies.

Struck by an unknown woman's legs in a laundry room (supposedly Nathalie Baye's), Bertrand has just enough time to write down her car's license plate. He makes a dent in his own car while tracking down her telephone number. Then he calls her under the pretense that she has caused this dent so that he may set up a meeting with her. A solitary hunter, Bertrand loves all women: a nanny whose number he had copied off a bulletin board in a department store, a car rental agent, a movie usherette, a bar waitress, a lingerie store owner, and a wake-up call telephone operator whose voice is the only tangible source of seduction. A female phone operator awakens him every morning

Charles Denner (Bertrand) and Brigitte Fossey (Geneviève) in François Truffaut's *The Man Who Loved Women* (*L'homme qui aimait les femmes*, 1977), (Courtesy of BIFI/ © Dominique Le Rigoleur).

and, although he is half-asleep, he relentlessly begs her to meet him. While constantly on the prowl for new adventures, Bertrand decides to write an autobiographical compilation of the accounts of his love adventures. The book, first entitled *Le cavaleur* (The flirt or the skirt chaser), is changed to *The Man Who Loved Women* and is eventually published. On Christmas Eve, unable to spend the holidays alone, Bertrand, in his relentless search for a female companion that night, is hit by a car while crossing a street (he had just recognized a former lover). As he regains consciousness in the hospital, he notices at a distance the elegant features of a nurse's legs. As he tries to get out of bed, he falls badly and dies doing what he has done his entire life: pursuing a woman.

Truffaut chose Charles Denner, an actor he had long admired for his natural intelligence, to avoid succumbing to the "handsome" stereotype of the traditional Casanova, which would have irrevocably changed the nature of the hero. Instead, the ordinary looks of Bertrand Morane win over our sympathy. The anxious, introverted, and serious nature of the hero, in addition to his ordinary look, gives the film all the force it requires to impart Bertrand's credo: a man who values the

love of women above everything else in his life. Far from being sala-
cious, the impulsive behavior of the protagonist actually reveals the
joy found in innumerable relationships and sexual quests. Denner
brought an interesting dimension to his character that would have
been absent with a more conventionally handsome leading man. His
physical presence emphasizes just how irrelevant a role physical beauty
can play in the game of seduction. With the character of Bertrand,
everything turns on creativity and experience, as he announces early in
the narrative: "Women's legs are compasses which circle the globe,
giving it its equilibrium and harmony."[43] For him, lovemaking is a
matter of technique, preparation, and will. Sex, jealousy, envy, and
revenge are so chaotic in his mind that he hardly bothers to separate
these strands. His impulse, simply, is to exert his influence in his little
world of women; how he exerts himself is almost beside the point. He
uses his power willfully, whenever and wherever he likes, without a
thought for consequences. In Montpellier, Bertrand lives the life of a
single man. When he goes out to restaurants or to the movies in search
of a possible conquest, the pursuit of an idea or an image takes over.
The more the road presents obstacles, ambushes, and deceptions, the
more the quest becomes mystical.

Through an earthy yet detached cinematography, Truffaut's fantasy
blurred with reality and beautifully rendered an atypical protagonist
driven to the edge of his obsession. What happens for the viewer is
mirrored in the changes in the characters, and what begins as amusement deepens into tragedy. The richness at the conclusion of the film
is not quite what is expected at the beginning, which features the
lightness of Truffaut's cinematography. Truffaut was able to achieve a
persuasive meditation on the theme of human obsession—obsession to
seduce and to create (as in literature), which eventually transformed a
personal and intimate experience into a singular language.

Later in the story, Bertrand manages to get the phone number of
Martine (Nathalie Baye). Although she lives in another city, Bertrand
drives there and finally reaches her by phone, only to confess immediately the true purpose of his phone call. Five minutes later, they meet
in a bar, and to his great disappointment he understands that the
woman he saw was actually Martine's cousin, who was just visiting at
the time. Once back in Montpellier, Bertrand stops by the car rental
agency to thank the employee who helped him and invites her for
dinner. After a romantic evening, she reveals why she accepted his
invitation so quickly: "I think it's hard to refuse you anything. You
have a special way of asking. It is as if your life depended on it. But
then, maybe, it's just a trick on your part—the playboy who doesn't
look like one, the wolf with a worried look."[44] It is precisely this
anxiety that is the basis of his obsession.

Bothered by his personal problems created by his fascination for women, Bertrand seeks help through a self-imposed therapy, writing an autobiographical novel of his innumerable conquests. Unlike the traditionally represented Casanova and other celluloid heroes, for whom love corresponds more to an unadorned serial quest for lust, Bertrand's seduction is just the opposite. An introverted and restless hunter, Bertrand strives to seduce women despite the most difficult obstacles that make the venture an intricate passion, a convoluted way of life on which the very purpose of his existence depends. Beleaguered by the presence of all the letters and photos of his ex-lovers that he has stocked for years, Bertrand finally decides to write his memoir to vent his obsession but also to avoid oblivion. He does not want to forget the women's names. As he locks himself in his bathroom to avoid the distraction of daylight, the first-time author resuscitates his childhood memory (which indirectly recalls Antoine Doinel's) before setting his imagination free and confessing the most intimate details about the women who have crossed his path. He writes: "Some are so beautiful from the back that I prolong the moment to catch up so as not be disappointed. But I'm never disappointed. When they turn out to be ugly, I feel somehow relieved . . . since it's out of the question to have them all!"[45]

Even failures are counted as victories. One day he witnesses an attractive young woman who just left her baby sitting job. He calls to hire her services, and when the young woman enters his apartment, she wonders where the baby is. Bertrand, who pretends that the baby is sleeping in his room, gets caught by the babysitter, who discovers a big baby doll tucked in the cradle. Another day the lingerie-store owner, Catherine, who sees him regularly, reveals after an intense flirting game, her secret attraction for younger men, much to Bertrand's dismay.

Once Bertrand's book is finished, the manuscript is sent to a Parisian publisher. At first the publishing committee, mainly made up of men, express no interest in the book. One of the editors, Geneviève (Brigitte Fossey), however, takes up the defense of the first-time author and finally persuades the rest of the group that with some necessary changes the book is meant to be published. The new title of the book, *The Man Who Loved Women*, suits Bertrand, but one detail puzzles him, namely, the use of the past tense. For Geneviève, the particular use of this tense suggests the ephemeral course of love in man's existence and, therefore, its preciousness. Geneviève is the ultimate woman in Bertrand's life:

Amid these kaleidoscopic fragments of Bertrand's amorous universe, one woman does emerge as the most significant—as well as Truf-

faut's most intelligently engaging female characterization. Geneviève
Bigey is an editor who convinces her publishing house to accept Bertrand's autobiographical novel, *The Man Who Loved Women*. Her structural importance is evident from the film's opening scene, as she is the
first (and last) narrator; her voice-over is the frame and the vehicle for
his story. Even before we know who is speaking, Geneviève is visually
set apart from the crowd of women at Bertrand's funeral: she stands
above the rest, and is occasionally given her own frame in close-up. . . .
She is a professional and therefore liberated woman . . . Geneviève is in
a sense an even more hopeful character . . . since romance is integrated
into her work: after being close to a text, she grows closer to its
author.[46]

Truffaut succeeded with the difficult task of making a film that
captures the background and ethos of a particular male behavior, a
social group for which manipulation and sexual-power games are often
a way of life. According to Diana Holmes and Robert Ingram, Geneviève's role as master narrator "does not negate the 'phallocentric' tone
of much of the film, but it did confirm that the film is also about the
problematic nature of conventionally andocentric sexual relations."[47] It
is also important to note that the central theme is not the portrayal of
innocent women, exploited and betrayed by a corrupt, decadent, and
discredited man. This confusion of behaviors, although often misunderstood by audiences, captured the spirit of the times and the breath
of social and artistic liberalism. It was a metaphor for total masculine
control over sexuality and an extreme expression of the basic subconscious attitude of many men toward women.

Truffaut's films were also known for their surface charm, which
often concealed highly paradoxical nuances, as he even occasionally
took leading or supporting roles in his own films (in *The Man Who
Loved Women*, he is an extra in the opening funeral scene). Despite the
appearance of both traditional and "on the spur of the moment" aspect
of the film, *The Man Who Loved Women* might very well be Truffaut's
most personal film (excluding *The Four Hundred Blows*).[48] Truffaut
repeatedly chose dazzling and strong leading ladies: Jeanne Moreau in
Jules and Jim and *The Bride Wore Black* (*La mariée était en noir*, 1967),
Catherine Deneuve in *Mississippi Mermaid* (*La sirène du Mississippi*,
1969) and *The Last Metro* (*Le dernier métro*, 1980), Jacqueline Bisset in
Day for Night, Isabelle Adjani in *The Story of Adele H.*, and Fanny
Ardant in *The Woman Next Door* (*La femme d'à côté*, 1981) and *Confiden-
tially Yours* (*Vivement dimanche*, 1983). But when *The Man Who Loved
Women* opened in April 1977, the French feminist press hammered it
for Truffaut's unequivocal misogynistic elements. Despite this negative
publicity, however, the film was a commercial and critical success,
with a screening totaling twelve weeks that year. Interestingly enough,

François Truffaut and Jean-Pierre Léaud (Photo courtesy of the Museum of Modern Art/Film Stills Archive).

the film met with greater success in northern Europe while it remained largely misunderstood in Latin countries where "ostentatious woman-izing" is traditionally a more overt theme in cinematic pop culture.[49]

One of the least known of Truffaut's films from the 1970s, *The Green Room* (*La chambre verte,* 1978), was solemn and serious in tone and dealt principally with the subject of death. Truffaut himself played the death-obsessed chronicler who created a pantheon devoted to the memory of the people he loved. The pivotal questions of life versus death and love versus the memory of those who have passed away were treated both rationally and emotionally.

More than ten years after the end of World War I, Julien Davenne (Truffaut), an unassuming newspaper reporter, specializes in the obit-uary section. He lives a peaceful life in a small provincial town. Deeply moved by the death toll of the war, he is constantly haunted by the idea of death, especially the memory of his wife, who passed away shortly after they were married. On the first floor of his house, Julien has created a room for his lost loved ones. One day in an auction room, Julien meets Cécilia (Nathalie Baye), who helps him find the ring that Julie, his late wife, used to own, and a sort of mutual feeling begins to flourish between them. Julien receives permission from the ecclesi-astical authorities to rehabilitate an abandoned chapel close to a cemetery. Julien, whose only wish is to join Julie in death, gives up on life and gradually weakens. And among all the photographs of those who gave their lives during the war, he peacefully dies.

One of the motivations for the film was a peculiar declaration made by the director, who said that, as the years go by, the number of one's acquaintances become smaller and smaller, until eventually one realizes that there are more people who are dead than alive in one's life. The director in part was inspired by several of Henry James's novels and tales, including "The Altar of the Dead," but mostly the film narrated a considerable part of his own life, his own reality and existential torments, reinforcing the centrality of his points of view. This particular aspect of "anticipated" autobiography (the fascination with death) is evidenced in the final scene when Julien's obsessions overwhelm him and lead him to death. For him, lost ones fall into oblivion when no one honors them; detached from the ideas of the Catholic church, the dead are alive and closer than what religion suggests as long as one remembers them and commemorates their names. Despite Truffaut's limitations as an actor (he lends little credibility to the words and existential sufferings of his character), his deeply personal involvement with the material conveyed an important constituent to the overall performance. Other features of the film helped convey the appropriate mood. The carefully crafted setting gave the narrative an element of solemnity and prevented the film from being overwhelmed by unnecessary lyricism and heavy symbolism. The editing was technically predominant, although misleading, with its mix of contemporary sources and staged dramatizations.

A year later, with *Love on the Run* (*L'amour en fuite,* 1979), Truffaut put an end to the series featuring Antoine Doinel's[50] sentimental tribulations. Through the use of extensive flashback to previous features, the film examined the ways in which art and passion could dispose of one's existence and happiness. The last episode of Antoine's vicissitudes, *Love on the Run* depicted the new relation between Antoine (Jean-Pierre Léaud), now thirty, and Sabine (Dorothée), a young salesperson in a record store. Antoine also runs into Colette (Marie-France Pisier), a former teenage love, who bought Antoine's first published autobiographical novel. Criticized for using too many former episodes of Antoine's past (*The Four Hundred Blows, Stolen Kisses,* and others), *Love on the Run* gave the series a captivating dimension to the memories of Antoine, thanks to the inimitable quality of the montage. Antoine Doinel displayed consistency in his character during the four episodes of the saga, and each time conveyed cinematographic intelligence and the sensitivity of the filmmaker.

*   *   *

The art of Eric Rohmer is a rather special case in the history of French cinema.[51] Born Jean-Marie Maurice Scherer in 1920, Rohmer has used perhaps some of the most humble mise-en-scènes in all of filmmaking history with his simple, low-budget films while exploring the dynamics and secrets of human relationships. Rohmer's narrative style explored in a calculated manner only those aspects of life that seemed most engaging to him, particularly between protagonists with his own idiosyncratic universe, a literary and philosophical background, all wrapped in an evocative narrative environment. Despite the recurrent format of their content (usually gathered in feature series such as *Moral Tales/Contes Moraux* and *Comedies and Proverbs/Comédies et proverbes*), Rohmer's romantic tales possess a refined and consistent talent that has been inspirational to many contemporary film directors. In his films, the visual lightness and informality of camera motions and the evocative treatment of the camera's relationship with reality revealed the presence of a number of cinematographic styles, such as intellectualism in *My Night at Maud's (Ma nuit chez Maud*, 1969), tenderness in *Pauline at the Beach (Pauline à la plage*, 1983), and sensuality in *Claire's Knee (Le genou de Claire*, 1970) and *Chloé in the Afternoon (L'amour l'après-midi*, 1972), as well as the "myth of youth" in an idiosyncratic vision of Chrétien de Troyes's *Perceval le Gallois (Perceval le Gallois*, 1978). Due to his deeply embedded lyrical personality, Rohmer's cinema intentionally limited its spectrum of concerns, and deliberately excluded certain human issues, involving social and political subject matter. For his detractors, Rohmer's cinema limited itself to the insubstantial, as part of a larger artistic and intellectual scheme, which, as a result, often failed to convey a persuasive artistic message. His narratives usually overlooked a possible contact with the spectator's deeper mental universe, and, as a result, the presence of unremitting melancholy in Rohmer's films has always had a limited impact on French popular audiences.

As undeniable as it is that Rohmer's cinema is a secluded one, it is also important to recognize the impact his films have had over some four decades. The fidelity of Rohmer's supporters has always assured his films reliable production; this is an unprecedented record of success in French cinema. The latest Rohmer cycle, *Contes des quatre saisons*, includes *A Tale of Springtime (Un conte de printemps*, 1989), *A Winter's Tale (Un conte d'hiver*, 1992), *A Summer's Tale (Un conte d'été*, 1996), and *Autumn Tale (Un conte d'automne*, 1998).

Rohmer earned numerous international prizes over the years, including the Silver Bear at the Berlin Film Festival for *The Collector (La collectionneuse*, 1966), an Oscar nomination for Best Foreign Film and Best Screenplay at the 1970 Academy Awards for *My Night at Maud's*, the Special Jury Prize at the 1976 Cannes Film Festival for *The Mar-*

quise of O (La marquise d'O, 1976), and the prize for Best Screenplay at the 1998 Venice Film Festival for *Autumn Tale.*

THE STORYTELLERS: BERTRAND BLIER AND BERTRAND TAVERNIER

Bertrand Blier (b. 1939), son of the popular French actor Bernard Blier (1916–89), began his career as assistant to Georges Lautner and as an adept of "direct cinema" shorts (*Hitler, connais pas,* 1963). Blier the director is seen as the most truculent maker of French films of the 1970s, a time that he generally considered stale and too conventional. He promoted a mode of cinema that would allow the director to write intimate dialogues, invent stories, and, in general, produce a film as an artistic whole in his or her own style. In the 1980s and 1990s, Blier produced several of the most popular films at the French box office: *Stepfather (Beau-Père,* 1981), *Ménage (Tenue de soirée,* 1986), *Too Beautiful for You (Trop belle pour toi,* 1989), *Thank You, Life (Merci la vie,* 1991), *My Man (Mon homme,* 1996), and *Actors (Les acteurs,* 2000).

Following a "false" start in 1963 with *Hitler, connais pas,* Blier had to wait an entire decade to make a full-length feature. Unsuccessful in his repeated attempts to persuade producers with the first-draft scenario of *Going Places (Les valseuses,* 1974), Blier successfully published it as a novel and then, once it was recognized, remodeled it for cinema. When the film premiered in France in March 1974, *Going Places* was one of the major cinematographic events of the decade. With it came much more than simply a new type of filmmaking; it also corresponded to the starting point of a new generation of actors. Although far from making a *cinéma d'auteurs,* Bertrand Blier offered an innovative look at reality, reevaluating the supposedly "liberated" society of the early 1970s with a sharp psychological approach and a good dose of cynical eroticism.

Going Places, which mirrored the disaffected, anarchic mood of France's youth of the time, propelled Blier all the way to the Oscars. The action-packed "country" road movie set in a sort of postapocalyptic near future narrates the idle existence of two young ex-cons who rapidly become aimless thugs: Jean-Claude (Gérard Depardieu) and Pierrot (Patrick Dewaere). The pair bully, harass, and steal from the residents of surrounding neighborhoods for entertainment. During an attempt to swipe a car, the owner injures Pierrot. After finding a surgeon for Pierrot's wound, he and Jean-Claude decide to rob the surgeon of his money and make their way across France, pulling petty crimes and accosting women whenever possible. They eventually meet Jeanne (Jeanne Moreau), also an ex-con, who happens to have just gotten out of jail. Disregarding common decency, Jean-Claude and

Pierrot travel the length and breadth of the country in stolen cars, in pursuit of hedonistic freedom. They are joined by a hairdresser, Marie-Ange (Miou-Miou), who ends up their lover, domestic, and confidante.

Dehumanization and isolation are at the center of almost every film by Bertrand Blier, and can readily be seen in *Going Places*. What makes this story compelling is not the violence itself, but the film's suggestion that passion is an inherently human characteristic; once taken away, it will make the individual less human. Blier presented violence in an unremitting, heightened manner, rendering the film alarmingly evocative and overpowering. With close, handheld camera shots, he invited viewers to critically observe Pierrot and Jean-Claude stealing and pillaging through the cities and countryside of France, and ultimately displayed to them that violence and power could be portrayed as inherently seductive. Blier's film made millions of viewers all the more uncomfortable as they found themselves sympathizing with such morally adverse characters. Blier never gave Pierrot and Jean-Claude any excuse for their behavior. There is no doubt that *Going Places* painted an extremely disturbing portrait of society as the viewers found themselves understanding the position of the two main protagonists. It is a brilliant, darkly poetic work that is able to enrapture and disgust viewers simultaneously. The stoic humanistic portrait in *Going Places* was emblematic of Blier's discomfort, and faithfully represented the arduous difficulty for the outsider of French cinema to communicate his individualistic conviction. Always concerned with the process as well as the end product, Blier has maintained his role as critic and commentator throughout his filmmaking career, as proud of his books as he is of his films.

Going Places was not concerned with the representation of events, the narration of fates, or the adventures of chosen characters. Instead Blier's films focused on the presentation of individuals' basic situations, presenting intuition in its daily situations as his characters experienced it. Pierrot and Jean-Claude are isolated, static, and motionless; thus, they express themselves from the inside. In *Going Places,* the whole universe reveals the psychological state of the characters who are parts of it. Blier's characters were expelled from the stream of successive life events, which created the illusion of time that could stop at one single moment, to reveal a static, unceasing, incongruous, and cruel world of absurdity.

Yet despite all the innovations of his work, Blier remained surprisingly consistent and limited in the targets of his social satire: the Catholic church, bourgeois culture, and totalitarianism. Blier's oeuvre was also one of frustrating inconsistency. Unlike Jean-Luc Godard and Jacques Rivette, he never made an "unwatchable" movie; but he would never approach the brilliance or innovation of their best works either.

Going Places is regarded as one of the pioneering films that carried the film industry into the next decade, and its important legacy is a testament not only to the talent of its cast, filmmaker, and crew but also to the cinematographic renewal that has undoubtedly stood the test of time. *Going Places* is one of those classics that simply cannot be remade better than the original. As Ginette Vincendeau describes it, Blier's work possesses an ability to capture *l'air du temps*[52] with all its crude language (constant use of French suburban slang/argot of the *banlieues*), obscenity (*Going Places*), cold objectivity (*Stepfather/Beau-Père* 1981, and *Too Beautiful for You/Trop belle pour toi,* 1989), exteriorization of the angst of urban existence (*Cold Cuts/Buffet froid,* 1979), and sexual obsession (*Get out Your Handkerchiefs/Préparez vos mouchoirs,* 1978, and *Ménage/Tenue de soirée,* 1986). His regular attempt to screen the bitter truth about sexual conduct in modern-day society is perhaps a heralding signal of the dead end in which modern society has unfortunately entered, leaving the weakest ones to their own fate. As amoral as his narratives may be, Blier somehow managed to capture a raw and compelling vision of modern social decadence. While one must look elsewhere for a critical examination, Blier remained an authoritative and revelatory film artist whose permissive/transgressive cinematographic semantics remind the spectator of the extremely narrow line between order and chaos, *libération des moeurs* or pure provocation, erotic energy and provocative exploration of sexual extravaganza.

In establishing a new-style male protagonist in French cinema, *Going Places* consequently boosted the reputations of Gérard Depardieu and Patrick Dewaere, which grew considerably during the rest of the decade. One of Bertrand Blier's favorite actors was Patrick Dewaere (1947–1982), who undeniably was one of the most talented and popular French players of the 1970s. Following his debut at the famous Café de la Gare[53] (a stand-up comedy club that featured such future film stars as Gérard Depardieu), Dewaere (born Jean-Marie Bourdeau) landed his first important role in *Going Places.* Despite five César nominations for Best Actor and several participations at the Cannes Film Festival—in particular, for Alain Corneau's *Thriller Story* (*Série noire,* 1979) and Blier's *Stepfather*—Dewaere was never awarded a prize. For many directors, including Jean-Jacques Annaud, Claude Lelouch, and Bertrand Blier, Dewaere's vast psychological complexity was one of the most interesting and attractive facets of his talent, leading him toward unusual protagonists who are violent in their quest for love and desperately in search of sentimental comfort. In the second half of the 1970s, he was the symbol of a generation of actors, representing a certain discomfort and agitation expressed with no ambiguity. He gave expression and reality to characters destined to emptiness and oblivion. Despite Dewaere's obvious talent for comedy, he was often

Patrick Dewaere (Stéphane) and Gérard Depardieu (Raoul) in Bertrand Blier's *Get out Your Handkerchiefs* (*Préparez vos mouchoirs*, 1978), (Courtesy of BIFI/© Ariane).

successfully cast as fragile, neurotic individuals playing a wide variety of roles on both sides of the social order—for example, a judge in Yves Boisset's *Le juge Fayard dit "le Shérif"* and a thug in *Série Noire*. Dewaere was notable for projecting a screen image of masculine strength that was nevertheless imbued with gentleness and sensitivity. By the late 1970s he had become the most popular actor in France and had achieved international fame. From his first appearance in *Going Places,* Dewaere's roles in film, theater, and television grew steadily in prominence. Shortly after the release of *Paradis pour tous* (*Paradise for All,* 1982), a black drama in which his character commits suicide, Patrick Dewaere shot himself on July 16, 1982, during the making of Lelouch's *Edith et Marcel.* The Patrick Dewaere Award was established in 1983. In 1992, the actor was the subject of the French documentary *Patrick Dewaere,* which was screened at the Cannes Film Festival.

Blier's other favorite actor, Gérard Depardieu (b. 1948), went from the provincial town of Châteauroux, where he grew up to Paris, where he studied acting. He made his screen debut in the short film *Le beatnik et le minet* (1965) and began to appear in full-length films in the early 1970s. Following his lead performance as a juvenile delinquent in *Going Places,* Depardieu was soon noted for his versatility and his unusual combination of gentleness and physicality. He subsequently appeared in such films as Bernardo Bertolucci's *Nineteen Hundred* (*1900,* 1976), Truffaut's *The Last Metro,* for which he won the César for Best Actor, Daniel Vigne's *The Return of Martin Guerre* (*Le retour de Martin Guerre,* 1981), Andrzej Wajda's *Danton* (*Danton,* 1982), and Claude Berri's *Jean de Florette* (*Jean de Florette,* 1986). In 1984, Depardieu also directed himself in stage and screen versions of Molière's *Tartuffe.* In 1988 he starred in *Camille Claudel,* and in 1990 he won the prize for Best Actor at the Cannes Film Festival for his exceptionally energetic role in *Cyrano de Bergerac* (*Cyrano de Bergerac,* 1990), which also received an Oscar nomination the following year. An international star due to his gift for performing an unlimited range of characters, Depardieu is today in a position to claim the title of greatest French actor of all time (before him, Jean Gabin was the only actor to have had such an aura).

Other significant films starring Depardieu include Sautet's *Vincent, François, Paul and the Others*; Blier's *Get out Your Handkerchiefs, Cold Cuts, Ménage,* and *Too Beautiful for You*; André Téchiné's *Barocco* (*Barocco,* 1976); Alain Resnais's *My American Uncle* (*Mon oncle d'Amérique,* 1980); Truffaut's *The Woman Next Door* (*La femme d'à côté,* 1981); Jean-Jacques Beineix's *The Moon in the Gutter* (*La lune dans le caniveau,* 1983); Philippe Labro's *Right Bank, Left Bank* (*Rive droite, rive gauche,* 1984); Alain Corneau's *Choice of Arms* (*Le choix des armes,* 1981), *Fort Saganne* (*Fort Saganne,* 1984), and *All the Mornings of the World* (*Tous les matins du monde,* 1991); Maurice Pialat's *Under the Sun of Satan* (*Sous le soleil de Satan,* 1987); Claude Berri's *Uranus* (*Uranus,* 1990) and *Germinal* (*Germinal,* 1993); Yves Angelo's *Colonel Chabert* (*Le Colonel Chabert,* 1994); Giuseppe Tornatore's *Una pura formalità* (*A Pure Formality,* 1994); Jean-Paul Rappeneau's *The Horseman on the Roof* (*Le Hussard sur le toit,* 1995); Claude Zidi's *Asterix and Obelix vs. Caesar* (*Astérix et Obélix contre César,* 1999); his own *The Bridge* (*Un pont entre deux rives,* 1999); Pitof's *Vidocq* (*Vidocq,* 2001); and Alain Chabat's *Astérix and Obélix: Mission Cléopatre* (2001), starring as Obélix.

The early 1990s were also Depardieu's introduction to American films, with his participation in Peter Weir's romantic comedy *Green Card* (1990), for which he received a Golden Globe Award, Ridley Scott's *1492: Conquest of Paradise* (1992), and Steve Miner's *My Father, the Hero* (a 1994 remake of Depardieu's 1991 French film *Mon père ce héros*). Depardieu received many international film awards and can best be described as one of France's most active professional actors in the

Gérard Depardieu (Alphonse Tram) and Geneviève Page (the widow) in Bertrand Blier's *Cold Cuts* (*Buffet froid*, 1979), (Photo courtesy of the Museum of Modern Art/Film Stills Archive/© Studio Canal).

industry as well as the champion of the so-called French cultural exception with his involvement in the international production of motion pictures (for example, coproducing in 1991 Satyajit Ray's last film, *Agantuk,* and financing the French distribution of the complete works of the American independent director John Cassavetes).

Blier's next important achievement in the 1970s was *Get out Your Handkerchiefs,* a film in which he self-consciously experimented with narrative form. The story opens in a Parisian bar where a young and depressed married couple, Raoul (Gérard Depardieu) and Solange (Carole Laure), struggle in their love life. Raoul is desperate because his apathetic wife will not give him a smile. Sunk in deep thought, she spends most of her days knitting pullovers: she barely looks at Raoul and does not talk much. To cure Solange's boredom and to release her from her sexual coma, Raoul unpredictably decides to offer her to the first stranger in the restaurant. This happens to be Stéphane (Patrick Dewaere), and Raoul begs him to become his wife's lover until she regains happiness. At first reluctant, Stéphane, a young physical education teacher (who, like Raoul, is a Mozart fan), eventually befriends the couple. Stéphane, however, fails to cheer up Solange. The two men's greatest mistake is to constantly attempt to offer her what they think she desires without ever giving her the freedom to express herself. Because they believe that the presence of a child in Solange's life is the key to her happiness, the three decide to work as summer camp counselors. Indeed, for the first time, Solange's mood seems to improve. She is particularly attracted to a precocious thirteen-year-old boy. Together, a new friendship and love begin, which finally quench her erotic longing; she has regained her laughter. Sentimental yet extremely sarcastic, the story of *Get out Your Handkerchiefs* was a success in the United States—a success all the more surprising since American society is not usually open to the depiction of love stories featuring such an age discrepancy (preteen-student and older teacher) and therefore seemed to have adapted to the discomfort of the story's moral landscape. Now more than ever the film is a rare testimony to the free spirit of the 1970s which contrasts with the 1980s and even more with today's sensitivity. Highly provocative, Blier's film cannot be easily characterized: it does not follow prescribed cinematographic conventions, instead achieving success because of its uniqueness. The music of Mozart, omnipresent throughout the film, contributed to the Best Score (by Georges Delerue) award at the Césars. *Get out Your Handkerchiefs* also earned the Oscar for Best Foreign Film in 1979 and the award for Best Screenwriting and Best Direction at the New York Film Critics' Circle in 1978.

One year later, it was again the on-screen personality of Gérard Depardieu that stood at the center of Blier's next film, *Cold Cuts*. The film heralded the director's movement into the Surrealist sphere. It also belonged to the black comedy genre and clearly epitomized, through the escapades of three men, the alienation and dehumanization process of the modern world and the pace of urbanization.

In a deserted Parisian subway station an unemployed young man, Alphonse Tram (Depardieu), finds an unknown man (Michel Serrault) stabbed to death with his own knife. As the film progresses, several deaths occur as Alphonse comes across other odd individuals with connections to the universe of death and alienation. Later, he meets an anomalous character who happens to live alone in his empty high-rise apartment block in the ultramodern district of La Défense. This man is a bored chief inspector, Morvandieu (Bernard Blier), a crooked individual who killed his wife years ago because he could not put up with her music. Soon after, Alphonse's wife is murdered, and although the psychotic killer (Jean Carmet) immediately begs Alphonse for forgiveness, neither the new widower nor the police inspector seems to be troubled. The three men now live together in a dehumanized universe of wide-open spaces, devoid of people or animals, and their eccentric demeanor is uniformly bleak and lacking in compassion. Indifferent to manslaughter (even of their own spouses), Alphonse and Morvandieu appear incapable of circumventing their existential anguish. Unable to sustain the stress of urban life, they decide to retreat to the countryside to calm their nerves. The bleak ghost-town background of the beginning of the film sets the tone and deliberately grants a disquieting gap with respect to the rural scenes of the epilogue. But there, too, a professional hit man tracks them down. The inspector and Alphonse, who now chase the killer, are eventually helped by a beautiful stranger (Carole Bouquet). While on a barge, Alphonse discovers that the police inspector does not know how to swim and immediately pushes him overboard in order to be left alone with the stranger. Alphonse's hope to elope with the mysterious woman is obliterated after she reveals her true identity. She is in fact the daughter of the victim stabbed in the metro. She shoots him and leaves.

Cold Cuts certainly reevaluated the standards of the crime thriller. As a distinctive film with a strong identity and clarity of purpose, it displayed an obvious moral indifference through images of urban paranoia and many discussions of sex and death. The film also provided a statement about the morality of power and contained an avalanche of affectionate references to the noir genre (Blier's favorite). Although the plot is ponderous, it defies the conventions of noir storytelling by not being open to a literal interpretation. The ambiguous, almost unintelligible nature of the dialogue, cryptic and literate at the same time, recalled Surrealism. The film received the César for Best Original Screenplay in 1980.

As a self-conscious moral satirist, Blier was not interested in a conventional narrative. According to film historian Jacques Siclier,[54] *Cold Cuts* was a pioneering film and inspired many filmmakers. Although the film evoked a situation similar to those found in the theater of the absurd of Eugène Ionesco, Blier never indulged in filmed theater, which would have meant possible rejection by audiences. The popular success of Blier's humor thus lay directly in its melodramatic subtext and the constant unpredictability of his characters.

Although radically different in style, the cinema of Bertrand Tavernier (b. 1941) also took its first steps in the mid 1970s. Discouraged by the obscurantism of certain auteurs, new directors, such as Blier and Tavernier began their careers with an already-established concept of storytelling. While working as a film critic for such journals as *Positif* and *Les cahiers du cinéma,* Tavernier wrote important books on American cinema and was hired as assistant director for Jean-Pierre Melville. His first feature film assignment, *The Clockmaker of St. Paul (L'horloger de Saint-Paul,* 1973), allowed him to impose his new "concept" on

French cinema. Surprisingly he collaborated with Jean Aurenche and
Pierre Bost (the two screenwriters of the postwar era who were vehemently criticized by Truffaut in *Les cahiers du cinéma*) to direct *The
Clockmaker of St. Paul,* which was also dedicated to Jacques Prévert.
This collaboration was all the more surprising in that Tavernier was
usually considered a New Wave critic. Although the screenplay was
adapted from the novel *L'horloger d'Everton* by Georges Simenon, several
producers had originally refused the project until Raymond Danon
accepted it. In Simenon's novel, the action actually took place in an
American town, where no one actually embodies the role of the enemy
or of the villain. However, due to a small budget, the scene was
transferred to Tavernier's native city of Lyon. The re-creation of an
American town would have involved a much more significant budget
and most likely would have diminished the credibility of the plot.

In *The Clockmaker of St. Paul,* Tavernier unveils the complex relationship that Michel Descombes (Philippe Noiret) faces with his passionate
twenty-year-old son and the bourgeois society that has fostered his
son's anger. Despite being divorced, Michel has a peaceful life. He
meets his friends at restaurants in the district of Saint-Paul in the
Vieux Lyon, where he enjoys his work, until tragedy steps in. Although not interested in politics, Michel respects the laws of society
as he peacefully maintains his existence as a good citizen. The serene
bliss comes to an end when his son, who lives with him, commits
murder. Since the son (Sylvain Rougerie) is now a fugitive, Police
Inspector Guiboud (Jean Rochefort) seeks Descombes to retrace the
young man's steps and make him surrender. Between the two men, a
confidential relationship grows. Eventually, the son surrenders, and
after an "expeditious" trial, he is condemned to twenty years in prison.
Despite their lack of intimacy, at the end of the story the father and
son realize that a sincere tie unites them for good, as Michel begins to
feel that he is unable to put the blame entirely on his son. Winner of
the 1974 Prix Louis Delluc, and the Silver Bear at the Berlin International Film Festival for that same year, *The Clockmaker of St. Paul* is a
brilliant authentication of introspection and humanity, through progressive and compassionate figures.

The strong elements of the narrative were the unique relationships
between completely opposite characters and the irreducibility of social
barriers. These helped model Tavernier's next feature film, *The Judge
and the Assassin (Le juge et l'assassin,* 1975). The narrative compares two
social portraits to prove that they are both the result of a social order
dominated by absurdity and injustice. There are references to the
intolerant climate at the end of the nineteenth century: Zola's books
are burned in public, anti-Semitic posters are displayed in the street,

and there is an exaltation of colonial grandeur. In 1893, Joseph Bouvier (Michel Galabru)[55] a former sergeant in the French military, is repudiated by his fiancée, Louise (Cécile Vassort). After attempting to murder her and botching his own suicide, Bouvier is sent to a hospital in Dole. The two bullets that the doctors are unable to remove from his skull cause him insurmountable pain. Although officially recognized as healthy and sound, Bouvier, once released from the hospital, commits a dozen atrocious crimes over the next few years all over southern France, attacking, raping, and killing isolated shepherdesses. Apparently mentally ill, he believes himself to be God's anarchist, assigned to reestablish justice on earth. Meanwhile, in Privas, provincial Judge Rousseau (Philippe Noiret), who is determined to solve the case to promote his own stagnant political career, suspects the murders are linked. When Bouvier is finally arrested, the judge begins to enact his plan. Convinced that Bouvier is faking his mental illness, he gradually becomes the murderer's confidant, uncovering more and more revelations as he convinces him that his madness will eventually be sufficient reason to rule out the death penalty. Once all the irrefutable proof is gathered, the trial begins, and Bouvier is condemned to death.

Directly inspired by a true story, the case of Joseph Vacher, the film was shot partly in the same region as the actual murders. The film probed the intriguing relationship between the condemner and the condemned, which echoed the circumstances of the late-nineteenth-century Dreyfus scandal, the anarchist movement, the division between church and state, and the difficult birth of trade unions as a latent social and historical background. In his second feature, Tavernier's narrative skills were characterized by the absence of stylistic excess and predominance for a simple discourse in order to reach emotion rather than visual impression. *The Judge and the Assassin* was critically acclaimed and enjoyed considerable success at the 1977 French Césars with the award for Best Actor to Michel Galabru, Best Music to Philippe Sarde, Best Original Screenplay to Jean Aurenche[56] and Tavernier.

Tavernier continued to produce solid quality work, with *Deathwatch* (*La mort en direct*, 1980), *Clean Slate* (*Coup de torchon*, 1981), *Mississippi Blues* (1983), *A Sunday in the Country* (*Un dimanche à la campagne*, 1984), *'Round Midnight* (*Autour de minuit*, 1986), *Life and Nothing But* (*La vie et rien d'autre*, 1989), and *It All Starts Today* (*Ça commence aujourd'hui*, 1999). He has been president of the Institut Lumière in Lyon since its creation in 1982.

Closely associated with Tavernier's career is the presence of actor Philippe Noiret (b. 1930). Part of the group of great actors able to perform a wide variety of different characters without ever having to relinquish the proper individuality, Noiret achieved several of his best performances in Tavernier's works. He is also one of the few French comedians to collaborate regularly with the best Italian directors, such as Marco Ferreri in *La Grande Bouffe* (1973), Mario Monicelli in *Amici miei* (*Mes chers amis*, 1975), and Giuseppe Tornatore in *Cinema Paradiso* (1989). Noiret began a successful career in Louis Malle's 1960 *Zazie dans le Métro*. He won a César for his performance in *The Old Gun* (*Le vieux fusil*, 1975), an honor he again earned for his portrayal of a World War I major in *Life and Nothing But*. Recipient of the Best Actor award at the 1976 New York Film Critics' Circle for *The Clockmaker of St. Paul*, Noiret also performed in Oscar-winning movies such as Michael Radford's *The Postman* (*Il Postino*, 1994).

It is important to keep in mind that despite the highs and lows of the industry throughout the decades, comedies have always been faithful economic boosters for French cinema. In part due to the sudden absence of veteran comedians Bourvil and Fernandel—who died in 1970 and 1971, respectively—the 1970s produced a number of mediocre comedies the majority of which, ironically, happened to be considerable commercial successes. Despite their sociological and cultural contents, French comedies are still neglected by film anthologies, film studies conferences, and, in particular, film festivals all over the world. The success of Gérard Oury at the beginning of the decade can be easily explained by the "commercial" stature of his first two successes (*Don't Look Now We're Being Shot At/La grande vadrouille* and *The Sucker/ Le corniaud*), but also by the better quality of the scripts when compared to average comedies. More sophisticated and sharper in its vocabulary, the plot gave access to very large means to complete its goals, which surpassed the average French comedies of the time. One of the most celebrated successes of French comedy is Edouard Molinaro's *La Cage Aux Folles* (*La cage aux folles*, 1978). Adapted from a play written by Jean Poiret, the story depicts the vicissitudes of a happily settled homosexual couple, Renato Baldi (Ugo Tognazzi), manager of the travestite nightclub La Cage aux Folles in Saint-Tropez, and his long-time life companion, Albin (Michel Serrault), also the club's biggest attraction, Zaza Napoli, professional female impersonator. Laurent, Renato's son, announces to his father his future marriage to Andréa, daughter of an ultraconservative senator (Michel Galabru). As Andréa's parents come down to Saint-Tropez to meet Renato for the first time, Laurent attempts to persuade Albin to step out of the family picture. But because Laurent's mother, Simone, (Claire Maurier) refuses to attend the dinner, Albin decides at the last minute to replace her in his role as Zaza.

In the late 1970s, the gay subtext of the film helped bring about a new outlook among audiences who for the most part were unpredictably swept away by the new energy of this comedy. Using the classic stratagem of vaudeville, the authors were able to redirect the plot toward a parade of frenetic and ingenious situations rather than a display of low and derisive vulgarity. The success of *La Cage Aux Folles* generated the completion of two sequels, *La Cage Aux Folles II* (1980) and Georges Lautner's *La Cage Aux Folles III,* and earned Michel Serrault the César for Best Actor in 1979. In 1996, the American remake of the film, Mike Nichols's *The Birdcage,* was similarly quite a success in American theaters. It starred Robin Williams, Nathan Lane, Dianne Wiest, and Gene Hackman.

Chapter 7
The Cinema of the 1980s

The film industry of the 1980s reacted to a major technological advancement in the entertainment business that originated outside of cinema itself. Video technology and cable distribution progressively altered overall film consumption, supplying new markets and targeting at that time a limited but well-secured audience.[1] The 1980s were characterized by the shift from eclectic independent films to more profitable commercial films, the beginning of the frenetic rise in production costs (dividing big productions with remaining national productions), and the increasingly more powerful position of French television over cinematographic production. From now on, the French film industry had to consider television ratings, accentuated by the introduction of TV commercials during the screening of films. More than ever, the obligation for sound financial profit became the major criterion in decision making. Consequently, the constant *rapport de force* between the big and small screen reined in filmmakers' initiative and shaped an aesthetic model with a common mold.

It is a daunting task to attempt an overall description of French cinema of the 1980s. Traditional film categories, usually recognized by general audiences, began to dissolve by the early part of the decade, rapidly substituted by a cinema of new young directors. For present purposes, the decade has been divided into three categories: experienced directors (Maurice Pialat, Bertrand Tavernier, Eric Rohmer, François Truffaut, Agnès Varda, Bertrand Blier), new directors (Jean-Jacques Beineix, Luc Besson, Leos Carax), and big-production directors (Claude Berri, Jean-Jacques Annaud). The 1980s was also a determining decade for feminist cinema. More women directors were represented at film festivals, and more women filmmakers graduated from French film schools. This particular trend accelerated in the 1990s.

Despite the move toward more commercial productions, film festivals around the world, like Cannes, strove to preserve the artistic ideals of filmmaking. Considered the most important film showcase in the world, Cannes had long been promoting European coproductions, Asian films (formerly little known in the West), and French New Wave. Moreover, it presented to the world a different image from the traditional Oscar iconography. At the end of the 1970s, the mission of Cannes seemingly moved toward the promotion of "courageous productions," rewarding films such as the Taviani brothers' *Padre Padrone* (1977), Francis Ford Coppola's *Apocalypse Now* (1979), Andrzej Wajda's *Man of Iron* (1981), Yilmaz Güney's *Yol* (1982), and even Wim Wenders's *Paris, Texas* (1984).

FRANCE IN THE 1980s

Following a twenty-three-year conservative regime, the 1980s began with one of the most extensive political changes in contemporary French history: the election of socialist François Mitterrand to the presidency on May 10, 1981. It brought the first Left-coalition government in some forty-five years, following Léon Blum's ephemeral Popular Front alliance. Despite the significant liberalization of French society, which occurred during the Giscard years, from 1974 to 1981 (the voting age was lowered to eighteen, the enrollment of female students at the university level increased, the decisive Simone Veil Act legalizing abortion and divorce by common consent passed in 1975), the female and youth vote favored the candidate of the Left. The apparent stability of the French presidential regime clearly indicated that the Fifth Republic's constitutional issues played an essential role in the political agenda since it was created in 1958. Taking advantage of an unprecedented movement of national enthusiasm, Mitterrand promptly dissolved the Assemblée nationale, and the consequent legislative elections that took place in June confirmed the inclination for political change, giving a wide majority to the Socialist Party alone

(269 of the total 491 seats). Mitterrand's "sovereignty," corroborated by his successful campaign slogan *La force tranquille,* began with a rush of socialist fervor all over France. Because of the Communist Party's endorsement before the second round of the election, four members of that political party were appointed to the cabinet of Prime Minister Pierre Mauroy (the first time since the Liberation's coalition government).

With a political victory, which evidently appeared to be the voters' mandate, Mitterrand gained the confidence to rapidly carry out major economic and social reforms. (Radical change, however, did not occur in 1981, any more than it did in 1968, as the foundations of French institutions remained unchanged.) Some of the very first decisions, for which the new government was widely praised among the working-class population, were the significant raise in the minimum wage (the minimum wage, called SMIC, was raised 10 percent in June 1981), increased social security benefits, increased welfare compensations, a fifth week of paid vacation, the working week shortened to thirty-nine hours, and the subjecting of layoffs to state control. On the judiciary side, a historical reorganization took place under the close scrutiny of the new administration, and in September 1981, Justice Secretary Joseph Badinter, following a speech of great magnitude before the French Parliament, led the vote for the abolition of the death penalty. (France was actually the last country in the EEC to ban capital punishment officially.)

In addition to the political transformations, economic measures defined the future direction of the new government's agenda: a dozen major industries, national banks, and insurance companies were nationalized within a couple of years; a ban on nuclear testing was imposed; several projects for the construction of nuclear power plants were deferred; and taxes on the highest social brackets were implemented. In addition, the government decentralized, giving more power to the regions. In an effort to create a new dynamic for smaller companies, a substantial degree of economic delegation shifted part of the state's authority to regional and local councils. The new organization of state cultural interventions played a major role in the daily lives of the French people. In September 1981, the first TGV (high-speed train) connection between Paris and Lyon was inaugurated. Two hours was now all the time needed to reach the capital from its second largest metropolis. Consequently, this new technical advance directly created an intense competition with French airline companies.

But while the socialist administration was focusing on some gigantic socioeconomic tasks, the majority of European nations had already begun the program to counter the European Economic Community's[2] most urgent problem at the time, inflation. In France, inflation rose to

14 percent and unemployment to almost 10 percent. By 1982, the economy had deteriorated in most European countries (an average 12 percent inflation rate), and most governments imposed a controlled growth of wage caps and unpopular price freezes among small businesses despite tax concessions to business. Finance Minister Jacques Delors indicated that the present economic and social projects were ultimately undermining the national economy. The so-called period of economic austerity began with the devaluation of the French franc. Austerity measures were adopted in June 1982 and March 1983, including major cuts in public expenses.

The first socialist administration came to an end with the legislative elections in 1986 and the victory of the right coalition, which regained a slim majority in the parliament. This episode was the first time in the history of the Fifth Republic that the majority in the assembly did not endorse the president's party. The new government, formed mainly by center-right democrats (RPR, Rassemblement Pour la République, and UDF, Union pour la Démocratie Française), was led by newly appointed Prime Minister Jacques Chirac, who began a policy of privatizing state-owned companies, decreasing income tax rates at the upper levels, and removing the wealth tax. Allowing the prime minister to conduct domestic matters, Mitterrand focused on international relations.

Meanwhile, within the turmoil of the so-called cohabitation, a new political figure emerged on the French political scene. This was Jean-Marie Le Pen, who headed the National Front Party (Front National), which scored successes with its xenophobic-themed crusade to expel illegal or unemployed immigrant workers. The party's platform also strongly opposed the residency and electoral rights granted to certain categories of immigrants.

If it was true that social tensions in most large suburban areas rapidly caused a redefinition of the political debate around the mid-1980s, it was also apparent that despite the escalation of those conflicts, new associations, such as S.O.S. Racisme, were proving the solidarity and cohesion of French people. Stand-up comedian and film actor Coluche, followed by a myriad of French artists and celebrities, created an unprecedented association—Les Restos du Coeur—which to date symbolizes the awareness triggered by the spreading of a new kind of poverty in major French urban areas: *les nouveaux pauvres*.

The period of "cohabitation" between Chirac and Socialist president Mitterrand lasted only a couple of years, until Mitterrand's reelection on May 8, 1988. Despite the fact that a significant segment of the French population that was profoundly disillusioned with the social changes and economic reforms (they were often labeled *les déçus du socialisme*/the disillusioned ones), against all odds Mitterrand was able to regain the confidence of the majority. What he had actually put in place, years before announcing his candidacy for a second mandate, can best be described as an understated reverence of the persona, an authentic "cultification" of the (or his own) presidency. Mitterrand's political career, indeed, extended over half a century, and his fourteen years as president of the French Republic made him France's longest reigning politician since Napoléon III.[3] However, despite the social reforms and historical decisions, the socialist administration's experience never quite succeeded in transforming French society's fundamental nucleus, capitalistic structure, or social profile.[4]

In France, the 1980s began with an assertive new cultural trend clearly defined as "cultural pluralism." One of the best examples of the new consensus occurred on March 6, 1980, as writer Marguerite Yourcenar became the first woman to enter the highly select society of the Académie française. In the field of popular music, the 1980s was marked by the rediscovery of cosmopolitan artists, particularly African artists (e.g., Touré Kounda, Manu di Bango, and Mori Kante), this time not exclusively by connoisseurs, but by large and diverse popular audiences. In the field of radio entertainment, and before the advent of video, there were new horizons for radio broadcast with the legalization of private and local stations in 1982. A multitude of new radio stations surfaced, along with traditional public radio stations on FM. Music stations, such as the newly created NRJ, Fun Radio, and Skyrock, were immediately popular among young audiences. The novelty led to the long-awaited reorganization of the radio networks. Unfortunately, the hope of seeing small radio stations finally emerge following decades of negation and sequestrations was squashed as the largest private radio companies (e.g., NRJ) promoted themselves as the new and exclusive leaders for young audiences. Created in 1981 by Jean-Paul Baudecroux, NRJ reached an audience between fifteen and thirty years of age. With its strong public relations strategy and organization of concerts in France, the company rapidly created a large network of provincial radio stations throughout the country.[5]

Outside the traditional fields of entertainment (music and cinema), France of the 1980s represented a new era for individual well-being. As the American trend for jogging invaded Europe and France, the French gradually developed a new awareness of physical fitness. In sports, France, one of the few western nations hitherto never to win any international title in team sports, came away with its first in June 1984: a victory in the European soccer championship. On water, Gérard d'Aboville was the first man to row across the Atlantic Ocean, and in space, astronaut Jean-Loup Chrétien was the first Frenchman to participate in an international space exploration project, spending seven days in the company of Soviet cosmonauts on *Soyuz T6* in 1982.

This success was echoed by another technological sensation. First launched in September 1982, Ariane began a long string of successful commercial contracts in the satellite market. In the field of architecture and national construction, the 1980s proved an exceptionally prolific period under the tutelage of President Mitterrand, whose decisions for the most part triggered fierce opposition from political adversaries and urban representatives, and as the years went by ultimately brought about a national reconciliation. Since Baron Georges Haussmann's architectural enterprises a century before, Paris had never undergone such extensive construction and architectural development. The following achievements asserted French cultural leadership by adorning Paris with a glittering collection of cultural monuments that included the Opéra Bastille (1989), I. M. Pei's pyramid of the Louvre (inaugurated in 1988), the Grand Louvre (1989), the new National Library (1995), a science and technology complex at La Villette (1985), and the gigantic Arche de la Défense (1989), making a spectacular visual and linear alignment with the Arc de Triomphe, the Champs-Elysées, the Tuileries, and the Louvre.

For cinema, as well as the arts in general, the nomination of Jack Lang as the new minister of culture within the socialist government would be of considerable importance for the rest of the century. With his nomination, the status of the Ministre de la Culture, traditionally secondary, even unknown at times, suddenly became the cultural window of a new nation in a new decade, and Lang served as the spokesman for the new political disposition. During the two socialist mandates, Lang was the only member of the government to be twice appointed to his position (1981–86 and 1988–93). Spectacular cultural manifestations, combined with a great communicative savoir faire, best define Lang's gift for popular appearances. Lang's agenda began immediately with a coup de théâtre, which occurred via his declarations toward Deauville's American Film Festival. Lang, who refused to attend the event, made several remarks emphasizing the desire for economic independence of French cinema from what was again perceived as American-cultural hegemony, which, according to observers at the time, was interpreted as outspoken anti-Americanism.

Despite some difficult episodes like the 1981 closing of the legendary Victorine Studios in Nice, French cinema was in part assisted by several encouraging initiatives, such as the foundation of the Lumière Institute in Lyon (1982), the inauguration of the flamboyant Palais des Festivals in Cannes (1983) to replace the old movie theater by then too small for the annual event, and the inauguration of the first annual French Film Festival in Sarasota, Florida (1989). And while Lang's popularity never wavered, particularly after organizing the first annual Fête de la musique in 1982, as well as the Fête du cinéma, the beginning of the 1980s was synonymous with growing economic difficulties and with the dramatic and sudden increase in production costs in French cinema. As a result, Lang decided to create eight regional cinema centers (Grenoble, Nantes, Quimper, Le Havre, Bobigny, Vitrolles, Villemur-sur-Tarn, and Nanterre), known as *maisons de la culture,* all financed by the state. Despite the strong commitment of the government, however, regional cinema never took off commercially, and Paris continued to be, and still remains, the only generator of full-length features and new filmmakers.

FRENCH CINEMA OF THE 1980s: OVER ONE THOUSAND FILMS PRODUCED

Compared to the preceding decade, which valued a certain type of militant cinema representative of the spirit of the time, French cinema of the 1980s could in retrospect be described as the era of the *"neopolar."* Although still inspired by the New Wave, French directors instigated an eloquent return to more traditional storytelling reminiscent of the postwar era. If a dependable and critical debate on the war in Algeria was absent during the early 1960s (as well as the militant spirit of the post-'68 era), this new decade suggested a wide variety of different aesthetic styles and theories just as if each director claimed his or her own school or *politique.* Inventive fictions juxtaposed with aesthetic chronicles and spirituality took over (e.g., Alain Cavalier's *Thérèse,* 1986, earned six César awards). One of the many reasons why political and militant cinema productions began to slow down at the end of the 1970s, and clearly during the first couple of years of the 1980s, was the shift of power to the new socialist administration. Many filmmakers, adherent to socialist political ideas, most likely did not feel a need to pursue a more politically engaged cinema while no longer in a position of opposition. Except in rare cases, most political films did not represent contemporary French society. Film historian Susan Hayward explains the reason for the trend:

> The primary reason for this evaporation of authenticity in cinema was tied in with the overall meaning of disaffection with ideology. When the Left came to power in 1981, they did so on a platform of social reforms. The Left's discourse was embedded with the rhetoric of social justice and as such was far removed from the politics of liberalism that had so valued capitalism, free-marketing ideology, and implicitly, the individual. In simple terms the socialist platform amounted to a credo in society. But by 1982–83—and to the electorate's mind at least—this credo, because of the effects of recession, had all but evaporated, and to all appearances the Left was instituting policies that did little to distinguish it from the Right. It is in the centering of these discourses

that one can perceive the evaporation of authentic cinema. As with the political arena, the 1980s witnessed a centering of cinema's ideological discourses from the "left-Marxist-inflected" and "anti-American hegemonic praxis" films of the 1960s and 1970s, from a political cinema that was politically made to an apolitical cinema that was designer and consumer led. With rare exceptions, the cinema of the 1980s and early 1990s has been one that says "since there is nothing here (no ideology, etc.), let's imitate."[6]

With the decline of political films in the 1980s, contemporary social observation was less likely to be found in the subject matter of new filmmakers. On an economic level, the financial aid committees clearly would not approve of a militant cinema. Therefore, it is true that soon after the beginning of the Mitterrand years, political cinema, as well as the subject of politics in films, rapidly disappeared, with rare exceptions.[7] Unlike the artistic trend of the preceding decade, French cinema of the 1980s never quite seemed to reflect the spirit of its time. The reason for this was most likely a combination of the growing economic and humanitarian crises and difficulties, the catastrophe of Chernobyl, the outbreak of AIDS, the eruption of a new type of urban poverty, and the never-ending growth of unemployment. If the decade began with the people's visible aspiration to social change, the 1980s certainly ended with a sky full of clouds over French society in general. "In the 1980s," observes Hayward, "the authentic cinema evaporated in the face of pastiche,"[8] and it was no surprise to perceive the decline of original auteur cinema. Although in financially dire straits, French *cinéma d'auteurs* nevertheless was still present in the 1980s, but in a large part in productions that never reached an audience and remained without distribution. The celebrated *cinéphiles'* cinema was going through a difficult period. One of the most dramatic aftermaths of the ruthless competition between television and the seventh art was, paradoxically, the declining importance of the *qualité* cinema. Television productions, although lacking technical mastery and credibility, step by step gained popularity among general audiences and eventually secured access to a much wider spectatorship. For the French television industry, mass viewership was the number one preoccupation, whereas for the French film industry, the notion of the art of film continued to supersede the importance of financial viability and audience fulfillment.

For the audiences of the 1980s, mainly by then television spectators, the star system began to change. Actors were no longer "movie stars" as in the past. With all the festivals, press conferences, promotional tours, TV talk shows, and magazines, French actors such as Gérard Depardieu, Catherine Deneuve, Nathalie Baye, Richard Berry, and Isabelle Adjani no longer embodied the hero or cult figure of their predecessors. Consequently, the devaluation of their *médiatique* images became unavoidable.⁹

TRANSFORMATIONS IN THE FRENCH FILM INDUSTRY

The debate over Hollywood hegemony versus French cinema corresponds to a general debate in France and throughout Europe regarding the growing supremacy of American culture. The main point of contention is the American system of mass production, as defined by most major US studios. Taking into consideration the higher cost effectiveness of the typical American production, the central point of the debate is whether to accept the system or to seek salutary alternatives. Although the issues around this old economic predicament were mostly a French concern in the first half of the century, it progressively became a European matter during the postwar era. Already suggested on many occasions by government officials as early as 1945 (Blum-Byrnes Agreements), the actual initiative to build up a European substitute for the Hollywood production system only began to take shape under the patronage of Jack Lang. In the end, the 1980s represented the realization of a distinct European production system.

Lang's endeavors were oriented toward preserving the identity of French cinema (and indirectly the European film industry in general) and making it prosper financially, despite the overpowering volume of American films and the menace of GATT (General Agreement on Tariffs and Trade) on the international film industry.¹⁰ To protect the French film industry from foreign competition, the government reasserted the doctrine of protectionism for national productions, via a complex set of quotas and state subventions. Logically, the best and most efficient way to accomplish preset goals, and to protect European cinema, was to encourage better and more productions. By persuading other European governments that quality cinematographic productions could also help reassert European economic and cultural authority, Lang indirectly implemented a rebirth in most European nations' efforts to subsidize their national film productions. Meanwhile, endowed with essentially worldwide comprehensible narratives and characters, American films quickly progressed within the European market, reaching fifty-six percent of the films shown in French movie theaters and over seventy percent in European movie theaters by 1990. Although incessantly providing leading new talent (film directors, actors, and technicians) with cutting-edge artistic scope, the French-film industry, in comparison to Hollywood's, was never able to sustain the necessary financial commitment and backing. As long as leading French filmmakers and critics firmly believed in cinema as an art form rather than popular entertainment, the gap between the US and French film industries widened each year. From the first generations of the postwar era until the 1980s, ending with the GATT in 1993, Hollywood expanded the "commerciability" of films. In contrast, the French system maintained the sacrosanct idea of *cinéma d'auteurs* and the highly protected artistic prerogative of its filmmakers.

In 1978, production costs began to increase dramatically (by seventeen percent in just one year) and rose by 35 percent in 1988.[11] This increase represented an attempt to keep up with the overwhelming pace of Hollywood. As a result, many successful actors (e.g., Alain Delon, Gérard Depardieu, and Jean-Paul Belmondo) became producers and were eventually able to survive the tide.

Long before production costs increased, however, several French filmmakers and producers understood that in order to keep up with American turnout, French cinema had to join forces with other national cinemas. For many, due to new technologies (e.g., satellites and cable access), which internationalized by force the *paysage audio-visuel,* the key was no longer to protect national borders but rather to think in terms of a real and efficient European policy (if not global economy). As a result, 1989 became the first year in which the majority of feature films were actually coproductions. The project was all the more difficult for Jack Lang to submit, since most European countries, in similar fashion to the United States, did not have an authentic representative for "cultural affairs" in their government. The sudden escalation in production costs directly penalized the *cinéma d'auteurs* (more than doubling during the decade).

Every stage of production was now to be taken into account: from the cost of materials (camera, lighting equipment, editing, and studio time) to the stipends of technical crews who, less often employed, required higher compensations every year. Because of these financial difficulties, small-budget productions slowly began to disappear from the film market. Inspired by the Hollywood model, French producers began to organize their film commercialization no longer around the film itself but rather through a series of marketing products and media appearances by actors and directors. Visibility in post-production was by then more than just a commercial necessity. It was a solid guarantee for a producers' next project. Many French producers, like Claude Berri, reflecting on the reason for the commercial success of American films in France, came to the conclusion that the key component of profitable movies was the size of their budget. By the very nature of their financing, Hollywood super productions were in a position to conquer new European markets. Some French producers, less fearful of financial risk, took up the challenge, giving birth to multinational giant productions (interestingly enough, gratis mainly American financing). Eventually, some French filmmakers, in order to secure necessary funding, chose English and English-speaking actors. This was mainly because most investors, especially distributors, were American, and their decisions were based on American versions of films. This gave an edge to those productions whose language was already English, such as Jean-Jacques Annaud's *The Name of the Rose* (*Le nom de la rose,* 1987) and Luc Besson's *The Professional* (*Léon,* 1994).

Meanwhile, the progression of American cinema seemingly continued to conquer the French market. In 1983, French films still constituted fifty percent of the market, as opposed to thirty-six percent for American films; three years later, in 1986, French spectatorship began for the first time to shift its preferences in majority for American films (over French films). The propensity worsened during the next couple of years, and in 1989 French films represented less than forty percent of the market, in comparison to fifty-eight percent for American films. This shift, however, was among regular film viewers and not among the occasional viewers whose attendance remained relatively stable. But despite the visible decline of its film industry (with an average of 180 million tickets sold annually in the 1970s, going down to 123 million by 1994), French cinema, compared to other European national cinemas, was still one of the best represented in its national market, with 34 percent in 1993.

A new phenomenon began to surface with the concentration of commercial successes in the French film market. In the 1970s, the most important commercial successes generally represented twenty percent of the market. But with the influence of Hollywood, French film viewing began to diversify, and big commercial productions grew to fifty percent of the markets. Especially among young audiences, American motion pictures became more and more popular, often perceived as more entertaining and more accessible when compared to the average French productions. In 1982, French cinema recorded more than 200 million spectators; attendance decreased by almost half the number at the end of the decade. Despite this crisis, because of its innovation and pragmatic energy, the French film industry somehow managed to limit its losses, especially when compared to countries like Italy, where the decrease in viewership reached 70 percent.

Momentarily leaving aside comparative assessments of US productions, the French film industry remains, at the beginning of the twenty-first century, the most dynamic in Europe, with the largest distribution network of more than 4,000 theaters. According to the CNC, the attendance (in millions) at French theaters in the 1980s was 179 (1980), 189 (1981), 202 (1982), 199 (1983), 191 (1984), 175 (1985), 168 (1986), 137 (1987), 125 (1988), 121 (1989), and 122 (1990).

Finally, despite the growing presence of American films, the French film industry saw some profitable results, with productions such as

Claude Pinoteau's *The Party* (*La boum*; more than four million tickets sold in 1980), Georges Lautner's *The Professional* (*Le professionel*; four million in 1981), Gérard Oury's *L'as des as* (almost 5.5 million in 1982, with 2.45 million during the first screening week), Jean Becker's *One Deadly Summer* (*L'été meurtrier*, five million in 1983),[12] Claude Berri's *Tchao Pantin!* (three million in 1983), Michel Blanc's *Marche à l'ombre* (5 million in 1984), Claude Zidi's *My New Partner* (*Les ripoux*, 5.8 million in 1984), Patrice Leconte's *Les spécialistes* (five million in 1984), Coline Serreau's *Three Men and a Cradle* (*Trois hommes et un couffin*, ten million in 1985), Claude Berri's *Jean de Florette* and *Manon of the Spring* (seven million and six million, respectively, in 1986), and Luc Besson's *The Big Blue* (*Le grand bleu*, nine million in 1988).

In light of growing US competition, French cinema relied heavily on the government's leadership and modernism in terms of coordinating a new system of financing national productions. For Jack Lang, the prevailing perspective of vertical integration (i.e., all phases of cinematographic production, from shooting, to marketing strategies, to distribution, to television rights), traditionally owned or controlled by a single investor or group of producers, had to be reorganized in order to liberate the market from the asphyxiating commercial conditions being created, which sooner or later would compel the French film industry to orient the very identity of its productions toward the Hollywood model. To supplement the *avances sur recettes* system, Jack Lang created the SOFICA (Sociétés de financement des industries cinématographiques et audiovisuelles) program in 1985. These investment companies were mostly created to acquire capital from private individuals or companies in exchange for fiscal advantages. As a result, more than fifty films were completed by the early 1990s. Contrary to common belief, the *avances sur recettes* system was not implemented solely to encourage new talent, but to provide sufficient financial help for already accomplished and even notorious filmmakers. Despite its numerous imperfections, the system was able, since its creation in the early 1960s, to set in motion some of the most important projects of the decade. Set against royalties from French box office revenues, the system directly benefited many other filmmakers and came to the assistance of some of France's most prestigious artists, such as Claude Lanzmann (*Shoah/Shoah*, 1984), Agnès Varda (*Vagabond/Sans toit ni loi,* 1985), Robert Bresson (*Money/L'argent,* 1983), and Alain Resnais (*L'amour à mort,* 1984).

In addition to its patron-of-the-arts image, one of the other objectives of the *avances sur recettes* institution was eventually to reinvigorate the film industry. As such, the regulation stipulated that movie companies benefiting from these incentives (mainly film producers) engage in all aspects of film activity, including post-production, distribution, and establishing studios and cinema houses. On the one hand, French producers generally argued that companies established under this regulation were more inclined to conduct distribution activities at the expense of production and the establishment, and running of studios. On the other hand, French industry representatives accused these film companies of swamping the local market with American movies. Although the government doubled the budget of the *avances sur recettes* system in 1982, and consequently facilitated the first feature films of many young film directors, a number of them were precluded from pursuing a successful movie career for several reasons. These reasons included the evolution of the market with the rapid escalation of production costs, the disaffection of a public, more and more oriented toward the American-star system, and the lack of support of French television companies which were not always open to endorsing "unknown" films, much less coproducing them. When they would consent to participate in a production, television companies committed to only a certain percentage of the project, which often turned out to be a relatively negligible amount. Compared to their seniors, the main difficulty young filmmakers had to negotiate was that for the first time television represented a major obstacle to the beginning of a film career. Many young and talented directors were able to achieve only one film before disappearing from the movie business.

Unlike the early 1960s, when the general public went to movie theaters to see Jean-Luc Godard's *Breathless* or Claude Chabrol's *Bitter Reunion,* the same general public twenty years later could choose to wait several months and view new directors' films at home on the small screen. One of the major problems for the French film industry in its effort to ensure a new generation of filmmakers was the producers' trust in the old-school directors, such as Maurice Pialat, Bertrand Tavernier, and François Truffaut. Investments were difficult during the economic crunch of the early 1980s, and investors would usually bet on sure values rather than venture to endorse unknown projects. As a result, young directors were more or less in the same situation their seniors faced thirty years before them: only a providential professional connection could launch their professional careers. Despite the innumerable obstacles, however, a respectable number of new French directors were able to achieve a first full-length feature film each year (between fifteen and twenty annually).

A NEW PARTNER: TELEVISION

In France, the 1980s represented a unique socio-economic phase, essentially dominated by the drastic acceleration in the consumption of cultural goods. Since its first broadcasts in the early 1950s, French television had never undergone a major organizational transformation. The single state-owned channel, ORTF (Office radio-télévision française), slowly evolved into several channels without ever changing its purpose or mission. As the number of TV channels expanded from three to six, then later seven, television became the dominant medium in the world of images. The year 1984 saw a revolution in French television with the birth of Canal+, whose mission was to broadcast recently released films. Soon imitated by the creation of two other private television companies two years later (La 5 and M6), the government allowed another major breakthrough with the privatization of the oldest state-owned channel, TF1. With a total of six channels by 1985 (four of which were private companies), French viewers for the first time enjoyed a relatively broad choice in television entertainment. The first and direct victim of this expansion was, logically, cinema production, since both the television and film industries were by now, for better or worse, closely interconnected. Cinema was no longer the only "image" distributor around.

The aesthetic requirements and economic realities of French television deeply influenced the production of French films during the 1980s. More inclined toward general public and family entertainment, TV producers gradually moved their expectations toward a more refined aesthetic, emphasizing clear-cut commercial products, closer to the one of the *qualité* era rather than the post-'68 era (deeply embedded in a political and militant behaviorism no longer in demand among general audiences). From now on, a substantial part of French cinematographic production was conceived for TV. This not only affected the choice of subject matter, but also seriously limited the creativity of filmmakers. Many film historians, like Jacques Siclier, argue that the sudden shift toward more televised filmmaking explains the emergence, or reemergence, of more visually inclined directors, who, for the most part, came from the world of advertising (e.g., Jean-Jacques Annaud and Luc Besson).

Despite a solid financial situation and increasing profits,[13] due mainly to healthy advertisement contracts, French television companies continued to increase their participation in cinema productions and films rights. The turning point of the evolution of film consumption occurred in 1985, when for the first time a larger number of movies were screened on national television than in theaters (consequently, American films became predominant when compared to French films). Paradoxical as it may seem, television cinema—films whose rights were bought by television companies—was by far the cheapest and most popular source of programming, since the production costs for a TV film were usually higher when compared to the purchase of the film's rights. In addition, American television series, which since the late 1970s had continued to overwhelm the European market with low prices (since already amortized in the US), indirectly slowed down the production of French TV films as well as French TV series. Because of this, national and European quotas were rapidly established. In 1985, the revenue of a film screened in theaters represented twenty-five percent of the total revenue; in 1990, less than twenty percent, with forty percent from television rights, eight percent from videos and fifteen percent from international sales.

In parallel with television, one of the largest society phenomena, which characterized so well the evolution of the 1980s, was a sudden and revolutionary shift in viewing format, which shaped the economic prediction of the cinematographic industry forever: television and VCRs, both accessible at home, became the new decisive adjuncts.[14] Born in the 1960s, the first tentative VCR models from the Sony Corporation initiated the market with the first affordable VCR in 1969, followed a few years later by the expansion of two viewing devices: the Betamax format by Sony and the VHS format by the Matsushita Corporation. Videocassette recorders gradually became less exclusive and consequently entered the homes of millions of families. In 1976, the VHS system was commercialized worldwide but its progression was somewhat relatively discreet in France. A rather small number of people at the time, mainly professional, clearly realized that this new format was about to revolutionize the concept of cinéphilie forever—the VCR would bring to the homes of millions a medium that had almost exclusively been presented in commercial houses since the invention of motion pictures. From the late 1970s on, the importance of video in the entertainment industry, as well as in art and education, grew. The accessibility to films on videocassette further affected attendance at the numerous *ciné-clubs* in France by offering the public its own selection of films. Although feared by film producers and distributors for its potential threat to exhibition profits (the sales of films on videocassette had increased steadily since the coming of VCRs, with a jump of 75 percent in 1993), the video market actually had the opposite effect: not only did it not dramatically affect attendance at theaters, but it also significantly prolonged the commercial time span of most French productions.

The 1980s were unquestionably the beginning of an important new viewing era, with more and more French households owning VCRs: over 200,000 VCRs in 1980; one million in 1982; three million in 1983; five million in 1988; and more than ten million in 1990. This trend parallels the growth in the number of televised films (over 800 feature films in 1986 and close to 1,300 films screened on French television by the end of the decade). With an increasing number of feature films screened on the six French channels (913 films in 1988, for example), the number of VCRs continued to grow, allowing viewers to record movies at no cost and watch them at their leisure.

The creation of the first private TV channel, Canal+, brought a small revolution in the history of French-television viewing and symbolized the beginning of the end for the state monopoly over the marketing of images. As early as the first season, the new subscription channel, accessible only with a decoder system, immediately offered nonconforming competitive programs with one feature film per day (usually screened one calendar year after the release in theaters). This was a considerable advantage since the other national channels had a three-year interval period, unless they coproduced the film (which meant a one-year delay). Quickly, Canal+ improved its programming and began to screen films six times in a two-week period. Because of the creation of free private television channels (La Cinq and TV6), the development of Canal+ slowed briefly before taking off again in the late 1980s and early 1990s. With such incentives as a record screening of 320 films per year, the number of subscribers began to increase dramatically, from 230,000 in 1987 to 3 million in 1990. Another advantage, which indirectly contributed to the success of Canal+, was the gradual implementation, on other channels, of regular interruptions in films for commercial spots. This phenomenon, absent at Canal+, not only outraged filmmakers but also attracted new viewers to the uninterrupted viewing mode offered by the new company.

The 1980s also brought an important change in the French film industry regarding financing. In the early 1980s, French television coproduced just over twenty percent of French films and ended the decade coproducing more than fifty percent. In November 1987, Canal+ signed an agreement with major producing companies, which indirectly affected the production and distribution network all over France. Canal+ became by far the most active participant, and is still the major partner for the financing of French feature films (e.g., eighty percent of French productions benefited from Canal+ financial aid in 1993). Later on, Canal+ pledged to use one-fifth of its commercial and subscription revenue to finance full-length feature films, 50 percent of which were to be French productions. This was a daunting task indeed, since more than a quarter of the company's budget was allocated to screening copyrights.

THE OLD SCHOOL OF FILMMAKERS: FRANÇOIS TRUFFAUT, BERTRAND TAVERNIER, BERTRAND BLIER, AND MAURICE PIALAT

Although experienced directors such as Maurice Pialat, Bertrand Tavernier, Bertrand Blier, Eric Rohmer, and François Truffaut were still active in the early 1980s, they represented their own cinematographic style. Despite their unshakable popularity among general audiences, they no longer epitomized the "young generation" of filmmakers. The case of François Truffaut is all the more interesting in that his career, although often celebrated for its phenomenal beginnings, finished with one of the greatest critical successes in French cinema history: *The Last Metro* (1980). The inspiration for the film came to Truffaut via Jean Marais's memoir on the splendor and pains of the Parisian stage during World War II. With a script written with Suzanne Schiffman, Truffaut again appealed to audiences with his multiple layers. He combined a delicate blend of artistic ambitions, popular storytelling, and excellence in the cinematographic tradition. *The Last Metro* was a realistic contemplation on the artistic mood during the Nazi Occupation. The film investigates the dynamics in the relationships between the actors of a theater company in a climate of antagonism and terror. Truffaut employed only recognizable significances from the plot's main implication. As the story unfolds, the emotional element progressively comes to imply another issue—the power of the artist even when confined to silence and isolation.

The double plot narrates the story of the struggles of the theater during the Occupation and Bernard Granger's fight for the French Resistance. In 1942 Lucas Steiner (Heinz Bennent), a stage director in the Montmartre district of Paris, takes refuge in the basement of his own theater to escape the Gestapo. Before his departure, he has left all the stage directions as well as the manuscript of his latest play to Jean-Loup Cottin (Jean Poiret), a fellow director. His wife, Marion (Catherine Deneuve), must persuade the French authorities not to close the theater. Meanwhile, the company hires a new actor, Bernard Granger (Gérard Depardieu). A parallel story evokes the double game played by Marion and Bernard, who hide their love affair as best they can, as well as the double game they play on the French censor. Although the gloomy environment of the theater echoes with the disorder of the Occupation and the tracking of the Jews, it also functions as a surreptitious device for solidarity among the stage actors. Through the theater's ventilation ducts, Lucas is able to continue to direct his play from a distance. When the police finally come to investigate the building, Bernard, who has learned that Marion's husband is living in the basement, decides to help the struggling couple.

With a large box-office profit of 3.3 million tickets sold and a record ten Césars (Best Film, Best Director, Best Scenario, Best Actor/ Gérard Depardieu, Best Actress/Catherine Deneuve, Best Photography, Best Montage, Best Set, Best Music, and Best Sound), *The Last Metro* proved a triumph for its director. Truffaut overcame a difficult challenge, namely, to associate the work of two artistically diverse actors, the most popular female actress from the 1960s with the biggest male actor from the 1970s. The shooting began January 28, 1980, and the film opened in Paris on September 17, 1980. *The Last Metro,* like most of Truffaut's films, was a subtle picture in the way its intrigue explored the characters, dexterously revealing individual layers of their psyche. The director's devotion to film, combined with his personal interest in male–female relationships, is omnipresent in the many elements of the plot. The film was a significant illustration of Truffaut's modus operandi: communication depends principally on sight and scent in order for the cinematography to create a faultless environment. This faultless mise-en-scène was actually re-created by stage decorator Jean-Pierre Kohut-Svelko and chief lighting operator Nestor Almendros through an unusual series of almost monochromatic colors, eventually rendering the mood of the Occupation more realistic for the everyday reality of artists during this time and tediously artificial to accompany the theatrical representation.

Truffaut's next film, *The Woman Next Door* (*La femme d'à côté,* 1981),[15] was a "frightening" love story where passion surpassed common neurosis. On a cinematographic level, the narrative of fatal attraction could be viewed as a psychoanalysis of contrasting implications behind the form of long takes, numerous cross-cutting, and fluid-camera movements. From start to finish, the intrigue reveals the phys-

Gérard Depardieu (Bernard) and Catherine Deneuve (Marion) in François Truffaut's *The Last Metro* (*Le dernier métro,* 1980), (Courtesy of BIFI/© Jean-Pierre Fizet).

ical hindrances between the couple. A sense of isolation and abandon grows stronger until the final explosion of energy recaptures what had been lost. Bernard (Gérard Depardieu) and Arlette Coudray (Michèle Baumgartner), a young couple, live a peaceful life outside Grenoble with their young son. One day, a new couple, Philippe (Henri Garcin) and Mathilde Bauchard (Fanny Ardant), move in next door. After a seven-year separation, destiny brings Bernard and Mathilde back together. At first reluctant even to behave like friends, the couple inevitably has an affair. Bernard and Mathilde begin their secret rendezvous in town as their passion grows mercilessly. One day, Bernard cannot control himself any longer. Life must go on as each couple pretends to live with the indiscretion and forgive the past. Meanwhile, however, Mathilde is hospitalized suffering from depression. Philippe and Mathilde move out of town, but one night Mathilde returns to visit their deserted house. Bernard overhears the noise and reencounters her one last time. As passion again becomes all-consuming, Mathilde shoots Bernard before killing herself.

With *The Woman Next Door,* as he did with *The Man Who Loved Women* and *The Story of Adele H.,* Truffaut acquainted his public with another saga of passionate love, this time with the looming sensation evolving in an apparently convivial-bourgeois environment, chronicled by the peaceful village outside the innumerable disturbances of city life. Interestingly, many of Truffaut's films used a narrative frame under a voice-over, like the puzzling prologue of Madame Jouve, (Véronique Silver) during the opening shot, who instructs the spectator that the featured story not only is authentic but also a reminder that everybody's life is at some point unstable. Once more with Truffaut, who was still dealing with the emotional aftermath of *The Green Room,* the idea of death was equally present as the symbol of love in the final adage of the narrative: reminiscing temptation can eventually lead human beings to a fatal finale.

On August 1, 1984, François Truffaut had a cerebral stroke from a brain tumor and died a month later at the age of fifty-two at the American Hospital in Neuilly. Exactly thirty years earlier, Truffaut had entered the arena as a turbulent critic for *Les cahiers du cinéma* and as a fierce opponent of the *tradition de qualité.*[16] He ruthlessly fought cinematographic academicism and its overpowering literary adaptations, as well as its anti-intellectual character. For Truffaut and the young critics-turned-directors of the *nouvelle vague,* the aspiration to film corresponded to a poeticized but still realistic representation of contemporary France, and was a cinematographic revolution in all its artistic and production aspects. According to film critic David Walsh, Truffaut's cinema with its "self-consciously Bressonian austerity, still retains its essential eloquence."[17] Heir to the humanistic cinematic tradition of Jean Renoir, Truffaut is remembered by both popular audiences and film historians as a unique filmmaker known for his contagious, exuberant celebration of filmmaking. Always involved with the production of his films as well as the well-being of his profession, Truffaut was also active as a film critic and commentator until the very end.[18] Two of his most noteworthy manuscripts include a long interview with Alfred Hitchcock[19] and a collection of critical essays, *Les films de ma vie* (*The Films in My Life*, 1975). Physically hampered during the last months of his life, Truffaut had already planned numerous projects, including an adaptation of Paul Léautaud's *Petit ami* and *Le Comte de Monte Cristo* for American television. In addition, he had completed the screenplay for *La petite voleuse*, which Claude Miller directed in 1988.

Following in Truffaut's footsteps, director Bertrand Tavernier, although active in filmmaking since the early 1970s, quickly appeared as an experienced filmmaker in the following decade. The success of *Clean Slate* (*Coup de torchon*, 1981), followed by his immaculate impressionistic composition *A Sunday in the Country* (*Un dimanche à la campagne*, 1984), confirmed Tavernier's position as an artist of considerable influence. Adapted from a short novel by Pierre Bost, entitled *Monsieur Ladmiral va bientôt mourir*, *A Sunday in the Country* narrates a bittersweet portrait of a man's life as he relives personal triumphs, family comedies and tragedies, the volatile politics of a war-torn world, and, most importantly, the people and passions that changed his life.

During the last peaceful years before World War I, Monsieur Ladmiral (Louis Ducreux), a retired painter, lives at his country home with the memory of his late spouse. On a beautiful Sunday, he receives a visit from his son, Gonzague (Michel Aumont), with his wife and three children, Emile, Lucien, and Mireille. Realizing that his son has slipped into a conformist bourgeois existence despite himself, Monsieur Ladmiral is disappointed with Gonzague's lack of ambition and adventure. But the peaceful family also receives a surprise visit that day from Monsieur Ladmiral's daughter Irène (Sabine Azéma), a thoroughly modern and independent young Parisian woman. Irène's contagious stamina and energy begin to spread to the whole family. Unfortunately, she must rush back to Paris after a phone call from her lover, who waits for her. Following his children's visit, Monsieur Ladmiral then returns to his studio to examine a painting that he has been working on for years, and reminisces on the passions and risks of life never taken.

Continuing the theme of *A Week's Vacation* (*Une semaine de vacances*, 1980), Tavernier concentrated his interest on the rapport among the three generations within a family, much like Ettore Scola had done in *The Family* (*La famiglia*, 1987). In addition to the poetic evocation of paternal love, *A Sunday in the Country* is an insightful analysis of a family's interior dynamics and a moving account of an aging artist's consciousness that his "masterpiece" may not survive the passage of time. Here Tavernier's visual narrative centers on the presentation of individuals' basic situations (which belong to daily life). It presents individual human beings' intuition of their daily situations as they experience them. Tavernier's protagonists are isolated, static, and motionless, and thus express themselves especially from the inside; they are recognized through a picture of the world that the filmmaker designed for the spectator. The whole peaceful *champêtre,* or pseudo-pastoral universe, is a symbol of the mental world of the characters who are organic parts of it. The reality of the situations in which the characters appear is a psychological reality expressed in images that are the outward projection of Monsieur Ladmiral's state of mind. Often described as a filmmaker of the past, traditionally extolling cinematographic academicism in all its forms, Tavernier provided a rare impressionistic taste for atmosphere in this transgenerational portrait of a common family. He displayed an obvious mastery of stage direction. With numerous shots focused on one figure before slowly tracking to another angle, the cinematography was able to reveal in each take a different aspect that placed a new spin on the set and directly enhanced a mood of hidden undercurrents. At the 1984 Cannes Film Festival, *A Sunday in the Country* won Best Director (Prix de la mise en scène). It also won Césars in 1985 for Best Actress (Sabine Azéma), Best Adapted Screenplay (Bertrand Tavernier), and Best Photography (Bruno de Keyser).

After the success of *A Sunday in the Country,* Tavernier developed a parallel interest in jazz. Following contacts with American filmmakers Martin Scorsese and Irwin Winkler, the idea of a feature film narrating the tribulations of American jazzmen in France came to light. *'Round Midnight (Autour de minuit,* 1986) and its international success demonstrated that a well-organized cinematography (assisted by Alexandre Trauner for the set) coordinated with a judicious pace and a strong musical score (Herbie Hancock earned an Oscar for Best Score)[20] could do well at the box office, in particular among general audiences not necessarily keen on or even knowledgeable about jazz. The film is a virtual homage to the jazz world: the music and the musicians who lived and played in France. Dexter Gordon (who was nominated for an Oscar) plays a disheartened tenor saxophone player living in self-exile in 1959 Paris. A young amateur, Francis Paudras (François Cluzet), who first surreptitiously listens to the musician in the rain (since he cannot afford to pay admission to the Blue Note Club), is disappointed at the way this jazz great is treated and decides to help his idol. The story is a compelling reflection on the phenomenon of appreciation toward artists and their subsequent interaction with fans. The title, taken from a Thelonious Monk piece, conveys the genuine atmosphere more than a literal narrative scheme.

Author of numerous articles, Tavernier also wrote, with Jean-Pierre Coursodon, a historical overview of American cinema from the postwar era, entitled *50 ans de cinéma américain* in 1995.[21] Today, Tavernier remains one of the most important and popular French filmmakers. His other significant contributions are *Deathwatch* (*La mort en direct,* 1980) and *Life and Nothing But* (*La vie et rien d'autre,* 1989), a pacifist film starring Philippe Noiret as a World War I major obsessed with making amends for the wartime carnage in which he took part. It is a persuasive investigation of the absurdity of war. Tavernier's career awards include the Prix Louis Delluc in 1974 for *L'horloger de Saint-Paul* and two Césars for Best Director in 1976 for *Let Joy Reign Supreme* (*Que la fête commence*) and in 1997 for *Captain Conan* and Best Original Screenplay for *The Judge and the Assassin* (*Le juge et l'assassin*) in 1977.

Compared to filmmakers such as Tavernier, François Truffaut, or even Jean-Luc Godard, Bertrand Blier can be considered, in his own style, a very conscientious observer of psychological conflicts. Like the others, Blier concentrated his work on a great deal of stage direction rather than subjective expression. In comparison to the film directors of the early 1960s, who found inspiration and artistic encouragement mostly within their inner selves or favorite literature, Blier goes as far as to capture inspiration from around him (e.g., *Going Places* and *Get Out Your Handkerchiefs*). With *Beau-père* (*Beau-Père*, 1981), selected for the 1981 Cannes Film Festival, the continuity in his endeavor to direct confrontational films is still noticeable. Often viewed as a nonconformist, whose vulgarity and provocation go beyond understanding, Blier is either rejected by the French public and critics or adored. Blier's infuriating scripts were obviously written to astound spectators as early as the first scene, when unexpected situations diffused a recurrent-corrosive humor. Built on paradoxical situations, the plots were then pushed to the limits of cinematographic frenzy, according to a logic of absurdity that could be best described as a blend of Surrealist fantasy and Existentialist uneasiness. Blier's characters usually evolve in dramatic situations, sometimes in despair and sometimes in absolute derision. In *Beau-père,* love and sex, breaking the bourgeois rules by their unbalanced and extreme nature, begin to take the form of a comedy of despair. For film historian René Prédal, Blier's concept in filmmaking, and storytelling in particular, is the antithesis of artistic malleability since "Blier's cinema is incongruous as it tracks down emotions with a bulldozer and incise pain with a needle."[22] Despite the depth of the implied sexuality, *Beau-père* mixes a significant dimension of humor with a tragic story.

The plot centers on Rémi (Patrick Dewaere), an almost-thirty-year-old composer and a philosophically disposed nightclub pianist who yearns to embrace a successful life before his next birthday. Discouraged by the melancholy of his professional career, Rémi limits himself to playing at night in fancy restaurants in order to survive financially. His longtime companion, Martine (Nicole Garcia), dies in a car accident, leaving her fourteen-year-old daughter, Marion (Ariel Besse), without a parent. Charly (Maurice Ronet), the child's biological father, wants to take her back home. Although extremely attached to her, Rémi takes Marion back to her father. After several weeks away, Marion, who has missed her "stepdad," suddenly stops by Rémi's apartment with her belongings. A romance begins to blossom immediately in the young teenager's imagination, but Rémi refuses to cede to temptation. He soon realizes that she in fact offers him emotional support. Meanwhile, Marion, desperate by his denial, loses her appetite for life and begins a slow slide into depression. She kisses Rémi one day, however, as he is taking her on the train for a ski trip. The romance takes a new turn, as both protagonists cannot live without each other, until Rémi meets Charlotte, a single woman his age. Marion finally understands that her future will be separate from Rémi's and reluctantly goes back to her father.

Often banal and even somewhat mediocre in nature, Blier's characters are meticulous studies in psychology, much as François Truffaut or Bertrand Tavernier do with their own protagonists: they all possess and communicate the flavor and pathos of life. Despite his congenial front, his humanist heart illustrated in its broad vision and bold courage, Rémi is actually a disturbed man. His fascination with Marion increasingly betrays his fragile self. Tender and violent, Blier goes beyond the tolerable limit on every occasion, and his visual insolence places his protagonist in impossible situations. For many French critics, Blier has always been an astonishing and influential director due in part to his representation of situations inspired by the theater of the absurd and outrageous dialogues rich in new colloquial expressions. The film does not lack the scope of many of his previous films, and the dose of hypnotism may be even more persuasive than *Get out Your Hankerchiefs*.

Five years later, Blier achieved a determinant picture with his very controversial *Ménage* (*Tenue de soirée,* 1986), for which he wrote the script and assigned the music score to trendy musician and songwriter Serge Gainsbourg. Overpowering in its unlimited audacity, *Ménage* is the most drastic and unprecedented depiction of the love triangle in motion-picture history. This time, it is the man who is conquered when a stranger comes to insert himself in the privacy of a couple. Antoine (Michel Blanc) and Monique (Miou-Miou), a young, struggling couple, often argue about their poverty. Between fights and tenderness, they exist without any direction. One night, however, their lives change drastically when they meet Bob (Gérard Depardieu) in an outdoor bar. What Monique strives for is simply a life of leisure and luxury. Bob impresses Monique and persuades Antoine to befriend him. After initiating the young couple to his lifestyle (of professional burglary), Bob, who first gave the impression that he was attracted to Monique, slowly makes his move on Antoine, who ultimately will become no less than his sexual-domestic slave. Bob is not so much concerned with sexuality as he is in manipulating the pair, in order to have them go along with his disturbing plans. Far from being jealous, Monique is complacent as long as her new glamorous lifestyle continues. As the ménage à trois progresses, Monique's plight becomes more and more difficult as she becomes unwanted by the two men. She eventually leaves for another man. Within a matter of days, Monique and Antoine have been removed from their dull middle-class universe and parachuted into a gloomy sexual and criminal predicament. Now liberated from the feminine presence, the male couple spend their days in a Paris suburban home until one night, when Bob meets a younger man in a disco. The end of the film enters the domain of frenzy as Monique, who by then, having gotten rid of her man (who was no more than a pimp), meets up with Bob and Antoine again. By now, Antoine's submission to Bob's desire is so strong that he freely dresses in drag. Thirteen years after the controversy of *Going Places,* Blier's *Ménage* triggered considerable controversy once again. The manner in which Antoine and Bob appear in their startling final exposure makes the characters of *La cage aux folles* look like neophytes. The role of Antoine, no longer possible for Patrick Dewaere, who died in 1982, was offered to Bernard Giraudeau, who declined due to the sardonic tone of the film, and finally went to Michel Blanc, who not only accepted the role but also earned the award for Best Actor (along with Bob Hoskins for Neil Jordan's *Mona Lisa*) at the 1986 Cannes Film Festival.

The key to understanding Blier's films is to be found in his treatment of the absurd. In what circumstances, then, does absurdity appear in Blier's scenarios? If spectators accept the possibility of common sense, and convenient logic may be absent, the dialogues consequently become entirely irrational and even absurd. The conflict between the world and human beings, who begin to be disillusioned with it, arises here. Can a simple fictional story, Blier suggests, be written about a topic that defies ridicule and the absurd? What Blier tried to capture in *Ménage,* however, was the feeling of absurdity inherent in the human condition as such, independent of personal motives. Blier's sense of the

absurd emerges from daily life as an anecdote that relates to Every-
man's seemingly, banal existence.

Despite an element of the uncanny that is always part of the intrigue, we never leave the domain of realism. Often labeled a misogynist artist, especially by American film critics, Blier, whose
protagonists often display unconventional attitudes toward women,
does not promote an uninhibited worldview of erotic chauvinism or
anarchy. The principal idea is to be found in social experimentation,
as fiction usually allows viewers to do so. Strong with solid elements
of social insurrection and provocation, Blier's visual paradigm centers
on the love triangle to understand its sexual options, from heterosexu-
ality to homosexuality. For Blier, comic tales, expressed on the screen,
are the result of these options and discrepancies. Rather small and
balding, with a discontented gaze, Antoine is the less plausible lover,
just as the crude and conceited Bob is the less plausible of kindhearted
lovers. Therefore, life is not absurd in itself, it only appears so. The
nature of this discrepancy has to be carefully understood as Antoine
progressively uncovers the "feminine condition." On the threshold of
Blier's universe lies the promise of grasping a knowledge far beyond
the regions of frustrated feelings; this new awareness neither contra-
dicts nor offsets the absurd but balances it, following the author's
intuition.

What can be seen as Blier's greatest quality as a storyteller is his
relentless ability to put his own beliefs at risk. This active humility
disarms his detractors and their label of "macho" or misogynist cinema.
Visually speaking, the trademark of Blier's style is best described as a
cinema of constant provocative close-ups blended with unbelievable
pieces of reality and prosaic truths. Blier's next film, *Too Beautiful for
You* (*Trop belle pour toi,* 1989), conquered the forty-second Cannes Film
Festival in 1990 with the Special Jury Prize (shared with Giuseppe
Tornatore's *Cinema Paradiso*). In France, *Too Beautiful for You* received
a series of awards, including Césars for Best Film, Best Director, Best
Actress (Carole Bouquet), Best Scenario (Bertrand Blier), and Best
Editing (Claudine Merlin).

The story narrates the extraordinary relationship that has suddenly
been brought to passion between ordinary-looking interim secretary
Colette Chevassu (Josiane Balasko) and automobile dealership manager
Bernard Barthélémy (Gérard Depardieu). After fourteen years of marriage, Bernard seems to have it all: a beautiful wife, Florence (Carole
Bouquet), two lovely children, and a very prosperous livelihood. However, he is immediately caught up in an intense love-at-first-sight
situation. Through the glass walls of his office, Bernard's eyes meet
Colette's, and the passionate couple begin to meet secretly in motel

rooms. All of his friends are astonished, since Bernard's wife, Florence, is beautiful. She is not disposed to let go of Bernard and battles back with a vehement arrogance. Although challenged in person by Bernard's wife, Colette, still "quivering" with bliss, manages to ask the unthinkable in an atypical wife–mistress altercation: "Vous pouvez pas me le prêter encore un tout petit peu? Il est bien avec moi, il est calme, il se repose. Quand je vais vous le rendre, il sera tout neuf; vous repartirez comme au premier jour." (Can you lend him to me a bit longer? He likes it with me; he's calm, he rests. I'll return him to you like new. You can start all over again.)

Introducing a hyper reality composed of phantasmagoric images and photographed with great passion by Philippe Rousselot (Jean-Jacques Beineix's *Diva,* Stephen Frears's *Dangerous Liaisons*), the narrative flashbacks and flash-forwards take the viewer from Bernard's wedding to Florence after he begins the relationship with his new mistress. Blier has converged many of his film subjects representing male sexuality— sometimes to the detriment of women, as most American critics like to remind—but this time he shows signs of moving more toward a compassionate and balanced psychoanalysis. The film is a disquieting tale, unsettling for the conservative minded, mixing burlesque comedy with drama, phantasms with the absurd. Once more, as in *Ménage,* the element of absurdity does not reflect on yesterday or tomorrow. Bernard is also a typically absurd hero, personifying the real quality of an absurd life. He is absurd through his passion for Colette, his suffering through his eternal fate, and his timeless quest for an idyllic love that can never be grasped. Although he is offered furtive moments with Colette, as an absurd character, Bernard misses any hopes, plans, and troubles about his future: so argues Bertrand Blier. One can see the great effort in him, recurring as he tries to move the expectation and push it up to the very last day. The film is laced with liberal amounts of offbeat humor and follows an unusual reverse order of melodramatic intrigue, since it begins within the domain of comedy, only to end as a more serious representation of the human condition. The two thematic threads are interwoven with great artistic gusto, and are finally emotionally fused in a climactic sequence that links the comedy to the drama. Gérard Depardieu, who plays the character of an ordinary man in a midlife crisis, communicates credibility in one of the most difficult roles in cinema. Depardieu makes his love obsession convincing because he never overacts it, and because the movie communicates it generally through the point of view of the actresses, Bouquet and Balasko. Blier's *Too Beautiful for You* was the third time Gérard Depardieu and Carole Bouquet performed together after *Cold Cuts* and Philippe Labro's *Rive droite, rive gauche* (1984).

A fourth director of the post-'68 era who was still a force in the 1980s is Maurice Pialat. Pialat unpredictably spun his contemporary films in a style borrowed from classic films and cinéma vérité. He deconstructed, systemized, and reinvented processes by breaking the rules of aesthetics with minimum lighting and austere realism. The spectator had the impression that the director invited audiences to share his fascination with melodrama but at the same time provided him with the necessary conditions to remain in full control. Often considered a chronicler more than a creator, Pialat's strength resided in the sincerity of the script as he alternated extremely diverse sequential shots: strong moments captured with a mobile hand camera—to best grapple with the behavior and the language of the characters—interspersed with rather banal excerpts of everyday life. Pialat was also known for his demanding treatment of actors and his memorable bursts of wrath, which explains why, in the director's universe, the individual always lived within close ties with society.

One of the most socially and politically charged of all French productions of the early part of the decade was undeniably Pialat's *Loulou* (*Loulou,* 1980). This film was all the more paradoxical for a filmmaker who always refused the title of political cineast. Although a love story in theory, Pialat's *Loulou* took advantage of each scene to remind viewers of the prominence of class awareness in modern French society. Nelly (Isabelle Huppert) is a middle-class woman married to a well-off publicist named André (Guy Marchand). Together, they live in a comfortable and spacious Parisian apartment. One night at a ball, Nelly meets Loulou (Gérard Depardieu), a tough *loubard* (thug), and immediately falls in love with him. Because Loulou seems so far away from reality, she is irresistibly attracted to this hoodlum and eventually leaves André for Loulou, sacrificing her current lifestyle to pursue her inner desire. While Loulou lives off Nelly's money in exchange for sexual and emotional fulfillment, she becomes pregnant. Nelly's brother attempts to assist the young couple by suggesting employment possibilities for Loulou, but much to his dismay, the future father is in no hurry to begin a full-time job. Often described as an "erotic revolution" in the American press, Pialat's love story is far from representing a radical change from 1970s sexuality. Trapped between two decades, the film actually serves a rather smooth transition between the sexual freedom of the post-'68 era and the return to storytelling of the 1980s.

However, the true innovation of Pialat at the dawn of the 1980s was the value he gave to the still often-underestimated importance of sex in social interactions and human patterns. Interestingly enough, *Loulou* addresses the notion of social abuse and the ambiguous affinity of a couple whose bond corresponds to the dialectical behavior of reciprocal exploitation. The thin line that separates the exploiter and the exploited reminds the spectator that social barriers, although temporarily put aside, may ultimately haunt any couple in the end. Far from a purely political or socially rhetorical approach, the plot indulges in a witness of two individuals in love and their downfall in a hostile world, eventually leading to violence, boredom, deception, alcoholism, and, finally, love. Arlette Langmann's scenario, offering the two different languages, gave a vital force to the film. Pialat's work may be considered a slice of life, without a real beginning or a real ending; but it certainly is a compelling testimony of the "conflictual" predicament of class struggle in the 1980s. Included in the French Official selection at Cannes in 1980, the film gained international fame, although it was excluded from the final award list (with a similar fate at the César Awards ceremony, as a result of the phenomenal success of Truffaut's *The Last Metro*).

After the success of Pialat's next film, *A nos amours* (1983), French critics were eager to see if Pialat could continue and confirm his earlier successful accomplishments. *Under the Sun of Satan* (*Sous le soleil de Satan,* 1987) divided critics while reassuring fans with the triumph of the precious Palme d'or at the fortieth Cannes Film Festival in 1987. Endowed with a self-consciously Bressonian austerity, Pialat's cinematography retained its essential eloquence, despite an excessive exposition—the evident vicissitudes of the dispirited priest who fails to save souls, including his own. For the first time in nine films, Pialat confronted a literary adaptation, with Georges Bernanos's first novel. To this date, no French film had received the prestigious Palme d'or since Claude Lelouch's *A Man and a Woman* (*Un homme et une femme,* 1966). With a continuous use of narrative ellipses, Pialat's script examines the fall of a young country priest in the north of France who falls prey to doubts of his own spiritual vocation.

In a small Artois village, Germaine Malorthy, an adolescent also called Mouchette (Sandrine Bonnaire), is the mistress of the marquis de Cadignan. One night, she reveals her pregnancy to her lover, and following his indifferent reaction, she kills him with his hunting gun. The police conclude it is an act of suicide. Meanwhile, Donissan (Gérard Depardieu), an unpretentious and frail priest, is struggling with his ecclesiastical assignment. In many instances, he confesses to his father superior, the abbot Menou-Segrais (Maurice Pialat), a request to abandon his faith and his methodical recourse to self-flagellation. One night, as he walks along a country road, he is confronted by Satan, who appears in front of him as a peasant. Once freed from his psychological onslaughts, Donissan continues his journey to the village. There he meets Mouchette, who confesses to him her abortion. Donissan, touched by the depth of the tragedy that unfolds before him, tries to help her, but to no avail. One day later, she is found dead, her throat slit. Back at home, Donissan is sent to a new parish in Lumbres, where he suddenly dies inside a confessional booth, on his way to sanctity.

The film generated a great deal of controversy, and at the 1987 Cannes Film Festival, Pialat received the Palme d'or under the insults and contemptuous growls of the crowd at the awards ceremony. He responded immediately by raising his fist in the air and saying: *"Si vous ne m'aimez pas, je peux vous dire que je ne vous aime pas non plus!"* under the compassionate, yet discomforted, smile of Yves Montand, president of the jury. For many of his opponents, Pialat's cinema proved to be too academic as he all too willingly injected his own interpretation of the novel, resulting in a movie far removed from filmed prose. What all Robert Bresson admirers expected to see (like Pialat, Bresson adapted a novel from Bernanos in the 1950s; see chapter 4) was perhaps a coherent narrative plot, which through its complexity and depth would have exposed a certain visual eloquence with sincere subjectivity. For many critics, Pialat's stoic portrait is an emblem of Bernanos's spiritual investigation, the exhausting obstacles a born outsider encounters in communicating his faith to and for others. For them, it is simply a betrayal of Bernanos's legacy or a pale imitation of Bresson's cinema.

Uncompromisingly rigorous and harsh, Pialat's high-powered adaptation of Bernanos's novel is undoubtedly a dark film, both literally and figuratively. It follows the chilling but compassionate atmosphere and the fight of mystical anguish against evil forces—much like Robert Bresson's 1951 *Diary of a Country Priest, Mouchette* (*Mouchette,* 1967) or even Philippe Agostini and Raymond-Léopold Bruckberger's *Le dialogue des carmélites* (1960)—mixed with the omnipresence of the French countryside, under ominous gray skies that serve to accentuate the twin sentiments of isolation and a hostile environment.

THE SUPER PRODUCTIONS: CLAUDE BERRI AND JEAN-JACQUES ANNAUD

Although often commonly regarded from an American point of view as great contributions to cinematography, French critics usually like to remind moviegoers that big-budget productions mostly concentrate on less serious narratives, complex stage productions, and highly structured camera movements to the exclusion of heavy content. Although sporadic when compared to American cinema, French big-budget films did well at the box office during the 1980s. One of the major figures of the moment was producer-director Claude Berri. Born in Paris in 1934, Berri entered the industry in small parts such as Chabrol's *The*

Girls (*Les bonnes femmes,* 1960) and Clouzot's *The Truth* (*La vérité,* 1960). By 1967, he had significantly advanced his career as he directed *The Two of Us* (*Le vieil homme et l'enfant*), his first feature. Producing the majority of his films, Claude Berri also began to coproduce other directors' films, such as Jacques Rivette's *Celine and Julie Go Boating* (*Céline et Julie vont en bateau,* 1974) and Claude Zidi's *Inspector La Bavure* (*L'inspecteur la bavure,* 1980). His most significant productions as a filmmaker were *Le maître d'école* (1981), *Tchao Pantin!* (1983), *Jean de Florette* (1986), *Manon of the Spring* (*Manon des sources,* 1986), *Uranus* (*Uranus,* 1990), *Germinal* (1993), and *Lucie Aubrac* (1997).

The case of *Tchao Pantin!* demonstrates that any cinematic enterprise implies aesthetic choices. Berri, like many other artists of his time, imposed an authentically personal universe and a private vision of French society in a close observation of human tragedy. Adapted from a novel by Alain Page (his first literary adaptation in ten films, since Berri usually brought his own script to the screen), the movie won five Césars in 1984: Best Actor (Coluche), Best Supporting Actor and Best Newcomer (Richard Anconina), Best Photography (Bruno Nuytten), and Best Sound (Jean Labussière and Gérard Lamps).[23]

Lambert (Coluche) works the night shift at a suburban gas station. He tries to forget the dullness of his existence by drinking. Resigned to an existence of alcohol and *attentisme,* he does not expect much from life until he meets Bensoussan (Richard Anconina), a young man who one night stops to refill his moped. The friendship develops as both men realize that their solitude in life is not unique. Half Jewish and half Arab, Bensoussan lives off drug dealing. Although disappointed in Bensoussan (his own son died of a drug overdose), Lambert still maintains an unyielding friendship. One night, the young man is killed by rival drug dealers in front of Lambert, who swears to avenge his friend. With Bensoussan's death, the dreadful past suddenly re-emerges in Lambert's mind. Emotionally destroyed, Lambert, also a former cop, conducts his own investigation. He meets Lola (Agnès Soral), an acquaintance of Bensoussan, who will eventually lead him to Rachid (Mahmoud Zemmouri), a bar owner also heavily implicated in Parisian drug-traffic circles. Finally, Lambert kills Rachid to avenge his young friend and indirectly the memory of his son.

Chief operator (photography) Bruno Nuytten gave the movie a dreamlike quality, a kind of dark sensuality that permeated every frame. There was depth in the images as well as a kind of mystical sense that made the suburban Parisian underworld and the individuals who lived within it as important to the story as the actors. The urban stylization and blue back lighting combined to retain a uniquely Parisian feel. With sets by Alexandre Trauner,[24] representing the familiar mood of Belleville, the film was able to re-create, on its own terms and atmosphere, a piece of the 1930s poetic realism associated with the dramatic tension of film noir.

Although Berri had no guarantee for the success of the film, he heavily emphasized the importance and visibility of the central player, Coluche. Known as the most popular stand-up comedian in France, Coluche had never had the opportunity to fully reveal his acting talent in the field of pure drama. Berri's fascination with actors and real acting allowed Coluche, who was struggling with drugs in real life, to endow the entire film with a special resonance. In a style reminiscent of Jean Gabin in the prewar era (e.g., *Daybreak, Port of Shadows, Lover Boy, They Were Five*), the character of Lambert bewilders and at the same time seduces viewers with his immobile gaze while indirectly exuding from within an aptitude for his character's communicability. Humanitarian craftsmanship, visual perspicacity, and refined sentiment are the hallmarks of Claude Berri's visual cinema. Even perfect acting, Berri acknowledged, can be covered with the smallest movements:

> I wanted Coluche's face to radiate with more and more light and be more and more handsome. I asked Bruno Nuytten, my cameraman, to light him and choose angles to favor this metamorphosis. For Coluche, the relief in having almost finished the film and knowing he was at the end of his work combined with the relief of Lambert who finishes with revenge, in the depths of which the hope of love is reborn. What I'm talking about is not directing an actor but a more intimate relationship between an actor and a director.[25]

The end result of the film corresponds to an epic variation on Berri's continual evocation that love can be indispensable, desirable, punishing, and destructive all at the same time. *Tchao Pantin!* was a deceptively composed film with an inherent connotation of modern-times poetic realism that eventually materialized through its visual surface, erupting in the emotional violence of thwarted and misdirected love. The César for Best Actor awarded to lead actor Coluche was the crowning touch for the comedian. Born Michel Colucci in Paris, Coluche (1948–86)—thanks to the support of actor Romain Bouteille—participated in the famous *Café de la Gare* (a renowned cabaret for stand-up comedians) with future celebrities such as Miou-Miou and Patrick Dewaere. Coluche began as a seasoned nightclub performer, and used the one-hour format to reveal more of himself as he often addressed the problems that the show endured in his audacious monologues (audacious for some, outrageous for others). In 1974, his solo career took off. Coluche often took questions from the audience, which frequently led to some uproarious exchanges and gave him a chance to exhibit his sharp wit. The sketches were better than the usual-variety

Coluche (Lambert) and Richard Anconina (Bensoussan) in Claude Berri's *Tchao Pantin!* (1983), (Courtesy of BIFI/© Renn Productions).

Gérard Depardieu (Jean de Florette) in Claude Berri's *Jean de Florette* (*Jean de Florette*, 1986), (Courtesy of BIFI/© Renn Productions).

fare, with Coluche walking off the set in the middle of routines over differences with the producers, and generally acting the petulant, spoiled superstar role. His tell-it-like-it-is humor influenced French comics of his own generation, as well as those who came later (Les Inconnus, Muriel Robin, Smaïn, etc.). Anticipating the liberalization of the 1980s, Coluche believed humor was to some extent the key to curing the prejudices of society. Coluche immediately captured the hearts of television viewers in the most adventurous radio and TV shows of the 1970s and early 1980s. It was his starring performance in one of the great music halls that made Coluche a household name in French cinema. In 1980, Coluche truly made national headlines. After announcing his candidacy for the presidential elections, he was credited with between 10 and 16 percent of the votes in the polls.

Meanwhile, despite putting on hold his comedic vocation, Coluche forged a successful acting career with commercial films such as Claude Zidi's *The Wing or the Thigh* (*L'aile où la cuisse*, 1976), *Inspector La Bavure, Le maître d'école* (1981), and *Banzai* (1983); Jean Yanne's *Quarter to Two before Jesus Christ* (*Deux heures moins le quart avant Jésus-Christ*, 1982); Bertrand Blier's *My Best Friend's Girl* (*La femme de mon pote*, 1983); and especially *Tchao Pantin!*

Taking everyone by surprise in the mid-1980s, the actor created an unprecedented charitable initiative, which to this day remains one of France's foremost humanitarian enterprises: the Restos du Coeur.[26] In addition to his efforts to create a new fiscal law that would ease taxes on companies in exchange for donations to his association, Coluche secretly offered 1.5 million francs to l'Abbé Pierre, one of France's greatest advocates for the homeless.[27] But Coluche's career tragically came to an end one afternoon in June 1986. In a motorbike accident, he hit a truck on a road in southern France. At his funeral on June 24, 1986, at the famous Père Lachaise cemetery, a myriad of film actors and directors (Yves Montand,[28] Roman Polanski, Miou-Miou, Michel Leeb, Richard Berry, Josiane Balasko, Richard Anconina, Thierry Le Luron, l'Abbé Pierre, Michel Blanc, Gérard Jugnot, Dominique Lavanant, Michel Boujenah, among others), as well as celebrities from all political and artistic backgrounds, gathered to salute one of France's most popular artistic figures. In the true tradition of the court jester, Coluche defied religious and political institutions, racism, and political correctness in all their forms and opened the gates for an entire generation of new comedians. With the psychology of a clown, he had the ability to invert the rapport of confrontation, of derision, and of ridicule. Coluche was the hero of a whole generation, not only the post-68's but also the entire youth of the 1980s.

Three years after the success of *Tchao Pantin!*, Claude Berri embarked on another challenge: Marcel Pagnol's *L'eau des collines*. Based on a folk tale of his native Provence, Pagnol's novel directly inspired Berri to remake what only Pagnol seemed to have been able to direct flawlessly: *Jean de Florette* and *Manon des sources*. Thirty-five years earlier, Pagnol had himself attempted to make a feature film out of *Manon des sources* (1952), which included only the second part of the novel, and whose main protagonist was his spouse, Jacqueline Pagnol. It was with her consent—mostly due to the anticipated presence of actor Yves Montand—that Berri obtained permission to readapt the novel to the screen. In the same way Pagnol did with his Provençal characters three decades earlier, Claude Berri's efforts deliberately focused particular attention on his personages' disposition and language, partly with the assistance of the actors' southern accents.

The first "act," *Jean de Florette,* is set between the two world wars in a small village in Provence called Les Bastides, where César Soubeyran (Yves Montand) is the last guardian of his family's heritage. Under pressure to carry on the lineage through his simpleminded nephew, Ugolin (Daniel Auteuil), he covets his neighbor's land for its natural-flowing spring. The land belongs to Jean de Florette (Gérard Depardieu), a hunchback tax collector and newcomer from the city, who settles in the country with his wife, Aimée (Elisabeth Depardieu), and daughter, Manon (Ernestine Mazurowna), to begin life afresh. He decides to raise vegetables and rabbits on the property, which, according to the map, contains the aforementioned freshwater source. The Soubeyrans must acquire the land at all costs and thus develop a Machiavellian stratagem. Manipulated by his scheming uncle, Ugolin secretly blocks the spring with concrete, covering its site and hoping to ruin the value of the property, since the summer will bring little rain. Meanwhile, they both pretend to support Jean's efforts. By forcing him to get his water miles away, they hope to discourage him from staying in this hostile nature and consequently resell his property. At the beginning, the frequent rains favor the growth of the vegetables, and the rabbits multiply. Then comes the drought, and Jean is compelled to carry water from a neighboring well, using his own strength, and consequently literally transforming himself into a beast of burden. César sends Ugolin to befriend the optimistic Jean. Facing the adversity of an extended drought, Jean is desperate to borrow a mule to help haul water from a nearby spring, but his efforts are to no avail. All day long, the man transports water under the burning sun of Provence. But Jean is much more tenacious than both expected, as he decides to intensify his work until the day when, exhausted by the inhumane amount of work, Jean is killed by a charge of dynamite. His death means victory for Ugolin and his uncle and the realization of their carnation-growing project. As the widow and daughter are about to leave the house, Manon comes upon the two men singing in victory while unclogging the spring. Her whole life unfolds before her as she instantly understands the devilish plot to which she and her family have been victim.

The second "act," *Manon of the Spring,* unfolds the suspense with the calculated pace of a Greek tragedy toward the inexorable resolution of justice. The account takes place a decade later when Manon (Emmanuelle Béart), by now a beautiful young woman who lusts for revenge, has returned to the hills of Provence to shepherd goats on the mountainside while living in poverty, rather than staying with her mother in Marseille. After the aging César and Ugolin become owners of the land, she reveals the long-silenced crime to the villagers. Ugolin, who has noticed the beautiful shepherdess on the hills, falls hopelessly in love with her. On the brink of despair, he publicly declares his love for her on the square of the village, but she directs hers to the local schoolteacher, Bernard (Hippolyte Girardot). One day, the entire village wakes up without water. No one knows that Manon has clogged the spring in order to avenge her father's death. During a gathering in the village shortly after, Manon accuses César and Ugolin of her father's death and reveals their stratagem. César denies the accusation, but Ugolin, first driven by ambition, then torn apart with remorse and love, publicly accepts the guilt and associates it with his love for her. Destroyed by her refusal and his guilt, Ugolin commits suicide the next day, hanging himself on a tree. As for César, he too no longer wishes to live, but before he passes away, one of the village patriarchs recounts the story of Florette, the young girl he was in love with in his youth. César then understands that the child she gave birth to, while he was in Africa, was the hunchback boy. Manon and Bernard, now her husband, unblock the spring. Prosperity comes anew.

Berri's main ambition was not to narrate a sequence of melodramatic episodes. Since most of the motives were disclosed early on, the outcome of Jean de Florette's fateful destiny appears quite predictable. Berri also did not intend to create a suspenseful plot devoid of any real psychological element, but rather to incorporate the ruthlessness of human voracity: the land and water are commodities worth dying for. The calculated pace of the multilayered and pervasive murder story emphasizes the abomination of the characters' wrongdoing. These two epic thrillers, shot but three months apart and totaling nine months of shooting, not only met with considerable success in the United States but also confirmed Claude Berri as one of the most talented producer-filmmakers in France.

For actor Daniel Auteuil (b. 1950), the collaboration with Claude Berri represented a decisive turning point in the actor's career, one of the premier examples of a sudden career takeoff in French cinema history. In 1975, Gérard Pirès assigned him a supporting role to

Emmanuelle Béart (Manon) in Claude Berri's *Manon of the Spring* (*Manon des sources*, 1986), (Courtesy of BIFI/© Renn Productions).

Claude Brasseur, Catherine Deneuve, and Jean-Louis Trintignant in *Act of Agression (L'Agression)*. Before *Jean de Florette*, Auteuil was considered the archetypal B-picture actor, working in Claude Zidi's *Bêtes mais disciplinés* in 1979, and later *Les sous-doués* in 1980 and Charles Nemes's *Les héros n'ont pas froid aux oreilles* in 1978. Virtually no film critic could ever have imagined that the rest of his film career, following the success of *Jean de Florette*, would include illustrious awards such as the Césars for Best Actor in *Manon of the Spring* in 1987, and Patrice Leconte's *The Girl on the Bridge (La fille sur le pont* in 1999). Interestingly, Auteuil gave up a part in Coline Serreau's *Three Men and a Cradle* to play the role of the unattractive Ugolin, which secured him the César. From then on, Auteuil's roles have been a long series of successful choices, including work in Michel Deville's *Le paltoquet* (1986), and Claude Sautet's *Quelques jours avec moi* (1988) and *A Heart in Winter (Un coeur en hiver,* 1992). His participation on the stage was also crowned by success with Molière's *Les fourberies de Scapin* at the Festival d'Avignon and at the Théâtre Mogador during the 1990–91 season. As the years went by, Auteuil endorsed even more serious roles in André Téchiné's *My Favorite Season (Ma saison préférée,* 1993), *Thieves (Les voleurs,* 1995), Coline Serreau's *Romuald and Juliette* (1989), a convincing Henri IV in Patrice Chéreau's *Queen Margot (La reine Margot,* 1993), Berri's *Lucie Aubrac,* and Jaco Van Dormael's *The Eighth Day (Le huitième jour,* 1996)—for which he received the Prix d'interprétation at the Cannes Film Festival, shared with Pascal Duquenne, his young Down syndrome costar. Despite a rather "delayed" career revelation that did not occur until his mid-thirties, the magnitude of Auteuil's accomplishments promoted him as one of the most artistic and multitalented actors of his generation. The key to Daniel Auteuil's triumphs may actually be his uncommon maturity, which allowed him to endorse challenging performances with rare sensitivity and eloquence.

The series *Jean de Florette* and *Manon of the Spring* was also the springboard for Emmanuelle Béart (b. 1963). Daughter of the famous songwriter and singer Guy Béart, the actress mostly appeared in minor roles, primarily on TV, until being cast as a call girl in Edouard Molinaro's *Date with an Angel (L'amour en douce,* 1985). Although only present in the sequel *Manon of the Spring,* the intensity of her performance impressed the French cinema academy to such a degree that she received two awards, Best Supporting Role and Best New Talent, for her work in the film. Like Daniel Auteuil, whom she married shortly thereafter, Emmanuelle Béart expanded her career on screen as well as on the theatrical stage (Marivaux's *La double inconstance* in 1988 and Molière's *Le misanthrope* with actor Jacques Weber in 1989). Her most recent pictures are Claude Sautet's *Nelly and Mr. Arnaud (Nelly et*

Daniel Auteuil (Ugolin) in Claude Berri's *Manon of the Spring (Manon des sources,* 1986), (Courtesy of BIFI/© Renn Productions).

Monsieur Arnaud, 1995), Brian De Palma's *Mission: Impossible* (1996), Danièle Thompson's *La Bûche (La bûche,* 1999), Olivier Assayas's *Les destinées (Les destinées sentimentales,* 2000), and François Ozon's *Huit femmes* (2002).

Along with Claude Berri, director Jean-Jacques Annaud must be regarded as a filmmaker dedicated to an international market, as he has often described himself as a "French man" who makes movies and not a "French filmmaker." Born in 1943, Annaud came to film via a strong advertising background from the 1970s. A graduate of the national film school, the Ecole de Vaugirard, he achieved his first short feature at age nineteen with *Les sept péchés capitaux du cinéaste.* He later obtained a licence de lettres, which allowed him to enter the prestigious IDHEC. Annaud practiced his artistic talents in *Paris-Match* and TV commercials (more than 400 spots). After his first full-length feature film in 1976, *Black and White in Color (La victoire en chantant),* a satire of the colonial period that did not do well at the box office (despite its Oscar for Best Foreign Film/Ivory Coast), his name began to be associated with the promising expectations of new French directors. Although rather mediocre, *Coup de tête* (1979), his second film, was another step toward "cinematographic consecration." But it was only with *Quest for Fire (La guerre du feu,* 1981), an enormous commercial success, that Annaud met with international fame. The Anglo-

Canadian production, whose total cost reached $12 million, gathered international actors such as Everett McGill, Ron Perlman, Namir El Kadi Gaw, Rae Dawn Chong, and Gary Schwartz, and won Césars for Best Film and Best Director in 1982.

Quest for Fire was the real breakthrough for Annaud; the film has defined his style ever since. Adapted from Joseph-Henri Rosny's 1911 novel,[29] the film is an allegorical tale narrating a tribal struggle for survival after its only source of fire has died. The tribe members know how to preserve it and spread it but not how to re-create it. Some of the tribe are sent on an expedition to discover the secret of fire. The story begins with the vicissitudes of three Homo sapiens in search of fire, which ultimately gives power to their tribe. Fire is not only a fearful weapon but a symbol of evolutionary superiority. Despite the unusual deploy of technical means for a French director, Annaud took the crew on a "similar" expedition around the globe as they began shooting in Kenya in 1980, Scotland, and ultimately in Canada in 1981.[30]

Five years later, Annaud successfully adapted the difficult novel *The Name of the Rose* (*Le nom de la rose,* 1986), written by the Italian novelist and semiologist Umberto Eco. With a budget of $17 million, a Franco-Italian-German coproduction team, and three years of planning, the film also took four screenwriters attempting to master Eco's novel.[31] These medieval chronicles, beautifully photographed by cinematographer Tonino delli Colli, fully came to life, eventually winning the César for Best Foreign Film in 1987. This psychological thriller retraces the memoir of Adso of Melk (Christian Slater) and his visit in 1327 with his master, the Franciscan monk William of Baskerville (Sean Connery), to a Benedictine abbey in northern Italy. Outside its walls, starving peasants battle for leftovers thrown down from the monks' kitchens. William is sent to investigate the mysterious death of one of the monks. Despite the silence and oddity of many of them, he makes measured but effective progress. However, while the investigation continues, a second murder occurs. William is convinced that the key to the mystery, which will lead to the true murderer, resides inside the scriptorium of the main library, at the pinnacle of which stands a great tower arranged as a labyrinth. Brother Berenger (Michael Habeck), now the third assassinated monk, is found drowned in a wine barrel with once more a recurrent particularity: a black spot on one of his forefingers as well as on his tongue. The progress of the investigation is hampered by the arrival of Bernardo Gui (Murray Abraham), an officer of the Holy Inquisition, who immediately condemns several suspicious monks to be put on trial. Meanwhile, William discovers the source of all the deaths—a translation of Aristotle's *Poetics,* a forbidden manuscript in medieval times, which defines the importance of human laughter. An old monk, Jorge de Burgos (Feodor Chaliapin), placed poison in the corner of each page, thereby indirectly killing anyone who dared to read the blasphemous book. Once trapped, the old monk sets the tower on fire and dies in the flames. William has just enough time to exit alive. Meanwhile, the peasants gathered around the gallows start an upheaval, which ends in the death of the inquisitor.

Despite his international fame and contribution to world cinema, many French film critics tend to systematically categorize Annaud's movies exclusively as part of the French-film legacy. To this, Annaud usually answers by asserting his international endorsement, whether financially or artistically, by the very makeup of his cast of actors and technical crews. Annaud wrote the scenario of most of his films with the collaboration of Gérard Brach[32] (b. 1927), and the scores were by various French artists. In an interview with cultural attaché Laurent Daniélou, Annaud spoke of his philosophy regarding national cinema:

> I think that one should not identify the nationality of a film with its language, as if it were literature. The art of film corresponds to the art of the image, and language is a secondary issue. When a French novel becomes an international success, it is because it conveys the thoughts of the French author and not his language. For films, it is the same.[33]

Thus, Annaud explained his decision to work in the United States. With the regulations imposed on French directors working in France, Annaud preferred to keep his artistic freedom even if this meant working abroad. Annaud is fond of mentioning to the international press that all of his films have been financed in different countries (e.g., *The Name of the Rose* was financed by American, German, Italian, and French backers).

> This is a good occasion to change mentalities and to explain to the French that Americans are not trying to kill French cinema. They are just businessmen whose goal is to make good movies. . . . We, professionals, think that with the American community, French people get the wrong idea about what is going on in Los Angeles. It is a much friendlier world and open to foreign influences than one thinks. We are here to help our French colleagues to understand the evolution of Hollywood cinema and to allow Americans to get acquainted with French technicians. The goal is to help contacts and eventually to create a friendly climate between the two communities.[34]

In 1991, Claude Berri offered Annaud the complex adaptation of Marguerite Duras's best-seller *The Lover* (*L'amant*), which proved to be a box office and critical success. Also successful at the box office was *Seven Years in Tibet* (*Sept ans au Tibet,* 1997), which took its inspiration from the autobiographical story of Heinrich Harrer, a war prisoner

Jean-Jacques Annaud and Sean Connery during the shooting of *The Name of the Rose* (*Le nom de la rose*, 1986), (Courtesy of BIFI).

held by the British in India during World War II, who escaped through the Himalayas and settled in Tibet, eventually becoming the preceptor of the Dalai Lama. Annaud's most-recent film, *Enemy at the Gates* (*Stalingrad*), depicting the Eastern front in epic scope through the character of the Russian sniper Vassili Zaitsev (interpreted by the rising British movie star Jude Law), was released in the United States in March 2001.

NEW DIRECTORS FOR A NEW GENERATION: JEAN-JACQUES BEINEIX AND LUC BESSON

As film historian René Prédal once observed, "After the cinema on weddings (the 1950s), the erotic cinema (1960s), cinema on sex (1970s), the cinema of the 1980s speaks about love as Beineix, Besson and Carax emphasize the comeback of the couple, following the *libertinage* of the New Wave and the sexual freedom of the following generation."[35] The new generation of young filmmakers was early characterized by the innovative style of Jean-Jacques Beineix. Beineix began his career as first assistant to filmmakers Claude Zidi and Claude Berri. His first feature-length film, *Diva* (*Diva,* 1981), can be considered both an auteur film and a commercial thriller. After a catastrophic debut in March 1981, due to slow attendance and some bad press by unenthusiastic critics, the film took off slowly. The success of *Diva* in the US allowed a commercial second chance in France, as it took four Césars the next year (Best First Feature, Best Music Score, Best Photography, Best Sound), consequently becoming an exceptionally fashionable movie.

Adapted from Delacorta's novel, *Diva* narrates the tranquil existence of young moped postman Jules (Frédéric Andrei), who, passionate for opera, declares an infinite admiration for his idol, the American opera star Cynthia Hawkins (Wilhelmenia Wiggins Fernandez). During one of her rare recitals in Paris, he records her live performance with a tape recorder surreptitiously placed on his lap. To make matters worse, he steals one of her dresses while waiting for an autograph backstage. Although universally celebrated, Cynthia Hawkins has refused to become a recording artist. Therefore, any pirated recording becomes priceless on the black market. A second story, so far unrelated to the previous one, concerns the murder of a prostitute by two hit men, who before dying leaves in Jules's motorcycle bag a compromising tape-recorded confession that will help indict a drug ringleader and head of the prostitution network, who also happens to be one of the chief officers in the police force, Saporta (Jacques Fabbri). Later, Jules meets Alba (Thuy An Luu), a young Asian girl, who, also interested in opera, asks to listen to his secret recording. Overcome by guilt, Jules decides to take the dress back to Cynthia. A friendship begins, as well as a platonic-love relationship. The tape Jules possesses of the diva's finest performance falls into the mob's hands, and soon they threaten to release major bootleg copies of it unless Cynthia signs exclusively with them. Meanwhile, Saporta and his hit men are after Jules to find the cassette left by the prostitute. On the brink of being killed, Jules is saved by Gorodish (Richard Bohringer), who takes him away to Normandy. In a suspenseful finale, Gorodish invites both parties (the Asian gangsters and Saporta) to recoup their long-awaited prize.

The action scenes, including a remarkable chase through the Paris Metro, are powerfully contrasted with the languorous setting of Garadish's immense apartment as well as Jules and Cynthia's romantic walk through the park. This new type of visual contrast, so characteristic of the late 1980s, with its strong visual aesthetics, colors, and conflicting tones, contributed to *Diva*'s reputation as a breakthrough film. Philippe Rousselot's cinematography[36] accounts for the numerous visual effects, in particular the film's stylized noirlike sense, an amalgamation of a significant emotional background with idiosyncratic personages like Jules. Constantly finding himself navigating worlds whose borders appear prohibitive and mysterious to him, Jules is relentelessly chased by the police, the mob, record companies, and ultimately his own conscience. The result is an effective enterprise of assimilation of the Romanesque element with the visual. With some innovative cinematography and direction, and the action becoming increasingly frenetic but at the same time always under control, Beineix was able to challenge the conventional rhythms of the thriller. A model of pacing for some, while too slow for others, the film, with its complicated plot, survives without falling prey to the usual damagingly excessive levels of exposition. Vladimir Cosma's score and, of course, Wilhelmenia Wiggins Fernandez's voice anchored the film, giving it an extrasensory element that separates *Diva* from the run-of-the-mill light thriller or melodrama.

Spurred to renew his successful, and by then widely praised creativity, Beineix's next attempt was a clear commercial failure. Disapproved by the critics and ignored by disenchanted audiences, *The Moon in the Gutter* (*La lune dans le caniveau*, 1983) surprised viewers with its tone and format. With some of the biggest names in European cinema (Nastassja Kinski, Gérard Depardieu, and Victoria Abril, among others), the film does not really succeed in capturing the mood of the times despite the impressive sets of Hilton McConnico (winner of the 1984 César for Best Set). However, it was *Betty Blue* (*37,2° le matin*, 1986) that confirmed the expectations of this promising filmmaker. Beineix decided to produce this film himself on a more modest budget. Adapted from Philippe Djian's novel, the story takes place in the south of France and centers on the relationship between Zorg (Jean-Hugues Anglade),[37] a young handyman who lives in a beach house, and his girlfriend, Betty (Béatrice Dalle). Painting houses by day and making love by night, the couple seem to live a fulfilled and hedonistic existence. One day, Betty clashes with Zorg's boss, violently insulting him before burning down several of his beach cottages. Zorg then loses his job. They now both work at Eddy's (Gérard Darmon) pizzeria. One day, Betty discovers a manuscript written by Zorg. She comes to believe that he is a great writer and spends hours typing the manuscript, then mailing it to several publishers. Following a string of rejections, Betty loses her confidence. Later, the couple move into an old house in a small village, where Zorg finds a job as a piano salesman. The story turns tragic when Betty lapses into schizophrenia. While hoping to become pregnant, she becomes depressed and ultimately goes mad. Following a suicide attempt, she is sent to an asylum while in a coma. Compassionate and desperate himself, Zorg decides to soothe her pain by choking her to death. The outcome of free-spiritedness is not uplifting success but madness, self-destruction, and ultimately death.

Beineix's primary goal for the film was to show the extraordinary relationship of this struggling couple from a compassionate perspective. Without being overbearing, the film succeeds in portraying the simple motivations of young people amid the obstacles of a complicated world. The director's visual talents (colorful style, spectacular crane shots, sliding camera movements) are combined with the fantastic photography and the tragic story line: "I had known Betty for a week. The forecast was for storms," reminds viewers of the implicit narrator in an early scene. Much like *Diva,* the film captured the mood and the sequential tensions as well as underscored the plot's inherent sexuality and absolute visual effervescence. Beineix's characters are creatures of pure will, given to ostentatious romantic obsessions. (Betty wanders without focus for her deep emotional energy.) Though the story was not atypical, it was already the expression of a new cinematographic trend. In its extraordinary narrative element, *Betty Blue* can come across as being both analytical and "swept away" in equal measure, and here the desolate poetry of Beineix's mise-en-scène is both unique and fully realized.

The other great revelation of the 1980s was director Luc Besson who experienced his first commercial success in 1984, with *Subway.* Born in Paris in 1959, Luc Besson grew up by the ocean, where his parents were diving instructors for the famous Club Méditerranée. After a brief stay in Hollywood, he returned to France, where he began to produce shorts. His first experiences were as an assistant in Lewis Gilbert's *Moonraker* (1979) and in Maurice Pialat's *Loulou* (1980). Winner of the Avoriaz International Film Festival, *Le dernier combat* (made in 1983, with a budget of 17 million francs) gave Besson the financial security he crucially needed to convince future producers. This success allowed him to win prestigious assignments, such as Isabelle Adjani's video "Pull marine" (music by Serge Gainsbourg) and some ad spots for the Dim brand. First perceived as neo–New Wave, Besson's so-called young cinema typically represents a heavily graphic world dehumanized by money and power, where the flight of human imagination and realism meet in a choked-up, overpoweringly oppressive environment. With the collaboration of Pierre Jolivet, Besson wrote the script for *Subway,* a film that was knocked by film critics for its lack of "real" characters. The public, on the other hand, not only ensured the success of the film but was also indirectly responsible for the César Awards in 1986 for Best Actor (Christophe Lambert), Best Set (Alexandre Trauner), and Best Sound (Harald Maury, Luc Périni, and Gérard Lamps).

Largely confined to the Paris Metro, the story narrates the vicissitudes of Fred (Christophe Lambert), an eccentric young man, who meets Helena (Isabelle Adjani) in the strange world of the Parisian subway. Besson explores the compositional alternatives for his wild, bright-yellow spiky punk haircut personage who, after stealing some compromising documents from Helena's husband in his residence, takes refuge from his pursuers, her husband's thugs, in the Paris underground. Bored by her life of wealth, Helena agrees to meet him. Fred demands a ransom in exchange for the documents, but what he secretly desires is to see Helena again. Fred does not give her the documents immediately. Helena, with the assistance of a police inspector, and her husband's private militia all chase him. Nevertheless, as the manhunt intensifies, Helena experiences a change of heart. The combination of visual "punk," intensely drawn actors from the mean streets, and the mesmerizing beauty of Isabelle Adjani epitomize a sort of postmodern fusion of frames of reference that ultimately gives the film a Surreal, cinematic dimension. For the general movie public this specialized segment is enchanting, as the film possesses a factual plot and an execution that is so neo-romantic as to approach visual opulence.

After the suffocating universe of the Parisian subway, Besson moved on to his next project, this time embracing the world he knew best, that of the ocean. *The Big Blue (Le grand bleu,* 1988) is considered one of the most significant cult movies of the 1980s, a true manifesto of youth. Besson presented a compelling meditation on the fascinating spell that the great oceans cast on humans (Besson himself once aspired to be a marine biologist).

The story begins with the childhood of two friends, Jacques Mayol (Jean-Marc Barr) and boisterous and cocky Enzo Molinari (Jean Réno), who share a passion for snorkeling. The friends spend wonderful moments during makeshift-diving competitions as they challenge each other to see who can stay underwater the longest, braving danger and possibly death. Obsessed with the idea of outdoing each other, the boys spur each other on to more daring feats of physical skill. But one day tragedy srikes as Jacques's father, an experienced diver, dies at sea. As an adult, Jacques still keeps in mind this tragic accident. Johanna (Rosanna Arquette), an American insurance claims adjuster, sees Jacques diving in a frozen Peruvian lake and immediately falls in love with him. She then follows him from New York to Europe to pursue a difficult romance (Besson ultimately sets up the real competition: Johanna versus the dolphins). What the young woman does not anticipate is the hypnotic enchantment the ocean has on Jacques and the way it incessantly appears to pull him deeper and deeper. Enzo, who has not seen Jacques for twenty years, is by now a world-class diver but is still haunted by knowing there is indeed someone out there

Isabelle Adjani (Helena) in Luc Besson's *Subway* (*Subway*, 1984), (Courtesy of BIFI/ © Gaumont).

better than he. During the world free-diving competition in Taormina, Sicily, both companions set world records that no competing divers can break. For his part, Jacques desires to put behind him the memory of his father's loss and earn Enzo's respect at a sport they have been playing for years. The contest between Jacques and Enzo keeps intensifying, with the two driving the other farther down to the depths of the sea. Although changed with time, their friendship remains strong until one day Enzo, surpassing his own limit in a dive, dies in the arms of Jacques when he returns to the surface. Distressed by Enzo's last request to leave his body at the bottom of the ocean, Jacques becomes depressed until the day he decides to dive for eternity. Once at the bottom of the sea, surrounded by the blueness, he slowly and silently lets go. With his cinematic storytelling style, Besson pondered the cosmos through his free-diving[38] hero Jacques Mayol,[39] a world-record holder, who stood at the center of the project. The role of Jacques was actually first offered to Christopher Lambert, Mickey Rourke, and Mel Gibson, before going to Jean-Marc Barr.[40]

Despite the apparent simplicity of the screenplay and the sagacity of the dialogue (the lack of complexity in the characters was unexpected), Besson, who is not considered a master storyteller, succeeded by virtue of his highly stylized use of imagery and his underwater scenes (*The Big Blue* oozed with a sensuous beauty unlike any other film at the time). *The Big Blue* was nonetheless intriguing, with the originality of its photography (by Carlo Varini) of Mediterranean waters. Eric Serra's score (*Golden Eye, The Fifth Element*) captured the director's ambitions with its pre–New Age music. In the American format, containing a drastically revised "happy" ending, a separate music score replaced the original sound track (by composer Bill Conti). The images and the music brilliantly intermingled as the eye of the camera plunged into the deep, generating a visual blend that could not be separated: vibrant hues and sound seem to glow off the screen.

Although French film directors and critics often address the hot-button issue of the "malevolent" Hollywood influence on their nation's cinematographic ethos, Luc Besson can be most accurately described as one of the few French filmmakers who has set out to compete head to head with heavyweights such as George Lucas and Steven Spielberg. But Besson's style also corresponds to a visual challenge that ultimately reevaluates the criteria of appreciation and visual coherence. In fact, Besson's main cinematographic force is his ability to capture the moment in vibrant images, to create a beautiful tapestry of emotions and sights. Distinctly un-European, Besson's productions are generally directed to the broad American public, yet they have still mostly pro-

Jean-Marc Barr (Jacques) in Luc Besson's *The Big Blue* (*Le grand bleu*, 1988), (Courtesy of BIFI/© Gaumont).

Roland Giraud (Pierre), Michel Boujenah (Michel), and André Dussollier (Jacques) in Coline Serreau's *Three Men and a Cradle* (*Trois hommes et un couffin*), 1985 (Courtesy of BIFI/© Flachfilms).

voked a lack of sympathy on the part of American critics and much apathy from other overseas moviegoers.

The shooting of *The Big Blue* took more than nine months, in Italy, Greece, the Virgin Islands, the United States, and Peru. One of the major problems in post-production was cutting the 200-minute film to 132 minutes. (A 168-minute director's cut was released in the US market twelve years later.) First screened at the 1988 Cannes Film Festival, the film went on to garner seven nominations for Césars, winning the award for Best Music Score (Eric Serra). Despite a certain disappointment when compared to Jean-Jacques Annaud's *The Bear* and Bruno Nuytten's *Camille Claudel*,[41] the film's popular success in France and distribution in the United States remained a rare example of a *phénomène de société*. Luc Besson's career continued to flourish with *La Femme Nikita* (*Nikita*, 1990), *The Professional* (*Léon*, 1994), *The Fifth Element* (*Le cinquième élément*, 1997), and *The Messenger: The Story of Joan of Arc* (*Jeanne d'Arc*, 1999).

THE REBIRTH OF POPULAR COMEDIES: COLINE SERREAU AND CLAUDE ZIDI

The *café-théâtre* phenomenon, born outside the world of stand-up comedy at the end of the 1960s, evolved into a new type of *comédies de boulevard*, or popular comedy, a decade later. The 1980s thrived on its legacy and promoted the performance of its actors—aside from the predominant humor instigated by Coluche with such films as Michel Blanc's *Marche à l'ombre* (1984) and Gérard Jugnot's *Pinot simple flic* (1984).

Against all expectations, the greatest comedy success of the 1980s, as well as the fifth biggest commercial hit ever, came from an almost-unknown female director, Coline Serreau (b. 1947), with *Three Men and a Cradle* (*Trois hommes et un couffin*, 1985). The film, a persuasive testimony to the change in mentality which occurred in the 1980s, was produced during a sociological evolution toward a more liberal and progressive society. Three single men, Pierre (Roland Giraud), egomaniacal Jacques (André Dussollier), and Michel (Michel Boujenah), live a life of leisure in their luxurious apartment. One rule prevails: women are strictly forbidden. Jacques, an Air France flight attendant, accepts an unknown package the day he must leave for Asia. One Sunday, Pierre and Michel find a cradle in front of their door, a basket with an infant girl Marie, and a letter from the baby's mother, Sylvia (Philippine Leroy Beaulieu), Jacques's ex-girlfriend. The note says she must go to the United States and wants Jacques to take care of the infant for "just" six months. Life for the bachelors is immediately and drastically changed. In a series of comic scenes, they learn about baby formulas and diapers. After three weeks, Jacques finally comes home, and the three men become Marie's three dads. When Sylvia returns to take Marie away, the men feel an immense relief that is soon followed by an inexplicable void in their lives. The finale is quite unexpected, as Sylvia, a professional model, asks her companions to help rear the child, since her professional career cannot allow her the time. The script, which tracks the men's relationship with the baby, explores the hidden desire for fatherhood from men who typically avoid making commitments. This American-style comedy although generated on a small budget won an impressive series of awards: Césars for Best Film, Best Scenario, and Best Supporting Role (Michel Boujenah). The American remake, Leonard Nimoy's *Three Men and a Baby,* shot in 1987 (with Tom Selleck, Ted Danson, and Steve Guttenberg), was also successful at the American box office.

Also widely acclaimed as one of the best comedies of all time was *My New Partner* (*Les ripoux,* 1985) by Claude Zidi (b. 1934). Never before had a mainstream comedy been rewarded so handsomely at the French Academy Awards as this one was in 1985. With Césars for Best Film, Best Director, and Best Montage (Nicole Saunier), *My New Partner* confirmed the rehabilitation of comedy among general audiences as well as film critics. Zidi's idea came from a meeting with a young police officer during the 1982 Cannes Film Festival. From a series of authentic anecdotes, Zidi developed the plot into a full-length feature film (the title, *Les ripoux,* is French slang for "crooked cops"). The story is a confrontation between two schools in the Parisian police force. Corruption in *My New Partner* seems to be the natural state of law enforcement.

René (Philippe Noiret), a police inspector who thrives on fraudulent kickbacks and racketeering, is joined by a young newcomer, François ('Thierry Lhermitte), who arrives straight from the police academy. The movie is primarily about the process of the conscientious, law-abiding officer and his "reeducation" under René. René has a hard time associating with his new partner since François disapproves of all his corrupt methods. Hoping to win François's loyalty, René's companion (Régine) finds a friend, Natacha (Grace De Capitani), an attractive call girl, who succeeds at least in changing his look. Both police officers enter a world of corruption as they get involved in drug trafficking. Ultimately François pulls it off, but not René.

Zidi is known for mainstream burlesque comedies and standard-bearers of Sunday cinema (purely commercial French cinema that normally never crosses the Atlantic). *My New Partner* was his first national commercial success. Except for *Three Men and a Cradle,* rarely has a comedy managed to win the best film award at the Césars. The success of *My New Partner* triggered a no less successful sequel in 1990, *Ripoux contre Ripoux*. Other films from Claude Zidi include *The Wing or the Thigh, Inspector La Bavure, The Jackpot!* (*La Totale!*, 1991), which inspired James Cameron's *True Lies* (1994), and *Asterix and Obelix vs. Caesar* (*Astérix et Obélix contre César*, 1999).

Chapter 8
The Last Decade and Beyond

French cinema of the 1990s is characterized by three consecutive trends: the persistence of economic difficulties in the early part of the decade due to the declining attendance of general audiences; the assertion in 1993 of the "cultural exception" to promote cinematographic pluralism against the growing presence of American productions in Europe; and finally, in the mid-1990s the unprecedented financial revival of French cinema due to the significant investments of television companies in film production, which moves beyond the twentieth century into the present time.

Following the declining attendance of the mid-to-late-1980s, French popular audiences continued to decrease in size during the first part of the 1990s. But contrary to popular predictions, the French film industry, during the second part of the decade, experienced a sudden revitalization thanks to the increased investments of television companies. This not only reversed declining attendance but also ensured French cinema's prosperity and independence. The return of comedies to the box office with films such as Jean-Marie Poiré's *The Visitors* (*Les visiteurs*, 1993) and Francis Veber's *The Dinner Game* (*Le dîner de cons*, 1998) confirmed the financial recovery for the entire industry. In addition, throughout the 1990s French cinema reestablished itself as an international critical success earning recognition with films such as Jean-Paul Rappeneau's *Cyrano de Bergerac* (*Cyrano de Bergerac*, 1990), which garnered a Best Actor at the Cannes Film Festival, Régis Wargnier's *Indochine* (*Indochine*, 1992), winner of the Oscar for Best Foreign Film, and more recently, Jean-Pierre Jeunet's *Amélie* (*Le fabuleux destin d'Amélie Poulain*, 2001).

French Cinema's strength today is in large part due to the active role of Canal+—a division of Vivendi Universal, the world's second-largest media company, present in 100 countries with over 300,000 employees—which in terms of growth and profit has become omnipresent and indispensable to French film production. By the end of the decade into the present, it has become clear that the French film industry is regarded as the leader of European productions in great part due to its recently remodeled infrastructure. At the turn of the new millennium, French cinema is represented by many original conceptions and imaginative creations like Pitof's *Vidocq* (2001). The industry as a whole is able to adapt to the rapid technological developments of modern filmmaking, along with the demands of popular audiences for more entertaining films, without losing its unique French spirit.

FRENCH SOCIETY IN THE 1990s

Elected for a second term (1988–95), François Mitterrand appointed Michel Rocard as the new head of government in May 1988. An accomplished financial consultant and a promoter of government by bilateral consent (left and center), Rocard contributed to the renovation of the social security system, helped organize the European Union at the beginning of the new decade, and ultimately qualified France for the European monetary union, which was achieved in 1999. On January 1, 2002, France and most European nations adopted the euro as their official currency.

Following the winds of change and hope, which mainly originated in Eastern Europe, the French government also reevaluated itself in May 1991. One of these changes was the replacement of Rocard with Edith Cresson, the first female prime minister. Despite the persistent high unemployment rate, drawn-out workers' strikes, and financial scandals that temporarily beleaguered the Socialist government, Mitterrand's vision to fortify the status of France in the European Union was exemplified by his participation in drafting the Maastricht Treaty in 1991, with a pledge to endorse closer economic connections between France and its European partners. Despite antagonistic criticisms, Mitterrand, who counted on a popular referendum to increase the coalition, won it with only 51 percent of the votes. In March 1993, Mitterrand did not participate in the resulting political infighting of the legislative election, which gave conservative forces a clear majority in the Assemblée nationale. Although the triumphant conservatives called on Mitterrand to resign, the president refused to leave office and carried on his presidential term until the end. He died on January 8, 1996, at age seventy-nine, just six months after leaving political life. Edouard Balladur, a Gaullist whose political mentor had been Georges Pompidou, became premier in March 1993. Although his platform to reduce unemployment and clandestine immigration and his promise to end an epidemic of political corruption won applause, subsequent financial scandals left Balladur's government vulnerable as well.

Like Mitterrand, who ran for three presidential elections before finally winning, Jacques Chirac's third attempt was a victory as he defeated Socialist candidate Lionel Jospin in May 1995. He immediately appointed Alain Juppé prime minister. Chirac's political win brought an end to the fourteen-year-long Socialist presidency, but only temporarily, since in the summer of 1997, the elections for the National Assembly gave the Socialist coalition a clear majority. Much to the surprise of many, the conservative parties lost control of the House, and Socialist leader Lionel Jospin became prime minister in 1997, serving in Matignon until the spring of 2002. On May 5, 2002, Chirac was reelected president and appointed conservative Jean-Pierre Raffarin as the new prime minister.

THE IMPROVING HEALTH OF FRENCH CINEMA

The visual lyricism, which had best described French cinema from the 1930s through the French New Wave and even into the 1970s, appeared at the turn of the last decade to have lost its mythological presence in contemporary movies. While attempting to capture the new look of French contemporary society, with its changing racial makeup, economic hardships, and growing apathy among young people, French filmmakers of the 1990s such as Marc Caro, Jean-Pierre Jeunet, Luc Besson, Leos Carax, Eric Zonca, Mathieu Kassovitz, Cédric Klapish, Olivier Assayas, Jean Becker, Patrice Leconte, and Dominik Moll emerged as the artists best able to reunite these apparently conflicting trends. Despite the political and economic bleakness of the country, new realities emerged: filmmakers successfully conciliated the technological evolutions in modern filmmaking with the increasingly challenging demands of popular audiences.

With a serious lack of original and innovative scripts, combined with a prevailing and almost stylish morose tone, much of French cinema of the early 1990s presented a new form of hyperrealism, a new trend for psychological realism as well as the romantic tale. But because of their high degree of pessimism, usually involving forlorn individuals evolving in an unsympathetic atmosphere, these films challenged the basic conventions of classic movies of the prewar poetic realism era. Even when killed at the end of macabre and doomed plots, Jean Gabin, unlike modern-day protagonists, usually appeared to secure a certain degree of deliverance in movies such as *Daybreak, Pépé le Moko,* and *The Human Beast.* This tendency among new and accomplished film directors and scriptwriters generated, as illustrated by Leos Carax's *Les amants du Pont-Neuf* (1991), starring Juliette Binoche,[1] an alarming fissure between French general audiences and regular *cinéphile* moviegoers.

Although healthier on paper when compared to other European film industries, the French film industry did not show any optimistic signs of renewal during the first half of the 1990s. The overall economic situation, with the power struggle involving global trade issues in the background, directly affected the morale of investors. As a result, more and more productions were directly achieved through government assistance and the cosponsorship of television companies.

From an average 180 million tickets for French films sold each year in the 1970s to a record 202 million in 1982 (half the 1960s' figures), attendance continued to decrease dramatically, reaching an all-time low of 116 million in 1992. But against all pessimistic prognostications, the French film industry was about to create the biggest revolution of the decade not only by reversing the decreasing-attendance trend but also by triggering one of the most vigorous and unprecedented waves of new productions. In order to appreciate the different rationales of the economic accomplishments of French cinema in the 1990s (both in domestic and foreign markets), it is helpful to understand the situation France and other countries faced in 1993 during the difficult GATT negotiations.

In the early 1950s, GATT (General Agreement on Tariffs and Trade), was the only international pact on world-trade and advocated three main principles: nondiscrimination between lateral parties, economic consolidation, and, above all, trade negotiation. Since it was only an agreement in principle, GATT never imposed any specific regulations, but rather suggested guidelines for a liberal economy and a free market. In 1994, the newly created World Trade Organization (WTO) officially replaced GATT. The European protection quotas,

TABLE 1: TICKETS SOLD (IN MILLIONS) AND BOX OFFICE REVENUE (MILLION FRANCS)

YEAR	TICKETS SOLD (IN MILLIONS)	BOX OFFICE REVENUE (BILLION FRANCS)
1990	121.92	3,826.12
1991	117.50	3,881.22
1992	116.00	3,941.15
1993	132.72	4,519.02
1994	124.42	4,286.80
1995	130.24	4,526.93
1996	136.74	4,762.11
1997	149.02	5,175.03
1998	170.57	6,013.96
1999	153.53	5,476.13
2000	165.54	5,858.78
2001	184.42	N/A

(*Source:* CNC)

established to limit the import of American films (see chapter 7), broke new ground in benefiting the French film industry (but not for all European-national cinemas). In addition to the motion-picture market, the entire audiovisual industry was directly affected by new minimums in television programming for instance. French television companies had to include in their primetime programming a minimum of 60 percent European films and 40 percent French-language films. Anticipating the new contretemps, the American delegation argued (to no avail) that the politics of heavy government-funded subventions, state intervention, and protective quotas promoting the "cultural exception," as well as national productions, were against the spirit of GATT and the global market.

What has been commonly called the "cultural exception" against the American domination (*l'exception culturelle,* incongruously dubbed the "French exception" by its numerous detractors) corresponded to an oral agreement, suggested after innumerable heated discussions, by which governments were entitled to decide which categories of "goods" should remain outside the accord (for example, cinema and audiovisual productions in general which could be considered "cultural goods"). This suggestion, voiced by French representatives, became very popular among European governments. Five years later, in November 1999, at the WTO conference in Seattle, the central question of "cultural exception" was never addressed. Many French filmmakers, like Claude Berri, promoted the imperative responsibility of the French administration to defend cultural "pluralism" via the sponsorship of new legislation and public funding to assist cinematographic production and international exports. For Berri, like many European filmmakers, movies were not to be considered common commercial merchandise, and political leaders were expected to become accountable for shielding and sustaining the efforts of the entire audiovisual sector (the European film market is the equivalent in size to that of the American). More than just a cultural venture, the world-film industry is also a political and economical asset. Beyond modestly promoting pluralistic-cultural supply, the French government must face the difficult challenge of successfully continuing its effort to co-finance local productions and stimulate quality as well as quantity, and more importantly to ensure the commercialization of these productions on foreign markets.

A UNIQUE FINANCIAL-AID SYSTEM

As discussed in the preceding chapter, the self-regulated financial assistance for filmmakers and producers initiated by the CNC in the early 1960s, and enhanced in the early 1980s, was in full swing in the early 1990s (Jack Lang doubled the allocation during his first term, in 1982). Each year over a hundred full-length feature films were produced in France, making it the leading film industry in Europe. Despite the successful *avances sur recettes,* the main mission of which was to set funds against royalties from box office revenues for quality, auteur, and experimental films, French cinema has always been in search of new subsidy opportunities. The financial aid system *aide sélective à la production* was money given directly to producers, once approved by the CNC, often as a long-term loan, since most of those films generally did not do well at the box office. In fact, only 10 percent of those films have been able to earn out and reimburse the initial credit. In the 1990s, state subsidies encouraged productions for international audiences as well as films by major foreign filmmakers, whose home countries did not create such favorable financial environments. In addition, several fiscal incentives, like the tax shelter named Sociétés de financement des industries cinématographiques et audiovisuelles (SOFICA), also created by Jack Lang in the 1980s, boosted investments in films and established a closer link between the movie industry and the world of finance.

Subtantial financial help also came from French-television companies, which slowly became the principal partners for coproductions. In 1993, their participation through public and private channels, (called *aide automatique,* or automatic financial aid) reached 35 percent of the overall volume of investments, or around $150 million. Joint productions included Claude Berri's *Germinal* (*Germinal,* 1993), Jean-Marie

TABLE 2: EVOLUTION OF FILM PRODUCTION IN THE 1990s

	REGISTERED FILMS	FRENCH INITIATIVE	COPRODUCTIONS MAJORITY FOREIGN	FOND ECO/SUD
1990	146	106	37	3
1991	156	108	36	12
1992	155	113	31	11
1993	152	101	36	15
1994	115	89	22	4
1995	141	97	32	12
1996	134	104	27	3
1997	163	125	33	5
1998	183	148	32	3
1999	181	150	31	/
2000	171	145	26	/

(*Source: CNC*)

Poiré's *The Visitors* (*Les visiteurs,* 1993), Francis Veber's *The Dinner Game* (*Le dîner de cons,* 1998), Gérard Pirès's *Taxi* (*Taxi,* 1998), Claude Zidi's *Asterix & Obelix vs. César,* and Luc Besson's *The Messenger: The Story of Joan of Arc* (*Jeanne d'Arc,* 1999). In addition, the four major national television stations (TF1, France2, France3, and M6) had to comply with a financial obligation, called *soutient automatique,* which constrained them to advance a minimum of 3 percent of their annual operating turnover toward future film productions and to broadcast a minimum of sixty percent European films. As ironic as it may seem, although French television debilitated French cinema in the 1980s, a decade later it helped to resuscitate it. In 2002, it is clear that, economically, French television needs French films, and French films need the funds of French television. After years of struggle, the financial-aid system established in the early 1980s was finally taking off. Nineteen-ninety-five was the first successful year, which immediately triggered spectacular growth in French cinema.

In the mid-1990s, for the centennial of the seventh art (1995), many statistics and rankings were published on the health of the French film industry. The figures showed that the film industry in France had now established itself as the largest, most successful market in Europe, with France the leading film producer (e.g., 134 films produced in 1996, up from 124 in 1995). France also had the largest distribution network in Europe, with more than 4,000 movie theaters (4,297 screens registered by the CNC in 1992, 4,762 screens in 1998). But the assessment of movie theaters' economic activity cannot rely simply on unsystematic statistics. Therefore, to assess the theaters'

TABLE 3:   MARKET SHARES OF BOX OFFICE
REVENUE

YEARS	FRENCH	EUROPEAN	AMERICAN	OTHERS
1990	37.4	5.3	56.6	0.7
1991	30.1	9.9	58.7	1.3
1992	35.1	4.3	58.3	2.3
1993	34.8	4.1	57.6	3.4
1994	28.3	8.6	61.3	1.9
1995	35.2	8.4	54.0	2.4
1996	37.3	6.0	54.7	2.0
1997	34.2	10.0	52.2	3.5
1998	27.2	7.2	64.0	1.7
1999	32.0	11.2	54.1	2.8
2000	38.3	12.2	35.7	13.8

(*Source: CNC*)

numbers accurately, the CNC established an annual review of *salles actives* (active theaters) in 1992. Each movie theater participates, releasing its revenue reports for the assessment of automatic financial aid and for the production of an entire array of statistics on theater distribution. Theater owners provide weekly statistics, per screen, per film. This system indicates a new approach in distribution: film copies circulate more easily from one screen to another during the same week, especially in multiplexes, and movie programming adapts to the customs and immediate reactions of audiences.

French cinema is one of the fastest growing sectors of the national economy, and official projections for the year 2005 predict a doubling of employment in the film business compared to the 1990s. According to Daniel Toscan du Plantier, chairman of Unifrance, the French film industry "is not to be the second-cinema industry worldwide, trailing the first, but to be the leader of an alternative to the monopoly." The relentless endeavors, articulated by the Ministère de la Culture in the early 1980s and film industry professionals did indeed preserve the identity of French cinema (and ultimately European cinema). Despite the overwhelming volume of American films, the French film industry appears more than ever the champion of European filmic creativity.

Despite their popularity among French audiences, American movies do not, as they do for the rest of the European market, pose a critical commercial or financial threat to the French film industry (even though action and animated films from Hollywood remain the most popular genres among the French public). In 1999, American films were seen by more than 70 million spectators, representing a steady market share at 54.1 percent and 34 percent of all films distributed; whereas

TABLE 4: NATIONALITY OF FILMS
DISTRIBUTED IN FRANCE IN 2000

	NUMBER OF FILMS	MARKET SHARE (%)
United States	194	35.7
100% France*	144	26.5
France majority**	33	6.1
Great Britain	37	6.8
France minority***	31	5.7
Japan	17	3.1
Italy	9	1.7
Spain	5	0.9
Germany	9	1.7
Canada	11	2.0
Other countries	48	8.7
TOTAL	544	100.0

(Source: CNC)

*Films entirely financed by French investors
**Films coproduced, with a majority of French investment
***Films coproduced, with a minority of French investment

French films represented almost 39 percent of all films distributed, 32 percent of all revenues, which was up almost 5 percent from the previous year. These statistics, although showing France as a distant second to the United States in the world market, underscore the strength of the French film industry in Europe as well as its growing appeal worldwide.

Coproductions with French partners have been an effective way for Hollywood studios and production companies to increase their market share, but this method has proved problematic, especially when compared to the British or Italian film industry. For instance, Great Britain's national cinema is now one of the most vulnerable in western Europe.[2] In 1992, one of its least productive years for example, national productions in Great Britain totaled 17 full-length feature films, compared to 155 films in France that same year. (Subsequent to the dismantlement of the financial-aid system initiated at the end of the 1970s, investments in the British film industry decreased almost 50 percent over the course of the 1980s.)

At the turn of the new century, European film industries have experienced one of their most challenging periods ever. In fact, if European governments do not comply with what filmmakers and the major professional organizations petition for, an effective pan-European policy on film production, promotion, and distribution, the entire future of European cinema could be compromised or in serious jeopardy.

FRENCH TELEVISION

Since 1982, the Conseil supérieur de l'audiovisuel (CSA), an independent council known for its autonomous decision making, regulates private and public television and radio companies, and gives necessary authorization to broadcast and to edit programs, supervises the freedom of expression, and assigns airtime for political debates and campaigns (the regulation also applies to the time allowed for publicity and airtime for broadcasting). Although sound in its structure, the dilemma for the French film industry remains the discrepancy between the profits of television companies and the ethical principles of the CSA. The evolution of technology makes it difficult for both parties to conciliate economic choice to fairness, and consequently the profitable logic of the film and television markets usually stands in opposition to the ethic of the high authority's regulations.

As an active component of the Paysage Audiovisuel Français, French television in the early 1990s had become, over the course of three decades, as much a cultural barometer as cinema was throughout the century. As a popular cultural catalyst, television, because of its accessibility, could very well become *the* new medium for artistic discourse due to its accessibility, thus outpacing the esteemed and powerful cinematographic medium as sole or primary architect of visual aesthetics. So one question arises: Is today's French cinema on the verge of progressively becoming a *telefilmic* medium? The tradition of public service and the role of the state as principal partner in social and economic life remain a strong characteristic in Europe. Despite the explosion of private-television companies in the late 1980s and digital broadcasting in the 1990s, France is still in search of an equilibrium between the necessary freedom for the development of new markets and the support of regulations guaranteeing a certain pluralism. However, the alliance between film and television does facilitate the collaboration of the two industries. In France, private television companies thrive in an almost paradoxical situation. They offer programs as worthy as the ones screened on public television while profiting from advertising revenues derived from a large market. Today, the competition posed by the growing purchase of videos and now DVDs (which doubled from the 1980s to the 1990s), and especially the strong influence of American television, has threatened the quality of programming, its coherence, and the professionalism of both sectors. As a result, most French television companies have reshuffled their documentary, news, and entertainment programming, while reducing overall film productions.

In this era of growing communication, it appears more crucial than ever for a national medium like cinema to relate to the global-communication network. As of 2002, the management of television programs and artistic images already signals a new cultural, political, and economic competition. To be part of the frontrunners in digital distribution, the successful companies will have to become part of the fastest-growing communications networks and technologies (Internet, music, film, sports, education). Such is the case with the television company Canal+. Its commitment to the French film industry reveals the success of a strategy initiated a decade before. *Diversification* had been the buzzword during the 1990s and resulted in a significant rise in viewership, with more than 14 million subscriptions currently in eleven countries throughout Europe, 7.3 million outside France. In addition, more and more customers are making the switch to digital, with the number of subscribers to digital services rising to 4.5 million (50 percent of all subscribers have now opted for digital service). Canal+ commits actively, in terms of growth and profit, to the television and movie division of Vivendi Universal, the world's second-largest media company, and remains Europe's leading multiservice pay-television operator. In addition, Canal+ has become omnipresent as well as indispensable for French film productions, as the following statistics in Table 5 (page 360) reveal.

In comparison, the rest of French television companies (France2, France3, TF1, M6, and Arte) financed a total of eighty-eight films in 1999, thus confirming the predominance of Canal+, in particular its production studio called Le Studio Canal, in terms of financial commitment within the French film industry. Each year, 50 percent of all French films are produced by Canal+. In addition, Canal+ has created a European film distribution network in partnership with the Pathé Film Company.

For the French film industry, the arrangement between Universal Pictures and Canal+ created the second-largest film library in the world—9,000 feature films in all—breaking new ground in distribution of the motion-picture business. Due to its recent European success, Le Studio Canal's next ambition is a greater involvement in the United States. Throughout the 1990s, Le Studio Canal's situation, as a growing foreign producer in the US, generated much interest among independent filmmakers (e.g., David Lynch's *Mulholland Drive,* 2001, and *The Straight Story,* 1999; Jim Jarmusch's *Ghost Dog: The Way of the Samurai,* 1999; and Sofia Coppola's *The Virgin Suicides,* 2000). Since the mid-1990s, Le Studio Canal has played a dominant role in the production of European films. It has indirectly led to the domination of French film within the European market. Through inspired diversification strategies, Le Studio Canal entered into a joint venture in England with its longstanding associate Telema (Toc Films) to develop and produce English-language films, to coproduce Italian

TABLE 5: EVOLUTION OF THE INTERVENTIONS IN PRE-PRODUCTION BY CANAL+

YEAR	FRENCH FILMS	COPRODUCTIONS	TOTAL
1992	102	22	124
1993	80	16	96
1994	76	16	92
1995	79	22	101
1996	85	22	107
1997	108	26	134
1998	117	22	139
1999	121	19	140

(*Source: CNC*)

films (e.g., Ettore Scola's *The Dinner/La cena* in 1998, Roberto Benigni's *Life Is Beautiful/La vita è Bella* in 1998, Michael Radford's *Il postino* in 1994, and Nanni Moretti's *Dear Diary/Caro diaro* in 1994), and to produce or coproduce twenty to thirty French feature films each year, through its subsidiaries and in conjunction with a number of independent filmmakers and producers (producing films for commercial audiences as well as young auteur films).[3] One of the most reliable partners of the group is producer Alain Sarde, who has made many films, including Jacques Doillon's *Ponette* (*Ponette,* 1997), Jean-Pierre Salomé's *Restons groupés* (1998), Jean-Pierre Ameris's *Bad Company* (*Les mauvaises fréquentations,* 1999), Danièle Thompson's *La bûche* (1999), Pierre Jolivet's *Ma petite entreprise* (1999), and Bertrand Blier's *Les acteurs* (2000). Important also are three associate producers, Alain Rocca, Adeline Lecallier, and Christophe Rossignon, who constitute Lazennec Films.[4] In 1995, 9 percent of Canal+'s operating turnover had to be reinvested to support French cinema as well as foreign film coproductions, not including other large-scale productions sponsored by its subsidiary, Le Studio Canal. Canal+'s financial-backing structure was designed to sponsor many productions in the French film industry and to promote the completion of first-feature films as well as to assist big-budget productions of proven cultural value (80 percent of French films each year are presold to Canal+). The omnipresence of the television company is all the more valuable for French national cinema since most French productions today appear incapable of attaining any profitability without public subventions.

Led by Jean-Marie Messier (former chairman and CEO of Vivendi) and Pierre Lescure (former chairman and CEO of group Canal+), the Group Canal+/Vivendi[5] was able to achieve a uniquely powerful growth.[6] With the support of Seagram and Canal+, Vivendi's position in global-communications is significant with, for instance, the aforementioned film library, the production studio, theme parks, and PC-based software game publishing through Vizzavi. As for distribution, Group Canal+/Vivendi provides Internet access through Vivendi/Vodafone Mobile to 60 million customers in Europe, and has become the principal partner of Internet consumers, business-to-business information, and other entertainment universes. Its Internet division, CanalNumedia, was created in January 2000. The new millennium opens important new markets for the Canal+ Group, and as the Internet allows extensive development of the recorded-music market (particularly among a growing young audience population using the MP3 format), by offering straightforward consumer experience, the Group Canal+/Vivendi has enormous potential, involving Europe's most influential wireless and wired trademark with the worldwide network.

FRENCH CINEMA ABROAD

In 1949, the CNC created the production company Unifrance to help in the commercialization and distribution of French movies in other countries. Since its creation, results have often exceeded expectations. For example, Jean-Paul Rappeneau's *Cyrano de Bergerac* made 50 million francs in the foreign market, twice its total production costs. Unifrance regularly indicates the fundamental magnitude of film exports as vital to the strength of the French-cinema industry since 85 percent of the total revenues of French films are generated abroad: Western Europe represents 40 percent of box-office revenues, while the United States alone accounts for 26 percent, followed by Germany and Japan with 16 percent, and Italy at 10 percent. Concurrently, the market share for French films abroad is regularly projected at around three to four percent, an apparently inconsequential stature which, nevertheless, still places France as the number-two film producer behind the United States. Foreign-language films inevitably face an additional challenge before distribution in the American market, namely, language subtitles. Because of the general reluctance among the average American audiences to view subtitled films over English movies, the perspective of commercial success in the US market is limited (in addition to the constraint of any commercial representation outside Europe).

Toward which future is French cinema moving? Unlike most French filmmakers, Jean-Jacques Annaud defends the future relationship between films and cultural identity:

TABLE 6:   MAIN MARKETS FOR FRENCH FILMS (MILLION FRANCS)

	1990	1991	1992	1993	1994	1995	1996	1997	1998	1999
United States	47	26	51	32	65	41	36	74	21	168
Japan	25	31	37	40	45	44	43	108	52	68
Germany	89	70	80	69	71	56	46	106	50	73
Italy	25	33	52	20	18	26	34	69	35	36
United Kingdom	18	11	9	9	14	9	5	53	10	23
Spain	17	17	34	15	18	14	25	42	30	51
Belgium	22	17	23	30	19	23	28	23	38	26
Australia	3	3	4	4	3	3	4	23	3	14
Argentina	2	1	5	7	2	1	2	25	4	14
Netherlands	3	2	5	3	4	4	3	3	5	17
Total (main markets)	251	211	300	229	259	221	226	626	248	490

(*Source:* CNC)

> Today's cinema is a global art form, it is impossible to make movies for a market the size of France, representing no more than four percent of the world's total. When Americans shoot movies, they aim at the entire planet. When the French make movies, they aim at Paris. I think that it is about time we stopped putting little flags on movies. When you create a movie, you create something in your image.[7]

This assertion, despite being in the minority among French film-makers, confirms the international image that French cinema has embodied through its one hundred years. If it is true that many French directors and animators have gone abroad, especially to Hollywood (Jean-Jacques Annaud, Luc Besson, Claude Autant-Lara, Jean Renoir, Maurice Tourneur, and Julien Duvivier, among others), many foreign artists have been able to profitably utilize the competent, professional, and rather unique modus operandi in France. Traditionally, France has fostered many foreign filmmakers. Carl Dreyer, Luis Buñuel, Robert Altman, Marco Ferreri, Volker Schlöndorff, Ettore Scola, Nagisa Oshima, and Wim Wenders, among others, have expressed a preference for French modalities of production and the French creative system of subsidies and co-productions that have been perfected over the years. This tradition began in the silent era of the 1920s when Russian immigrants (Ladislav Starevitch, Victor Tourjanski, Ivan Mosjoukine, and Nathalie Lissenko) became famous among French audiences. Along with them, Carl Dreyer came from Denmark to shoot *The Passion of Joan of Arc* (1928). In the late 1920s, Luis Buñuel directed such coproductions as *An Andalusian Dog* and *The Golden Age*. In the 1960s, and after a long absence abroad, Buñuel returned to France with *The Diary of a Chambermaid* (*Le journal d'une femme de chambre,* 1963), with Jeanne Moreau; and *Belle de jour.* Like many artists of his time,

Table 7:   MAIN FOREIGN PARTNERS IN FRENCH
COPRODUCTIONS (NUMBER OF FILMS)

	1997	1998	1999	2000
Spain	12	16	16	7
Belgium	10	18	10	10
Italy	13	12	8	11
Switzerland	11	10	7	6
Canada	8	5	7	8
Portugal	6	5	6	4
United Kingdom	7	4	6	6
Germany	7	5	4	8

(*Source: CNC*)

German-born Max Ophuls chose to live in France in the early 1930s and directed movies such as *La ronde* and *Lola Montès* (*Lola Montès,* 1955). Still attracting foreign artists and film professionals, French cinema of the 1970s welcomed new Polish directors such as Roman Polanski, Andrzej Zulawski, and Walerian Borowczyk, and more recently Krzysztof Kieslowski, with his famous trilogy *Trois couleurs: Bleu* (1993), *Blanc* (1994), and *Rouge* (1994).[8]

As the second-largest exporter of feature films after the United States, France, as noted, has become the preeminent producer of European cinema. Throughout the 1990s, French productions only initiated their commercial operation once set up on the distribution market abroad, where French films have regularly attracted a broader worldwide audience. This growth was facilitated by the creation in November 1989 of the Sarasota Film Festival, which besides screening, in competition, French movies to the American public, also gathers French film directors along with American distributors. Every year, several French films are able to cross the Atlantic and make profitable revenues at the box office: Rappeneau's *Cyrano de Bergerac* ($15 million), Annaud's *The Lover* (*L'amant,* 1992; $4.9 million), Régis Wargnier's *Indochine* (*Indochine,* 1992; $5.7 milion), and Jean-Pierre Jeunet's *Amélie* (*Le fabuleux destin d'Amélie Poulain,* 2001).

Perhaps one of the most successful and regular representatives of French cinema abroad (although far from representing its "Frenchness") is Luc Besson (b. 1959). Along with Leos Carax and earlier Jean-Jacques Beineix, Besson is considered one of the key propagators for the emergence of the *cinéma du look* of the late 1980s and early 1990s. In 1990 *La Femme Nikita,* starring Anne Parillaud, presented new possibilities for French action movies, which were usually behind the fast pace of Hollywood productions. Warner Bros. bought the rights and assigned direction of the American remake to filmmaker John Badham as *Point of No Return* (1993), which starred Bridget Fonda. In 1994, Besson directed *The Professional* (*Léon,* 1994) in New York, with the emerging star of French cinema of the 1990s, Jean Réno. This story of a hit man who befriends a little girl made $20 million in three weeks and altogether tallied more than $32 million at the American box office.

Acclaimed by international commentators and film historians, and screened at countless international film festivals throughout the second part of the 1990s, French films seem to have recaptured the powerful spirit of the times—somehow lost in the early 1980s—plus the favor of audiences and, more importantly from a financial point of view, the cutting edge on a faster-paced-motion-picture market. This thriving spirit and achievement, both in France and in the United States, can best be seen in the broad variety of genres offered to an evermore diverse and seemingly fragmented public, from comedies (*The Dinner Game*), to flamboyant dramas (*Cyrano de Bergerac,* Nicole Garcia's *Place Vendôme*), to film noir and action pictures (Besson's *The Messenger,* Annaud's *Enemy at the Gates*).

Despite the apparent omnipresent Americanization of the international-movie scene, French cinema clearly remains an industry for which the rules and regulations are radically different. Because of the customs and tastes of its audiences, French cinema is still considered a singular catalyst of cultural messages. For the French public, cinema, above all, is an art, and its most important mission, despite the pace of technology and other trends, is to remain creative and culturally relevant.

French cinema finished the first year of the new millennium—and the start of its third century—in a healthy position, encouraged by higher box-office revenues in the United States, as the following revenues (in million francs) illustrate: 50 (1995), 53 (1996), 184 (1997), 33 (1998), and 192 (1999). With such an international aura, it is no surprise to see many American producers and scriptwriters looking for new inspiration from already accomplished and guaranteed European successes. Considered more a commercial product, the "author" of which is the producer (certainly at the opposite end from the scriptwriter or even the director), American cinema finances each year, motivated by pure commercial logic, a certain number of remakes, and in particular French remakes such as *Dinner For Schmucks* (2002) after Francis Veber's *The Dinner Game* (*Le dîner de con,* 1997); Jean-Marie Poiré's *Just Visiting* (2001), after his own *The Visitors* (*Les visiteurs,* 1993); Ivan Reitman's *Father's Day* (1997), after Veber's *Les compères* (1983); John Pasquin's *Jungle 2 Jungle* (1997), after Hervé Palud's *Un Indien dans la ville* (1994); Donals Petri's *The Associate* (1996), after René Gainville's *L'associé* (1979); Jeremiah Chechik's *Diabolique* (1996), after Henri-Georges Clouzot's *Les diaboliques* (1954); Mike

Nichols's *The Birdcage* (1996), after Edouard Molinaro's *La cage aux folles* (1978); Chris Colombus's *Nine Months* (1995), after Patrick Braoudé's *Neuf mois* (1994); James Cameron's *True Lies* (1994), after Zidi's *La totale* (1991); John Badham's *Point of No Return* (1993), after Besson's *Nikita* (1990); Jon Amiel's *Sommersby* (1993), after Daniel Vigne's *Le retour de Martin Guerre* (1982); Leonard Nimoy's *Three Men and a Baby* (1987), after Coline Serreau's *Trois hommes et un couffin* (1985); Blake Edwards's *The Man Who Loved Women* (1983), after Truffaut's *L'homme qui aimait les femmes* (1977); Jim McBride's *Breathless* (1983), after Jean-Luc Godard's *A bout de souffle* (1960); Bob Rafelson's *The Postman Always Rings Twice* (1981) and Tay Garnett's *The Postman Always Ring Twice* (1946), after Pierre Chenal's *Le dernier tournant* (1939); Otto Preminger's *The Thirteenth Letter* (1951), after Henri-Georges Clouzot's *Le corbeau* (1942); and Anatole Litvak's *The Long Night* (1947), after Marcel Carné's *Le jour se lève* (1939).

NEW ARTISTS, NEW CREATORS: JEAN-PIERRE JEUNET AND MARC CARO

Two of the most stylish, outlandishly original French filmmakers of the decade, endowed with an entirely original inspiration, Jean-Pierre Jeunet (b. 1955) and Marc Caro (b. 1956), stand as seminal figures in French cinema history for the scope and artistic vision of their productions. During the 1980s, both artists began their careers in music videos and animated shorts like *Le Manège* (1980), only to rapidly make their mark on international filmmaking. By creating elaborate storyboards, including unique futuristic fantasies, and balancing simple and likable characters with ingenious special effects, the work of Jeunet and Caro resulted in a style that will not likely soon be surpassed or even well-imitated. Their films are an inspiring series of visual effects blended with Orwellian paranoia, then embedded within production designs seemingly pieced together from the shared dreams of Franz Kafka. Jeunet's *Things I Like, Things I Don't Like* (*Foutaises*, 1989) won the César for Best Short Film Fiction in 1990. *Delicatessen* (*Delicatessen*, 1991) was Jeunet and Caro's first full-length feature (Jeunet directed, while Caro controlled the visuals and the design production). The film earned numerous awards in 1991: Césars for Best Editing (Hervé Schneid), Best First Film (Marc Caro and Jean-Pierre Jeunet), Best Original Screenplay (Gilles Adrien, Jean-Pierre Jeunet, and Marc Caro), and Best Production Design (Jean-Philippe Carp and Kreka Kljakovic).

The story of *Delicatessen* comes straight out of a Gothic comic book and uses cartoon-style visual design. But with Caro and Jeunet, the story becomes eccentrically original. Gilles Adrien led the plot and the characterization of the protagonists: an imaginary journey to the edge of sanity, questioning the nature of human identity. In a possibly alternate 1950s, postapocalyptic-imaginary time, the people of a small town have turned to cannibalism to survive. A malevolent butcher named Clapet (Jean-Claude Dreyfus) secretly kills unsuspecting tenants, and serves the meat to supplement the lentils that have taken over as hard currency in the famished town. The butcher's ritual is to hire a new maintenance worker, kill him, and sell the meat to the tenants of the decadent apartment building he owns. The sinister edifice is filled with the presence of eccentric characters, including Monsieur Potin, who lives in a cellar filled with water frogs and snails, and Madame Interligator, a woman who is constantly and unsuccessfully committing suicide. One day, the butcher-landlord hires Louison (Dominique Pinon), an unemployed clown grieving over the death of his monkey (a chimpanzee named Dr. Livingstone, who has recently been devoured by famished circus spectators), who will work as a repairman in exchange for room and board. But the butcher has grisly plans for him, and of course the real reason for his employment is to eliminate him. In the meantime, Louison befriends Julie (Marie-Laure Dougnac), the butcher's nearsighted daughter and the only character who remains untouched by the omnipresent carnivore frenzy. She falls in love with him and tries to save her new lover from his horrific fate. Their grotesque and unsophisticated romance offers an interval of rationality and optimism from the many dark themes of the film. Determined to fill his empty shelves with freshly butchered clown parts, the butcher plans to kill Louison the next night. To save him, Julie must seek the help of the Troglodytes, a rebellious group of vegetarians who live underground and circulate through the endless sewage network. At first, they are reluctant to help her, anticipating an ambush, but she persuades them by revealing the existence of an astronomic amount of lentils in her father's cellar. The Troglodytes plan their collective assault the same night that the butcher has decided to kill the unsuspecting Louison. Following a climactic rescue, the butcher is killed and a normal life begins anew.

The nightmarish atmosphere was well suited to the story, immersing the audience in the same sense of paranoia that recalls the visceral power of Terry Gilliam's *Brazil* (1985). Despite dealing with the unsettling subject of cannibalism, *Delicatessen* is poised between farce and horror. With an invading and almost ominous presence, borrowed from the poetic realism of the prewar era, the representation of a postapocalyptic nightmare was viewed as a surreal black comedy too dark for mainstream audiences in the United States. Caro and Jeunet fashioned an exceptionally detailed world, as the film seemed both high-tech and curiously quaint. The technique had the ability to turn

Jean-Pierre Jeunet and Marc Caro's *City of Lost Children* (*La cité des enfants perdus*, 1994), (Courtesy BIFI).

Judith Vittet (Miette) and Ron Perlman (One) in Jean-Pierre Jeunet and Marc Caro's *City of Lost Children* (*La cité des enfants perdus*, 1994), (Courtesy BIFI).

cinematographic preconceptions around: shocking and ominous visual predicaments are comical, and amusing witticisms become alarming. With subjective and imaginative viewpoints, *Delicatessen* appeared as if its narratives had concealed explanations, which, while they may be part of a futuristic universe, fit into the framework of conventional linear narrative. Scripted by noted comic book writer Gilles Adrien, the film was rife with comic devotion to a series of vignettes about minor characters. According to film historian Susan Hayward, Caro and Jeunet succeeded in the difficult task of bringing innovation to the comedy genre: "What is significant is that the renewal is being attempted in comedy, the most conservative of all genres."[9]

Thanks to Darius Khondji's impressive camera skills, the film was particularly noteworthy on a visual level, with many pictorial landscapes bursting with vibrant colors (e.g., series of gray hues among the claustrophobic urban sprawl). Not only does the apartment building feel oppressive to a Kafkaesque degree, but every indoor set created a claustrophobic sensation, enough to evoke the feeling of being trapped in a universe where death is literally the only escape. *Delicatessen* is a story of originality and creativity that effortlessly blends special effects. Many observers considered the innovation a type of cinematographic challenge that cleverly manipulated action and special effects instead of being controlled by them. Among the most memorable cinematic ventures of the 1990s, with its complex camera movements and shots, *Delicatessen* used a deliberate technique designed to unsettle the audience, making it difficult to believe what any protagonist said or thought. But what makes the film seminal is not only its look and artistic vision, but also its hypnotic, haunting, and dark photography, which constantly evokes new angles and strange developments. The film was framed in disquieting moments that seemed strangely contemporary, and simultaneously conveyed a futuristic science-fiction noir quality, which transported the viewer beyond conventional spheres of imagination.

The filmmakers' next assignment, *The City of Lost Children* (*La cité des enfants perdus,* 1994), was once again sheer imaginative creation, full of visual wonders, this time capturing the magic of Georges Méliès's *Trip to the Moon*: dark phantasmagoria combined with hallucinatory nightmares and striking imagery also reminiscent of Gustave Doré's illustrations. Their artistic inspiration—the advertising industry for Jeunet and comics for Caro—appeared to be firmly rooted in so-called underground comix, whose characters come to life by the unique use of wide angles, mobile frames, and fantastic visual effects with computer imagery. *The City of Lost Children* resourcefully assumes a life and a flow of its own. Screened as the Grand Opening Night picture at the

1995 Cannes Film Festival, *City of Lost Children* was nominated for several awards, including the Palme d'or.

With a screenplay by Gilles Adrien, Jean-Pierre Jeunet, and Guillaume Laurant, this futuristic tale transports the spectator to an unidentified seaport, a synthetic but stylized world devoid of adults where young orphans mysteriously disappear. When captured, the unfortunate children are sent to an abandoned offshore oil rig, erected on stilts in the middle of the sea and protected by countless submerged mines. The mastermind is a prematurely aging scientist, named Krank (Daniel Emilfork),[10] who, tormented by having lost the ability to dream, has invented a device to steal children's dreams through a thought-transfer apparatus. Krank, which means "ill" in German, directs the systematic kidnapping by contracting a crew of blind fanatics, known as the Cyclopes, in order to capture young children from the nearby harbor town. Once brought onto the sea platform, the scientist ties each child in sleeping sarcophagi, wires them to download their dreams, then invades these little internees' mind. Little does Krank know that altering children's dreams will not provide him with the answers for which he so desperately searches. The experiment continues to fail as the children's slumber is invaded by unpleasant nightmares. Convinced of the existence of a psychologically poised child who is not afraid of him, the mad scientist continues to exploit more and more children with the help of his brutish henchmen. One day, Denrée (Joseph Lucien), a three-year-old orphan adopted by a circus strongman named One (Ron Perlman),[11] is kidnapped by the Cyclopes, who organize the trade with Krank. Desperately searching for his adopted brother, One eventually discovers a sinister orphanage held by the tyrannical Siamese-twin sisters Zette and Line (Geneviève Brunet and Odile Mallet), a.k.a. *la Pieuvre* (the Octopus). In order to be sheltered, the children are taught the art of robbing and become pilfering street urchins. Precocious nine-year-old Miette (Judith Vittet), the oldest girl of the orphan gang, understands One's tragedy and decides to assist him in his doomed quest. One night, as they discover the location of the trade between the Cyclopes and Krank's accomplices, they attempt to intervene, but to no avail. Captured, they are immediately sent to death. Their hands and feet tied, they are pushed into the canal. As they both fall into the water, One is rescued by Marcello (Jean-Claude Dreyfus), a circus director who once owned the Siamese sisters as a popular attraction. Gutsy little Miette's destiny is also providential when a lonely deep-sea diver (Dominique Pinon) rescues her in the murky waters of the harbor. He was once a scientist himself working for Krank, but was chased off the platform. But the malevolent sisters are still after One and Miette. Using a sinister device, a flea

3 7 0 FRENCH CINEMA

carrying poison that ultimately develops aggressivity within its victim, they achieve their goal by having One turn against Miette. Just as One is about to strangle her to death, a colliding boat comes into the port and pushes them into the water. Marcello, who had planned to eliminate the tyrannical sisters years ago, arrives in time to send another deadly flea, this time contaminating the sisters themselves and eventually forcing them to kill each other. After discovering the existence of the platform at sea, Miette and One embark on a barge to discover its location. Krank's lieutenants, six genetically engineered clones (all played by Dominique Pinon), quarrel among themselves about which among the group is the "original." Irvin (voiced by Jean-Louis Trintignant), Krank's philosophical brother, who subsists as a submersed disembodied brain in an aquarium with a lens for sight and a gramophone for hearing, is the only wise individual on the platform. As One and Miette arrive, they successfully outsmart the team of clones and find Denrée asleep and connected to the diabolical machine. For Miette, the real challenge begins. To save Denrée, she must penetrate Krank's dream, fight against his will, age prematurely (while sending him back to childhood), and bring Denrée back to reality. The nature of the nightmare is too strong for Krank, who dies of a heart attack. Thanks to the deep-sea diver—the authentic "original"—Krank's empire is destroyed and all the children are liberated.

In the *City of Lost Children,* the oneiric representation is deliberately related through the icons of childhood, bliss, and purity, which explains the reason why the evil scientist's elaborate scheme focuses on young, unspoiled children (e.g., the opening scene representing the "ominous" arrival of several Santa Clauses through the chimney bringing toys). As true visionaries, Jeunet and Caro, who conceived the film some fourteen years before, achieved one of the most audacious and original films of the decade. The eerie grandeur of this film, in addition to the countless dazzling special effects designed to overwhelm audiences, relied on the awareness of imagination and of the importance of protecting a child's faculty to dream. Mythic childhood innocence is also represented as the narrative's emotional focal point—the poignant sentimental rapport of One and Miette. Assisted by careful lighting and framing, Miette's ingénue personage displayed an almost adult performance with a touching cynical facade to conceal her solitude. Although elaborated with thoughtfulness and unadulterated feeling, the team of One and Miette share a minimal but clearly ephemeral erotic attraction. The character of Miette even sees in One and Denrée an opportunity for the traditional family she has never experienced, but throughout the narrative the ambiguities of this relationship never draw near the sordid or perverse.

The City of Lost Children is both intuitive and cerebral, and its lucid story line is backed by a series of stunning sets and special effects. The imaginative set construction of the Studios de France[12] (supervised by designer Jean Rabasse,[13] who won the César for Best Production Design in 1995) corresponded to a dark configuration that visually borrowed Jules Verne's turn-of-the-century illustrations. Caro's Surrealistic art direction and production designs can be experienced as excursions into a hypnotic world with illusory colors that are highly reminiscent of Verne's representations of fantastic underworlds as well as Marcel Carné's atmosphere in *Port of Shadows*. Jean-Marie Vivès's contributions for the *peintures numériques*/matte paintings (the first digital matte paintings in France) offered a seamless transition between matte painting and set, and a subtle combination of real characters, model, and matte painting. This expensive high-tech production (120 million francs and one gigantic set mainly made of styrofoam), using more special effects than any other films at that time, was a rarity and really a world of its own. Whereas the film manages to strike a perfect balance between dreamlike Surrealism and real-world reference points, the unconventional camera angles and wide-angle lenses in a sense call to mind a wide-eyed child's innocuous way of looking at life. Darius Khondji's cinematography and dark fantasy (*Seven, Evita, The Beach, Stealing Beauty*) created a gloomy world by assembling his most salient visuals on top of one another in shot-by-shot editing (Hervé Schneid), thereby magnifying the scope of the nightmarish view of this post-apocalyptic world.

With a big budget for a European film, the movie included an impressive series of "numeric" special effects[14] (40,000 digitalized images, 17 minutes of special effects, orchestrated in 144 sequences out of the 800 included in the final version of the film), as well as technical innovations like the first use of accelerated and slowed-down speed in the same take. The post-production technique known as "warping" made the opening and final dream sequences intriguingly Surreal compared to conventional representations. The dream sequences were artistically well inspired and developed gradually darker in tone as the plot progressed. The inventive editing changed speed during the same shot—motion control process; at the same time, the music and voices slowed independently from the images (e.g., in the final-dream sequence). Another feature of the film was the fine use of *images de synthèse* (digital-image system; e.g., the flea shot with a steady cam; the metamorphoses occurring between Miette and Krank in the dream sequence, forty-eight sequences representing ten months' work), under the supervision of Pierre Buffin and his unit known as Buf Compagnie. In addition, the digital special effects of Pitof *(Les visiteurs, Alien IV,*

The Messenger: The Story of Joan of Arc, Vidocq), who the previous year had done the special effects for Michel Blanc's comedy *Dead Tired (Grosse fatigue),* proved influential for the rest of the decade. The costumes by Jean-Paul Gaultier (Luc Besson's *The Fifth Element*) generated a real sense of childish/impertinence within this eccentric humanity. The richly atmospheric music of Angelo Badalamenti (*The Beach, The Straight Story, Twin Peaks*) triggered intense and utterly Surreal emotions. Far from being an experimental film (despite its radically different artistic approach relating dreams to creativity), *The City of Lost Children* followed a rather conventional narrative format. Although too pessimistic for the general public, and unfortunately often misconstrued as a picture for children due its fairy-tale quality, the final message of the film reminded audiences of the dreadful prospect of losing one's imagination, encouraging individuals to protect idealism and creativity. More of a fantasy than a macabre comedy, *City of Lost Children* did not hit big at the American box office as general audiences most likely aspired to see a little more "light at the end of the tunnel."

A couple of years later, following the completion of *Alien: Resurrection,* in 1997, Jeunet's career took a new turn with *Amélie,* an "authentic" fairy tale "made in Montmartre," which was released in France on April 25, 2001, and in the United States on November 4 of the same year. Its release appeared to be much more than just a commercial blockbuster but an authentic *phénomène de société.* The poetry and satire that had been missing from French film during the last part of the 1990s returned to the screen with this feel-good movie, much lighter and more engaging than *Delicatessen* or *The City of Lost Children.* Jeunet's decision to return to France after a relatively successful Hollywood experience can be compared to the so-called French cultural exception, as *Le fabuleux destin d'Amélie Poulain* is another compelling reminder of the comparative strength and vitality of contemporary French cinema.[15] *Amélie* echoed the trend in increased attendance figures for French productions, which at the time grew by 24 percent when compared with the previous year, and French films finally surpassed the 50 percent market share.[16] Despite its rather small budget (76 million francs, one-tenth that of *Alien IV),* the rights of *Amélie* were rapidly sold in forty countries.[17]

During an austere childhood, young Amélie witnesses many strange episodes that forever shape her personality. Both of her parents are averse to outward signs of emotion, and Amélie endures difficult hours. Her goldfish, unsuccessfully and repeatedly attempting suicide, is finally released in a municipal fountain. Amélie's neurotic mother, Amandine, who had educated her at home, is accidentally killed on the front steps of Notre Dame when Amélie is eight. Her nonchalant and unemotional father, Raphael (Rufus),[18] a family doctor, secludes

Audrey Tautou (Amélie) in Jean-Pierre Jeunet's *Amélie* (*Le fabuleux destin d'Amélie Poulain*, 2001), (Courtesy of Victoires Productions/UGC).

Mathieu Kassovitz (Nino) and Audrey Tautou (Amélie) in Jean-Pierre Jeunet's *Amélie* (*Le fabuleux destin d'Amélie Poulain*, 2001), (Courtesy of Victoires Productions/ UGC).

himself and devotes his affection to a garden gnome, repainting it endlessly. He rarely communicates with his daughter except via stethoscope while conducting medical check-ups. He eventually misdiagnoses her condition and believes that her heart beats faster in these unusual moments of physical contact. Unfortunately for Amélie (Flora Guiet), the only treatment her father can think of is to be confined at home, and the little girl grows up without playmates and in a world of her own colorful dreams. Once disallowed any emotional and physical contact with children her age, Amélie begins to compensate with her fertile imagination.

The film moves to an adult Amélie (Audrey Tautou),[19] who lives on her own in Paris and works as a waitress in a bar in the Montmartre district.[20] Shy by nature, and a troublesome ingenue, Amélie nurtures a unique penchant for the small pleasures of life. She loves to dig her hand deep into a bagful of beans, break the crust of crème brûlée with the back of a spoon, and compulsively collect stones to skim off the canal Saint-Martin. The young woman continues to develop an unconditional taste for imaginative romance. In conclusion, she lives her life within her daydreams while discovering the wonders of humanitarianism. Amélie, with her girl-next-door looks, is depicted as an extraordinary being with a mind of her own concealed in an imaginary universe.

As the story unfolds, the heroine becomes conscious that the shorter path to happiness entails taking her destiny into her own hands by reaching out to others. One of Amélie's greatest gifts is her ability to observe the people of Montmartre around her. She has not been corrupted by bliss, nor compromised by desire. One day, stunned by the news of Princess Diana's death, Amélie inadvertently drops a bottle and, stooping down, discovers a tin box of old toys behind the bathroom wall in her apartment. She makes up her mind and decides to return it to the now-grown owner, Dominique Bretodeau (Maurice Benichou), to whom it once belonged. After tracking him down, Amélie is able to offer him one of life's greatest sensations: an impromptu vision of one's childhood treasures.

Proud of her success, the new *marchande de bonheur*, decides to turn her kindness toward the people around her. She begins with the janitor of her building, Madeleine Wallace (Yolande Moreau), an inconsolable widow abandoned by her husband. Amélie is fond of Lucien (Jamel Debbouze), a young produce grocer at the fruit stand called Marché de la Butte, and the way he delicately hands the endives to customers: his own way of expressing his love for his job. Because he is relentlessly patronized by his tyrannical boss (Urbain Cancelier),[21] she decides to help him out. Amélie also looks after Raymond Dufayel (Serge Merlin),[22] an aging artist whose frail bones have compelled him to live in an entirely padded apartment for the past twenty years. His only pastime is to paint a copy of Renoir's *Le déjeuner des canotiers* every year. Despite his unfriendly appearance, he quickly becomes her mentor and guardian angel. At the Café-Tabac des Deux Moulins, Amélie succeeds in setting up two lonely people, Georgette (Isabelle Nanty),[23] an employee of the establishment and entertaining hypochondriac, and Joseph (Dominique Pinon),[24] a bitter customer in search of black humor. Amélie's endeavors are finally rewarded by a providential encounter in a subway station with Nino Quincampoix (Mathieu Kassovitz),[25] a secluded sex-shop salesperson and recreational spook-show ghost at the Foire du Trône who collects discarded photo-booth pictures all over Paris. Because she suddenly recognizes him as a kindred soul, she begins to search for him. Her timidity compels her to stay hidden, and only the firm admonition of Raymond will convince her to step forward.

Jeunet's plot and characterization of the protagonists are entirely original and inspired from the insight that inhabits his own fruitful mind. What is cutting edge in his filmmaking? How can one consider Jeunet's concept of mise en scène numérique groundbreaking? He fashions a detailed world, and the film seems both high-tech and curiously quaint. With its subjective and imaginative perspectives, *Amélie* looks as if its narratives have concealed explanations, which, while they may be a part of reality, do not quite fit within the framework of a conventional linear narrative. It effortlessly blends special effects and traditional cinematography. Far from being a purely experimental film (despite its radically different artistic approach relating dreams to creativity), the movie presents, in many ways through its nonlinear plot, a rather mesmerizing and eccentric worldview.[26] The central asset of this self-indulgent Montmartre fairy tale, light years away from the universe of their previous independent experiments, is that the scenario writers Guillaume Laurant and Jean-Pierre Jeunet were able to insert an idea behind each shot and sequence (e.g., the recurrence of inventories, Prévert style, and an extreme sense of detail for the sad and the absurd). More of a fantasy than a comedy, *Amélie* hit the French box office (more than eight million tickets sold) just at the moment French audiences were thirsting for, and finally ready to see, more uplifting pictures. The film garnered five Academy Award nominations, including Best Foreign Film.

Jeunet's first three feature films were shot exclusively in the studio, which allowed him to exert absolute artistic control over the direction as well as the special effects. With *Amélie,* however, he went outside the studio to shoot in an all-zinc and marble café of Montmartre, the Café des Deux Moulins, an authentic Parisian café, which is now an authentic landmark among filmgoers. The Café des Deux Moulins, one of eighty Paris locations in the movie, reveals a new facet of Jeunet's aesthetic. In an interview with Jean-Marc Lalanne and Didier Péron,[27] Jeunet confesses his passion for the look of the 1940s: *Un micro-ondes aujourd'hui, c'est moins beau qu'une télé des années 40!* (A modern-day microwave oven is not as nice as a television set from the 1940s!) Passionate about the Paris of the 1940s and 1950s, Jean-Pierre Jeunet emphasized the scarce presence of automobiles in his outdoor shorts in the streets of Paris, without the so-called mobilier urbain and graphics of the 1990s. Jeunet's work is a blend of national nostalgia, of a postcard-Paris reminiscent of Robert Doisneau's work, combined with marvelous post-production special effects. These special effects are the work of Alain Carsoux and Thomas Duval of the Duboi Company, the team responsible for more than 150 digital special effects (also in Pitof's *Vidocq*). On the set, special effects were achieved by Yves Domenjoud of the Société des Versaillais.

Working independently of Marc Caro, Jeunet was able to exploit his sensitive and sentimental side, rather than being influenced by Caro's typically artistic gloom (claustrophobic apartment, rundown building, disquieting underground paths). *Amélie* is the first film to present a realistic universe—far from *Delicatessen, The City of Lost Children,* or even *Alien IV,* despite the numerous instances of intertext sequences with the first two films (the squeaking of the box springs; the teddy bear left outside the home).

THE EPICS: RÉGIS WARGNIER AND CLAUDE BERRI

According to the artistic ambience of each decade or era, certain genres or cinematographic themes suddenly disappear from the screen only to reemerge when there seems to be a new public appeal or when artistic circumstances permit or sponsor their resumption. This is very true of epic productions, which became popular again in the early 1990s, especially those that dealt with the suddenly fashionable topic of the old French-colonial empire. One such film, Régis Wargnier's *Indochine* (*Indochine,* 1992), was a $20 million epic, a huge budget for a non–Hollywood film. *Indochine* opened in France on April 15, 1992, and premièred in the United States on Christmas Day of the same year. For French cinema, 1992 saw a return to the colonial period in its themes as several major films took a retrospective look at the country's colonial legacy in Southeast Asia, the others being Jean-Jacques Annaud's *The Lover* (*L'amant*)[28] and Pierre Schoendoerffer's *Diên-Biên-Phu* (*Diên-Biên-Phu*). At the 1992 Academy Awards, *Indochine* came away with the Oscar for Best Foreign Film, as well as a nomination for Best Actress (Catherine Deneuve). It also won for Best Foreign Language Film at the 1993 British Academy Awards. At the 1992 Césars,

Indochine was the recipient of an avalanche of awards: Best Actress (Catherine Deneuve), Best Cinematography (François Catonné), Best Production Design (Jacques Bufnoir), Best Sound (Dominique Henne-quin, Guillaume Sciama), and Best Supporting Actress (Dominique Blanc). Director Régis Wargnier, who began his career as second-unit director and assistant director for films such as Patrice Leconte's *Viens chez moi, j'habite chez une copine* (1981) and Alexandre Arcady's *Le grand pardon* (1981), had his first and greatest success with *Indochine*. He became a celebrated international filmmaker overnight. His credits also include *A French Woman* (*Une femme française,* 1995), again starring Catherine Deneuve, and *East-West* (*Est-ouest,* 1999), with Sandrine Bonnaire and Catherine Deneuve.

Set in 1930s French Indochina and picturing the last twenty years of French presence, *Indochine* opens as a recollection with a voice-over narration by Deneuve that tells the story of Eliane Devries (a tailor-made role for the actress), a single woman who manages a profitable rubber plantation. Camille (Linh Dan Phan), her adopted Vietnamese daughter, an Annam princess educated in French schools, is her only joy in life. While facing the rising tide of nationalistic sentiment, Eliane is able to survive thanks to the assistance of her longtime friend, Guy Asselin (Jean Yanne), the Saigon chief of police. Mother and daughter are inseparable until their semipeaceful existence is suddenly altered by the arrival of a dashing young naval officer, Jean-Baptiste Le Guen (Vincent Pérez). Eliane's conservative outside appearance con-founds her own passion, which becomes evident when Jean-Baptiste enters her life for a brief romance. Eliane falls for him in spite of herself. Her daughter, Camille, later falls in love with him too. Believ-ing that she is acting in her daughter's own good, Eliane manages through her connections to have Jean-Baptiste reprimanded for his behavior, at an upper-class gathering, by having him reassigned to a faraway outpost on the Island of the Dragon. But Eliane misjudges Camille's tenacity. Although betrothed since birth to her cousin Tanh (Eric Nguyen), the young woman is still in love with Jean-Baptiste and flees the comfort of her dwelling in search of the man she loves. During her perilous expedition, Camille, who undertakes a strenuous journey, learns immensely about Indochina and realizes the true depth of misery among her people. She eventually ends up in the camp where Jean-Baptiste was assigned.

The pace of the story suddenly picks up as the film shows how the French army organized the slave trade, separating families and keeping the population in fear. Outraged, Camille kills an officer in charge of the slave traffic. Jean-Baptiste immediately decides to desert the navy in order to protect her. For years both flee through the wilderness of Indochina, seeking refuge from the armed forces that still want to

entangle them. As they hide during the day with a traveling-theatrical
group, Camille gives birth to their son, Etienne. Their run comes to
an abrupt end when the army captures the baby and the father, sending
Camille to prison. Eliane is able to get the child back and rears him
after the sudden, mysterious death of Jean-Baptiste. In 1936, Camille
is released from the penitentiary of Poulo-Condor, where she was
imprisoned, but despite the comforting presence of her mother at the
door, she decides to join the resistance against the French-colonial
power. Eighteen years later, in Geneva, Eliane has just finished her
story to Etienne. She reveals to him that among the Communist
Vietnamese delegation is his mother, who came to sign the peace
treaty with France.

Inspired by the established genre of colonial narratives, the film has
been criticized for its "Eurocentric" point of view, contributing to a
so-called cinematic neocolonialism.[29] Unlike the British, the French
have generally been reluctant to look back critically at their past: the
war in Algeria, the loss of Indochina (Vietnam), or even the collaboration during World War II. Director Régis Wargnier, however, did
present French imperialism with a radically deadening spiritual isolation. Although accused of presenting a sanitized version of colonialism,
the corrupt and cruel colonial establishment is clearly represented at
every stage of the film. After nearly a century of French-colonial
control, Vietnam, then known as Indochina, was tormented by decades
of violence in pursuit of independence. The political turmoil in the
dying days of the French colonial regime functions as a backdrop.
Although the story steers away from political opinions, its measured
pace evokes the poignant fading of the empire as well as the exploitation of the people of Indochina. Sympathies—obviously against French
occupation—and political viewpoint remain somewhat understated,
however, since, in many instances, "the colonized are never characterized in an individual manner."[30]

In its depiction of this episode in French colonialism, the film offered a vague chronology of events. Reminiscent of Sydney Pollack's
Out of Africa, Indochine was a well-photographed motion picture, the
main quality of which was to capture striking images of a magnificent landscape with local colors. This lack of historical precision was
overshadowed by the film's striking photography (François Catonné)
and lush orchestration (Patrick Doyle). From the opening shot to
the very last frame, audiences were presented with stunning images.
The dramatic beauty of places like Saigon, along with the beauty of
the tropical rain forest (all the scenes were shot on location in Vietnam), granted the film a matchless atmosphere and a unique post-
card look.

Catherine Deneuve (Eliane) and Vincent Pérez (Jean-Baptiste) in Régis Wargnier's *Indochine* (*Indochine*, 1992), (Courtesy of BIFI/© Jean-Marie Leroy).

A year after the release of *Indochine,* another epic came to French theaters: Claude Berri's 1993 *Germinal* (*Germinal*).

Germinal was the fourth[31] adaptation of Emile Zola's 1885 novel. At the time it was the most expensive French production ever, with a budget of 172 million francs (around $20 million, a third of which served for the construction of the gigantic mine set). Since the novel is considered one of the greatest works of French literature, movie producers were far from being discouraged by the astronomical production cost (almost five months of shooting in the very same mining region near Valenciennes where the story took place one hundred years before), and an entire legion of extras were recruited (most of them unemployed miners). Berri's ambitious epic, produced with the support of government agencies as well as television companies (France2 and Canal+), premiered in Lille on September 1993 with national publicity in the presence of President François Mitterrand, Jack Lang, and Jacques Delors. Claude Berri's political involvement extended beyond national borders; his seminal role for the defense of European cinema during the 1993 GATT negotiations made him one of the spokespersons for the entire film industry. This super production, French style, was awarded Césars for Best Cinematography (Yves Angelo) and Best Costume Design (Bernadette Villard, Caroline de Vivaise, Sylvie Gautrelet) at the 1993 French Academy Awards. This period drama set in the late nineteenth century and adapted by Arlette Langmann, was a naturalistic depiction of the lives of coal miners and their families in northern France as they attempt to organize themselves for the first time to overcome their ubiquitous poverty. This was far from a simple, sanitized version of history, but rather a critical and unswerving look at a dark time, as one critic observed: "The film's representation of the nation's immediate history to itself seeks an accommodation with past mistakes rather than confrontation."[32] For many film critics, the inner strength of Berri's period re-creation relied on the consentual attempt to present a novelistic discourse rather than indulging viewers with a conflictual and ideological discourse.

Recently dismissed from the railroad company, central character Etienne Lantier (popular singer and working-class icon Renaud) comes to a mining community looking for work. Hired at the Voreux Coal Mine in Montsou, the out-of-work machinist must immediately face a new challenge as he descends into the pit to discover the harsh working and living conditions of the miners. He is assigned to the team of Toussaint Maheu (Gérard Depardieu), and the two rapidly become friends. Maheu takes Lantier into his digging crew to replace a deceased worker, and later at the end of the day invites him to stay at his home (barracks provided by the mining company). What Etienne sees around him during that first day is chaos: the workers, whose plight stands between servitude and starvation, strive to maintain even simple humanity in the face of their grim working and living conditions. Becoming more hazardous by the moment, the state of the mineshaft roof with sturdy wooden beams becomes the main concern of the workers. Engineers constantly reprimand miners for not fixing the timbering (since, in the case of fatal accidents, owners must pay benefits to families). Yet miners who spend time fixing the timbering are penalized for not bringing out enough coal. Workers scramble to load as much coal as possible, neglecting their own well-being while hoping to provide more bread on the table.

As the working conditions in the mine worsen, and pay is cut back, Etienne persuades Maheu to organize a strike. Etienne becomes a rebellious leader against his will, and as an outsider he is considered the perfect man to speak up in defense of the miners' rights. While the idea of a hypothetical trade union develops during the end of the nineteenth century, Etienne closely participates in the organization of a strike. He relentlessly emphasizes the outrageous interdependence between the starving miners and their well-fed overlords. When the mining organization lowers the workers' wages, the miners finally decide to strike. At first nonviolent, the labor unrest rapidly becomes more intense, with predictable consequences. As the strike takes a new turn, miners at other sites decide to return to work. Immediately alerted, the miners at the Voreux mine sabotage the installations to prevent work from resuming. But the work stoppage is not resolved, and the situation turns sour. The mining company decides to hire Belgian miners as replacements and thus continue with production. The result is a chain reaction of tragic events. Maheu, who believes in the inherent goodness of man, cannot accept that French soldiers brought in to defend the mine would fire on their own countrymen. The angry crowd attempts to oppose their arrival but the armed forces shoot at them. Maheu dies under fire, and his wife, la Maheude (Miou-Miou), is determined to take up and continue the fight. Lacking unanimity and cohesiveness, the striking-miners' resentment turns to all-out insurrection as they begin tearing apart the mines. For one of them, Souvarine (Laurent Terzieff), a Russian anarchist, the only solution is to burn down all of the mines and factories created by human-kind and from this, he believes, deliverance will come. One night, Souvarine descends into one of the mines by himself and undoes a water duct, hoping to flood the entire network of galleys. The chilling climax shows terror and desolation, as the mine floods and the workers are trapped inside. Etienne leaves the troubled mining community and a mourning town, convinced that the ideas he fomented will eventually germinate in the future.

Berri's reworking of Zola's classic novel was much more than a heritage film tailored as a big-production epic. Zola's denunciation of the miners' plight appeared simple and moving as the subtext in part 1 meticulously described the growing threat of the strike. An authen-tic and powerful look into the tumultuous, ill-fated existence of the nineteenth-century French coal mining community, *Germinal* is far from being a model epic tale. But it is impossible not to sense the realism that pervades the enormous project. Whereas Zola's fervent and uncompromising call for social reform lie at the heart of the novel, the relations between each individual protagonist symbolize the very essence of the film. The movie tackles every theme pertaining to a conventional drama (from love and death to labor relations and class warfare to destructive violence). Yves Angelo's cinematography, as-sisted by an impressive production design, put every theme and shot in sharp contrast, faithfully rendering the ultimate hopelessness of the human condition. Audiences were transfixed by the visual veracity, not only via the translucently illustrated protagonists who inhabit this universe, but also by the ability of the cameras to conjure up the labyrinth of the coal-mines with claustrophobic genuineness. Berri's meticulously detailed account of inherent social inequalities and despondent living conditions remains ever faithful to the original naturalist description made one hundred years before.

Born Claude Langmann in 1934, Berri began his acting career with small roles in Claude Autant-Lara's *Good Lord without Confession (Le bon Dieu sans confession,* 1953) and *The Game of Love (Le blé en herbe,* 1954), Claude Chabrol's *The Girls (Les bonnes femmes,* 1960), and Henri-Georges Clouzot's *The Truth (La verité,* 1960). He later appeared in Patrice Chéreau's *The Wounded Man (L'homme blessé,* 1983), and more recently in Didier Bourdon and Bernard Campan's *The Three Brothers (Les trois frères,* 1995). However, Berri's principal career has been as producer and director. His first short, *The Chicken (Le poulet,* 1965), which won an Oscar for Best Live Action Short Film that same year, was followed by his first feature film, *The Two of Us (Le vieil homme et l'enfant,* 1967), starring veteran actor Michel Simon. In 1980, the most popular artistic celebrities of France, such as Catherine Deneuve, Gérard Depardieu, Jean-Louis Trintignant, Serge Gainsbourg, and Alain Souchon appeared in Berri's *I Love You All (Je vous aime).* Berri is also remembered as the first and only director who gave a dramatic role to France's most popular comedian, Coluche. Berri's movies include a long list of popular successes: *Tchao Pantin!* (1983), *Jean de Florette* (1986), *Manon of the Spring* (1986), *Uranus* (1990), *Germinal,* and *Lucie Aubrac* (1997). Producer of a variety of films from popular comedies to high-budget historical epics, Berri worked with such internationally known filmmakers as Roman Polanski, *Tess* (1979), Pierre Schoendoerffer, *Le Crabe-tambour,* (1977), Claude Sautet, *A Simple Story (Une histoire simple,* 1978) and *Garçon!* (1983), Claude Miller, *The Little Thief (La petite voleuse,* 1989), Jean-Jacques Annaud, *The Lover,* (1991), Patrice Chéreau, *Queen Margot (La reine Margot,* 1994), Christian Vincent, *The Separation (La séparation,* 1994), Josiane Balasko, *French Twist (Gazon maudit,* 1995), Claude Zidi, *Asterix and Obelix vs. Caesar* (1999) and *La boîte* (2001), and Alain Chabat, *Astérix and Obélix: Mission Cléopatre* (2002).

PERIOD DRAMAS: PATRICE CHÉREAU, ALAIN CORNEAU, JEAN-PAUL RAPPENEAU, AND PATRICE LECONTE

Patrice Chéreau's *Queen Margot (La reine Margot,* 1994), was a long anticipated, prestigious French production (with a huge budget totaling 120 million francs). Far from being a Shakespearean tragedy or a romanticized historical adaptation, the screenplay, written by Danièle Thompson and Patrice Chéreau, was an adaptation of Alexandre Dumas's grandiose historical novel of the same name. (Dumas of course also wrote *The Count of Monte Cristo* and *The Three Musketeers*.) Originally involved with theater and opera as, most notably, the Piccolo Teatro di Milano, Patrice Chéreau (b. 1944) began his career in film with the adaptation of Jacques Offenbach's *Les Contes d'Hoffmann* (1978). As codirector, with Roger Planchon, of the Théâtre National Populaire de Lyon/Villeurbanne and director of the Théâtre des Amandiers in Nanterre, Chéreau discovered many unknown talents who ultimately dominated the 1990s, such as Vincent Pérez, Valeria Bruni-Tedeschi, Agnès Jaoui, and Isabelle Renauld. Chéreau's major productions are *The Wounded Man* (*L'homme blessé*, 1983), *Those Who Love Me Can Take the Train* (*Ceux qui m'aiment prendront le train*, 1998), *Intimacy* (*Intimité*, 2000), and *Betsy and the Emperor* (2002). The filmmaker has also performed in various films, such as the voice of Marcel Proust in Raoul Ruiz's *Time Regained* (*Le temps retrouvé*, 1999); Berri's *Lucie Aubrac*; Michael Mann's *The Last of the Mohicans* (1992), as General Montcalm, and Andrzej Wajda's *Danton* (*Danton*, 1982) as Camille Desmoulins.

Sumptuously rich visuals and a story of doomed love characterize *Queen Margot*. Imprisoned between Eros and power, Margot's character is ambivalent regarding her union with the future Henri IV, since their marriage is simply for the purpose of ending religious hostilities. Viewers are introduced to the religious persecution that occurred in sixteenth-century France, a country rife with violence and dominated by the French exile of Catherine de Medici (Virna Lisi). Catholics and Protestants live under difficult circumstances as a result of the political machinations in the court of the ineffectual King Charles IX (Jean-Huges Anglade).[33] Influenced by the queen mother, Catherine de Medici, the king compels his own sister, Marguerite de Valois, known as Margot (Isabelle Adjani), to marry a Protestant prince, Henri de Navarre (Daniel Auteuil), leader of the Huguenots in an ostentatious wedding in order to secure a fragile reconciliation between the religious communities (and, it is hoped, to tease the Huguenot community away from the Spanish Crown). The film explores King Charles's limited and immoral efforts to end the divisive religious hatred of this time, and thereby overcome the many plots, both within his own court and overseas, to usurp him. Whereas this artificial concord is intended to guarantee peace between the rival religious factions, it is a marriage of convenience. Despising her new husband, Margot openly chooses a lover, the dashing Huguenot Boniface de la Môle (Vincent Pérez). Six days later, the "religious" marriage proves to be a political failure: the repression against the Protestants increases until the night of Saint-Barthélemy, with the gruesome slaughter of thousands of Protestants, among them, the king's counselor, Coligny (Jean-Claude Brialy). Thousands of Protestants die, including most of the guests whom Henri de Navarre had brought to the wedding. Much of the story then revolves around the newlyweds being held captive in the Palais du Louvre as implicit prisoners.[33]

It is in this climate of bloody schemes and last-minute political alliances that Margot becomes acquainted with power. To save the life of many of his subjects, Henri is forced to convert to Catholicism. Margot decides to assist her husband (by now advisedly converted to Catholicism). La Môle's assignment, under the influence of Annibal de Coconas, is to gather an army of Protestants to fight the treacherous Papists. The events take a turn when Henri de Navarre strikes an alliance with Charles IX. Meanwhile, conspiracies against the king develop within his court and abroad. Although both men seem to trust each other, Catherine de Medici prepares a poison for her son-in-law, but it is the king who takes it and dies. As the Medici family crumbles, the revenging brothers accuse La Môle, and with one swing the new king will have gotten rid of two tormentors. Margot avoids death at the last minute, but La Môle is arrested and executed with his companion Coconas. The new king is crowned, and Margot departs from Paris, exiling herself to Navarre. Henri III, Margot's brother, ascends to the throne and consolidates his power, as his most immediate challenge now is to calm religious strife.

The title of the film can be misleading since *Queen Margot* is the complex story of many protagonists, not simply Margot. Although usually represented as fanatical and even nymphomaniacal, Margot despised the thought of being reliant on any man, and to a certain extent showed how she played her rivals off one another by entertaining many marriage offers without accepting any of them. (What must be taken into account is that Margot came from what may be the most dysfunctional family in French history!) The dramatic disposition of Margot is a compelling combination of strength and weakness. The character is admired for her freedom of thought and self-determination, yet seen as chained by her repressed emotion. All who have loved her unsuccessfully—including her own brothers who are believed by historians to have been involved to the point where incest is suspected— or whose love has been thwarted by cowardice, find in her their fateful toll. Eventually, the viewer is left to reach the conclusion that Margot, who did not become an adult with the healthiest deference for the institution of marriage, sees her union to Henri de Navarre as the main *raison d'être* to maintain her independence.

The ageless Isabelle Adjani took on the mythical role that was interpreted with an unarguable screen presence by the great Jeanne Moreau some forty years before (in Jean Dréville's *La reine Margot,*

1954). Adjani's sensual features truly embodied the sexually dynamic character of Margot. Known for portraying independent if not ill-fated historical figures (e.g., *The Story of Adèle H., Camille Claudel*), Adjani expressed with style, composure, and aptitude Margot's disposition as a scheming, influential, advanced thinker, who was far too conscious of her own extraordinary nature to bow to any man. Adjani's Margot is no exception. Also of note is the performance by Italian actress Virna Lisi, a worldwide sex symbol in the 1960s, who outstandingly concealed her striking features as the court matriarch Catherine de Medici, the very embodiment of wickedness and malevolence. Like most monarchs before them, the Valois's reign was constantly threatened mainly because they did not have absolute power. Still, Charles IX was faced with a rising sea of troubles, both internal (powerful religious and political enemies) and external (superior powers Spain and England were threatening invasion). It is how he confronted and conquered these threats that forms the compelling center of this film. During the reconstitution of the Saint-Barthélémy massacre, the violent, yet dazzling scenes of religious warfare were cleverly shot with visual aptitude. With historians differing about which faction started the massacre, the audience is left to decide on its own (around 3,000 were massacred that day in the capital and many more all across the kingdom). The important set production for this sixteenth-century period piece included several historic locations, such as the famous apartments of the Louvre, the Cathedral of Saint-Quentin (Margot's wedding), some streets in old Bordeaux, the forest of Rambouillet (for a memorable hunting scene), the Palace of Mafra in Portugal, and the Théâtre des amandiers de Nanterre, so dear to Patrice Chéreau.

Film critics argue that period movies inevitably reflect more on the times in which they are shot than on their subject, and *Queen Margot* is no exception. When classified with the big-screen productions of the decade, *Queen Margot,* which covered the years 1572–76, is remembered as a top-quality historical epic featuring immaculate costumes and a carefully re-created historical background. But the accuracy of the movie setting became immediately less preponderant as a cinematographic issue; the film generated its own historical context within a complex network of conspiracies and wide variety of personalities, sceneries, and action even though many historical events were altered, compressed, and juxtaposed for dramatic effect. (Understandably, it may be difficult for some historians to benefit from a fictional narrative set in such a decipherable historical context if it is weakened by what would appear to them as noticeable historical errors.)

On one level, *Queen Margot* was obviously a grand epic reminiscent of Jean-Paul Rappeneau's *Cyrano de Bergerac,* but the mise-en-scène clearly portrays a character-driven story line that indirectly elucidated various events and vengeance acts from the very beginning of the film. One of the most staggering features of this multi-character historical film was that it opened on a bewildering assortment of individuals whose motives were to be guessed by the spectator. Indeed, many observers in America noted that a chart of the succession to the throne placed in the opening credit would have helped audiences, less familiar with French history, interpret the tortuous series of political arrangements, betrayals, coalitions, warring religious factions, secret plots, poisonings, purges, executions, and, of course, love-affairs. The plot possesses enough cinematic vigor, however, to progressively drive the sequencing of the different sword fights and battle scenes, and Chéreau, to the satisfaction of many, did not indulge in filming too many scenes with only the two main protagonists. As a renowned stage and opera director, Chéreau successfully got his players to act without any degree of bodily limitation. The film never appears wearisome despite its running length. More than thirty minutes were edited by Miramax from the 164 minutes of the 1994 Cannes Film Festival original cut. For a nonspecialist spectatorship, the editing of certain scenes found compensation in the long explanatory clarifications at the opening of the film. Some observers declared that the cuts did indeed trigger a certain element of clarity, while others considered the drastic editing a narrative oversimplification.[34]

Philippe Rousselot's camera movements were tight on the characters much of the time while capturing the dazzling visual-feast background to create an intense imagery. The dark interior of the Louvre settings generated a claustrophobic intensity that underscored the emergent sense of paranoia and the brothers' ominous maneuverings in a battle for the crown. This darkness also implied the inflexible social structure of the time, with its internal strife between the political and religious aristocracy who regarded the masses as pawns to be sacrificed for the greater good of the kingdom. Rousselot (*Diva, Dangerous Liaisons, A River Runs through It, The Tailor of Panama*), who painstakingly re-created the period, maximized the period costumes at his disposal and utilized the inspired device of candlelight, thereby overwhelming the senses with the inimitable royal apartments and floors of the Louvre. His photography was in constant motion and generated an ominous dynamic and depth, working in tandem with the somber colors and heavy-stone interiors of the set to create a dark, Gothic look that befit the lush dramatics of the piece. Like the momentum of the final plot, the beauty of Moidele Bickel's striking costumes blended and harmonized with the overpowering sound track (Goran Bregovic), thereby elevating the dramatic tension even further. With all of this, at the 1994 Cannes Film Festival *Queen Margot* took the Prix de la mise en scène (Jury Prize) and the Prix d'interprétation féminine (Best Actress to Virna Lisi as Catherine de Médicis, despite the fact that Isabelle Adjani was widely expected to win a Best Actress Award for the film's main character). At the 1994 French Academy of Cinema Awards, the film received the Césars for Best Actress (Isabelle Adjani), Best Cinematography (Philippe Rousselot), Best Costume Design (Moidele Bickel), Best Supporting Actor (Jean-Hugues Anglade), and Best Supporting Actress (Virna Lisi), as well as a nomination for Best Foreign Language Film at the 1995 Golden Globe Awards and one for Best Costume Design at the 1994 Oscars.

Another highly anticipated project was *All the Mornings of the World* (*Tous les matins du monde,* 1991) by Alain Corneau (b. 1943). The film is a transparently nostalgic vision of what an accomplished filmmaker such as Corneau, had in mind for years. In addition to his musical background in jazz, Corneau is mainly known as one of the most successful advocates of the French-style thriller of the 1970s. After graduating from IDHEC, Corneau became an assistant director to Costa-Gavras on *The Confession* (*L'aveu,* 1970), and soon imposed himself as an assistant director working in particular with filmmakers Marcel Camus and José Giovanni. Corneau's first feature film, *French Anonymity Society* (*France société anonyme,* 1973), revealed his talent for police thrillers. This talent grew throughout the 1970s, with films such as *The Case against Ferro* (*Police Python 357,* 1976), a movie that marked his debut in big productions with actors such as Yves Montand, Simone Signoret, François Périer, and Italian actress Stefania Sandrelli; *Série noire,* an adaptation of Georges Perec's novel, eventually selected for French representation at the 1979 Cannes Film Festival with Patrick Dewaere; and finally, one of his largest critical and popular successes, *The Choice of Arms* (*Le choix des armes,* 1981), with Gérard Depardieu, Yves Montand, and Catherine Deneuve. In 1984, Corneau moved from the police thriller to the so called heritage film as he directed the biggest stars of the decade: Depardieu, Deneuve, Sophie Marceau, and Philippe Noiret in *Fort Saganne,* an adaptation of Louis Gardel's novel. For the occasion of the centennial of the invention of motion pictures, Corneau and Jacques Perrin directed *The Children of Lumière* (*Les enfants de Lumière,* 1995), and recently *The Prince of the Pacific* (*Le Prince du Pacifique,* 2000).

One of his most significant contributions to the heritage genre, however, is undeniably *All the Mornings of the World* (*Tous les matins du monde,* 1991). After seventeen versions of the scenario, drafted by Alain Corneau and Pascal Quignard, who is also known as a scholar of baroque music, the film is the realization of a rather difficult task: namely, it makes the beauty of baroque music apparent to contemporary audiences. Although a film for a musically inclined spectatorship, the success among popular audiences sparked a national revival of interest in French baroque music. Recipient of the prestigious Prix Louis Delluc, the film garnered eleven César award nominations, and won for Best Film, Best Director (Alain Corneau), Best Supporting Actress (Anne Brochet), Best Cinematography (Yves Angelo), Best Costume Design (Corinne Jorry), Best Music (Jordi Savall), and Best Sound (Pierre Verany, Anne LeCampion, Pierre Gamet, and Gérard Lamps).

The story begins with a voice-over narrative by the aging Marin Marais (Gérard Depardieu), a retired viol musician-courtier and virtuoso composer, reminiscing with his students on his first music teacher. His voice-over begins a series of flashbacks about his master the Jansenist[35] Monsieur de Sainte-Colombe[36] (Jean-Pierre Marielle), teacher of the viol, or viole de gambe. Following the death of his wife (Caroline Sihol) in the spring of 1660, Sainte-Colombe secludes himself into silence in an eremetic lifestyle with just one goal in mind: to attain musical perfection (which he will not share). Detached from the outside world and psychologically alienating himself, Sainte-Colombe rears two daughters by himself, Madeleine (Anne Brochet) and Toinette (Carole Richert), while teaching them the rudiments of music literacy and the techniques of the viol. As the years go by, Sainte-Colombe and his daughters give rare trio performances in his house for the privileged nobility. Unavoidably, their exquisite but infrequent performances become famous and attract the attention of the court. At Versailles, the cultural and artistic center of the Western world, King Louis XIV gets wind of Sainte-Colombe's reputation and sends an emissary, summoning him to play at the court. Without subtleties, the disconsolate musician turns down the request, offended by the thought of entertaining for prestige or money. This does not endear him to the court.

Sainte-Colombe spends hours each day in a recluse cabin, rehearsing his viol. One day, an adolescent, Marin Marais (Guillaume Depardieu), visits him and begs to be his student. After a long deliberation, Sainte-Colombe accepts, but the lessons turn out to be laborious. When, after a few rehearsals, Sainte-Colombe recognizes that his novice may eventually rise above his art, he simply declares that he has nothing more to teach. The music teacher becomes denigrating, as he tells Marais that his virtuosity, though brilliant, is limited and cannot compensate for a lack of spirit: "You make music, you are not a musician," says the unimpressed teacher. But Sainte-Colombe's daughters successfully intercede on behalf of the handsome young man until the day the relationship between the two men ends in a feud. The tempestuous and vile-tempered master does not see any talent in the young aspirant, and in a rage he breaks Marin's instrument. Meanwhile, Madeleine, a talented violist herself, and already in love with Marais, allows him to spy on her father's secret rehearsals and teaches him everything she has learned. Marais cedes to the temptations of fame and fortune, and decides to go to Versailles to become court conductor, abandoning Madeline. Sainte-Colombe asks him to return, but to no avail. Filled with remorse, Marais eventually returns to Sainte-Colombe. Madeleine wishes to listen to a piece he has composed for her. But as Marais again departs, Madeleine is overcome with grief and hangs herself. Devastated by this second loss, Sainte-Colombe fantasizes that his deceased wife visits him as he witnesses a series of her apparitions. During his later years, Marais realizes that his emotional bond to his master was more powerful than he had ever thought. All that he has left are memories and thoughts of what might have been.

Musicologists know little about the life of Sainte-Colombe. Besides being known as Marin Marais's spiritual father, Sainte-Colombe was an ascetic, grieving, metaphysical personage, isolated from the outside world, who mainly rejected unheard musical lavishness. But in 1966, a manuscript containing sixty-seven pieces for the viol attributed to Sainte-Colombe was discovered among the belongings of French pianist and conductor Alfred Cortot. A tribute to an underrated artist, *All the Mornings of the World* was a challenge to investigate the artist's muse from a privileged angle. By portraying both talented musicians, demonstrating to each other their expertise of the viol, first through the canons of classicism (discipline, grace, respect for rules), and then through flamboyant talent, the film illustrates the symbolic conflict between art and commercial success. The serious, slow-paced, sadly beautiful music that pervades the film reveals the tragic and terrifying nature of the mourning artist's haunting memory of his wife. The two main characters stand in sharp contrast, and the film presents an interesting melodramatic fictionalization of the relationship between the two men. Sainte-Colombe, with his cold, dour appearance (usually wearing black clothing), despises the trappings of Versailles and epitomizes the antithesis of young Marais's hedonistic quest for recognition. Marin Marais, on the other hand, aspires to a position that will bring him prominence and wealth. For Sainte-Colombe, Marais's compositions are musical fragments, the very essence of which is to please others. Faith, without which no genuine art can be achieved, is at the center of Sainte-Colombe's philosophy. Unlike Marais, he plays because he is driven to do so. Every day, the divine melody generated from the heart of his instrument is destined for no receptive audience, nor is it to be rehearsed endlessly; it is instead a private and intimate communion with the self, unique and never quite to be repeated as the title of the film, an excerpt from a sentence in the novel suggests: *Tous les matins du monde sont sans retour* (All the mornings of the world are without return). Assisted by inspired editing, the interplay between the haunting baroque music and the pastoral scenery brought the somber and underrated viol to the public's attention (compositions by Sainte-Colombe, Marais, Lully, and Couperin, in arrangements and performances by Spanish viol master Jordi Savall). In the absence of dialogue, a resonant and mesmerizing musical score took over in a steady flow of baroque requiems. Everything appeared to be nuanced musically or in visual hues. Corneau's narrative entirely disassembled the notions of time and space; the story was interrupted by flashbacks, which consequently gave no accurate suggestion of where the current action stood in relation to the chronology.

The frail lighting reproduced the period's visual atmosphere with great precision. Yves Angelo's photography—a series of long head shots, fixed camera angles, and detailed period accuracy (reminiscent of paintings by Georges de la Tour and others)—embraced a wealth of visually decorative details. Between the reclusive master, illustrated by austere and monotonous colors, and the flamboyant Marais, represented by an explosion of light as he leaves Sainte-Colombe for the glamour of the court, *All the Mornings of the World* is far from a simple parable. The film does not step out of the semantic frame it has chosen for itself (heritage film, that is), and it would be difficult for contemporary viewers to overlook the filmmakers' endeavors to present a specific vision of the seventeenth century.

Also set in the seventeenth century, Jean-Paul Rappeneau's *Cyrano de Bergerac (Cyrano de Bergerac,* 1990) was a greater success than Corneau's production as the film won the 1990 Oscar for Best Costume Design (Franca Squarciapino), with nominations for several other categories, such as Best Actor, Best Art Direction–Set Decoration, Best Makeup,[37] and Best Foreign Film. At the 1990 Cannes Film Festival, Gérard Depardieu won the prize for Best Actor. The production also earned the award for Best Foreign Film at the 1991 Golden Globes. In France, this costly epic ($17 million) received an impressive series of awards (ten in all, equaling the record held by François Truffaut's *The Last Metro*), such as the 1991 César for Best Film, Best Director (Jean-Paul Rappeneau), Best Actor (Gérard Depardieu), Best Supporting Actor (Jacques Weber), Best Cinematography (Pierre Lhomme), Best Costume Design (Franca Squarciapino), Best Editing (Noëlle Boisson), Best Music (Jean-Claude Petit), Best Production Design (Ezio Frigerio), and Best Sound (Pierre Gamet and Dominique Hennequin).

Jean-Paul Rappeneau (b. 1932) began as a screenwriter for Yves Robert's *Signé Arsène Lupin* (1959), Louis Malle's *Zazie dans le métro* (1960), and Philippe de Broca's *That Man from Rio (L'homme de Rio,* 1964, written with Alain Cavalier and Claude Sautet). His directing debut was *A Matter of Resistance* (*La vie de château*, 1965). His second feature film, *The Swashbuckler* (*Les mariés de l'an II*, 1971), confirmed an inclination toward comedy as well as costume epic productions. With his most successful production, *Cyrano de Bergerac*, Rappeneau showed a talent for high-budget literary adaptations narrowly fluctuating between both cinematic substance and enunciation, preserving the essential theatricality of the play.

Rostand's flamboyant tale evokes the turbulent yet passionate life of poet-swordfighter Savinien Cyrano de Bergerac (1619–1655)[38] in seventeenth-century France, and presents the atypical love triangle between Cyrano, his companion of arms, Christian, and the woman they both love, Roxane. Endowed with a protuberant nose, Cyrano leads a life of poetry and battles. Since the only way Cyrano secures the admiration of women is through poetry and physical feats of skill, he is astonishingly brilliant as he battles one hundred men single-handedly. Cyrano seeks refuge in his persuasive eloquence, while concealing his repulsiveness behind his mental powers. The opening sequence in a theater acquaints the viewer with Cyrano's character in medias res, as he generates a famous fight, which eventually results in a duel with his rival, the Vicomte de Valvert (Philippe Volter). During the duel, Cyrano lively extemporizes alexandrines to ridicule the young nobleman until defeating him by the sword. He strikes his rivals with his sword, but it is his verses that touch the heart of others.

At the request of his cousin Roxane (Anne Brochet), Cyrano (Gérard Depardieu) takes Baron Christian de Neuvillette (Vincent Pérez) under his wing at the cadet regiment of Gascogne. Roxane is infatuated with the young cadet, whom she thinks is trying to reach her. Christian is in love with her too, but he blatantly lacks the words to convey his love. Roxane ignores the passion, which burns Cyrano secretly. He believes himself too repulsive to win the affection of women. But his eloquent poems prove successful, since Roxane immediately falls in love with Christian. One night, as Christian struggles with some verse to seduce Roxane, it is Cyrano who comes to the rescue of the intrepid lover and, hidden behind a tree, whispers the sweet poetry he has always wanted to declare. Christian climbs up to seek his reward, while Cyrano walks away in the rainy night, alone. That same night, a monk brings a letter from the Comte de Guiche (Jacques Weber), who has arranged a secret rendezvous with Roxane. To avoid the impending tragedy, Roxane decides to marry Christian immediately. When the Comte de Guiche arrives, it is too late. To avenge himself of this insult, the comte sends the regiment of cadets to the front against the Spanish troops who besiege the city of Arras. Hope suddenly resurfaces when Cyrano realizes he may have seduced Roxane, who has fallen in love with the soul behind the alexandrines. While in battle, Cyrano writes to Roxane daily and signs, as usual, Christian's name. But one day Christian realizes that Cyrano has gone so far as to risk his own life to convey the letters across enemy lines, and understands that Cyrano really loves Roxane. Discouraged, Christian comprehends that Roxane loves only his physical features, not his soul. He loses hope and fights to the death.

Fourteen years go by, Roxane has retreated to a convent, while Cyrano has come to visit her every Saturday afternoon. Following a deadly ambush, Cyrano, now critically wounded, finds the strength to come to his weekly appointment. As he sits down, knowing that he is about to die, he requests one final favor from Roxane. He asks her to let him read the last letter "Christian" wrote to her. As he begins to read, Roxane is struck by the beauty of the voice, which comes through the verses. She turns and realizes that it is too dark for Cyrano to read but that his voice still goes on as if he had written the letter himself. She understands and declares her love to the dying Cyrano. The disconsolate poet reveals to Roxane the truth about his and Christian's deception, and of his lifelong love for her.

Adapted from Edmond Rostand's drama (written, when he was twenty nine), *Cyrano de Bergerac* has been the inspiration for several more-or-less successful versions (e.g., Michael Gordon's Oscar-winning version *Cyrano de Bergerac,* starring Jose Ferrer in 1950, and more recently, in 1987, the modernized popular retelling of the story by Steve Martin in Fred Schepisi's *Roxanne*). On stage, many productions attempted to re-create the genius of Rostand, in particular, the popular production by Robert Hossein, with lead actor Jean-Paul Belmondo at the famous Théâtre Marigny. The daunting task for Jean-Paul Rappeneau and Jean-Claude Carrière was to maintain control of the versification of the original play, which made difficult, even impossible, to keep the poetic nature of the drama within the cinematographic requirements of the screenplay, deconstructing and reconstructing each scene while leaving the play's sharp verses unbroken. Although reduced in length, the spirit and poetic dimension of each act survived and resulted in an unexpected emotion among popular audiences. Indeed, the public's endorsement of the story's enchanting romanticism showed a recognition of the audacity of the screen-writers in retaining the alexandrines from the original play. Film critics discovered a version of Cyrano matching up as intimately as possible to a truthful, uncontentious visualization of the celebrated play rather than the imaginative reshapings often found on stage. Rappeneau's mise-en-scène complies with Rostand's general narrative development, despite the few oversights of particular occurrences or secondary personages and the reworking of poetic verses. The screenplay conveys this roman-

Gérard Depardieu (Cyrano) in Jean-Paul Rappeneau's *Cyrano de Bergerac* (*Cyrano de Bergerac*, 1990), (Courtesy of BIFI/© Hachette-Première).

tic intrigue in a series of court adversities and outrages, with Cyrano always evolving as the main protagonist yet also a character of shadows.

Cyrano's famous self-descriptive verse, *j'ai été toujours l'ombre* (I have always been the shadow), laid the groundwork for the success of the film. Furthermore, the richly evocative verse translation by the English author Anthony Burgess is succinct yet filled with atypical literary audaciousness. It thereby contributed to the triumph of the film in America. Cinematographer Pierre Lhomme worked to keep the film from feeling like a filmed play. With his lively camera work, exuberant intelligence, and tragic poignancy, Rappeneau allowed the logical process of sequencing to flow without visually disengaging viewers. The rich costumes, sets, and lighting kept it from feeling heavy or fossilized. In a similar vein to how Cyrano dies at the end of the play, this film deserves to be remembered for its panache. *Cyrano de Bergerac* was ultimately a tragedy of grand scale, the final scene being reminiscent of French poet André Chénier's memorable verses *L'art ne fait que des vers, seul le coeur est poète.*

The *siècle des lumières* (the Enlightment era), especially the Revolution, has always been a favorite among French audiences. Therefore, it is no surprise to see Patrice Leconte's *Ridicule* (*Ridicule,* 1996) emerging as one of the true successes of the 1990s.

Born in 1947, Patrice Leconte began specializing in film studies in 1967 at IDHEC, where he met future cinematographer and director Bruno Nuytten. After graduation, he went into cartoon publications, thanks to designers Marcel Gotlib and especially René Goscinny, who hired him for the magazine *Pilote*. Several years later, Leconte made his first full-length feature film with Coluche, *Les vécés étaient fermés de l'intérieur* (1975). Still in the comedy genre, Leconte wrote the scenario for his next film with L'Équipe du Splendid, a group of comedians known in the *café-théâtre* circle, who looked to adapt their latest success to the big screen, *Amours, coquillages et crustacés,* a satirical parody of the Club Méditerranée resorts. This immediately became a double success with *French Fried Vacation* (*Les bronzés,* 1978), followed by *Les bronzés font du ski* (1979).

In 1984, Leconte changed direction along with an action movie with Gérard Lanvin and Bernard Giraudeau called *Les spécialistes*. One of the most interesting films of his career was a remake of Julien Duvivier's *Panique* (1946), an adaptation of a thriller from Georges Simenon's *Les fiançailles de M. Hire,* starring Michel Blanc and Sandrine Bonnaire. *Monsieur Hire* (*Monsieur Hire,* 1989) was an official selection at the 1989 Cannes Film Festival. Following growing popular success, Leconte took more initiative in the choice of screenplays as he successfully directed *The Hairdresser's Husband* (*Le mari de la coiffeuse,* 1990)

Anne Brochet (Roxane), Vincent Pérez (Christian) and Gérard Depardieu (Cyrano) in Jean-Paul Rappeneau's *Cyrano de Bergerac* (*Cyrano de Bergerac*, 1990), (Courtesy of BIFI/© Hachette-Première).

and *Tango* (*Tango*, 1993) both reminiscent of Bertrand Blier's absurdist comedies. Leconte has also directed *The Girl on the Bridge* (*La fille sur le pont*, 1999), *The Widow of Saint-Pierre* (*La veuve de Saint-Pierre*, 2000), and *Rue des plaisirs* (2001).

At the opening of the 1996 Cannes Film Festival, *Ridicule* met with terrific popular and critical success, winning a year later Césars for Best Art Direction (Ivan Maussion), Best Costume Design (Christian Gasc), Best Director (Patrice Leconte), and Best Film. It also was nominated for Best Foreign Language Film at the 1996 Academy Awards. The story narrates Grégoire Ponceludon de Malavoy's futile pursuit of royal favor against the decadent disciples of a mean-verbal sport, which ultimately symbolizes man's struggle against the forces that contain him. An overwhelmingly powerful film with many inspired moments, *Ridicule* shows viewers in Laclos's fashion how deception is something inflicted by one person on another, inevitably defying reason and logic.

Set at the Versailles court of Louis XVI in 1783, the film tells the story of Grégoire Ponceludon de Malavoy (Charles Berling),[39] a young, serious-minded aristocrat who makes a trip to the capital in order to petition and to persuade King Louis XVI (Urbain Cancelier) to drain the festering marshlands of his estate, which holds his people in a state of poverty in the Dombes region where disease is killing the peasants. To see his plan succeed, he must be introduced to the life of the prerevolutionary court and master its protocols. With no access to the king's court, however, he is resigned to his fate and decides to return to his rural province. On leaving Paris, however, he is robbed and left semiconscious. The Marquis de Bellegarde (Jean Rochefort) rescues Grégoire and decides to help him by giving him access to the court and to a file he has kept of every witty remark he has ever heard at the court. The young baron is immediately attracted to Mathilde de Bellegarde (Judith Godrèche), the marquis's daughter, who is also a scientist experimenting with a rudimentary diving suit. Having inherited her father's yearning for scientific knowledge, she reveals her disgust toward life at the court, and her attraction to the spirit of the Lumières. Nevertheless, she is about to enter into a wedding of convenience with a rich nobleman, Monsieur Montalieri (Bernard Dheran), and will be able to use his wealth to support her experiments.

As the protégé of the Marquis de Bellegarde, Grégoire discovers the true nature of the court, for instance, the influential Madame de Blayac (Fanny Ardant) and the Abbot de Vilecourt (Bernard Giraudeau). Both are expert at plots, compromises, and other Machiavellian subtleties. Unfortunately, the characters talk about wit much more than they exhibit it. With the viciously competitive pressures of the court, the young baron surprisingly survives the verbal games in this fortified and sophisticated system of humiliations, a world constantly permeated by a Machiavelian atmosphere. Grégoire must be taught to play the delicate games of wit at a place where the aristocrats show an indifference to social concerns other than the ones that please their own vanity. The alternately calculating, seductive, and manipulative Madame de Blayac, a flirtatious woman of the world, thought to be the mistress of the king, favorably notices the unusual presence of Grégoire and becomes his mistress. She is a powerful ally, especially for this novice seeking to meet the insulated king. Although a man of compassion and reason, Grégoire is determined to beat the king and his court at their own game. In a parallel story, Mathilde is in dismay since she had renounced her marriage. As Grégoire finally wins a private audience with the king, he is forced into a duel that proves fatal for his adversary, an eminent officer who is close to the king. While his mischievous counterparts view Ponceludon with mocking disdain, Grégoire ultimately chooses Mathilde over Madame de Blayac, leaving behind the arena of power and a world of characters unaware of the apocalypse toward which they are heading.

Conceived from Rémi Waterhouse's screenplay,[40] this engaging costume drama featured spiritual dialogues and a beautifully designed mise-en-scène. Art director Ivan Maussion (*Monsieur Hire, La fille sur le*

Judith Godrèche (Mathilde de Bellegarde) and Charles Berling (Ponceludon de Malavoy) in Patrice Leconte's *Ridicule* (*Ridicule*, 1996), (Courtesy of BIFI/© Epithète Productions).

pont, La veuve de Saint-Pierre, Felix et Lola) oversaw the countless interiors, exteriors, costumes, and artifacts that contributed to the tone of the film. In addition, cinematographer Thierry Arbogast skillfully recreated the lavishness of 1783 Versailles through his impressive production designs, and a colorful setting for captivating period detail. But beyond the common portrayal of a corrupt court universe, with its visual splendor and pathos, the film emphasized a variety of literary elements. The power of words was passionately evoked with the arch dialogue, turning the whole experience into exhausting conversational games and matches of the soul. This unusually literate comedy-drama offered subtle ironies and acid-laced dialogue as if from the best theatrical plays. Again, the film was a visual feast and a semantic tour de force. With the linguistic exercise of style of eighteenth-century fashion, the camera frequently lingered on rituals of the courtesan's day (the powdering of Madame de Blayac, played with utter finesse by Fanny Ardant). One of the most compelling aspects of *Ridicule* was the representation of the two deceitful main characters and their ultimate humiliation. They arbitrarily thrived on control and manipulation, and it is not until the climax that viewers are shown their frail and apprehensive side.

Of special note is the performance of Fanny Ardant as Madame de Blayac, a Parisian courtisane whose living is spent concocting sophisticated erotic intrigues. With her malevolent smile, she seems majestically corrupt, like an evil queen in a fairy story, and she openly recognizes that "her life is governed by intrigue and that her power is indistinguishable from her sexual attraction."[41] The Countess de Blayac's compulsive destructiveness makes her a character with true classical grandeur. With that opening glance, she draws viewers into her confidence, making them party to her contemptuous conspiracies. Along with unscrupulous and dark characters, such as the sly, suave, sexual predator Abbot de Vilecourt, she is a devious powermonger who, with a single impulse, can devastate the lives of anyone around her. Her boudoir expertise, which the film underlines in basic terms, is to exert her persuasive powers in the world (how she exerts herself seems almost beside the point). And she deliberately exploits her powers, whenever and however she desires, without contemplation for the consequent harm. But she lacks the devilish charm and seductiveness necessary to carry off all her conquests, much like Valmont, her corresponding character in Stephen Frears's *Dangerous Liaisons* (1989). Along with her comes the main protagonist of the film, Grégoire. Ignorant and ill equipped to face the social protocol of Parisian nobility, Grégoire must first learn the rules of the grotesque and hypocritical game and find his way through the courtesans to accomplish his goal. In order to advance, he needs more than simple logic and benevolent reason: he needs wit. But it must be a particular malicious kind of verbal amusement to leave one's victim in a state of ridicule and disgrace. The thriving continuance of his new lifestyle begins to supersede his reasons for coming to Versailles in the first place. Yet Grégoire and Mathilde, in their naively optimistic state of mind and youth, are threatened by imminent corruption: Grégoire by having to ward the countess's ruses in order to advance his plans; Mathilde by a union to an aged, wealthy suitor whom she sees as the only way to fund her study. Grégoire finds an eccentric despotism at court, dominated by wit and aristocratic genealogy. Whereas his mentor advises him not to laugh at his own jokes, to exclude all usage of puns and, whenever he laughs, not to do it with his mouth open, the young baron, deliberately oblivious to the rules, rises through the ranks and the machinations of the court. Taking a critical distance from the distribution of characters, only Mathilde, who personifies the scientific spirit of the Enlightenment, can be considered one of the rare characters not to indulge in this "dangerous liaisons" style Russian roulette and voyeuristic game. Interestingly, the behavior of most characters seems completely logical in relation to their own motivations, as the game reduces them to a form of dishonor through verbal dueling.

Supremely caustic, like *Dangerous Liaisons*, *Ridicule* is an enlightening costume drama with much modern relevance that simultaneously functions as a period satire and a kind of contemporary metaphor. According to the logic of this decadent universe, if bright individuals are evil, then virtuous people must be dull and without character.[42] But what began as a luscious spiritual game deepened into a double-edged tragedy. From the salons to the boudoirs, humor is used as a disarming device or form of verbal fencing, as audiences are reminded with a quotation from the duke of Guines: "In this country, vices are without consequence, but ridicule can kill." Each successful riposte opens doors, an advantage that money and noble birth could not provide. Louis XVI himself sets the tone, encouraging or rejecting his spellbound cohorts according to his evaluation of their individual wit. What dominates at court is not the art of subtle diplomacy but rather an effective talent for repartee, the ability to make clever and humorous comments and ultimately cruel witticisms, especially ones that damage others' reputations. Although wittiness appears to be the most precious apparatus for aspiring courtesans, each individual's fate and character could be made or ruined in parlors, at card games, or even at dress balls over the influence of a single observation uttered in front of one's peers. Once ridiculed, the unfortunate victims' influence instantaneously declines among king and courtiers, courtesans and assorted other players. In *Ridicule*, "the body's skill and elegance are just as important as the mastery of language and the latter can actually damage the former."[43] As Mireille Rosello remarks, the film can be seen as "a convincing heritage film while commenting on cultural and political issues of immediate relevance to a contemporary French audience; that is, its ability to invent a particular past to construct a particular present."[44] With poignant veracity, *Ridicule* captures the ethos of an elite social group, a group for which manipulation and sexual power struggles turn into a game of chess. It is the France of Louis XVI, and French aristocrats are entertaining themselves at the edge of the abyss, ignoring all but themselves.

THE RETURN OF COMEDIES AT THE BOX OFFICE: JEAN-MARIE POIRÉ AND FRANCIS VEBER

In the 1990s, French comedy appeared best able to resist (at the box office) the assaults of Hollywood blockbusters. The uncontested money-making winner of the 1990s was Jean-Marie Poiré's *The Visitors* (*Les visiteurs*, 1993), the second-biggest film in French history, with

13.6 million tickets sold (second only to Gérard Oury's *Don't Look Now We're Being Shot At,* with 17.2 million). This commercial success was all the more remarkable since it belonged to the select list of five films to exceed the bar of ten million spectators: Julien Duvivier's *The Little World of Don Camillo* (*Le petit monde de Don Camillo*), with 12.7 million; Gérard Oury's 1965 *The Sucker!,* with 11.7 million; and Coline Serreau's *Three Men and a Cradle* in 1985, with 10.2 million.[45] Despite its enormous popularity, *The Visitors* was awarded only a single César (Best Supporting Actress, Valérie Lemercier).

The story begins in the Middle Ages during the reign of King Louis VI in 1122, as Count Godefroy de Montmirail (Jean Réno)[46] is about to marry Frénégonde de Pouille (Valérie Lemercier). On his way to the wedding ceremony, the count accidentally kills his future father-in-law while under a spell cast by a sorceress. Unable to marry his betrothed, he is devastated by the idea of not having any heirs. The magician Eusaebius conjures a potion to transport the count into the past and eventually give him the necessary time to change the course of history. Unfortunately, he forgets to include quail eggs inside the potion and the magician mistakenly sends the count and his squire, Jacquouille la Fripouille (Christian Clavier), into the future instead. Once in modern-day France, the two men meet upper-class Béatrice Goulard de Montmirail (also played by Valérie Lemercier), a descendant of Frénégonde, and slowly realize that they have jumped a thousand years into the future. Béatrice mistakes Godefroy for her long-lost cousin Hubert. Much to his dismay, she reveals to him that the chateau no longer belongs to their family. The new owner, Jacquart (also played by Christian Clavier), a descendant of Jacquouille, runs it as a luxury hotel. Appalled to see the feudal world upside down, Godefroy pledges to restore the family honor. As for Jacquouille, he adapts quickly to his new lifestyle and does not pay attention to his master's concerns. He even falls in love with "Dame" Ginette (Marie-Anne Chazel), a small-time artist, unemployed and homeless, who is convinced that he is an actor shooting a movie in medieval times. To return to the past, Godefroy must find an old parchment with the magician's secret potion. In the chateau, he discovers a secret path leading to the dungeon. There, he finds a message urging him to see Ferdinand Eusèbe, a descendant of Eusaebius. After countless tribulations, creating confusion in a contemporary small town and other misunderstandings, Godefroy forces his squire to return with him to the past. As they both land safe and sound back in the twelfth century, Jacquart (Jacquouille surreptitiously evades his master's orders and stays in the present by interchanging Jacquart at his place while asleep) wakes up among an angry crowd of starving peasants. As for Godefroy,

Jean Réno (Godefroy de Montmirail) in Jean-Marie Poiré's *The Visitors* (*Les visiteurs*, 1993), (Courtesy of BIFI/© J. Prébois).

he arrives just in time to change the target of his arbalest and save the life of his father-in-law.

Despite the long prologue, the weak composition of its structure, and its ad hoc style, which recalls, albeit less successfully, the delirious antics of Monty Python, *The Visitors* enjoyed great word-of-mouth approbation. The apparent popular consensus around the film came from the long-established comic device of the culture shock in moving ahead eight centuries, as well as the sheer new style of the film. Imaginative witticisms and more importantly, the enormous intertextual network of popular-culture references inform this unique and memorable scenario. With allusions to other comedies (e.g., *Le Père Noël est une ordure, French Fried Vacation*), television celebrities, and popular icons—ignorance of the two medieval protagonists indiscriminately triggered a similar derisive and comical reaction among audiences' collective imaginary, attesting to the utterly evident "Frenchness" of the film. In *The Visitors,* comedy is shifted from plot development to the individual comic reliance on greater physical and personality traits. For instance, the character Jacquouille embodies self-deprecating humor and also plays with language, learning contemporary slang. In addition to collective awareness, the most spectacular multifaceted aspect of his personality was mirrored by the mutation of his language skills (another sign of social emancipation). Jacquouille's catchphrases have become especially popular among young audiences (e.g., *dingue* for "crazy" and the new intonation of "OK"). As one of the most eagerly anticipated releases, the sequel, entitled *The Corridors of Time: The Visitors II* (*Les visiteurs II,* 1998), had the biggest opening day in French-film history, breaking the record set by *Men in Black* and again generating an array of inventive sight gags. This in a country where few films ever received the "sequel treatment." At $23 million, the second film cost three times as much as *The Visitors,* and its success, although less impressive than the first, allowed Jean-Marie Poiré to pursue the American remake, *Just Visiting,* which was released in the United States in April 2001. The nature of this overwhelming success continues to amaze, and like all similar pop-culture phenomena, no one knows the true reasons for the craze. Like Luc Besson's *The Big Blue* and Jean-Jacques Beineix's *Betty Blue,* word of mouth resulted in enormous success.

Born in 1945, Jean-Marie Poiré, son of Alain Poiré, a successful film producer, began his career as first assistant to the operator of the Gaumont newsreels. Later, he worked for directors such as Claude Autant-Lara, Edouard Molinaro, and Gérard Oury. One of his most providential moves was to cast actress Josiane Balasko, who connected him with the increasingly popular café-théâtre actors L'Équipe du Splendid. In the early 1980s, he coauthored *Men Prefer Fat Girls* (*Les hommes préfèrent les grosses,* 1981) with Balasko. Similar to what Patrice Leconte did with *French Fried Vacation,* Poiré adapted the group's latest comedy, *Le Père Noël est une ordure,* inspiring the Hollywood remake directed by Nora Ephron, *Mixed Nuts,* in 1994. *Le Père Noël* immediately became a hit in 1982 and remains to this date one of the most celebrated comedies in France. Since then, Poiré has regularly cast Christian Clavier, Gérard Jugnot, Thierry Lhermitte, and Josiane Balasko in his films. But it was only in the 1990s that Poiré was able to make history at the French box office by successively achieving top box-grossing records: *Opération Corned-Beef* (1991), *The Visitors, The Guardian Angels* (*Les anges gardiens,* 1995), and *The Corridors of Time: The Visitors II.*

Although not quite the social phenomenon of Poiré's comedies, Francis Veber's *The Dinner Game* (*Le dîner de cons,* 1998) was no less a commercial success. Adapted from his own stage comedy, which was directed in 1993 by Pierre Mondy at the Théâtre des Variétés with actors Claude Brasseur and Jacques Villeret, *The Dinner Game* became a huge success at the box office and won Césars for Best Actor (Jacques Villeret),[47] Best Screenplay (Francis Veber), and Best Supporting Actor (Daniel Prévost). Not surprisingly, the rights to *The Dinner Game* have been sold to DreamWorks for the announced American version, entitled *Dinner for Schmucks* (2002) to star Kevin Kline and Steve Martin.

A master of French high-concept comedy, Francis Veber (b. 1937) has always displayed a talent for comic scenarios. He wrote some of the most memorable scripts for stand-up comedian Guy Bedos. Veber can be best characterized as the French filmmaker or artist who has been, like Robert Bresson—although working in a radically different genre—one of the most studied and imitated. Veber was one of the writers of *La cage aux folles* and cowrote the American remake, *The Birdcage*. Although Veber's productions have been consistently disregarded (in terms of critical consensus), Hollywood producers have repeatedly purchased or borrowed his ideas for American remakes. These include films such as *The Man with One Red Shoe* (1985), a remake of *The Tall Blond Man with One Black Shoe (Le grand blond avec une chaussure noire,* 1972); *My Father the Hero* (1994), a remake of *Mon père ce héros* (1988); *The Toy* (1982), a remake of *Le jouet* (1976); *Three Fugitives* (1989), a remake of *Les fugitifs* (1986); and *Father's Day* (1997), a remake of *Les compères* (1983). With eight films remade in Hollywood, Francis Veber has since declared residence in California, where he released his latest production, *The Closet (Le placard,* 2000).

An insightful journey into social-class differences, identity misunderstanding, and arrogance characterize Veber's work. Indeed, for twenty years Veber has relished in associating on screen unlikely and antagonistic main protagonists with divergent personalities—all for comedic purpose. *The Dinner Game* tells the story of Pierre Brochant (Thierry Lhermitte), a successful and arrogant publisher who organizes, with other well-off executive friends, a weekly practical-joke nicknamed *dîner de cons.* The rule is simple enough: the winner is the one who finds, invites, and sponsors the most stunning "idiot" for one evening. The uninformed guests are led to believe that it is their honor to share their hobbies and leisurely pursuits. Brochant makes the acquaintance of François Pignon (Jacques Villeret), a humble financial controller at the Department of Finance, who spends most of his time building models of towers and bridges out of matchsticks (his Eiffel Tower uses exactly 346,422 matches). Brochant believes he has found the perfect "idiot" for the next competition. Deluding Pignon with the idea of publishing a book on his matchstick masterpieces, Brochant manages to invite him to dinner. But shortly after, Brochant hurts his back while playing golf and must cancel the dinner party. Unfortunately, it is too late and the guest is at the door of his lavish Parisian apartment. Pignon, however, insists on staying in order to help Brochant, resulting in a sequence of catastrophic events that leaves Brochant's sheltered existence a wreck. Pignon desperately attempts to astound his new friend, whereas Brochant, appears more and more malicious in his voracious need for amusement at the expense of Pignon. Brochant's wife, Christine (Alexandra Vandernoot), leaves in protest of the cruel sport, announcing her decision for an immediate separation. Devastated at the idea of having sent his wife into the arms of an ex-lover, Brochant is at a loss. To compound his predicament, Pignon offers his services and agrees to play the role of a Belgian film producer in order to find out whether or not Christine is with Brochant's old friend, Just Leblanc (Francis Huster). As the attempt fails miserably, they both find out that she may be with Pascal Meneaux, a notorious Parisian womanizer. Unexpectedly, Christine changes her mind and comes home, only to find Pignon, who sends her away, mistaking her for Marlène (Catherine Frot), Brochant's mistress. When Marlène enters the apartment soon after, Brochant realizes that Pignon has thrown out his own wife. Pignon's primary intuition was to lend a hand in every way he possibly could, but he is seemingly a magnet for every mix-up and injudicious decision. Convinced that his wife is now with the famous advertising tycoon Pascal Meneaux, Brochant is discouraged since he does not know Meneaux's address. With the help of Cheval (Daniel Prévost), Pignon's cynical colleague, who supervises Meneaux's tax audit, they obtain the address. The plot generates even more momentum toward its climax, when a visit to Brochant's by the tax auditor finds all of Brochant's undeclared artwork in a back room. Pignon then learns that Meneaux is not in the company of Christine but rather Cheval's wife. In conclusion, over the course of the night, Pignon essentially devastates Brochant's marriage, inadvertently invites Brochant's mistress over, and discloses his private and undeclared art collection to an overzealous tax inspector. The story, as expected, provides a moral ending, allowing Brochant to learn a lesson about using spitefulness as malicious entertainment.

Reminiscent of the popular comédie de Boulevard dear to Georges Feydeau, this fast-paced comedy of errors contains all the essential elements of the traditional farce: odd-couple relationships, mistaken identities, near collisions of people who should not meet, slapstick physical humor, situational absurdity, and shrewd wordplay. Assembled as a screwball comedy, *The Dinner Game* relies heavily on timing and a continuous intensification of comic momentum. For each problem there corresponds a solution, but Pignon and Brochant are clearly unable to remedy the situation as they create more chaos by the minute. The two protagonists thrive to surpass each other's limitations and eventually find common ground at the conclusion of the story (this may explain why characters like Pignon subconsciously remind viewers of Jerry Lewis, perhaps one of the most beloved American comics among the French). The humor is imaginative and unapologetically idiosyncratic and can be viewed as an antidote to the Gallic predisposition to wry comedies, even with the presence of a nonsentimental ending. Modestly staged in high-sitcom style, this low-budget production reveals Veber's ability for effective stage direction as well as the artistry of the actors themselves. The presence of the one-room apartment setting, the use of the telephone as a comic device, and the dependence on rich and elaborate dialogue are all evident signs of the theatrical genesis of this film. (On stage Jacques Villeret played the comedy more than 900 nights.) In particular, Villeret gives the character of François Pignon a true presence, a bittersweet emotional life, and an understandable desire to be accepted by his new acquaintances rather than making him a two-dimensional object of pity or ridicule.

With the resounding successes of *The Dinner Game* and *The Visitors,* character comedics made a spectacular comeback. The trend continued with Hervé Palud's hit, *An Indian in the City (Un indien dans la ville,* 1994), scoring over eight million spectators and distributed through 43 countries since then. With 5.5 million tickets sold, Josiane Balasko's *French Twist (Gazon maudit,* 1995) was nominated for Best Foreign Film at the 1996 American Academy Awards, and Jean-Marie Poiré's *The Guardian Angels,* with the team of Depardieu and Clavier, remains one of France's most successful productions.

THE NEW FRENCH CINEMA—*LE JEUNE CINÉMA:* MATHIEU KASSOVITZ AND ERIC ZONCA

Mathieu Kassovitz (b. 1967), son of filmmaker Peter Kassovitz, began his movie career as an actor before stepping behind the camera. He can be seen in roles such as the ephemeral apparition in the initial scene of Jean-Pierre Jeunet's *The City of Lost Children,* as the lead in Jacques Audiard's *A Self-made Hero (Un héros très discret,* 1996), in international productions such as Luc Besson's *The Fifth Element (Le cinquième élément,* 1997), his father Peter Kassovitz's *Jakob the Liar (Jakob le menteur,* 1999), and most recently in Jean-Pierre Jeunet's *Amélie.* But it is not so much his acting career as his contributions as a director that have helped to create the new French cinema: *le jeune cinéma.* Of special importance is his film *Hate (La haine,* 1995). His filmography also includes *Café au Lait (Métisse,* 1993), *Assassin(s)* (1997), and *The Crimson Rivers (Les rivières pourpres,* 2000).

Hate managed to carry off its premise and characters with amazing visuals and a self-conscience aesthetic, combining varied camera angles and black-and-white lighting. When *Hate* was first screened in French theaters in 1995, it caused mixed reactions among audiences as a result of its purposefully ambiguous exploration of escalating racial tensions. The story was seen by some as a truly eye-opening account of life in troubled communities outside Paris, and simultaneously was criticized by others as a vicious commercial misuse of the same issue.

In a Parisian *banlieue* (suburb), racial tensions and urban violence explode in reaction to police brutality. Most young people of the surrounding low-income housing projects have sporadic altercations with the police. Unemployed, with no real tangible economic independence, they survive through a routine of petty crimes and drug dealing, and consequently serve time in prison. This becomes a badge of honor while handguns are deemed with the highest regard. As a result, riots and general chaos emerge to protest against the increasingly epidemic poverty. Abdel, a sixteen-year-old teenager, is near death in a hospital after being beaten during a police interrogation. His friends Hubert (Hubert Koundé), an aspiring boxer eager to escape the violence and the *banlieue* he lives in, Saïd (Saïd Taghmaoui), a small-time crook, and Vinz (Vincent Cassel), a rash character who alternates between turbulent temper and an emotionless state, learn that Abdel is in a coma and might not survive. The film is the journey of the three *banlieusards* in Paris during their twenty-four-hour stroll as they heighten hostilities among each other and seek their own justice. Vincent confesses that he has a handgun, a chrome-plated Smith and Wesson .44, that was lost by a police officer during the riot. Each of them feels the thrill of power. During their Parisian spree, they manage to sneak into an art gallery vernissage, from which they are later expelled, winding up in a confrontation with a gang of skinheads before stealing a car. While sitting in front of the Eiffel Tower, the most idealized monument in France, Hubert, more mature than his friends, relates an anecdote he once heard from an old rabbi, about a man who fell off a skyscraper: on the way down, he says to himself, "So far, so good." The line seems to fit the protagonists in the suburb: so far, so good. But how will they land?

Later, Saïd and Hubert are picked up by the police and tortured by an unscrupulous cop, who wants to teach the coercive technique of terrorization to his new partner. Ironically, while the banlieue is an austere battle zone of impending misfortune, a commercial street billboard illustrating Planet Earth says *Le monde est à nous* (The world is ours). During their aimless wandering through early morning Paris, the young men learn that their friend Abdel has died in the hospital. Hubert and Saïd worry that the news will enrage Vinz, although by now it occurs to them that Vinz does not want to kill anyone; he just does not know how to deal with his growing frustration. Returning to the *banlieue,* they are intercepted by a police patrol. During the check, an officer unintentionally kills Vinz. Hubert seizes Vinz's .44 and holds it against the officer. Suddenly, a gunshot is heard.

Hubert Koundé (Hubert), Saïd Taghmaoui (Saïd), and Vincent Cassel (Vinz) in Mathieu Kassovitz's *Hate* (*La haine*, 1995), (Courtesy of BIFI/© Productions Lazennec).

Constructed as a visual time bomb (the gunshot is the very last frame), *Hate* was one of the most eagerly anticipated screenplays at the 1995 Cannes Film Festival. Although focusing on the lives of three youngsters in a twenty-four-hour period, the ultimate implication of this film went beyond the conventional documentary. The rendering of today's generation of aggravated, disenchanted youths shows that violence in itself is a reaction to social powerlessness. Seemingly aimless, their solidarity lent the film both incongruity and poignancy. Presented by Jodie Foster and Egg Pictures Film Company, *Hate* drew an austere visual rendering of the grim reality of French *banlieues*. According to Phil Powrie, Kassovitz's production was "undoubtedly one of the major films of the 1990s by its focus on contemporary issues of youth alienation, and accordingly much attention was lavished on it, extending to government ministers watching it as to understand what might be ailing the disaffected youth of the *banlieues*."[48]

One of Kassovitz's strengths is keeping situations genuine and characters authentic. *Hate* neither glamorized nor trivialized its anxious antiheroes, and although some characters may have appeared more in focus than others, no one is seen as a stereotype or as an uncompromising character, with the exception of the local-police officers. Through the device of intensive characterization, the film brought a sense of impulsive realism. Occasionally, this realism was used for comic relief, as when the three young men instigate a vigorous exchange, which quickly becomes a dispute, at the art gallery, and end up in the street. *Hate* also portrays the protagonists' intensity without dwelling on emotional values, and at the same time underscores their limitation without being condemnatory. This is what made the film thoroughly engaging and compelling. By sharing twenty-four hours in each character's life, and detailing each of their personalities and their relations with one another, the film helps viewers come to realize the process through which the unfortunate protagonists arrive at their final predicament and become caught up in the passion of the inferno that mercilessly surrounds them.

Hate belongs to the category of films in which script and direction are so on-target that it appears difficult to evaluate the real quality of the actors (although Vincent Cassel already had extensive acting and directing credits in France).[49] Besides the evident acting talent of most of its nonprofessional actors, the good reception of the movie essentially relied on its simplicity: *Hate* consists of a series of events, not quite a homogeneous plot. Kassovitz approached his canvas in an Expressionist manner, as the film includes many characters and several narratives told simultaneously. However, the major strength of the opening narration helps draw audiences quickly into the story. This alone revealed Kassovitz's creative abilities, since he did not concentrate so much on the narration and plot as he did on character development and atmosphere. The result is an insightful, thematic film, even if the themes are ostentatiously involved. The film benefits from a sound script and direction, which capture the look, feel, and gritty language of the *banlieue* with real compassion.

Hate is also an introverted inquiry of the different lines of social power. What appears fundamental is the awareness that the three youths, representative of most French suburban areas, emerge at times alienated from one another, not so much by ethnic background and religious identity but by a simpler separation of those who have power and those who do not. When Vinz gets hold of the gun, he too is convinced that he can shift the balance of power. Vincent Cassel captures the hostile feelings teens have for adults and society, their street smarts, and code of honor among friends. The account is a riveting and intense denunciation of urban predicaments and police brutality, seen through the perceptive sensibilities of youngsters who are inclined to violence. In this Parisian suburb, racial bigotry, although never openly realized on the screen, is omnipresent but subtly so, and while the impression of racial anxiety and despondency pervades each and every shot of the Parisian journey, the representation of the heroes' spiritual psyche (hate, opportunism, and nonviolent conciliation), help the viewer to sympathize with the impending tragedy of the heroes.

By 1995, Kassovitz was already a director of promising talent. His expert camera work, character-driven story lines, and incisive dialogue in *Hate* and *Café au Lait* recalled the best films of Spike Lee and Quentin Tarantino. In addition to Scott Stevenson's editing (mostly jump cuts, "argumentative" intertitles to lead the audience, and prompt zooms), the omnipresent montage faithfully renders the boiling passion that grip Vinz, Hubert, and Saïd. Each frame is seemingly filled with implications of which the characters are not aware. The film constantly moves in the rhythm of real time. Cinematographer Pierre Aim's camera jumped and tracked down its leading characters, but never really called attention to its own technical feats of skill. The remarkable illusory-visual minimalism, a series of deceiving kinetic exploits, marked the emergence of Kassovitz's new style. He used a handheld camera and indulged in a certain—perhaps fashionable—stylistic looseness that corresponded to a tragic, deterministic narrative. The black-and-white cinematography of *Hate* suggests cinéma-vérité, and captures the raw energy of the streets by using real locations along with hyper realistic dialogue (the latest French urban slang). Interpreting the linguistically "insubordinate" dialogue was undoubtedly a rather difficult undertaking for English subtitles' authors Alexander Whitelaw and Stephen O'Shea. Their translation, however, successfully made the most of American rap lyrics in order to bring a certain level of comprehension to US audiences. Kassovitz made excellent use of music (Iam, FFF, McSolaar) to create tension and to echo the action. As a result, the art direction turned out to be a vivid, dynamic work that truly crossed the boundary between entertainment and art. This aspect of new French cinema clearly motivated the choice of the 1995 Cannes Film Festival Jury for Kassovitz's directing debut: the prize for Best Director at the 1995 Cannes Film Festival as well as the 1996 Césars for Best Film and Best Editing (Scott Stevenson).

For new and emerging French directors, such as Kassovitz, Eric Zonca, Cédric Klapish, Olivier Assayas, and Dominik Moll, a new type of film directing had to fashion heroes whose lives heavily relied on a mundane, almost monotonous type of happiness. One of the best examples of these successful filmmakers is Eric Zonca. Born in Orléans in 1956, Zonca came to Paris to study acting when he was only sixteen, and at the age of twenty he moved to New York City to pursue a new chapter in his apprenticeships in dance, theater, and documentary filmmaking. After working odd jobs on both sides of the

Atlantic for many years, he returned to France, and it was only at age thirty that Zonca entered the film industry where he secured an apprenticeship. He became an assistant, then a director of TV commercials and television documentaries, and later made three shorts (*Rives,* 1992; *Eternelles,* 1994; and *Seule,* 1997). For the producers as well as the film critics, the result was unambiguous. For each short, Zonca displayed maturity in his delicate and desperate studies of the human condition.

Zonca has clearly established himself as one of the most significant and farsighted new filmmakers in French cinema. In competition at the 1998 Cannes Film Festival, Zonca's first full-length feature, *The Dreamlife of Angels* (*La vie rêvée des anges,* 1998), earned the prize for Best Actress (Elodie Bouchez and Natacha Régnier). In 1999, it went on to win Césars for Best Film and Best Actress (Elodie Bouchez), as well as the César for Most Promising Young Actress (Natacha Régnier). Bouchez and Régnier repeated their Cannes success at the European Film Awards. In 1999, Zonca released a second feature, *The Little Thief* (*Le petit voleur*), which premiered at the 1999 Cannes Festival. His latest contribution was the script for Virginie Wagon's *The Secret* (*Le secret,* 2000).

In the opening scene of *The Dreamlife of Angels,* which recalls Agnès Varda's heroine Mona in *Vagabond* (*Sans toit ni loi,* 1985), twenty-year-old Isabelle Tostin (Elodie Bouchez)[50] arrives in Lille in the middle of winter with a backpack and bedroll, expecting to stay with a friend. But since her male friend has long moved on, in order to survive she must sell handmade cards on the street and in the bars of the city. The next day, she finds a job as a seamstress in a sweatshop. There she meets Marie Thomas (Natacha Régnier), a hard-edged woman constantly caught between a lack of affection and a fearsome revolt against life. Since Isabelle does not have a home, Marie temporarily invites her to share her apartment. (She actually stays in the apartment while the owner and her daughter, Sandrine, gravely injured in an auto accident, are in a coma at the hospital.) Isabelle moves in with her, and stays on even after she is fired for inefficiency and for her tempestuous free spirit. Shortly after, Marie quits. Due to their mutual solitude, their friendship takes on a new dimension, as both their lives are thrown together by difficult circumstances, and the two kindred spirits rapidly become inseparable. They wander at night, provoking random men in a mall as well as two leather-jacketed bouncers at a local nightclub, Fredo (Jo Prestia) and Charly (Patrick Mercado). Warm and good-natured beneath their brusque exteriors, the two men later become attracted to the girls. Generally at odds with those around her, Marie somehow becomes attached to them and begins dating physically

Elodie Bouchez (Isabelle) and Natacha Régnier (Marie) in Eric Zonca's *The Dreamlife of Angels* (*La vie rêvée des anges*, 1998), (Courtesy of BIFI/© Productions Bagheera).

unattractive but affectionate Charly. Marie is apprehended in a depart-ment store while attempting to steal a leather jacket, but Chriss (Grégoire Colin), the son of a wealthy nightclub owner, spontaneously rescues her from the police, volunteering to pay for the jacket. In-stantly hostile to the untrustworthy individual, her emotional barriers fall. She pretends for a while not to attach any great significance to his generosity, but decides to see him again. Chriss takes her to the hotel owned by his father, and an intimate relation, although tempestuous at times, begins. Immediately in love with Chriss, although aware that he has other girlfriends as well, Marie loses touch with reality and deludes herself into believing that she and Chriss can make a life together. But the differences that make their friendship also threaten its fragile balance. In the meantime, the waitressing-job prospect that Marie and Isabelle both expected turns out to be only sandwich-board-jobs distributing flyers in the street on roller skates. Only Isabelle accepts the humiliation, while Marie grows bitter. One day, Chriss stops by the apartment to inform Isabelle that he no longer wishes to see Marie and asks her to transmit the news. Isabelle must now face a difficult challenge: letting her best friend know about the illusion of her relationship without hurting her feelings and jeopardizing their friendship. Her rapport with Marie soon begins to unravel. Meanwhile, Marie enters a self-destructive phase; she no longer displays intervals of lucidity. She becomes increasingly withdrawn and emotionally secluded. She does not understand Isabelle's lifestyle, in particular, the hours she spends at the hospital keeping company with Sandrine while holding her hand to assist the young girl, who apparently has no other visitors. Isabelle, knowing how devastating the news will be, tells Marie of Chriss's decision. Marie, in despair, commits suicide. Back to her initial life of solitude, Isabelle goes to another factory to assemble electronic components.

With *The Dreamlife of Angels,* the "great plot versus great character" debate seems irrelevant. The characters are in service to style, and the result is a movie adhering to the classic rules of storytelling. Zonca's minimalist script direction never interferes with the performance of the actors, who work with a great deal of self-abandonment. The narrative develops around two young working/idle women of contrasting temperament: Isabelle, with her animated face that reveals her youthful optimism and survival instincts (even though all her possessions fit into a backpack) conveys a childlike sense of discovery, while the unenthusiastic and rebellious Marie, always reluctant to show affection, indirectly persuades the viewer that Isabelle would be enthralled with someone as introverted as she is outspoken. Although some argue that Zonca clearly displayed more interest in the character of Isabelle (due to more screen time), and consequently utilized Marie literally as a "supporting" function to prop up the film's dramatic dimension, the real quality of the movie must be found in its treatment of relationships (especially the ill-fated friendship between these two women). While shooting the film, Zonca neither moderated his approach nor mainstreamed his visually striking vision, as he explained the method (or more precisely, the absence of method) for his inspiration:

> It is from these two encounters, from these two feminine characters, that I built my story. It took me two years to write it and to develop it from the initial four-hour project to what the film actually is today. My approach to the text is mainly a visual one. The starting point of my scenarios is always my imagination. Any didactic approach does not suit me. I do not start from a theme or a theoretical point of view; rather, I let myself be guided by my only imaginative inspiration. The introduction of the significance and coherence is a device that occurs after a intuitive phase randomly initiated.[51]

This sincere assertion shows the director's inclination toward straightforward communication of motions and confirms that the final version of Zonca's scenario surfaced in post-production. The well-defined main characters are shaped and highlighted by Zonca's lucid and economical screenplay. As for the dialogue (written by Zonca and Roger Bohbot), it is reminiscent of the outspokenness of Eric Rohmer's scripts. Although most of the characters' discourses take up little screen time, they are complex enough to maintain a true sense of realism. With its courageous plot, ultimately about the power of friendship and the disastrous consequences of unwanted solitude, the film tells a tragic tale with great attention and compassion. Seemingly photographed with minimal technique by accomplished veteran cinematographer Agnès Godard, the deceptively casual rhythms of the film—each scene reaching the perfect balance between a controlled and naturalistic outcome—won over the audiences at Cannes. Godard's unassuming camera work involved frequent close-ups, natural light set-ups, and the aforementioned cinema-verité techniques to impart a genuine organic feel to the film. Additionally, the cinematography, efficiently done with super-16 cameras, allowed for more visual agility in the pseudodocumentary format; the grainy film stock added convincing realism to the actors' performances. The photography accompanied the performances with austere, washed-out pastel hues, adding a dour atmosphere to the narrative but ultimately offering "cheerful" blues to counterbalance the bleak world of saturated whites. Although highly sophisticated characterization remained the strong element of the narrative, the atmosphere, authenticated by the score of Yann Thiersen, was equally eloquent in Zonca's cinematography.

One of the challenges for the new French cinema is to combine authentic ideas and feelings without failing to pursue ideas artistically to their end. *The Dreamlife of Angels* offers glimpses of a story that exists in the imagination as well as in daily life, and it is not necessarily dependent on the established realism it means to promote. Yet Zonca refuses to emotionalize his characters beyond what is necessary, taking the narrative to an unusual level of truthfulness and consequently realism. Whereas many detractors could indeed argue that the film is merely about the dreams and illusions of young working-class women and about their emotional struggle when a man comes between them, the intensity of the film's aestheticism proves just the opposite. In fact, the picaresque elements that displace the psychological interpretation of the characters give the story a highly realistic image and display a true ability (at least for a male) to enter the female psyche. Zonca presents a uniquely touching rapport that essentially modifies both women's awareness of existence, as Marie and Isabelle are both imagining a better life for themselves, making this psychological drama the kind of film that the French have always thrived in making. The utter sense of realism is often heartbreaking to witness as Marie, affected by her uncommunicative mind-set and unsentimental spirit, quickly spirals into a violent emotional descent. Moreover, despite the same film critics' disapproval—in particular, that the character study takes a premature and unnecessarily melodramatic turn—the dynamic between the two central characters remains the key component of the film's success among French audiences. The movie is about the permanence and the disruption of a friendship. Zonca's zealous passion for the splendor of the quotidian is reminiscent of *The Four Hundred Blows* in the way that it represents two people spellbound by the burdens of reality as they live (though temporarily) amorally, stealing what and where they can as well as the prewar poetic-realism concept with its stream of the "Popular Front" picturing the tragic destiny of heroic loners.[52]

The title casts a reservation on the actual ending of the film (who is dreaming, and who are the angels?), and the viewer is left to wonder if the title of the film should be understood as "Life Dreamed by Angels." Indeed, the heroines' dreams never come into focus: there is no dream life, and there are no angels in the narrative. *The Dreamlife of Angels* leaves an aftertaste of irony since not only is the narrative about veracity and realism, but both girls appear to be unsophisticated. Irritated by the idea that Isabelle constantly fantasizes about a better life away from poverty, Marie says to her: "You're torturing yourself, and you dream a lot." However, the only moment that the characters' dreams come into view in a rather concrete manner is when Isabelle, in return, writes a farewell note to her friend: "I wish you the life you want, the one you're dreaming of, each day, each second." The note will never be read in time, and Marie's chaotic obsession is never fully explained. Viewers who address the issue of Isabelle's plight without having the opportunity to verify the filmmaker's intent will of course be quite limited in their appreciation.

With just three full-length feature films to his credit, Zonca appears to possess one of the most compelling visions of contemporary social discourse. His narrative about life is practically isolated in reflecting a sense of discomfort in today's society. Since his works display the outward signs of visual invention and an evident revelation of the inner investigation of the meaning of film language as sign, Eric Zonca will most likely be one of the historic icons of the present century, as his films will have an effect on other filmmakers, both mainstream and avant-garde.

THE DIGITAL REVOLUTION AND THE HIGH-DEFINITION SYSTEM: PITOF

The high-definition digital system made its shooting debut in France in May 2000, with *Vidocq,* the first 100-percent digitalized film (before

George Lucas's second episode of *Star Wars*).[53] *Vidocq* was the first feature film of Jean-Christophe Comar, also known as Pitof (*City of Lost Children, Alien IV*). This thriller takes place in 1830 Paris and narrates the story of Vidocq (Gérard Depardieu), a legendary Parisian detective, who disappears while fighting against the Alchemist, a ruthless serial killer responsible for several crimes in the capital. On the brink of death, Vidocq asks the murderer one last favor, which is to reveal his identity by removing his mask. Following his death, a young journalist, Etienne Boisset (Guillaume Canet), who swears to avenge Vidocq, tries to solve the mystery surrounding his murder. The most insane rumors begin to spread all over Paris, asserting that the killer, a man without a face, could very well be the reflection of the soul of more than one hundred faces.

The digital camera used in the film is the Sony HDF-F900, which unequivocally is meant to replace the traditional 35mm cameras, although it is no longer incompatible with the older format. Before the advent of digital cinema, due to the overpowering heaviness of the 35mm camera, the complexity of operating it, and the necessary technical support, filmmakers had to overcome countless obstacles to realize their projects. Soon enough, digital cameras will be light enough to capture images from the comfort of the filmmaker's hand and at the complete disposal of the artist, in part due to the separation of the monitor and the lens, which allows greater manipulation and motion freedom. Fifty years after the invention of the concept of the *caméra stylo,* a second revolution in cinema has arrived (in other words, the reinvention of the "camera-pen"). Although problems with funding and distribution will still be part of the production process, it is clear that filmmakers will gain considerable initiative in their choices, control, and especially artistic vision, virtually as if they were to hold their own pen in the palm of their hand. In short, this means no more celluloid film stocks, but instead high-resolution video.

As a universal format (two million pixels), the new system is compatible with television and film, and stands as a major step forward for the international-film industry as well as for the world of science. Broadcast and television companies are collaborating on a time-saving, cost-efficient high-definition film process that offers filmmakers daily video viewing and optical transitions inserted for preview screenings in high definition. The history of the development of cinematographic techniques, as in television, is really viewed as a quest for greater realism. With the progress in image quality and sophistication of techniques, general audiences have become more aware and educated, and consequently more passionate and demanding in terms of visual and sound requirements (e.g., colorization of old black-and-white films, and the commercial success of the DVD system and home

Gérard Depardieu (Vidocq) and Ines Sastre (Preah) in Pitof's *Vidocq* (2001), (Courtesy of RF2K Productions).

theaters). The pace of high-definition technology is accelerating each year, and by 2005, it is expected that more than 10 percent of homes in France and 20 percent of all European homes will subscribe to digital services.

This high-definition system reduces costs, saves time, and provides a result that gives filmmakers an equivalent if not better rendering (mainly through superior preview screenings) than film; and in particular, it provides the ability to recognize defects and shooting predicaments immediately. One significant advantage of the new system is that the cinematographer and the director can view takes at the shooting location itself, and consequently avoid waiting for rushes (formerly, monitors could help the director in the framing of the takes, but could not reveal the quality of the photography). The new system allows technicians to remaster a film digitally, store it in a computer, then screen it via a digital projector. Virtual montage also allows editors to manipulate—through disc recording and computer memory—images, special effects, lighting, sound track, and sequencing at will. Consequently, the movie is scored via the desired sequencing of scene, which presents a major advantage: a reduction of time in the editing room and cost for post-production. In addition, several versions of a film can

Opposite: Pitof's *Vidocq* (*Vidocq*, 2001). Sequence 32 representing a view of nineteenth-century Paris with first a sketch from Jérôme Fournier (Matte painter) then its corresponding view in 3D and lastly the final version in digital video, (Courtesy of RF2K Productions).

be shaped without having to recut the entire film stock and remix the sound from the start. The fast-developing systems of production using digitally processed images have already significantly reduced post-production costs, and consequently are meant to allow "non-producing" markets to build self-sufficient production structures customized to their own cultural regulations.

Abbreviations

ACE	Alliance Cinématographique Européenne
ACI	Alliance du Cinéma Indépendant
AEAR	Association des Ecrivains et Artistes Révolutionnaires
BIFI	Bibliothèque du Film
CFDT	Confédération Française Démocratique du Travail
CGT	Confédération Générale du Travail
CLCF	Comité de Libération du Cinéma Français
CNC	Centre National de la Cinématographie
CNR	Conseil National de la Résistance
COIC	Comité de l'Organisation de l'Industrie Cinématographique
CSA	Conseil Supérieur de l'Audiovisuel
EEC	European Economic Community
FEMIS	Ecole Nationale Supérieure des Métiers de l'Image et du Son
FLN	Front de Libération Nationale
GATT	General Agreement on Tariffs and Trade
GFFA	Gaumont-Franco-Film-Aubert
IDHEC	Institut des Hautes Etudes Cinématographiques
MGM	Metro-Goldwyn-Mayer
MLF	Mouvement de Libération de la Femme
MOMA	Museum of Modern Art
ORTF	Office Radio Télévision Française
PCF	Parti Communiste Français
RKO	Radio-Keith-Orpheum Corporation
RPR	Rassemblement Pour la République

SCAGL	Société Cinématographique des Auteurs et des Gens de Lettres
SEG	Société des Etablissements Gaumont
SFP	Société Française de Production
SMIC	Salaire Minimum Interprofessional de Croissance
SNEG	Société Nouvelle des Etablissements Gaumont
SOFICA	Sociétés de Financement des Industries Cinématographiques et Audiovisuelles
SOGEC	Société de Gestion et d'Exploitation du Cinéma
SRF	Société des Réalisateurs de Film
STO	Service du Travail Obligatoire
TNP	Théâtre National Populaire
UDF	Union pour la Démocratie Française
UFA	Universum Film A.G.
UGC	Union Générale Cinématographique
WTO	World Trade Organization

Appendix
Awards and Box Office

AWARDS FOR FRENCH CINEMA AT THE CANNES FILM FESTIVAL

1946
Grand prix for Jean Delannoy's *La symphonie pastorale* (ex-aequo)

Special Jury Prize for René Clément's *Battle of the Rails* (*La bataille du rail*)

Best Director, René Clément for *Battle of the Rails* (*La bataille du rail*)

Best Actress, Michèle Morgan for Jean Delannoy's *La symphonie pastorale*

Best Music for Georges Auric for Jean Delannoy's *La symphonie pastorale*

1947
Grand prix for Jacques Becker's *Antoine and Antoinette* (*Antoine et Antoinette*)

Grand prix for René Clément's *The Damned* (*Les maudits*)

1949
Best Director, René Clément for *The Walls of Malapaga* (*Au-delà des grilles*)

Best Set Design for Claude Autant-Lara's *Look After Amelie* (*Occupe-toi d'Amélie*)

1951
Best Music, Joseph Kosma for Marcel Carné's *Juliette or Key of Dreams* (*Juliette ou la clé des songes*)

1952
Special Jury Prize for André Cayatte's *We Are All Murderers* (*Nous sommes tous des assassins*)

Best Director, Christian-Jaque for *Fan-Fan the Tulip* (*Fanfan-la-Tulipe*)

1953

Grand prix du festival international du film for Henri-Georges Clouzot's *Wages of Fear* (*Le salaire de la peur*)

Best Actor, Charles Vanel for *Wages of Fear* (*Le salaire de la peur*)

1954

Best Director, René Clément for *Monsieur Ripoix*

Prix internationaux (International Recognition Award) for André Cayatte's *Before the Deluge* (*Avant le déluge*)

1955

Best Director, Jules Dassin for *Rififi* (*Du rififi chez les hommes*) and Serge Vassiliev for *Le héros de Chipka* (Bulgaria)

1956

Palme d'or–Golden Palm for Jacques-Yves Cousteau's *The Silent World* (*Le monde du silence*)

Special Jury Prize for Henri-Georges Clouzot's *The Mystery of Picasso* (*Le mystère Picasso*)

1957

Best Director, Robert Bresson for *A Man Escaped* (*Un condamné à mort s'est échappé*)

1958

Special Jury Prize for Jacques Tati's *My Uncle* (*Mon oncle*)

1959

Golden Palm–Palme d'or for Marcel Camus's *Black Orpheus* (*Orfeu Negro*)

Best Director, François Truffaut for *The Four Hundred Blows* (*Les quatre cents coups*)

Best Actress, Simone Signoret for Jack Clayton's *Room at the Top*

1960

Best Actress, Jeanne Moreau for Peter Brook's *Moderato Cantabile* and Melina Mercouri for Jules Dassin's *Jamais le dimanche* (Greece)

1961

Golden Palm–Palme d'or for Henri Colpi's *Such a Long Absence* (*Une aussi longue absence*) and Luis Buñuel's *Viridiana* (Spain)

1962

Special Jury Prize for Robert Bresson's *The Trial of Joan of Arc* (*Le procès de Jeanne d'Arc*) and Michelangelo Antonioni's *The Eclipse* (Italy)

1963

Best Actress, Marina Vlady for Marco Ferreri's (*Una storia moderna: l'ape regina*)

1964
Golden Palm for Jacques Demy's *The Umbrellas of Cherbourg* (*Les parapluies de Cherbourg*)

1965
Best Screenplay, Pierre Schoendoerffer's *317th Platoon* (*La 317e Section*)

1966
Golden Palm for Claude Lelouch's *A Man and a Woman* (*Un homme et une femme*) and Pietro Germi's *The Birds, the Bees and the Italians* (Italy)

1967
Best Screenplay, Alain Jessua's *The Killing Game* (*Jeu de massacre*) and Elio Petri's *We Still Kill the Old Way* (Italy)
Special Jury Prize for Robert Bresson's *Mouchette*

1969
Best Actor, Jean-Louis Trintignant in Costa-Gavras's *Z* (Z)
Jury Prize for Costa-Gavras's *Z* (Z)

1970
Prize for First Feature Film for Raoul Coutard's *Hoa-Binh*

1972
Best Actor, Jean Yanne for Maurice Pialat's *We Will Not Grow Old Together* (*Nous ne vieillirons pas ensemble*)

1973
Special Jury Prize for Jean Eustache's *The Mother and the Whore* (*La maman et la putain*)
Special Prize for René Laloux's *The Fantastic Planet* (*La planète sauvage*)

1974
Best Actress, Marie-José Nat in Michel Drach's *Violins at the Ball* (*Les violons du bal*)

1975
Best Director, Costa-Gavras for *Special Section* (*Section spéciale*) and Michel Brault for *Les ordres* (Canada)

1976
Best Actress, Dominique Sanda for Mauro Bolognini's *L'eredità Ferramonti*
Special Jury Prize for Eric Rohmer's *The Marquise of O* (*La marquise d'O*)

1977
Best Actress, Monique Mercure for Jean Beaudin's *J. A. Martin, Photographer* (*J. A. Martin Photographe*)

1978
Best Actress, Isabelle Huppert in Claude Chabrol's *Violette Nozière* and
   Jill Clayburgh in Paul Mazursky's *An Unmarried Woman* (USA)

1979
Prix du jeune cinéma for Jacques Doillon's *The Hussy (La drôlesse)*

1980
Best Actress, Anouk Aimée for Marco Bellocchio's *Le saut dans le vide*
Special Jury Prize for Alain Resnais's *Mon oncle d'Amérique*
Best Actor, Michel Piccoli for Marco Bellocchio's *Le saut dans le vide*
Grand Prix de la Commission supérieure Technique Gérard Calde-
   ron's *The Risk of Living* (*Le risque de vivre*)
Special Golden Camera Prize for Jean-Pierre Denis's *Histoire d'Adrien*

1981
Special Jury Prize for Alain Tanner's *Light Years Away* (*Les années
   lumière*), (Switzerland–France)
Best Actress, Isabelle Adjani for James Ivory's *Quartet* (Great Britain)
   and Andrzej Zulawski's *Possession* (Germany–France)
Prize for Contemporary Cinema for Juliet Berto and Jean-Henri
   Roger's *Snow* (*Neige*)
Grand Prix de la Commission supérieure technique for Claude Lel-
   ouch's *Bolero* (*Les uns et les autres*)

1982
Best Cinematography for Bruno Nuytten in Peter Del Monte's *Invita-
   tion au voyage*
Grand Prix de la Commission supérieure technique for Raoul Coutard
   in Jean-Luc Godard's *Passion* (France-Switzerland)
Special Golden Camera Prize for Romain Goupil's *Mourir à 30 ans*

1983
Best Director, Robert Bresson *Money* (*L'argent*), and Andrei Tarkov-
   sky's *Nostalghia* (Italy)

1984
Best Director, Bertrand Tavernier for *A Sunday in the Country* (*Un
   dimanche à la campagne*)

1985
Best Director, André Téchiné for *Rendez-vous*

1986
Best Actor, Michel Blanc in Bertrand Blier's *Ménage* (*Tenue de soirée*),
   and Bob Hoskins for Neil Jordan's *Mona Lisa* (Great Britain)
Jury Prize for Alain Cavalier's *Thérèse*

1987
Golden Palm, Maurice Pialat's *Under the Sun of Satan* (*Sous le soleil de Satan*)

1988
Special Golden Camera Prize for Mira Nair's *Salaam Bombay*

1989
Special Jury Prize for Bertrand Blier's *Too Beautiful for You* (*Trop belle pour toi*), and Giuseppe Tornatore's *Cinema Paradiso* (Italy-France)

1990
Best Actor, Gérard Depardieu in Jean-Paul Rappeneau's *Cyrano de Bergerac* (*Cyrano de Bergerac*)
Best Photography for Pierre Lhomme in *Cyrano de Bergerac* (*Cyrano de Bergerac*)

1991
Special Jury Prize for Jacques Rivette's *The Beautiful Troublemaker* (*La belle noiseuse*)
Jury Prize for Maroun Bagdadi's for *Hors la vie*
Best Actress, Irène Jacob for Krzysztof Kieslowski's *La double vie de Véronique*

1993
Grand Prix de la Commission supérieure technique for Bartabas's *Mazeppa*

1994
Best Actress, Virna Lisi for Patrice Chéreau's *Queen Margot* (*La reine Margot*)
Jury Prize for Patrice Chéreau's *Queen Margot* (*La reine Margot*)
Grand Prix de la Commission supérieure technique for Michel Blanc's *Dead Tired* (*Grosse fatigue*)
Special Golden Camera Prize for Pascale Ferran's *Petits arrangements avec les morts*
Best Screenplay for Michel Blanc's *Dead Tired* (*Grosse fatigue*)

1995
Jury Prize for Xavier Beauvois's *Don't Forget You're Going to Die* (*N'oublie pas que tu vas mourir*)
Best Director, Mathieu Kassovitz for *Hate* (*La haine*)

1996
Best Actor, Daniel Auteuil and Pascal Duquenne in Jaco van Dormael's *The Eighth Day* (*Le huitième jour*)

Best Screenplay for Jacques Audiard's *A Self-Made Hero* (*Un héros très discret*)

1997
Jury Prize for Manuel Poirier's *Western*
Special Golden Camera Prize for Bruno Dumont's *Life of Jesus* (*La vie de Jésus*)

1998
Best Actress, Elodie Bouchez and Natacha Régnier for Eric Zonca's *The Dreamlife of Angels* (*La vie rêvée des anges*)
Jury Prize for Claude Miller's *The Class Trip* (*La classe de neige*) and Thomas Vinterberg's *Celebration* (Denmark)

1999
Grand Prize for Bruno Dumont's *Humanity* (*L'humanité*)
Best Actor, Emmanuel Schotte for Bruno Dumont's *Humanity* (*L'humanité*)
Best Actress, Severine Caneele for Bruno Dumont's *Humanity* (*L'humanité*) and Emilie Dequenne, *Rosetta* (Belgium)

2001
Grand Prize for Michael Haneke's *The Piano Teacher* (*La pianiste*)
Best Actor, Benoît Magimel for Michael Haneke's *The Piano Teacher*
Best Actress, Isabelle Huppert for Michael Haneke's *The Piano Teacher*

2002
Golden Camera Prize for Julie Lopes-Curval's *Bord de mer*

The César Awards

BEST FILM

1976   Robert Enrico's *The Old Gun* (*Le vieux fusil*)

1977   Joseph Losey's *Mr. Klein* (*Monsieur Klein*)

1978   Alain Resnais's *Providence*

1979   Christian de Chalonge's *Other People's Money* (*L'argent des autres*)

1980   Roman Polanski's *Tess* (*Tess*)

1981   François Truffaut's *The Last Metro* (*Le dernier métro*)

1982   Jean-Jacques Annaud's *Quest for Fire* (*La guerre du feu*)

1983   Bob Swaim's *The Nark* (*La balance*)

1984   Ettore Scola's *The Ball* (*Le bal*), ex aequo with Maurice Pialat's *To Our Loves* (*A nos amours*)

1985   Claude Zidi's *My New Partner* (*Les ripoux*)

1986   Coline Serreau's *Three Men and a Cradle* (*Trois hommes et un couffin*)

1987   Alain Cavalier's *Thérèse*

1988   Louis Malle's *Au Revoir, Les Enfants* (*Au revoir, les enfants*)

1989   Bruno Nuytten's *Camille Claudel* (*Camille Claudel*)

1990   Bertrand Blier's *Too Beautiful for You* (*Trop belle pour toi*)

1991   Jean-Paul Rappeneau's *Cyrano de Bergerac* (*Cyrano de Bergerac*)

1992   Alain Corneau's *All the Mornings of the World* (*Tous les matins du monde*)

1993   Cyril Collard's *Savage Nights* (*Les nuits fauves*)

1994   Alain Resnais's *Smoking/no smoking*

1995   André Téchiné's *Wild Reeds* (*Les roseaux sauvages*)

1996   Mathieu Kassovitz's *Hate* (*La haine*)

1997   Patrice Leconte's *Ridicule* (*Ridicule*)

1998   Alain Resnais's *Same Old Song* (*On connaît la chanson*)

1999   Eric Zonca's *The Dreamlife of Angels* (*La vie rêvée des anges*)

2000   Tonie Marshall's *Venus Beauty Institute* (*Vénus beauté*)

2001   Agnès Jaoui's *The Taste of Others* (*Le goût des autres*)

2002   Jean-Pierre Jeunet's *Amélie* (*Le fabuleux destin d'Amélie Poulain*)

BEST DIRECTOR

1976   Bertrand Tavernier for *Let Joy Reign Supreme* (*Que la fête commence*)

1977   Joseph Losey for *Mr. Klein* (*Monsieur Klein*)

1978   Alain Resnais for *Providence*

1979   Christian de Chalonge for *Other People's Money* (*L'argent des autres*)

1980   Roman Polanski for *Tess* (*Tess*)

1981   François Truffaut for *The Last Metro* (*Le dernier métro*)

1982   Jean-Jacques Annaud for *The Quest for Fire* (*La guerre du feu*)

1983   Andrzej Wajda for *Danton*

1984   Ettore Scola for *The Ball* (*Le bal*)

1985   Claude Zidi for *My New Partner* (*Les ripoux*)

1986   Michel Deville for *Peril* (*Péril en la demeure*)

1987   Alain Cavalier for *Thérèse*

1988   Louis Malle for *Au Revoir, Les Enfants* (*Au revoir, les enfants*)

1989   Jean-Jacques Annaud for *The Bear* (*L'ours*)

1990   Bertrand Blier for *Too Beautiful for You* (*Trop belle pour toi*)

1991   Jean-Paul Rappeneau for *Cyrano de Bergerac* (*Cyrano de Bergerac*)

1992   Alain Corneau for *All the Mornings of the World* (*Tous les matins du monde*)

1993   Claude Sautet for *A Heart in Winter* (*Un coeur en hiver*)

1994   Alain Resnais for *Smoking/no Smoking*

1995   André Téchiné for *Wild Reeds* (*Les roseaux sauvages*)

1996   Claude Sautet for *Nelly and Mr. Arnaud* (*Nelly et M. Arnaud*)

1997   Bertrand Tavernier for *Captain Conan* (*Capitaine Conan*) and Patrice Leconte's *Ridicule* (*Ridicule*)

1998   Luc Besson for *The Fifth Element* (*Le cinquième élément*)

1999   Patrice Chéreau for *Those Who Love Me Can Take the Train* (*Ceux qui m'aiment prendront le train*)

2000 Tonie Marshall for *Venus Beauty Institute* (*Vénus beauté*)

2001 Dominik Moll for *With a Friend Like Harry* (*Harry, un ami qui vous veut du bien*)

2002 Jean-Pierre Jeunet's *Amélie* (*Le fabuleux destin d'Amélie Poulain*)

BEST ACTRESS

1976 Romy Schneider for Andrzej Zulawski's *The Main Thing Is to Love* (*L'important c'est d'aimer*)

1977 Annie Girardot for Jean-Louis Bertucelli's *No Time for Breakfast* (*Docteur Françoise Gailland*)

1978 Simone Signoret for Moshe Mizrahi's *Madame Rosa* (*La vie devant soi*)

1979 Romy Schneider for Claude Sautet's *A Simple Story* (*Une histoire simple*)

1980 Miou-Miou for Daniel Duval's *La dérobade*

1981 Catherine Deneuve for François Truffaut's *The Last Metro* (*Le dernier métro*)

1982 Isabelle Adjani for Andrzej Zulawski's *Possession*

1983 Nathalie Baye for Bob Swain's *The Nark* (*La balance*)

1984 Isabelle Adjani for Jean Becker's *One Deadly Summer* (*L'été meurtrier*)

1985 Sabine Azéma for Bertrand Tavernier's *A Sunday in the Country* (*Un dimanche à la campagne*)

1986 Sandrine Bonnaire for Agnès Varda's *Vagabond* (*Sans toit ni loi*)

1987 Sabine Azéma for Alain Resnais's *Mélo*

1988 Anémone for Jean-Loup Hubert's *The Grand Highway* (*Le grand chemin*)

1989 Isabelle Adjani for Bruno Nuytten's *Camille Claudel* (*Camille Claudel*)

1990 Carole Bouquet for Bertrand Blier's *Too Beautiful for You* (*Trop belle pour toi*)

1991 Anne Parillaud for Luc Besson's *La Femme Nikita* (*Nikita*)

1992 Jeanne Moreau for Laurent Heynemann's *The Old Lady Who Walked in the Sea* (*La vieille qui marchait dans la mer*)

1993 Catherine Deneuve for Régis Wargnier's *Indochine* (*Indochine*)

1994 Juliette Binoche for Krzysztof Kieslowski's *Blue* (*Trois Couleurs: Bleu*)

1995   Isabelle Adjani for Patrice Chéreau's *Queen Margot* (*La reine Margot*)

1996   Isabelle Huppert for Claude Chabrol's *The Ceremony* (*La cérémonie*)

1997   Fanny Ardant for Gabriel Aghion's *What a Drag* (*Pédale douce*)

1998   Ariane Ascaride for Robert Guédiguian's *Marius and Jeannette* (*Marius et Jeannette*)

1999   Elodie Bouchez for Eric Zonca's *The Dreamlife of Angels* (*La vie rêvée des anges*)

2000   Karin Viard for Solveig Anspach's *Chin Up!* (*Haut les coeurs!*)

2001   Dominique Blanc for Roch Stéphanik's *Stand By*

2002   Emmanuelle Devos for Jacques Audiard's *Read My Lips* (*Sur mes lèvres*)

BEST ACTOR

1976   Philippe Noiret for Robert Enrico's *The Old Gun* (*Le vieux fusil*)

1977   Michel Galabru for Bertrand Tavernier's *The Judge and the Assassin* (*Le juge et l'assassin*)

1978   Jean Rochefort for Pierre Schoendoerffer's *The Crab Drum* (*Le crabe tambour*)

1979   Michel Serrault for Edouard Molinaro's *La Cage Aux Folles* (*La cage aux folles*)

1980   Claude Brasseur for Robin Davis's *The Police War* (*La guerre des polices*)

1981   Gérard Depardieu for François Truffaut's *The Last Metro* (*Le dernier métro*)

1982   Michel Serrault for Claude Miller's *Under Suspicion* (*Garde à vue*)

1983   Philippe Léotard for Bob Swain's *The Nark* (*La balance*)

1984   Coluche for Claude Berri's *Tchao Pantin!*

1985   Alain Delon for Bertrand Blier's *Notre histoire*

1986   Christophe Lambert for Luc Besson's *Subway* (*Subway*)

1987   Daniel Auteuil for Claude Berri's *Manon of the Spring* (*Manon des sources*)

1988   Richard Bohringer for Jean-Loup Hubert's *The Grand Highway* (*Le grand chemin*)

1989   Jean-Paul Belmondo for Claude Lelouch's *Itinéraire d'un enfant gâté*

1990   Philippe Noiret for Bertrand Tavernier's *Life and Nothing But* (*La vie et rien d'autre*)

1991   Gérard Depardieu for Jean-Paul Rappeneau's *Cyrano de Bergerac* (*Cyrano de Bergerac*)

1992   Jacques Dutronc for Maurice Pialat's *Van Gogh*

1993   Claude Rich for Edouard Molinaro's *The Supper* (*Le souper*)

1994   Pierre Arditi for Alain Resnais's *Smoking/no smoking*

1995   Gérard Lanvin for Nicole Garcia's *The Favorite Son* (*Le fils préféré*)

1996   Michel Serrault for Claude Sautet's *Nelly and Mr. Arnaud* (*Nelly et M. Arnaud*)

1997   Philippe Torreton for Bertrand Tavernier's *Captain Conan* (*Capitaine Conan*)

1998   André Dussolier for Jean Becker's *Children of the Marshland* (*Les enfants du marais*)

1999   Jacques Villeret for Francis Veber's *The Dinner Game* (*Le dîner de cons*)

2000   Daniel Auteuil for Patrice Leconte's *The Girl on the Bridge* (*La fille sur le pont*)

2001   Sergi Lopez for Dominik Moll's *With a Friend Like Harry* (*Harry, un ami qui vous veut du bien*)

2002   Michel Bouquet for Anne Fontaine's *Comment j'ai tué mon père*

Biggest Box-office Successes in France (in million-tickets sold)

DIRECTOR	US TITLE	FRENCH TITLE	YEAR	
Gérard Oury	Don't Look Now We're Being Shot At	La grande vadrouille	1966	17.27
Jean-Marie Poiré	The Visitors	Les visiteurs	1993	13.78
Julien Duvivier	The Little World of Don Camillo	Le petit monde de Don Camillo	1952	12.79
Gérard Oury	The Sucker	Le corniaud	1965	11.74
Coline Serreau	Three Men and a Cradle	Trois hommes et un couffin	1985	10.25
Gérard Krawczyk		Taxi 2	2000	10.24
Jean-Paul Le Chanois		Les misérables	1958	9.94
Yves Robert	The War of the Buttons	La guerre des boutons	1962	9.88
Francis Veber	The Dinner Game	Le dîner de cons	1998	9.22
Luc Besson	The Big Blue	Le grand bleu	1988	9.19
Jean-Jacques Annaud	The Bear	L'ours	1988	9.14
Claude Zidi		Astérix et Obélix contre César	1999	9.09
Just Jaeckin	Emmanuelle	Emmanuelle	1974	8.89
Alexander Esway	Sky Battalion	Le bataillon du ciel	1947	8.65
Jean-Pierre Jeunet	Amélie	Le fabuleux destin d'Amélie Poulain	2001	8.17
Jean-Marie Poiré	The Visitors 2	Les visiteurs 2	1998	8.03
Hervé Palud	An Indian in the City	Un indien dans la ville	1994	7.88
Thomas Gilou	Would I Lie to You? 2	La vérité si je mens 2	2001	7.87
Jean Girault	The Gendarme of St. Tropez	Le gendarme de Saint-Tropez	1964	7.81
Robert Vernay	The Count of Monte Cristo	Le comte de Monte-Cristo	1955	7.78
Luc Besson	The Fifth Element	Le cinquième élément	1997	7.70
Claude Zidi	Bookies Run Amok	Les bidasses en folie	1971	7.46
Julien Duvivier	The Return of Don Camillo	Le retour de Don Camillo	1953	7.43
Gérard Oury	The Adventures of Rabbi Jacob	Les aventures de Rabbi Jacob	1973	7.30
Claude Berri	Jean de Florette	Jean de Florette	1986	7.22
Francis Veber	The Goat	La chèvre	1981	7.08
Maurice Cloche	Monsieur Vincent	Monsieur Vincent	1947	7.06
Jean Girault	The Big Vacation	Les grandes vacances	1967	6.99
Sacha Guitry	Royal Affairs in Versailles	Si Versailles m'était conté	1954	6.99
Henri-Georges Clouzot	Wages of Fear	Le salaire de la peur	1953	6.94

French Films at the Oscars®

1949 Maurice Cloche's *Monsieur Vincent (Monsieur Vincent)*

1951 René Clément's *The Walls of Malapaga (Au delà des grilles)*

1953 René Clément's *Forbidden Games (Jeux interdits)*

1958 Jacques Tati's *My Uncle (Mon oncle)*

1960 Marcel Camus's *Black Orpheus (Orfeu Negro)*

1960 Simone Signoret, Best Actress for Jack Clayton's *Room at the Top*

1962 Serge Bourguignon's *Sundays and Cybele (Les dimanches de Ville-d'Avray)*

1966 Claude Lelouch's *A Man and a Woman (Un homme et une femme)*

1969 Costa Gavras's *Z (Z)*

1972 Luis Buñuel's *The Discreet Charm of the Bourgeoisie (Le charme discret de la bourgeoisie)*

1973 François Truffaut's *Day for Night (La nuit américaine)*

1977 Moshe Mizrahi's *Madame Rosa (La vie devant soi)*

1978 Bertrand Blier's *Get out Your Handkerchiefs (Préparez vos mouchoirs)*

1992 Régis Wargnier's *Indochine (Indochine)*

1996 Juliette Binoche, Best Supporting Actress for Anthony Minghella's *The English Patient*

Notes

CHAPTER 1: THE INVENTION OF MOTION PICTURES AND THE
SILENT ERA OF FILM

1. The association of cinema with public entertainment, as well as being a common cultural and popular landmark, goes back to the early days of the Cinématographe, when it was projected for the first time on screen in Paris in December 1895 (although one century later its "collective" concept may very well shift back toward a more individualistic entertainment form with the development of home theater equipment among the general population and the DVD computerized viewing systems).

2. Thomas Edison met Eadweard James Muybridge on February 25, 1888, and contracted him to design a camera patent in October 1888.

3. Edison's next invention, the kinetophonograph, was able to display animated pictures in synchronization with recorded music.

4. R. W. Paul publicly and formally displayed his theatrograph at Finsbury Technical College in London during that same year. Subsequently, he produced a series of short views of political events as well as newsreel footage of the royal family. In England, Paul's theatrograph was the most popular projecting machine on a commercial level.

5. With the rapid development of the international film market, the battles over the question of patent monopoly increased in number and circumvented endless legal pursuits. The nine major producers of the time settled in 1909 to joint venture in the Motion Pictures Patents Company.

6. For an extensive study on the beginning of motion pictures and in particular a partial observation of the war of patents, see Gordon Hendricks's *The Edison Motion Picture Myth* (Berkeley: University of California Press, 1961), as well as his *Beginnings of the Biograph: The Story of the Invention of the Mutoscope and Biograph and Their Supplying Camera* (New York: The Beginnings of the American Film, 1964).

7. There were initially three versions filmed that day (or at least during the spring of 1895). The actual first version was discovered in Lyon in 1985.

8. In 1876, Emile Reynaud developed the first of a long series of preponderant inventions for the twentieth century, the Praxinoscope. The new instrument made it possible to reconstruct the illusion of movement and was composed mainly of a central piece (twelve mirrors and a metal drum), inside of which

a hard-bound tape representing twelve installations of a subject or a scene moving. By looking at the image reflected in the mirrors, viewers could see animated scenes. This invention was all the more noticeable as a spectacle since it was visible by several people at the same time, who could enjoy the clearness and the luminosity of the images all designed and painted by hand by Reynaud. In 1880, he developed the Praxinoscope with a projection device; the principle remained the same except for a magic lantern, which, once added, enabled a projection of the animation on a screen. On October 28, 1892, three years before the advent of cinema, Reynaud projected the first animated pictures in front of a public at the Grévin museum in Paris. In 1907, he developed another derivative of the Praxinoscope, the Stéréocinéma, which projected animated flight strips in relief.

9. The view already included the major fundamentals of modern-day comedy.

10. Although most films at the time were made in a single and continuous take, because the immobile camera was set up in one position only, the innovation of Eugène Promio, who first installed his camera on a moving gondola in Venice, rapidly created a revolution in the aesthetic of the image. Later that same year Promio renewed his experience in *Panorama of the Banks of the Nile* (*Panorama des rives du Nil*).

11. In addition to color photography, the Lumière brothers developed a technique to achieve hand-painted color films.

12. Many film historians and film rhetoricians, such as André Bazin, refer to the duality of French cinema and illustrate this concept by contrasting the Lumière element, which promoted a dose of realism and documentary of the world as it was, with the Méliès fantasy, which advocated the re-creation of the world through the author's imagination.

13. As the length of films grew longer and featured more complex story lines, the typology of these films helps film historians to understand the targeted audiences.

14. Jeancolas, p. 21.

15. Cineast, producer, and scenarist Albert Capellani (1874–1931) entered the film profession as a stage actor and eventually became the manager of Firmin Gémier, then the administrator of the variety show Alhambra in 1903. In 1905, he was hired by Pathé as a film director with Ferdinand Zecca. Promoted artistic director of the newly created SCAGL (Société cinématographique des auteurs et des gens de lettres), he adapted many prestigious oeuvres of French literature to the screen (Victor Hugo's *Notre Dame de Paris* and a much celebrated version at the time of Emile Zola's *Germinal* in 1913). With the realities of World War I in 1914 paralyzing the Pathé Company, Albert Capellani was sent to the United States to reinvigorate the small community of French filmmakers under the leadership of Maurice Tourneur. Capellani continued his career in the United States, then returned to France in 1923. An indefatigable and impassioned innovator, Capellani left behind him a considerable oeuvre of burlesque films, literary adaptations, and important sociological films.

16. For more on the subject of the Gaumont enterprise, see François Garçon's *Gaumont: A Century of French Cinema* (New York: Harry Abrams, 1994).

17. Alice Guy Blaché (1873–1968) was the first woman screen-writer as well as

the first female director. In December 1894, she entered the film industry as a twenty-one-year-old secretary, and soon undertook the direction of cinematographic productions for Léon Gaumont. She began to supervise scenarios, the casting of actors, background sets, costumes, and so forth. She hired future prestigious film directors such as Ferdinand Zecca, Emile Cohl, Victorin Jasset, and Louis Feuillade, who ensured the successful destiny of the film company. On a technical level, Alice Guy worked with all the significant researchers of the time: Marey, Light, Demenÿ, and utilized their contributions to film with sound, color tinting, and enhanced photography. In 1907, she married the British cinematographer Herbert Blaché Bolton, and both pursued their career in the United States, later creating their own film company, Solax, in 1910, as well as several studios. Film historians have attributed more than six hundred indexed films to Alice Guy Blaché: comedies, action films, dramas, westerns, fantastic films, science fiction, operas, documentaries, war pictures, and historical movies. Guy Blaché ended her career in 1920. During more than fifty years, her films disappeared only to resurface in 1972, four years after her death. For more on the life of Guy Blaché, see Alison McMahan's *Alice Guy Blaché: Cinematic Visionary* (New York and London: Continuum, 2002).

18. Around 1905, Pathé in Vincennes and Gaumont in Buttes de Chaumont built their first studios, and a few years later, in 1916, seeking a warmer environment, Gaumont built the Victorine Studios in Nice in order to better exploit natural lighting.

19. Before becoming "talking" pictures, films of the silent era were sometimes referred to as "singing" pictures.

20. Born Emile Courtet (he took the pseudonym of Cohl much later), the French animation pioneer Emile Cohl (1857–1938) began his interest in cinema only at age fifty as scenario writer and film director, first with the Lux Company, then with Gaumont, which he joined after a year of independent work. Following a short passage at Pathé (1911), he pursued his directing career mainly with Eclair and managed animation at the company's American studio in Fort Lee, New Jersey (1912–1914). Shortly after his return to Paris, Cohl opened the first animation studios with Raoul Barré and J. R. Bray. Walt Disney himself recognized Emile Cohl as the forefather of cinematographic cartoons. Cohl invented cinematographic cartoons with *Fantasmagorie* (1908), an innovative experiment featuring technical and aesthetic novelties, and a year later an entertaining film entitled *The Joyous Microbe* (*Le microbe joyeux,* 1909), in which minuscule microbic entities floated on the screen to represent the diseases they supposedly caused. Cohl applied the cinematic tricks that Méliès employed with the natural world of animated drawings. Many film critics saw in his oeuvre the direct influence of Cubism, Dadaism, and Surrealism. Cohl's major achievement was the creation of the first hero of animated pictures (Fantoche), the first animated drawings in advertising (Campbell Soups, 1912), and the first animation film drawn from comic strips (*Les aventures des pieds nicklés,* 1917). Emile Cohl stopped his cinema career in 1923, after having directed more than three hundred short films (many of which are lost today), mostly working alone. Financially ruined and forgotten, he died in the hospital of Villejuif on January 20, 1938.

21. In addition to historical reconstitutions (André Calmettes and Charles Le Bargy's *The Assassination of the Duc de Guise-L'assassinat du duc de Guise,* 1908) and newsreels, the French public was very much enamoured with religious and biblical subjects as demonstrated by the success of Pathé's *La Vie et la passion du Christ* (1905) and Gaumont's *La Vie du Christ* (1906).

22. For a more detailed explanation of the concept of "filmed theater," see the section referring to the cinema of Marcel Pagnol in chapter 2.

23. In its own terms, silent cinema, just like literature and the press, discovered the potential of the serials and perfected the genre to become one of the most popular forms of entertainment of the century.

24. Indeed, during the 1920s, the purchase of an American film for small film companies was cheaper and consequently more profitable than producing a French film.

CHAPTER 2: THE GOLDEN AGE OF FRENCH CINEMA

1. It is worth keeping in mind that, although almost all 1930 films declared themselves to be 100 percent "talking," most merely corresponded to motion pictures elaborated as silent and later customized with a recorded music track.

2. Unlike silent film in the United States, French silent films were still present in France until well into the 1930s.

3. Both directors were actually not hostile to the new sound revolution, as they tried to adapt to it, but the new technology and the new expectations of the French public did not permit them to continue their career the same way.

4. Also sponsored by Noailles in 1930, *Le sang d'un poète,* Jean Cocteau's first feature film, was subjected to a difficult launch because of the disapproval of many Surrealist followers, although later critics credited it with images of an outstanding poetic command. It was an influential collection of works of compulsive inspirations and images out of which Jean Cocteau assembled his personal oeuvre.

5. In fact, *The Golden Age* obtained its first public distribution in France only half a century later, in 1981 by Gaumont.

6. René Clair had been surprisingly promoted even before he had received full recognition in France.

7. Annabella, a well-known French film actress of the 1930s and whose actual name was Suzanne Charpentier, made her movie debut in Abel Gance's silent classic *Napoléon* (1927). Her brilliant performance in René Clair's *The Million* (1931) and *Bastille Day* (1932) divulged her talent to the world and, in particular, Hollywood, where she starred with actors like James Cagney and Tyrone Power, with whom she eventually fell in love during the shooting of *Suez* in 1938. Some of her most memorable roles were *Under the Roofs of Paris* (1930), *La Bandera* (1935), and *Hôtel du Nord* (*Hôtel du Nord,* 1938). After her divorce from Power, Annabella did not continue her acting career but returned to France, where she died in 1996.

8. When *Modern Times* was completed in 1935, the Tobis Studios, under the direction of Josef Goebbels (in charge of the Third Reich propaganda), attempted to sue Charlie Chaplin, accusing him of plagiarism, in particular for

the scenes representing the assembly line René Clair dismissed the lawsuit by asserting that all directors owe Charlie Chaplin a great deal and that any remake, borrowing, or adaptation from Clair's own film would be an honor.

9. Many of these businesses never managed to produce more than one (or, in some cases, even one) motion picture.

10. The first five annual New York Film Critics' Awards for the Best Foreign Film, beginning in 1936, were repeatedly given to France: *Carnival in Flanders, Mayerling, Grand Illusion, Harvest,* and *The Baker's Wife.*

11. In 1691, Spain occupies Flanders, and the city of Boom is informed of the impending arrival of a Spaniards' regiment and consequently the men abandon the city. The women, on the other hand, hurriedly unite to divert and charm the militia. With a script by Charles Spaak and splendid sets by Lazare Meerson (justly credited with achieving a minor miracle in paying tribute to northern European masters such as Pieter Bruegel, Franz Hals, and Vermeer), the film is not only a skillful comedy but also an unusual example of the work of Jacques Feyder. In 1936, it won the New York Film Critics' Award for Best Foreign Film.

12. For an insightful study of the political situation and the cinematographic productions, the rise and the fall of Left filmmaking during the Popular Front, see Jonathan Buchsbaum, *Cinéma Engagé: Film in the Popular Front* (Chicago: University of Illinois Press, 1988), p. 21.

13. First pioneered by Charles Pathé, the French newsreels were for the collective memory of an entire nation an important and priceless testimony in terms of historical archives. Generally organized as a series of short reports of current events and unrelated documentaries, the newsreels were principally screened as additional feature besides the long feature-film programs. Ultimately with the advent of the television news coverage in the late 1950s, the newsreels slowly became obsolete among popular theaters.

14. Paul Léglise, *Histoire de la politique du Cinéma Français,* (vol. 1 Paris: Film Editions, 1970), pp. 29–32, 63.

15. The Alliance du Cinéma Indépendant also created a magazine with the same name and began its publication on May 20, 1936, just a few weeks before the vast strike overshadowed the whole country.

16. Roy Armes, *French Cinema* (New York: Oxford University Press, 1985), p. 72.

17. When the twentieth century brought with it the moving picture camera, it is to be noted that the very first motion picture ever made was entitled *Workers Leaving the Lumière Factory* by the French film pioneers Louis and Auguste Lumière. This historic view was one of the first realistic films ever achieved for its topic and was precisely what the title acknowledged.

18. For a complete study of the Gabin myth, see Claude Gauteur and Ginette Vincendeau, *Jean Gabin: anatomie d'un mythe* (Paris: Nathan, 1993), pp. 95–171.

19. With the advent of sound, many French directors took advantage of the popularity of the boulevard style and attempted an immediate adaptation to the big screen. Guitry, among others, was even able to overtake its archetypal modus operandi (love at first sight, adultery, reunions, coincidences, quid pro quo) to eventually impose his own style.

20. Gauteur and Vincendeau, p. 107.

21. Gauteur and Vincendeau, p. 17.

22. *Le Jour se Lève: A Film by Jacques Prévert and Marcel Carné* (New York: Simon & Schuster), p. 55. "Ecoutez . . . vous êtes bien gentille, mais quand vous aurez fini de faire le ménage, vous me le direz?"

23. Gauteur and Vincendeau, p. 133.

24. During the 1940s and 1950s, film noir was one of the most popular American cinematographic genres. Chronologically between German Expressionism and Hollywood hard-boiled detective narrative, French poetic realism represented the gloomy and exhilarating look of uncompromising heroes.

25. André Bazin, "The Disincarnation of Carné," in *Rediscovering French Film* (New York: Little, Brown, 1983), p. 131.

26. André Bazin, *Le Jour se Lève: A Film by Jacques Prévert and Marcel Carné.* (New York: Simon & Schuster), p. 12.

27. The film, considered too "demoralizing," was banned by the French censorship committee in its final distribution phase. After the war, Hollywood did not deem it necessary to keep the scene in which Arletty is seen naked in the shower, as well as the scene in which she and Gabin lie together in bed. The American remake, directed by Anatole Litvak, came out in 1947 with a happier ending (though film noir in essence) and was entitled *The Long Night,* starring Henry Fonda, Barbara Bel Geddes, Ann Dvorak, and Vincent Price. From a chronological perspective, it is clear that the depth of poetic realism and the aesthetic of *Daybreak* had a decisive influence on the expansion of the film noir genre of the 1940s.

28. For more on Marcel Carné's *Daybreak,* see Allen Thiher's *The Cinematic Muse: Critical Studies in the History of French Cinema* (Columbia: University of Missouri Press, 1979), pp. 113–128.

29. Luchino Visconti, who started his career in 1942 with *Obsession (Obsessione)*, was an intern on the set of Renoir's *Toni* in 1934.

30. Because of his Jewish origin, Marcel Dalio fled to the United States during the first days of the war and there accepted supporting roles from major directors. One of his most famous roles is in Michael Curtiz's *Casablanca* (1943) as Emil the croupier.

31. Marianne Alexandre and Andrew Sinclair, *Classic Film Scripts, Grand Illusion: A Film by Jean Renoir* (New York: Simon & Schuster) p. 89.

32. In *Grand Illusion,* Jean Gabin even wears Renoir's own air force uniform.

33. During the Venice Film Festival in 1937, violent reactions arose, which led to the film's being banned in France as well as in Italy.

34. An American remake of the film was released in 1954 under the title *Human Desire* and was directed by Fritz Lang.

35. In Renoir's *Human Beast,* the different shots were realized on a moving train, with the exception of the final scene, when Jean Gabin commits suicide and jumps from the train to his death.

36. Always present in Renoir's pictures, the classically trained Julien Carette imposed himself as the stereotype of the Parisian character, also called *titi parisien.*

37. André Bazin, *Jean Renoir* (New York: Simon & Schuster, 1971), p. 73.

38. The premiere of the film, on April 7, 1933, was a failure. An unsympathetic public's reaction severely contrasted with the weak support of French intellec-

tuals, for it fully lacked commercial qualities. It underwent ruthless commercial cuts and numerous censorship alterations. It was only in 1946 that *Zero of Conduct* was rereleased in France.

39. Interestingly enough, Vigo's style provoked just as much analysis and discussion as any other kind of artistic phenomenon.

40. The *ciné-club* initiative is representative of the beginning of a new awareness in the 1930s, still extremely minor in France, of the need to conserve films. Georges Franju and Henri Langlois created the Cinémathèque française in 1936. A genuine living memory of the *septième art,* its board of trustees consisted of some of the most prestigious personalities in the film industry and contains an immense collection of world feature films. Immediately following its creation, the new institution asserted a sincere objective by clearly discarding any form of thematic or aesthetic associations, preferences for a specific national cinema or particular genres. Moviemaking in France of the 1930s followed certain principles and artistic requirements that did not control the medium as in other national cinemas (combining literariness with the visual powers of moving pictures). Jean Vigo had a precise conception of motion pictures, cinema as art, a fundamental element toward creativity, and values of civilization. Despite the loss of Vigo and the absence of René Clair in 1934, French film production reached the edge of one of its episodic quandaries, even with some detectable indications of artistic rejuvenation.

41. Roy Armes, *French Cinema* (New York: Oxford University Press, 1985), p. 99.

42. J. P. Chartier and R. F. Desplanques, *Derrière l'écran* (Paris: Spes, 1950), 140–145. For an extensive study on cinematographic procedures and the stylistic transformations of French cinema during the 1930s, see Crisp, *The Classic French Cinema,* pp. 358–414.

43. Crisp, p. 372.

44. For a detailed account of *Le jour se lève,* see Maureen Turim, "Poetic Realism as Psychoanalytical and Ideological Operation," in *French Film: Texts and Contexts* (New York: Routledge, 1990), p. 113. In her article, the author investigates the role of poetry and memory through the film's realism and its physical representation: "While Trauner, and the Carné/Prévert team in general, may have set out to re-create in the space of the studio a corner of a working-class suburb, such descriptive mimesis immediately becomes appropriated by the symbolic structuration and interior vision of this film."

CHAPTER 3: FRENCH CINEMA OF THE OCCUPATION

1. The armistice was respected until November 1942, when the Allies invaded North Africa. At this time, Hitler annulled the 1940 armistice and occupied all of France.

2. During the years of the Occupation, the austerity of daily life along with the nonexistence of heating in homes and apartment buildings directly favored the growing popularity of "romantic" pursuits as a fashionable distraction for young couples, including attending movies.

3. Marcel Dalio (born Israel Blauschild) made several successful movies in the United States, among which was Michael Curtiz's *Casablanca* (1942).

4. Julien Duvivier directed *The Great Waltz* in 1938, as well as *The Impostor* (*L'imposteur,* 1944).

5. For detailed information on the Jean Gabin–Marlene Dietrich episode, see Marlene Dietrich, *Marlene D* (Paris: Grasset, 1984), p. 129.

6. See chapter 2, "The Golden Age of French Cinema."

7. Boyer's unique love story with Pat Paterson remains one of the most romantic in all of Hollywood's "offscreen" sentimental history. It was a marriage that lasted over four decades (quite rare in Hollywood). Boyer committed suicide two days after his wife's death in 1978.

8. For a more in-depth analysis of the emerging careers of young cineasts see Colin Crisp, *The Classic French Cinema, 1930–1960* (Bloomington: Indiana University Press, 1993), pp. 59. In his extensive research of French film industry, Crisp discloses one of the most important reasons for the sudden phenomenon: "The previous generation had mostly approached the cinema from outside it—from classical music, the theater, literature, or more generally from the complexity of cultural movement of the 1920s. For them, cinema had been one among a multitude of cultural passions, and one to which frequently no more than a happy accident led them to commit themselves. For the new generation, cinema was their life, their career, and their principal cultural experience" p. 59.

9. *The Fantastic Night* was a typical example of "escapist" movies presented to the audience of the Occupation, eager to mentally "desert," although temporarily, the troubles of the war. In this 1942 motion picture, Marcel L'Herbier's cinematography involved the audience within the limits between dream and reality through a succession of oneiric sequences (special effects, artistic mistiness, overimpression, and deformed images), which also conjure an earlier sagacity of Surrealist pictures. The rather simple plot (Irène, a lady veiled in white, is pursued by her lover) was enriched by the technique of the visual effects, distinctive of the Avant-garde directors of the 1920s. *The Fantastic Night* was a rather surprising film, in a large part discarded by the French public, which did not take advantage of the "retro" flavor.

10. See Jean-Pierre Bertin-Maghit, *Le cinéma français sous l'occupation* (Paris: Presses Universitaires de France, 1994), p. 76.

11. Marcel Pagnol's *The Well-Digger's Daughter (La fille du puisatier,* 1941) was one of the first films to resume after the outbreak of war. Responding to Marshal Pétain's discourse for a return to the land and the values of rural culture, Pagnol argued that the basis according to which he included the discourse of the events of June 17, 1940, in his film was to correct the exaggeration of the media, which often represented the armistice as a necessity and an event welcomed by the French population. The propaganda broadcast over the radio was indeed meant to influence the population by suggesting two possible explanations for the present dramatic situation: first, that the events were a logical consequence of the mistakes made in the past; and second, that the enemy was not as hideous as heretofore described before the war. Consequently, a friendly collaboration was the only solution. Pagnol was acquitted of collaboration on February 3, 1947.

12. In his survey of French cinema, Pierre Darmon quotes Marcel L'Herbier's article in *La Gerbe* in 1941: "How many times have we regreted that the

Americans . . . have considered French screens conquered territory . . ." or in the journal *France* in 1940: "Sometimes America weakens it [French cinema], sometimes Israeli emigrants, who took control in 1936, transform it to their image, which is certainly not ours." Bertin-Maghit, pp. 134, 145.

13. Ultimately, under a convoluted blend of French and Nazi regulation, millions of dollars of Jewish material goods were embezzled. The method was logical, practical, and, most of all, legalized. Many Jews sought advice with notaries and were able to safeguard their belongings through relocation, corporate rearrangement, or financial manipulation.

14. One must remember that, though often pressured by the Occupation, the Vichy regime drafted, established, and applied anti-Semitic legislation without direct pressure from the Germans and was certainly in no way entirely influenced by Nazi ideology.

15. It was a fact that Harry Baur's averseness for the Nazi occupation was one of the actor's evident characteristics from early on in the war.

16. See chapter 2, "The Golden Age of French Cinema."

17. In his book, Bertin-Maghit exemplifies the severity of French censorship at the time. The movie *Macao,* produced by an English company and directed by Jean Delannoy, whose central character was interpreted by Erich von Stroheim, was forbidden. It later obtained an exploitation visa under the condition that it reshoot all the scenes played by Stroheim. Pierre Renoir, who finally accepted the contract, demanded that the new version be destroyed at the end of the war. Bertin-Maghit, p. 40.

18. Crisp, p. 52.

19. Darmon, p. 323.

20. For instance, slang words like *flics* and *poulets* (cops) were no longer considered acceptable on screen.

21. Darmon, p. 141.

22. The film, which was released on May 16, 1944, was quickly banned after the Liberation.

23. Paul Riche's real name was Jean Mamy.

24. Crisp, p. 54.

25. In his autobiography, Marcel Carné proved the idea that room for negotiation with Greven (and Continental in general) was not as problematic as it may have seemed, or to a certain extent, easier than some American studios: "As for me, I insisted to have, first, the choice of the subject, or at least that the subject be chosen unanimously in order to avoid any propaganda or indirect propaganda film. Second, that the film had to be shot in its entirety in France. I did not want, one must understand, to have the obligation to shoot in Germany." Alfred Greven agreed to let Carné choose his actors, technicians, shooting locations, and scenarios in concert with Continental. Although Carné signed an official contract, he never directed a single film with Continental. Marcel Carné, *Ma vie à belles dents* (Paris: Jean Vuarnet, 1979), p. 175.

26. On January 26, 1945, Continental was sequestered by the state and became a new company with a new name, Union générale cinématographique (UGC), which welcomed two new partners, SOGEC and ACE, in 1947.

27. This film was Clouzot's second major directing experience. Although considered an emerging director in the early 1940s, Henri-Georges Clouzot was far

from being a novice, since by now he had already directed *The Murderer Lives at Number 21* (*L'assassin habite au 21*, 1942), as well as a short film in 1931, *La terreur des Batignolles*. In addition, he worked as a scriptwriter for several films, some of them made in Germany during the 1930s. In 1941, Clouzot signed a contract with Continental and became an expert within the thriller genre.

28. The CLCF was actually created as an underground movement at the end of 1943.

29. Among celebrities of the profession, Jacques Prévert, Jacques Becker, and René Clair came to Clouzot's defense.

30. The Hollywood remake of *The Raven,* entitled *The Thirteenth Letter* (1951), starred Charles Boyer and was directed by Otto Preminger.

31. A contact printer is the machine used to make a release print before sending its final negative for distribution to theaters.

32. This anecdote was quoted by Jean-Pierre Jeancolas in his article "Beneath the Despair, the Show Goes On: Marcel Carné's *Les enfants du paradis* (1943–1945)," in *French Film: Texts and Contexts* (New York: Routledge, 1990), p. 120.

33. Carné, p. 201.

34. Darmon, p. 262.

35. The three main centers of production during the Occupation were Paris, Nice (studios of Victorine) and Marseille (Marcel Pagnol's studios). In comparison with the thirty studios in Paris, the nine studios in Nice offered only limited access for filmmakers.

36. Jean-Pierre Jeancolas, p. 118.

37. Translated by the author from the film's original screenplay by Jacques Prévert and Pierre Laroche, *Les visiteurs du soir* (Paris: La Nouvelle edition-Les classiques du cinéma français, 1947), p. 100: "Oublié dans son pays, inconnu ailleurs, tel est le destin du voyageur."

38. Translated by the author: "Regardez comme les flames sont prévenantes pour moi . . . elles me lèchent comme le ferait un jeune chien," p. 99.

39. Edward Baron Turk, *Child of Paradise: Marcel Carné and the Golden Age of French Cinema* (Cambridge, MA: Harvard University Press, 1989), p. 195.

40. Turk, p. 206.

41. For a detailed account of the preparation of the set, see Jill Forbes, *Les Enfants du Paradis* (London: British Film Institute, 1997), pp. 11–34. The subtle technical qualities that made the boulevard du Temple the most famous set in French film history is unveiled by Jill Forbes: "The charm of Trauner's set in the harm of recognition, the pleasure deriving from the fact that the physical environment is exactly as the viewer somehow always expected it to be, a second-level recreation based on the impressions of other artists and illustrators already in wide circulation. Paradoxically, the success of the sets derives from their lack of inventiveness and their conformity to an ideal 'original,' which we already carry in our mind's eye. One of Trauner's specialisms (following Meerson) was the *trompe l'oeil* which is used in the crowd scenes of the film on the Boulevard du Temple where the last twenty metres of the set were painted, and child extras were brought in to increase the sense of perspective." Forbes, p. 21.

42. Parker Tyler, *Classics of the Foreign Film* (New York: Citadel Press, 1967), p. 143.

43. Initially a Franco-Italian production, *Children of Paradise* had its first scenes shot during the summer of 1943 but was almost terminated as a result of the sudden American invasion of Sicily in November 1943. Pathé, at the time eager to complete with its European rivals, agreed to take over the gigantic project. The shooting resumed in February 1944, and the picture was completed in March 1945.

44. Forbes, p. 45.

45. Forbes, p. 36.

46. André Bazin, "The Disincantation of Carné," in *Rediscovering French Film* (New York: Museum of Modern Art, 1983), p. 131.

47. Darmon, p. 343.

48. Bertin-Maghit, pp. 86–108.

49. In particular, it was Guitry's status of persona grata among Parisian intelligentsia, which at the time was enough for social collaboration.

50. For more details on Le Vigan's unfortunate vicissitudes, see Darmon, p. 299.

51. Roy Armes, *French Cinema* (New York: Oxford University Press, 1985), p. 124.

CHAPTER 4: THE POSTWAR ERA

1. On April 29, 1945, during municipal elections, women in France obtained the right to vote, exactly twenty-five years after their American counterparts.

2. The origins of film noir go back to the prewar period with poetic realism, which indirectly inspired many American directors and novelists.

3. The Monnet Plan in particular laid the groundwork for the future European community.

4. Jacques Prévert's *Paroles* was published in 1946.

5. Beyond the field of arts and humanities, France was thrust into the spotlight with such athletic achievements as boxer Marcel Cerdan's world championship in 1948 (he died tragically in a plane crash the following year), cyclist Louison Bobet's triple win of the Tour de France in 1953, 1954, 1955, and marathon gold medalist Alain Mimoun's 1956 Olympic Games in Melbourne. These athletic achievements made the headlines of French newspapers in the 1950s.

6. Prédal, p. 85.

7. The advent of new possibilities for the entertainment industry provided the French population with a growing variety of escapes, such as television, weekends in the country, vacations, tourism, and automobiles (the indefatigable Citroën 2 CV and Renault 4 CV).

8. According to film historian René Prédal, each year France accepted the entry of 186 foreign films, among which 121 were American, all dubbed. The original version releases, however were excluded from the above statistic since they were not significant in number. Prédal, p. 41.

9. The quota technically required French theaters to screen French films for a minimum of four out of every thirteen weeks. After 1948, it was increased to five weeks.

10. In addition, the CNC was in charge of monitoring box office receipts, assuring distributors accurate box office revenues and reporting on market trends.

11. Crisp, p. 78.

12. The main objective was evidently to counterattack the predominance of the colossal American productions with bigger financial means.

13. Mast, p. 365.

14. Colombat, p. 27.

15. Henri Alekan displayed the film's outstanding structuring of lights and shadows. He distinguished the opposed effects of focused spotlighting (*lumières uni-directionelles*) and diffused floodlighting (*lumières multi-directionelles*). The abstract dimension was finally palpable. Diffused lighting successfully created a psychological climate and blurriness.

16. Cocteau originally had in mind internationally renowned actress Greta Garbo or Marlene Dietrich for the role of Death-Princess.

17. Translated by the author from the original *Orpheus* screenplay (Heurtebise to Orphée): "Les miroirs sont les portes par lesquelles la mort vient et va; du reste, regardez-vous toute votre vie dans un miroir: vous verrez la mort travailler comme les abeilles dans une ruche de verre."

18. For a complete explanation of the special effects used in the film by Cocteau himself, consult André Fraigneau's *Cocteau on the Film* (New York: Dover, 1972), pp. 99–131.

19. Armes, p. 144.

20. In contrast to the thriller genre, the comedy, deeply influenced by several national cinemas, was able to remain 100 percent French.

21. The French also had their own process called Rouxcolor, which did not receive proper financial backing and consequently came too late on the international market to commercialize the color process. Marcel Pagnol was probably the only film director to attempt the new sophisticated technique in an unsuccessful film, *La Belle meunière* (1948).

22. Conceived in the early 1930s the Technicolor process functioned due to a beam-splitting optical cube at the level of the camera lens, to expose three black-and-white films. In theory the idea was simple. When the light beam entered the camera it was to be divided into three beams: one capturing green, one red, and the last one blue. The three strips were then developed independently before printing them through their corresponding coloring. Once juxtaposed together, the triple film fashioned a convincingly truthful approximation of natural color.

23. Crisp, p. 144.

24. Armes, p. 167.

25. Surprisingly enough, during the 1950s, Claude Autant-Lara appeared to the film critics as a "leftist bourgeois" whose tendencies for anarchy often shocked morality, religion, and bourgeois values.

26. Olivier Barrot and Raymond Chirat, *Noir et blanc: 250 acteurs du cinéma français, 1930–1960* (Paris: Flammarion, 2000), p. 434.

27. Sadly enough, after four marriages, the last years of Martine Carol's career were difficult due to an escalating dependence on drugs and alcohol.

28. André Cayatte (1909–1989) published six novels before entering the film profession. Through collaboration, he first wrote Marc Allégret's *The Curtain*

Rises (Entrée des artistes, 1938) and Jean Grémillon's *Stormy Waters (Remorques,* 1941). Thanks to the help of Jacques Prévert, Cayatte was noticed with the famous *The Lovers of Verona (Les amants de Vérone,* 1948), one of the innumerable versions of Shakespeare's *Romeo and Juliet.* In 1950, *Justice Is Done (Justice est faite,* 1950), whose scenarist, Charles Spaak, revitalized the plot with zeal, demonstrated how popular juries, despite freedom of conscience granted by the law, still remained prisoners of social and moral conditioning as well as upbringing. *We Are All Murderers (Nous sommes tous des assassins,* 1952) dealt with the problem of crime during wartime. Little concerned with showing the subtle flaw of modern judiciary systems, Cayatte's point of view relentlessly aimed at underlying with strength and sincerity his conviction against the weakness of the jury system, the absolute arbitrary nature of the death penalty, and the difficult, even impossible task, for an experience judge to render justice at the beginning of his career. Although never a cinematographic innovator, Cayatte's contribution to French cinema remained determinant in its critical view of French society of the postwar era and the French moral rule of conduct. No one remained indifferent to his films. His filmography includes *Before the Deluge (Avant le déluge,* 1953), *An Eye for an Eye (Oeil pour oeil,* 1956), and *The Miror Has Two Faces (Le miroir à deux faces,* 1958).

29. Prédal, p. 84.
30. Vincendeau, p. 26.
31. The same year Brigitte Bardot married Roger Vadim (both had known each other years earlier), but she wished to marry him when she was seventeen. The marriage lasted only five years.
32. Hollywood actor Curd Jürgens, imposed by Columbia Studios, featured in the film as an American millionaire due to the financing by the American company of both color and Cinemascope for the film.
33. Siclier, *Le cinéma français,* p. 156.
34. Prédal, p. 137.
35. In 1973, Brigitte Bardot officially announced her retreat from the screen and began to devote herself to what had become the major interest in her life, animal rights.
36. During the spring of 1960, Simone Signoret and Yves Montand were neighbors at the Beverly Hills Hotel of Marilyn Monroe and Arthur Miller. Monroe told her dresser (who later wrote a biography) that Miller enjoyed talking to Signoret and that after she went back to France to make another picture, he also left for New York to work on a play. Monroe and Montand did indeed have the *aventure* that was speculated about in the press.
37. Ginette Vincedeau, *The Companion to French Cinema* (London: Cassell–British Film Institute, 1996), p. 74.
38. François Truffaut, *The Films in My Life* (New York: Simon & Schuster, 1978), p. 172.
39. In 1956, Claude Autant-Lara temporarily regained critical esteem with productions like *Four Full Bags,* and prompted even moderate acclaim from François Truffaut himself. The film, an immediate success, was recognized as an audacious movie by Truffaut, who two years earlier had vehemently attacked Autant-Lara's style, stating "Autant-Lara seemed to me like a butcher

who insists on trying to make lace." Truffaut, *The Films in My Life,*
p. 171.

40. Unlike the United States, France does not differentiate between A- and B-
rated movies (usually determined by budget scales).

41. Buss, *French Film Noir,* p. 46.

42. Simenon's novels were even more often adapted to the big screen than nineteenth-century authors Emile Zola and Alexandre Dumas.

43. Marcel Carné adapted the novel to the screen with *Three Rooms in Manhattan
(Trois chambres à Manhattan,* 1965).

44. The remake of *Diabolique,* directed by Jeremiah Chechik, released in 1996,
featured Sharon Stone, Chazz Palminteri, and Isabelle Adjani. As an icy
femme fatale, Sharon Stone was ideally cast as the aloof schoolteacher, a role
made famous by Simone Signoret.

45. Despite the international success of the film at the Cannes and Berlin Film
Festivals, *Wages of Fear* was received with rather circumspect comment by
American film critics, who mainly reproached Clouzot for his indirect condemnation of American oil companies' hypothetical involvement in the so-
called banana republics.

46. Pierre Boileau and Thomas Narcejac's novel entitled *D'entre les morts* was
adapted to the screen and became Alfred Hitchcock's *Vertigo* (1958).

47. Born Angelo Borrini in Parma, Italy, Lino Ventura (1919–1987) came to
France as a child in the mid 1920s. When in 1953 Jacques Becker sought a
strong-minded, charismatic character to counteract the emotional weight of
Jean Gabin's presence in *Grisbi,* Lino Ventura appeared to be the appropriate
actor. His memorable role as Angelo set the agenda for the rest of his acting
career. Ventura's physical and authentic presence, mainly cast in gangster
roles, pervaded the screen with a rare magnetism of self-contained masculinity
in such films as Henri Decoin's *Razzia sur la Chnouf (Razzia sur la chnouf,*
1955), Louis Malle's *Elevator to the Gallows (Ascenseur pour l'échafaud,* 1958),
Claude Sautet's *The Big Risk (Classe tous risques,* 1960), Georges Lautner's
Monsieur Gangster (Les tontons flingeurs, 1963), Henri Verneuil's *Greed in the Sun
(Cent mille dollars au soleil,* 1963) and *The Sicilian Clan (Le clan des Siciliens,*
1969), Robert Enrico's *The Wise Guys (Les grandes gueules,* 1965), Jean-Pierre
Melville's *The Second Breath (Le deuxième souffle,* 1966) and *The Shadow Army
(L'armée des ombres,* 1969), Francesco Rosi's *Cadaveri eccellenti (Illustrious Corpses,*
1976), Claude Miller's *Under Suspicion (Garde à vue,* 1981), and José Gio-
vanni's *The Ruffian (Le ruffian* 1983).

48. Born Jean-Pierre Grumbach, Jean Pierre Melville (1917–73) took his surname
from novelist Herman Melville, whom he admired. He began his cinematographic career in 1945 by creating his own production company, OGC, with
independently made adaptations of major French literary works: Vercors (*Le
silence de la mer,* 1949) and Jean Cocteau's *The Strange Ones (Les enfants terribles,*
1950). Melville's *Bob the Gambler* paid homage to the old school of American
gangster movies and directly stimulated many future New Wave directors.
Co-written by the popular thriller novelist Auguste Le Breton (Jules Dassin's
Rififi), the story traces the vicissitudes of obsessive gambler Bob (Roger
Duchesne), who plans a hit at the Deauville casino by bringing together a
squad of old and new associates. (Despite the doubtful likelihood the gangster

boss does not change his mind). Unlike many *polars* of the decade, the general ambience, despite many stylistic and thematic allusions to American gangster films, remained indisputably French.

49. Truffaut, *The Films in My Life*, p. 180.

50. *Battle of the Rails* (*La bataille du rail*) received the Special Jury Prize at the 1946 Cannes Film Festival. *The Damned* (*Les maudits*) was honored with the Grand Prix at the 1947 Cannes Film Festival. In 1949, *The Walls of Malapaga* (*Au delà des grilles,* 1949) won the Best Director award at Cannes.

51. François Boyer's novel was first published in the United States under the title *The Secret Game* (1950) and was a best-seller during the early 1950s.

52. Brigitte Fossey continued her film career as an adult and appeared in Bertrand Blier's *Going Places* (*Les valseuses,* 1974), François Truffaut's *The Man Who Loved Women* (*L'homme qui aimait les femmes,* 1977), and Giuseppe Tornatore's *Nuovo Cinema Paradiso* (1988), among others.

53. Translated by the author from René Prédal's 50 *ans de cinéma français*: "Entre vingt et trente ans, le cinéaste s'use à jouer les garçons de courses alors qu'il vit sa période la plus créative. Mais le talent et les idées ne sont permis qu'aux anciens. De trente à quarante ans, il est alors second puis premier assistant ou coscénariste, mais on attend de lui de la technique, de l'habileté, de l'efficacité, et toujours pas de création." Prédal, p. 92.

54. Alain Resnais was the epitome of the so-called *artiste engagé* (politically dedicated artist). To date, *Night and Fog* (*Nuit et brouillard,* 1955) remains the best evocation of the horror of Nazi camps. Presented in the form of a short film documentary for the tenth anniversary of the liberation of the concentration camps, *Night and Fog* offers a disquieting look at life in the Nazi concentration camps after 1942. The screenplay was written by Jean Cayrol, a camp survivor. As he would do in his next feature, *Hiroshima Mon Amour* (*Hiroshima Mon Amour,* 1959), Alain Resnais manipulated the chronology with memory by alternating contemporary color sequences of the empty camps with black-and-white footage of Nazi documentaries. The film emphasized the fate of the victims more than the extermination of the Jews in general. Its conclusion suggested to the viewer that with the existing testimony, one must assume that history is never a sealed book. Censorship allowed release of the film only after one scene showing a French police officer guarding a concentration camp during the German Occupation was cut. At the 1956 Cannes Film Festival, the German embassy obtained in extremis the expulsion of the film from French selection. The film was still presented in Cannes but under the label *Hors competition*. *Night and Fog* won the Jean Vigo Prize in 1956.

55. Robert Bresson was a painter and photographer before he released his first short film, *Les affaires publiques* in 1934 (unexpectedly a comedy). This explains his use of graphic metaphor, which pervades his works. Bresson's original photography, based on a particular concept of the image (involving implication and sense rather than beauty), strove to express itself through the actors' minimalist acting and combinations of "flat" images rather than movement and skilled dialogue.

56. Ellis, p. 298.

57. Kristin Thompson and David Bordwell, *Film History: An Introduction* (New York: McGraw-Hill, 1993), p. 446.

58. In the Montluc Prison, more than seven thousand men had died during the Occupation under the Gestapo.

59. For more on Bresson's *A Man Escaped,* see Allen Thiher's *The Cinematic Muse: Critical Studies in the History of French Cinema* (Columbia: University of Missouri Press, 1979), pp. 129–142.

60. Commenting on Bresson's style, François Truffaut observed, "We know that Bresson directs his actors by holding them back from acting 'dramatically,' from adding emphasis, forcing them to abstract from their 'art.' He achieves this by killing their will, exhausting them with an endless number of repetitions and takes, by almost hypnotizing them." Truffaut, *The Films in My Life,* p. 192.

61. Truffaut, *The Films in My Life,* p. 193.

62. Truffaut, *The Films in My Life,* p. 178.

63. Translated by the author from the original screenplay: "Mom ami Jacques Becker a retracé dans tous les détails une histoire vraie: la mienne. Ça s'est passé en 1947, à la prison de la Santé."

64. René Clément's *Purple Noon* opened in New York in late August 1961.

65. In 1999, Anthony Minghella (*The English Patient*) directed another version of *The Talented Mr. Ripley.* After being out of circulation in the United States for many years, Martin Scorsese re-released *Plein Soleil* under the title *Purple Noon* in 1996.

66. At the time, Patricia Highsmith was renowned for *Strangers on a Train,* adapted to the screen by Alfred Hitchcock in 1951.

67. Translated by the author from the review *L'Avant Scène,* (261 February 1981).

CHAPTER 5: THE YEARS OF THE FRENCH NEW WAVE

1. Born Catherine Dorléac, Catherine Deneuve began her film career as a teenager using her mother's maiden name and appeared in several films, such as Jacques Poitrenaud's *The Doors Slam (Les portes claquent,* 1960), with her elder sister, Françoise Dorléac. Often associated with roles representing a "dependable" bourgeoise, Catherine Deneuve became internationally famous thanks to Jacques Demy's *The Umbrellas of Cherbourg (Les parapluies de Cherbourg,* 1964), followed by *The Young Girls of Rochefort (Les demoiselles de Rochefort,* 1967). Deneuve is well known for her photogenic, classic beauty. Her features have embodied France for decades, as her image has been used since 1985 in French city halls, succeeding Brigitte Bardot as a model for Marianne, the symbol of the French Republic. On screen, she has often represented strong, independent women, but she also has played memorable roles disclosing frailty and modesty, such as in André Téchiné's *My Favorite Season (Ma saison préférée,* 1993) and Régis Wargnier's *Indochine (Indochine,* 1992). In 1980, she won the César for Best Actress for François Truffaut's *The Last Metro (Le dernier métro,* 1980) in 1998 for Nicole Garcia's *Place Vendôme (Place Vendôme,* 1998), and in 1993, she obtained the César for Best Actress and a nomination at the Oscars for Best Actress as well.

2. When asked about the most important events of the decade, French people usually respond with the construction of the Berlin wall in August 1961,

which remained one of the uncompromising political barriers for the next three decades; US President John Kennedy's assassination in 1963; the feats of Soviet astronaut Yuri Gagarin, who was to orbit the earth in April 1961; and the revolutionary Ernesto "Che" Guevara, who became one of the most powerful symbols of a new generation. In the world of sports were Jacques Anquetil, who won five Tours de France (1957, 1961, 1962, 1963, and 1964), and Jean-Claude Killy, who won three gold medals in the Winter Olympics in Grenoble in 1968.

3. During the night of October 31, 1954, more than sixty bombing attacks occurred all over Algerian territory, which officially marked the beginning of the insurrection. The FLN (Algerian Liberation Front) became the main political party at the independence in 1962.

4. French state censorship was still very much unsympathetic with the cinematographic medium, despite the rapid social evolution of the 1960s.

5. The movie career of Jeanne Moreau (b. 1928) began in 1949. She acted in about twenty films, mostly in small roles. From a classical background (Conservatoire, Comédie-Française, Théâtre national populaire), Jeanne Moreau deeply influenced French contemporary sensitivity on eroticism and femininity. While she was still at the Comédie-Française, she starred with Jean Gabin and Lino Ventura in Jacques Becker's *Grisbi* (*Touchez pas au grisbi*, 1953). She had acted regularly in movies since 1949, but was already thirty before the New Wave found proper use of her image. Known for her sophisticated portrayals of amoral heroines, her real revelation as the supreme seductress was in Louis Malle's *Elevator to the Gallows* (*Ascenseur pour l'échafaud*, 1957), followed by *The Lovers* (*Les amants*, 1958) and François Truffaut's *Jules and Jim* (*Jules et Jim*, 1961). Moreau directed two films herself, *Light* (*Lumière*, 1976), which she also wrote, and *The Adolescent* (*L'adolescente*, 1979). Twice president of the Cannes Film Festival, in 1975 and 1995, she was one of the rare French actresses to be consistently solicited by great international names such as Orson Welles, Rainer Warner Fassbinder, Luis Buñuel. She is mostly remembered for her roles in Truffaut's *The Bride Wore Black* (*La mariée était en noir*, 1968), Jacques Demy's *Bay of Angels* (*La baie des Anges*, 1963), Malle's *The Fire Within* (*Le feu follet*, 1963) and *Viva Maria!* (*Viva Maria!*, 1965), Luis Buñuel's *Diary of a Chambermaid* (*Le journal d'une femme de chambre*, 1964), Bertrand Blier's *Going Places* (*Les valseuses*, 1974), Luc Besson's *La Femme Nikita* (*Nikita*, 1989), and for her memorable voice in Jean-Jacques Annaud's *The Lover* (*L'amant*, 1991). Moreau won for Best Actress at the 1960 Cannes Film Festival for Peter Brook's *Moderato Cantabile* and the César for Best Actress in 1992 for Laurent Heynemann's *The Old Lady Who Walked in the Sea* (*La vieille qui marchait dans la mer*, 1991).

6. Georges Poujouly (1940–96) first started his acting career as Michel in *Forbidden Games* (*Jeux interdits*, 1952), then appeared in supporting roles for several films, such as a schoolboy in *Diabolique* (*Les diaboliques*, 1955), as Jean-Louis Trintignant's younger brother in . . . *And God Created Woman* (*Et Dieu créa la femme*, 1956), and as the clumsy Louis in *Elevator to the Gallows* (*Ascenseur pour l'échafaud*, 1957).

7. Buss, *French Film Noir*, p. 46.

8. Alexandre Astruc (b. 1923) was one of the first critics to convert to film

directing and as a result insp~~~~~~~~~~~~~~~~~~~ng directors of the *nouvelle vague*. In his first important feature film, *The Crimson Curtain* (*Le rideau cramoisi*, 1952), he used the voice-over for the first-person narration. Although later drawn to a more formal literary cinema, he remained a pioneer of the spirit of the New Wave.

9. Truffaut's article was finally translated in English and published in January 1966 in the English version of the *Cahiers du cinéma*.

10. François Truffaut, *The Films in My Life* (New York: Simon & Schuster), p. 173.

11. Unlike the frequent pseudo-autobiographical aspect of New Wave films, the auteurs of the early 1960s were more stimulated by war issues, for example, Agnès Varda and the war in Algeria (*Cléo From 5 to 7*), or the atomic bomb, for example Alain Resnais (*Hiroshima Mon Amour*).

12. Claire Clouzot, *Le cinéma français depuis la nouvelle vague*, p. 48.

13. French New Wave, by conjugating the romanesque factor and documentary-like fiction, was consequently far off the line of work used by neorealist artists.

14. The notion of literary adaptation was also entirely reevaluated by Alain Resnais's *Hiroshima, Mon Amour* as "literature" was taken to a new type of transposition to the screen: conventional ideas were conveyed through a revolutionary medium.

15. These outdoor location shootings were made possible by the technological improvement of the 1950s, in particular the use of more sensitive film stocks (250 ASA). For more on these cinematic improvements see René Prédal's *50 ans de cinéma français*, pp. 123–25.

16. Although advocates of outdoor locations and natural lighting, French New Wave filmmakers had to work within certain technical constraints. In an art that principally involved the exhibition of vulnerable visual appearances, the presence of artificial lighting could not disappear overnight, especially in daylight shooting (outdoor locations); technical operators were compelled to rely on a certain amount of artificial light to lessen highlight effects or to brighten the natural darkness.

17. Also used in television, the invention of ultradirectional microphones allowed the source or the voice of the intended actor to be isolated in the general noise of an outdoor location.

18. Clouzot, p. 22.

19. Sardent was the actual village in the Creuse region where Claude Chabrol had spent part of his childhood.

20. Truffaut, *The Films in My Life*, p. 3.

21. Truffaut, *The Films in My Life*, p. 4.

22. *The Four Hundred Blows* conjured up Jean Vigo's *Zero for Conduct* (*Zéro de conduite*, 1933). The English translation of *Les quatre cents coups* could be "Raising Hell," recalling the pillow fight scene in the boarding school in Vigo's *Zero for Conduct*.

23. Although his childhood took place during the years of the German Occupation, François Truffaut did not feel comfortable enough for his first full-length film to re-create the particular ambience and background of the war, and consequently transferred the narrative to the 1950s. Strangely enough,

and despite Antoine Doinel's depiction, Truffaut never acknowledged making an entirely autobiographical film.

24. *Stolen Kisses,* whose score was a tribute to French singer Charles Trenet's evocative song "Que reste-t-il de nos amours?" narrated the urban chronicles of Antoine Doinel (Jean-Pierre Léaud), now a twenty-year-old in Paris, unsuccessfully trying to initiate a career as a private detective as well as an unadventurous romance. But his cumbersome behavior around women thwarts his plans. The film, although not Truffaut's best, earned more than a few awards, with a nomination for Best Foreign Film in the 1968 Academy Awards, the Prix Louis Delluc that same year, and prizes for Best Direction and Best Film in the 1969 New York Film Critics Circle.

25. One of the reasons for the fascination with American B-series gangster movies by New Wave directors was the obvious parallel (they liked to think) with their own situation as authors. Indeed, in a Hollywood where production left no personal trademark on films (especially for cinematographers, cameramen, and even directors) and where the mode of production relied heavily on tight script; B movies left an unusual amount of freedom for filmmakers.

26. James R. Paris, *The Great French Films* (Secaucus, NJ: The Citadel, 1983), p. 173.

27. Bellone, p. 125.

28. Tyler, p. 224.

29. A good illustration of the characteristic refusal of realism in the narration (long-established relation cause/effect) is the use of numerous and almost subliminal flash cuts in the characters' depiction, precision editing, which disrupted the habits of spectatorship.

30. The long tracking shots of grandiose settings, infused with a horizontal continuity (evoking the characters' stream of consciousness), made the different motions of the camera a beautiful combination of studio and outdoors shots (captured in Cinemascope by Alain Resnais's cinematographer, Sacha Vierny).

31. Francis Seyrig's hypnotically dreamlike music contributed to the overall mesmerizing performance of *Last Year at Marienbad.*

32. Jacques-Bernard Brunius, *En marge du cinéma français* (Paris: Arcanes, 1954), p. 130.

33. Jean-Paul Belmondo (b. 1933) started his acting career on the stage in 1951. His first film role was in Marcel Carné's *The Cheaters (Les tricheurs,* 1958). A year later, he landed his first important role in Claude Chabrol's *Double Twist (A double tour,* 1959), then starred with Lino Ventura in Claude Sautet's *The Big Risk (Classe tous risques,* 1960). In 1959, his destiny took a dramatic turn in Jean-Luc Godard's *Breathless,* and immediately after he imposed a face on French cinema that lasted for the rest of the century. His unusually unconcerned style and antiheroic disposition magnetized a young French public of the early 1960s and promoted him as one of the most popular male film stars. Early associated with the New Wave, Belmondo distanced himself from it with commercial movies such as Philippe de Broca's *That Man of Rio (L'homme de Rio,* 1963). Belmondo finally obtained critical acclaim with a César for Best Actor with Claude Lelouch's *Itinerary of a Spoiled Child (Itinéraire d'un enfant gâté,* 1988).

34. The remake of Jean Luc Godard's *Breathless* came out in 1983 with the same title, starring Richard Gere and Valerie Kaprisky and directed by Jim Mc-Bride.

35. By the turn of this new century actor Michel Piccoli (b. 1925) is one of French cinema's living legends, with an acting career that has spanned over four decades. Like most film actors of his generation, Piccoli was trained on the stage, starting with an apprenticeship at the prestigious Théâtre national populaire, which consequently triggered a future career shaped by every new twist of contemporary moods. However, he owes his existing notoriety in French cinema to Jean-Luc Godard for his role in *Contempt* (*Le mépris*, 1964), opposite Brigitte Bardot. Like Jean-Paul Belmondo and Alain Delon, Piccoli has not always performed in masterpieces, but he left his special trademark on every part of an inspired personal identity. As the architect and betraying husband in Claude Sautet's *The Things of Life* or the disillusioned physician and betrayed husband in *Vincent, Pierre, Paul and others*, Piccoli could rival and even surpass any of his celebrated fellow actors in indistinct intricacy between character study and real-life acting. In addition, Piccoli is one of the few French actors to have successfully worked with Italy's most prestigious directors for example, Marco Ferreri (*Blow Out/La grande bouffe*, 1973), Sergio Corbucci (*Neopolitan Thriller/Giallo napoletano*, 1978), and Lilana Cavani (*Beyond Obsession/Oltre la porta*, 1982). Piccoli won for Best Actor at the 1980 Cannes Film Festival for Marco Bellochio's *Salto nel vuoto* (*Le saut dans le vide*) and at the 1982 Berlin Film Festival for Pierre Granier-Deferre's *A Strange Affair* (*Une étrange affaire*, 1981).

36. Dialogue from Jean-Luc Godard's *Contempt* as translated by the author.
    CAMILLE: *Tu aimes mes yeux?* Paul: *Oui.*
    CAMILLE: *Tu aimes ma bouche?* Paul: *Oui.*
    CAMILLE: *Tu aimes mes seins?* Paul: *Oui.*
    CAMILLE: *Tu aimes mes fesses?* Paul: *Oui.*
    CAMILLE: *Alors, tu m'aimes?* Paul: *Oui.*

37. Dialogue from Agnès Varda's *Cléo from 5 to 7* as translated by the author. Cléo: "Ah, les hommes c'est pas pareil. Ils attendent toutes les femmes. Il les abordent, ils leur parlent. D'habitude je ne réponds pas, mais là, j'ai oublié. J'avais l'esprit ailleurs. Puis vous avez l'air si calme." Antoine: "Je suis en permission." Cléo: "Et ce costume?" Antoine: "Vous voyez, je suis à moitié en uniforme. A moitié parti, quoi. C'est que je repars ce soir. Oui, ce soir c'est fini. J'avais trois semaines et je n'ai rien fait, c'est trop court. Ça me fait plaisir de vous parler. Vous êtes mariée?"

38. Dialogue from Agnès Varda's *Cléo from 5 to 7* as translated by the author. Antoine: "Moi c'est plutôt mourir pour rien qui me désole. Donner sa vie à la guerre c'est un peu triste. J'aurais mieux aimé la donner à une femme, mourir d'amour." Cléo: "Vous n'avez jamais été amoureux?" Antoine: "Oh si, des tas de fois, mais jamais autant que j'aurais voulu, à cause des filles, vous savez comme elles sont. Elles aiment, et puis total, elles aiment qu'on les aime. Elles ont peur de tout, de se donner à fond, d'y laisser une plume ou deux. D'être marquées. Elles aiment à moitié, elles s'économisent. Leur corps c'est comme un joujou, ce n'est pas leur vie. Alors moi aussi je m'arrête en route et je débraye. Excusez-moi de vous dire tout cela, je ne vous connais pas."

39. Susan Hayward and Ginette Vincendeau, *French Film: Texts and Contexts* (New York: Routledge, 2000), p. 257.

40. Interestingly, Jean Gabin was reunited on stage, in 1936, with the most erotically glamorous actress of the 1930s, Viviane Romance, with whom he had not worked since Julien Duvivier's *They Were Five* (*La belle équipe*). Unfortunately, Viviane Romance's cameo role did not allow any mood for reminiscing, as her character disappears from the screen shortly after the beginning of the film.

41. "In critical situations, when one talks with a nice caliber in hand, no one argues. Check the statistics."

42. "Louis? His honesty is grotesque. He is almost unnatural, I mean . . . he never even got a speeding ticket."

43. Discontinued in February 1987, the Citroën 2 C.V. quickly became the French car of the century. It amusingly contrasted with the large American cars (preferably sporty convertible) usually featured in New Wave films (for example, Jean-Luc Godard's *Breathless* and Jean-Pierre Melville's *Le doulos*).

CHAPTER 6: THE CINEMA OF THE 1970S

1. Along with Bertrand Tavernier and Bertrand Blier, film directors Patrice Leconte, Alain Corneau, and Jean-Jacques Annaud still contribute regularly to French cinema.

2. Many film historians see the rise of erotic film as a result of more significant masculine susceptibility in conjunction with certain economic difficulties, as well as the collapse of traditional values.

3. *Emmanuelle* totaled almost nine million admissions in 1974.

4. Despite the TVA (value-added tax) set at 33 percent instead of the usual 17 percent, the erotic film industry moved forward through the decade. In fact, 1978 was the heyday of porn films in France, with a record 142 productions that year, corresponding to almost 5 percent of national cinematographic investments. On the production level, the average shooting length was from one to two weeks, and the general production costs remained very low in comparison to other commercial productions (especially since the entrance fee stayed the same). Under pressure from feminists the porn industry responded with more male nudity. In addition, in the mid-1970s, the determination and enforcement of what constituted pornography were turned over to the government at the same time that filmmakers were attempting to break away from production codes' bans on sexuality and violence.

5. The pornographic film industry was definitely a trend of the 1970s. By the mid-1980s, porn productions disappeared as a class from film statistics. With more than 150 films produced each year in the 1970s, only 4 were produced in 1986. Consequently, videos became increasingly more popular.

6. The 1970s were marked by a number of world tragedies and political improvements. In Europe, the post-68 era represented the end of the last right-wing dictatorships with the death of Franco in Spain in 1975, the overturn

of the military regime in Greece, and the revolution in Portugal terminating several long decades of military repression as well as the dramatic eradication of freedom's hope in Czechoslovakia. Alexander Dubcek's moderate socialism in Czechoslovakia appeared too dangerous to the Soviet Union, and in August 1968, Soviet tanks invaded Prague and reestablished an orthodox communist regime. Meanwhile, in the United States, while the situation in Vietnam worsened each year, the 1960s ended with a spectacular manifestation of youth and hope at Woodstock in August 1969, which inspired countless musicians throughout the rest of the century. Also mesmerizing was the journey of Apollo 11, achieving humankind's oldest dream, with the landing of the first men on the moon on July 21, 1969. The entire world watched the event live on television. Also of importance were President Richard Nixon's resignation following the Watergate scandal in the summer of 1974, the tragic fall of Saigon in 1975, and the alarming crisis in Cambodia, with revelations of the genocide by the Khmer Rouge. The world of sports saw its share of crisis and glory with the Mexico City Olympic games of 1968, with the display of Black power by some American athletes. That same year saw the assassination of Martin Luther King Jr. and Robert F. Kennedy. Four years later, political tension caused one of the most dramatic events in Olympic history, with the Munich hostage crisis in 1972 resulting in the death of eleven Israeli athletes. Finally, one of the greatest technological advancements of the century occurred in November 1971. This date is remembered as the birth of what was to revolutionize world technology and industry: the microprocessor.

7. Susan Hayward and Ginette Vincendeau, *French Film Texts and Contexts* (New York: Routledge, 2000), p. 244.

8. Jean-Paul Sartre intervened in favor of German anarchist Andreas Baader and eventually visited him in prison in Germany in 1974.

9. The 1970s were marked by the triple gold medal won by downhill skier Jean-Claude Killy at the Grenoble Winter Olympics in 1968. A few years later, the tribulations of soccer team Saint-Etienne who for the first time represented a French club in a final of a European cup. Although defeated in the final game on May 12, 1976, in Glasgow, Saint Etienne's exploits was highly celebrated as thousands of supporters gathered on the Champs Elysées, Saint Etienne remains to this date the most prestigious soccer team in French history. In the world of fashion, after the *mini-jupe* success of the 1960s, the topless vogue on French beaches, directly imported from northern Europe, became the rages. In music, the decade was marked by the advent of disco, which came to France through Anglo-Saxon and American music, as well as French newly reconverted singers such as Claude François, Joe Dassin, and Mike Brandt.

10. Following the Yom Kippur War between Israel and its surrounding Arab nations, the OPEC–oil embargo triggered the first oil crisis in 1973. Indirectly, unemployment rose for the first time. Immigration was also officially stopped for the first time since 1962, leading to underground immigration.

11. In 1972, a third channel (FR3) started to be broadcast in France.

12. In addition to the *cinéphilie* on the small screen, the French cinéma d'art et essai experienced a revival, with close to a thousand theaters in France by the late 1970s.

13. With approximately twelve million TV sets in France by the mid-1970s (in a population of fifty million), salvation came in part from the system of coproductions between European countries in addition to the French Film industry and French television.

14. Among the actors and directors of the French film industry, some prestigious names have never made it to the French Academy Award Hall of Fame; these include Patrick Dewaere, Lino Ventura, Claude Chabrol, Anouk Aimée, Jean-Louis Trintignant, Michel Piccoli, Maurice Pialat and Claude Lelouch (although both Palme d'Or), Danielle Darrieux, Claude Berri, Jacques Rivette, Jean-Pierre Mocky, Eric Rohmer, and Jean-Jacques Beineix. Luc Besson finally gained recognition with the César for Best Director for *The Fifth Element* (*Le cinquième élément,* 1997).

15. Since the postwar era, films that performed the best at the box office (except American and foreign productions) belonged to the commercial category. These include *La vache et le prisonnier* (1959), *La guerre des boutons* (1961), *Le corniaud* (1964), *La grande vadrouille* (1966), *Les aventures de Rabbi Jacob* (1973), and *Emmanuelle* (1974).

16. In *My American Uncle* (*Mon oncle d'Amérique*), Alain Resnais took reference from the behaviorist theories of scientist Henri Laborit, whose work and comments were at the basis of the project. Originally, a short for a pharmaceutical company, the film's script was elaborated by veteran screenwriter Jean Gruault and won the Prix spécial du jury at the 1980 Cannes Film Festival. This multifaceted story retraces the lives of Jean (Roger Pierre), whose political and literary career ultimately compels him to temporarily leave his wife and children, and to live with his new companion, Janine (Nicole Garcia), and René (Gérard Depardieu), a man with a rural and Catholic background who after becoming manager of a textile plant endures several professional demotions and humiliations. As the three itineraries proceed, the central idea of the film illustrates people's dependability on primitive instincts, which by its constant connection with the physical world, construct an understanding of reality based on experience rather than intellect. These laws of human behavior, based on brain study and animal physiognomy, explain how human behavior is conditioned by the development of early childhood.

17. One of the reasons for the poor condition of the films was the highly flammable texture of nitrate film stock, which was used in France until the late 1940s, then replaced with acetate, which was chemically unsafe. In addition, when the film stock ran through the projector, it became scratched or damaged. Even with limited selection, acquisition and storage were expensive and difficult, and nitrate film needed regular testing to determine whether it had deteriorated enough to require copying.

18. "La société française des années 70 ressemble à celle du Second Empire triomphant. Elle est dominée par le culte de l'argent, les grands travaux d'urbanisme, l'affairisme qui engendre des scandales immobiliers dans lesquels se trouve compromise la classe politique au pouvoir." Siclier, *Le cinéma français,* p. 26 (translated by the author).

19. "Et, au sein de ce cinéma du récit, la véritable nouveauté des films à 'sujets politiques,' celle qui caractérise cette période, est de ne plus chercher le plaisir du récit dans des valeurs collectives mais au contraire d'exalter les individus— ce qui passe aussi, alors, dans le jeu de faux-semblants et la rhétorique propres à l'époque, pour 'révolutionnaire,' " p. 246 (translated by the author).

20. Luhr, *World Cinema since 1945,* 1987. p. 203.

21. Frodon described the difficult relationship between the two directors after the screening of *Day for Night* in 1973. Frodon, pp. 384–387.

22. Born in Wisconsin, Joseph Losey cannot be categorized exclusively as an American filmmaker. After being blacklisted in the 1950s, he moved to England, where he enjoyed a brilliant new career that included major collaborations in European cinema. In the following years, he used a pseudonym for his films *The Big Night* (1951), *Blind Date* (1959), *The Criminal* (1960), *The Damned* (1963), *These Are the Damned* (1965), *Eva* (1965), *The Assassination of Trotsky* (*L'Assassinio di Trotsky,* 1972), and *Mozart's Don Giovanni* (*Don Giovanni,* 1979).

23. Born in Budapest, Hungary, Alexandre Trauner (1906–1993) came to France in the early 1930s and started to collaborate with Marcel Carné on early successes such as *Port of Shadows* (*Quai des brumes,* 1938), *Hôtel du Nord* (*Hôtel du Nord,* 1938), *Daybreak* (*Le jour se lève,* 1939), *The Devil's Envoys* (*Les visiteurs du soir,* 1942), *Children of Paradise* (*Les enfants du Paradis,* 1945), *La Marie du port* (1949), and *Juliette ou la clé des songes* (1950). He then worked for American cinema until the end of his career but still contributed to French films such as Jules Dassin's *Rififi* (*Du rififi chez les hommes,* 1955), Billy Wilder's *The Apartment* (1960), Joseph Losey's *Mr. Klein* (*Monsieur Klein,* 1976), Bertrand Tavernier's *Clean Slate* (*Coup de torchon,* 1981) and *'Round Midnight* (*Autour de minuit,* 1986), Claude Berri's *Tchao, pantin!* (1983), and Luc Besson's *Subway* (*Subway,* 1985).

24. Costa-Gavras became a French citizen in 1968.

25. Dan Mitrione, head of the Office of Public Safety in Montevideo, was alleged to have incited the practice of torture in Uruguayan prisons in the 1960s.

26. Philippe Noiret, Michel Piccoli, Marcello Mastroianni, and Ugo Tognazzi participated in this eccentric, decadent comedy, which immediately became a worldwide sensation. The four friends, victims of their lust for women and good food, decide to retire in a villa, where they fill their days with an excess of carnal delight until they pass out in a catharsis of orgiastic hedonism.

27. Clouzot, p. 132.

28. His first color film was *Magnet of Doom* (*L'aîné des Ferchaux,* 1962).

29. Melville purposely used composite characters as they represented several types of people in one. For instance, it is believed that the role of Luc Jardie interpreted by Paul Meurisse was partly based on Jean Moulin's and Jean Cavaillès's extraordinary roles in the French Resistance in Lyon.

30. *The Army of Shadows* was also published in New York a year later, in 1944.

31. Buache, p. 55.

32. Henri Verneuil employed the same actors as in *Any Number Can Win* (*Mélodie en sous-sol,* 1964).

33. The title of the counter operation, which eventually led Henry Volney to his death, was named after Icarus, from Greek mythology, who exited the laby-

rinth by attaching wings on his back with the help of wax. Flying high in the sky, Icarus gets too near the heat of the sun (or the truth). As the wax melts he falls into the sea.

34. Here Truffaut is referring to Sautet's first long feature films *Nous n'irons plus au bois* (1951) and *The Big Risk* (*Classe tous risques,* 1959).

35. François Truffaut, *The Films in My Life* (New York: Simon & Schuster, 1978), p. 341.

36. Truffaut, p. 340.

37. Truffaut, pp. 340–342.

38. The edit integrated additional material in the account, such as the presence of a compromising letter, in order to set the illusion of the story against the hard reality of other types of images. Sautet's choice in editing permitted the juxtaposition of very different kinds of material for a variety of rhetorical effects.

39. Jean Boffety, one of the most talented cinematographers of the 1970s, worked mainly with French filmmakers, Italian director Vittorio de Sica, and American Robert Altman. Some of his most important work was in Claude Goretta's *The Lacemaker* (*La dentellière,* 1977), Robert Altman's *Quintet* (1979), Claude Lelouch's *Bolero* (*Les uns et les autres,* 1981) and *Edith and Marcel* (*Edith et Marcel,* 1983), and Claude Sautet's *Waiter!* (*Garçon!,* 1983).

40. Claude Sautet offered Vittorio Gassman the role of César with Catherine Deneuve as Rosalie, but the Italian refused the role. Sautet's inadvertently chose Yves Montand, as both met during a film projection. The director, touched by the actor's features, immediately realized that Montand was perfect for the character of César.

41. Truffaut, p. 341.

42. The *Man Who Loved Women* was remade in 1983 by Blake Edwards, with Burt Reynolds as the "irresistible" hero.

43. "Les jambes de femmes sont des compas qui arpentent le globe terrestre en tout sens, lui donnant son équilibre et son harmonie" (translation taken from the American release).

44. "Je crois qu' on peut difficilement vous refuser quelque chose. Vous avez une façon spéciale de demander; c'est comme si votre vie en dépendait. Mais au fond c'est peut-être tout simplement une ruse de guerre: le dragueur qui n'en a pas l'air, le dragueur inquiet" (translation taken from the American release).

45. "Certaines sont si belles vu de dos, que je retarde le moment d'arriver à leur hauteur pour ne pas être déçu. A vrai dire je ne suis jamais déçu parce que celles qui sont belles de dos et moches de face me donnent une sensation de soulagement . . . puisqu'il n'est pas question de les avoir toutes" (translation taken from the American release).

46. Annette Insdorf, *François Truffaut* (Boston: Twayne, 1978), pp. 142–143.

47. Diana Holmes and Robert Ingram, *François Truffaut* (Manchester: Manchester University Press, 1998), p. 132.

48. For more on *The Man Who Loved Women,* see Gordon Gow, "The Man Who Loved Women," in *Films and Filming,* 24(8) (May 1978), p. 41, and Marsha Kinder, "The Man Who Loved Women," *Film Quarterly* 31(3) (Spring 1978), pp. 48–52.

49. See Antoine de Baecque, *Truffaut* (New York: Knopf, 1999) p. 335.

50. See chapter 5.
51. For a thorough study on Eric Rohmer, see Colin Crisp's *Eric Rohmer, Realist and Moralist* (Bloomington: Indiana University Press, 1988).
52. Vincendeau, p. 36.
53. Le Café de la Gare launched innumerable young comedians, such as Michel Colucci (Coluche), Sylvette Herry (Miou-Miou), Patrick Maurin (Dewaere), Rufus, Jacques Higelin, Renaud Séchan, Martin Lamotte, Thierry Lhermitte, and Michel Blanc. All went on to achieve success in the movies.
54. See Jacques Siclier, *Le cinéma français* (Paris: Ramsay, 1990), pp. 275–277.
55. A rather surprising presence of Michel Galabru in such an intense drama for an actor usually involved with comic roles, i.e., the Adjudant Gerber in Jean Girod's *The Gendarme of St. Tropez* (*Le gendarme de St. Tropez,* 1964), *La cage aux folles* (*La cage aux folles,* 1978), and *Papi fait de la résistance* (1983).
56. Pierre Bost was no longer collaborating. He died shortly before the shooting of the film in 1975.

CHAPTER 7: THE CINEMA OF THE 1980S

1. In France, satellite dish systems were still reaching a very small minority by the end of the 1980s.
2. European Economic Community (EEC) was the former name of the present European Union.
3. In 1965, Mitterrand ran unsuccessfully for the presidency against Charles de Gaulle and against Valéry Giscard d'Estaing in 1974, losing by a narrow margin.
4. Meanwhile, the 1980s were a turbulent period. From ex-Beatle John Lennon's murder in New York City in December 1980 to Egyptian president and peace advocate, Anwar Sadat's assassination in Egypt in 1981, to the Iraq-Iran war and the Falkland war between Argentina and Great Britain in 1982, to the massive starvation disaster in Ethiopia in 1986, the decade witnessed many misfortunes around the globe. With the state of emergency declared in Poland while General Jaruzelski took power in December 1983, the communist regimes of Eastern Europe saw their last demonstration of force before what became known as Mikhail Gorbachev's *glasnost* era after 1987. Perhaps the major event was the dismantlement of the Eastern bloc. In parallel with the worst environmental catastrophe of the decade occurring at Chernobyl in the Ukraine (April 1986), the communist bloc slowly dissolved. In June 1989, in Beijing, the Chinese regime ordered the termination of student protests at Tien-an-men Square, one of the most tragic (and definitely most forgotten) dramas of the century, as the United States became the first country to resume economic trade with China a few months later.
5. Today, the harsh competition between the *radios jeunes* and newcomers, such as Europe 2 and RTL 2, is the result of the nearly identical nature of the targeted audience and the similar music programming.
6. Hayward, pp. 232–233.
7. Except rare films like Romain Goupil's *Mourir à trente ans* (1982).

8. Hayward, p. 232.

9. Interestingly, popular actor Lino Ventura, who died in October 1987, became a movie legend based on his roles in mobster movies (e.g., *Grisbi, The Sicilian Clan*). Ventura's charisma and sincerity contributed to the fascination the French public had for the actor and illustrated the transformation of the French star system.

10. The General Agreement on Tariffs and Trade (GATT), which took effect on January 1, 1948, was primarily designed to eradicate quotas and tariff duties among countries participating in the agreement. However, despite a strong commitment against discrimination, the GATT merely contained protectionist measures. Following a failure to reach a decisive agreement in 1993, the World Trade Organization replaced GATT in 1995. Currently 125 nations are participants, representing more than 90 percent of world trade.

11. Jean-Michel Frodon, *L'âge modern du cinéma français: De la nouvelle vague à nos jours* (Paris: Flammarion, 1995), p. 657.

12. Jean Becker's *One Deadly Summer* (*L'été meurtrier,* 1983) was characteristic of the decade. By reflecting the spirit of the times, the film's ambition was not only to join two of France's most celebrated artists (Isabelle Adjani and Alain Souchon) but also to reinstate the thriller/crime story. Especially colorful, the film was a success in large part because of Adjani, who played her first sexually prominent part in a French film, more than for the disposition of the scenario and suspense element. At first reluctant to play the role, Isabelle Adjani postponed on several occasions Becker's offer for the part in the project written by Sébastien Japrisot. Finally, after four years of negotiations, Adjani accepted. The story line: In a small village in Provence, PinPon (Alain Souchon), a mechanic, falls in love with the promiscuous Eliane (Isabelle Adjani), a newcomer to the village. Although pretending to be interested in the romance, she is actually seeking revenge on men, since her mother was raped by three men years before and one of them might well have been Pinpon's late father. The two soon marry. Temporarily peaceful in her new marriage, Isabelle relapses to the furies of vengeance and slowly convinces Pinpon to murder the two remaining suspected rapists. They turn out to be innocent but it is too late, and ultimately she will end up in a mental hospital. At the 1984 Césars ceremony, *One Deadly Summer* earned awards for Best Actress (Isabelle Adjani), Best Supporting Actress (Suzanne Flon), Best Adapted Screenplay (Sébastien Japrisot), and Best Montage (Jacques Witta).

13. For more on television income and advertisement, see Prédal, pp. 458–64.

14. With VCRs came "zapping." Bored, or even frustrated, viewers could now switch channels easily using remote controls. A decade later, the effect of this phenomenon was seen in spectators' reduced attention spans which necessitated a new type of visual language.

15. Script by Suzanne Schiffman and Jean Aurel.

16. See chapter 4.

17. David Walsh, *The Films of François Truffaut* article published in October 1999 on wsws.org.

18. In the 1970s, Truffaut politically moved leftward, eventually supporting the ideas of the Socialist Party and the CFDT trade union (*Confédération Française Démocratique du Travail*).

19. Truffaut, *Hitchcock/Truffaut,* New York: Simon and Schuster, 1967.

20. Hancock was accompanied by musicians Billy Higgins, Wayne Shorter, Ron Carter, John McLaughlin, and Bobby Hutcherson, among others.

21. Bertrand Tavernier, *50 ans de cinéma américain,* Paris: Nathan, 1995.

22. Prédal, p. 605.

23. Charlélie Couture wrote the music for the film.

24. See chapter 2.

25. Claude Berri, *Le Matin,* Dec. 19, 1983.

26. Deeply touched by a spectator's comment on the situations of homeless people during a TV show appearance, Coluche took the project to heart and began to establish regular contact with Jacques Atali, François Mitterrand's adviser at the time. On December 1985, a television fundraiser show, unprecedented at the time in France, gathered actors like Yves Montand and Jean-Paul Belmondo and singers Michel Sardou, Enrico Macias, and Patrick Sébastien to generate more than 20 million francs in one night. Consequently, every winter, more than 600 restaurants are able to distribute 100,000 meals for the homeless all over France (to this date 36,000 volunteers of the Restos du Coeur serve up to 600,000 meals per day and 60 million meals per year).

27. The association Restaurants du Coeur has officially been recognized by the Comité de la Charité de Déontologie des organisations sociales et humanitaires. The "Coluche" law allows companies to benefit from a tax cut (up to 60 percent) for donations up to 2,050 francs, with a limit of 6 percent of total revenue.

28. In front of the TV cameras, Yves Montand, who had lost his wife, Simone Signoret, a year before, pronounced these memorable lines: "Je suis là aujourd'hui parce que ton ami Lederman m'a dit que tu partais en voyage et que tu aurais souhaité que je sois près de toi. Alors, voilà, je suis près de toi. Et comme on dit dans le Midi, ça me fait bien plaisir! Mais j'aurais préféré te rencontrer et te retrouver dans d'autres circonstances. Ceux qui t'aiment sont une minorité qui fait une drôle de majorité. Je ne sais pas qui de Simone ou de toi est le plus enfoiré, mais ce que je sais, c'est que vous ne perdez rien pour attendre."

29. Anthony Burgess, who wrote *A Clockwork Orange,* conceived an incomprehensible pseudo-language especially for Jean-Jacques Annaud's project.

30. The dialogue grunts were authored by Anthony Burgess and the precious "body language" provided by Desmond Morris.

31. Umberto Eco, a renowned semiology professor at the University of Bologna, ended his enigmatic novel with a Latin phrase, which gave the title to the book. The rose could be associated with the young girl saved by the mob.

32. Gérard Brach's filmography as screenwriter includes such films as Claude Berri's *Jean de Florette* and Annaud's *The Quest for Fire, The Name of the Rose,* and *The Lover.*

33. "Je crois qu'on a tort d'identifier le cinéma à la langue, comme si le cinéma était de la littérature. L'art du cinéma est l'art de l'image et la langue y est très secondaire. Quand un livre français est un succès international, il l'est parce qu'il véhicule la pensée de l'auteur français et non pas sa langue. Pour le cinéma, c'est pareil." Interview conducted by Laurent Daniélou, cultural attaché in Los Angeles.

34. "C'est une bonne occasion de changer les mentalités et d'expliquer aux français que les Américains ne cherchent pas à tuer le cinéma français. Ce sont tout simplement des hommes d'affaires qui ont envie de faire de bons films. . . . Nous pensons, nous professionnels qui travaillons depuis longtemps avec la communauté américaine, que les Français se font une fausse idée de se qui se passe à Los Angeles. C'est un milieu beaucoup plus amical et ouvert aux influences étrangères qu'on ne le pense. Nous sommes là pour aider nos collègues français à comprendre l'évolution du cinéma hollywoodien et pour permettre aux Américains de faire connaissance avec les techniciens et les gens de talent français. L'objectif est de favoriser les rencontres et de réinstaller un climat amical entre les deux communautés." Interview conducted by Laurent Daniélou, cultural attaché in Los Angeles.

35. Prédal, p. 548.

36. With cinematographers Raoul Coutard and Henri Decaë, Philippe Rousselot (b. 1945) is one of France's leading film artists. He was assistant cameraman for Eric Rohmer's *My Night at Maud's* (*Ma nuit chez Maud,* 1969), *Claire's Knee* (*Le genou de Claire,* 1970), and *Chloé in the Afternoon* (*L'amour l'après-midi,* 1972) and photographer for Diane Kurys's *Peppermint Soda* (*Diabolo menthe,* 1977), Jacques Doillon's *The Hussy* (*La drôlesse,* 1979), Beineix's *Diva,* and *The Moon in the Gutter* (*La lune dans le caniveau,* 1983), Jean-Jacques Annaud's *The Bear* (*L'our,* 1988), Bertrand Blier's *Too Beautiful for You* (*Trop belle pour toi,* 1989), and Patrice Chéreau's *Queen Margot* (*La reine Margot,* 1994). Rousselot also collaborated with American filmmakers in features such as Stephen Frears's *Dangerous Liaisons* (1988), Neil Jordan's *We're No Angels* (1989) and *Interview with the Vampire* (1994), Robert Redford's *A River Runs through It* (1992), Jon Amiel's *Sommersby* (1993), Milos Forman's *The People vs. Larry Flynt* (1996), Sydney Pollack's *Random Hearts* (1999), Boaz Yakin's *Remember the Titans* (2000), and Tim Burton's *Planet of the Apes* (2001).

37. As Zorg, Jean-Hugues Anglade revealed himself as a new type of romantic urban hero, highly representative of the spirit of the 1980s. He appeared again in Luc Besson's *La Femme Nikita* (*Nikita,* 1990) and in *Subway* (*Subway,* 1984).

38. The annual world free-diving competition persisted well into the 1980s before it was finally called to a halt when league officials concluded that competitors were diving too deep, making it practically impossible for anyone to make it safely to the surface.

39. Jean-Marc Barr's character is based on an actual free-diving champion, Jacques Mayol, who agreed to participate in the project.

40. Mayol's preference for the sea was evoked in Jean-Marc Barr's performance and the way the actor maintained an evocative look, much like the dolphins that were his "family" in the film.

41. Bruno Nuytten (b. 1945) re-created the tragic destiny of artist Camille Claudel (1864–1943), interpreted by Isabelle Adjani, who, as an adolescent, dreamed of becoming the student of Auguste Rodin (Gérard Depardieu). Her dreams become reality when Rodin accepts her as his apprentice. Soon enough, she becomes his mistress and discovers that his passion for the female body is his only source of inspiration. Losing her stamina, she devotes all of her strength to her love until Rodin abandons her following a stormy rela-

tionship. Hopeless and distressed, Camille begins a life of drinking, debauchery, and solitude. In 1913, her brother Paul sends her to a mental institution, where she stays until her death in 1943. The film was Bruno Nuytten's first full-length feature and won the César for Best Film in 1989. Nuytten had already experienced national recognition as a cinematographer, winning the César for Best Cinematography, first in 1976 for André Téchiné's *Barocco,* then in 1984 for Claude Berri's *Tchao Pantin!*

CHAPTER 8: THE LAST DECADE AND BEYOND

1. First discovered in Jean-Luc Godard's *Hail Mary* (*Je vous salue Marie,* 1984), Parisian actress Juliette Binoche (b. 1964) won acclaim a year later in André Téchiné's *Rendez-vous* (*Rendez-vous,* 1985), then in Philip Kaufman's *The Unbearable Lightness of Being* (*L'insoutenable légèreté de l'être,* 1987), starring Daniel Day-Lewis, adapted from a novel by Milan Kundera. She was also cast in Leos Carax's *Bad Blood* (*Mauvais sang,* 1987) and the memorable *Lovers on the Bridge* (*Les amants du Pont neuf,* 1991), Louis Malle's *Damage* (*Fatale,* 1992), Jean-Paul Rappeneau's *The Horseman on the Roof* (*Le hussard sur le toit,* 1995), and Patrice Leconte's *The Widow of Saint-Pierre* (*La veuve de Saint-Pierre,* 2000). One of her most dramatic roles, which evidently confirmed the shift of Binoche's acting career toward more mature roles was in Krzysztof Kieslowski's *Bleu* (*Bleu,* 1993), for which Binoche won the award for Best Actress at the French Academy Awards in 1993. With her radiant smile and energy, Juliette Binoche has not only become France's top actress but has started a second career with international productions such as Anthony Minghella's *The English Patient* (1996), for which she received an Oscar for Best Supporting Actress in 1996, and more recently Lasse Hallström's *Chocolat,* nominated for five Oscars in 2001.

2. Most American studios control an important part of British film distribution networks, by making favorable agreements and eventually screening exclusively American films. Having this virtual monopoly, they can undermine small theaters that may be more inclined to screen European art house productions.

3. In 1997, 40 percent of French full-length features produced or coproduced by Le Studio Canal were first films.

4. Mathieu Kassovitz's *La haine* (1995), Philippe Harel's *The Hikers* (*Les randonneurs,* 1997), Christian Vincent's *La discrète* (1990), and Eric Rochant's *Love without Pity* (*Un monde sans pitié,* 1989).

5. Headquartered in Paris, Vivendi, which holds a 49 percent stake in Canal+'s capital, operates in over one hundred countries with 260,000 employees.

6. Universal's Music Group is presently the world's largest music company.

7. Extract from the interview with cultural attaché Laurent Daniélou in Los Angeles. Jean-Jacques Annaud (b. 1943) came to filmmaking through army training documentaries and TV commercial ads. His film career started with an Oscar-winning feature, for Best Foreign Picture, *Black and White in Color* (*La victoire en chantant,* 1976) but only gave Annaud International stature with *Quest for Fire* (*La guerre du feu,* 1981) and *The Name of the Rose* (*Le nom de*

la rose, 1986) with big-name stars including Sean Connery. Since then, Annaud made international productions involving an array of different nationalities for his actors such as *The Bear* (*L'ours,* 1989), *The Lover* (*L'amant,* 1991) an adaptation of Marguerite Duras' best-selling novel, and more recently *Seven Years in Tibet* (1997) with Brad Pitt (which resulted in a permanent ban on the filmmaker from entering China) and *Enemy at the Gates* (*Stalingrad,* 2001) starring Jude Law and Joseph Fiennes.

8. Newcomers on French film sets were not always citizens of the Eastern block, searching for artistic freedom for example, American director John Berry fled the United States in 1951 to avoid the merciless witch hunt of the McCarthy era.

9. Hayward, p. 254.

10. Daniel Emilfork has an extensive film career and is mostly associated with European cinema (e.g., Federico Fellini's *Casanova,* 1976).

11. Ron Perlman is not unknown to French directors, as he appeared in Jean-Jacques Annaud's *Quest for Fire* (1980), *The Name of the Rose* (1986), and *Enemy at the Gates* (2001), and the last version of *Alien: Resurrection* (1997) with Jean-Pierre Jeunet.

12. The Studios de France set was unusually large, totaling 4,000 square meters, 40 meters long and 16 meters high.

13. Many scenes included a number of digital effects (supervised by the Duboi Company): for example a surprisingly reliant technical inventiveness, when allowing actor Dominique Pinon played six different parts on-screen at the same time the clones appearances and synchronized movements and final explosion of the platform.

14. The French film *Amélie* entered the UK box office charts in the top five, making it the biggest French-language opening in British cinema history.

15. French production reached 50 percent of national market during the first part of 2001 (US films accounted for 41 percent). A good indicator in parallel to the national success of several French productions: Thomas Gilou's *Would I Lie To You? 2* (*La vérité si je mens 2,* 2001), Christophe Gans's *The Brotherhood of the Wolf* (*Le pacte des loups,* 2001), and so forth.

16. The film was shown at a private screening for Jacques Chirac at the Palais de l'Elysée.

17. Rufus also appeared in *Delicatessen* and *The City of Lost Children.*

18. Audrey Tautou appeared in Tonie Marshall's *Venus Beauté Institut* (1999).

19. Jean-Pierre Jeunet's original choice for the character of Amélie was British actress Emily Watson. But it was only with Audrey Tautou that the director found the continuation of the heroine of *The City of Lost Children,* a sort of grown-up Miette.

20. Urbain Cancelier appeared in Patrice Leconte's *Ridicule* (1996) as Louis XVI.

21. Serge Merlin appeared in *The City of Lost Children.*

22. Isabelle Nanty appeared in Etienne Chatiliez's *Tatie Danielle* (1990) and Jean-Marie Poiré's *The Visitors* (*Les visiteurs,* 1993).

23. Dominique Pinon appeared in *The City of Lost Children* and Jean-Jacques Beineix's *Diva.*

24. Mathieu Kassovitz was the director of *Hate* (*La haine,* 1995).

25. But among the national fervor, the unenthusiastic critics converged around three main elements. First, that Jeunet's vision of an ideal cinematographic happiness was far from successful since intangible and even impossible by nature; second that the device which was to convey a rather simplistic narration through a giant clip using a technique reminiscent of commercials, in order to easily capture viewers' mind, was underhanded in a context of a so-called artistic cinema; and finally that the representation of the traditional values of Paris were distorted, erroneous and fake.

26. *Libération,* April 25, 2001.

27. In 1984, Marguerite Duras won the Goncourt Prize for her autobiographical novel *The Lover* (*L'amant*). Duras suggested the adaptation to Jean-Jacques Annaud. The film, first screened in January 1992, had a budget of $20 million.

28. Relentlessly introverted, the character of Eliane seems to enjoy a rather easy life, while exploiting the local people for her own prosperity. However, it is worthwhile to note that Wargnier gave the character an extra dimension, absent among her French colleagues, as she attempts to seek understanding and even intimacy with the local Vietnamese population.

29. Powrie, *French Cinema in the 1990s,* p. 41.

30. *Germinal* has been one of the most challenging adaptations in French cinema history. Because of the length of Zola's novel and the countless details in the presentation of the working conditions of miners, the film has remained a challenge for filmmakers: Victorin Jasset (1912), Albert Capellani (1913), and Yves Allégret (1963) also directed versions of Germinal.

31. Powrie, p. 19.

32. Jean-Hugues Anglade (b. 1955) has often been described as the *héros romantique* of French cinema for his roles in Jean-Jacques Beineix's *Betty Blue* (37°2 *le matin,* 1986) and Luc Besson's *Subway* and *Nikita.* He is one of the few French actors to work with American film directors, such as Roger Avary in *Killing Zoe* (1994). His filmography also includes Patrice Chéreau's *The Wounded Man* (*L'homme blessé,* 1983) and *Queen Margot* (*La reine Margot,* 1994), Alain Corneau's *Nocturne indien* (1989), Claude Sautet's *Nelly and Mr. Arnaud* (*Nelly and M. Arnaud,* 1995), and Beineix's *Mortal Transfer* (*Mortel transfert,* 2000).

33. Henri de Navarre, one of the most popular kings in French history, became the Court's captive until 1576, when he escaped. He later renounced Catholicism and took charge again of Protestant forces.

34. For the film's detractors, eager to maintain historical accuracy, none of the historical events and their possible impact on Margot's psyche were fully explored.

35. Jansenists disapproved of the Jesuits' worldliness and inclination for ostentation.

36. Composer–performer Monsieur de Sainte-Colombe revolutionized the usage of the viol (the viola de gamba, which ultimately became the cello), adding a seventh string to it, finding new fingerings, and designating Marin Marais as his direct disciple.

37. Unlike many other film versions that emphasized the absurdly deformed, even idiotic nose of the main character, in this *Cyrano de Bergerac* Depardieu's nose

looked startlingly real, as a result of the precious expertise of make-up artist Michèle Burke, who received on-screen credit.

38. Historians have asserted that the real Cyrano de Bergerac, an accomplished soldier, expert swordsman, poet, playwright, philosopher, and even science fiction writer (for *A Voyage to the Moon,* 1656), had in fact little in common with the Cyrano of Rostand's play.

39. Charles Berling (b. 1958) began his acting career on stage in 1982. Pascale Ferran's *Petits arrangements avec les morts* (1994) and his leading role in Patrice Leconte's *Ridicule* gained him international recognition. His roles in Claude Sautet's *Nelly et Monsieur Arnaud* (1995), in which he played Emmanuelle Béart's monotonous husband, and Cédric Kahn's *L'ennui* (1998), based on the novel by Moravia, as well as Patrice Chéreau's *Ceux qui m'aiment prendront le train* (1998), confirmed him as one of France's leading male actors at the turn of the century. Berling reteamed with Emmanuelle Béart to star in a period drama, *Les destinées sentimentales,* by Olivier Assayas, as well as Bernard Rapp's *A Question of Taste* (*Une affaire de goût,* 2000) and Olivier Douyere's *Crime Scenes* (*Scènes de crimes,* 2000).

40. Rémi Waterhouse was assisted by screenwriters Michel Fessler and Eric Vicaut.

41. Powrie, p. 86.

42. As paradoxical as it may seem, many pre-Revolutionary noblemen venerated the personage of Voltaire as the epitome of courage and wit, but their axioms outperformed his in vindictiveness while avoiding his genuine sense for social insurgence. This illustrates the well-known *preciosité* of eighteenth-century French aristocrats who engaged in spiritual jousting as a mean-spirited form of dishonor and repression, and ultimately to maintain class distinctions.

43. Powrie, p. 89.

44. Ibid.

45. Other leading comedies include Francis Veber's *The Dinner Game* (*Le dîner de cons,* 1998), 9.2 million; Henri Verneuil's *La vache et le prisonnier* (1959), 8.8 million; Jean-Marie Poiré's *The visitors II* (*Les couloirs du temps: Les visiteurs II,* 1998), 8 million; Hervé Palud's *Un indien dans la ville* (1994), 7.8 million; Jean Girault's *Le gendarme de Saint-Tropez* (1964), 7.8 million; Claude Zidi's *Les bidasses en folie* (1971), 7.4 million; Gérard Oury's *Les aventures de Rabbi Jacob* (1973), 7.3 million; Francis Veber's *La chèvre* (1981), 7 million; Gilles Grangier's *La cuisine au beurre* (1963), 6.4 million; Michel Blanc's *Marche à l'ombre* (1984), 6.1 million; Edouard Molinaro's *Oscar* (*Oscar,* 1967), 6.1 million; Claude Zidi's *My New Partner* (*Les ripoux,* 1984), 5.8 million; Claude Zidi's *L'aile ou la cuisse* (1976), 5.8 million; Jean-Marie Poiré's *Les anges gardiens* (1995), 5.7 million; Gérard Oury's *La folie des grandeurs* (1971), 5.5 million; Edouard Molinaro's *La cage aux folles* (*La cage aux folles,* 1978), 5.4 million; Thomas Gilou's *La verité si je mens,* (1997), 4.8 million; and Francis Veber's *Les compères* (1983), 4.8 million.

46. Born Juan Moreno in Casablanca, Morocco, Jean Réno (b. 1948) has regularly performed in American productions while maintaining a solid career in France. His career started in the early 1980s with small parts in Costa-Gavras's *Womanlight* (*Clair de femme,* 1979) and Jacques Rouffio's *The Passerby* (*La passante du sans souci,* 1982). Other roles included Luc Besson's *Subway* (*Sub-*

way, 1985), *The Big Blue* (*Le grand bleu,* 1988) and *La Femme Nikita* (*Nikita,* 1990), and *The Professional* (*Léon,* 1994). Reno also collaborated on several occasions with American filmmakers, such as Lawrence Kasdan (*French Kiss,* 1995), Brian De Palma (*Mission: Impossible,* 1996), Roland Emmerich (*Godzilla,* 1998), and John Frankenheimer (*Ronin,* 1998), with Robert De Niro. He was also in Mathieu Kassovitz's *The Crimson Rivers* (*Les rivières pourpres,* 2000).

47. Jacques Villeret, one of France most popular comedians, has starred in such films as Jean Becker's *Les enfants du Marais* (1999) and Thomas Gilou's *Black Mic Mac* (1986).

48. Powrie, p. 16.

49. Actor Vincent Cassel (b. 1966), originally from Paris and son of actor Jean-Pierre Cassel, has extended his acting talent oversees as well as in France. His international film career includes James Ivory's *Jefferson in Paris* (1995), as Camille Desmoulins, Shekhar Kapur's *Elizabeth* (*Elizabeth,* 1998), as the Duc d'Anjou, Luc Besson's *The Messenger: The Story of Joan of Arc* (Jeanne d'Arc, 1999), Mathieu Kassovitz's *The Crimson Rivers,* and Christophe Gans's *Brotherhood of the Wolf* (*Le pacte des loups,* 2001).

50. Elodie Bouchez has been acting in French films since the early 1990s, in particular in André Téchiné's *Wild Reeds* (*Les roseaux sauvages*). *The Dreamlife of Angels,* however, undeniably was her first major movie.

51. Eric Zonca, *Dossier de presse du film,* Cannes Film Festival, 1998.

52. Class barriers also are very much suggested, as both characters do not socially progress within the narration. Like vagabonds, both young women, although estranged from mainstream society, never enter the world of homelessness.

53. The release of the film (with a budget estimated around 160 million francs), foreseen for the 2001 Cannes Film Festival in May, was postponed in post-production until September of the same year.

Select Bibliography

GENERAL

Abel, Richard. *French Cinema: The First Wave, 1915–1929*. Princeton: Princeton University Press, 1987.

———. *French Film Theory and Criticism: A History/Anthology, 1907–1939*. Vol. 2. Princeton: Princeton University Press, 1988.

Alekan, Henri. *Des lumières et des ombres*. Paris: Le Sycamore/La Cinémathèque française, 1984.

Amengual, B. *Les français et leur cinéma, 1930–39*. Créteil: Losfeld, 1973.

Andrew, Dudley. *Film in the Aura of Art*. Princeton: Princeton University Press, 1984.

Armes, Roy. *French Cinema*. New York: Oxford University Press, 1985.

———. *French Cinema since 1946*. 2 vols. New Jersey: A. S. Barnes and Co., 1970.

Austin, Guy. *Contemporary French Cinema: An Introduction*. Manchester: Manchester University Press, 1996.

Bandy, Mary Lea, ed. *Rediscovering French Film*. New York: Museum of Modern Art, 1983.

Barrot, Olivier, and Raymond Chirat. *Les excentriques du cinéma français*. Paris: Veyrier, 1993.

Barsacq, Léon. *Le décor de film*. Paris: Seghers, 1970.

Bardèche, Maurice and Robert Brasillach. *Histoire du cinéma*. Paris: André Martel, 1954.

Bazin, André. *La politique des auteurs*. Paris: Cahiers du Cinéma, 1984.

———. *What Is Cinema?* 2 vols. Berkeley: University of California Press, 1967–71.

Bellone, Julius. *Renaissance of the film*. New York: Collier, 1970.

Biggs, Melissa. *French Films, 1945 through 1993: A Critical Filmography of the 400 Most Important Releases*. Jefferson, NC: McFarland & Company, 1996.

Billard, Pierre. *L'âge classique du cinéma français: Du cinéma parlant à la nouvelle vague*. Paris: Flammarion, 1995.

Borde, Raymond. *Les cinémathèques*. Lausanne: L'âge d'homme, 1983.

Braunberger, Pierre. *Cinémamémoire*. Paris: Centre Georges Pompidou, 1987.

Brunius, Jacques-Bernard. *En marge du cinéma français*. Paris: Arcanes, 1954.

Burch, Noël, and Geneviève Sellier. *La drôle de guerre des sexes du cinéma français (1930–1956)*. Paris: Nathan, 1996.

Buss, Robin. *French Film Noir*. New York: Marion Boyars, 1994.

————. *The French through Their Films*. New York: Ungar, 1988.

Cadars, Pierre. *Les séducteurs du cinéma français, 1928–1958*. Paris: Veyrier, 1982.

Chartier, Jean-Pierre and F. Desplanques. *Derrière l'écran: Initiation au cinéma*. Paris: Spes, 1950.

Chirat, Raymond. *Catalogue des films français de long métrage, films sonores de fiction, 1929–1939*. Luxembourg: Imprimerie Saint-Paul, 1981.

————. *Catalogue des films français de long métrage, films sonores de fiction, 1940–1950*. Brussels: Cinémathèque Royale de Belgique, 1975.

Chirat, Raymond, and Roger Icart. *Catalogue des films français de long métrage, films sonores de fiction, 1919–1929*. Toulouse: Cinémathèque de Toulouse, 1984.

Delpierre, Madeleine. *French Elegance in the Cinema*. Paris: Société de l'histoire du costume, 1988.

Ducout, Françoise. *Les séductrices du cinéma français, 1936–1956*. Paris: Veyrier, 1978.

Ellis, Jack. *A History of Film*. Englewood Cliffs, N.J.: Prentice-Hall, 1979.

Flitterman-Lewis, Sandy. *To Desire Differently: Feminism and the French Cinema*. Urbana: University of Illinois Press, 1990.

Forbes, Jill. *The Cinema in France*. Houndmills: Macmillan Press, 1992.

————. *Les Enfants du Paradis*. London: BFI Film Classics, 1997.

Ford, Charles. *Femmes cinéastes, ou le triomphe de la volonté*. Paris: Denoël, 1972.

Frodon, Jean-Michel. *L'âge moderne du cinéma français: De la nouvelle vague à nos jours*. Paris: Flammarion, 1995.

Garçon, François. *Gaumont: A Century of French Cinema*. New York: Harry Abrams, 1994.

Guérif, François. *Le cinéma policier français*. Paris: Veyrier, 1981.

Hayward, Susan. *French National Cinema*. New York: Routledge, 1993.

Hayward, Susan, and Ginette Vincendeau. *French Film: Texts and Contexts*. New York: Routledge, 2000.

Hughes, Alex, and James S. Williams, eds. *Gender and French Cinema*. Oxford: Berg Publishers, 2001.

Hugues, Philippe d', *L'envahisseur américain: Hollywood contre Billancourt*. Lausanne: Favre, 1999.

Jeancolas, Jean-Pierre. *Histoire du cinéma français*. Paris: Nathan, 1995.

Langlois, Henri. *Trois cents ans de cinéma*. Paris: Cahiers du cinéma and Cinémathèque française, 1986.

Lejeune, Paule. *Le cinéma des femmes*. Paris: Atlas, 1987.

Luhr, William. *World Cinema since 1945*. New York: Ungar, 1987.

Mazdon, Lucy, ed. *France on Film: Reflections on Popular French Cinema*. London: Wallflower Press, 2000.

Metz, Christian. *Film Language: A Semiotics of the Cinema*. New York: Oxford University Press, 1974.

————. *The Imaginary Signifier: Psychoanalysis and the Cinema*. Bloomington: Indiana University Press, 1982.

————. *Language and Cinema*. The Hague: Mouton, 1974.

Pallister, Janis. *French-speaking Women Film Directors*. Madison, NJ: Fairleigh Dickinson University Press, 1998.

Paris, James R. *The Great French Films*. Secaucus, NJ: The Citadel, 1983.

Powrie, Phil. *French Cinema in the 1980s: Nostalgia and the Crisis of Masculinity*. Oxford: Clarendon Press, 1997.

————. *French Cinema in the 1990s*. New York: Oxford University Press, 1999.

Prédal, René. *50 ans de cinéma français*. Paris: Nathan, 1996.

Roux, Jean, and René Thévenet. *Industrie et commerce du film en France*. Paris: Editions scientifiques, 1979.

Sadoul, Georges. *French Film*. London: Falcon Press, 1953.

Siclier, Jacques. *Le cinéma français*. Paris: Ramsay, 1990. 2 vols.

————. *La femme dans le cinéma français*. Paris: Editions du Cerf, 1957.

Thiher, Allen. *The Cinematic Muse: Critical Studies in the History of French Cinema*. Columbia: University of Missouri Press, 1979.

Thompson, Kristin, and David Bordwell. *Film History: An Introduction*. New York: McGraw-Hill, 1993.

Tyler, Parker. *Classics of Foreign Film: A Pictorial Treasury*. New York: Citadel Press, 1962.

Vincendeau, Ginette. *The Companion to French Cinema*. London: Cassell–British Film Institute, 1996.

————. *Stars and Stardom in French Cinema*. New York: Continuum, 2000.

Williams, Alan. *Republic of Images: A History of French Filmmaking*. Cambridge, MA: Harvard University Press, 1992.

Wilson, Emma. *French Cinema since 1950*. Lanham, MD: Rowman & Littlefield Publishers, 2001.

Zants, Emily. *Chaos Theory, Complexity, Cinema and the Evolution of the French Novel*. New York: Edwin Mellen Press, 1996.

FILM HISTORY

Abel, Richard. *The Ciné Goes to Town: French Cinema, 1896–1914*. Berkeley: University of California Press, 1994.

————. *French cinema: The First Wave, 1915–1929*. Princeton: Princeton University Press, 1984.

Andrew, Dudley. *Mists of Regret: Culture and Sensibility in Classic French Film*. Princeton: Princeton University Press, 1995.

Bazin, André. *Le cinéma français de l'occupation et de la résistance*. Paris: Union générale d'éditions, 1975.

————. *French Cinema of the Occupation and the Resistance: The Birth of a Critical Esthetic*. New York: Ungar, 1981.

Bertin-Marghit, Jean-Pierre. *Le cinéma français sous l'occupation*. Paris: Presses Universitaires de France, 1994.

————. *Le cinéma français sous Vichy: Les films français de 1940 à 1944*. Paris: Revue de Cinéma-Albatros, 1980.

Buache, Freddy. *Le cinéma français des années 60*. Paris: Hatier, 1987.

————. *Le cinéma français des années 70*. Paris: Hatier, 1990.

Buchsbaum Jonathan. *Cinéma Engagé: Film in the Popular Front*. Chicago: University of Illinois Press, 1988.

Chirat, Raymond. *La IVème République et ses films*. Paris: Hatier, 1985.

Clouzot, Claire. *Le cinéma français depuis la nouvelle vague*. Paris: Nathan, 1972.

Colombat, André. *The Holocaust in French Film*. Metuchen, NJ: Scarecrow Press, 1993.

Courtade, Francis. *Les malédictions du cinéma français: Une histoire du cinéma français parlant (1928–1978)*. Paris: Moreau, 1978.

Crisp, Colin. *The Classic French Cinema, 1930–1960*. Bloomington: Indiana University Press, 1993.

——. *The Genre, Myth, and Convention in the Classic French Cinema, 1929–1939*. Bloomington: Indiana University Press, 2002.

Darmon, Pierre. *Le monde du cinéma sous l'occupation*. Paris: Stock, 1997.

Douchet, Jean. *French New Wave*. New York: Distributed Art Publishers, 1998.

Ehrilich, Evelyn. *Cinema of Paradox: French Filmmaking under the German Occupation*. New York: Columbia University Press, 1985.

Garçon, François. *De Blum à Pétain: Cinéma et société française, 1936–44*. Paris: Editions du Cerf, 1984.

Greene, Naomi. *Landscapes of Loss: The National Past in Postwar French Cinema*. Princeton: Princeton University Press, 1999.

Jeancolas, Jean-Pierre. *Histoire du cinéma français*. Paris: Nathan, 1995.

——. *15 ans d'années trente: Le cinéma des français, 1929–1944*. Paris: Stock, 1983.

Kline, T. Jefferson. *Screening the Text: Intertextuality in New Wave French Cinema*. Baltimore: Johns Hopkins University Press, 1992.

Lanzmann, Claude. *Shoah: An Oral History of the Holocaust*. New York: Pantheon Books, 1985.

Martin, John. *The Golden Age of French Cinema, 1929–1939*. Boston: Twayne, 1983.

Monaco, James. *The New Wave*. New York: Oxford University Press, 1976.

Sadoul, Georges. *Le cinéma français (1890–1962)*. Paris: Flammarion, 1962.

Servel, Alain. *Frenchies Goes to Hollywood. La France et les français dans le cinéma américain de 1929 à nos jours*. Paris: Veyrier, 1987.

Siclier, Jacques. *La France de Pétain et son cinéma*. Paris: Veyrier, 1981.

Tarr, Carrie. *French Cinema and Post-Colonial Minorities*. New York: Routledge, 1997.

Tavernier, Bertrand. *50 ans de cinéma américain*. Paris: Nathan, 1995.

ACTORS AND DIRECTORS

Allen, Don. *Finally Truffaut*. New York: Beaufort Books, 1985.

Andrew, Dudley. *André Bazin*. New York: Oxford University Press, 1978.

Aumont, Jacques. *Amnésies: Fictions du cinéma d'après Jean-Luc Godard*. Paris: POL, 1999.

Austin, Guy. *Claude Chabrol*. Manchester: Manchester University Press, 1999.

Baecque, Antoine de. *Truffaut*. New York: Knopf, 1999.

Barrot, Olivier, and Raymond Chirat. *Gueules d'atmosphères: Les acteurs du cinéma français, 1929–1959*. Paris: Gallimard, 1994.

——. *Noir et blanc: 250 acteurs du cinéma français, 1930–1960*. Paris: Flammarion, 2000.

Bazin, André. *Jean Renoir*. Paris: Editions champ libre, 1971.

——. *Jean Renoir* (with an introduction by François Truffaut). New York: Simon & Schuster, 1973.

Bergala, Alain. *Nul mieux que Godard*. Paris: Editions Cahiers du Cinéma, 1999.

Bergan, Ronald. *Jean Renoir: Projections of Paradise*. Woodstock, NY: Overlook Press, 1994.

Bertin, Celia. *Jean Renoir: A Life in Pictures*. Baltimore: Johns Hopkins University Press, 1991.

Beylie, Claude. *Marcel Pagnol*. Paris: Seghers, 1974.

Blakeway, C. *Jacques Prévert: Popular French Theater and Cinema*. Madison, NJ: Fairleigh Dickinson University Press, 1989.

Bourgeois, Jacques. *René Clair*. Geneva and Paris: Roulet, 1949.

Braucourt, Guy. *André Cayatte*. Paris: Seygers, 1969.

Braudy, Leo. *Jean Renoir, the World of His Films*. New York: Columbia University Press, 1989.

Brown, Royal. *Focus on Godard*. Englewood Cliffs, NJ: Prentice-Hall, 1972.

Brownlow, Kevin. *Napoleon: Abel Gance's Classic Film*. New York: Knopf, 1983.

Carné, Marcel. *Ma vie à belles dents: Mémoires*. Paris: L'Archipel, 1996.

Catelin, J. *Marcel L'Herbier*. Paris: Jacques Vautrin, 1950.

Cauliez, Armand. *Jacques Tati*. Paris: Seghers, 1968.

―――. *Jean Renoir*. Paris: Editions Universities, 1962.

Cerisuelo, Marc. *Jean-Luc Godard*. Paris: Editions des Quatre-vents, 1989.

Charensol, Georges. *Un maître du cinéma: René Clair*. Paris: La Table Ronde, 1952.

Chazal, Robert. *Marcel Carné*. Paris: Seghers, 1969.

Clair, René. *Cinéma d'hier, cinéma d'aujourd'hui*. Paris: Gallimard, 1970.

Collet, Jean. *Jean-Luc Godard*. New York: Crown, 1970.

Crisp, Colin. *Eric Rohmer*. Indianapolis: Indiana University Press, 1988.

―――. *François Truffaut*. New York: Praeger, 1972.

Dixon, Wheeler. *The Films of Jean-Luc Godard*. Albany: State University of New York Press, 1997.

Douin, Jean Luc. *Jean-Luc Godard*. Paris: Rivages, 1989.

Durgnat, Raymond. *Jean Renoir*. Berkeley: University of California Press, 1974.

Ezra, Elizabeth. *Georges Méliès: The Birth of the Auteur*. Manchester: Manchester University Press, 2000.

Faulkner, Christopher. *Jean Renoir: A Guide to References and Resources*. Boston: G. K. Hall, 1979.

―――. *The Social Cinema of Jean Renoir*. Princeton: Princeton University Press, 1986.

Fischer, Lucy. *Jacques Tati*. Boston: G. K. Hall, 1983.

Fraigneau, André. *Cocteau on the Film*. New York: Dover, 1972.

French, Philip. *Malle on Malle*. London: Faber & Faber, 1995.

Gauteur, Claude, and Ginette Vincendeau. *Jean Gabin: Anatomie d'un mythe*. Paris: Nathan, 1993.

Gilliatt, Penelope. *Jean Renoir: Essays, Conversations, Reviews*. New York: McGraw-Hill, 1975.

Godard, Jean Luc. *Godard on Godard: Critical Writings*. New York: Viking Press, 1972.

―――. *Introduction à une véritable histoire du cinéma*. Paris: Albatros, 1980.

Hayward, Susan. *Luc Besson*. Manchester: Manchester University Press. 1998.

Holmes, Diana, and Robert Ingram. *François Truffaut*. Manchester: Manchester University Press, 1998.

Insdorf, Annette. *François Truffaut*. Boston: Twayne, 1978.

King, Norman. *Abel Gance: A Politics of Spectacle.* London: British Film Institute, 1984.

Kramer, Steven, and James Welsh. *Abel Gance.* Boston: Twayne, 1978.

Lacassin, Francis. *Louis Feuillade.* Paris: Bordas, 1995.

Leprohon, Pierre. *Jean Renoir.* New York: Crown, 1971.

Maddock, Brent. *The Films of Jacques Tati.* London: Scarecrow Press, 1977.

McGerr, Celia. *René Clair.* Boston: Twayne, 1980.

McMahan, Alison. *Alice Guy Blaché: Cinematic Visionary.* New York and London: Continuum, 2002.

Mouren, Yannick. *François Truffaut, l'art du récit.* Paris: Minard, 1997.

O'Shaughnessy, Martin. *Jean Renoir.* Manchester: Manchester University Press, 2000.

Perez, Michel. *Les films de Carné.* Paris: Ramsay, 1986.

Reader, Keith. *Robert Bresson.* Manchester: Manchester University Press, 2000.

Renoir, Jean. *Entretiens et propos.* Paris: Editions de l'étoile Cahiers du Cinéma, 1979.

———. *My Life and My Films.* New York: Atheneum, 1974.

———. *Renoir on Renoir: Interviews, Essays, and Remarks.* Cambridge: Cambridge University Press, 1989.

Rollet, Brigitte. *Coline Serreau.* Manchester: Manchester University Press, 1998.

Roud, Richard. *Jean-Luc Godard.* London: Secker & Warburg, in association with the British Film Institute, 1967.

Serceau, Daniel. *Jean Renoir, l'insurgé.* Paris: Le Sycomore, 1981.

———. *Jean Renoir: La sagesse du plaisir* (preface by Claude Chabrol). Paris: Editions du Cerf, 1985.

Sesonske, Alexander. *Jean Renoir, the French Films, 1924–1939.* Cambridge, MA: Harvard University Press, 1980.

Silverman, Kaja. *Speaking About Godard.* New York: New York University Press, 1998.

Smith, Alison. *Agnès Varda.* Manchester: Manchester University Press, 1998.

Sterritt, David. *The Films of Jean-Luc Godard: Seeing the Invisible.* Cambridge: Cambridge University Press, 1999.

Toubiana, Serge. "Au revoir les enfants de Louis Malle: Regards d'enfants." *Cahiers du Cinéma* 400 (1987): 18–22.

Trauner, Alexandre. *Cinquante ans de cinéma.* Paris: Flammarion, 1986.

Truffaut, François. *The Early Film Criticism of François Truffaut.* Bloomington: Indiana University Press, 1993.

———. *The Films in My Life.* New York: Simon & Schuster, 1978.

Truffaut, François. *Hitchcock/Truffaut.* New York: Simon Schuster, 1967.

———. *Truffaut by Truffaut.* New York: Abrams, 1987.

Turk, Edward Baron. *Child of Paradise: Marcel Carné and the Golden Age of French Cinema.* Cambridge, MA: Harvard University Press, 1989.

Vaugeois, Gérard. *Drôle de drame: Marcel Carné.* Paris: Balland, 1974.

Walz, Eugene. *François Truffaut: A Guide to References and Resources.* Boston: G. K. Hall, 1982.

Index